Masculinities in Contemporary American Culture

Masculinities in Contemporary American Culture offers readers a multidisciplinary, intersectional overview of masculinity studies that includes both theoretical and applied lenses. Keith combines current research with historical perspectives to demonstrate the contexts in which masculine identities have evolved. With an emphasis on popular culture—particularly film, TV, video games, and music—this text invites students to examine their gendered sensibilities and discuss the ways in which different forms of media appeal to toxic masculinity.

Thomas Keith received his Ph.D. in philosophy from Claremont Graduate University, Claremont, California, specializing in American philosophy with an emphasis on issues of race, gender, and class. He has published numerous articles on the intersection of gender, media, and popular culture, appeared on TV and radio programs, and produced two best-selling films for Media Education Foundation: *Generation M: Misogyny in Media and Culture* (2008), and *The Bro Code: How Contemporary Culture Creates Sexist Men* (2011). In 2015, Keith released his third film for MEF entitled *The Empathy Gap: Masculinity and the Courage to Change*, and continues to speak to audiences around the country on issues of masculinity, gender violence, media, and popular culture.

With this book, Thomas Keith has captured the essence of both long existing tensions and changing notions of masculinity in American culture. This is both an interdisciplinary and intersectional account of men's lives. Easy to read, comprehensive, and even entertaining, *Masculinities in Contemporary American Culture* is the most relevant Masculinities textbook on the market.
Eric Anderson. Professor of Sport, Masculinities and Sexualities, University of Winchester, England

Tom Keith's introduction to Masculinities Studies is a most welcome addition to a growing field. Sure-handed, level-headed, both judicious and clear, he gives us the next generation of introductory text: steeped in intersectional thinking, taking diversity as its starting point, not the "problem" to be explained.
Michael Kimmel Distinguished Professor of Sociology and Gender Studies, Stony Brook University

This volume offers a comprehensive compendium of the terms and concepts needed to analyze *Masculinities in Contemporary American Culture.* A valuable introduction to popular and academic approaches to understanding representations of masculinities and how men are engendered, full of up-to-date, engaging examples.
Harry Brod, Professor of Sociology and Humanities, University of Northern Iowa

Dr. Thomas Keith's new book is proof that there are a numerous amount of innovative ways to engage traditional material. With a philosopher's approach to unpacking complex material, yet through the lens of an ex-musician, Dr. Keith tells a profoundly lyrical story that feels like he himself authored the manual for making dysfunctional men, just so that he could tell us how to make repairs. If you are interested in acquiring the tools to create conversations that lead to deeper understanding, personal epiphanies, and yes, revelations for men to self-reflect and own the fact that we can actually be better, and more importantly, do better, then there is no better place to start your exploration than with Dr. Keith's intersectional approach. This is the new book that the academy will be talking about.
Dr. J.W. Wiley, Chief Diversity Officer and Lecturer, Philosophy & Interdisciplinary Studies, SUNY Plattsburgh and Author of *The NIGGER In You: Challenging Dysfunctional Language, Engaging Leadership Moments*

Masculinities in Contemporary American Culture

An Intersectional Approach to the Complexities and Challenges of Male Identity

Thomas Keith

NEW YORK AND LONDON

First published 2017
by Routledge
711 Third Avenue, New York, NY 10017

and by Routledge
2 Park Square, Milton Park, Abingdon, Oxon, OX14 4RN

Routledge is an imprint of the Taylor & Francis Group, an informa business

Library of Congress Cataloging-in-Publication Data
Names: Keith, Thomas, 1958- author.
Title: Masculinities in contemporary American culture : an intersectional approach to the complexities and challenges of male identity / Thomas Keith.
Description: New York, NY : Routledge, 2017. | Includes index.
Identifiers: LCCN 2016029549| ISBN 9781138818064 (hardcover : alk. paper) | ISBN 9781138818071 (pbk. : alk. paper) | ISBN 9781315745459 (e-book)
Subjects: LCSH: Men–United States. | Masculinity–United States. | Men–Identity.
Classification: LCC HQ1090.3 .K445 2017 | DDC 305.310973–dc23
LC record available at https://lccn.loc.gov/2016029549

ISBN: 978-1-138-81806-4 (hbk)
ISBN: 978-1-138-81807-1 (pbk)
ISBN: 978-1-315-74545-9 (ebk)

Typeset in Sabon
by Cenveo Publisher Services

To my wife Leslie, my son Jordan, and to the courageous men and women who have served in the military, faced combat, and returned to a nation that needs to better support them.

Contents

Preface

The early twenty-first century has witnessed a much more pronounced interest in issues of gender. An interest in masculinities, in particular, has emerged as desire for a more forensic account of masculinity has grown. One could say that since the arrival of the women's movement, questions about manhood and masculinity began to form around some basic concerns: Why do men dominate positions of power in America? Why do men commit far more violence than women? Why do men, on average, die younger than women? Why do men commit suicide at higher rates than women? Why are men incarcerated at higher rates than women? Why are men more emotionally stoic and less likely to seek out counseling than women? Why do men have difficulties going to a doctor for a routine checkup? As time passed, more questions arose: Why are men seemingly more homophobic than women? Why do men make up the majority of homeless people in America? Are men happy with their lives? These questions and others continued to be asked so that it was a foregone conclusion that, at some point, courses in men and masculinities would appear alongside courses in women's studies. Today, most universities have courses in gender studies that also include at least one course on men and masculinities. This text has been written to construct a disciplinarily diverse, intersectional account of masculinities that explores these forensic questions. The examination of men and masculinities, like the study of women and femininities, is complex and cannot be reduced to investigating only sociological, psychological, or theoretical accounts, although these disciplines provide important insight into American masculine construction. An understanding of the multiple factors that construct the various masculine performances and identities we witness today require an integration of a variety of disciplines that include sociology, psychology, anthropology, biology, communications and media studies, education studies, cultural studies, history, philosophy, political theory, economics, religious studies, and no doubt other areas of inquiry not taken up in this text. In fact, the word 'masculinity' is pluralized in the title of this text to acknowledge the fact that there is no one, guiding set of traits or influences that account for 'masculinity'. Increasingly, what is considered to be 'masculine' is undergoing nuanced changes in American culture that incorporates both traditional and nonconforming masculinities that are also responsive to differences in culture, religion, political alliance, generational variation, levels of education, socioeconomics, diverse gender identities, and sexual orientation. Needless to say, the notion of a traditional gender binary into which people can be neatly divided is no longer tenable if it ever was.

So, what accounts for the multitude of masculinities? As the multidisciplinary approach suggests, there is a complex set of influences that construct masculinities. From parental and family influence to the influences of media, sports and music culture, to niche cultural influences, to biology and more, masculine identities are rich, subtle, and diverse. This is not to say that hegemonic versions of masculinity do not continue to exist. There are, in fact, certain masculine templates that dominate popular culture, but these templates are becoming more varied and are seen more prominently within masculine subcultures than throughout American culture at large. Media is a good reflector against which to approximate the multiplicity of masculine styles on display in America. Even a casual look at media representations of men makes this point about masculine diversity abundantly clear. From the hyper-aggressive tough guys of action-adventure films to wealthy playboys who wield great power over others, media representations of men lionize affluent, powerful men as one of the most common masculine templates in contemporary popular culture. But there are also plenty of media depictions of men that diverge from the hypermasculine archetype and could even be considered antithetical to the tough-guy prototype found in most action-adventure, summertime movies aimed at teen audiences. Many if not most boys and young men actually do not connect with the prototypical media tough-guys that proliferate mediated popular culture, and for these boys and young men, alternate and sometimes nonconforming versions of masculinity feel more comfortable. So, at a time when issues of gender and sexuality have exploded onto college and university campuses, the many issues bound up in manhood and masculinities have found an equally robust interest among college students and academicians alike. This text is designed to stimulate, explore, and respond to the increase in interest over men and masculine identities that is intriguing students and faculty across America today. In so doing, an emphasis on intersectionality will be made to better understand the complexities and challenges that attend men of color, ethnic diversity, nonconforming gender identities, sexual orientation, and socioeconomic class.

Ideas on How to Use This Text

Masculinities in Contemporary American Culture: An Intersectional Approach to the Complexities and Challenges of Male Identity has been crafted to work as either a standalone textbook that takes students on a journey through the complexities of masculine identities or as a work that can be supplemented with readings from appropriate anthologies. The chapters are designed to provide requisite contemporary research on men and masculinities along with some historical perspective to better understand the contexts in which masculine identities have come about and evolved over time. This is particularly true in the chapter on patriarchy and the media chapters. But the text is also designed to spark discussion and thought on the many questions that remain for scholarship on masculinities, questions that students can address in organized class discussion and coursework. Throughout the text, "Thought Boxes" are found that can assist instructors in devising homework or in-class group work or individual assignments that can also create discussion topics for wider student participation. In addition, Inset Boxes are provided to highlight certain movements, individuals, streams of research, or specialty topics around which in-class discussions can be framed. The goal of the text is to integrate fact and theory within an intersectional framework so that the diversity of masculine expression and identities can be appreciated from both perspectives. Theory in the absence of fact becomes a labyrinth of speculation, while fact in the absence of theory can create a disparate collection of points in need of coherence. So, a profitable approach to using this text is to frame certain issues around several theories of gender and masculinities and to then use the research as support for or in opposition to certain theories as the case may be.

One of the most salient features of this text that makes it both original and relevant to young people is the emphasis placed on popular culture, and particularly the areas of popular culture that resonate with college-aged people, which include film, TV, video games, and music. This feature of the text allows students to bring into class instances of pop cultural media that appeal to them or that they view as toxic to issues of gender and masculinities in particular. Instructors can take advantage of student interest in this area to show and discuss TV or film clips, scenes from popular video games, or music videos and lyrics from popular songs or rhymes for analysis. Exercises can include group projects, media presentations, and actual debate in some cases. Since many college students qualify as media experts in terms of the number of hours they spend using media, this element of the text draws young people into discussions that a course steeped in complicated theory and technical terminology will not. In fact, since the visual aspect of gender identity is so pronounced, visual media partners well with pedagogy and course assignments to create a classroom environment ripe for student interaction.

The fact that this text has taken an intersectional approach to issues of masculinities also provides classroom opportunities for discussion and course work. Entire weeks of a quarter or semester can be devoted to analyzing LGBTQ and gender-nonconformist issues as they relate to men and masculinities. The ongoing evolution of popular culture is itself favorable to class discussions on the ways that masculinities are changing and adapting to the nuances of cultural change occurring in education, career, politics, international studies, military culture, social media, journalism, sports culture, fatherhood, fraternity and sorority life, sex, pornography, and many other areas of interest to students who are already immersed in gender studies as well as for those students for whom the course may be their first contact with issues of gender and masculinities.

Chapter Summaries

Chapter one begins with an investigation of patriarchy and the male privileges that men enjoy in patriarchal cultures. When men control governmental and economic power to the exclusion of most or all women, a society is patriarchal in nature. A patriarchal culture is not dependent on laws that mandate male power, but, as witnessed in America, can be the result of a de facto set of circumstances that maintain male power. In American culture, for instance, men outnumber women in governmental and executive business positions, including those industries such as banking, finance, and brokerage, where large sums of money are made and invested. Men also dominate certain occupations and enjoy executive positions in far greater number than women in almost every field of employment other than those considered to be traditionally female-centered careers such as nursing and primary school education. So, patriarchal cultures need not be cultures where men exclusively control power, but where men overwhelmingly control power. But it is not the case that all men enjoy male privilege to the same degree, since socioeconomics, race, ethnicity, gender identity, sexual orientation, bodied-abilities, cognitive status, and a host of potential factors influence and mitigate male privilege. But with these caveats in mind, the first chapter traces both the historical and contemporary factors that maintain patriarchy in America along with the many advantages that males enjoy in patriarchal cultures.

Chapter two takes up one of the most common explanations for higher levels of aggression and violence in men than witnessed in women: biology. In trying to understand why, on average, men are more violent than women, the default answer that springs from some quarters is the view that men possess more testosterone than women. This biological fact along with other biological and evolutionary factors purport to explain aggression as male dominant. The nature–nurture debate has been around for a long time when attempting to explain human behavior, but with men there has been less examination of the environmental factors that may be contributing to high levels of aggression and violence. The phrase "boys will be boys" sums up the most common way that biology-based explanations are expressed whether wittingly or not. This phrase serves as a conversation stopper that purportedly reveals why boys seem to play rougher than girls and then subsequently why men are more violent than women. Challenges to nature-based explanations for gendered behavioral differences have been around for a long time as well, but have had to wait until science created a body of evidence to see whether one explanation was better supported than the other. Today, the biological research into gendered behavior comes largely from endocrinology and neuroscience. Longitudinal studies have now been conducted to see whether higher rates of testosterone equate to higher rates of aggression and antisocial behavior. Similarly, neuroscientists have squared off over whether male brains and female brains are significantly different enough to account for gendered behavioral differences. This particular line of research has produced sharp and contentious disagreement. The chapter ends by attempting to understand why biological accounts are both fatalistic and defeatist in terms of successful intervention. If male brains are wired for violence, then little beyond surgical intervention can bring about progressive changes in male behaviors. If, on the other hand, observed gendered behaviors can be explained in terms of culture and environment, opportunities arise that increase the chance of more successful circumstantial intervention. In fact, even if gendered behaviors turn out to be the product of both nature and nurture, there would be greater variance in modes of intervention to counteract problematic behaviors than working from the assumption that biology is the lone efficacious factor in determining male aggression and violence.

Chapter three investigates men's organizations, starting with a critical examination of college fraternities, which have come under great scrutiny over the past couple decades for episodes of hazing and high rates of sexual assault. From there, the chapter takes up organizations that cater specifically to boys such as the Boy Scouts of America. It is important to understand the origins of the Boy Scouts, since it was founded on the view that cosmopolitan life was undermining masculinity. The idea was that city and suburban lifestyles were destroying the toughness associated with uncultivated, rural manliness. These sorts of views are still very much around today and are politicized with conservative pundits claiming that contemporary culture "wussifies" men by coddling boys too much, while also discouraging what they take to be natural aggressive play in boys. A more politically liberal perspective on masculine construction is the view that violence can be decreased only if boys are raised without aggression and violence as the presumed approach to conflict resolution. Given this background, the chapter goes on to examine a variety of contemporary men's groups, some of which can be identified as pro-feminist and others as anti-feminist, including men's rights activists who angrily defend the idea that men are under attack today by women and particularly feminist ideals that they view as undermining male authority. Pro-feminist men's groups respond by arguing that patriarchy is unjust and harmful to both women and men. There are other men's groups that straddle positions of feminism and anti-feminism, but the importance of this chapter lies in understanding how and why these groups formed along with the implications these groups have to the future of masculinities.

Chapter four takes up what many have called a "boy crisis" in America. Statistics suggest that compared to girls, boys are failing out of school, getting lower overall grades, entering colleges and universities at lower rates, getting into more trouble with the law and abusing substances at higher rates. Books have now been written that attempt to explain this boy crisis with ideas about how to turn it around. Some of the analysis places blame on education, claiming that current pedagogy is biased against boys. Others argue that an anti-feminist sentiment is to blame by getting boys to view education as having a softening effect on masculinity, that real men pursue careers of physical labor or specialized technical labor such as plumbing, electrical, construction, contractor, and other areas of the workforce that are dominated by men. Not everyone believes the boy crisis is as bad as critics make it out to be, and that the problems boys are facing have much more to do with boys living in socioeconomically-depressed environments than they do with educational pedagogy.

Chapter five takes up fatherhood and the many challenges and rewards that face fathers today. Beginning with teen fathers, the chapter traces the more common elements that place teen boys at risk for becoming teen dads and the associated issues that commonly arise for these young men. As with other chapters, the chapter on fatherhood takes an intersectional approach to fatherhood by noting some of the cultural differences in the ways that fatherhood is viewed and practiced. In addition, the challenges of being a single father are explored, including the complaints made by fathers' right groups. Many of the men who gravitate toward fathers' rights groups are angry in the wake of a contentious divorce coupled with what they believe to be injustice in the family court system. This chapter also covers the critiques of fathers' rights groups and most notably the criticisms of sociologist Michael Flood.

Beyond the many challenges for teen and single fathers, this chapter also takes up special challenges for black, Latino, Asian, and Native fathers who struggle with multiple identities beyond the status of "father." Those fathers who are gay also face numerous and unique challenges, not the least of which is dealing with a homophobic society that often condemns gay parenting. In addition to the challenges gay men face in being parents in homophobic America, the challenges can be intense for the sons and daughters who come out to their parents. This is also true for young transgender men and women who fear the reactions of their parents upon learning the gender identities of their children.

Chapter six is the first of three chapters on men and media. In chapter six, the focus turns to heteronormative male representation that also treats violent and aggressive masculinity as a mediated cultural norm. From the hypermasculine portrayals of John Wayne characters in the mid-twentieth century through the more contemporary versions of hypermasculine tough guy characters in action-adventure media, a particular brand of heteronormative masculinity has proliferated American media for generations. Leaning on the work of George Gerbner, chapter six traces the ways that media representation has had an effect on audiences and in this case male audiences. In line with Gerbner's *cultivation theory*, this chapter takes up the ways in which the notion of gender-normality is culturally constructed. If 'normal' is a social construct and if media play a role in shaping this construction, what does the research show about media's effect on boys and men?

In particular, chapter six explores how different versions of heteronormative masculinity are marketed to men of different socioeconomic backgrounds. Whether men hail from working, middle, or wealthy classes, the common themes found in the marketing of masculinity are power, control, autonomy, and an assumed sexual entitlement over women's bodies. Author and antiviolence educator Jackson Katz argues that many boys and men are conditioned by a variety of influences, including media, to adopt a hypermasculine performance Katz terms, *the tough guise*, which is found throughout American culture. The tough guise bifurcates gender and instructs boys that they are defined in large part by what they are not or should not aspire to be: feminine in any way. As boys and men are conditioned to define themselves through the prescription of non-femininity, a conspicuous concern immediately arises: how are boys and men trained to view girls and women?

Chapter six ends with an examination of gendered comedy, and particularly those comedies that purport to appeal to men. Infamously, some male comedians are on record claiming that men are funnier than women. Beyond this sexist quip, chapter six takes up some of the more insidious elements of so-called *guy humor*, a brand of humor that celebrates everything from dangerous risk-taking behaviors to unending vulgarity to homophobia to both mild and violent sexism and rape. In this way, comedy can actually be quite serious. It allows boys and men to bully others who do not enjoy alpha-male privilege and then excuse the bullying by claiming "it's just a joke."

Chapter seven continues the investigation of masculinities and media by focusing on the ways that differing media influence boys and men with respect to their views, choices, and behaviors. From adopting what author Richard Majors terms *the cool pose* to more readily accepting *rape myth* narratives, this chapter traces the various ways media affect men in their views about women. This latter point can be seen most vividly in advertisement, as the marketing of products through sexually objectifying women is commonplace. Authors such as Jean Kilbourne, Mary Pipher, and others have documented the many ways that ads of this kind hurt women; this chapter takes up how these sorts of ads influence men.

However, media as well as American culture in general have witnessed slow, progressive movement toward more diversity of male representation including more diverse depictions of gay and transgender men. At the same time, there has been a backlash to the greater media acceptance of gay and transgender men, and what has been termed the *metrosexual*. A decidedly indignant response to metrosexual masculinity has emerged through shows like *Duck Dynasty*, where a distinctly rustic masculine throwback version of manhood has come to represent a prevailing conservative view about what proper masculine identity in America should be. In a less direct way, some male comedians have found success by appealing to gender and sexual orientation stereotypes to a largely young, male audience.

Chapter seven then takes up video games and gamer culture, which continues to draw its main support from boys and young men. Video games notoriously gender their characters and avatars in wildly stereotypical ways. The male characters are inordinately muscular and violent, while the female characters are hypersexual and often violent as well. Beyond the physical and behavioral stereotypes of the avatars, this section examines gamers themselves to try to better understand whether games and gaming have an effect on the thinking and behaviors of gamers, and in particular whether male gamers internalize the sexist narratives embedded in the games they play.

The chapter ends by explaining the concept of media literacy and why proponents of media literacy believe it is crucial to teach children at the youngest ages the critical thinking tools they need to better understand the gendered messages they receive from media. Currently, primary education avoids discussions about media almost entirely, while children consume media each day at levels never before seen. The concern is that if media contain normative messages, while underage media consumers lack the critical thinking tools to process and understand these messages, how are young people able to critically examine these messages to parse out the regulating gender directives from the product endorsements, and how are these images and directives influencing their lives?

Chapter eight takes up the intersection of masculine identities, masculine performance, and music with an emphasis on the evolving nature of male music artists, lyrics, visual styles, attitudes, and artists' influence on boys and men in wider culture. Music has been and continues to be enormously popular and influential with young people, but the gender dichotomy and masculine representation found in lyrics, video, and artist persona is rarely examined. This chapter redresses this neglect by featuring a lengthy investigation of masculine expression and representation in music. Analyzing both the history and textual accounts of popular music artists, this section of the chapter intends to expose how music plays a normative role in constructing and reinforcing masculine archetypes, some of which are profoundly sexist, homophobic, and consistent with a pervasive cultural code of hypermasculine posturing and heteronormativity. But like all forms of media, music is diverse and male representation has been and continues to be disparate, particularly in some genres of music more than others.

Chapter nine takes up sports culture, beginning with the many ways that sports enhance the lives of boys and men. Beginning in childhood, many boys gravitate or are guided toward sports as part of a typical male upbringing and these experiences can have a decidedly positive effect on their lives. However, this chapter also investigates some of the negative facets of sports in men's lives, such as the line that some men cross in developing a sports obsession. There is scholarly speculation as to why some men form sports obsessions, while others place fandom in balance with other, more important aspects of their lives. What are the consequences for men who are preoccupied with sports fandom?

This chapter also takes up traumatic brain injury in sports and most notably in football and boxing. Beyond the medical concerns of head trauma and performance enhancing drug use, an important question for this section of the text is whether certain forms of normative masculinity play a role in encouraging men to engage in risk-taking athletic activities. Again, this particular issue like other issues involving men creates some political wrangling over whether boys are being weakened by being diverted away from contact sports. The resistance by many to mitigating sports injury, as one example, may be yet another sign of the conservative backlash to perceived male weakness in contemporary culture.

Another longstanding concern about sports is the locker room environment, where sexism and homophobia in the conversations, taunting, and joking between male athletes are thought to have free reign. The question is whether male team sports promote a sexist, homophobic environment where men feel comfortable to express what otherwise would be considered hateful and politically incorrect speech. A more expansive concern is whether male team sports promote an approval of sexism with cheerleaders that are hypersexualized for male viewing consumption along with the reinforcement of homophobia with the acceptance of slurs as a recognized part of male athletic banter. Several NFL teams have taken a stance against sexualizing cheerleaders and some cheerleaders themselves have expressed disdain for the ways they are treated. The NBA recently broadcast a PSA against the use of homophobic slurs in recognition of the fact that there has been and continues to be a problem, as part of acknowledging that male athletes have an influence on boys and young men.

A final concern for male team sports is the way that intimate partner violence and sexual assault have been handled by league and college officials around the country. With rates of intimate partner violence and sexual assault at exceedingly high levels, if male athletes are role models to boys and young men, how should university and league policy address cases of athletes who commit violence, including sexual violence? Is the answer to this question consistent with the ways that university and league policy currently address violence perpetrated by athletes?

Chapter ten takes up the intersection of men and violence. It is uncontroversial that men commit the lion share of violence in societies around the world. This chapter investigates why experts believe that men, starting in adolescence, engage in more violent acts than women. Since chapter two takes up some of the biological theories for male aggression and violence, this chapters focuses more on the theories that come from psychologists and child-development experts. If violence is not simply the product of biological factors over which little can be done, the obvious question is whether violence can be mitigated through cultural intervention. Specifically, this chapter investigates the power-control theory of delinquency and how hegemonic masculinity may contribute to rates of male violence.

In addition to violence in general, this chapter more specifically investigates sexual violence both in military and civilian populations, where men are overwhelmingly the perpetrators. The chapter continues by examining the interconnections between certain hegemonic forms of masculinity, alcohol usage, sexual assault, and rape. The chapter ends by examining intimate partner violence and how statistics are gathered including the deceptive ways that men's rights activists assemble and report statistics to make it appear that violence is gender equal. What is known is that men commit intimate partner violence at much higher rates than women and perpetrate on average much more severe levels of injury. Yet, a controversial scale is often used to document cases of intimate partner violence that make it appear as though violence between partners is not a gendered matter. Sociologist Michael Kimmel exposes the many flaws of this scale and explains why the conclusions drawn by men's rights activists are not only erroneous, but dangerous.

Chapter eleven takes up the relationship between men and pornography. The pornography industry has historically been an industry made by men for men. Beginning with the Playboy empire created by Hugh Hefner to today's internet pornography, this chapter begins by tracing the history of pornography in America and the early cultural and political backlash. But the main focus of the chapter is on the ways that pornography usage affects men and relationships. From the many forms of gonzo-pornography that exist online to the forms of rape-porn and other violent forms of pornography available today, the more prevailing questions include why so many men find this sort of porn entertaining and what effects might result from ritualized usage of these forms of pornography.

There are those, of course, who defend pornography and this chapter will take up the debates between pro-pornography feminists and anti-pornography feminists. But ultimately the chapter focuses on how porn usage affects men. From those who argue that pornography serves as a catharsis for sexual violence to those who claim that pornography is useful to couples, porn supporters continue to defend pornography on grounds of utility and agency, while critics view porn use by men not unlike substance abuse with similar sorts of fallout for men, women, and relationships.

The chapter ends with a brief examination of gay pornography along with the phenomenon of "gay for pay" pornography where heterosexual men engage in sex with other men for pay. Gay male scholars tend to view gay male pornography differently than their heterosexual colleagues view heterosexual porn. In most cases, although certainly not all, those scholars who are themselves gay men, and who have written about pornography tend to view it in a positive light. The reasons for this support are investigated along with the arguments offered by gay, male scholars who dissent from this majority view.

Chapter twelve closes out the text with an examination of men, health, and aging, beginning with an examination of the close relationship between men, capitalism, and the ways that material wealth are thought to define masculine success. For generations men were considered to be the bread-winners of the nuclear family, but in the twenty-first century the benchmark for success has increasingly been associated with personal wealth. As wealth and masculinity have been connected in popular culture, high levels of stress and the associated illnesses that are considered stress-related impact men's health. For decades, men have been pushed into believing that a defining role for men is found in their earning ability. Material success was also accompanied by the idea that one needed an outgoing, assertive, "Type-A" personality in order to succeed at peak efficiency. But critics have noted that there have been and continue to be a host of negative consequences for men who push themselves to conform to certain contemporary standards of masculine success.

Today, we also witness an increase in men who are concerned about their physical appearances as the "beauty industry" has begun targeting men with products and services. What was once an industry devoted to appealing to women is now trying to profit from men's insecurities about aging and losing sexual appeal. One of the more interesting parts of this redirection is that an industry that has targeted women has had to find ways to appeal to men without threatening their sense of masculinity. That is, because men have been socialized to view masculinity as non-femininity, and this is particularly true of older men, the beauty industry has had to meet the challenge of getting men to view beauty products and services as being consistent with a masculine identity.

Chapter twelve also focuses on the very high levels of male suicide in America. Men commit suicide at four times the rate of women. Health care professionals, psychologists, and psychiatrists have been trying to understand this phenomenon to see whether the way men are socialized to think of themselves as men is contributing to this problem. We see the same concerns in the military, where suicide rates are extremely high when compared to rates in civilian populations. Military commanders and those within the Pentagon who are entrusted to investigate the health of military personnel are seeking answers to this crisis, and some are taking a harder look at the ways that young men and women are being trained to cope with the pressures of being soldiers and the aftermath of having experienced combat.

The chapter ends with an analysis of what has been termed "mid-life crisis," which experts agree affects men more than women. The ages that most experts associate with mid-life crisis are mid-30s to late 50s, but individual contingencies make it difficult to narrow to any specific ages or birthdays. There are several identifiable triggering events that can cause some men to experience a more intense mid-life crisis, while others experience very little disruption or anxiety as they travel through middle-age and on to their senior years. One common concern that scholars agree is a constant for many men is the worry that with age they will lose independence, autonomy, and relevance. When asking men to identify some of the things that concern them as they cross certain pivotal birthdays, a frequent worry is that retirement will bring a loss of purpose and identity. One thing scholars agree upon is that when turning to the subject of men and aging, very little research has been conducted, so that almost all experts conclude that much more scholarship needs to be devoted to understanding the challenges that men face as they reach middle-age and beyond. In a culture that seems to worship youth, the current model for older men who are approaching their senior years through the lens of media and popular culture is one of genderless dependency, where their opinions and worth have less value than when they were younger. The challenge for older men is to find relevance and purpose in new, engaging ways.

*Many of the topics raised in one chapter of the text overlap with material covered in other chapters of the text for good reason; when covering patterns of male violence, for instance, the material in the chapter on biology will seep into the chapter on violence. In these cases, footnotes are often employed to refer the reader to other chapters where a topic is taken up again or taken up in more detail or from a different perspective. In covering the many theories in this textbook, many of the cited scholars themselves reviewed and approved of the explication and analysis of their work.

Acknowledgments

In composing this textbook, I would like to thank the following individuals for their input, suggestions, permissions, and guidance: Jack Halberstam (USC), Peggy McIntosh (Wellesley Centers for Women), bell hooks (Berea College), Eddie Moore Jr., Harry Brod (Northern Iowa University), E.O. Wilson (Harvard University), Judith Butler (University of California, Berkeley), Noam Chomsky (M.I.T.), Anne Fausto-Sterling (Brown University), Michael Messner (USC), Michael Kimmel (SUNY Stony Brook), Jackson Katz, Tony Porter, Michael Thompson, Leonard Sax, Diane F. Halpern (Claremont McKenna College), C.J. Pascoe (University of Oregon), Jean Kilbourne, Alison Bechdel, Anita Sarkeesian, Tessa Jolls, Mark Steven Greenfield, Dave Zirin, R.W. Connell (University of Sydney), Jesse Prinz (City University of New York), Dan Mahle, Robert Jensen (University of Texas, Austin), Gail Dines (Wheelock College), Michael Eric Dyson (Georgetown University), Elijah Anderson (Yale University), Catharine MacKinnon (University of Michigan), Rory Reid (UCLA), Robin Morgan, Randy Flood, Charlie Donaldson, Michael Addis (Clark University), Tiffany Christian (Washington State University), Michael Gill (Grinnell College), Michael Johnson Jr. (Washington State University), Eric Jorrey, Gayle Kaufman (Davidson College), Stacy Keogh, Natalie Kouri-Towe, John Landreau (The College of New Jersey), Daniel Lewis (Lewis & Clark), Bambi Lobdell (SUNY Oneonta), Michele Meek (University of Rhode Island), Scott Melzer (Albion College), Todd A. Migliaccio (Sacramento State), Alfredo Mirandé (UC Riverside), Justin Morgan-Parmett (Western Washington University), Michael Murphy (University of Illinois, Springfield), Freeden Oeur (Tufts University), Greg Phipps (University of Indiana Southeast), Rebecca Plante (Ithaca College), Jennifer Popple (Augustana College), Annegret Staiger (Clarkson University), Robert Strikwerda (Saint Louis University), Linda Van Ingen (University of Nebraska at Kearney), Jake Wilson (CSU-Long Beach), and Iraq and Afghanistan Veterans of America. I would like to especially thank J.W. Wiley (SUNY Plattsburgh) and Eric Anderson (University of Winchester) for their assistance and input in editing the content of several chapters.

Chapter

1

Patriarchy, Male Privilege, and the Consequences of Living in a Patriarchal Society

In us colored folks was the great desire to be able to read and write. We took advantage of every opportunity to educate ourselves ... the plantation owners were very harsh if we were caught trying to learn or write. ... Our ignorance was the greatest hold the South had on us.[1]

~excerpt from an interview with Dr. John W. Fields, ex-slave of the Civil War era

However much it may have been resented, women accepted the idea of their intellectual inequality. In education, in marriage, in religion, in everything disappointment is the lot of women. It shall be the business of my life to deepen that disappointment in every woman's heart until she bows down to it no longer.[2]

~abolitionist and nineteenth-century feminist Lucy Stone

LEARNING OBJECTIVES

After reading this chapter, students should be able to respond to the following questions with an understanding of the terms and expressions employed:

- *What is patriarchy? What is male privilege? How are the two related? What is the Marxist theory of patriarchy? How do radical feminist theories of patriarchy differ from Marxist theories? What is the post-structural solution to patriarchy? How do dual-systems feminists view patriarchy?*
- *What are female masculinities? How do they stand as a challenge to maleness, heteronormativity, and heterosexism?*
- *What is earned and unearned privilege? What is the common sense view of privilege? How does privilege differ between men and women? How do class distinctions affect privilege? How does patriarchy affect men and women of color? What is "benevolent patriarchy" and "violent patriarchy"? What is*

"repressed intersectionality"? What are some of the factors that account for why white men earn more money than black men?

- *What are the origins and early justifications for patriarchal practices? How did patriarchy manifest itself in colonial America? How did women respond to being subjected to patriarchal authorities and practices that deprived women of a multitude of rights possessed by men? What are the factors today that provide advantage for white men over men of color in the workforce?*
- *What are the effects of patriarchy in the workforce? How are women influenced by patriarchy today? What is "patriarchal capitalism"? Is there a contemporary pay gap between men and women, and how does patriarchy influence this gap?*
- *What is conscious and unconscious bias? How do these biases reinforce male privilege in academia? What is the difference between descriptive and prescriptive bias? With respect to businesses and law firms, what is meant by an inverse pyramid? What are some of the elements that sustain male privilege in politics, business, law, and academia?*
- *What is* benevolent sexism*?*
- *What is "the glass ceiling" versus "the glass escalator"?*
- *How does patriarchy and male privilege manifest themselves in language, visual media, and the representations of male and female politicians in journalism?*
- *In what ways is patriarchy being challenged today? Why do some deny the existence of male privilege? What does humanities professor Harry Brod mean by terming masculinities studies, "superordinate studies"?*

Before embarking on the material covered in this textbook, it is important to note that when evaluating boys, men, and issues of masculinity, along with matters of patriarchy and male privilege, the material in this text is not designed to attack boys and men. To the contrary, in many ways boys and men face challenges due to the existence and reinforcement of the same patriarchal structures that harm girls and women. In addition, as we work through the material in this text, it can seem that there is an attempt to point out the worst parts of male culture, particularly when covering media representation, violence, crime, sexual assault, and sexual harassment. While the text uncovers some of the forces that help shape these cultural problems, these same forces harm and limit men in untold ways. It is also important to note, when examining male privilege, that not all males receive privilege to the same degree or in the same way. Many boys grow up being bullied in school or abused at home, and these boys understandably do not connect with the idea that boys and men receive privilege simply from the fact that they are male. In some ways, bullying and other forms of coercion and violence are part of what has been termed *toxic masculinity*, a form of masculinity that creates hierarchies favoring some and victimizing others. Disrupting these forms of toxic masculinity benefits boys and men, rather than attacks and blames men for these behaviors. In fact, issues of masculinity are not always about boys and men. In the case of *female masculinities* we see that masculinity can be attributed to women. Furthermore, non-binary or nontraditional masculinities raise a host of issues that span far beyond mainstream masculinities. In addition, boys and men of color deal with obstacles and challenges that are not as pronounced or even present for most white boys and men. Socioeconomic factors also greatly impact one's opportunities, and these factors will be taken up in appropriate places in the text. Moreover, boys and men who are gay, queer, or transgender also face challenges that heterosexual, cis-males rarely face, unless as part of bullying, hazing rituals, or violence that can affect anyone. But there are also subjective differences in the ways boys and men, just like girls and women, are treated based on physical features such as height, weight, complexion, athletic abilities, and being able-bodied. In general, this text examines the many influences and pressures placed upon boys and men to conform, confront, and contend with gender-normative, culture-driven factors that face them throughout various stages of their lives. In essence, the criticism found in this text is aimed at patriarchal power structures, not individual men.

It is also important to note that "male" and "female" are not static, binary categories as covered in sections below. As transperson Jacob Anderson-Minshall notes, "transpeople, along with intersex people, threaten the conservative assumption that there are two, and only two, classes of human being—men and women—and radical assumptions that gender classes are entirely socially created, rather than having some biological roots."[3] This chapter, while taking up the concepts of patriarchy and male privilege, is looking only at a cultural and historical tradition of men possessing power over women along with the many consequences that flow from such a power differential without assuming that 'men' and 'women' are tightly defined naturally existing dualities. On the contrary, the longstanding assumption that such dualities are natural and immutable has been part of what has made patriarchy and male privilege such tenacious states of being. The gender essentialist notion that gender is established by nature will be examined and challenged in chapter two of the text. We begin, however, by understanding the concepts of patriarchy, male privilege, and the many ramifications of living in a patriarchal culture.

Patriarchy and Male Privilege

> It is the law of nature that woman should be held under the dominance of man.
>
> ~ Confucius[4]

What is Patriarchy?

There are several prominent theories about what patriarchy is and how it maintains itself in contemporary society. One of the most cited explanations of patriarchy is the **Marxist theory** which claims that patriarchy is a power-structure whereby one group of people (men) controls another group of people (women), and that this control depends on capitalism, since the control group holds financial power over the controlled group. According to Friedrich Engels, the nuclear family is predicated on a power dynamic:

> According to the division of labor within the family, it was the man's part to obtain food and the instruments of labor necessary for the purpose. He therefore also owned the instruments of labor, and in the event of husband and wife separating, he took them with him, just as she retained her household goods. Therefore, the man was also the owner of the new source of subsistence, the cattle, and later of the new instruments of labor, the slaves … in proportion as wealth increased, it made the man's position in the family more important than the woman's …[5]

This power dynamic between men and women that became the contemporary, monogamous family was, according to Marx, a development that came about after earlier versions of family structure receded in the wake of capitalism. In the Marxist model of family, women were responsible for bearing and raising children, which, while recognized as necessary work, was not valued under a capitalist structure of economics. As Engels explains, as agriculture and the domestication of animals became a chief source of economic prosperity, a division of labor was created. Men possessed land and controlled the means of cultivating the land, leaving women in the subordinated category of domestic servant. These (male) land owners became the forbearers of the bourgeoisie class, and patriarchy was established as a fundamental outgrowth of capitalism.

Radical feminist theories of patriarchy, while in no way exhaustive of feminist views of patriarchy since there exist Marxist or *materialist* feminists, reject the Marxist idea that patriarchy is dependent on capitalism, for, they argue, Marxism falsely assumes that exploitation takes place only under the capital/labor exchange. Radical feminists argue that another form of exploitation takes place under the patriarchal division of reproductive/productive labor binary. The feminist model accuses Marx of not recognizing the significance of reproductive labor as unpaid labor and that this fundamental inequality is a product of an unequal dynamic between working class men and women, independent of capitalism. In fact, a workforce, in the Marxist sense of the idea, is not possible without the unpaid reproductive work of women. Therefore, it is argued, the inequality between men and women is antecedent to the inequalities derived through capitalism.[6] In tandem with radical feminist critiques of patriarchy, **post-structural feminist** critiques of patriarchy emphasize the notion that all identities are contingent such that all gendered relationships are socially constructed. Gender inequalities, then, are not the product of any natural dominance/submission taxonomy. If correct, patriarchy can be overturned through a radical restructuring of society.

In an attempt to syncretize Marxist accounts with feminist accounts of patriarchy, **dual systems feminism** views the economic system of capitalism and the sex/gender system of patriarchy as interrelated concepts. The dual systems view considers patriarchy to be universal, but specialized in capitalist societies. The argument goes that the domestic division of labor restricts a woman's ability to receive pay in cases where her time and energies are bound to child bearing and raising, which converts into a woman's economic dependency on men who have no such limitations. Therefore, the two systems reinforce one another. In critical response, sociologist Silvia Federici agrees that capitalism depends on the exploitation of women as sources of unpaid labor, but that patriarchy proper has as a goal keeping women out of the paid workforce to assure their reliance on men.[7] When capitalist forces are required to employ women, the forces of patriarchy aim to keep them in positions of subordination by placing women in low-paying jobs or by creating glass ceilings that prevent women from economic upward mobility. Patriarchal policies and practices are, therefore, responsible for an unbalanced workforce where men hold greater authority and where a pay gap exists between men and women such that women receive less money for the same work regardless of equal or superior qualifications.

Male privilege is the logical outgrowth of patriarchy. With systems in place that assure the continued subordination of women in a host of ways and degrees, males gain advantages unavailable or less available to women. Advantages may be economic, political, social, educational, and even temporal and psychological if women are expected to work for a wage, care for children, and tend to housework at the same time, while men focus only on their revenue-earning jobs. In many cases, women find it more difficult to obtain high-paying jobs, despite qualifications, or to move higher within the ranks of their chosen occupations than men. This is the essence of male privilege, having advantage due solely to being born male as a result of structures in place that benefit men over women.

Male privilege can be found in a multitude of settings. Commerce, for example, until very recently has been controlled exclusively by men throughout cultures around the world for the entirety of human history. The power wielded by those who own and control land, capital, and other forms of wealth is perhaps the greatest source of power in any society. Those who possess wealth have a great deal of authority over employment and therefore a great deal of influence over the working classes. This means that in the absence of regulations to keep businesses in check with respect to hiring and firing practices, men have been able to hire other men, including through nepotistic traditions, for centuries, which is precisely what is witnessed when surveying the history of commerce around the world. Furthermore, when women are expected to bear sole responsibility for child care while working for companies that do not provide child care services, a burden is placed directly on women that is not placed on men and this unequal burden places women at much greater risk of being fired or simply not being advanced in their professions. Changes in gendered expectations of child care along with institutional changes to provide child care services would certainly mitigate the unequal burden, but those are not the present realities in which women live. As long as circumstances remain in place, these realities constitute a male privilege.

FEMALE MASCULINITIES

When writing of masculinities, most assume that the work will be exclusively about men. But in the book *Female Masculinity*, University of Southern California Professor Jack "Judith" Halberstam argues that a distinctive female masculinity is almost always left out of discussions about masculinity.[1] Female masculinity is typified by a masculine lesbian who, Halberstam reports, is often vilified in motion pictures and larger culture as well. Recognizing female masculinity opens the door to four realizations: (1) female masculinity challenges the notion that masculinity belongs solely to the domain of maleness, (2) female masculinity detaches misogyny from maleness and social power from masculinity, (3) female masculinity represents a

FIGURE 1.1: Jack Halberstam

Continued

disruption to compulsory heterosexuality, while offering a powerful model of what "inauthentic masculinity" can look like, and (4) female masculinity may force another look at male femininities and challenge the new politics of manliness that "has swept through gay male communities in the last decade."[2]

One of the interesting ways that Halberstam reveals the cultural resistance to female masculinity is in the ways that motion pictures depict the masculine lesbian. In particular, Halberstam exposes a theme found in certain romantic comedies or romantic dramas he terms "heterosexual conversion fantasies."[3] In these films a heterosexual person is attracted to a presumably unattainable gay person, yet in the end the conversion takes place. This conversion fantasy occurs in films such as *Chasing Amy* and *The Opposite of Sex*. But one particular version of this narrative introduces a heterosexual man, a bisexual woman, and a masculine lesbian with a plot of the heterosexual man and masculine lesbian competing for the affections of the bisexual woman, a plot found in the Wilkie Collins novel *The Woman in White*.[4] What is striking about this version of the heterosexual conversion fantasy is that the masculine lesbian character (Marian) is described as follows:

> Never was the old conventional maxim, that Nature cannot err, more fully contradicted – never was the fair promise of a lovely figure more strangely and startlingly belied by the face and head that crowned it. The lady's complexion was almost swarthy and the dark down on her upper lip was almost a moustache. She had a large, firm, masculine mouth and jaw; prominent, piercing, resolute brown eyes; and thick, coal-black hair, growing unusually low down on her forehead.[5]

Here, the starkness of the heteronormativity and heterosexism is astonishing. But the description of "Marian" reinforces a heteronormative view that lesbians should please the male gaze as much as cis-gender heterosexual women such that female masculinity is castigated as strange and unseemly. What are your thoughts?

---

1 Halberstam, Judith. *Female Masculinity* (Duke University Press, 1998).
2 Halberstam, Judith. "The Good, The Bad, and the Ugly: Men, Women, and Masculinity," in *Masculinity Studies & Feminist Theory: New Directions*, Judith Kegan Gardiner, ed. (Columbia University Press, 2002).
3 Ibid. 347.
4 Ibid. 359.
5 Ibid. 360.

In cultures dominated by religion, men have occupied positions of power within the vast majority of churches around the world. Liturgical authority, along with the rules of morality that influence the creation of law within many non-secular societies, has been exclusively in the hands of men. The role of women within religious hierarchies has been and continues to be limited to supporting roles to men. While there is movement toward women taking more egalitarian roles in certain splinter denominations of major religions,[8] and with the controversial exception of possible matriarchal religions in prehistory,[9] the vast majority of world religions continue to find men holding the highest positions of liturgical power and authority throughout the world.

Politics and law are other areas that have historically been controlled by men, and like religion, have a profound effect on the lives of individuals. Those who are empowered to create law and those empowered to enforce law obviously possess an incredible amount of power over the populace of any society. Lawmakers construct behavioral rules, the violation of which can lead to the imposition of penalties small and large. Members of law enforcement have been imbued with the ability to use physical force, if necessary, to uphold law. In both the construction and enforcement of law, men have enjoyed overwhelming authority. When nations collide, military forces are often called upon to wage war, and, again, overwhelmingly these forces are led and fought by men. Some view this part of male dominance as being a count against male privilege, since soldiers lose limbs, suffer from innumerable traumas, and die in battle in the service of their countries. If soldiering is numerically dominated by men, critics point out that there is little enviable about this aspect of male dominance. But the spoils of war, as they are often called, usually flow to men in political power who order war, as well as to those in positions of military command in terms of multiplied and solidified regional, national, or international power. It is also the case that war is fraught with instances of rape, which means that even though men suffer greatly in war, women are often targeted by soldiers who view them as part of the gains of military occupation.

Science and technology are also areas that have been historically dominated by men. Most of the early explorers, along with the great majority of scholars who populated the bygone academic halls of science have been men. Various fields of technology that are the practical outgrowth of the theoretical sciences have been and continue to be populated largely by men, who then benefit both in terms of professional stature and financial remuneration as patents are established and a consumer base is roused into purchasing the many products that come to market. Early inventor and industrialist Henry Ford became famous and wealthy by designing the Model-T automobile and installing an automated assembly line for mass production.[10] Thomas Edison held more than 1,000 patents for the many inventions he devised, inventions that also generated him great fame and fortune.[11] But the fact that men have dominated these areas of endeavor, as we will see in chapter two of this text, have little to do with the notion that men are endowed with certain natural capacities for science and technology, and more to do with the access and opportunities that have attended male privilege for centuries.

Earned and Unearned Privilege

In principle, a privilege of one kind or another is usually considered to be either earned or unearned, although in practice, it is much more complex. In a great oversimplification, earned privileges are advantages gained through effort, while unearned privileges are advantages not gained through effort. If, for example, someone is able-bodied, while another person suffers from a physical disability of some kind, it is overwhelmingly likely that the able-bodied person possesses an unearned privilege. It is extremely unlikely that the able-bodied person, through some effort on his part, earned his able-bodied stature. Likewise, it is usually the case that someone who possesses a disability did not do something to deserve that disability. On the other hand, if a person rode a motorcycle over 100 miles per hour in the rain without wearing a helmet and subsequently crashes and suffers a traumatic brain injury, his recklessness contributes to his injury. But if someone is afflicted with muscular dystrophy, her illness is not due to some negligence on her part. The question is whether these straightforward examples apply to other examples of privilege.

It is commonly thought that it is unproblematic to assume that privileges are earned if one's advantages are the result of one's labor. If, for instance, someone receives good grades in school and subsequently attends an Ivy League law school, graduates with honors, and afterward lands a partnership position at a major law firm, the ***common sense*** view of privilege considers this to be an earned advantage. But what if the young person in question comes from an extremely wealthy family with political connections within the university or within American politics at large? Add to this the further stipulation that this person is white and male. In the first case, coming from a family of wealth and political connection is an unearned advantage, although it is clearly an advantage. A young person of inherited wealth has access to a vast array of educational resources the young, working class person almost certainly does not possess. For example, if the wealthy family decides to donate a large sum of money to the university, the young person will receive donor preferences, an advantage the working class person's family will be unable to match. Furthermore, the young person of wealth would be able to take advantage of legacy preferences at his target university if one of his parents is an alumnus, an advantage few working class, young people enjoy.

But what of being white and male? The fact that a young person is white and male is also unearned, but does that constitute an advantage? Imagine your target university is Harvard. Statistically, Harvard University admits approximately 18% black, Latino, and Native American total applicants each year, but only 7% of those admits are accepted under legacy policies.[12] Nationally, underrepresented ethnic minorities make up approximately 28% of the collective university student applicant pool, but less than 7% of legacy admits come from that same pool.[13] This means that, statistically, it is much more likely that white students will receive legacy points than underrepresented minority students, and being a legacy student matters. In 2009, Princeton University admitted 41% of its legacy candidates, which is 450% higher than the admittance rate for non-legacy candidates.[14] Some have defended legacy policies by arguing that children of alumni have a better chance of performing at high levels, but one study of Duke University legacy candidates revealed that legacy students underperformed non-legacy students in their first year, and other studies revealed similar patterns at a number of elite universities.[15] In 2013, 62% of students at Yale University were white, while 8% of students were African-American, even though 13.5% of Americans are African-American.[16] [17] What about being male? It turns out that only 18% of senior law partners nationwide are women,[18] and only 31% of American Bar Association members are women.[19] Only 19% of attorneys sitting on executive boards are women.[20] This means that our hypothetical young, male, white law school graduate has statistics in his favor over a hypothetical black, female law school graduate, even if they both work hard and graduate in similar places in their class.

This unearned advantage for white males is not arbitrary or mysterious. In the 1930s, sociologist, historian, and social activist W.E.B. DuBois coined the term **psychological wage** to mean special status or social compensation that divided labor such that low-earning white laborers felt superior and received perks not available to low-earning black laborers.[21]

This privilege was imparted to low-earning white laborers strictly due to the color of their skin, and hence the expression ***white-skinned privilege*** has since been used to emphasize the fact that the advantage is unearned. The ways that white-skinned privilege found expression was in the fact that although socioeconomically these white workers were on a par with black laborers who occupied similar jobs, white laborers were admitted to "public functions, public parks, and the best schools ... the police were drawn from their ranks [and] treated them with such leniency as to encourage lawlessness."[22] Peggy McIntosh, associate director of the Wellesley Centers for Women, follows this theme and applies it to both race and gender. In what McIntosh terms the ***invisible knapsack***, those who enjoy unearned privilege are often oblivious to the fact that they possess this privilege and will commonly deny it.[23] Of all the invisible knapsacks in existence, the weightiest of them all belongs to white males:

> The weightless and invisible backpack carried by white males is the largest and most expansive of all, granting them access to the most spaces with the least doubts about their sense of place or authority.[24]

FIGURE 1.2: W.E.B. DuBois (1868–1963)

Throughout the history of America, McIntosh argues, the opinions of white men have been considered more credible and important than those of any other group, regardless of the value of the opinion itself. This is not to say, of course, that every white male has identical privilege, since white males as a group can be parsed into subgroups where those, for instance, with greater physical strength, athletic ability, wealth, or social status will possess greater advantage than white males who do not enjoy these privileges. Working class, white males have less privilege than wealthy white males, but all white males tap into a legacy and heritage that extends advantage to them for no reason other than their gender and white skin. This entails, as cited above, that being male and black, Latino, Native American, Asian, Pacific Islander, or other non-white ethnic categories does not bestow the same degree of privilege on one as being male and white. But the stratification of male privilege also means that there are men who have far less privilege within cultural boundaries. If you are a black, homosexual, working class male dealing with disabilities, you enjoy far less privilege than an able-bodied, black, heterosexual male of wealth. Thus, socioeconomic class, sexual orientation, gender, being able-bodied and other traits that distinguish individuals from one another mitigate or accentuate privilege.

If McIntosh is correct, male privilege should be viewed as an outgrowth of patriarchy. It is privilege that comes about through an accident of birth in the context of living in a patriarchal culture. It means that being male gives men a statistical advantage over women with respect to how much money they earn as compared to women in the same job, or their ability to rise to and hold positions of authority and financial power. Male privilege also means that as a man, your opinions will probably be taken more seriously than the opinions of women. It means that when looking to role models, men will see many more men than women in positions of authority, including a history of men exclusively holding the office of President or Vice President of the United States, Chief Justice of the Supreme Court, and Senate Majority Leader or Whip. It means that almost all athletic icons in America are men. It means that for

FIGURE 1.3: Peggy McIntosh, Wellesley Centers for Women

*The "thought boxes" are possible in-class or homework exercises for students. They can also be used to organize class discussions around topics raised in chapters, or simply to provide food for thought.

THOUGHT BOX

The following *Huffington Post* article documents that very few women occupy management positions in Fortune 500 companies: http://www.huffingtonpost.com/2013/12/11/women-in-leadership-roles_n_4418725.html. Before reading the remainder of this chapter, discuss why you believe so few women are in executive positions today.

the majority of organized faiths in America, if you are a man of faith, you have the ability to rise in the ranks of a church or denomination that will exceed any heights to which women may rise. In means that for adherents of Western religions, it is to be told all your life that God is male. It means that as a man, your character will not be questioned nearly as much as will be true of a woman if you are suspected of having multiple sex partners. It means that as a man, you will not be called "a slut" based on what you are wearing, or be blamed for having been sexually assaulted based on how much alcohol you consumed. It includes the knowledge that, statistically, the likelihood of a man being raped is less than it is for women. It means that it is less likely that as a man, you will be sexually harassed at work or on the street. It means that, as a man, your likelihood of being a victim of intimate partner violence is less or less severe than it is for women. This is, of course, only a partial list of the perks that come with being male in America.

Patriarchy and Repressed Intersectionality

Even though white men have enjoyed the most advantage through patriarchal policies and practices, that does not mean that men of color do not also gain advantage through patriarchy. Race and gender scholar Moya Bailey coined the term **'misogynoir'** to mean "hatred of black women." It is a type of misogyny that denotes the cultural fact that blackness has been placed at the bottom of the cultural hierarchy in America as a matter of white supremacist policies and practices, while also noting that women have struggled under the yoke of patriarchy. The consequence of misogynoir is that black women, and other women of color, have suffered more than white women under white, capitalist, patriarchal conditions.

To understand how patriarchy became a part of American, black masculinity, author, cultural scholar, and social activist bell hooks explains that patriarchy was taught to African men by witnessing the ways that white, male slave-owners treated women and then mimicking these white men, which included a combination of **benevolent patriarchy** (controlling women psychologically and economically without the use of physical force) and **violent patriarchy** (controlling women by use of force). hooks writes:

> Transplanted African men, even those coming from communities where sex roles shaped the division of labor, where the status of men was different and most times higher than that of women, had to be taught to equate their higher status as men with the right to dominate women, they had to be taught patriarchal masculinity. They had to be taught that it was acceptable to use violence to establish patriarchal power. The gender politics of slavery and white-supremacist domination of free black men was the school where black men from different African tribes, with different languages and value systems, learned in the new world, patriarchal masculinity.[25]

By the twentieth century, black, male intellectuals were calling on black men to support gender equality rather than taking on the patriarchal norms of American culture. In 1920, influenced by black, female activist Anna Julia Cooper, W.E.B. DuBois implored black men to think about the ways they were treating black women,

> We cannot abolish the new economic freedom of women. We cannot imprison women again in a home or require them all on pain of death to be nurses and housekeepers. ... The uplift of women is, next to the problem of color and the peace movement, our greatest modern cause.[26]

hooks notes that sexist black people believed that slavery and racist indignity emasculated "Afro-American" men and that black women had the responsibility to revitalize black men by supporting and submitting to them.[27] The result has been termed **repressed intersectionality,** whereby one is "unable to understand how one's own identity is intersectional. It prevents individuals from realizing that the experience of marginalization is not unilateral across an oppressed population, and it obscures the recognition of internal differences within a group that suffers from sociopolitical domination."[28] The revitalization of black men, if it was to happen at all, would come at the price of subordinating black women.

It is this fundamental awareness of subordination within subordinated groups that fueled the **womanism** movement. Coined by author and poet Alice Walker, womanism acknowledges the oppression that black women, and other women of color, face that is not faced by white women. The roots of this movement find expression in the words of nineteenth-century abolitionist and women's activist Sojourner Truth, who in 1851 at a women's convention in Akron, Ohio, delivered a speech that reminded listeners that patriarchy was a double-bind for women of color:

> That man over there says that women need to be helped into carriages, and lifted over ditches, and to have the best place everywhere. Nobody ever helps me into carriages, or over mud-puddles, or gives me any best place! And ain't I a woman? Look at me! Look at my arm! I have ploughed and planted, and gathered into barns, and no man could head me! And ain't I a woman? I could work as much and eat as much as a man – when I could get it – and bear the lash as well! And ain't I a woman? I have borne thirteen children, and seen most all sold off to slavery, and when I cried out with my mother's grief, none but Jesus heard me! And ain't I a woman? Then they talk about this thing in the head; what's this they call it? [member of audience whispers, "intellect"] That's it, honey. What's that got to do with women's rights or negroes' rights? If my cup won't hold but a pint, and yours holds a quart, wouldn't you be mean not to let me have my little half measure full?[29]
>
> (excerpt from "Ain't I A Woman?")

By noting that "yours holds a quart" while "my cup won't hold but a pint", Truth scenically and forcefully makes the point that the plight of white women and women of color were struggles that did not begin at the same place. While all women were subjected to patriarchal proscriptions against voting, owning property, or receiving a college education, Truth reveals a great difference in treatment white women enjoyed that women of color, due strictly to skin color, did not enjoy.

Today, concerns about the mistreatment of women of color continue, including worries about high rates of domestic and sexual violence.[30] In addition, while pay gaps between men and women will be discussed later in the chapter, for women of color the pay gaps are wider than between men and white women.[31] In 2012, ABC News show *20/20* posted identical resumes on a widely used career website, but used the "blackest" and "whitest" names as determined by the book *Freakonomics* as the names attached to each resume. The results revealed that the resumes with "white names" were downloaded at a 20% higher rate than those with "black names." According to *Forbes magazine*, two women, one African-American, and one Latina, after experiencing frustration at their highly qualified resumes not receiving much attention, changed their names on the resumes to reflect "whiter-sounding" names and received much more attention.[32]

But patriarchal practices in America also favor white men over men of color. Between white men and men of color, a pay gap exists due to a host of factors that include educational disparities, occupational distribution disparities (white and Asian men occupy more executive and managerial occupations, while black and Latino men occupy more blue-collar, low-wage skilled and service industry jobs), outsourcing of labor-industry jobs overseas, the redistribution of manufacturing jobs outside of inner-city locations creating a commute problem, client-channeling (white employers assigning white employees to white clients and minority employees to minority clients), and, of course, racial discrimination in hiring. The consequences to race-based socioeconomic disparity are great. The median annual income level for black men in America is $23,738 compared to the annual median income level for white men at $36,785.[33] College-educated Hispanic men earn wages at roughly 80% of college-educated white men.[34] For Native Americans, the U.S. Census Bureau reports that one in four live in poverty, as compared to one in eleven white people.[35]

Early Justifications for Patriarchy and Male Privilege

There is really no adequate way to discuss the male privileges that flow from patriarchy without also discussing the female paucity of privilege, since the two are inseparably linked. But it has often been asked, on what basis can patriarchy be defended? In one of the more scathing indictments of patriarchy and the subordination of women that accompanies patriarchal systems, nineteenth-century British philosopher John Stuart Mill in collaboration with his wife Harriet Taylor Mill authored the piece "The Subjection of Women" to expose the poverty of ethical support for men's subordination of women by comparing it to slavery,

> the slavery of the male sex has in all countries of Christian Europe at least been at length abolished, and that of the female sex has been gradually changed into a milder form of dependence. But this dependence, as it exists at present ... is the primitive state of slavery lasting on ... the inequality of rights between men and women has no other source than the law of the strongest.[36]

Invoking the specter of slavery was meant to emphasize the proprietary nature of the most familiar relationships between men and women. Men were in positions of ownership while women were in positions of being property. Mill could find only one reason why men have subordinated women to a lower stratum of power and importance for the majority of human history: the physical ability to do so. In ethics, this principle is abbreviated *might makes right*, which Mill notes had long ago been abandoned as a reputable premise in moral argumentation. It is the kind of thinking that permeates prison environments, where physical strength and prowess command respect and obedience from those who are physically weaker. And yet few cultures around the world have not employed this sort of thinking in their support of the enslavement and subordination of people who did not enjoy social, political, and economic privileges. This unequal gendered exchange of power went unchallenged from ancient human history through the eighteenth century, except in limited and highly contested forms,[37] [38] and certainly found its way into the fiber of early American culture.

With the justification of male supremacy exposed as fraudulent, Mill and Taylor-Mill called for a complete enfranchisement for women, not as a courtesy, but as a demand. As Harriet Taylor Mill forcefully states:

> the fact which affords the occasion for this notice makes it impossible any longer to assert the universal acquiescence of women in their dependent condition. In the United States at least, there are women, seemingly numerous, and now organized for action on the public mind, who demand equality in the fullest acceptation of the word, and demand it by a straightforward appeal to men's sense of justice, not plead for it with timid depreciation of their displeasure.[39]

The fight for gender equality that took place in the nineteenth and twentieth centuries was met with great resistance. America's history itself is a history of arduous upheaval in the pursuit of social justice with patriarchy being high on the list of roadblocks. Each attempt or even suggestion at gender equality experienced a backlash from those who enjoyed advantage. Men created and maintained the patriarchal systems that ruled American society with unchallenged authority and were not going to allow women access to that authority without a fight.

A Truncated History of American Patriarchy

> As long as she thinks of a man, nobody objects to a woman thinking.
>
> ~ Virginia Woolf[40]

America was built on the principles of liberty and equality, but not for all. From the earliest moments of the European colonization of what would become the United States of America, women were placed in subordinate positions to men. Gender discrimination, many would argue, was woven into the fabric of Jefferson's *Declaration of Independence*, the second paragraph of which begins, "We hold these truths to be self-evident, that all men are created equal..."[41] *The Declaration*'s concept of equality has long been considered problematic in the face of slavery and the unequal treatment of men who were not land owners, along with the so-called "three-fifths compromise" included in Article I, section 2 of the U.S. Constitution.[42] But the exclusion of women from every position of political power when, in 1776, 56 men signed *The Declaration* speaks to a gender-literal interpretation of the phrase, "all men are created equal."

In the wake of the signing of the *Declaration of Independence*, discussions grew about the proper role of women in this new political alliance. Thomas Jefferson steadfastly refused to entertain the idea of women holding political office, claiming, "The appointment of a woman to office is an innovation for which the public is not prepared, nor I."[43] On education, Jefferson noted, "a plan for female education has never been a subject of systematic contemplation with me. It has occupied my attention so far as only the education of my own daughters occasionally required."[44] On the occasion of his oldest daughter's wedding, Jefferson wrote, "The happiness of your life now depends on continuing to please a single person. To this all other objects must be secondary, even your love for me."[45] In what he believed to be a compliment to American women, Jefferson stated, "Our good ladies, I trust, have been too wise to wrinkle their foreheads with politics. They are contented to soothe and calm the minds of their husbands returning from political debate."[46]

Jefferson was, of course, not alone in his views about women. When Abigail Adams, wife of second U.S. president John Adams, wrote to her husband to get him to consider giving voice and representation to women, John Adams sarcastically responded, "As to your extraordinary Code of Laws, I cannot but laugh. Depend upon it, We know better than to repeal our Masculine systems and rather than give up this, which would completely subject Us to the Despotism of the Petticoat, I hope General Washington and all our brave Heroes would fight."[47] John Quincy Adams, sixth president of the United States and son of John Adams, was known generally to have a dismissive attitude about the intelligence of women,[48] although in a speech given in 1838, he touted the right of people, men *and women*, to petition the government.[49] The inclusion of women into Adams's speech on rights and freedoms reveals a tension within the thinking of some colonial men of leadership with respect to their views on women. For instance, in a letter written to educator Albert Picket upon Picket's inquiry to James Madison about educating women in light of plans to build a women's college in Maryland, Madison wrote, "The capacity of the female mind for studies of the highest order cannot be doubted, having been sufficiently illustrated by its works of genius, of erudition, and of science."[50] Like today, there were men in colonial America who went against the tide of male, majority opinion, although those dissenting voices did not garner enough strength to bring about enfranchisement for women or an opening of doors to women in academia. The wheels of progressive change moved very slowly over the next several decades as patriarchy dominated almost every aspect of the early American political landscape.

By 1848, 68 women and 32 men signed ***The Declaration of Sentiments*** at the first women's rights convention to be organized by women, often referred to as the Seneca Falls Convention.[51] Along with key organizers Elizabeth Cady Stanton, Lucretia Coffin Mott, and Martha Coffin Wright, abolitionist Frederick Douglas attended and signed the *Declaration* in solidarity with women as individuals who, like people of African descent, suffered oppression and discrimination in America. As an attempt to point out the discriminatory content of the *Declaration of Independence*, the *Declaration of Sentiments* begins with the lines:

> We hold these truths to be self-evident: that all men *and women* are created equal; that they are endowed by their Creator with certain inalienable rights; that among these are life, liberty, and the pursuit of happiness; that to secure these rights governments are instituted, deriving their powers from the consent of the governed.[52]

The *Declaration* goes on to list the many rights and liberties denied to women by men, including voting rights, property rights, and rights to an education.[53] But against this call for equality, many voices rose in opposition to the notion that women should possess the same rights and privileges enjoyed by men. The most common reasons offered against women's suffrage included themes of male supremacy mixed with vague warnings about the alleged dire consequences of political power getting into the hands of women:

> It means competition of women with men.
> In some states more voting women than voting men will place the government under petticoat rule.
> It is unwise to risk the good we already have for the evil which may occur.[54]

Referring to a woman's undergarment, the expression "petticoat rule" was coined to derisively describe a gynocentric government where men were under the political dominion of women, which, it was assumed, would weaken men in incalculable ways. To add greater insult to women, anti-suffrage pamphlets were handed out to women that included statements like, "You do not need a ballot to clean out your sink spout."[55] Depicting suffragettes as angry, man-hating women was also a common theme to anti-suffragist propaganda.

University of Northern Iowa professor of communications and women's and gender studies Catherine Palczewski argues that even though concerns about men being feminized was not one of the central points being made against the suffrage movement,[56] postcards of the era were disseminated showing men taking on domestic work considered to be proper to women with the clear connotation that women would now be found running the household, placing men in subordinate and dignity-defying domestic positions.

The anti-suffrage propaganda was supposed to serve as a scare tactic to get men to fear what may happen if women receive voting power, but also points to the unapologetic

FIGURE 1.4: Anti-suffrage Propaganda Poster, circa late nineteenth century

FIGURE 1.5: Anti-Suffrage Postcards, circa early twentieth century

patriarchy of the day, since men thought nothing of their wives having to do the very same household chores considered to be work beneath their dignity as men.

In 1870, in the wake of the end of the Civil War and as part of the Reconstructionist Amendments, the fifteenth amendment to the constitution was ratified after a contentious debate ensued over extending voting rights to those who had previously been denied those rights due to "race, color, or previous condition of servitude."[57] Excluded from this debate and newfound enfranchisement were women, sparking a 50-year-long debate on women's suffrage that, in 1920, would terminate in the ratification of the nineteenth amendment to the constitution.[58] What was once thought to be a naïve dream was finally a reality: women had achieved the constitutional right to vote. But, of course, sexism and gender exclusionism did not end with the ratification of the nineteenth amendment. The right to vote was only a prelude to women's ongoing struggles to gain political, economic, educational, and social empowerment. It was not until 1949 that a woman served as a U.S. District Judge,[59] and as covered in chapter three of this text, many American universities did not admit women until the latter part of the twentieth century.[60]

Among the many legal watershed moments that have continued to push America toward greater levels of gender equality is the 1963 Equal Pay Act, which requires employers to provide equal pay for equal work regardless of gender.[61] Title VII of the Civil Rights Act of 1964 banned gender discrimination by private employers,[62] and contraceptives became available to married women in 1965[63] and to single women in 1972.[64] Also in 1972, The Equal Rights Amendment, which declared, "Equality of rights under the law shall not be denied or abridged by the United States or by any State on account of sex," passed through Congress, but fell three state votes short of ratification.[65] In 1973, the historic decision to grant a woman the right to an abortion was made in the now famous case of *Roe v. Wade*.[66] The slow march toward gender equality continues today, but as with runners held back in a race, there is a documented lag-effect that many work to bridge. The categories in the remainder of this chapter represent some of the more salient areas of inequality that continue to exist between women and men, and that are considered by many to be the accumulative effects of centuries of patriarchy.

MARGINALIZED MASCULINITIES

When we speak about masculinities, it is important to note that there are many versions of masculinity that do not enjoy dominant, hegemonic status. That men enjoy privilege in many areas of cultural life is abundantly clear and will be discussed in sections below. But as covered in sections above, this does not mean that all men share equally in privilege. There are hierarchies of privilege that are mitigated or enhanced by race, ethnicity, socioeconomic class, sexual orientation, gender identity, and other factors that are not always part of the mainstream discussions about male privilege, such as being able-bodied, enjoying cognitive health, being tall in stature in a culture that prizes tall men, being athletic in a culture that values athletics, being cis-gender in a culture that denigrates trans and queer identities or those who identify as agender.

For many boys and men who do not conform to culturally approved masculine standards, life can be difficult. American culture has long reinforced a very specific gendered-binary structure. As a thought experiment, how many different traits can you list that are considered to be favorable male traits in American culture and how many different traits can you list that are considered to be adverse male traits in American culture? Are there cultures within cultures that view these traits in a more positive or negative light? When looking at the following images, are some male representations considered to be more acceptable than others by mainstream, contemporary cultural standards? Why? Who within American culture, in your opinion, are making these rules?

FIGURE 1.6:

FIGURE 1.7:

Continued

FIGURE 1.8:

FIGURE 1.9:

If you acknowledge that gender nonconformist men are often mistreated, why do you believe this is? Why is gender conformity so important to mainstream culture? More importantly, what must happen, in your opinion, for these marginalized masculinities to be accepted and respected in American culture?

Male Dominance in Business and Economics

> Rail as they will about 'discrimination,' women are simply not endowed by nature with the same measures of single-minded ambition and the will to succeed in the fiercely competitive world of Western capitalism.
>
> ~ Pat Buchanan, senior advisor to Presidents Richard Nixon, Gerald Ford, and Ronald Reagan[67]

When you mix the patriarchal value of placing men in favored positions in society with the survival of the fittest values of free-market economics, you get **patriarchal capitalism**, whereby the rich tend to get richer and the rich tend to be men. Surveying the Fortune 500 companies in America, there are currently 25 that have a female CEO, which equates to 5% of all F-500 corporations.[68] Another way of stating it is that 95% of Fortune 500 corporations are run by men. If we examine the finance and insurance industry, we find that 23.1% of all senior officers are women, while 76.9% are men.[69] While these levels actually represent strides that women have made in business as compared to percentages a decade ago,[70] the gender gap in business and finance is tremendous. Additionally, according to statistics compiled by the Bureau of Labor, the median weekly salary for men who occupy full-time management positions is $1,349 as opposed to women who earn $973 weekly in the same positions.[71] This means that women earn approximately 72% of what men earn for doing the same job.[72] If we calculate these numbers out to represent annual salaries, men in full-time management positions average approximately $70,148 per year as opposed to women in the same positions who earn $50,596 per year.

Breaking these numbers down into more specific fields, male chief executive officers in the U.S. earn a median weekly income amount of $2,266, while female chief executive officers earn a median weekly income amount of $1,811.[73] Male financial managers earn a median weekly amount of $1,518, while female financial managers earn a median weekly amount of $1,064.[74] These amounts represent 79% and 70% respectively for women who are doing the same job as their male counterpart despite the legal precedents set in the past. Male human resource managers earn a median weekly salary of $1,536 compared to female human resource managers who earn a median weekly salary of $1,240.[75] Male marketing and sales managers earn a weekly median salary of $1,658, compared to females in the identical job who earn $1,124 per week.[76] In fact, in every category of employment that has to do with business and financial management taken collectively, women earn approximately 75 cents on the dollar that men earn.[77] Multiplied out over an entire year, men who work in business and financial management average approximately $73,424 in wages, while women in identical jobs earn approximately $54,548.[78]

Many women's advocates have been pointing out for years that there is a pay gap for women who hold identical jobs to men, but have been largely ignored or ridiculed. One way that skeptics attempt to undermine the pay gap is to purport that women work fewer hours than men,[79] or that women pursue low-paying jobs in fields where there is already a glut of women,[80] or that women having children impedes their earning potential,[81] or that women do not possess as much ambition as men or do not push as hard as men for raises and career advancement.[82] This latter assessment was offered by Chief Operating Officer for social media giant Facebook, Sheryl Sandberg, in her 2013 book *Lean In: Women, Work, and the Will to Lead.*[83] Sandberg argues that both external and internal obstacles conspire to prevent women from achieving the goals in business that men routinely enjoy. Sandberg's advice on overcoming the internal obstacles is for women to be more proactive in pursuing goals, less concerned with appearing to be pleasant, taking greater risks for greater rewards, and "not checking out of work mentally" when planning a family.

The criticisms of Sandberg's advice to women have been numerous. But one of the more persistent objections comes from those who argue that the rules of corporate America are the same rules that govern most patriarchal systems,[84] and that Sandberg is informing women that the key to women's success is for women to play a man's game by men's rules that were invented to sustain men's power. NYU sociologist Robert Max Jackson explains that to understand male power in the corporate realm is to first understand that the history of capitalism and industrialization is a history of men having a monopoly over capital and resources, so that anyone who hopes to ascend to economic prominence must receive the support of those men who control capital and resources.[85] Referring to "**powerful men**" as distinguished from "**ordinary men**," Jackson argues that "gender inequality is an instance of status inequality."[86] For inequality to maintain itself, systems must be in place to "deny subordinate people the means to overcome their disadvantages," without which, inequality becomes unstable.[87] A problem for "powerful men" is that subordinated people will inevitably attempt to overcome their subordinate status.

However, the early advances into corporate America by women were principally into positions of dead-end jobs that did not promise upward mobility, as a result of stereotypical thinking about women by the men who held corporate power.[88] A persistent view held by many corporate executives in 1965, for instance, according to a Harvard Business Review survey, was the view that women are not capable of commanding the necessary respect and confidence to lead a corporation, while half of the men surveyed went even further to state that women were "temperamentally unfit for management."[89] These sorts of preconceived notions about women do not exist in a vacuum. Jackson sites three main social conditions that historically kept women from achieving positions of economic power, and which many argue continue to obstruct women from achieving professional success:

1. Men were unwilling to promote women into positions of power due to concerns about their own futures, based in large part on prejudiced views about women's abilities to lead.
2. Discriminatory views about women have a cumulative effect. Each step up the corporate ladder eliminated a round of male candidates. The upward mobility of men into positions of power was usually the result of competition between men, which creates a disadvantage for women who, by the end of the competitive process, make up less than 1% of those men still in the running for an upper management position.
3. Women did not aspire to positions of political and economic power because they were not socialized as were men to prove themselves in this way.[90]

This three-pronged account created a cycle of male privilege that systematically prevented women from reaching leadership positions in government and business. But the third of these accounts, that women are not socialized to compete in the same ways as are men, speaks to the advice given by Sandberg. If women are taught to be reticent in challenging male power from girlhood to adulthood, it would make sense that they would not feel comfortable asserting themselves into positions historically and presently dominated by men. But this does not discount the fact that men's power is due in part to men's continued prejudicial belief, whether consciously or unconsciously, that women are not designed to lead or to make quick, sharp decisions in the face of complicated predicaments or under the pressures of demanding deadlines. If men sustain these views about women, it would explain why men tend to offer advancement more readily to other men, even if a woman is as qualified or even more qualified than her male counterpart.

With respect to jobs that are traditionally or predominantly held by men, research has shown that women with identical qualifications are routinely evaluated lower than men.[91] One of the more visible areas of male domination in the workforce is found on Wall Street, where women make up only 16% of senior management and 0% of Chief Executive Officers.[92] Former stock analyst for Paine Webber, Margo Epprecht reports that women were cut substantially in the wake of the 1987 stock market crash, cuts that have been painstakingly slow to rehabilitate in the wake of the market recovery.[93] According to Epprecht, "on Wall Street, to advance, women must fit into the male-dominated, hierarchical world of Wall Street—or leave." Epprecht cites the many anecdotal stories of women who worked in Wall Street careers and later left after dealing with sexism and outright harassment.[94] Business psychologist Sharon Horowitz agrees stating, "Wall Street is a specific culture; it is a specific culture of men."[95] When critics note that there are many women working jobs on Wall Street, Epprecht points to the fact that the EEOC reports that more than half of those jobs are in a clerical capacity, while only 16% of those jobs are in positions of management.[96] When other critics claim that men are better suited for the fast-paced, fast-thinking environment of Wall Street, Epprecht notes that when Wall Street legend Jack Rifkin instituted a gender-egalitarian policy of management hiring in the equity research division of Lehman Brothers, many more women were hired, sending Lehman Brothers in four years from the fifteenth ranked research department to the number one ranked research department on Wall Street. Boris Groysberg of Harvard Business School, citing the Rifkin case as one example, states:

> The biggest beneficiaries of having more women are men. If you embrace diversity of perspective, you will get more men and women with fresh perspectives. If we think about performance of an organization, we are going to do so much better if we embrace different perspectives. [97]

Yet when men on Wall Street are asked why a gender gap persists at the management level, they report that there are not enough qualified women to occupy the available positions, to which Groysberg scoffs, "We cannot find a couple of hundred qualified women to sit on boards? I think it's outrageous."[98]

In fact, the number of women taking the GMAT exam (the admissions test for entry into MBA programs and other business graduate programs) is at all-time highs.[99] *Fortune* magazine reports that the number of women pursuing graduate degrees in business has increased as business schools actively recruit women to address the shortages of female students in business programs overall.[100] Women now make up approximately one-third of MBA recipients each year, which represents a substantial increase from a decade ago, but still points to an overall underrepresentation of women receiving graduate business degrees compared to men.[101] Yet even after graduating, women are receiving job offers at half the rate of men despite submitting 20% more job applications than men.[102]

One of the many ways that corporations remain male-centric is found in the interviewing process, where different questions are asked of female versus male job candidates. One study uncovered familiar trends in interviewing practices that create an uneven playing field for women.[103] Even though it is unlawful under Title VII to ask a female job applicant if she has children or is planning to have children,[104] women are routinely asked about their family lives and whether the demands of their families would impede their ability to give their all to the job for which they applied, questions that male applicants rarely if ever face. Those in positions of hiring often violate the law by asking women about their families or potential families, because they know that it is virtually impossible to prove that not receiving a job was the result of discrimination along with the fact that there are no recording devices in place during interviews to document the questions being asked.

But even in the absence of actual legal infractions, there are other aspects of the interviewing process that favor men over women. In an *ABC News* report citing a Yale University hiring experiment, actors were employed to go into job interviews with identical resumes and identical interview scripts to see whether the applicants would be evaluated differently on the basis of gender.[105] For instance, in one rehearsed answer to questions about computer operating system literacy, both the male and female applicants responded to hiring personnel, "I know the Windows operating system like the back of my hand." In hundreds of evaluations by those in hiring positions, the female job applicant was later assessed as being arrogant, aggressive, and bossy, while the male job applicant was viewed as being competent, knowledgeable, and more hirable. The fact that both males and females in positions of hiring evaluated the male candidate as being superior to the female candidate suggests that gender bias is engrained in the perceptions of both men and women in advance of interviews taking place, and that gender bias in hiring is an equal opportunity discriminatory practice.

There is little doubt that a gender gap exists both in human resource percentages, salary range in the fields of business and finance, and the ways that women are treated in the workplace as opposed to men. When asked "why?" many note that patriarchal systems infused with prejudicial beliefs about women must be ranked high on the list of candidates for an answer. If money equals power in capitalist America, and if men overwhelmingly occupy positions of economic power, while viewing women as mentally inferior, overly emotional, or at least unsuited for fast-paced, competitive environments, then as long as men of these kind occupy positions of leadership in high finance, the strides women make into management fields, where multi-million or multi-billion dollar accounts are considered to be commonplace, change will be slow and arduous.

Male Privilege, Politics, and Law

> To promote a woman to bear rule, superiority, dominion or empire, above any realm, nation, or city, is repugnant to nature; it is the subversion of good order, of all equity and justice.
>
> ~ sixteenth-century theologian John Knox[106]

Often going hand-in-hand with business and finance are the realms of politics and law where political and legal decisions regularly impact business. Many people today view politics as a changing, gendered realm that can no longer be considered in the control of men, while others note that men continue to be greatly overrepresented in U.S. politics. A joint study conducted by American University professor Jennifer L. Lawless and Loyola Marymount University professor Richard L. Fox, shows current percentages of women in government to be as shown in Table 1.1.[107]

In their study, Lawless and Fox identify seven factors they believe contribute to the ongoing gender gap in politics:

1. Women are substantially more likely than men to perceive the electoral environment as highly competitive and biased against female candidates.
2. Hillary Clinton and Sarah Palin's candidacies aggravated women's perceptions of gender bias in the electoral arena.
3. Women are much less likely than men to think they are qualified to run for office.
4. Female potential candidates are less competitive, less confident, and more risk averse than their male counterparts.
5. Women react more negatively than men to many aspects of modern campaigns.
6. Women are less likely than men to receive the suggestion to run for office—from anyone.
7. Women are still responsible for the majority of childcare and household tasks.

TABLE 1.1

U.S. Senate:	18%
Members of the House of Representatives:	16.8%
State Governors:	12%
Statewide Elected Officials:	22.4%
State Legislators:	23.6%
Mayors of the 100 largest U.S. Cities:	8%

Lawless and Fox conclude that women are turned off by the toxic, negative campaign ads, the gendered scrutiny female candidates receive, and the overall hostile climate of contemporary, American politics. These things, coupled with a general lack of support, lead fewer women to climb into the political arena.

An example of the blowback some women receive who become politically active can be illustrated in the case of Sandra Fluke, a social justice attorney who in 2012 testified before congress about the importance of contraception coverage in health insurance.[108] Within days, right-wing radio talk show host Rush Limbaugh took to the airwaves calling Ms. Fluke a "slut" and a "prostitute" for what Limbaugh viewed as her promotion of casual sex.[109] Limbaugh was castigated for this sexist and mean-spirited attack and later apologized to Fluke, although many viewed the apology as insincere.[110] Yet, in a report by *USA Today*, the effects of sexist name-calling have been linked to voter approval ratings.[111] In a survey of 800 likely voters who were asked to evaluate two hypothetical congressional candidates, one male, one female, after sexist name-calling was used by the male to refer to his female opponent, including characterizing her as a "prostitute," the female candidate lost twice as much support as she had before the sexist taunts.[112] The use of sexist name-calling, then, may have a two-pronged effect: (1) fewer women will want to jump into politics, knowing that they will be subjected to this sort of personal attack, and, (2) fewer female candidates will win elections if sexist name-calling has an efficacious effect on voters.

In terms of international percentages of women as national legislators, the U.S. ranks ninety-first in the world, three percentage points lower than the international average of all nations taken collectively.[113] Cynthia Terrell, chairperson for the Representation 2020 Project, notes that given the extremely slow rate of progress, "women won't achieve fair representation for nearly 500 years." Columbia University economist Howard Steven Friedman agrees and reports:

> It took more than 130 years for American women to gain the right to vote and it wasn't until 1933 that the U.S. saw its first female Cabinet secretary, yet there still hasn't been a female vice president or president.[114]

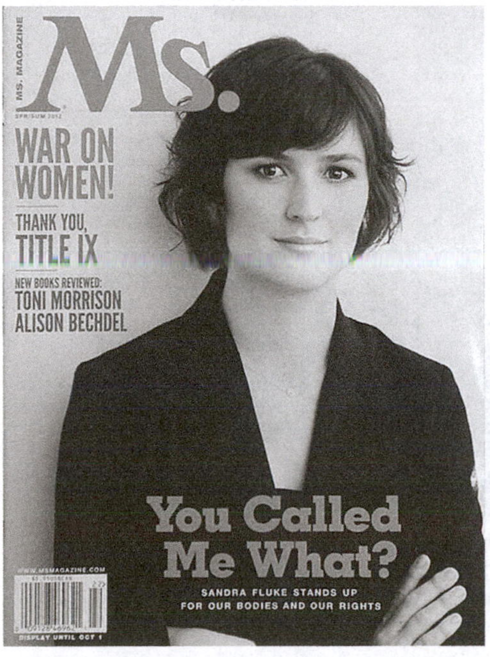

FIGURE 1.10: Sandra Fluke on the cover of Ms. Magazine

Friedman wonders whether advancement for women in American politics may actually be in decline and admits that gender quotas will not be accepted in American politics as they are in Belgium, Korea, Portugal, and Spain, nor voluntary party quotas as found in Australia, Canada, France, Germany, Greece, Italy, Netherlands, and the U.K. What he proposes is the idea of a voting process that adopts a **proportional representation** method, whereby "the number of seats won by a party or group of candidates is proportionate to the number of votes received," which might encourage more women to enter politics, instead of the current winner-takes-all approach.[115]

Turning to the legal profession, according to the American Bar Association, men outnumber women in the legal profession by a ratio of two to one, and women are receiving J.D. degrees at slightly less than half the rate of men.[116] When turning to federal court judges, three of the nine Supreme Court justices are women, 31% of Circuit Court of Appeals judges are women, and 24% of Federal Court judges are women.[117] Turning to state courts, 27% of all state court judges in the U.S. are women.[118] Taking all judges in the U.S. collectively, at both state and federal levels, women make up 27.1%.[119] The *Wall Street Journal* reports that women make up only 17% of equity partners with ownership stakes at the 200 top-grossing law firms in America and that, overall, female attorneys earn approximately 25% less than their male counterparts.[120]

Joan C. Williams, professor at the University of California, Hastings College of Law asks us to imagine a law firm partner.[121] So let's do so. Our typical image, Williams suggests, is that of a white man. In fact, white men make up the majority of law firm partners in America. But this means that many people will judge an individual against this ideal, which is a case of what Williams terms **descriptive bias**, forming a preconceived image.[122] One concern about descriptive bias is that it can often convert into **prescriptive bias**, whereby one may come to believe that a law firm partner *ought* to resemble the preconceived image. If white males are the default presumption of what law partners should look like, the consequences to women and men of color is fairly obvious. Williams also informs readers that in a survey of 700 female law firm partners conducted by the Project for Attorney Retention and the Minority Corporate Counsel Association, one-third of the women reported having been bullied, threatened, or intimidated out of origination

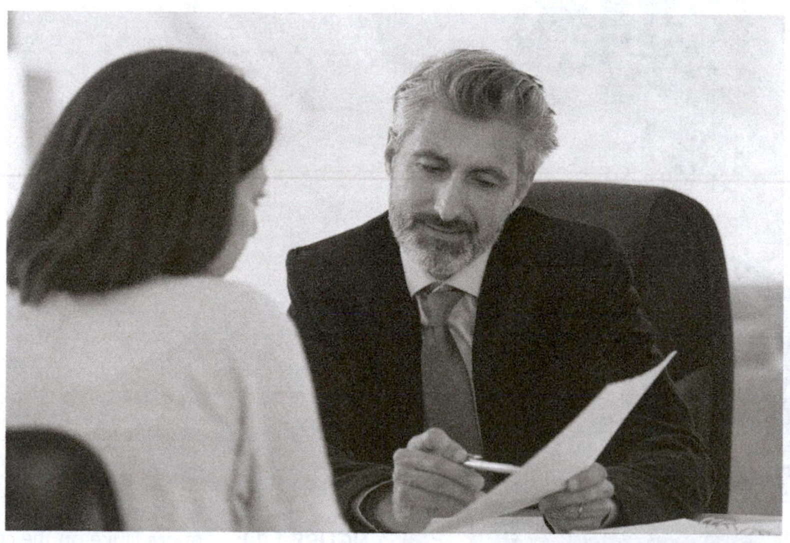

FIGURE 1.11:

credit, a key factor in setting compensation.[123] In addition, the survey found that 20% of women who are law firm partners report that no women sit on compensation committees for their firms.[124] MCCA Executive Director Veta Richardson explains that "with few women on compensation committees and in top management positions, female law firm partners' ability to influence compensation decisions and address salary differentials is limited."[125] Attorney and partner at Fine, Kaplan, and Black, Roberta D. Liebenberg also views as troubling the trend by many law firms to use staff attorneys, who, while being made up overwhelmingly of women, receive substantially lower pay, have less job security, and possess no real opportunities for advancement.[126] Liebenberg identifies this trend as being responsible for what she terms an **inverse pyramid** for women in law careers, whereby the higher up in a law firm you go, the less women you will see.[127]

But there are also concerns about gender bias in the workplace once women receive employment in professional careers. In a memo entitled "Presentation Tips for Women," from international law firm Clifford Chance, female attorneys were given the following advice on their courtroom appearances:

> Use harder words … pretend you're in moot court, not the high school cafeteria … don't giggle … don't squirm … if wearing a skirt, make sure the audience can't see up it … wear a suit, not your party outfit … think Lauren Bacall, not Marilyn Monroe … no one heard Hillary the day she showed cleavage.[128]

Calling the memo 'patronizing' and questioning the condescending and paternalistic language of the piece, attorney Marilyn Stowe stated, "I hope I speak for other female lawyers when I say this: when it comes to the contents of our wardrobes, stop worrying about the size of our earrings and leave us to get on with doing a good job."[129] The law firm responded by claiming that the sexism found in the memo was "unintentional" and sought exoneration by insisting that the memo was drafted by a female partner.[130]

Academia and Gender Bias

> When a woman turns to scholarship, there is usually something wrong with her sexual opportunities.
>
> ~ Frederick Nietzsche

The history of the teaching profession has been one that favors women over men, but this is only with respect to K through 12 education, and particularly elementary and middle school where women currently make up 80% of teachers.[131] One theory for this disparity is that women view themselves as childcare providers, while men do not.[132] In fact, a slew of pieces have been written that denigrate public school teaching as "glorified babysitting."[133] [134] Also, at a median annual salary of $40,000 nationally, primary education does not pay well compared to other occupations.[135] However, Susan H. Fuhrman, president of Teachers College at Columbia University, views the gender disparity in teaching as involving much more than low wages:

> Women went into it without other options and it was a low-status profession that was associated with women, and the fact that it's now dominated by women inhibits the status from increasing. [136]

That teaching does not carry a great deal of status in contemporary society may be a central reason why men do not seek careers in teaching. In fact, principals around the country are made up of 50% men, a profession that carries more status.[137] When turning to college professorships, men outnumber women at a ratio of approximately 60% to 40% nationally.[138] There is little doubt that the prestige of being a college or university professor is considered by many to be greater than being a K through 12 teacher. When coupled with the fact that males are socialized away from childcare as being "women's work,"[139] the gender disparity found in both primary education and higher education makes sense. Yet some educators argue that boys need to see more male teachers at the primary levels of education to serve as role models for boys who currently do not view men in the roles of working with children.[140] Still, even though women are now graduating college and attending graduate school at higher rates than men,[141] women still find it difficult to receive advancement within their disciplines at the same rate enjoyed by men. A study by the University of Maine revealed that women take up to 24.2% longer to advance to the rank of "full professor" within their given areas of specialization.[142] Why this is has become the focus of a number of studies around the nation.

In what has been called **implicit** or **unconscious gender bias**, one now famous study was conducted by researchers at the University of Wisconsin to see whether there existed gender bias in hiring based on reviews of the curricula vitae of two tenure candidates.[143] In the study, 238 professors of psychology in positions of hiring were given for review the curricula vitae of tenure candidates. They were asked to assess the candidates on teaching, research, and service experience in an attempt to discover which candidates were more qualified, more hirable, and at what appropriate opening salary the individual should be paid. The psychology professors were given two CVs for review; one identified the applicant as "Brian Miller," the other identified the applicant as "Susan Miller," when in fact the two CVs were identical in content. Nothing whatsoever was different between the two CVs other than the names cited at the top of the page. In the majority of cases, "Brian Miller" was considered to be better qualified, more hirable, and better situated to open at a higher salary than "Susan Miller." When the reviewers were

FIGURE 1.12: "Teacher"

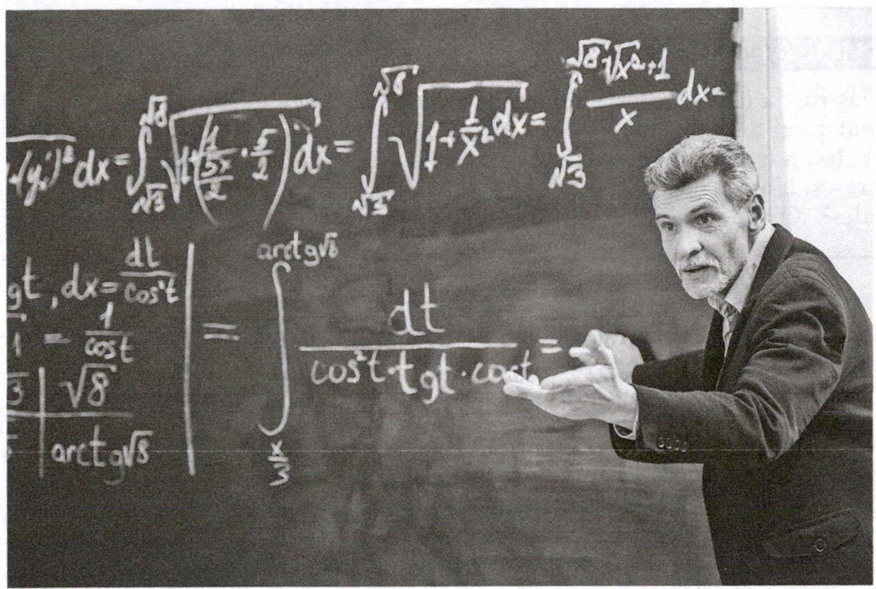

FIGURE 1.13: "Professor"

informed that they had reviewed identical CVs with only the names being different, they were shocked. Even though approximately half of the reviewers were women, the results were consistent. Both male and female reviewers had either consciously or unconsciously selected a male over a female as being more qualified and deserving of a higher salary. These results have been replicated in other, similar studies.[144]

In another study of over 300 recommendation letters for medical faculty at a large U.S. medical school, letters for female applicants were shorter (less than 10 lines) than male applicants (over 50 lines), provided minimal assurance, and raised more doubt about their abilities than male applicants.[145] The letters also more frequently mentioned women's personal lives than did the letters written for men. The specific language used for female applicants referred to "her teaching" or "her training," while language used for male applicants referred to "his research," or "his career," making male candidates appear to be more confident and competent. As expected, in academic medicine, female physicians advance more slowly toward seniority than male physicians and earn less than their male counterparts.[146]

In a joint study conducted by researchers from Rice University and the University of Houston, similar investigations demonstrated that the language used to describe male job applicants and female job applicants for academic positions was remarkably gendered in nature.[147] The authors of the study note, "(a) that women were described as more communal and less agentic than men and (b) that communal characteristics tend to have negative significance with hiring personnel in academia that are based on letters of recommendation."[148] In describing female applicants, communal comments such as "'She's very nice,' 'She's outgoing,' 'She's so helpful to the students'" abound, while comments supporting male candidates stress the applicants' leadership and administrative abilities. As University of Pennsylvania's chair of legal studies Janice Bellace notes, "You can tell the people writing letters actually support the women. It's just that when you compare them to the letters written about men, you begin to see differences."[149] Bellace argues that these differences, while unconscious and coming from well-intentioned individuals, create gender bias that extend an advantage to men over women in academic employment.

THOUGHT BOX

Construct a list of words and phrases that are agentic in quality (pro-active, self-regulating) and another list that are communal in quality (nurture-based). Find articles, advertisements, and other materials that make use of these words and phrases. How many of the words are describing females; how many are describing males? What do you conclude from your investigation?

In 2012, researchers at Yale University were interested in seeing whether this same pattern of implicit gender bias was present in the hiring of applicants for positions in science.[150] Researchers asked 127 scientists to evaluate job applications for science-related job openings. Identically qualified applicants were rated for competency and hire-ability. Both male and female evaluators ranked male applicants higher than female applicants in both categories.[151] Jo Handelsman, professor of molecular, cellular, and developmental biology at Yale University decided to take the study further. In coordination with colleagues, Handelsman provided 200 academic researchers with an application from a senior undergraduate student to evaluate for a position as lab manager.[152] Unbeknownst to the researchers, they had all received the same application with a randomly selected male or female name identifying the applicant. Once again, both male and female researchers ranked the male as being more competent and were willing to pay him $4,000 more than the female applicant.[153]

In 1998, social scientists introduced the Implicit Association Test (IAT) to measure **implicit cognition** (cognitive processes of which one has no conscious awareness).[154] The way it works is to show a subject a picture with words in the upper left and right corners, or words with other words in these positions in order for the subject to associate words with objects or words with other words. The test purports to be able to demonstrate whether a subject holds implicit or unconscious bias. In the case of the Gender-Career

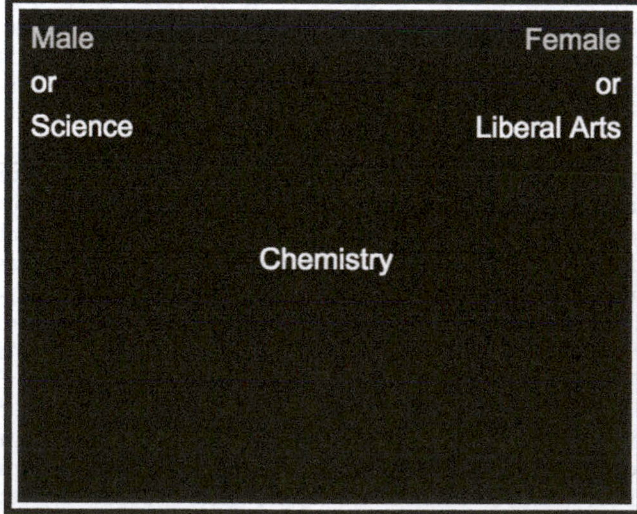

FIGURE 1.14: Example of an Implicit Association Test (IAT) applied to gender

IAT, most people associate 'women' with liberal arts and 'men' with science. Similarly, most people associate 'women' with 'family' and 'men' with 'career'.[155] Supporters of the IAT argue that a similar process is occurring when women or men are interviewed for a job or when memos, such as the Clifford Chance memo noted above, are disseminated to a workforce without malicious intent.

Researchers from Harvard University, University of Washington, and University of Virginia note that the IAT has been given to hundreds of thousands of people via computer and that implicit bias has been found in subjects as young as four years of age. A further finding reports that "those people who show stronger IAT-measured biases against a target social group are also more likely to discriminate against that target group and its members,"[156] a finding that has clear implications for job interviews, advancement, retention, and voting patterns.

STUDENTS

IAT tests can be taken online at https://implicit.harvard.edu/implicit/ to check to see whether you hold unconscious bias.

Yet another way that male privilege seeps into academia is in the way that scholars are invited or accepted to speak at conferences. In a study conducted by researchers at the University of California, Davis, an analysis of 21 annual meetings of the American Association of Physical Anthropologists revealed that within the subfield of primatology, women give more poster presentations than talks, whereas men give more talks than posters.[157] A poster presentation is a conference presentation that makes use of a poster often in tandem with a Power-Point visual aid. A conference "talk" is considered to be more prestigious than a poster presentation. When applying for a spot at a conference, applicants must determine whether to submit their contribution as a "talk" or a "poster," which means that self-selection is part of the process of deciding who will receive the more distinguished spot in the schedule. Otherwise, the identity of the applicant remains blinded to those sitting on the conference panels, individuals who will ultimately determine which talks or posters will be included at the conference. The highest level of esteem goes to those contributors who are invited to speak at the conference. The findings of the U.C. Davis study demonstrate that when the conference panel members are made up entirely of women, there was no difference between the number of women speaking at a conference and the percentage of women in the field.[158] However, "male-organized symposia have half the number of female first authors (29%) that symposia organized by women (64%) or by both men and women (58%) have, and half that of female participation in talks and posters (65%)."[159] Writing for *Psychology Today*, Kristian Marlow suggests that the tendency for men to invite other men to speak at conferences may be the result of what he terms **homophily**, the view that some men feel more comfortable working with other men in the belief that they will have more in common.[160]

Stanford University researchers, working with the National Science Foundation, identified a host of studies that demonstrate the many ways that gender bias finds its way into academic sciences.[161] The collective studies found the following pervasive problems:

- Women who were assertive were perceived as competent, but not pleasant, which convert into women facing prejudice in leadership evaluations.
- Decades of "draw-a-scientist" research indicate that children tend to depict scientists as men, reinforcing a persistent stereotype that scientists are men.

- Male associate professors are two and a half times more likely to be advanced to full professorship, even when age, time since Ph.D., field, and measures of academic productiveness (such as output of books and peer-reviewed articles) are controlled for.
- Gendered beliefs about competency may influence career choice. Boys tend to evaluate their abilities in math higher that do girls, even when test scores are equal. Self-rated competency has a direct effect on students selecting majors in college.
- Male professors are judged to be more competent by students than female professors, even when actors implementing identical scripts posing as guest professors were hired to speak to students in physics classes.
- Sexual harassment continues to exist within academic sciences.

When taken together, a pattern of obstacles emerges for women in academia and science that are not in place for men, and that have the potential for long-term, negative consequences for women who work at colleges and universities. In fact, the sixth obstacle for women in academia (sexual harassment) is one that is foreign to the experiences of most male professors. If anything, stories continue to appear in mainstream news coverage that uncover yet another investigation into allegations or findings confirming that a male professor has sexually harassed students.[162] Furthermore, assertive women are often interpreted as pushy and unpleasant, while the same trait in men is commonly viewed as a strength and grounds for leadership consideration. These double-standards are more evidence of male privilege that is a mainstay in contemporary academia.

THE "BENEVOLENT SEXISM" OF CONSERVATIVE CHRISTIANITY

In October, 2014, Kristen Davis Eliason, Dr. Elizabeth Lewis Hall, and Tamara L. Anderson published an article entitled, "Benevolent sexism's manifestation and expression in conservative Christianity: Measurement issues and religious correlates" that exposed the sexist practices found in Evangelical Christian colleges and universities.[1] By "benevolent sexism," the authors mean "sexism that is not overtly hostile."[2] In fact, benevolent sexism, they inform us, usually comes in the form of a warm, friendly environment, but undermines opportunities for women due strictly to the fact that they are women. Within Evangelical Christian populations, women are believed to be designed to nurture and raise children, while men are believed to be designed to lead, protect, and provide for their families. Specifically, Dr. Hall argues in an interview with *Christianity Today*,

> Many women faculty on the evangelical campus in the study reported feeling undermined at work by implicit assumptions that they should be home with their children, or that the qualities that are valued in academia—intelligence, assertiveness, and confidence—are not traits appropriate for Christian women.[3]

The consequences of this sexist treatment is that female faculty members at conservative Christian universities are often passed over for advancement, which, argues Hall, explains why there is such a disparity between male and female faculty who reach the level of "full professor" and who gain access to sabbaticals, funding, and course release for research. Male and female colleagues are also discouraged from socializing with one another over coffee or meals in the fear that sexual temptation will overcome them. These concerns and the disadvantages for women in these settings that include pay inequality spring from what Hall terms "a dominant theology of gender hierarchy."[4]

1 http://www.apadivisions.org/division-36/publications/newsletters/religion/2014/10/conservative-christianity.aspx
2 http://www.christianitytoday.com/ct/2012/november-web-only/benevolent-sexism-at-christian-colleges.html
3 Ibid.
4 Ibid.

The Glass Ceiling versus The Glass Escalator

In essence, the foregoing material highlights what some scholars have termed *the glass ceiling*, which is a metaphor that represents advancement obstacles for women in certain professions strictly due to gender bias. In her piece, "The Glass Escalator," University of Texas, Austin sociologist Christine L. Williams argues that while many women face obstacles to success in male-dominated occupations, the opposite is true for men who pursue careers in traditional female-centered occupations.[163] In interviews with men who entered careers in nursing or library sciences, areas of endeavor traditionally occupied by women, Williams was told that men are encouraged to seek advancement in their chosen professions by administrators.[164] This is what Williams means by a *glass escalator*. It is glass because there are no stated policies that reinforce discrimination in either direction, but the de facto consequences for women and men are very different from one another. Add to this the fact that men rarely experience sexual harassment at work as compared to women, and the escalator for men is a smooth, upward ride that is not fraught with daily challenges as a result of gender bias. In fact, Williams found that the discrimination occurring against men who work in non-traditional male occupations comes mainly from "outsiders," people they meet outside of work who ridicule them as being "wimpy" or "feminine" for working in fields historically associated with women.

Washington University, St. Louis professor of sociology Adia Harvey Wingfield, while also finding that men who work in traditional women's occupations are pushed into leadership roles, notes that the glass escalator is racialized such that black, male nurses, for instance, do not receive the same support and encouragement as do white, male nurses.[165] Wingfield found that black men, in particular, are not as welcomed as white men and often report tense interactions with female colleagues, while rarely encouraged to seek leadership positions.[166] Male nurses who are black more commonly report that both colleagues and patients treat them with surprise and curiosity over their decision to become nurses. Wingfield attributes much of these reactions to issues of masculinity and racist stereotypes. Where white men have historically enjoyed the perception of being competent and non-threatening, black men have traditionally been regarded as threatening and lacking competency.[167] The apprehension held by many patients, and particularly white women, Wingfield attributes to age old stereotypical racialized imagery and narratives about black men. Wingfield found a similar effect in place for gay, male nurses who are also rarely encouraged to seek leadership positions in the numbers found among heterosexual, male nurses. If the nurse is male, black, and gay, the glass escalator, argues Wingfield, is not operative.[168]

Patriarchy and Language

The preceding sections trace the history and continuance of patriarchy and male privilege in a wide range of occupations. But a supporting cog of male privilege and a realm sometimes not considered as readily is the way language is gendered, which contributes to the deprecation of women. Scholar and author J.W. Wiley, in his book, *The Nigger in You: Challenging Dysfunctional Language, Engaging Leadership Moments*, raises the concern that the language we use reinforces patriarchy, particularly in the way that women are addressed by men.[169]

In a section of his book entitled "Girl Talk," Wiley argues that "calling a grown woman 'a girl' contributes to an expectation that her voice is not as pertinent, not as resonant, not deserving of the respect normally afforded a man."[170] The hope is that if we can get men to understand and care about the problem of referring to women as 'girls', as well as other derisive terms men often apply to women, men may consciously adjust their language thereby creating the residual effect that more men will begin to take women seriously.[171]

The use of insulting jargon to refer to women also introduces a double-standard that attorney Philip Galanes noticed in his law firm, where female attorneys were routinely referred to as 'girls' even if they were middle-aged women.[172] Galanes states that even if no harm is intended, the fact that male attorneys are not referred to as 'boys' highlights a socialized norm that uncovers a deeply entrenched patriarchal pattern in our use of gendered terminology. Writer Tabby Biddle agrees and notes that the feminist movement worked hard for women to be called 'women' instead of 'girls'.[173] Kashmir Hill, writing for *Forbes* magazine, comically observes that no one blinked an eye at the title of the film 'The Girl with the Dragon Tattoo' that featured a strong and even violent woman in the role of protagonist, yet it is hard to imagine Robert Downey Jr. signing onto a film entitled "Iron Boy."[174]

FIGURE 1.15: J.W. Wiley, Chief Diversity Officer, State University of New York, Plattsburgh

In addressing why this distinction matters, particularly when the person identifying women as 'girls' appears to mean no harm, Law professor Kate Galloway argues, "Attitudes to women that are subtly reflected in how we use language ... reinforce gender stereotypes."[175] As women fight to achieve respect in business, academia, science, journalism, law, law enforcement, military, politics, fire/rescue work and many other areas of public life where women have been historically excluded, being referred to as a 'girl' is yet one more way of undermining credibility in realms where credibility is of paramount importance. A similar form of sexism occurs when a group comprised of women and men is collectively referred to as "you guys." In a study conducted by J.C. Becker and J.K. Swim, many men claim that they do not perceive these subtle forms of sexism as discriminatory or harmful to women, no doubt because they do not view these sexist expressions as carrying consequences.[176]

The infantilizing and hypersexualizing of women have been pervasive practices in language and are also commonly found in the ways that women are depicted in marketing imagery as opposed to men (see Figures 1.16–1.19).

Visual media is yet another form of communication. It is a measure of male privilege that the male models are visually depicted in authoritative, serious, and dignified manners, while the female models are portrayed in childlike or exaggeratedly silly poses, while underscoring a more conspicuous sexuality. This gendered imagery along with the messages they convey radiate out to generations of boys, girls, men, and women with normative connotations about power, competency, and authority.

In a similar vein, referring to women as 'hysterical' or 'overly emotional' or simply 'crazy' are terms that pathologize women. As noted by writer Harris O'Malley, labeling women 'hysterical' or 'crazy' have been ways for men to minimize women's concerns and accomplishments, without having to think about the validity of the points made.[177] Name-calling of this kind is a fairly straightforward way to reinforce patriarchy, since

FIGURE 1.16:

FIGURE 1.17:

FIGURE 1.18:

FIGURE 1.19:

women are judged incompetent by the sensibilities of men, who are by default, 'normal'. It reduces the credibility of women and further serves to marginalize and stereotype women who are attempting to be taken seriously in male-dominated professions. O'Malley goes further to argue that what he terms **gaslighting** (minimizing the feelings of others by reframing them as unreasonable) is classic abusive behavior.[178] It is telling a person that their feelings are wrong or irrational. If you can take away one's rights to one's feelings, manipulation and abuse are much easier to facilitate. This is a ploy some men use to justify their abuse after the fact.

One of the more conspicuous places to find gender bias in language is in the way female politicians are characterized in the press as opposed to the characterization of male politicians. Thus, Nancy Pelosi ***whines*** while Paul Ryan ***levels a blistering attack*** (Figures 1.20 and 1.21).

In a patriarchal society, these sorts of double standards often go unnoticed, since patriarchy sets up expectations about male leadership and female subordination. As another example, one article reports that "Hillary Clinton ***complains*** about being broke and high tax rates,"[179] while another article reports that "Ted Cruz ***demands*** votes to stop IRS targeting."[180] Characterizing one person as "complaining" is a way of marginalizing that person and their views, while characterizing another person as "making demands" is a way to depict that person as authoritative and worthy of respect.

There is little doubt that men continue to enjoy privileges that are not enjoyed by women. One person who knows what it feels like to experience male privilege and who also knows what it feels like not to receive this privilege is author Jacob Anderson-Minshall, who was born female and elected to have genital reassignment surgery to

FIGURE 1.20: "Pelosi whines: "We never treated President Bush the way they treat President Obama." ~Red Flag News

FIGURE 1.21: "Paul Ryan levels blistering attack against IRS boss over lost emails explanation." ~Fox News

become male. In his piece, "The Enemy Within: On Becoming a Straight White Guy," Anderson-Minshall discusses the noticeable differences in the way people have responded to him now that his outward appearance is male:

> As soon as I changed my name from Susannah to Jacob, I started to be treated differently … Men grant me greater respect and are willing to see me as an authority. Women and men alike stopped being courteous. Traits like being outspoken that were formerly lauded as feminist, are now seen as just another guy's propensity for interrupting and valuing their own opinions over women's.[181]

Anderson-Minshall wonders out loud whether this newfound privilege will change him as a person. But he admits that he enjoys the respect he now receives as a result of being male. For the rest of us, it may not be evident that we, as men, receive privilege of this kind, having no knowledge about what it is feels like to be a woman in America. This no doubt accounts, in part, for why many men claim they do not feel that they possess privileges unavailable to women, or that their successes are due purely to hard work without any advantage from their being male.

EXERCISE

Compile a list of ways that men benefit due strictly to their being male, or, conversely, compile a list of ways that women are disadvantaged due strictly to their being female. That these lists prove the existence of male privilege seems beyond critique, although we will see below that some dispute this claim. What do you believe it will take to create authentic gender equality in a patriarchal society that currently supports male privilege and female subordination?

Denials of Male Privilege

Resistance to the idea that men enjoy privilege simply from being male was given a face when, in 2014, Princeton University student Tal Fortgang wrote a piece for *The Princeton Tory*, later republished by *Time Magazine* where he argues that claims of white, male privilege diminish his accomplishments.[182] Fortgang acknowledges that he benefitted from having parents who instilled in him values of hard work and the importance of education, but believes it is irresponsible to blame social and economic inequalities on gender or race privileges that abate the hard work he put into his studies along with the sacrifices made by his parents. *The American Conservative* magazine praised Fortgang's boldness,[183] while other conservative authors dismissed critics of Fortgang as being champions of political-correctness.[184] But criticism of Fortgang's denial of male privilege came from those who rhetorically asked, "How must he account for the gendered pay gap? Is it that women are not working hard enough, or something else?"[185] Others noted that acknowledging male privilege does not discount hard work.[186] Mychal Denzel Smith, writing for *The Nation* reports:

> When people with privilege hear that they have privilege, what they hear is not, "Our society is structured so that your life is more valued than others." They hear, "Everything, no matter what, will be handed to you. You have done nothing to achieve what you have."[187]

If men hear that they have done nothing to achieve their success, they will naturally balk at the idea of male privilege. But Denzel-Smith notes that acknowledging male privilege is not to claim that he has done nothing to achieve whatever success he may enjoy, but to acknowledge that the privileges he experiences includes the absence of barriers that exist for other people.[188] Denzel-Smith also points out that those men who are poor, unable to receive a college education, or simply finding it difficult to land a good paying job are not in their predicaments due to wholesale, institutionalized discrimination practices against men, particularly white men. Nor are their struggles necessarily the result of their having done something wrong. It can even be understandable when men who are experiencing obstacles to success rebel against the concept of male privilege, which would naturally be a foreign idea to someone who is experiencing affliction in his life. But again, while many men are not living lives of privilege, their challenges and hardships are not the result of their being male. For the many men who are living lives of privilege, they may have no ill intent toward women while still benefitting from the discrimination in place against women. University of Northern Iowa Professor of Humanities Harry Brod agrees and states,

> Those in the dominant group need not have any intention to discriminate against or take advantage of anyone to benefit from being in the mainstream.[189]

Terming masculinities studies ***superordinate studies***, Brod argues that men's studies necessarily investigate male privilege as a superordinate group (men) having privileges over a subordinate group (women) and how this power inequality is found in contemporary culture. Of this power inequality, Brod writes,

> While it is true that a talented and energetic woman may be able to break through the ceiling, it is equally true that a man need only be average to move upward on the escalator.[190]

Following and extending this analogy, for a talented and energetic man, particularly a white, heterosexual man, there are no glass ceilings to break through and the very heights of executive power are within his grasp without having to deal with the sexism that confronts women seeking the same positions of executive power. While the majority of both men and women must work hard to gain positions of authority in business, government, military, law, education, and other areas of executive power, men do not face the same institutional barriers that women face, and this is what Brod and others argue when defending the idea that male privilege is a reality in a patriarchal society like America.

Male privilege and patriarchy go hand-in-hand. If a culture is patriarchal in nature, it is simply one where males enjoy advantages over females. Males may then refuse to acknowledge their privilege if doing so would appear to undermine their success or appear that their success was unfairly obtained in a culture that purports to care about fairness. It is likely that as long as this denial remains in place, patriarchy and male privilege will go largely unchecked. However, White Privilege Conference founder Eddie Moore Jr. remains optimistic, stating:

> America is very, very different in the 21st century than it was the 20th century. We need to build skills and prepare for that kind of society by having diversity and cultural competency skills. But we can't stop there. We also have to understand dynamics and issues of power and privilege so that we can be competent, confident and action-oriented leaders and 21st-century citizens.[191]

The challenge to patriarchy comes overwhelmingly from feminism, which has attempted to disrupt the unearned privilege and power that men possess over women, to

FIGURE 1.22: Harry Brod

level what has been an unlevel playing field. But the challenge to patriarchy also comes from those men who acknowledge and are willing to work to reverse the fact that our culture extends unearned rewards to some over others, while placing obstacles to success in the path of some who work hard and do everything in their power to succeed.

Summary

Patriarchy comes in degrees. While some nations, like the United States, make it difficult for women to achieve at the same level as men, other nations prohibit women from enjoying the access and opportunities America frames as basic rights. This prohibition, and the less severe but grossly inequitable glass ceilings that are in place making it difficult for women to achieve at the highest levels of executive power, is created and maintained by men. It is not that one society is patriarchal and the other is not. Rather, it is that some societies have made progress toward creating gender equality, while others have much further to go, and whatever gains have been made are due to strong, capable women, in alliance with some men, fighting hard to secure the basic rights denied to women who came before them. But as this chapter uncovers, the fight for equal rights in America was, and continues to be, an arduous fight against the patriarchal structures and male privileges that are entrenched in American culture. Some of the sexism in America is overt, while other instances of sexism are covert and may be unconscious in nature when both women and men internalize the idea that women are less competent than men when it comes to positions of leadership and authority. Many men deny their privileges, particularly when suffering hardship, while others view the concept of male privilege as a notion that denies effort and tenacity. But male privilege is an outgrowth of patriarchy, where men are afforded greater opportunities and greater overall status than women. Those who raise awareness about male privilege and who work to create a gender-equal society are not anti-male, but instead attempting to build a culture that rebukes discrimination and lives up to America's claimed value of equality for all.

Notes

1 www.loc.gov/teachers/classroom-materials/connections/narratives-slavery/file.html.
2 http://womenshistory.about.com/od/quotes/fl/Lucy-Stone-Quotes.htm.
3 Anderson-Minshall, Jacob, "The Enemy Within: On Becoming a Straight, White Guy," in *Men Speak Out: Views on Gender, Sex, and Power*, 2nd edition (Routledge, 2013).
4 Source: http://escholarship.org/uc/item/43d8m3fk.
5 Engels, Friedrich, "The Origin of the Family, Private Property and the State" (1884), in *Marx/Engels Selected Works*, Volume Three, *MEW* [Marx-Engels Werke] Volume 21, (Dietz Verlag, 1962).
6 Federici, Silvia, "A Feminist Critique of Marx," http://endofcapitalism.com/2013/05/29/a-feminist-critique-of-marx-by-silvia-federici/.
7 Ibid.
8 See The Episcopal Church of Los Angeles, where the presiding bishop is Katherine Jefferts Schori and the Evangelical Lutheran Church where Elizabeth A. Eaton is the presiding bishop: www.episcopalchurch.org/.
9 www.nytimes.com/books/first/e/eller-myth.html. (There is debate over whether matriarchal religions ever existed in human history. Johann Jakob Bachofen, Jane Ellen Harrison, and Marija Gimbutas have argued for such religions, while some contemporary figures dispute whether any such religions existed. http://en.wikipedia.org/wiki/The_Myth_of_Matriarchal_Prehistory.)
10 www.eyewitnesstohistory.com/ford.htm.
11 http://edison.rutgers.edu/patents.htm.
12 Kahlenberg, Richard D., *Affirmative Action for the Rich: Legacy Preferences in College Admissions* (The Century Foundation, 2010).
13 Ibid. See statistics uncovered by Daniel Golden.
14 Ibid. See statistics uncovered by Daniel Golden.
15 Jaschik, Scott, "Legacy Admits: More Money, Lower Scores," *Inside Higher Education*, August, 2008. www.insidehighered.com/news/2008/08/04/legacy.
16 Yale University Fact Sheet. http://oir.yale.edu/yale-factsheet.
17 United States Census Bureau, 2013. http://quickfacts.census.gov/qfd/states/00000.html.
18 "Law firm diversity wobbles: Minority numbers bounce back while women associates extend two-year decline," National Association for Law Placement (NALP) Press Release, November 3, 2011, www.nalp.org/2011_law_firm_diversity.
19 Ibid.
20 Ibid.
21 DuBois, W.E.B., *Black Reconstruction in America* (1935) (Free Press, 1995), pp. 700–701.
22 Ibid.
23 McIntosh, Peggy, "White privilege: Unpacking the Invisible Knapsack," *Peace and Freedom* (July/August 1989), 9–10; repr. in *Independent School*, 49 (1990), pp. 31–35.
24 Ibid.
25 hooks, bell, *We Real Cool: Black Men and Masculinity* (Routledge Press, 2003).
26 DuBois, W.E.B., *Darkwater: Voices from Within the Veil* (1920) (Dover Publications, 1999).
27 hooks, *We Real Cool.*
28 http://africanakaleidoscopes.com/2014/03/17/450/.
29 Truth, Sojourner. "Ain't I A Woman?," www.fordham.edu/halsall/mod/sojtruth-woman.asp.
30 www.wcsap.org/african-american-community.
31 www.nwlc.org/sites/default/files/pdfs/closing_the_wage_gap_is_crucial_for_woc_and_their_families.pdf.

32 www.forbes.com/sites/dailymuse/2013/03/20/the-other-pay-gap-why-minorities-are-still-behind/.
33 *U.S. Census Bureau.* Statistical Abstract of the United States: 2012 *(PDF).*
34 Council of Economic Advisers for the President's Initiative on Race, "Changing America: Indicators of Social and Economic Well-Being by Race and Hispanic Origin" (2009). https://www.gpo.gov/fdsys/pkg/GPO-EOP-CHANGINGAMERICA/pdf/GPO-EOP-CHANGINGAMERICA.pdf.
35 www.epi.org/publication/bp370-native-americans-jobs/.
36 Mill, J.S., "The Subjection of Women," in *Three Essays* (Oxford University Press, 1975).
37 See: Mary Wollstonecraft. "A Vindication of the Rights of Women" (1792). http://oregonstate.edu/instruct/phl302/texts/wollstonecraft/woman-a.html.
38 On the reception and vilification of Wollstonecraft's work: www.jstor.org/discover/10.2307/2708781?uid=3739560&uid=2129&uid=2&uid=70&uid=4&uid=3739256&sid=21104274732623.
39 Taylor-Mill, Harriet, "The Enfranchisement of Women," *Westminster & Foreign Quarterly Review* (1851), p. 27.
40 Source: Woolf, Virginia, *Orlando: A Biography* (Hogarth Press, 1928).
41 www.archives.gov/exhibits/charters/declaration_transcript.html.
42 The Three-fifths Compromise, www.digitalhistory.uh.edu/disp_textbook.cfm?smtID=3&psid=163.
43 Miller, John Chester, *The Wolf by the Ears: Thomas Jefferson and Slavery* (University Press of Virginia, 1995), p. 184.
44 Padover, Saul K., *A Jefferson Profile* (The John Day Company, 1956), p. 297.
45 Nock, Albert Jay, *Jefferson* (Hill and Wang, 1966), p. 58.
46 Ellis, Joseph J., *American Sphinx: The Character of Thomas Jefferson* (Alfred A. Knopf, 1997), p. 91.
47 Adams, John. April 14, 1776. http://history.hanover.edu/courses/excerpts/165adams-rtl.html.
48 www.firstladies.org/biographies/firstladies.aspx?biography=6.
49 Archives, https://archive.org/details/speechofjohnquin00adam.
50 Madison, James. September, 1821. www.montpelier.org/blog/%E2%80%9C-capacity-female-mind%E2%80%A6can-not-be-doubted%E2%80%A6%E2%80%9D%E2%80%93james-madison-1821.
51 http://en.wikipedia.org/wiki/Declaration_of_Sentiments.
52 *Modern History Source book: Seneca Falls: The Declaration of Sentiments*, 1848.
53 Ibid.
54 *The Atlantic*, November 6, 2012. www.theatlantic.com/sexes/archive/2012/11/vote-no-on-womens-suffrage-bizarre-reasons-for-not-letting-women-vote/264639/.
55 Ibid.
56 Palczewski, Catherine H., "The Male Madonna and the Feminine Uncle Sam: Visual Argument, Icons, and Ideographs in 1909 Anti-Woman Suffrage Postcards," *Quarterly of Speech* 91 (2005), pp. 365–394.
57 The Library of Congress. www.loc.gov/rr/program/bib/ourdocs/15thamendment.html.
58 National Archives, www.archives.gov/exhibits/charters/constitution_amendments_11-27.html#19.
59 https://en.wikipedia.org/wiki/Burnita_Shelton_Matthews.
60 Princeton – Brookings, *The Future of Children,* "The Changing Landscape of Higher Education," Spring, 2010. http://futureofchildren.org/publications/journals/article/index.xml?journalid=72&articleid=523§ionid=3589.
61 The U.S. Equal Employment Opportunity Commission, The Equal Pay Act of 1963, www.eeoc.gov/laws/statutes/epa.cfm.
62 Ibid. Title VII of the Civil Rights Act of 1964. www.eeoc.gov/laws/statutes/titlevii.cfm.
63 Griswold v. Connecticut, 1965. 381 U.S. 479.
64 *Eisenstadt v. Baird*, 1972. 405 U.S. 438.
65 http://countrystudies.us/united-states/history-131.htm.
66 *Roe v. Wade.* 410 U.S. 113 (1973). http://en.wikipedia.org/wiki/Roe_v._Wade.
67 Source: http://fair.org/press-release/pat-buchanan-in-his-own-words/.
68 Catalyst Knowledge Center, June, 2014. www.catalyst.org/knowledge/women-ceos-fortune-1000.
69 Catalyst Knowledge Center, March, 2014. www.catalyst.org/knowledge/women-financial-services.
70 Grant Thornton Business Report, 2013. ForbesInsight, www.gti.org/files/ibr2013_wib_report_final.pdf.

71 Bureau of Labor Statistics, 2013. www.bls.gov/cps/cpsaat39.htm.
72 Ibid.
73 Ibid.
74 Ibid.
75 Ibid.
76 Ibid.
77 Ibid. (Percentage derived from dividing women's average median, weekly salary by men's average median, weekly salary.)
78 Ibid. (Dollar amount determined by multiplying weekly salary by 52.)
79 "The White House's Use of Data on the Gender Wage Gap," *The Washington Post*, www.washingtonpost.com/blogs/fact-checker/post/the-white-houses-use-of-data-on-the-gender-wage-gap/2012/06/04/gJQAYH6nEV_blog.html.
80 *New York Times*, March 22, 1981, www.nytimes.com/1981/03/22/business/l-readers-dispute-why-women-earn-less-050809.html.
81 AAS Committee on the Status of Women, "Women who have Children early in their Careers Hurt Their Chances to Achieve Tenure," Thomas Bartlett, June, 2002. www.aas.org/cswa/status/2002/JUNE2002/HavingChildren.html.
82 *New York Times*, Book Review by Anne-Marie Slaughter of Sheryl Sandberg's Book *Lean In: Women, Work, and the Will to Lead*. March 7, 2013. www.nytimes.com/2013/03/10/books/review/sheryl-sandbergs-lean-in.html?pagewanted=all.
83 Sandberg, Sheryl, *Lean In: Women, Work, and the Will to Lead* (Knopf-Double Day, 2013).
84 Garcia, Vanessa, "Why I Won't Lean In," *Huffington Post*, July 19, 2003. www.huffingtonpost.com/vanessa-garcia/why-i-wont-lean-in_b_3586527.html.
85 Jackson, Robert Max, *Down So Long: Why It Is So Hard to Explain Gender Inequality* (Working Draft, 2014), pp. 87–89.
86 Ibid., p. 90.
87 Ibid., p. 90.
88 Moss-Kanter, Rosabeth, *Men and Women of the Corporation* (Basic Books, 1993).
89 Jackson, *Down So Long*, p. 99.
90 Ibid., p. 118.
91 Isaac C., Lee B., Carnes M., "Interventions that affect gender bias in hiring: a systematic review," *Academic Medicine*, October, 2009. http://facultyhiring.uoregon.edu/files/2011/05/Isaac-Lee-Carnes-2009-26cqtlj.pdf.
92 Sheelah Kolhatkar, "In Times of Trouble, Wall Street Women get the Boot," *Bloomberg Businessweek*, September, 2013. www.businessweek.com/articles/2013-09-09/in-times-of-trouble-wall-street-women-get-the-boot.
93 Epprecht, Margo, "The Real Reason Women are leaving Wall Street," http://qz.com/121085/the-real-reason-women-are-opting-out-of-wall-street/#/h/10269,4/.
94 Ibid.
95 Ibid.
96 Ibid.
97 Ibid.
98 Marjorie Censer, "Women Influencing Corporate Boards, Despite Shortage of Numbers," *The Washington Post*, September 22, 2013. www.washingtonpost.com/business/capitalbusiness/women-influencing-corporate-boards-despite-shortage-of-numbers/2013/09/22/8fa9ad10-16f4-11e3-804b-d3a1a3a18f2c_story.html.
99 http://fortune.com/2011/04/22/more-female-mbas-but-little-gains-for-equal-pay/.
100 Ibid.
101 Ibid.
102 Ibid.
103 Tienari, Janne, Merila, Susan, Holgersson, Charlotte, and Bendl, Regine, "And then there are none: on the exclusion of women in the processes of executive search," *Gender in Management: An International Journal*, 28, 1 (2013), pp. 43–62. www.emeraldinsight.com/1754-2413.htm.
104 The U.S. Equal Employment Opportunity Commission, Title VII, Pregnancy Discrimination in Job Interviews, www.eeoc.gov/eeoc/foia/letters/2007/pregnancy_discrimination.html.
105 ABC News, "Women Endure Surprising Bias in the Workplace." http://abcnews.go.com/WNT/video/women-endure-surprising-bias-workplace-21186867.
106 Source: John Knox (1505–1572), Scottish Presbyterian leader. Pamphlet. *First Blast of the Trumpet Against the Monstrous Regiment of Women* (1558).
107 Women & Politics Institute, American University; and Center for American Women and Politics, Rutgers University, in, "Men Rule: The Continued Under-Representation of Women in U.S. Politics," Women & Politics Institute, School of Public Affairs, Washington D.C., 2012.

108 www.politifact.com/truth-o-meter/article/2012/mar/06/context-sandra-fluke-contraceptives-and-womens-hea/.
109 www.huffingtonpost.com/2012/02/29/rush-limbaugh-sandra-fluke-slut_n_1311640.html.
110 www.policymic.com/articles/5019/rush-limbaugh-apology-toward-sandra-fluke-means-nothing-he-s-insanely-sexist/.
111 http://usatoday30.usatoday.com/news/politics/2010-09-22-sexist-insults-female-politicians_N.htm.
112 Ibid.
113 Inter-Parliamentary Union, "Women in National Parliaments," as of August 31, 2011.
114 Friedman, Howard Steven. "America Lagging Behind in Female Political Representation," *Huffington Post*, August, 2012. www.huffingtonpost.com/howard-steven-friedman/women-in-politics_b_1804390.html.
115 Ibid.
116 American Bar Association, 2013. www.americanbar.org/groups/women/resources/statistics.html.
117 Ibid.
118 Ibid.
119 Ibid.
120 http://online.wsj.com/news/articles/SB10001424052702303948104579537814028747376.
121 Williams, Joan C., "Eliminating Gender Bias in the Law." www.dailyjournal.com/cle.cfm?show=CLEDisplayArticle&qVersionID=66&eid=884867&evid=1.
122 Ibid.
123 Williams, Joan C., "New Millennium, Same Glass Ceiling? The Impact of Law Firm Compensation Systems on Women," Minority Corporate Counsel Association, July, 2010. www.mcca.com/index.cfm?fuseaction=page.viewPage&pageID=2095&nodeID=.
124 Ibid.
125 Ibid.
126 Liebenberg, Roberta D. "Has Women Lawyers' Progress Stalled?" http://ms-jd.org/blog/article/has-women-lawyers-progress-stalled.
127 Ibid.
128 http://abovethelaw.com/2013/10/biglaw-memo-from-top-firm-advises-that-women-dont-giggle-dont-show-cleavage/.
129 *The Guardian*, November 11, 2013. www.theguardian.com/women-in-leadership/2013/nov/11/clifford-chance-memo-how-to-dress.
130 http://thinkprogress.org/justice/2013/10/27/2841901/sexist-law-firm-memo-advises-women-lawyers/.
131 www.nytimes.com/2014/09/07/sunday-review/why-dont-more-men-go-into-teaching.html?_r=0.
132 Ibid.
133 http://education.penelopetrunk.com/2012/09/17/public-school-is-a-babysitting-service/.
134 www.nea.org/home/53540.htm.
135 www.nytimes.com/2014/09/07/sunday-review/why-dont-more-men-go-into-teaching.html?_r=0.
136 Ibid.
137 Ibid.
138 http://iwl.rutgers.edu/documents/njwomencount/Faculty%20Diversity-3.pdf.
139 www.theguardian.com/lifeandstyle/2013/jul/05/childcare-men-pull-weight.
140 www.nytimes.com/2014/09/07/sunday-review/why-dont-more-men-go-into-teaching.html?_r=0.
141 www.usnews.com/news/blogs/data-mine/2014/10/31/women-more-likely-to-graduate-college-but-still-earn-less-than-men.
142 http://umaine.edu/advancerisingtide/files/2013/08/Report-on-Experiences-in-the-Process-of-Promotion-to-Full-P.pdf.
143 http://advance.cornell.edu/documents/ImpactofGender.pdf.
144 http://gender.stanford.edu/news/2014/why-does-john-get-stem-job-rather-jennifer.
145 Trix, Frances and Psenka, Carolyn, "Exploring the color of glass: Letters of recommendation for female and male medical faculty," *Discourse & Society* 1, 2 (2003), pp. 191–220.
146 Ibid.
147 Madera, Juan M., Hebl, Michelle R., and Martin, Randi C., "Gender and Letters of Recommendation for Academia: Agentic and Communal Differences," *Journal of Applied Psychology* 94, 6 (2009), pp. 1591–1599.
148 Ibid.
149 The Daily Pennsylvanian, January, 2011. www.thedp.com/article/2011/01/study_shows_gender_bias_in_rec_letters.
150 Yale News, September, 2012. http://news.yale.edu/2012/09/24/scientists-not-immune-gender-bias-yale-study-shows.
151 Ibid.

152 Ibid.
153 Ibid.
154 https://implicit.harvard.edu/implicit/uk/.
155 Nosek, B.A., Banaji, M.R., and Greenwald, A.G., "Harvesting implicit group attitudes and beliefs from a demonstration website," *Group Dynamics*, 6, 1 (2002), pp. 101–115.
156 Carney, Dana R., Nosek, Brian A., Greenwald, Anthony G., and Banaji, Mahzarin R., "Implicit Association Test," http://faculty.haas.berkeley.edu/dana_carney/IAT.encyclopedia.drc.ban.agg.mrb.final.doc.
157 Isabell, Lynn A., Young, Truman P., and Harcourt, Alexander H. "Stag parties linger: Continued gender bias in a female-rich scientific discipline," DOI: 10.1371/journal.pone.0049682, November, 2012. www.plosone.org/article/info:doi%2F10.1371%2Fjournal.pone.0049682.
158 Ibid.
159 Ibid.
160 Marlow, Kristian, "The Academic Gender Bias," *Psychology Today*, November, 2012. www.psychologytoday.com/blog/the-superhuman-mind/201211/the-academic-gender-bia.
161 http://genderedinnovations.stanford.edu/institutions/bias.html#anchorfour.
162 "Northwestern University professor under investigation for sexual harassment." www.slate.com/articles/news_and_politics/education/2014/02/northwestern_university_found_professor_peter_ludlow_violated_the_sexual.html. "Arizona State University professor investigated for sexual harassment." www.statepress.com/2014/04/14/asu-honors-college-clams-up-over-sexual-misconduct-allegations/. This is a sampling only; there are too many of these sorts of stories to cite them all.
163 Williams, Christine L., "The glass escalator: Hidden advantages for men in the 'female' professions," in *Men's Lives*, 9th edition, ed. Michael S. Kimmel and Michael A. Messner (Pearson Education, 2013).
164 Ibid.
165 Wingfield, Adia Harvey, "Racializing the glass escalator: Reconsidering men's experiences with women's work," in *Men's Lives*, 9th edition.
166 Ibid.
167 Ibid., pp. 174–175.
168 Ibid., p. 177.
169 Wiley, J.W., *The Nigger in You: Challenging Dysfunctional Language, Engaging Leadership Moments* (Stylus Publishing, 2013).
170 Ibid., p. 75.
171 Ibid., pp. 74–75.
172 Galanes, Philip, "Girls Not Allowed," *New York Times*, August 1, 2013. www.nytimes.com/2013/08/04/fashion/girls-not-allowed.html?_r=0.
173 Biddle, Tabby, "Woman vs. Girl," *Huffington Post*, January, 2010. www.huffingtonpost.com/tabby-biddle/women-vs-girl_b_415745.html.
174 Hill, Kashmir, "'Girls? Ladies? Folks?' Here's A Visual Guide To What You Should Call That Group Of Individuals," *Forbes*, January, 2013. www.forbes.com/sites/kashmirhill/2013/01/30/girls-ladies-folks-heres-a-visual-guide-to-what-you-should-call-that-group-of-individuals/.
175 Galloway, Kate, "Don't Call Me Girl. I'm a Woman," *Amicae Curiae*, August, 2012. http://amicaecuriae.com/2012/08/01/dont-call-me-girl-im-a-woman/.
176 J.C. Becker, J.K. Swim, "Seeing the unseen: Attention to daily encounters with sexism as way to reduce sexist belief," *Psychology of Women Quarterly* (2011); DOI: 10.1177/0361684310397509.
177 O'Malley, Harris. "On Labeling Women 'Crazy'," *Huffington Post*, November, 2013. www.huffingtonpost.com/harris-oamalley/on-labeling-women-crazy_b_4259779.html.
178 Ibid.
179 www.campaignforliberty.org/national-blog/hillary-clinton-complains-broke-high-tax-rates/.
180 www.breitbart.com/Breitbart-Texas/2014/05/06/Ted-Cruz-Demands-Vote-to-Stop-IRS-Targeting.
181 Anderson-Minshall, "The Enemy Within."
182 Fortgang, Tal, "Why I'll never apologize for my white, male privilege," *Time Magazine*, May 2, 2014. http://time.com/85933/why-ill-never-apologize-for-my-white-male-privilege/.
183 *The American Conservative* on Tal Fortgang. www.theamericanconservative.com/dreher/tal-fortgang-yes/.
184 *Los Angeles Times*, May 23, 2014. www.latimes.com/opinion/opinion-la/la-ol-white-privilege-tal-fortgang-princeton-harvard-20140522-story.html.
185 Nicholas J. Bonstow writing for the *Harvard Crimson*, May 10, 2014. www.thecrimson.com/article/2014/5/10/fortgang-princeton-controversy/.

186 Denzel-Smith, Mychal, "No one cares if you never apologize for your white male privilege," *The Nation*, May 5, 2014. www.thenation.com/blog/179675/no-one-cares-if-you-never-apologize-your-white-male-privilege.
187 Ibid.
188 Ibid.
189 Brod, Harry. "Studying masculinities as superordinate studies," in *Masculinity Studies & Feminist Theory: New Directions*, ed. Judith Kegan Gardiner (Columbia University Press, 2002).
190 Ibid., p. 172.
191 Moore Jr., Eddie, "Privilege and Power: Dr. Eddie Moore, Jr. Launches SPSCC Lecture Series," September, 2013. www.thurstontalk.com/2013/09/14/dr-eddie-moore-jr-spscc-lecture-series/, reprinted with permission from the author.

Chapter

2

Masculinity and the Nature–Nurture Debate

Mickey: I realized my true calling in life.
Wayne Gale: What's that?
Mickey: Shit, man, I'm a natural born killer.

~ *Natural Born Killers*, 1994[1]

LEARNING OBJECTIVES

After reading this chapter, students should be able to respond to the following questions with an understanding of the terms and expressions employed:

- *What is evolutionary psychology and how does it pertain to alleged differences between masculinity and femininity? Why do arguments based on biology tend to favor men with respect to power and privilege? How do evolutionary psychologists account for gendered differences in rates of sexual assault? What are STEM fields and why do some scientists believe that men are better at STEM than women? What are the counterarguments to this belief?*
- *What is the warrior gene and what importance was it thought to have with respect to men? Why was warrior gene theory abandoned by most neuroscientists and geneticists?*
- *Why do some neuroscientists believe that men have less empathy than women? What criticisms have been leveled toward neuroscientific accounts of gender difference? What does Cordelia Fine mean by 'neurosexism'?*
- *What have testosterone studies taught us about men and aggression? Why has so much of the work in testosterone studies been conducted on animals?*
- *What is socialization? What is cultural conditioning? How do social scientists distinguish between sex and gender? What is social learning theory? What does feminist philosopher Judith Butler mean by* gender performativity*?*
- *What are the main implications and concerns about the phrase 'boys will be boys'? What is the domestication syndrome?*

- *What does Anna Fausto-Sterling mean by "Developmental Systems Theory" and "Brain-Building" and what are the implications to gender? What do the concepts 'naked sex' and 'naked culture' mean and how does Fausto-Sterling refute them?*

A consensus among many researchers is that nature and nurture combine to create the rich and complex tapestry known as human behavior. The question before most researchers is not whether nature *or* nurture, as though mutually exclusive to one another, is responsible for human behavior, but rather the extent to which we can successfully explain how nature *and* nurture contribute to the equation without oversimplifying what can be a very complex interaction. Few scholars believe that the *mind*, which cognitive scientists reduce to the brain, is an utterly blank slate upon which nature and nurture imprint their respective content. However, nature advocates place greater emphasis on so-called ***innate capacities*** or ***innate cognitive preferences*** than do their social science colleagues, who place greater significance on environmental influences that include the many socializing influences in our lives from earliest ages. When discussing gender and gendered behavior, this debate is particularly important. Those who side with nature as the main contributor to gendered behavior will turn to evolution as the theoretical framework that informs gendered preferences or gendered capacities, while those who side with nurture as the central contributor to gendered behavior will turn to more contemporary, culture-bound influences in attempting to understand gendered preferences. No one doubts that there are individual differences between people, both natural and environmental, that account for behavioral differences. The debate heats up when claims are made about ***group differences***, which convert into generalizations about race, culture, sexual orientation, or gender. This chapter will examine some of the more salient arguments found in the nature–nurture debate as they pertain to gender in general and masculinity specifically.

Background

Throughout recorded history in the vast majority of cultures around the world, men have held the available positions of authority and power, and justified the gendered power dichotomy on what they believed to be a foundational truth, that women are *by nature* inferior to men. The ancient Greek philosopher Plato is often credited with having challenged this power dualism by asserting that women were suited for political leadership alongside men.[2] But it would be a mistake to then assume that Plato held remarkably progressive views about women for his time. In other passages Plato denigrates women, writing, "one finds all kinds of diverse desires, pleasures, and pains, mostly in children, women, household slaves, and in those of the inferior majority who are called free."[3] In *Republic,* Plato rhetorically asks his brother Glaucon, "Do you know of anything practiced by mankind in which the masculine sex does not surpass the female?" to which Glaucon responds, "You are right; the one sex is far surpassed by the other in everything."[4] Plato's protégé Aristotle on the nature of women, opined:

> [woman is] more mischievous, less simple, more impulsive ... more compassionate[,] ... more easily moved to tears[,] ... more jealous, more querulous, more apt to scold and to strike[,] ... more prone to despondency and less hopeful[,] ... more void of shame or self-respect, more false of speech, more deceptive, of more retentive memory [and] ... also more wakeful; more shrinking [and] more difficult to rouse to action.[5]

These views were espoused over 2,300 years ago by men considered by some to be among the most advanced thinkers in human history. To many contemporary scholars, these sexist views seem to be the backward product of an ancient mentality that did not have the benefit of contemporary insights about sex and gender, until you consider the twentieth-century enrollment policies of some of the most prestigious universities in America.

It was not until 1963 that Harvard University allowed women to enroll in courses, although until that year they were formally matriculated into Radcliffe Women's College.[6] In 1969, Princeton and Yale followed suit,[7] while Columbia University did not open its doors to women until 1979.[8] The thinking behind the exclusionary practice of not allowing women admittance to Ivy League institutions was fueled by the persistent stereotype that women were incapable, by nature, of competing with men at the collegiate level, particularly when it came to the physical and biological sciences, coupled with the normative social trope that women belonged at home raising children, doing household chores, and taking care of their husbands.

A longstanding belief about sex and gender involved the view that nature had designed men and women for different tasks, thereby creating different aptitudes and preferences. This conventional view about gender went largely unchallenged except by revolutionary thinkers like Simone de Beauvoir, who, in arguably her most famous work, *The Second Sex,* stated that "One is not born, but rather becomes, a woman."[9] At the time, so controversial was this view that the Vatican placed *The Second Sex* on its "List of Prohibited Books,"[10] viewing the notion that gender is a social construct as a subversion of the generally accepted, non-secular view that gender roles are immutable and originate from divine will as part of a natural order.

More famously, neurologist and founder of psychoanalysis, Sigmund Freud, considered male gender identity to be determined by the dynamics found in early stages of child development. In what he termed the ***oedipal complex***, boys feel inferior to and in competition with their fathers while falling in love with their mothers. The oedipal struggle is resolved when boys identify with their fathers, break away from their mothers, and eventually gain their own identities as men by embracing strength and aggressiveness, while shunning passivity and nurturance.[11] When it came to girls and women, Freud viewed females as "incomplete men," who suffer from "penis envy" and who "oppose change, receive passively, and add nothing of their own."[12] [13] Like many who examined issues of sex and gender in his day, Freud believed that gendered characteristics were determined so that males and females are largely locked into patterns of traditional gendered behaviors and traits that weigh in favor of male superiority and female inferiority. This brand of deterministic gender inequality dominated most of the early- to mid-twentieth-century thinking about men and women, which served as the background for the exclusion of women in many academic disciplines, most notably within the areas of science and technology.

The controversy was renewed in 2005, when then Harvard University president Lawrence Summers opined that differences in aptitude explain why boys outperform girls in math and science stating, "Research in behavioral genetics is showing that things people previously attributed to socialization weren't due to socialization after all,"[14] adding that there are innate differences between men and women that cause women to underperform in math and science careers.[15] Lawrence provided, as evidence, the anecdotal story of giving his daughter toy trucks, upon which, he reported, his daughter treated them like dolls and named them 'mummy' and 'daddy' trucks.[16] The backlash to Summers's impromptu musings was immediate and resounding.[17] In February, 2005, the American Sociological Association published findings documenting the fact that women flourish in science when given opportunities in a supportive environment.[18] The counterexamples of Nobel prize winning physicist Marie Curie, nuclear physicist Lise Meitner, chemist Ida Noddack,

FIGURE 2.1: The Solvay Conference on Physics in 1927 with only one woman (Marie Curie) in attendance, bottom row, third from left

mathematician and physicist Emmy Noether, and many others were also duly noted, but dismissed by critics as being female oddities who did not represent the vast majority of women.[19]

THOUGHT BOX

Are there any conclusions to be drawn from the fact that men dominated math and science in the past? Does it help nature over nurture supporters or does it simply reflect the cultural norms of the past that encouraged boys to pursue the disciplines of math and science while systematically excluding women from many institutions that prepared students for careers in math and science? After reading this chapter, do your answers to the above questions change?

The view that STEM fields (Science, Technology, Engineering, and Math) are uniquely suited for men continues to flourish and reverberate throughout the editorial pieces of conservative pundits,[20] even as contemporary studies show that girls now match the scores of boys on standardized mathematics assessment tests.[21] Stanford University professor of mathematics Jo Boaler quips, "When boys are more successful than girls in math and science, everybody says it's because boys are genetically suited to math and science. But when girls are doing better, people say it's because they work hard."[22] Yet the stereotypical view that males are better suited by nature to excel in science and math than females is stubbornly entrenched in the minds of both laypersons and many STEM experts themselves. Those who defend the idea that men are better suited for STEM often rely on the view that nature has constructed male brains more than it has female brains to better comprehend spatial relationships, which permeate science. Underlying this notion is the belief that there are observable gendered preferences based on gender-aptitude that explain differences between men and women with respect to personality, aptitude, temperament, risk-taking, sexual interest, aggression, violence, and crime. The locus of the nature argument rests on the model that evolution shapes biology and biology shapes abilities, interests, and behavior.

Evolutionary Psychology and Gendered Behavioral Traits

The origin of the idea that human behavior, including the many nuanced complexities of human psychology, is the result of evolutionary factors can be traced to Charles Darwin, who, in his groundbreaking work *The Origin of Species* (1859) wrote, "In the distant future I see open fields for far more important researches. Psychology will be based on a new foundation, that of the necessary acquirement of each mental power and capacity by gradation."[23] The notion that adaptation by natural selection would extend beyond biological traits to that of psychological traits would usher in the discipline known today as ***evolutionary psychology***. The fundamental assumption underlying evolutionary psychology is the view that behaviors, interests, preferences, and talents are conditioned responses to environmental contingencies that convert into heritable traits. If, for example, we wish to understand why human beings prefer sweets, the answer would presumably lie in our ancestors' need for energy-dense foods rich in carbohydrates in pre-agricultural environments. In savannah environments, our ancestors began to transition to grain-based diets or what are called C-4 diets,[24] which would apparently explain shifts in dietary preferences for populations inhabiting certain geographical regions. In a similar fashion, evolutionary psychology might explain athletic talent as a set of inherited traits passed down from ancestors who

FIGURE 2.2: "I am inclined to agree with Francis Galton in believing that education and environment produce only a small effect on the mind of any one, and that most of our qualities are innate." ~ Charles Darwin, in Nora Barlow, *The Autobiography of Charles Darwin: 1809–1882* (W.W. Norton & Company; Revised ed. 1993).

developed running speed or jumping abilities in response to environmental conditions that benefitted individuals who possessed these talents, ultimately bestowing on those individuals a better chance of passing on their genes. The next logical step in this argument is to explain sexual dimorphism (gendered physical differences) as a response to past environmental conditions. If, for instance, hunting was conducted primarily by males and if successful hunters required highly-developed upper body muscularity, then the differentiation of muscle mass in men and women would be explained against this ancestral condition.

Evolutionary psychologists argue that like hearts, eyes, kidneys, liver, and the immune system, the brain has evolved through a series of adaptations by natural selection and that, as theoretical biologist Edward H. Hagen notes, "there is no fundamental distinction between physiological adaptations and psychological adaptations."[25] Hagen suggests that the similarity in our adapted biology is good evidence to suppose that psychological states are experienced in similar fashion across human populations. Pain, for example, is believed to be felt universally across human populations such that pain is considered to be a "genetically determined human universal."[26] This does not account for individual differences between people, but applies to generalized experiences over human groups. Evolutionary psychologists argue that an understanding of evolutionary factors can enrich our understanding of things like violence, homicide, and war.[27] If correct, traits such as aggression, violence, nurturance, empathy, and altruism may be viewed as inherited traits that were shaped by environmental pressures over potentially long periods of time.

When turning to gender, evolutionary psychologists argue that observable behavioral differences between males and females are the result of evolutionary adaptations. An adaptation is defined as

> an inherited and reliably developing characteristic that came into existence as a feature of a species through natural selection because it helped to directly or indirectly facilitate reproduction during the period of its evolution.[28]

If, for instance, there are discernible differences between males and females with respect to levels of aggression, the evolutionary account of those differences would be traced to a chain of events whereby measurable hormonal differences between males and females arose from differences in genetic markers, which are themselves the product of environmental pressures placed on ancestral populations. The resulting adaptation converts into biological distinctions in terms of hormone production or brain chemistry, which then become heritable traits found in offspring, cashed out in terms of observable behavior, and all of this in the service of successfully facilitating reproduction.

In understanding gendered traits, psychologist Barry X. Kuhle offers the evolutionary explanation, "In domains in which the sexes recurrently faced different adaptive problems, selection is likely to have fashioned different adaptive solutions."[29] This evolutionary framework allows evolutionary psychologists to explain, for example, why men sexually assault women in far greater number than women sexually assault men by pointing to things like differing levels of testosterone production or different sizes of certain brain structures between women and men. If correct, the evolutionary account does not mean that changing gendered behavior is impossible, but it does make it far more difficult, for it involves having to get men to resist preferences that nature has embedded in them. It also does not mean that morally abhorrent or criminal behavior must be accepted or excused, but it does purport to explain why men as a group are more violent and commit far more sexual crimes than do women.

THOUGHT BOX

THE "IS–OUGHT" FALLACY.

Scottish philosopher David Hume noted that some writers attempt to argue how things ought to be based on how they believe things are in actuality. But Hume claimed that it is not obvious how prescriptive claims can be based on descriptive claims. If, for instance, we learned that rape was part of sexual practices for some animals (is), it would not then be legitimate to conclude that rape is good (ought). Is there a sense in which evolutionary psychology can be used to commit this fallacy? Are you able to find accounts where authors appear to state that a behavior is good, or at least should be excused, because it evolved as part of a natural process?

One way evolutionary psychologists attempt to prove that there are inherent gendered behavioral differences is to observe primate populations under controlled conditions. The reason that researchers use nonhuman primates in their studies of behavior is to preemptively strike against the criticism that boys and girls, at even very young ages, have already been subjected to the shaping forces of ***socialization***, which is the rich and complex interaction of individuals with their parents, siblings, relatives, friends, teachers, clergy, media, and cultural mores that influence one's values and beliefs. The idea is that within nonhuman primate communities, there are no normative, gendered scripts being played out and reinforced by parents and other community members, as there often are within human communities. If, therefore, preferences by gender can be observed in nonhuman primate communities, the assumption is that these differences must be the result of natural inclinations rather than socialized influences.

An example of an evolutionary psychological account of gendered difference comes from a 2008 study, where researchers from Emory University conducted experiments with vervet monkeys to determine whether these monkeys would exhibit gender-specific toy preferences.[30] In the study, what were considered to be "male-toys" such as trucks and other vehicles and "female toys" such as dolls and stuffed animals were displayed in an outdoor area. Individual monkeys were released into the area and observed. Male rhesus monkeys preferred to play with the "male toys" while female rhesus monkeys were less specialized in their preferences. These results parallel results found when boys and girls are given similar toy options. Given that the play behavior was conducted in the absence of other community members who could conceivably bias the results, along with the assumption that vervet monkeys are not socialized with normative gendered scripts, the researchers concluded that there are inherent gendered preferences, at least with males, when it comes to play-activities.

Turning to human communities, evolutionary psychologists also point to the fact that in almost no cultures in human history have women taken a sexually aggressive stance over men or created harems of men for their sexual gratification. Added to this observation is the acknowledgement that men account for the majority of violence and violent crime in societies around the world, including physical assault, sexual assault, and violence against women.[31] The argument then concludes that when you witness male violence in far greater numbers than female violence across differing cultures and regions of the world, and that this tendency can be found throughout history, it must be the case that males, by nature, are more prone to aggression and violence than are females.

FIGURE 2.3: Rhesus monkeys playing with toys. Photo Credit: Gerianne Alexander, photo

But science must connect physical dots in order to proclaim a theory to be sound. Anecdotal experiences and *ad hoc* observations do not rise to the requirements of scientific theory. So, for many who hold an evolutionary view of gender, the search has been and continues to be an investigation to locate a biological basis of gender that would prove once and for all that men are designed by nature to be more aggressive, physically and sexually, than women. What was needed was a hormone or gene in whose presence aggression arises. Several candidates were studied, when in 1991 an enzyme was isolated that seemed to be that crucial link researchers had been looking for that would finally demonstrate that male aggression is caused by inherent biological, instead of sociological, factors. That biological factor was the enzyme, monoamine oxidase A, known as MAO-A, which is encoded by the MAOA gene.[32] This gene became known as "the warrior gene."

The Warrior Gene

With the discovery of the function of MAO-A within the MAOA gene, scientific journals exploded with announcements of there being a biological basis for aggression. *Science Daily*, citing a study from Brown University, declared, "'Warrior Gene' Predicts Aggressive Behavior after Provocation."[33] The study was conducted by asking subjects to inflict physical pain on those who they were told had taken money from them by orally administering varying amounts of hot sauce to the alleged thieves. The published results claimed that those with lower MAOA activity demonstrated slightly higher levels of aggression than those with higher MAOA activity. The finding set off a number of optimistic articles that suggested we may be closer to understanding the links between biology, aggression, violence, and crime. This optimism was tempered, however, by the fact that the Brown

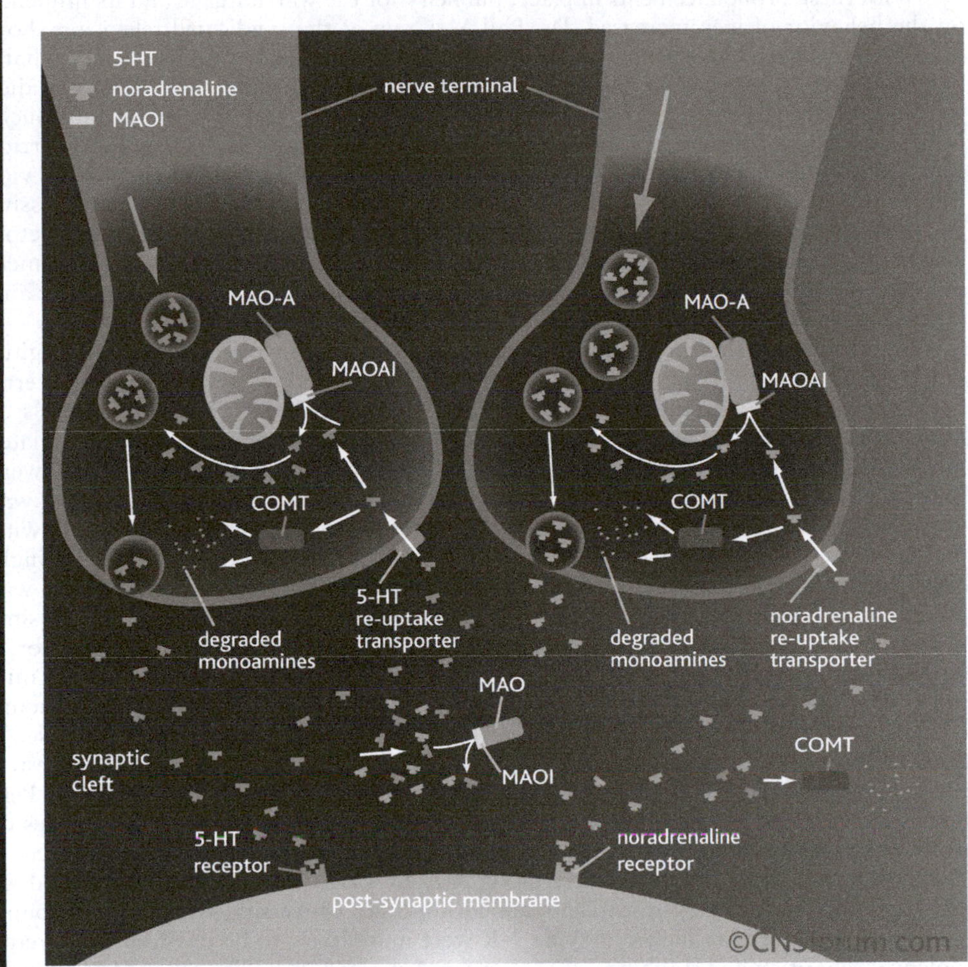

FIGURE 2.4: MAO-A Mechanism

University study did not cite its findings in gender specific language so that conclusions could not be drawn about whether MAOA levels affected men differently than women. A closer look at the research conducted at Brown University revealed that while 75% of warrior gene carriers exhibited "meted out aggression" in the "hot sauce experiment," this was also true of 62% who did not carry the warrior gene.[34] When the test subjects were told that the amounts of money stolen were smaller, there were no observable aggression differences detected between carriers and non-carriers whatsoever.[35]

However, by 2012, data suggested that lower MAOA activity exhibited itself differently in men than in women. While men with lower MAOA activity were found to be more aggressive, women with lower MAOA activity reported feeling happier than women with higher MAOA activity.[36] Henian Chen of the University of South Florida expressed surprise by this finding, since lower levels of MAOA had been consistently linked to negative behaviors such as higher levels of alcoholism and antisocial behavior.[37] But now, it seemed, there was biological proof to support the generalization that males, or at least low-level MAOA males, are prone to more aggression and violence than females.

With these pronouncements in place, publicity for the warrior gene and its influence on the behavior of men increased. Dr. Phil McGraw of the syndicated television show "Dr. Phil" informed his viewing audience that "about one-third of all men carry what's been called the warrior gene"[38] even as research continued to show that MAOA studies were not panning out as originally hoped. Harvard University professor Joshua Buckholtz argued that "there is not now, nor could there ever be any such thing as a warrior gene. Why not? Enormous variability. It takes more than one bad allele to produce a violent person."[39] Buchholtz was claiming what many researchers suspected, that aggressive and violent behavior cannot be reduced to a single gene, or perhaps even one single factor. The longstanding view has been and continues to be that violence is a product of numerous factors, some of which may be common to those who repeatedly act out violently and others that may be specific to the individual.

In a study published in the *British Journal of Psychiatry* involving a 30-year longitudinal study of the connection between MAOA and antisocial behavior, critical concerns began to mount.[40] The study confirmed earlier findings that those with lower levels of MAOA activity, coupled with abuse in their childhood, were more likely to offend in later life, which itself tempered optimism since the childhood environments of the subjects were acknowledged to be integral to the results. However, the study also reported that it was possible to generate false-positives and that it was time to replace single-gene studies with multiple-gene studies combined with multiple environmental factors. It was increasingly clear that the optimism of reducing antisocial and violent behavior to a single gene was premature at best, and in all likelihood mythical. It was, in essence, a notification that simplistic, biological reductionism is naïve when attempting to understand human behavior.

Further problems for the warrior gene theory came from the fact that there are millions of people who are not violent or antisocial who also possess the low-producing enzyme variety of the MAOA gene.[41] In 2010, National Geographic Explorer released a documentary film entitled, *Born to Rage*, in which 18 men with violent pasts were tested for the low-producing MAOA gene. Only nine of the 18 tested positive for the gene. Perhaps most notable was the finding that three Buddhist monks who had chosen lives of peace and nonviolence, all tested positive for the "warrior gene."[42]

In another study, the 2-R variant of MAOA (MAOA-2R) was investigated in African-American men by researchers at Florida State University, where it was found that "African-American males carrying 2-R were more likely to be involved in extreme violence—shooting and stabbing—than African American men with other MAOA variants." [43] [44] African-American men were selected for the study because the 2-R variant was found in African-American men at five times the rate it was found in Caucasian American men.[45] Yet Kevin M. Beaver, lead researcher in the study, also notes, "Even if *MAOA-2R* is causally linked with antisocial behaviors, it is not common enough in African-Americans to solely account for crime rates in blacks."[46] This means that the "African American male 2-R rate of five times that of white men" is not statistically important enough against the population to draw generalizations. Beaver continues, "It is probably correct to assume that social behaviors are due to gene-environment interaction."[47] Medical anthropologist Alondra Oubre states of research designed to draw conclusions about the effects of genetics on an individual's behavior:

> A heritability estimate does not pertain to the amount of genetic influence on a particular trait in a particular person … Heritability estimates can change, depending upon the strength or weakness of environmental factors, which along with various genes, shape social behaviors.[48]

Today, the reductionism of the warrior gene theory of violence has been effectively debunked so that even though it is likely that biology influences aggressive behavior to some degree, including propensities for violence in some, there is no way to divorce environment from the behavioral equation. A person living under violent conditions is more likely to get caught up in violence than is a person who is living in peaceful conditions whether or not he possesses the warrior gene.

A similar flurry of excitement was generated in the 1960s in the wake of discovering that some men possess an extra Y-chromosome, which was termed *XYY syndrome*.[49] Found in approximately one in one thousand male births, boys with an extra Y-chromosome possess 47 total chromosomes or a 47 karyotype. A physical trait associated with XYY males is being slightly taller than average and it is also the case that slightly over 50% of XYY males demonstrate learning difficulties.[50] But the early studies also suggested that XYY males were more aggressive, violent, and prone to crime.[51] Drawing almost entirely on the work of biochemist Mary Telfer, articles in the *New York Times*,[52] *Newsweek*, and *Time* magazine[53] reported that several notorious murder trials at the time were planning to use XYY syndrome as mitigating factors in the defense of the accused.

However, in December of 1968, Michael Court Brown, director of the MRC Human Genetics Unit, published a report documenting that no overrepresentation of XYY males were found in prison populations or in patients of hospitals for developmentally disabled persons.[54] He found that Telfer's results were likely due to selection bias, whereby one is careful to report only those cases that conform to one's conclusions.[55] Subsequent studies were unable to find a strong correlation between XYY men and higher rates of aggression and violence.[56] In their book, *Criminology: Theory, Research, and Policy*, criminologists Gennaro Vito and Jeffrey Maahs conclude that early studies that reported a connection of XYY men to violence were "simplistic, clumsy" and that no link between XYY men and violence has ever been established.[57]

Neuroscience and Gender

The connection between biology and gender popped onto the radar of many laypersons in 1992, when self-proclaimed relationship counselor John Gray authored the best-selling book *Men are from Mars, Women are from Venus: The Classic Guide to Understanding the Opposite Sex*.[58] In 2008, Gray followed this title up with the book *Why Mars and Venus Collide: Improving Relationships by Understanding How Men and Women Cope Differently with Stress*, where he appealed to brain science to explain the purported differences between male and female cognition.[59] According to Gray, differences in the IPL (inferior parietal lobe) of the brain in men and women account for differences in cognitive traits.

> The IPL is often larger on the left—or logical, analytical, and objective—side of the brain in men, prompting them to be action-oriented with high focus on task and achievement ... In women, the IPL is often larger on the right—or intuitive, thoughtful, and subjective—side of the brain. Women are inclined to measure themselves by their successes in relationship-building.[60]

Gray is not a neuroscientist, but he employs neuroscience, the study of the brain, to support the old-fashioned notion that men are driven by rational thinking, while women are driven by emotion. He relies on the neuroscientific work of others such as the research conducted at the University of Pennsylvania's Perelman School of Medicine where it was found that inter-hemispheric connectivity is stronger in girls and women, while intra-hemispheric connectivity was stronger in boys and men,[61] although researchers did not draw the generalizations about gender, cognition, and emotion drawn by Gray.

Criticism of Gray's views comes from many in the social sciences who note that Gray perpetuates gender stereotypes, downplays the many similarities found in male and female brains, draws vast generalizations on little evidence, universalizes gender differences by falsely assuming that his conclusions apply to all men and all women, and ignores the increases in women who are drawn to and succeeding in science and engineering, long believed to be paradigmatic disciplines that require so-called left-brain thinking.[62] As a critical response to Gray and others who promote gendered neurological difference, Lise Eliot of the Chicago School of Medicine argues,

> Most of those differences are far smaller than the *Men Are from Mars, Women Are from Venus* stereotypes suggest. Nor are the reasoning, speaking, computing, emphasising, navigating and other cognitive differences fixed in the genetic architecture of our brains. All such skills are learned, and neuro-plasticity—the modifications of neurons and their connections in response experience—trumps hard-wiring every time.[63]

Those neuroscientists who research alleged differences in male and female aptitude base much of their conclusions on brain activity as recorded by functional magnetic resonance imaging (fMRI), which measures changes in blood flow to different areas of the brain. Neuroscience also works under the assumption that evolutionary factors account for human behavior, including instinctive sex drives and differences in sexual arousal for males and females. Among the many conclusions drawn from neuroscience is the view that men have a stronger sex drive than women due to the relative size of the amygdala, two small (left and right), almond-shaped subcortical structures located deep within the temporal lobes of the brain. Sex drive has been linked to the size of the amygdala,[64] which on average is larger in men than in women.[65] Other gendered sexual differences associated with the amygdala is the finding that sexual arousal is more closely connected to visual stimulation in men than it is in women.[66]

Neuroscientific research has also revealed that, on average, males have 8% to 13% larger total brain volume than females,[67] although a 2012 study found that women are now scoring slightly higher on IQ tests than males after almost a century of men scoring slightly higher than women.[68] James R. Flynn, who conducted the research, speculates that the rise in female IQ's is likely due to what Flynn terms the "characterological trait" that women have a greater ability to focus during tests just as they do in classrooms.[69] Other brain differences in men and women can be found in the fact that the frontal area of the cortex is larger in volume and more organized in women than in men, which led University of Missouri cognitive behavioral psychologist David C. Geary to speculate that if using language skill was beneficial to organizing relationships over evolutionary history, this might explain why women "gossip and manipulate information."[70] It is this kind of speculation and characterization of female communication practices that lead critics to argue that even men who are educated in science are sometimes unable to keep their sexist prejudice out of their work.

In 2011, neuropsychiatrist Louann Brizendine published the book *The Male Brain* as a follow up and companion to her 2006 book *The Female Brain*.[71] Brizendine draws generalizations about men based on anecdotal stories of stereotypical male behavior that include aggression, competition, increased sexual pursuit, and dominance. Arguing that brain chemistry and hormones create these common male behavioral patterns, Brizendine capitalizes on the well-traveled notion that men and women are very different from one another by first attaching prototypical male, pet names to testosterone ("Zeus") and vasopressin ("The White Knight") and female, pet names to estrogen ("The Queen") and oxytocin ("The Fluffy, Purring Kitty") to take readers on a less than scientific journey to the conclusion that innate differences between men and women are grounded in biology. Drawing on discussions with patients she counseled, Brizendine argues that alleged emotional differences between men and women are based in brain differences between men and women, with the predictable conclusion that women are innately more empathetic, better negotiators, and conciliators than men, while men are innately better fighters and more prone to being loners.

The basis of this distinction, Brizendine argues, is found in the difference between the ***mirror neuron system (MNS)***, which appears to be responsible for the human capacity to learn by imitation[72] and the ***temporoparietal junction system*** (*TPJ*), which is located in the region between the temporal and parietal lobes of the brain and thought to be involved in information processing and perception.[73] In the early 1990s, neurophysiologist Giacomo Rizzolatti discovered "mirror neurons" while observing the activity of individual nerve cells in the brains of macaque monkeys.[74] These nerves were observed to be active in the brain of the monkey performing an activity, but also in the brain of a separate monkey observing the first monkey, hence, the establishment of the phrase "mirror neurons."

Brizendine receives some support from University of California, San Diego neuroscientist V.S. Ramachandran who argues that while there are many factors in bringing about empathy in human beings, mirror neurons are required to experience empathy by breaking down the barrier between self and other.[75] Mirror neurons activate when one person views another person performing an activity, which, as noted, may help us to learn particular tasks through imitation. In his TED talk of 2009, Ramachandran boldly stated that mirror neurons are responsible for human civilization as we know it.[76] As the fanfare for mirror neurons grew, more neuroscientists began to chime in with claims that extended to gendered differences that reinforced enduring generalizations about women and men, since studies have shown that mirror neuron activity is more pronounced in females than males when exposed to the same visual stimuli.[77]

Cambridge University psychopathologist and author of the book *Zero Degrees of Empathy*, [78] Simon Baron-Cohen also touts the connection between mirror neurons and empathy, arguing that empathy is distributed over society in a bell curve with women scoring slightly higher than men. Baron-Cohen revealed that at 24 hours old, 100 babies were tested by having them look at two objects: a human face and a mechanical mobile. More boys than girls looked at the mechanical mobile, while more girls than boys looked at the human face.[79] While noting that this pattern was not true of all male and female newborns, a statistical trend could be established. Terming his view the ***empathizing-systematizing theory***, Baron-Cohen concludes that the female brain is predominantly hard-wired for empathy, while the male brain is predominantly hard-wired for understanding and building systems.[80]

Baron-Cohen also points to observations of boys and girls at play. When boys and girls are together in a play environment and given a movie player with only one eye piece, boys will demonstrate less empathy and more self-centeredness by nudging girls out of the way to receive more time with the player. Given a play area with plastic toy cars, boys will begin deliberately ramming one another while girls are more careful to avoid hitting other cars.[81] Boys, he notes, also display more *direct aggression* by hitting, pushing, and punching, while girls display more *indirect aggression* that includes, "gossip, exclusion, and bitchy remarks."[82] Baron-Cohen goes some way in aligning himself with the views of Lawrence Summers by concluding that these innate, gendered capacities explain why men dominate careers in math, physics, and engineering, and other industries where construction is involved, while, he states, "women are more likely to go to the magazine rack featuring fashion, romance, beauty, intimacy, emotional problems, agony aunts, counseling, relationship advice, and parenting."[83] Like Geary, Baron-Cohen resorts to sexist descriptors to describe the observational differences witnessed between males and females and to support his version of biological determinism, but he backtracks by acknowledging that the environmental factors of abuse and neglect can erode empathy.[84] He also notes that empathy can be used as a tool to build equality between people and nations,[85] lending weight to the notion that empathy can be built and developed, rather than viewed as a static feature of neurobiology. This latter feature of Baron-Cohen's work also disrupts the view that women and men are locked into empathy–apathy dichotomies as part of sex-differentiated, neurological imperatives. Still, researchers like Baron-Cohen, Brizendine, and Ramachandran emphasize nature over nurture, in large part, to explain what they see as innate behavioral differences between the sexes.

One criticism of neuroscience as a basis for making generalizations about gendered behavior comes from psychologist Cordelia Fine, who argues that much of the research springing from neuroscience comes from those who hold stereotypical views about gender, such that their work can be termed ***neurosexism***.[86] In Fine's view, those who attempt to reduce gendered behavior to brain science allow their theories and biases to influence the research. If I am a neuroscientist who believes that men are less empathic than women, I may look for signals in the brain to confirm that belief, rather than impartially allowing the facts to create the theory. The problem is compounded when the researcher bases his findings on small samples without also controlling for important variables. In a criticism specifically aimed at Baron-Cohen's work, Fine points out that the research on day-old infants did not control for the gendered views of those adults holding the babies. If a participant holding an infant believes boys are wired to care more about spatial objects, and he is holding a male infant, he may be inclined to subtly position the baby toward the mechanical mobile than the human face. In the presence of bias, poor methodologies, and what Fine terms "leaps of faith," researchers grasp onto conclusions that suit their preconceived beliefs about and women and men:

> The sheer complexity of the brain lends itself beautifully to over-interpretation and precipitous conclusions. It's a compelling story that offers a neat, satisfying explanation, and justification, of the status quo.[87]

Fine concludes that the brain is a product of nature in combination with "your physical, social and cultural environment, your behaviour and your thoughts," such that gendered differences cannot be reduced to congenital biological differences.[88]

A further criticism of the view that differences in brain physiology between men and women create different aptitudes and preferences comes from Gina Rippon, professor of cognitive neuroimaging at Aston University, Birmingham, who argues that gendered behavioral and preference differences, if they occur at all, come from environmental rather than innate factors. Rippon begins by noting that differences between the brains of males and females are miniscule and insignificant compared to the similarities.[89] Emphasizing the permeability of the human brain over the course of a lifetime, Rippon terms 'neuro-hype' the attempts to use neuroscience to support longstanding stereotypes about women and men that purport to explain social roles and status.[90] Rippon argues that cultural expectations placed on males and females often lead men and women to pursue traditional gendered interests and vocations, which in turn make use of different parts of the brain.[91] If this account is correct, it would make sense that researchers would find different parts of the brain to be more active in men or women, as the case may be, but it would explain those differences in environmental rather than in purely biological terms. If, for instance, more male students are majoring in engineering while more female students are majoring in psychology, fMRI scans are going to show that blood flow is directed to different areas of the brain for those men and women with differing majors and occupations, but this evidence would count only toward *ad hoc* neurological explanations of gender difference rather than evidence supportive of innate biological differences between men and women. In such cases, environment would trump biology in terms of providing an efficacious causal explanation of gendered preference.

Testosterone and Male Aggression

Anyone who has investigated contemporary masculinity from an academic standpoint has had to respond to the bio-determinist point about higher levels of testosterone (T-levels) in males as opposed to females as the causal agent of increased rates of aggression and violence in men. The testosterone argument rides on the coattails of evolutionary psychology, since it is assumed that higher levels of testosterone in males are the product of male ancestral activities such as hunting and defending one's tribe, even though these activities are no longer required for survival. It is then argued that it is *natural* for boys and men to be more aggressive and violent than girls and women so that attempts to construct more compassionate and sensitive men are difficult to impossible.

Testosterone is a steroid hormone, which is produced in men in amounts seven to eight times higher than amounts found in women,[92] although when metabolic consumption of testosterone is considered, which is higher in men, the production of testosterone in men is closer to 20 times that of levels found in women.[93] Testosterone is well known to increase muscle and bone mass,[94] but is also thought to be responsible for increased rates of aggression and violence.[95] If, it is argued, men produce more of a substance that leads to aggressive and violent behavior, biology explains men's increased levels of violence.

Cross-species studies have been a favorite tool in the biological sciences to investigate claims about gendered behavior and this is especially true when it comes to endocrinological accounts of gendered aggression. Biologist David Anderson of the California Institute of Technology studies fruit flies to determine the biological basis for aggression in male flies. It turns out that male fruit flies are more aggressive than females and that male flies possess a cluster of neurons in their brains that are not found in the brains of female flies.[96] It is believed that activation of these particular neurons coupled with

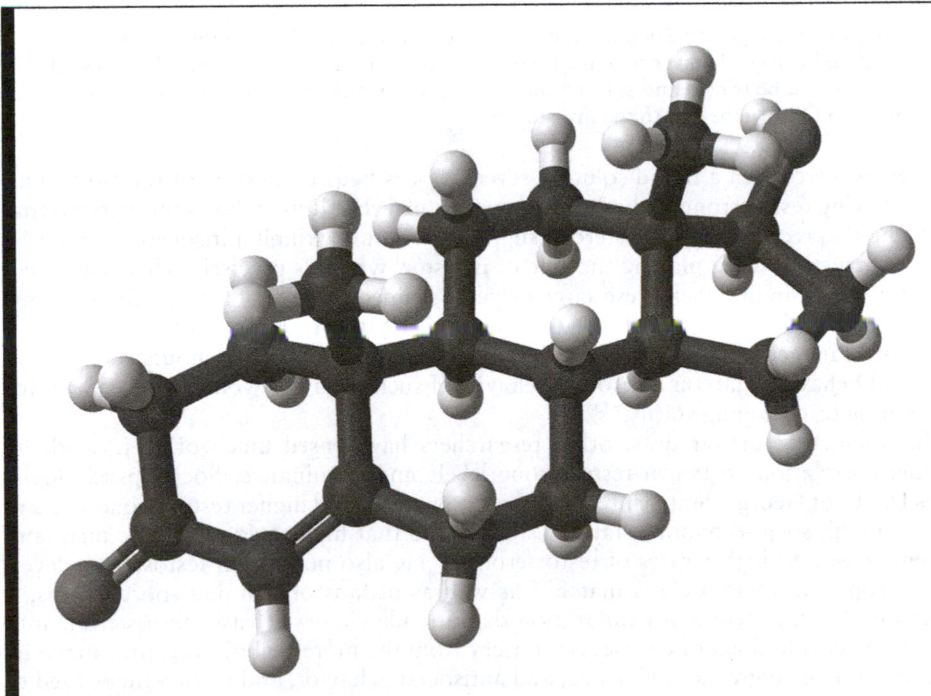

FIGURE 2.5: $C_{19}H_{28}O_2$, better known as testosterone

the expression of the gene that creates the neuropeptide Tk within those cells lead to increased aggression so pronounced that the flies can be provoked to attack inanimate objects.[97] The hope for researchers is that understanding the mechanisms that underlie aggression at the genetic, hormonal, and neurobiological levels in other species will better assist our understanding of human aggression, particularly in males.

Similar studies have been conducted with birds. Neuroscientist Kazuyoshi Tsutsui of Waseda University discovered that the neuropeptide GnIH inhibits aggression in quail.[98] He and his research team injected GnIH into the brains of male quail, which are famously aggressive. Researchers then injected concentrated estrogen into the birds and observed that aggressiveness in males greatly decreased.[99] The study concluded by noting that future work should be designed to investigate whether there is a similar mechanism in human beings so that spikes of male aggression might be regulated to create a more peaceful and orderly society.[100]

The focus on bird aggression is based on the famous studies of nineteenth-century German zoologist Arnold Berthold who discovered that testicular secretions were required for normal aggression patterns in roosters.[101] Berthold observed that hens, by comparison, were not aggressive, and he concluded that there must be something inherent in roosters that cause their increased levels of aggression. As research extended to songbirds and eventually to rodents and other vertebrates, it was not long before conclusions were drawn that neuroendocrine mechanisms must be responsible for aggression patterns in most if not all vertebrates including humans, and that the key to understanding male aggression, in particular, would be found in these mechanisms.[102]

Turning to humans and extending the focus of research beyond behavioral aggression, studies have also linked testosterone levels to competition.[103] These findings inspired researchers to see whether increased testosterone levels in humans would lead to increased competitiveness when subjects were asked to play an investment game.[104] In the game,

> participants were given €20 and were instructed that they could keep the amount they wanted and invest whatever remained with a trustee (another participant). The invested portion would be tripled and split by the trustee, who would keep whatever portion she wanted and return the rest to the investor.[105]

Players were given a liquid solution several hours before the start of the game with some receiving testosterone and others receiving a placebo. Researches hypothesized that those who had received the testosterone supplement would exhibit antisocial behavior by being less trusting when playing the role of investor, which is precisely what happened. However, surprisingly, when these same players assumed the role of trustee, they became more generous. This unexpected result led researcher Maarten Boksem of the Rotterdam School of Management to note that "testosterone has had a more pronounced effect on pro-social behavior than on antisocial behavior if such behavior would be beneficial for maintaining or obtaining status."[106]

In connecting similar dots, other researchers have based much of their work on drawing correlations between testosterone levels and dominance. Social psychologist James Dabbs of Georgia State University famously associated higher testosterone levels in men with high socio-economic status. Dabbs found that high socio-economic men (and women) possessed higher rates of testosterone.[107] He also noted that testosterone levels rise in people who win a chess match[108] as well as in fans of winning sports teams,[109] suggesting that the feeling of exhilaration that attends victory releases testosterone into the system. This finding, of course, is a far cry from the more ambitious claims made by some about men, aggression, violence, and antisocial behavior, and is sometimes used to demonstrate how difficult and complex it is to draw reductionist connections between biology and male behavior.

In a study on generosity and selfishness conducted by Claremont Graduate University neuroeconomist Paul Zak in tandem with a team of endocrinologists, men with artificially raised T-levels, compared to those given placebos, were found to be 27% less generous with strangers in a computerized economics game devised by Zak and his research team.[110] The generalization Zak draws from this and similar studies is that younger men, with greater levels of testosterone, are more self-centered, imbued with feelings of entitlement, and driven to succeed, than older men, who tend to be more generous[111] and whose levels of testosterone diminish at an approximate rate of 1% per year starting at age 30.[112]

The results of the Rotterdam experiment, coupled with the research of Dabbs and Zak, are consistent with other testosterone studies. Increased levels of testosterone have not been correlated to antisocial behavior, per se, but have been found to be correlated to competition and status. Problems emerge when scholars and authors extrapolate from this body of research a particular speculative generalization about boys and men, such as Zak concluding that his findings inform us why younger men join the military while younger women decide to pursue careers in nursing or teaching.[113] Generalizations of this sort do not consider the multitude of factors that go into vocational pursuits for men and women, let alone support the view that testosterone levels provide the critical etiology to explain gendered preferences, and, in fact, inconsistencies abound. From one study that claims enhanced testosterone levels increase "gaze aversion from angry faces outside of conscious awareness,"[114] to studies that contradict the view that increased levels of testosterone lead to increased levels of competition and selfishness,[115] the general view that higher levels of testosterone increase aggressive and antisocial behavior or explain alleged male patterns of behavior has not found a consensus in science, and in fact led neuroscientist Christoph Eisenegger of the University of Cambridge to state, "The preconception that testosterone only causes aggressive or egoistic behavior in humans is clearly refuted."[116]

Sexual arousal has also been shown to be especially affected by rates of testosterone.[117] As testosterone is eliminated from the system of nonhuman, male primates, sexual interest appears to diminish. Findings of these kind lead some to conclude that higher levels of testosterone are responsible for men's increased sexual interest, which in turn leads to some men committing higher rates of sexual assault. Sexual desire is often associated with a family of hormones that include testosterone, estrogen, progesterone, oxytocin, and vasopressin, leading some who search for solutions to male sexual violence to suggest therapeutic, invasive intervention to reduce serum-T levels in men.[118] In one particular noteworthy study of 501 convicted male sex offenders who volunteered for a psychotherapy treatment program, it was found that those who had committed the most invasive sexual crimes also had higher levels of serum testosterone.[119] Researchers also concluded that sex offenders who possess higher levels of serum testosterone have a greater likelihood for recidivism.[120] Unsurprisingly, treatment of recidivist sex offenders often revolves around reducing levels of serum testosterone. Forensic psychiatrists Harvey Gordon and Don Grubin note, however, that while endocrinological factors cannot be dismissed, there are a multitude of other factors that contribute to male sexual violence such as substance abuse, personality disorders including schizophrenia and other related psychoses, dysmorphic mood disorder, the preoccupation with deviant sex fantasies that emphasize violence, distorted beliefs about rape, and other factors that can be revealed through clinical interview and psychometric testing.[121] Once again, attempting to reduce behavior, in this case sexually violent behavior found principally in men, is fraught with complications.

FIGURE 2.6: "Homo sapiens, the first truly free species, is about to decommission natural selection, the force that made us … Soon we must look deep within ourselves and decide what we wish to become." ~ E.O. Wilson, *Consilience, The Unity of Knowledge* (Vintage, 1999).

Socialization and Environment

The above quote by E.O. Wilson, the founder of the discipline known as sociobiology, may be somewhat surprising, because it seems to contradict one of the commonly held beliefs about sociobiology, the view that behavior is determined by biology. But Wilson does not subscribe to this deterministic view and instead holds that there is a strong cultural element that must be considered in explaining human behavior.[122] By identifying us as "truly free," Wilson is suggesting that we are capable of thwarting whatever biological impulses we have through the conscious urgings of our will or perhaps through the ways we determine to socialize children or other cognizant environmental changes we choose to develop.

The central criticisms of evolutionary psychological accounts of human behavior have come mainly from sociologists and social scientists who point out that unlike other primates, and especially birds and insects, human beings are socialized by identifiable social constructs that include cultural norms and practices that are often specific to gender. According to this view, normative gender scripts are introduced by those around us and reinforced from early childhood by rewarding what are considered to be appropriate gendered interests and behavior, while punishing what are considered to be inappropriate gendered interests and behavior. Researchers have found that in many cases, parents of children as young as 13 months of age begin the socialization process by engaging sons in "rough play," while being much more gentle with their daughters.[123] In these same studies, researchers found that parents are more responsive to male infants when the boys demand attention through crying, screaming, or behaving aggressively than they are to female infants. This same gendered response by parents was observed when language-routed behavior was involved. Parents are more responsive to female infants when the girls use language or gestures to communicate than they are when boys use this same approach.[124]

Parental reinforcement of gender norms is an example of what psychologists term ***operant conditioning***, whereby, in its most basic form as applied to child development, a child receives a positive or negative reinforcement by the parent according to the gendered behavior being produced by the child. Negative reinforcements can be meted out in two ways. A parent can apply a punishment of some kind to the child or the parent can withdraw attention from a child rather than inflicting an actual punishment in an attempt to get the child to abandon an unfavorable behavior for a favorable behavior, which can then be rewarded in some way. As a child ages, further positive and negative reinforcements come from siblings, friends, teachers, coaches, and other persons of influence. By the time a child has reached adolescence, a system of rewards and punishments from multiple sources contribute to a process sociologists and social psychologists term ***social*** or ***cultural conditioning***.[125] With respect to gender, sociologists argue that while ***sex*** is a biological classification that is assigned by gametes during prenatal sex specialization processes, ***gender*** is mainly a socially constructed and personal view that is laden with subjectivity and fluidity.[126]

The notion that gender is socially constructed finds roots in the work of self-titled sexologist John Money. In discussing differences between males and females, Money distinguished between ***sex-derivative traits***, ***sex-adjunctive traits***, and ***sex-arbitrary traits***. A sex-derivative trait is a physical trait that is produced from hormones such as the physical trait of men being, on average, taller than women. A sex-adjunctive trait is a trait not directly caused by hormonal influences, but by sex-derived effects such as women having to be sedentary during breast-feeding or more stationary in order to care for children. Money believed that these traits explain why women are expected to be responsible for "domestic work," while men are expected to gain employment outside of the home. Finally, sex-arbitrary traits are those found to be entirely constructed by culture such as assigning the color 'blue' to boys and 'pink' to girls.[127]

Money is also responsible for creating the expression ***gender role***, which he took to be an umbrella expression that covers genitalia, erotic sexual roles, and cultural conventions assigned to males and females. But Money expanded the notion of gender to include one's own personal conception of being male or female, a concept today known as ***gender identity***.[128] Money, in fact, viewed gender roles and gender identity as such closely interwoven concepts that he abbreviated the two as G-I/R.[129]

Money believed that gender identities are fixed after age three, and that socializing influences from birth to age three determine gender identity. Drawing on this view, Money supervised the sex-reassignment surgery of David Reimer, who was born physiologically male but whose penis was destroyed during circumcision. Money argued that it would be best to reconstruct Reimer's genitalia to resemble a vagina and then socialize Reimer as a female. As a result, Reimer was renamed 'Brenda," given hormone therapy, and socialized as a girl. The reconstruction was touted as a success and Money became famous in his day for having *proven* that gender is socially constructed. In 1959, drawing largely on endocrinological and biological evidence, anatomist and reproduction biologist Milton Diamond challenged Money, arguing that gender identity is essentially hard-wired into the brain from conception.[130] Diamond and Money engaged in one of more acrimonious public disputes on gender identity in the history of the subject. Diamond accused Money of confirmation bias and ignoring contrary evidence in coming to his conclusions. Reimer, it turns out, did not identify as a female and by age 13, told his parents that he would commit suicide if they sent him to visit John Money again. At 14, 'Brenda' renamed himself 'David' and began what would become many treatments to reverse the gender reassignment. He eventually revealed his story to Diamond, who along with Reimer, went public with his account leading Money's work on gender to be widely regarded in disrepute. In 2004, David Reimer committed suicide.

However, those who argued that environment plays the dominant role in gender identity were not deterred. Relying on socialization as the key process through which gendered behavior and gendered preferences are constructed, social psychologists identify two basic sorts of socialization that impact gender identity: ***natural socialization***, which occurs when infants and children explore the world around them, including their contact with social norms, and ***planned socialization***, which is the mainly human phenomenon of people taking a proactive approach to teaching or training infants and children to adopt certain prescribed norms of behavior. The working assumption is that infants are born without any cultural or normative regulations in place so that determinations about which behaviors are acceptable within a given culture are entirely learned. An example of the socialization process is learning the native language spoken within one's culture, which is largely a feature of guided imitation. With respect to gender norms, many cultures are imbued with rules on how properly to train girls to be daughters, wives, and mothers, while training boys how to be sons, husbands, and fathers. Along with these community roles come lessons on appropriate vocational and avocational pursuits for girls, boys, women, and men.

These gendered lessons can be distinct for different cultures. For instance, the Semai tribesmen of the central Malay Peninsula of Malaysia avoid aggressive and hostile people and subsequently teach their boys to be gentle, while the Yanomamo Indians who reside in the border area between Brazil and Venezuela train their boys to seek out hostile and even violent paths to conflict resolution.[131] Anthropologists have discovered that ***gender training*** is widely divergent in varying cultures around the world as part of what is termed ***informal education***, which involves imitating and practicing what others in your culture say and do. This informal process can pass through many generations, particularly in the absence of contact with other cultures, an increasingly unlikely reality.

Cultural Learning Theory and Gender Performativity

In one of the more notable studies of the 1950s, Harvard anthropologists John and Beatrice Whiting coined the phrase ***cultural learning environment*** to denote "all of the dimensions (macro and micro) of the context of everyday life, which create normative patterns of child socialization and development."[132] These notions have been modified today by a host of researchers including Charles Super and Sara Harkness who introduced the idea of a ***developmental niche***, which "provides a framework for examining the effects of cultural features on child rearing in interaction with general developmental parameters."[133] Super and Harkness outline three distinct elements involved in the socializing process of child development:

1. the physical and social setting in which a child lives, learns, grows, and develops,
2. parenting practices, which include the culturally regulated routines of child care as well as the training used by child caregivers,
3. the cultural belief system in place that caregivers hold and bring to their interactions with children.[134]

This last element is particularly noteworthy when turning to the distinct gendered scripts that are taught to boys and girls. As child caregivers interact with children, the theoretical framework informing culturally approved gender norms will be reinforced from caregiver to child with each behavioral opportunity that presents itself. In many cultures where gender dichotomies are strictly enforced, boys will be discouraged from playing with play-items considered in the culture to be suited for girls and instead directed to toys and activities that caregivers view as being appropriately masculine, while girls will be encouraged to play with culturally approved feminine toys and directed away from toys and activities considered to be masculine. Given the gendered framework of the culture from which the caregiver is socialized, boys are taught to mow the lawn and take out the garbage, while girls are taught to bake and clean house. Boys may be encouraged to play contact sports such as football and basketball, while girls, if encouraged to play sports at all, may be directed toward non-contact sports such as volleyball, golf, softball, or tennis.

GENDERED TOYS AND ACTIVITIES

Many have pointed out that boys and girls are routinely socialized to be different from one another in terms of appropriate toys, behaviors, activities, and interests. Sociologists note that these gendered interests are part of a process of socialization that begins in early childhood. As such, gendered toys and interests are shaped and reinforced. Girls are routinely encouraged to play with dolls and learn to apply makeup:

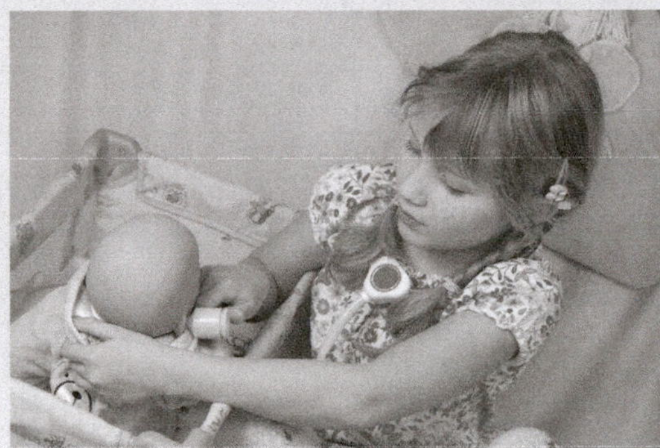

FIGURE 2.7:

FIGURE 2.8:

Continued

Toys and interests for boys are commonly reinforced in very different directions, guided typically toward mechanical toys, military, and other spatial-locomotive play.

FIGURE 2.9:

FIGURE 2.10:

Those on both sides of the nature–nurture debate will often use these same images to show that either boys and girls are naturally drawn to certain activities or to show that boys and girls are socialized by parents and others to gravitate toward certain activities. Those on the side of nurture note that when boys and girls are left to their own devices, they will often play with toys considered to be made for the other gender. In the U.K., the campaign "Let Toys Be Toys" was launched to encourage children to explore a variety of interests while attempting to eliminate gender stereotypes: www.lettoysbetoys.org.uk. What is your opinion?

But beyond these extracurricular activities, gendered socialization also involves the ways that boys and girls are expected to view career paths. In American culture, there has been a tradition of viewing math, science, technology, and construction-related fields as vocational areas pursued by men, while careers in nursing, teaching, and other fields thought to require nurturance have been coded female in orientation. The subtleties can be numerous, but often based on status distinctions; so while cooking has been traditionally viewed as an activity proper to females in domestic settings, being a chef has been traditionally viewed as a career for men. It is also impossible to ignore the power dynamics of these distinctions. Becoming an R.N. or L.V.N. has been considered a career path for women, with the attending assumption that women are naturally better at providing care and following orders, while becoming an M.D. has been historically considered the career domain of men, who it was assumed are naturally adapted for understanding the complexities of science and possessing the diagnostic skills required for a clinical environment where mental acuity and quick, accurate decisions are needed. All of these cultural assumptions feed into the various ways boys and girls are raised by parents and other caregivers in what are considered to be gendered proclivities, which are then converted into educational and vocational directions boys and girls are encouraged and expected to take.

As further rebuttal to the notion that gender is an immutable state of affairs grounded in biology, in 1961 Albert Bandura introduced ***social learning theory***, which maintains that children acquire novel behaviors by observing and imitating others.[135] Bandura and his colleagues were able to show that children will imitate aggressive behavior when witnessed on video. On the other hand, when children were shown a character being punished for exhibiting aggressive behavior, the aggression in children decreased.[136] Bandura concluded that learning is a cognitive process that occurs within a social context such that one will imitate the behaviors one is exposed to unless negative consequences are associated with that behavior. The connection these studies have to gendered behavior is fairly obvious. If a child is repeatedly exposed to behaviors modeled by mentors or peers as proper masculine or feminine behavior, the likelihood increases that the child will begin to imitate and eventually adopt those behaviors. This also suggests that if the observed behaviors are attended with negative consequences, the likelihood decreases that the child will adopt those behaviors. So, if a boy witnesses his father, caregiver, or male peers engaging in aggressive or violent behavior, particularly in the absence of palpable negative consequences to the perpetrator, social learning theory predicts that the boy will begin to adopt these behaviors as well. High rates of generational violence are often explained through social learning theory in what is termed ***intergenerational transmission of violence theory***.[137] [138] Social learning theorists view this cycle of violence as a predictable pattern of behavior given the repeated violent behaviors boys are exposed to in the home.

In yet another way of explaining gender identity, feminist philosopher Judith Butler introduced ***gender performativity*** as the view that gender is a stylized repetition of acts, an imitation of the dominant cultural conventions of gender. According to Butler, gender identity is not simply a matter of arbitrary choice nor a matter of immutable forces of nature, but rather involves complexities that include:

> the tacit collective agreement to perform, produce, and sustain discrete and polar genders as cultural fictions [is] obscured by the credibility of those productions—and the punishments that attend not agreeing to believe in them.[139]

Because this "tacit collective agreement" is so powerfully a part of our introduction to and reinforcement of our gender identities, Butler argues that we begin to believe that masculine and feminine identities are polar opposites, and that these identities are

FIGURE 2.11: Feminist philosopher Judith Butler

natural, when they are in fact a product of the many socializing forces that instruct us what it means to perform as male or female. When one is immersed in a heteronormative culture that has very specific rules on proper masculine or feminine behaviors, there will be a good deal of gender-policing by members of that culture toward those who are not performing their masculine or feminine script to code. Punishments of various kinds will then be doled out to gender nonconformists to assure compliance with the gender script leading to the foreseeable result of widespread adherence to culturally-approved gender norms.

In their article "Doing Gender," sociologists Candace West and Don Zimmerman argue that gender is performed in response to interactions with others based on socially accepted norms of gender within a given culture.[140] Gender becomes structured through these interactions, which, again, fuel the common notion that gender is a static classification rooted in biology, even though this structure is a product of an untold number of social influences. With respect to men, masculine performance becomes visible through appearance, fashion, styles of conversation, word choice, handshake conventions, and dozens of mannerisms consistent with societal expectations of masculinity. Similarly, feminine performance is observable in a host of behaviors, styles, and fashions coded female by the culture. As these performances become codified over time, gender polarization is widely fortified and accepted as a conspicuous truth, when in fact gender may be more fluid and accommodating to change in cultural attitudes. In American popular culture, as witnessed in the Calvin Klein ads pictured in Figures 2.12 and 2.13, it is much more common to view men and women depicted in terms of gendered power binaries where men are shown to be in positions of dominance while women are shown to be in positions of submission.

Gender polarity may be more pronounced and caricatured in popular culture, which includes the mass-media avenues into which youth culture is immersed, but the pervasiveness of these cultural tropes is part of the reinforcing process that is the signature of gender performance for boys and girls who look to cultural archetypes to determine how to conduct their male or female performances. These archetypal performances are then

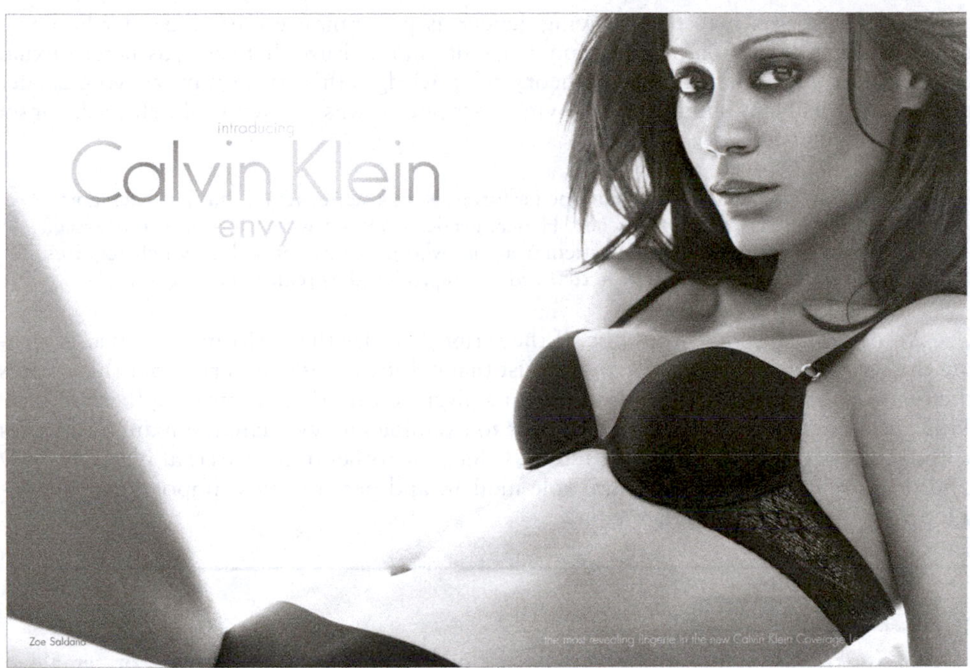

FIGURE 2.12: Actor Zoe Saldana in Calvin Klein ad

FIGURE 2.13: Actor Mark Wahlberg in Calvin Klein ad

reproduced on campuses, malls, and other environments where boys and girls interact. Some people will rebel against gender conformity or simply feel uncomfortable assuming the gender roles imparted by their cultures, but the archetypes will serve as templates for the majority who are trying to fit in with their respective peer groups.

Queer theorists note that viewing gender as performance creates gender-homogeneity, which in turn promotes heteronormativity in a culture that rewards heterosexual expression. Butler's performativity theory acknowledges this concern by viewing gender performance as being similar to following a script that was written well before the onset of the performance:

> The act that one does, the act that one performs, is, in a sense, an act that has been going on before one arrived on the scene. Hence, gender is an act which has been rehearsed, much as a script survives the particular actors who make use of it, but which requires individual actors in order to be actualized and reproduced as reality once again.[141]

An obvious question would be, if the script precedes the performance, who is writing the script? West and Zimmerman insist that cultures write the script, but this creates the further question, who are those within a given culture that are writing these scripts? This question will lead us later in the text to examine and evaluate the many influences within culture that shape customs, mores, values, and other influences that include family traditions, religious ideals, cultural role models, and perhaps most importantly in contemporary American culture, media.

THOUGHT BOX

Identify trends, styles, and fashions that are distinctively coded male or female throughout culture. Bring some pictures to class of these styles and discuss why you believe some have been classified male and others female. For instance, the backward baseball cap is worn almost entirely by boys and young men. Why do you think this is? What are the origins of the reverse cap? What does it allegedly say about the wearer?

Examine these two ads by Carl's Jr./Hardee's. Beyond selling fast-food, do you believe the ads are saying something about men and women?

FIGURE 2.14:

FIGURE 2.15:

Boys will be Boys?

The expression "boys will be boys" is a longstanding expression meant to describe the sorts of behavioral dispositions and activities to which boys naturally gravitate, and this

FIGURE 2.16: "Eruptions of rage in boys are most often deemed normal, explained by the age-old justification for adolescent patriarchal misbehavior, 'Boys will be boys'" ~ bell hooks[142]

alleged natural inclination has always been considered to be rougher, more physical, and prone to higher rates of aggression and violence than what is thought to be true of girls. But there is another sense of the phrase "boys will be boys" that is fraught with resignation. In the spirit of biological determinism, "boys will be boys" means that there is nothing that can be done to change male behavior even if we have the desire to do so. It means that the higher rates of aggression and violence found in male behavior is an immutable masculine trait that we just have to deal with, and by "deal with," it is sometimes meant that we will probably have to build more prisons and prepare for more wars.

Some scholars are now recognizing the dangers of the "boys will be boys" assumption. Dr. Elizabeth Meyers, professor of education at California State Polytechnic University, San Luis Obispo, identifies four main problems with the expression *boys will be boys*:

1. it prompts students to construct and reinforce gender stereotypes,
2. gender stereotypes allow unconscious biases to form and proliferate,
3. it is misinformed thinking that oversimplifies the problem,
4. it limits the full expression of children.[143]

The proliferation of stereotypes creates expectations, in this case negative expectations about boys, that can convert into self-fulfilling prophesies. If boys are told repeatedly that there is something inherent in them as males that causes them to act out in hostile and destructive ways, boys can internalize those stereotypes and believe there is innate justification for doing so. This same expectation can influence the way others view and treat boys. Parents who buy into the notion that boys are "naturally disruptive" may treat boys with harsher disciplinary measures. Educators who believe boys are inherently unruly and troublesome may adjust their pedagogy to adapt to this convention. The stereotype also sets up a peer environment where boys who do not adhere to the aggressive, unruly expectation are targeted for ridicule and bullying.

Writer and researcher, Rachel Brandt Fisher adds to the list of dangers the fact that buying into the *boys will be boys* missive leads to lessening efforts to help boys find constructive ways to deal with anger and other emotions.[144] Serious issues like depression, impulsive anger, bullying, physical and sexual violence, and high rates of male suicide are chalked up to *male tendencies* about which very little other than punitive measures can be done. Richard A. Mendel, researcher for the American Youth Policy Forum, reports that the most common way society deals with male youth violence is to lock up more boys and young men, including trying more boys as adults in criminal courts, while feeding the notion to a fearful public that not doing so will result in a generation of *superpredator* that will terrorize the streets of America.[145] Policy-makers employ these scare tactics to gain political mileage from a largely conservative public that believe only tough tactics will have an impact on male violence. These caricatures are often racialized as well, which feeds into a racist stereotype about boys and men of color. When alternative methods of dealing with male violence that focus on prevention and rehabilitation are suggested or promoted, the *boys will be boys* incantation is wheeled out as an indisputable fact about boys and men that only incarceration can hope to contain.

In what many viewed as a particularly outrageous case, a prosecutor in Montana explained to the mother of a 5-year-old girl who had been raped, "boys will be boys."[146] In line with the endocrinological account of male sexual urges, this sense of the expression *boys will be boys* reinforces the view that males are naturally more interested in sex so that along with having to deal with violence, society will have to endure high rates of sexual violence as a byproduct of the inordinate degree of male lust. This idea actually found academic favor by two scholars, anthropologist Craig T. Palmer and zoologist Randy Thornhill in their coauthored book, *A Natural History of Rape: The Biological Bases of Sexual Coercion*,[147] where they argue that rape is an evolutionary byproduct of ancestral sex practices. In a review for the *New York Times*, distinguished Emory

University primatologist Frans de Waal mockingly retitled the book, "survival of the rapist,"[148] noting that Palmer and Thornhill's solution to high rates of rape is to warn girls and women to stop dressing provocatively. But this advice underlines the problem with the phrase *boys will be boys*; it creates an intractable problem that can be met only by society taking measures to protect itself against men.

THE BELYAEV FOX EXPERIMENT

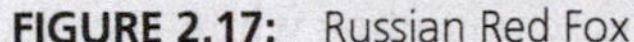

FIGURE 2.17: Russian Red Fox

FIGURE 2.18: Through domestication, the red fox's coat turned white and behavior changed

During the 1950s, Russian geneticist Dmitry Belyaev domesticated wild foxes by carefully selecting individuals that demonstrated an eagerness to establish human contact.[1] These "social foxes" were allowed to breed, while those that exhibited antisocial behaviors were not. The experiments were fueled by Belyaev's evolutionary contention that behavior can be modified through selective breeding. This phenomenon is known as ***domestication syndrome***, a syndrome that relies on the notion that "reduced stress levels in animals living in a protected anthropogenic environment cause multiple changes in hormonal responses that reset patterns of gene expression."[2] This means that serene environments and the encouragement of prosocial behaviors can actually alter the expression of genes including those genes that are marked for aggression. This new genetic arrangement is then heritable and the domestication of otherwise wild, aggressive, and violent animals is mitigated for future generations. The speculative consequences for masculinity and human societies are obvious: the transition from hostile, aggressive, and highly competitive environments to more tranquil and cooperative environments holds the promise of less violent men. But this eugenically adapted utopian world where violence has been contained is not the world in which most human beings live, and selective breeding is not considered to be an ethical response to human behavioral problems. Furthermore, human beings are not foxes; our communities and influences are obviously much more complex. Still, those who tout the study as a groundbreaking study believe that it has shown there to be an interaction between genetics and environment that can be modified to accomplish behavioral goals.

1. http://cbsu.tc.cornell.edu/ccgr/behaviour/history.htm.
2. www.genetics.org/content/197/3/795.full.

Not all authors agree that the *boys will be boys* model of masculinity is a negative model. In his book *Raising Cain: Protecting the Emotional Lives of Boys*, child psychologist Michael Thompson argues that rough, physical play is a feature of boyhood in every society on Earth.[149] Thompson calls it "an urban myth" that boys who play rough will become desensitized to violence and more prone to act out violently later in life.[150] Thompson blames women for overreacting to boys' rough play on the view that females do not grow up playing the way that boys play and so do not understand the dynamic of healthy, rough play.[151] Author and professor of education at Wheelock College, Diane Levin, disagrees.[152] Levin argues that beginning in the 1980s, due in part to FCC deregulation, aggressive play escalated into what she terms "war play," with boys imitating what they saw in media. Levin argues that violence is marketed to boys, while prettiness and sexiness is marketed to girls, with marketers defending these dichotomies as being natural. Thompson sides with marketers, stating, "Boys are innately wired for dominance and that is going to affect the kinds of stories they like and the kind of games they play."[153]

In line with Thompson's view that boys need rough, physical play, Falling Creek Camp in North Carolina was founded in 1969 by Jim Miller as a Christian boys' camp where boys can explore and play in the woods.[154] Featured in a *Time Magazine* article in July of 2007, Falling Creek subscribes to the view that the *boys will be boys* model of masculinity should not be taken in a negative sense, but should be embraced and channeled in constructive ways. Promoting a view they term "structured freedom," boys are allowed to explore and engage in supervised tasks that include pounding white-hot pieces of metal, clinging to a zip line two stories over a lake, backpacking, and white-water rafting. Camp organizers argue that these activities build character, self-confidence, and teach boys the importance of working within a team environment. Boston College evolutionary psychologist Peter Gray agrees and argues that physical play is educational and helps children develop empathy and cooperation.[155] Of boys, aggressive play, and nature, Gray writes:

> Children—especially boys—play this way because Mother Nature knows that they have to learn how to control not just their fear but also their anger. In this play, they experience anger within the limits of what they can manage.[156]

Gray frames aggressive play in boys as part of developing the inner tools of anger management. According to this view, boys learn their anger limits in the safety of friendly fighting with close friends so that lessons are learned without any real dangers or harms befalling them.

FIGURE 2.19: Falling Creek Camp, North Carolina

> **THOUGHT BOX**
>
> List five traits you think of when considering the phrase, "Boys will be Boys." How many of these traits are positive? How many negative? What, then, do you believe the phrase "boys will be boys" states about being male?

In her book, *Boys Will Be Boys*, author and former professor of philosophy at Rutgers University, Myriam Miedzian, sides with Levin arguing that we must change male culture if we hope to reverse the rates of aggression and violence found in men.[157] Emphasizing the importance of instructing boys on how to navigate conflict without violence, encouraging fathers to be more involved in the nurturing of their sons, while raising awareness about the harms of glorifying violence in media are the focal points of Miedzian's approach to turning the tide of destructive masculinity. Getting to boys early in life is also a central concern, since socializing forces can be difficult to overcome later in life. A recurring theme in Miedzian's work is the worry that boys who practice aggression and violence as a means of conflict resolution, even in the context of play, have little else to draw upon in the face of actual conflict. If a boy has been taught since early childhood that conflict with others is best addressed through hostility and aggression, and the tools of cooperative resolution or empathetic compromise are not part of a boy's socialization with respect to negotiating conflict, boys will not suddenly discover these tools in the heat of contentious disagreement with others. Instead, the *boys will be boys* model of masculinity restricts the range of options boys and men have at their disposal to resolving difference, and if anything, promotes and excuses aggressive response with all of the attending problematic consequences that come with it. When coupled with the glorification of violence by media, Miedzian concludes that current societal norms are a blueprint for creating violent men who see no other choice but to act out violently in the face of conflict.

Nature–Nurture Revisited

Professor of biology and gender studies at Brown University, Anne Fausto-Sterling argues that instead of pitting nature against nurture, we should abandon the search for root causes and look to an individual's behavioral capacities as "a web of mutual interactions between the biological being and the social environment."[158] Scholarship of the past has segregated sex and gender by viewing what Cynthia Kraus terms 'naked sex' as what remains when gender is stripped away,[159] creating impermeable boundaries between the contributions of biology and the contributions of culture. Fausto-Sterling cautions that this sort of thinking oversells the idea that biological contributions are immutable, while cultural contributions are permeable.[160] Instead, Fausto-Sterling constructs a syncretic view of sex-gender she terms ***Developmental Systems Theory (DST)***, which rejects the notion of 'naked sex' or 'naked culture' (what remains after any influence of nature has been eliminated), and argues rather that differences in brain development are impacted by environmental differences, which entails that biology is not immutable. Fausto-Sterling views the future of sex–gender dialogues as dialogues between members of different academic disciplines addressing the following sorts of questions:

> What childhood experiences and behaviours contribute to the developing anatomy of the brain? Are there particular developmental periods when a child's brain is more or less responsive to functional stimuli? How do nerve cells translate externally generated information into specific growth patterns and neural circuits? Answering these latter questions will require the skills of molecular biologists and cell biologists as well as psychologists, sociologists, and cultural theorists.[161]

Cultural contributions, through the lens of DST, would not be as malleable as originally thought, since social experiences would be "interpreted and integrated by a differently functioning brain."[162] This means that the flexibility thought to be intrinsic to cultural contributions to the overall gender equation would have certain *soft* biological restrictions in place.

But Fausto-Sterling goes further to state that she finds nature–nurture interactionism to be unsatisfying as well, because it sets up a mysterious dualism not unlike the old-fashioned mind–body problem of the past.[163] Instead, Fausto-Sterling opts for the idea that nature and nurture are inextricable parts of a whole that evolves continuously throughout our lives.[164] The problem is that, for many researchers, the nature–nurture debate is viewed as a zero-sum game, where one side wins at the direct expense of the other. Fausto-Sterling argues that studies have shown maternal caretaking to affect the expression of certain genes, which shape the density of hormone receptors in the brains of rats.[165] This means that nurture has a direct effect on what Fausto-Sterling terms ***brain-building***, a phenomenon that results due to the influence of nurturing behavior on the new and developing brain. Synaptic density in neonate brains is quite low but becomes increasingly dense throughout the first two years of life.[166]

For Fausto-Sterling, there is an important take-away point:

> The general lesson: greater stimulation [leads] to greater nerve development in the brain and spinal cord; diminished stimulation [produces] diminished connectivity.[167]

One example of the importance of environment to gender may be found in vocalization patterns for male and female infants. Some neuroscientists report differences in language proliferation between boys and girls and have used these differences to defend the idea that gendered brain differences exist by nature. Fausto-Sterling argues that it is an exaggeration to state that there are pronounced language-skill differences between males and females, and points to the fact that the small differences that do exist may be accounted for by noting that in studies where infants babbled, "the mother's vocal responses to boys' babbles decreased, while maternal vocal responses to girls' babbling

FIGURE 2.20: Anne Fausto-Sterling

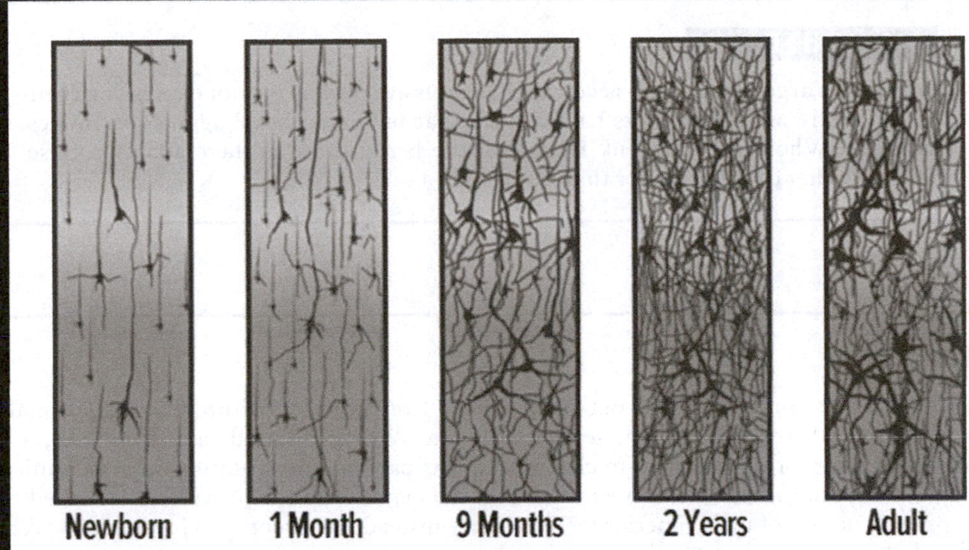

FIGURE 2.21: Synaptic Density Over Time

increased," concluding that there is a "touch, talk, hold connect nexus [that] may differ for adult-boy and adult-girl dyads, which could lead to different patterns of speech development."[168] Early behavioral gender asymmetries may result, therefore, from "the dynamic interplay of systems such as hearing, sound production and emotional attachment as they play out for girl and boy infants and their caregivers."[169]

Yet, for the foreseeable future, the nature–nurture debate will likely continue with each side claiming victory over the other. At the same time, those defending nurture as the primary factor in bringing about gender norms argue that their side is empowering, while noting that the nature defense locks us into more rigid, less mutable gender assignments, without, perhaps, the aid of neurosurgery or other biologically intrusive interventions. That is, if gender is determined chiefly by nature, our ability to modify problematic behaviors may be constrained by forces immune to cultural change. On the other hand, if gender is largely constructed, then altering cultural mores about gender creates an opportunity to redefine gender and thus creates an opportunity for innovation that includes, for instance, the construction of more empathetic and compassionate men. At the same time, those who subscribe to the notion that gender is socially constructed usually note that change of the sort necessary to bring about a less violent, more cohesive society is anything but easy. It would amount to changing some of the most foundational views currently held on masculinity. Oakland University professor, therapist Thomas W. Blume, argues that the requisite change needed to bring about a more peaceful society involves a ***system change***, which involves a partnered effort of individuals in communities with cooperation from policy-makers, parents, teachers, producers of media, members of law enforcement, social workers, child care providers, and other key contributors who hold positions of influence in society, particularly those who hold credible sway over boys and men.[170] Changing current models of manhood would involve an adjustment not just of facts and perspectives, but of values; and this sort of transformation may require nothing less than a revolution of male culture.

THOUGHT BOX

Some have argued that boys need rough, aggressive play as part of expressing their inner nature as boys. Others have argued that indulging boys' aggression invites violence. Whom do you think is making the better case? Is there a compromise available that could be better than either side alone?

EXERCISE

Individually, or in groups, seek out claims pulled from popular culture that suggest male aggression, whether physical or sexual, is innate. Whether found in ads, articles, TV shows or films, bring examples to class to share as part of a presentation on masculinity, aggression, and innateness. Do you feel that the claims you found were constructed to support a notion of male superiority? Were they instead constructed to insult men? Were the claims made as part of a larger claim about violence?

Summary

The debate over whether aggression and violence in men are natural or culturally learned traits has been taking place only over the past century or so. Before the advance of sociological accounts of violence, it was assumed that men are violent than women by nature. The proof for this *fact* was found in *post facto* observation: it was simply perceptible to anyone who investigated the subject that men are more violent than women. Given that animals functioned on the basis of natural instincts, it was assumed that the same must be true for human beings, and this notion was then extended to noticeable differences in the behaviors of men and women. This same reasoning led many early philosophers to assume that not only is aggression in men natural, but that the qualities of rationality, strength of mind, and leadership were natural to men, unnatural to women. Very few thought to ask whether these observed gendered behavioral and allegedly aptitudinal differences might be taught and learned. Once it was discovered that men had higher serum levels of certain hormones than women, and particularly testosterone, it was all but agreed that aggression, violence, intellect, and leadership qualities were a predetermined gift of nature bestowed upon men.

Today, much of the gendered nature–nature debate has fallen to neuroscience as the science best qualified to opine about differences in gendered capacities and aptitudes. Predictably, however, neuroscientists do not agree whether sense can be made of there being a male brain and female brain that explain alleged differences in the capacities of men and women. The hope of endocrinological and neurological studies deciding the matter is no longer held high, although several prominent neurologists continue to focus their work in this area and continue to maintain that neurological features explain why, they claim, men are less empathic and nurturing than women. But much of this work has been criticized by other neurologists who argue that confirmation bias, conflicting data, over-reaching conclusions on insufficient evidence, and explicit sexist assumptions have poisoned the research.

Even though the nature–nurture debate is not close to being over, much of the most promising research begins with the assumption that both nature and nurture play a role in constructing behavior, including whatever gendered behaviors exist. Those critical to this research point out that there is far too much variation between individuals to generalize about gender and that even if both nature and nurture contribute to human behavior, it is highly unlikely that conclusions can be drawn about each element's relative contributions to the matter. In addition, critics note that the biological determinist views espoused by those who see nature as the central or lone contributor to behavior leave us in the untenable position of having to accept with little recourse other than surgical intervention the behaviors society would like to change. When coupled with the documented successes of various forms of cultural conditioning, those on the nurture side of the debate ask that we try to produce beneficial change instead of assume that nothing can be done.

Notes

1 www.imdb.com/title/tt0110632/quotes.
2 Plato, *Republic*, 454d.
3 Ibid., 431c.
4 Ibid., 455c–d.
5 Aristotle, *History of Animals*, 608b 1–14.
6 *Encyclopaedia Britannica*. www.britannica.com/EBchecked/topic/256300/Harvard-University.
7 "The History of Women at Princeton University," www.princeton.edu/mudd/news/faq/topics/women.shtml, and "Landmarks in Yale's History," www2.yale.edu/timeline/1969/index.html.
8 "The Record." www.columbia.edu/cu/news/record/coeducation.html.
9 De Beauvoir, Simone, *The Second Sex* (1949) (Vintage Press, 1989). The H.M. Parshley translation from French to English is widely considered to be a poor translation. An updated translation can now be obtained through Vintage Press.
10 http://en.wikipedia.org/wiki/Index_Librorum_Prohibitorum.
11 Freud, Sigmund, *The Ego and the Id*, 1923 (Create Space Independent Publishing Platform, 2013).
12 Freud, Sigmund, "The Psychical Consequences of the Anatomic Distinction Between the Sexes" (1925). www.aquestionofexistence.com/Aquestionofexistence/Problems_of_Gender/Entries/2011/8/28_Sigmund_Freud_files/Freud%20Some%20Psychological%20Consequences%20of%20the%20Anatomical%20Distinction%20between%20the%20Sexes.pdf.
13 "Compare and Contrast Freud and Horney's View of Women," StudyMode.com. 04 2006. www.studymode.com/essays/Compare-And-Contrast-Freud-And-Horney%27s-85593.html.
14 *Boston Globe*, January, 2005. www.boston.com/news/local/articles/2005/01/17/summers_remarks_on_women_draw_fire/.
15 Ibid.
16 *The Guardian*, January, 2005. www.theguardian.com/science/2005/jan/18/educationsgendergap.genderissues.
17 *The Harvard Crimson*, January 2005. www.thecrimson.com/article/2005/1/14/summers-comments-on-women-and-science/.
18 American Sociological Association. "Statement of the American Sociological Association Council on the Causes of Gender Differences in Science and Math Career Achievement: Harvard's Lawrence Summers and the Ensuing Public Debate," February, 2005.
19 Ogilvie, Marilyn Bailey, "Marie Curie, Women, and the History of Chemistry," in *Celebrating the 100th Anniversary of Madame Marie Sklodowska Curie's Nobel Prize in Chemistry* (Sense Publishers, 2011), pp. 105–118.
20 Unz, Ron, "Meritocracy: Almost as Wrong as Larry Summers," *The American Conservative*, March 9, 2013.
21 *U.C. Berkeley News*. http://berkeley.edu/news/media/releases/2008/07/24_math.shtml.
22 Stanford Report, "No Evidence of Innate Gender Differences in Math and Science," February 9, 2005.
23 Darwin, Charles, *The Origin of Species* (1859), p. 449.
24 Wynn, Jonathan G., Sponheimer, Matt, Kimbel, William H., Alemseged, Zeresenay, Reed, Kaye, Bedaso, Zelalem K., and Wilson, Jessica N., "Diet of *Australopithecus*

afarensis from the Pliocene Hadar Formation, Ethiopia," *Proceedings of the National Academy of Sciences of the United States of America*, 2013.
25 www.anth.ucsb.edu/projects/human/epfaq/determinism.html.
26 Ibid.
27 Liddle, James R., Shackelford, Todd K., and Weekes-Shackelford, Viviana A., "Why can't we all just get along? Evolutionary perspectives on violence, homicide, and war," *Review of General Psychology*, November 2011.
28 Buss, David M., Haselton, Martie G., Shackelford, Todd K., Bleske, April L., and Wakefield, Jerome C., "Adaptations, exaptations, and spandrels," *American Psychologist*, 1998.
29 *Psychology Today*, May, 28, 2012. www.psychologytoday.com/blog/evolutionary-entertainment/201205/giving-feminism-bad-name.
30 Hassett, Janice M., Siebert, Erin R., and Wallen, Kim. "Sex preferences in rhesus monkey toy preferences parallel those of children," *Hormones and Behavior*, August, 2008.
31 World Health Organization, "WHO Multi-country study on women's health and domestic violence against women." www.who.int/gender/violence/who_multicountry_study/en/.
32 Hotamisligil, G.S. and Breakfield, X.O., "Human monoamine oxidase A gene determines levels of enzyme activity," *American Journal of Human Genetics* 49, 2 (1991), pp. 383–392.
33 Brown University. "'Warrior Gene' Predicts Aggressive Behavior After Provocation." *Science Daily*, January 23, 2009.
34 *Scientific American*. http://blogs.scientificamerican.com/cross-check/2011/04/26/code-rage-the-warrior-gene-makes-me-mad-whether-i-have-it-or-not/.
35 Ibid.
36 *Progress in Neuropsychopharmacology and Biological Psychiatry* 40 (January 2013), pp. 122–125.
37 Ibid.
38 "Dr. Phil" July 26, 2011, CBS.
39 Buckholtz, Joshua W., "Neuroprediction and Crime," *NOVA science NOW*, October, 2012.
40 Fergusson, David M., Boden, Joseph M., Horwood, L. John, Miller, Allison L. and Kennedy, Martin A., "MAOA, abuse exposure and antisocial behavior: 3-year longitudinal study," *The British Journal of Psychiatry*, 198 (2011), pp. 457–463.
41 Buchholtz, Joshua W., "Neuroprediction and crime," *NOVA scienceNOW*, October, 2012.
42 National Geographic Explorer, *Born to Rage*, 2010.
43 Beaver K, Barnes J. and Boutwell B., "The 2-repeat allele of the MAOA gene confers an increased risk for shooting and stabbing behaviors," *Psychiatric Quarterly* 85 (2013), pp. 257–265.
44 https://scientiasalon.wordpress.com/2014/07/31/the-extreme-warrior-gene-a-reality-check/.
45 Ibid.
46 Ibid.
47 Ibid.
48 Ibid.
49 http://en.wikipedia.org/wiki/XYY_syndrome.
50 Walzer, Stanley, Bashir, Anthony S., and Silbert, Annette R., "Cognitive and behavioral factors in the learning disabilities of 47,XXY and 47,XYY boys," *Birth Defects Original Article Series* 26, 4 (1990), pp. 45–58.
51 Jacobs, Patricia A., Brunton, Muriel, Melville, Marie M., Brittain, Robert P., and McClemont, William F., "Aggressive behavior, mental sub-normality and the XYY male," *Nature* 208, 5017 (December 25, 1965), pp. 1351–1352.
52 Stock, Robert W., "The XYY and the criminal." *The New York Times Magazine*, October 20, 1968, SM30.
53 "Of chromosomes & crime," *Time Magazine* 91/18 (May 3, 1968), p. 41.
54 Court Brown, W. Michael, "Sex chromosomes and the law," *Lancet* 280, 7254 (1962), pp. 508–509; "William Michael Court Brown," Lancet 293, 7584 (1969), pp. 57–58.
55 Court Brown, W. Michael. "Males with an XYY sex chromosome complement," December, *Journal of Medical Genetics* 5, 4 (1968), pp. 341–359.
56 Witkin, Herman A., Mednick, Sarnoff A., Schulsinger, Fini, Bakkestrøm, Eskild, Christiansen, Karl O., Goodenough, Donald R., Hirschhorn, Kurt, Lundsteen, Claes, Owen, David R., Philip, John, Rubin, Donald B., and Stocking, Martha, "Criminality in XYY and XXY men," *Science* 193, issue 4253 (August 13, 1976), pp. 547–555. doi:10.1126/science.959813.
57 Vito, Gennaro and Maahs, Jeffrey, *Criminology: Theory, Research, and Policy*

(Jones and Bartlett Publishers, 2011), pp. 83–84.

58 Gray, John, *Men are from Mars, Women are from Venus: The Classic Guise to Understanding the Opposite Sex* (Harper-Collins, 1992).

59 Gray, John, *Why Mars and Venus Collide: Improving Relationships by Understanding How Men and Women Cope Differently with Stress* (Harper Perennial, 2008).

60 Annis, Barbara and Gray, John, *Work with Me: The 8 Blind Spots between Men and Women in Business* (Palgrave Macmillan, 2014), p. 63.

61 Ingalhalikar M., Smith A., Parker D., et al., "Sex Differences in the Structural Connectome of the Human Brain," *Proceedings of the National Academy of Sciences of the United States of America* 111, 2 (2013), pp. 823–828.

62 *The Guardian*, February, 18, 2014. www.theguardian.com/education/2014/feb/18/female-students-science-engineering-sixth-formers-stem-subjects.

63 Eliot, Lise, "Out with pink and blue: Don't foster the gender divide," *New Scientist*, 19 July 2010.

64 Hamaan S., "Sex differences in the responses of the human amygdala," *The Neuroscientist* 11, 4 (2005), pp. 288–293.

65 http://languagelog.ldc.upenn.edu/myl/ldc/llog/Brizendine/Hamann2005.pdf.

66 Ibid.

67 Ruigrok, Amber N.V., Salimi-Khorshidi, Gholamreza, Lai, Meng-Chuan, Baron-Cohen, Simon, Lombardo, Michael V., Tait, Roger J., and Suckling, John, "**A meta-analysis of sex differences in human brain structure**," *Neuroscience & Biobehavioral Reviews*, 2013.

68 Flynn, James R. *Are We Getting Smarter?* (Cambridge University Press, 2012).

69 *Psychology Today*, July 20, 2012, http://www.psychologytoday.com/blog/beautiful-minds/201207/men-women-and-iq-setting-the-record-straight.

70 WebMD, "How Male and Female Brains Differ," David C. Geary quoted within piece, www.webmd.com/balance/features/how-male-female-brains-differ?page=2.

71 Brizendine, Louann, *The Male Brain* (Harmony Books, 2011); *The Female Brain* (Harmony Books, 2006).

72 Rizzolatti, G. Craighero, L., "The Mirror-Neuron System," *Annual Review of Neuroscience* 27 (2004), pp. 169–192.

73 Abu-Akel, A and Shamay-Tsoory, S., "Neuroanatomical and neurochemical bases of theory of mind," *Neuropsychologia* 49, 11 (2011), 2976.

74 Di Pellegrino, G., Fadiga, L., Fogassi, L., Gallese, V., and Rizzolatti, G., "Understanding motor events: a neurophysiological study. Experimental Brain Research," 91 (1992), pp. 176–180.

75 Ramachandran, V.R., *The Tell-Tale Brain: A Neuroscientist's Quest for What Makes Us Human* (W.W. Norton, 2012).

76 V. S. Ramachdran, TED talk, 2009. www.brainfacts.org/brain-basics/neuroanatomy/articles/2013/vs-ramachandran-the-neurons-that-shaped-civilization/.

77 Cheng, Yawei, Lee, Po-Lei, Yang, Chia-Yen, Lin, Ching-Po, Hung, Daisy, and Decety, Jean, "Gender differences in the mu rhythm of the human mirror-neuron system," *PLOS ONE*, May 7, 2008. www.plosone.org/article/info%3Adoi%2F10.1371%2Fjournal.pone.0002113.

78 Baron-Cohen, Simon, *Zero Degrees of Empathy* (Allen Lane Books, 2011).

79 Edge Video featuring Simon Baron-Cohen, 2014. http://edge.org/conversation/do-women-have-better-empathy-than-men.

80 Baron-Cohen, Simon, *The Guardian*, April, 2003. www.theguardian.com/education/2003/apr/17/research.highereducation.

81 Ibid.

82 Ibid.

83 Ibid.

84 Baron-Cohen, Simon, *The Science of Evil: On Empathy and the Origins of Cruelty* (Basic Books, 2011).

85 Baron-Cohen, *Zero Degrees of Empathy*.

86 Fine, Cordelia. *Delusions of Gender: How Our Minds, Society, and Neurosexism Create Difference* (W.W. Norton, 2010).

87 "Gender gap a scientific myth, says psychology expert," *The Guardian*, September 10, 2010.

88 Ibid.

89 *The Australian*, quoting Gina Rippon, September, 2010. www.theaustralian.com.au/news/world/theories-that-mens-and-womens-brains-are-wired-differently-are-a-myth-say-experts/story-e6frg6so-1225919328066.

90 Ibid.

91 www.telegraph.co.uk/science/science-news/10684179/Men-and-women-do-not-have-different-brains-claims-neuroscientist.html.

92 Torjesen P.A. and Sandnes L., "Serum testosterone in women as measured by an automated immunoassay and a RIA," *Clinical Chemistry* 50, 3 (2004), pp. 678–679.

93 Southren, A.L., Gordon, G.G., Carmody, N.C., and Isurugi, K., "Plasma production rates of testosterone in normal adult men and women and in patients with the syndrome of feminizing testes," *The Journal of Clinical Endocrinology and Metabolism* 25, 11 (1965), pp. 1441–1450.

94 Mooardian, A.D., Morley, J.E., and Korenman, S.G., "Biological Actions of Androgens," *Endocrine Reviews* 8, 1 (1987), pp. 1–28.

95 *New York Times* archives, 1990. www.nytimes.com/1990/07/17/science/aggression-in-men-hormone-levels-are-a-key.html.

96 Asahina, K., Watanabe, K., Duistermars, B., Hoopfer E., González C., Eyjólfsdóttir E., Perona P. and Anderson D., "Tachykinin-expressing neurons control male-specific aggressive arousal in drosophila," *Cell*, 156, 1–2 (2014), 221–235. DOI: 10.1016/j.cell.2013.11.045.

97 Ibid.

98 Takayoshi Ubuka, Shogo Haraguchi, Yasuko Tobari, Misato Narihiro, Kei Ishikawa, Takanori Hayashi, Nobuhiro Harada, and Kazuyoshi Tsutsui, "Hypothalamic inhibition of socio-sexual behaviour by increasing neuroestrogen synthesis," *Nature Communications*, 2014, 5. DOI: 10.1038/ncomms4061.

99 Ibid.

100 Ibid.

101 Berthold, Arnold. *Natürliche Familien des Thierreichs* (1827).

102 Soma, K.K. "Testosterone and aggression: Berthold, birds, and beyond," *Journal of Endocrinology*, July, 2006.

103 Booth, A., Shelley, G., Mazur, A., Tharp, G., and Kittok, R., "Testosterone, and winning and losing in human competition," *Hormones and Behavior*, December, 1989.

104 Boksem, M.A.S., Mehta, P.H., Van den Bergh, B., van Son, V., Trautmann, S. T., Roelofs, K., Smidts, A., and Sanfey, A.G., "Testosterone inhibits trust but promotes reciprocity," *Psychological Science*, 2013.

105 *Science Daily*. www.sciencedaily.com/releases/2013/09/130930113955.htm.

106 Ibid.

107 Dabbs, J.M. Jr. and Dabbs, M.G., *Heroes, Rogues, and Lovers: Testosterone and Behavior* (McGraw-Hill, 2000)

108 Dabbs, J.M. Jr. "Testosterone, smiling, and facial appearance," *Journal of Nonverbal Behavior*, 21 (1997), pp. 45–55.

109 Bernhardt, P.C., Dabbs, J.M. Jr., Fielden, J.A. and Lutter, C.D., "Testosterone changes during vicarious experiences of winning and losing among fans at sporting events," *Physiology & Behavior*, 65 (1998), pp. 59–62.

110 Zak, P.J., Kurzban, R., Ahmadi, S., Swerdloff, R.S., Park J, et al., "Testosterone Administration Decreases Generosity in the Ultimatum Game," *PLoS ONE*, 4, 12 (2009), e8330. doi:10.1371/journal.pone.0008330.

111 Zak, Paul, "Center for Neuroeconomics Studies determines testosterone affects generosity," Claremont Graduate University, December, 2009, www.cgu.edu/pages/4546.asp?item=3556.

112 "Testosterone therapy: Key to male virility?" The Mayo Clinic, www.mayoclinic.org/healthy-living/sexual-health/in-depth/testosterone-therapy/art-20045728.

113 Ibid.

114 Terburg, David, "Testosterone affects gaze aversion from angry faces outside of conscious awareness," *Journal of the Association for Psychological Sciences*, November, 2011.

115 Eisenegger et al. "Prejudice and truth about the effect of testosterone on human bargaining behavior," *Nature*, 2009.

116 www.sciencedaily.com/releases/2009/12/091208132241.htm.

117 James, P.J., Nyby, J.G., and Saviolakis, G.A., "Sexually stimulated testosterone release in male mice (Mus musculus): roles of genotype and sexual arousal." *Hormones and Behavior* 50, 3 (2006), pp. 424–431.

118 "Pharmacological interventions with adult male sexual offenders," *ATSA*, August, 30, 2012. www.atsa.com/pharmacological-interventions-adult-male-sexual-offenders.

119 "Testosterone, sexual offense recidivism, and treatment effect among adult male sex offenders," *Sex Abuse*, 17 (2005), pp. 171–181.

120 Ibid.

121 Gordon, Harvey and Grubin, Donald, "Psychiatric aspects of the assessment and treatment of sex offenders," *Advances*

in Psychiatric Treatment, 10 (2004), pp. 73–80. doi: 10.1192/apt.10.1.73.
122 Wilson, E.O., *On Human Nature* (Harvard University Press, 1978).
123 McDonald, K. and R.D. Park, "Parent-child physical play," *Sex Roles*, 15 (1986), pp. 367–378.
124 Fagot, B.I., "Differential reactions to assertive and communicative acts by toddler boys and girls," *Child Development*, 56 (1995), pp. 499–505.
125 Young, Kendall, "Childhood and early social conditioning," in *Social Psychology: An Analysis of Social Behavior* (Alfred A. Knopf, 1930), pp. 233–270.
126 It should be noted that many members of the transgender community disagree with this analysis: www.soc.ucsb.edu/sexinfo/article/trans-identities.
127 Money, John. *Gay, Straight, and In Between: The Sexology of Erotic Orientation* (Oxford University Press, 1988), pp. 76–77.
128 Money, John and Ehrhardt, Anke A., *Man and Woman, Boy and Girl: Gender Identity from Conception to Maturity* (University of Michigan Press, 1972).
129 Online Archives of California, "Finding aid of the John Money Papers." www.oac.cdlib.org/findaid/ark:/13030/kt4779q9bb/entire_text/.
130 Diamond, Milton, "Prenatal Androgen and Sex Behaviour," *Endocrinology*, 65 (1959), pp. 369–382.
131 Palomar University, department of anthropology. http://anthro.palomar.edu/social/soc_1.htm.
132 Edwards, Carolyn P. and Bloch, Marianne, "The Whitings' concepts of culture and how they have fared in contemporary psychology and anthropology," Faculty Publications, Department of Psychology, University of Nebraska, Lincoln, 2010.
133 Harkness, S. and Super, C. M., "The developmental niche: A theoretical framework for analyzing the household production of health," *Social Science and Medicine*, 38, 2 (1992), pp. 217–226.
134 Ibid.
135 Bandura, A., Ross, D., and Ross, S.A., "Transmission of aggression through the imitation of aggressive models." *Journal of Abnormal and Social Psychology*, 63, 3 (1961), pp. 575–582.
136 Bandura, Albert, "Influence of models' reinforcement contingencies on the acquisition of imitative responses," *Journal of Personality and Social Psychology*, 1, 6 (1965), pp. 589–595.
137 www.crisisconnectioninc.org/justformen/generational_cycle_of_violence.htm.
138 Black, David S., Sussman, Steve., and Unger, Jennifer B. "A further look at the intergenerational transmission of violence: Witnessing interparental violence in emerging adulthood," *Journal of Interpersonal Violence*, 25 (2010), pp. 1022–1042, first published on October 2, 2009.
139 Butler, Judith, *Gender Trouble: Feminism and the Subversion of Identity* (Subversive bodily acts, IV Bodily Inscriptions, Performative Subversions) (Routledge, 1999) [1990]), p. 179.
140 "Accounting for Doing Gender, by Candace West and Don H. Zimmerman," *Gender & Society*, 23, 1 (2009), pp. 112–122.
141 Butler, Judith, "Performative acts and gender constitution: An essay in phenomenology and feminist theory," *Performing Feminisms: Feminist Critical Theory and Theatre*, ed. Sue-Ellen Case (Johns Hopkins University Press, 1990).
142 www.goodreads.com/quotes/295252-emotional-neglect-lays-the-groundwork-for-the-emotional-numbing-that.
143 Meyer, Elizabeth, "Gender and schooling: Ending bullying and harassment, and promoting sexual diversity in schools," *Psychology Today*, March, 2014.
144 Brandt, Rachel, "How 'boys will be boys' hurts everyone," February, 2014. http://feminspire.com/how-boys-will-be-boys-hurts-everyone/.
145 Mendel, Richard A., *Less Hype, More Help: Reducing Juvenile Crime, What Works and What Doesn't* (Diane Publishing, 2000).
146 *New York Daily News*, February, 2014. www.nydailynews.com/news/national/boys-boys-mont-prosecutor-tells-5-year-old-rape-victim-mom-report-article-1.1616670.
147 Thornhill, Randy and Palmer, Craig T., *A Natural History of Rape: The Biological Bases of Sexual Coercion* (Bradford Books, 2001).
148 De Waal, Frans, *New York Times Online*, Book Review, April 2, 2000. www.nytimes.com/books/00/04/02/reviews/000402.002waalt.html.
149 Thompson, Michael and Kindlon, Dan, *Raising Cain: Protecting the Emotional Lives of Boys* (Ballantine Books, 2000).

150 Parry, Wynne. "Bring It: Boys may benefit from aggressive play," NBC News.com, 2010.
151 Ibid.
152 Levin, Diane and Carlsson-Paige, Nancy, *The War Play Dilemma: What Every Parent and Teacher Needs to Know*, 2nd edition (Teacher's College Press, 2005).
153 Parry, "Bring It."
154 Falling Creek Camp. www.fallingcreek.com/.
155 Gray, Peter, *Free to Learn: Why Unleashing the Instinct to Play Will Make our Children Happier, More Self-Reliant, and Better Students for Life* (Basic Books, 2013).
156 Gray, Peter, "Free play is essential for normal emotional development: Why mother nature motivates our children to play in emotionally exciting ways," *Psychology Today*, June, 2012.
157 Miedzian, Myriam, *Boys Will Be Boys* (Doubleday Press, 1991).
158 Fausto-Sterling, Anne. *Myths of Gender: Biological Theories about Women and Men* (Basic Books, 1992).
159 Kraus, Cynthia, "Naked sex in exile: On the paradox of the 'sex question' in feminism and in science," *NWSA Journal*, 12, 3 (2000).
160 Fausto-Sterling, Anne. "The problem with sex/gender and nature/nurture," in *Debating Biology: Sociological Reflections on Health, Medicine, and Society*, ed. Simon J. Williams, Lynda Birke, and Gillian Bendelow (Routledge, 2003).
161 Ibid.
162 Ibid.
163 Fausto-Sterling, Anne, "Nature VERSUS Nurture (Part 1): It's time to withdraw from this war!," *Psychology Today*, July 29, 2010. www.psychologytoday.com/blog/sexing-the-body/201007/nature-versus-nurture-part-1-it-s-time-withdraw-war.
164 Ibid.
165 Ibid.
166 Fausto-Sterling, Anne. "Nature VERSUS Nurture (Part 2): Building Brains," *Psychology Today*, August 30, 2010. www.psychologytoday.com/blog/sexing-the-body/201008/nature-versus-nurture-part-2-building-brain.
167 Ibid.
168 Fausto-Sterling, Anne. "Nature VERSUS Nurture Part 3: QUACK?," *Psychology Today*, March 11, 2011. www.psychologytoday.com/blog/sexing-the-body/201103/nature-versus-nurture-part-3-quack.
169 Ibid.
170 Blume, Thomas W., "Social Perspectives on Violence," *Michigan Family Review*, Spring, 1996, pp. 9–23.

Chapter

3

Men's Movements and Organizations

Simply put, if you go out and get drunk, hook-up with someone, and then regret your decision the morning after, news flash: That is not rape. Do you know what it is, though? It's called life, and life is messy and full of mistakes.

~ open letter from a men's rights activist[1]

When I say "rape," I'm not talking about jumping someone in a dark alley. I'm talking about going on a date, thinking about "getting some," hoping the female is interested or too wasted to decide. But, the guy [has] sex with her anyway, even though she never says yes.

~ open letter from a feminist to college-aged men[2]

LEARNING OBJECTIVES

After reading this chapter, students should be able to respond to the following questions with an understanding of the terms and expressions employed:

- *In what ways do researchers contend that fraternity life contributes to sexual assault and rape on college and university campuses and off-campus parties? What are rape myths and how are these alleged "myths" contested? How do some defend hazing rituals? Why are so many fraternity parties thrown with sexist and racist themes? What are the arguments in support of joining a fraternity?*
- *What were the founding ideas that led to the creation of the Boy Scouts? What are some of the ideological differences between Boys Scouts and Girl Scouts? What are the governing views of the YMCA?*
- *What were the founding ideas of the Men's Liberation Movement?*
- *What are the fundamental views of the Mythopoetic Men's Movement? What is the ManKind Project? What are the criticisms of these movements?*

- *What are the founding ideas of the Men's Rights Movement? What are the issues taken up by the Father's Rights movement? What are the criticisms of this movement? What is the 'manosphere'?*
- *What were the views and goals of the Million Man March?*
- *Who are the Promise Keepers and what are their central views? What are the criticisms of this group? Who are the King's Men?*
- *What are the guiding principles of NOMAS? What are the guiding principles of the American Men's Studies Association?*
- *What is the White Ribbon Campaign? What is the "monster myth"?*
- *What are the central views of Mentors in Violence Prevention? What is the Bystander Program?*
- *What are the views of the organization A CALL TO MEN? What does Tony Porter mean by "The Man Box"?*

There is a rich history involving groups organized specifically for and by men, often constructed around unifying principles developed by group founders. Foundational doctrines and interests can range from shared hobbies to shared political or religious views. But what bonds many of these organizations together is the belief that boys and men are better served in groups that restrict membership to males. Other groups have been formulated around men's interests, but do not restrict membership to men. This chapter will examine the views of some of the more salient boys' and men's groups in America; but because there have been so many men's movements and organizations, the focus will be on those groups that have been organized either in harmony with or in opposition to feminist principles. This chapter will begin, however, by taking up the hotly contested contemporary debate surrounding the utility of college fraternities, with special attention given to the many allegations aimed at fraternity members for having committed sexual assault, rape, hazing, and episodes of racism.

Fraternal Groups

Throughout history there have been many notable groups that either prohibited women from membership and retain that policy today or that began as organizations that restricted membership to men and later offered memberships to men and women. From longstanding fraternal organizations such as Knights of Columbus and the Order of Freemasons to college fraternities, organizations have been established to bond men around common principles defined by the organizing body. The Freemasons are a good example of an organization that couches itself in secrecy and extends membership exclusively to men. On their official website, they note:

> Masonic Lodges maintain today a long-standing tradition of restricting membership in Freemasonry to men. This tradition is based on the historical all male membership of stonemasons guilds. During the Middle Ages, men traveled far from home and lived in lodges while constructing great cathedrals throughout Europe.[3]

Most Masonic lodges require that the candidate for membership declares belief in a divine being and usually only admits members who affiliate exclusively with Christianity.[4] During the initiation ceremony, the candidate is required to swear an oath of allegiance to the Masonic order and to agree to fulfill certain obligations.[5] Like many fraternal orders, Masons are built on hierarchies and secrecy. From initiates to lodge officers to deacons to wardens to "Worshipful Master," a structured hierarchy is in place, each with its own set of responsibilities.[6] Dan Brown author of *The Lost Symbol* states that whatever role Masons may have played in the past with respect to politics and economics, today, "It's largely, at this point, a social organization [where] people enjoy each other's company."[7]

College Fraternities, Hazing, Racism, and Rape

College fraternities recruit members during "rush week" and require that new members pledge the fraternity, a tradition that borrows from the Masonic tradition the idea that members are sworn to secrecy so that knowledge about what transpires within the fraternity is strictly limited to sworn members. Imparting secret information would be grounds for expulsion from the fraternity. Like Freemasons, a fraternity pledge gains full membership after participating in a formal and secretive ritual of initiation.[8] It is during these initiations that hazing rituals may be undertaken. Julian Hawthorne, son of American novelist Nathaniel Hawthorne, wrote in his memoirs of his initiation into the fraternity *Delta Kappa Epsilon*:

> I was initiated into a college secret society—a couple of hours of grotesque and good-humored horseplay, in which I cooperated as in a kind of pleasant nightmare, confident, even when branded with a red-hot iron or doused head-over heels in boiling oil, that it would come out all right. The neophyte is effectively blindfolded during the proceedings, and at last, still sightless, I was led down flights of steps into a silent crypt, and helped into a coffin, where I was to stay until the Resurrection ... Thus it was that just as my father passed from this earth, I was lying in a coffin during my initiation.[9]

FIGURE 3.1: Epsilon Pi fraternity house, University of Illinois, Urbana

Even though officially prohibited by national fraternity organizations, hazing is a common practice for initiates.[10] Hazing rituals run the gamut from relatively benign pranks to humiliating behaviors to abuse and criminal misconduct with the alleged purpose of building solidarity among members.[11]

Since 2005, 59 students have died in incidents involving fraternities.[12] From alcohol-related death and injury to the use of weapons and fight-club imitations, fraternity behaviors and stunts have led to hundreds of hospitalizations, investigations, and sanctions. In addition, racist themed parties, such as a Dartmouth University fraternity party where attendees donned afro-wigs, dressed like bloods or crips, carried toy guns, and advertised the event as a "ghetto party," have sprung up around the country.[13] At Tulane University, five men were arrested for pouring boiling water on initiates and then rubbing cayenne pepper into the wounds produced as part of a hazing ritual.[14] Other hazing rituals have included the ingestion or submersion in buckets of vomit, urine, and excrement.[15] Author Benjamin Radford writes that the thinking behind these dangerous or disgusting rituals is that hazing represents,

> a ritualized way to turn someone from an outsider into a group insider through shared traumatic experiences. The idea is that people who suffer together form stronger bonds than those who do not; it's the trial-by-fire mentality, initiation with a sadistic edge.[16]

Similar initiation rites are found in entering gang life where initiates are beaten up to show their fortitude and commitment to the gang. But many fraternity hazing rituals have been described as sadism, torture, and degradation, which surpasses many of the initiate rituals for entrance into a gang. Radford notes that with fraternities, there is a "twisted element of fairness" involved, where older members feel that since they had to endure these humiliating and painful rituals, the new initiates ought to do so as well.[17] John Tally, writing for *International Business Times*, actually defends hazing, claiming that enduring hazing rituals made him a better, stronger person.[18] Calling it a "tried and true method of developing young people" and comparing it to Marine Corps boot camp, Tally claims that hazing makes men out of boys and women out of girls.[19]

Beyond hazing rituals, college fraternities have come under scrutiny for being environments dangerous to women, and, in particular, that women have a greater chance of

FIGURE 3.2: Frat guys

being raped or sexually assaulted at parties thrown by fraternities than any other college environment.[20] [21] A study conducted by Oklahoma State University professor John Foubert found that members of fraternities are responsible for rape at a rate of three times that of non-fraternity men.[22] [23] Other studies have revealed similar findings and reported that fraternity men are more accepting of *rape myth* and *rape supportive attitudes* that accompany higher rates of sexual assault and rape than are non-fraternity men.[24] **Rape myth** is the view that rape does not occur very often and that reports of rape are usually cases of false reporting by women who are angry after consensual sex when realizing that the man involved has no desire to be in a romantic relationship with the woman.[25] Rape myth supporters also routinely blame women for inducing men to have sex with them through women's choices of clothing, flirtatious behaviors, and alcohol consumption so that the sexual contact is not considered by perpetrators to be "real rape."[26] Critics point out that a 2015 Association of American Universities (AAU) Campus Survey of 150,000 students coming from 27 different universities revealed that over 20% of female undergraduates and 5% of male undergraduates surveyed report having been victims of nonconsensual sexual contact since entering college.[27] When coupled with the many reports of nonconsensual sexual contact made by former students years later who were afraid or ashamed to report the assaults at the time of the offense, critics note that rape myth narratives cannot begin to account for the rates of sexual assault in these numbers, and are nothing other than feeble attempts to avoid responsibility by blaming victims for men's violations.[28] [29] [30]

The existence of fraternity bystanders who are not committing rape but who know it is occurring and do nothing to prevent it from happening has also been the subject of scholarly research and found to contribute to high rates of rape.[31] Many victim advocates blame fraternities for promoting an environment that encourages bystander behaviors.[32] Within fraternity culture, the *pledge* agrees to keep secret the activities of the fraternity, while promoting a party atmosphere that centers around alcohol and sex.[33] [34] Beyond the attitudinal climate of many fraternities, others point out that there is pressure on victims not to report cases of sexual assault and rape out of fear of reprisal by fraternity members in the form of threats, blame, and shame.[35] Pressures of these sort applied to victims is thought to explain why so many victims remain silent after being assaulted. In 2015, the film *The Hunting Ground* was released by filmmakers Amy Ziering and Kirby Dick to document the ongoing problem of rape and sexual assault on college campuses, and what they believe to be inadequate university administration response.[36] Some universities have taken action including San Diego State University, which suspended Delta Sigma Phi after fraternity members harassed members of an anti-rape rally.[37] Yale University suspended Delta Kappa Epsilon for five years after a video emerged of fraternity members marching through campus chanting:

> No Means Yes, Yes Means Anal! My name is Jack, I'm a necrophiliac, I fuck dead women and fill them with my semen.[38]

But many anti-rape organizations and activists are not satisfied with what they view as either non-action or sluggish and non-transparent actions on the part of many universities.[39] Some critics of fraternities argue that the problems have become so immense that they recommend the shutting down of fraternities altogether in universities across the nation.[40] [41] Writing for *The Wall Street Journal*, Caitlyn Flanagan states,

> If you want to improve women's lives on campus, the first thing you could do is close down the fraternities. The Yale complaint may finally do what no amount of female outrage and violation has accomplished. It just might shut them down for good.[42]

Flanagan notes that a 2007 National Institute of Justice study found that fraternity men drink alcohol more heavily and frequently than nonmembers and "are more likely to perpetrate sexual assault than non-fraternity men," a finding that has been supported by numerous studies.[43]

Critics of banning fraternities point out that most fraternity men do not rape women and that some fraternities are actively combatting rape and sexual assault. In 2014, the *Fraternal Health and Safety Initiative* (FHSI) was adopted by a consortium of colleges to fight against rape, sexual assault, relationship misconduct, binge drinking, and hazing on college campuses.[44] The FHSI curriculum, explains Justin Buck, CEO of Pi Kappa Alpha,

> [establishes] a uniform language, skill set and decision-making framework, the FHSI makes it exponentially easier for undergraduates across fraternal organizations to apply these skills in a practical setting and use the influence of their peer groups for good.[45]

The FHSI guidelines are thought to provide training to young men who enter fraternities to direct them away from the mindset and conditions that create a climate of rape acceptance. Some fraternities are actually ending the longstanding tradition of pledging including Sigma Alpha Epsilon, the second largest fraternity in the U.S., although skeptics claim that the practice of pledging continues.[46]

Those who defend fraternity life often point to five reasons why joining a fraternity is a positive thing for young men:

- companionship and lifelong friendships are formed;
- social opportunities to meet people and have fun;
- academic achievement, since studies have shown that those in fraternities have higher rates of graduation due in part to greater access to tutors;
- opportunities for leadership by being part of organizing committees;
- access to student housing.[47]

Others have pointed out that while some fraternity members have engaged in behaviors that bring shame to their organizations, the majority of fraternity men do not engage in those behaviors and that their fraternity affiliations have helped them in developing social skills and prepared them for successful post-collegiate lives and careers.[48] [49] Since 2005, according to the North American Interfraternity Conference, fraternity membership has risen 40% nationwide.[50]

Black Fraternities and Racism within White Fraternities

Several fraternities that have long traditions of being part of *black Greek letter organizations* making up "The Divine Nine and the National Pan-Hellenic Council" include Alpha Phi Alpha, Alpha Kappa, Kappa Alpha Psi, Omega Psi Phi, Delta Sigma Theta, Phi Beta Sigma, Zeta Phi Beta, Sigma Gamma Rho, and Iota Phi Theta.[51] Writing for *The Atlantic*, Walter M. Kimbrough notes that black fraternities face different issues than white fraternities due mainly to less disposable income.[52] As a result, there are less reports of alcohol abuse, but hazing rituals are still employed, which have led to injuries and arrests.[53] Supporters of black fraternities note that since 1990, after the death of a pledge at Morehouse College, black fraternities cracked down on hazing and instituted a new intake process whereby pledging was officially ended, although some claim that pledging, including violent hazing rituals, continues to take place.[54] Others note that black fraternities provide guidance for young black men who have traditionally been excluded from the perks of fraternity affiliation, which include forming alliances with businesses and corporations, access to tutoring, and a social support network.

Critics of racially segregated fraternities, and particularly white-only fraternities, note that when fraternities are not racially and ethnically diverse, racism often proliferates. In 2015, members of Oklahoma State University's chapter of Sigma Alpha Epsilon were caught on video chanting "There will never be a nigger SAE; you can hang him from a tree, but he can never sign with me."[55] University of Connecticut professor of sociology Matthew Hughey argues that we should not be surprised by such racist outbursts, given that fraternities in America were founded on exclusionary practices. At the University of Cincinnati, Sigma Alpha Epsilon threw a Martin Luther King Jr. party where partygoers were asked to bring canceled welfare checks, radios "bigger than your head," and other racist imagery.[56] The Clemson University chapter of Sigma Alpha Epsilon threw a similar party titled "Cripmas party," where white students dressed as gang members and touted stereotypical clothing, handcuffs, and images of famous black rappers.[57] Other university chapters have organized parties around black-face makeup with themes such as "jungle fever," where racial slurs and epithets are common.[58] Still, many do not favor an all-out ban on fraternities. Benjamin Reese Jr., president of the National Association of Diversity Officers in Higher Education and vice president of institutional equity at Duke University, states,

> There are fraternities that are deeply engaged, but also many that operate in a similar way to how they operated half a century ago. But I would shy away from painting all fraternities with a broad brush. This is an area where perhaps we haven't done as good a job.[59]

Hughey, however, responds that it is a mistake to attribute these behaviors to a few outliers and adds,

> The Greek system is talked about as though it's full of good, upstanding young gentleman and then there's these bad apples. While that may be true at some chapters, it turns the conversation into a matter of good versus bad, and ignores all the ugly that surrounds the whole system.[60]

In 2015, 30 fraternities in America were shut down for misconduct as zero-tolerance policies have begun to be implemented. Some of these cases of misconduct include the use of a stun gun to intimidate new members, the destruction of hotel rooms, the circulation of nude photos of unconscious women, the discovery of roofies (a date-rape drug) in member dorms, and racist behaviors captured on film.[61] What to do about these ongoing problems is being contentiously debated, but it is expected that stronger sanctions and more closures will be part of the solutions.

THOUGHT BOX

After reading about college fraternities, what are your thoughts about joining a fraternity? Do you believe the risks outweigh the rewards or the other way around? Why do you believe some hazing rituals are steeped in extreme pain or extreme degradation? Do you believe there are ingredients within fraternity culture that make it particularly open to rape myth and committing higher rates of sexual assault and rape than non-fraternity college men? What solutions do you think are appropriate to address the high rates of sexual assault and ongoing racism on college campuses?

In addition to college fraternities, some of the early American organizations to restrict membership to men were country clubs that catered to wealthy clientele. One of the most famous of these is the Augusta Country Club in Augusta, Georgia, a private and exclusive country club that does not accept applications so that new members are admitted through invitation only. Unsurprisingly, Augusta garnered notoriety for not accepting black members until 1990 (although early rules of the club required that all caddies were black[62]) and allowed its first two female members in 2012 in the persons of former Secretary of State Condoleezza Rice and investment banker Darla Moore.[63] Private organizations have traditionally defended their discriminatory practices by invoking the First Amendment right of peaceful assembly, which is why, for example, white supremacist groups like the Ku Klux Klan are not required by law to integrate membership by race or ethnic background.

A long tradition of fraternal organizations can be found throughout American and world histories, a tradition that often defends the view that male bonding is important to the healthy development of boys and young men. Others argue that gender exclusionary practices do not prepare men for societal integration of men and women. How best to equip boys for the challenges of adulthood and the tools needed to successfully navigate life has been the subject of centuries of discussion and debate. Today, there continue to be large contingencies that believe boys are best served through boys-only organizations that instill values specific to males. Precisely which set of values are important to boys more than girls or to boys exclusively is strongly contested, but the belief that boys require training that is specific to their special needs is an assumption that is maintained in a number of male-only organizations. In that tradition, two organizations stand out as having survived the test of time, but not without controversy, *The Boy Scouts of America* and the *YMCA*.

FIGURE 3.3: National Boy Scouts Jamboree

Boy Scouts of America

One of the more interesting histories involving male-only organizations is the history of the *Boy Scouts of America*. Incorporated in 1910, the Boy Scouts of America extended honorary titles of president and vice president to U.S. presidents William Taft and Theodore Roosevelt, respectively,[64] and has been praised by presidents past and present including President Obama. But more central to the early teachings of the Boy Scouts were the views of Lord Robert Baden-Powell, who founded scouting organizations in his native England and who wrote the influential manual *Aids to Scouting*, which became a best-seller and a template for the scouting movement.[65] Baden-Powell emphasized the need for Christian faith in boys' and men's lives, arguing that "God made men to be men," adding that "we badly need some training for our lads if we are to keep up manliness in our race instead of lapsing into a nation of soft, sloppy, cigarette suckers."[66] The early twentieth century sustained the continuation of a class of men known as "dandies," a title bestowed in the nineteenth century on George Bryan "Beau" Brummell in British society, Charles Baudelaire in French society, Irish poet Oscar Wilde, and American artist James McNeill Whistler.[67] [68] The **dandy** was a man who took great care in his physical appearance and about whom French philosopher Albert Camus claimed "lived and died in front of a mirror."[69] Lurking beneath this title was the implication that the dandy was homosexual, not a real man. The notion "men should be men" meant to Baden-Powell that boys need to learn to be rugged, independent, tough, physically and mentally strong, and imbued with traits of leadership and dominance. The Boy Scouts were founded, then, with the explicit purpose of guiding boys away from what was believed to be an effeminate form of masculinity and toward what was considered to be God's intended form of tough, independent, resilient manhood.

Unsurprisingly, given this history, the Boy Scouts of America, until very recently, disallowed gay members. In 2000, the United States Supreme Court, in a five to four decision, supported the Boy Scouts of America's right to forbid membership of homosexuals, citing their constitutional right of association.[70] The case of ***Boy Scouts of America et al. versus Dale*** was brought before the Supreme Court by the Boy Scouts after New Jersey's Supreme Court ruled that the organization must reinstate openly gay Scoutmaster James Dale. In 2013, over 60% of Boy Scouts of America members voted that membership would not be denied or revoked on the basis of sexual orientation, although this provision was extended only to youth and not to men in leadership positions.[71]

Not everyone was happy with the 2013 vote. For many, the Boy Scouts of America represent a conservative, Christian boys' and men's organization such that, according to Robert Knight of the *Washington Times*, allowing homosexual Scouts "presents a danger to boys," adding, "The Scout oath requires boys (and leaders) to be 'morally straight.' Putting openly homosexual men and boys into Scout troops would be a direct violation of that oath. The Scout leadership needs to man up."[72] The entire Boy Scout Oath states:

> On my honor I will do my best
> To do my duty to God and my country
> and to obey the Scout Law;
> To help other people at all times;
> To keep myself physically strong,
> mentally awake, and morally straight.[73]

Boy Scouts of America's President Wayne Perry responded, "No matter how you feel about this issue, kids are better off in scouting. Our mission is to serve every kid."[74] Other critics of the decision, however, felt that the Boy Scouts did not go far enough in allowing gay scouts, leaving Eagle Scouts, scout leaders, and parents out of the new policy.[75] [76]

The overall mission statement of the Boy Scouts is to enhance confidence in boys by teaching them to overcome obstacles through personal achievement and to "prepare every eligible youth in America to become a responsible, participating citizen and leader who is guided by the Scout Oath and Law."[77] Scouts obtain merit badges by accomplishing certain requirements within areas of study that include business, astronomy, art, animal and plant sciences, geology, and law, but also achievement in fields of vocational and avocational interests such as archery, swimming, photography, welding, home repair, electronics, and aviation. According to their fact sheet, Boy Scouts, ages 11 to 17, total just under one million in number.

By contrast, ***Girl Scouts of the USA*** was formed in 1912 by Juliette "Daisy" Gordon as a girl-centered organization that focused on helping girls develop "physically, mentally, and spiritually."[78] Today, Girls Scouts tout the goals of increasing girls' involvement in science, technology, engineering, and math (STEM), strengthening financial literacy and entrepreneurial skills, and reducing bullying and relational aggression.[79] Interestingly, the girl scouts, unlike the boy scouts, have become associated with what some term liberal, progressive politics.[80] State Representative Bob Morris (R-Indiana) called the Girl Scouts, "a tactical arm of Planned Parenthood," and refused to sign a resolution honoring the Girl Scouts' 100-year anniversary.[81] Author Kate Tuttle quips that while the boys of Boy Scouts are in an environment "steeped in straight, male Christianity," the girls of Girl Scouts "soak up messages about empowerment, diversity, and social activism."[82]

YMCA

Founded in 1844 in London by George Williams, the YMCA (Young Men's Christian Association) was established on the idea of developing in men a healthy, "body, mind, and spirit," the three principles captured visibly in the triangle of their logo.[83] U.S. chapters of the YMCA formally adopted the core values of honesty, respect, and responsibility in the early 1990s. The organization was established to, in their words, "provide low-cost housing in a safe, Christian environment for rural young men journeying to the cities."[84] The prevailing view of YMCA founders was that young men who made their way from rural environments to urban centers would be tempted into the vices of prostitution, gambling, and alcohol consumption without the guidance of men who can train them in what they view as the virtues of living a clean, Christian-centered life.

Like Boy Scouts of America, the YMCA had its own controversy when, in 1978, singing group The Village People released the song "YMCA," which hit number 2 on U.S. charts and number 1 on British charts.[85] Early on, the YMCA did not know whether to view the song as a tribute, a copyright infringement, or satire.[86] The band and the record company worried that a lawsuit would be issued by the YMCA, but to their surprise, the men's organization eventually viewed the song as free advertisement and reported that membership increased because of the song.[87] But because most members of The Village People were gay and the fact that the song became an anthem in gay, male culture along with lyrics that were purportedly inside jokes within the gay, male community, many began to view YMCA locations as places where gay men met one another to engage in sexual hook-ups.[88] Those who valued the historical traditions of the YMCA as a Bible study group for men were not pleased with the new association to gay culture.

In 2010, the YMCA rebranded its name to "The Y," emphasizing family involvement and community-building with a lowered emphasis on being an exclusive men's organization. Its guiding principles are now stated,

FIGURE 3.4:

Lasting personal and social change comes about when we all work together. That's why, at the Y, strengthening community is our cause. Every day, we work side-by-side with our neighbors to make sure that everyone, regardless of age, income or background, has the opportunity to learn, grow and thrive.[89]

Yet the "C" (Christian) part of YMCA is still touted by the mission statement as an important part of the organization's goals: "To put Christian principles into practice through programs that build healthy spirit, mind and body for all," but going on to note, "In that Christian principles are caring and inclusive, we will be respectful of various expressions of religion. We serve people from all faith traditions and perspectives."[90]

The **YWCA**, like the Girl Scouts of the U.S.A., emphasizes empowering women, with the additional stated goal of eliminating racism.[91] This latter aspect of the YWCA is not one they view as in conflict with YMCA goals, but as an extension of the core values of youth development and social responsibility. The YWCA notes that its organization was involved in "every aspect of the Civil Rights Movement" and today supports the furthering goals of affirmative action, while opposing racial profiling and hate crimes.[92] YWCA goals very much reflect the progressive goals of Girl Scouts of the USA:

- We seek to increase the equal protections and equal opportunities of people of color.
- We work to increase economic opportunities for women and girls of color, recognizing the importance of addressing the race and gender inequities that exist for this historically and contemporarily marginalized community.
- We strive to improve the often disproportionately negative health and safety outcomes for women and girls of color by making sure they have access to high-quality health and safety resources and support systems.[93]

In 2011, the YWCA in Great Britain dropped its official affiliation with Christianity and changed its name to *Platform 51* to denote the fact that 51% of people are women.[94] It then changed its name once again to *Young Women's Trust*, stating,

Young Women's Trust supports and represents over one million women aged 16–30 trapped by low pay or no pay and facing a life of poverty. We provide services and run campaigns to make sure that the potential and talents of young women don't go to waste.[95]

Critics of the YWCA are much like critics of Girl Scouts of the U.S.A. When the YWCA named former president of the *National Organization for Women*, Patricia Ireland, chief executive officer, Andrea Lafferty, executive director of the *Traditional Values Coalition*, stated, "I think basically the Y.W.C.A. has come out of the closet," as a not so veiled allusion to NOW's support of a women's right to an abortion and particularly lesbian rights.[96] Peter LaBarbera, a senior policy analyst at *Concerned Women for America's Culture and Family Institute*, added of new YWCA CEO Ireland that she is "a strong advocate for radical feminism, abortion, and—due to her lifestyle—homosexuality."[97] Like Girl Scouts of the U.S.A., conservative critics have maintained that the YWCA is a Christian organization that should maintain the values they view as being Christian in order to uphold the traditions of the organization, to which Ireland responded, "I'm not the head of a Christian organization; I'm the head of a social justice women's organization."[98]

In addition to these historic boys' and young men's organizations, men's movements in America have offered an assortment of perspectives on men and masculinity with some groups promoting a more traditional view of masculinity as tough, adventurous, autonomous, and sometimes aggressive, and other groups promoting a more progressive way of viewing contemporary masculinity. In general, and without necessarily a discreet divide in every case, contemporary men's groups can be divided into pro-feminist groups and anti-feminist groups. But interestingly, the groups known today for being either staunchly pro-feminist or antifeminist had their origins in an early men's movement that sought solidarity with and empathy for the early women's movement. These men organized around what became known as the men's liberation movement.

THOUGHT BOX

For class discussion, do you believe there are benefits to male-only organizations or do male-exclusive organizations lessen their impact and miss out on important insight by excluding women?

The Men's Liberation Movement

The women's movement of the 1960s was characterized by the push for women's liberation, which meant that many women were tired of being shackled by society's expectations and mores to the view of women as exclusively home-bound servants to men and family. The notion that women should stay at home, clean the house, take care of children, and prepare for their husband's return from work by preparing dinner and readying themselves aesthetically for his arrival was met with contemptuous disdain by millions of women who asked why they could not enter the workplace, earn a living of their own, and become autonomous in the same way that men expected and assumed for themselves. Predictably, many men met this challenge as a threat to what they believed was their natural dominance and supremacy, but some men considered women's liberation as an opportunity for men who, like women, felt they were forced to conform to traditional expectations placed on them. The expression "men's liberation" was coined by Jack Sawyer in the 1970 article, "On Men's Liberation,"[99] where Sawyer considered the expectations placed upon men to be part of a stereotype that was fraught with negative consequences for men's lives. For Sawyer, patriarchy harmed men as well as women by reinforcing the idea that men should be emotionally stoic, bill-paying workaholics who become slaves to mind-numbing careers.

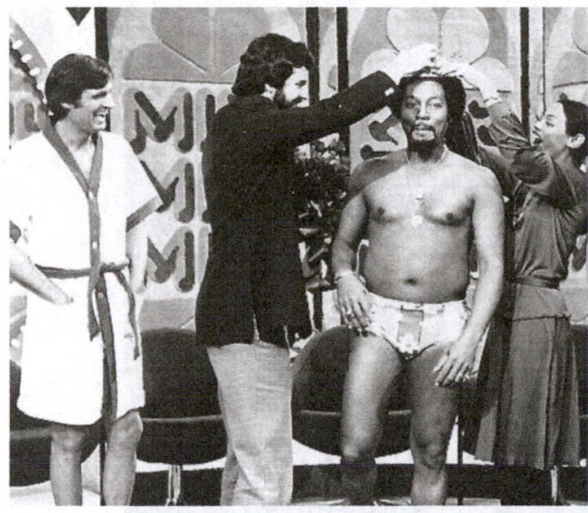

FIGURE 3.5: Actor, Alan Alda joins Warren Farrell in creating a male beauty contest, 1976

In 1974, author Warren Farrell published the book "The Liberated Man,"[100] a profeminist work that espoused the virtues of reformulating family structures to accommodate working women, while supporting the need for more caring and nurturing men. Farrell argued against the paradigm that viewed women as sex objects and men as what he termed "success objects."[101] Farrell also became famous for going on TV shows to reverse traditional gendered roles in order for men to get a glimpse into what it is like to be a woman in contemporary society. So, for instance, he would create faux-beauty contests for men so that men could understand what women go through every day when being judged on the basis of their physical appearances. At the time, Farrell was the only elected male board member of the National Organization for Women.[102]

However, in 1993, Farrell authored the book *The Myth of Male Power*, arguing that it is an error to view women as economically down-trodden and men as economically advantaged.[103] Claiming that men occupy the worst sorts of jobs, including the most dangerous jobs, as well as arguing that men do not get to retain much of the money they make due to family obligations or spousal and child support in the event of divorce, Farrell concluded that men are actually the economically disadvantaged gender when the entire economic picture is considered. Farrell also noted that men are trained to feel obligated to work long hours to succeed at levels at which they are taught to succeed, driving many men to early deaths. In the lessons on love that men receive, Farrell argued that heterosexual men are taught that making enough money is how you are able to find and keep love, which means, he states, "men's weakness is their facade of strength; women's strength is their facade of weakness."[104] When coupled with the fact that it is men who make up the majority of military casualties in the many wars that are fought, Farrell concluded that men are the "disposable sex."

One way that Farrell purports to show that men's lives are viewed as less valuable than women's lives is found in his claim that the U.S. spends six times more on research and treatment to fight breast cancer than it does prostate cancer. Farrell also criticized the family court system, where he argues, women are given child custody in divorce settlements over men in a disproportionate number of cases. What Farrell had tapped into was a growing dissatisfaction among men who felt both beaten down by unfulfilling jobs and emotionally estranged from their children and most relationships in general. The dissatisfaction Farrell hoped to expose inspired several reactionary men's groups. One branch of this tree was typified by an angry lashing out toward women and a system they viewed as stacked in favor of women, while the other branch focused on an inward exploration of what it means to be a man. Taking these two movements in order, the inward journey

FIGURE 3.6: The real man smiles in trouble, gathers strength from distress, and grows brave by reflection. ~ Thomas Paine[105]

turned into the mythopoetic men's movement, while the angry backlash against women and particularly feminism became what is today known as men's rights activism.

Mythopoetic Men's Movement

The Mythopoetic men's movement began in the early 1980s as an effort to get men in touch with their "true masculine natures," a movement that viewed modern society as toxic to authentic manhood by creating feminized men. The idea was that contemporary societies produce practical men of reason who are alienated from their inner masculine emotions. What men allegedly needed to do was to reawaken their "deep masculine selves" by bonding with other men in a celebration of men's differences from women.

One of the founders of the mythopoetic men's movement is poet Robert Bly, who, in 1990, published the book *Iron John: A Book about Men*[106] as a self-help guide to assist men in transforming themselves into more of what he considered to be authentically masculine men. Bly viewed one of the biggest problems in contemporary society as being the decline in traditional fathering. Without a strong masculine guide through the more challenging stages of boyhood, Bly argued, boys are adrift in a culture that will seduce them toward dangerous paths. It is up to older men to train boys and young men, he insisted, on how to be authentic men in a culture that is largely devoid of such training.[107]

Bly argues that if you do not have fully-fledged, mature men training boys how to become men, you are left with what he termed "half-adults" attempting to teach boys what it takes real men to teach.[108] You have, essentially, created a cycle of unprepared men training boys, who will in turn become unprepared men teaching their sons someday to be unprepared men. This cycle, according to Bly, leaves a void that is filled by women who soften boys and men by instructing men to be sensitive and caring without acknowledging other traits that boys need in order to become strong, creative leaders.

FIGURE 3.7: Poet, Robert Bly

The solution to reversing the "softening" of men, according to Bly, is to look to the myths and stories of the past that reveal how boys become mature men through heroic confrontations with nature and spiritual journeys where men remove themselves from women to tap into the rich and pure meanings of authentic manhood. Without this vital separation from modern culture and the women who weaken men, Bly believes that many men are lost to lives of alcoholism, alienation, depression, and disillusion. This needed maturation assumes that men will not simply become hypermasculine chauvinists who deal with their feelings of emptiness by subordinating and sexually objectifying women. The mythopoetic man is one who is properly masculine, by their definitions of what constitutes being properly masculine, but who respects and treats women with consideration.

These themes of masculine renewal were embraced by the mythopoetic men's groups around the country where an assortment of activities and rituals were established that resemble those found in tribal societies to assist in constructing what are considered to be mature, naturally masculine men. Older men instruct younger men through the use of stories and fables along with rituals of male initiation that purport to allow men to feel accepted and encouraged without fear of humiliation.[109]

Sociologist Michael Messner evaluates the attractiveness of the mythopoetic men's movement to white, college-educated, middle-class, middle-aged men as not being due to it breaking with traditional masculinity, but because it is consistent with the contemporary, popular shift in adopting the *soft essentialist* view that men and women are fundamentally different.[110] The "men are from Mars, women are from Venus" conception of gender has permeated much of the popular discourse on gender and inspired men's groups to find ways to segregate themselves in the interest of finding their hidden, inner male selves. Writing about Bly's work and the ethos that drives the mythopoetic movement, Messner argues,

> Bly assumes a natural dichotomization of "male values" and "female values" and states that feminism has been good for women, in allowing them to reassert "the feminine voice" that has been suppressed. But Bly states (and he carefully avoids directly blaming feminism for this), "the masculine voice" has now been muted—men have become "passive, tame—domesticated." Men thus need a movement to reconnect with the "Zeus energy" that they have lost. And "Zeus energy is male authority accepted for the good of the community."[111]

When heralded as "male authority accepted for the good of the community," Messner argues that mythopoetic gender dichotomies are anything but pro-feminist in nature. In fact, while mythopoetic men may find nurturance and empowerment in acknowledging that they possess mutual pain and need for validation from one another, Messner notes that

> unlike feminism, it does not confront men with the reality of how their own privileges are based on the continued subordination of women and other men. In short, the mythopoetic men's movement may be seen as a new form of hegemonic masculinity—a masculinity that is less self-destructive, that has revalued and reconstructed men's emotional bonds with each other, and that has learned to feel good about its own "Zeus power."[112]

Today, an offshoot of the mythopoetic men's movement is the **ManKind Project,** which touts a training program for men they term the *New Warrior Training Adventure.*[113] The NWTA is a weekend men's retreat where rituals take place in three stages: descent, ordeal, return. For the weekend, men surrender all communication devices, weapons, and jewelry. Groups of 20 to 30 men participate in the weekend with the assistance of 30 to 40 staff members. The men who participate are sworn to secrecy about the actual occurrences of the weekend, but are encouraged to discuss openly their feelings about the experience. The NWTA is advertised at costing between $575 to $750 depending on one's location with the advisory caution, "Be prepared to face your shadow and be called on your 'stuff,' expect to be physically and emotionally spent by the end of the weekend, but rewarded with a hero's journey."[114]

Criticism of the ManKind Project is similar to the criticism of mythopoetic men's groups in general, that it sells a repackaged form of hegemonic masculinity to men who do not confront their own male privilege such that women continue to be viewed as a weaker sex that need men to protect them. In addition, some criticism has focused on the notion that the ManKind Project uses coercion and intimidation tactics more reminiscent of the sorts of things employed by cults, where individuality is replaced by group-thinking in the guise of therapy.[115] [116] Like mythopoetic men's groups, the men of the ManKind Project do not openly criticize feminism and feminist principles, but do not view feminism as the proper place for men.

The Men's Rights Movement

Also splintering off from the early men's liberation movement, the men's rights movement openly blames feminism for what they consider to be the plight of contemporary men. Credit is often given to Richard Doyle in the U.S. for having started the movement in 1973,[117] and according to Boyle's biography he was shocked to see what he viewed as anti-male prejudice in the courts.[118] In 1977, Free Men, Inc. was formed in Maryland, which itself spawned what became known as the National Coalition for Men, which identifies as an organization dedicated to "removal of harmful gender based stereotypes, especially as they impact boys, men, their families and those who love them."[119] [120] But as with other men's rights activist groups, the NCFM focuses on what they view as "paternity fraud," "fathers' rights," "female privilege," women as perpetrators of violence against men, and a host of actions and laws they view as discriminatory against men.[121]

There are a multitude of issues men's rights activists raise in an attempt to show that males are actually the gender being discriminated against in a society they believe has been appropriated by feminist thinking. Their issues include:

- spousal support men are forced to pay under divorce settlements;
- rates of child custody given to mothers over fathers;
- the underreporting of domestic violence committed by women;

- false claims of domestic violence reported by women about men;
- false claims of sexual assault and rape reported by women about men;
- boys being discriminated against by teachers in the classroom;
- females being the beneficiaries of privilege in many areas;
- men's shorter life span;
- men's higher suicide rates;
- paternity fraud perpetrated by women;
- men receiving longer prison terms;
- men paying more into social security, while women receiving greater benefits.

According to men's rights activists, feminism has been successful in biasing the courts, educators, and even other men into believing that women are disadvantaged, when, they argue, the reverse is true. According to Paul Elam, one of the more prominent men's rights activists and founder of the website *A Voice for Men*,

> What used to be cooperation between sexes is now gynocentric parasitism that inhabits every level of men's existence, from cradle to coffin. The efforts to enhance the rights of women have become toxic efforts to undermine the rights of men.[122]

Even though Elam insists that his organization is not political, neoconservative groups have aligned themselves with many of the themes found in men's rights rhetoric, including Christina Hoff Sommers, resident scholar at the neoconservative think tank American Enterprise Institute,[123] who declared in her 2000 book *The War Against Boys: How Misguided Feminism is Harming Our Young Men*,[124] that boys are being shortchanged in education as part of wrong-headed policies that view girls as a downtrodden gender that require encouragement and assistance at the expense of boys. As evidence, Hoff Sommers points to rising dropout, failure, and learning disability rates among boys.[125] [126] This is one of the common talking points for men's rights groups where the feeling is that in education, boys do not matter as much as girls. So, they argue, resources and teacher attention are focused on helping girls succeed, while boys are written off and neglected. It is also a neoconservative talking point to argue that feminism has softened men and that men need to "man up" in the face of this alleged emasculation. Conservative television personality Elizabeth Hasselbeck, in fact, suggested that men weakened by feminism were threatening the national security of America, although neither she nor her guest, author Nick Adams, in discussing this point on the show *Fox and Friends*, explained why this is the case.[127]

Another central point for men's rights activists is what they see as a fundamental unfairness in the treatment of men in family court. In fact, there are now attorneys and law firms that specialize in representing men who believe they are not being treated fairly in family court. The two main issues of contention are what men's rights activists view as unreasonable alimony rates and biased child-custody laws.[128] With respect to alimony, Elam would like to see alimony eliminated altogether unless part of a prenuptial agreement.[129] But perhaps an even more pressing matter for men's rights activists is parental rights, with a focus on paternity, custody, and visitation arrangements. Sociologist Michael Kimmel, while interviewing men across the country for his book *Angry White Men*, found that many divorced fathers are upset because they view family court judges as being biased in favor of women and against men, reducing a father's involvement in his children's lives to a child-support check and bimonthly visitation rights.[130] This group of disgruntled men, while part of men's rights activism, have narrowed the focus of their anger to what they now term **fathers' rights**.[131]

The fathers' rights movement has grown over the past decade. Using what they term 'tactics' to show men how to reduce child support, how to win custody decisions, overturn visitation denial, and fight charges of domestic violence, fathers' rights groups and attorneys claim to help men who are not being treated fairly by the family court system,[132] which they view as stacked in favor of mothers over fathers. Sociologist Michael Flood disagrees. In a piece entitled, "What's Wrong with Fathers' Rights?" Flood begins by citing three ways that the fathers' rights movement has had a damaging effect on efforts to combat violence against women and children:[133]

- "right to contact" overrides the more important principle "safety from violence";
- fathers' rights groups have had a negative impact on community understandings of violence against women and children by attempting to discredit victims;
- fathers' rights groups have attempted to erode the protections available to victims of domestic violence, which harms female and male victims alike.

Flood argues that visitation rights should be made strictly on a case-by-case basis with histories of violence taken into consideration, while Flood views fathers' rights advocates as making children less safe by insisting that a violent father is better in a child's life than no father. Flood also notes that in cases of domestic violence, rather than false reporting being the norm, no reporting is the actual norm since many victims of domestic violence live in fear of violent reprisal from the abuser should they seek police intervention. Finally, by stripping away the protections in place to help victims of domestic violence, father's rights advocates help facilitate victimization by assuming the account given by the perpetrator is true. By so doing, father's rights supporters deny violence exists, blame the victim, and falsely report the interpersonal violence as being reciprocal, when, in fact, governmental statistics find men to be guilty of perpetrating violence in the vast majority of cases of domestic violence and also find injuries to women to be, on average, much more severe than injuries sustained by men.[134]

Another criticism of the men's rights movement that critics claim reveals their hatred toward women is their pervasive use of misogynistic and sexist language in presenting their views. On the splash page of Elam's website, for instance, he writes, "The old saying goes, you can't fight city hall. That may be true, but it's nothing compared to fighting *titty* hall. Not even close."[135] This quote is mild by comparison to other statements made by Elam aimed at feminists:

> I find you, as a feminist, to be a loathsome, vile piece of human garbage. I find you so pernicious and repugnant that the idea of fucking your shit up gives me an erection.[136]

Critics note that Elam often avoids responsibility for his hatred of women by claiming that his inflammatory language is meant to be taken as satire to draw attention to the oppression of men and not as an actual reflection of his views about women. Elam is not alone in his violent rhetoric and victim-blaming. Fellow men's rights activist and rape apologist W.F. Price takes a similar tactic by blaming the high rates of rape in the military on women:

> fighting men are more passionate by nature, and then there's the fact that these men also turn women on more ... add to that the fact that our personnel are serving in a remote Muslim country with no access to local females to speak of, and things are bound to happen.[137]

to which another fellow men's rights activist blogged:

> Once they invaded the workplace the last vestige of male-only space was the military. Now even this is no longer true. I don't know where men can go and work with other men without female interference anymore.[138]

Some men's rights activists claim that these misogynistic rants do not represent their core views and values, but critics respond that the vitriol present in the language of men's rights activism is consistent with a general hatred and contempt of women. On the topic of sexual assault and rape, Elam, on his site *A Voice for Men*, writes,

> all the outraged PC demands [that state] nothing justifies or excuses rape won't change the fact that a lot of women who get pummeled and pumped are stupid enough to walk through life with a I'M A STUPID, CONNIVING BITCH—PLEASE RAPE ME neon sign above their empty little narcissistic heads.[139]

While defining a men's rights group as "an egalitarian, equity-oriented organization" and boasting of his past work in the "mental health field,"[140] Elam vowed that "Should I be called to sit on a jury for a rape trial, I vow publicly to vote not guilty, even in the face of overwhelming evidence that the charges are true."[141]

One particular men's rights group, *The National Center for Men*, argues, "Only women have the extraordinary freedom to enjoy sexual intimacy free from the fear of forced parenthood."[142] The NCM argues that women will often defraud men about contraception and then force fatherhood on men with all of the attendant economic responsibilities that come with it.[143] In addition, they view women as "sexual celebrities" who seduce men into pursuing and paying for the privilege of their sexual company.[144] The men's rights websites that have materialized on the internet have collectively earned the name "**the manosphere**," which includes the blog-site, "Boycott American Women," where American men are encouraged to boycott having relationships with American women. The site *informs* men that "American women are generally immature, selfish, extremely arrogant and self-centered, mentally unstable, irresponsible, and highly unchaste. The behavior of most American women is utterly disgusting."[145] The MRA blog-site *The Counter Feminism* declares, "The female-supremacist hate movement called 'feminism' must be opened to the disinfecting sunlight of the world's gaze and held to a stern accounting for its grievous transgressions."[146] MRA site *A Voice for Male Students* asserts, "Female students are systemically taught that sex is rape when it is not; [women are] essentially being taught to make false rape accusations."[147] *SAVE Services* is a site that purports to be working for legal reform that will stop false allegations of men's violence, stating, "female initiation of partner violence is the leading reason for the woman becoming a victim of subsequent violence," and goes on to state that most domestic violence is actually committed by women.[148]

The loosely organized men's rights movement is united in its rage toward feminism, pro-feminist men, and the family court system, while blaming victims when women come forward in the wake of being raped, sexually assaulted, or battered. They even voice outrage when Hollywood makes movies that feature strong female protagonists.[149] They long for a return to a time when men indisputably and unapologetically dominated women with impunity, while insisting that they do not hate women. Yet many of their comments belie this view. Elam has dubbed October "Bash a Violent Bitch Month,"[150] going on to clarify,

> I mean literally to grab them by the hair and smack their face against the wall till the smugness of beating on someone because you know they won't fight back drains from their nose with a few million red corpuscles. And then make them clean up the mess.[151]

The assumption Elam makes about women violently abusing men is rectified, in his mind, by calling on men to inflict violent abuse to these same women. Beyond this violent rhetoric, the backlash to feminism created by men's rights activism is often seen as a defense of traditional patriarchy. Men's rights activist Mike Buchanan argues that feminists are "female supremacists, driven by misandry, the hatred of men and boys," and continues, "feminists have worked through the state to attack many of the pillars of civilized society, becoming the defining ideology of the political establishment."[152] By once again viewing gender relations as a zero-sum battle of the sexes, and viewing feminism as a challenge to the patriarchal traditions of American society, men's rights activists view the struggle for gender equality as a war against men and what they take to be men's natural supremacy and entitlement to dominate society and the world.

The Million Man March

On October 16, 1995, Minister Louis Farrakhan of the Nation of Islam organized a march of African-American men to the National Mall in Washington D.C. In coordination with a number of civil rights leaders and local chapters of the NAACP, African-American men were invited to gather "to convey to the world a vastly different picture of the Black male" as well as to help unite African-American communities in America in coming together to fight against the economic and social persecution that persisted against African-American people in the post-civil rights era.[153] Among the luminaries who spoke at or attended the March were poet **Maya Angelou**, Rev. **Jeremiah Wright**, Rev. **Jesse Jackson, Rosa Parks,** and **Martin Luther King III.**

Germane to the March was exposing media stereotypes of African-American men as violent criminals and irresponsible fathers by the over-coverage of figures such as Willie Horton and O.J. Simpson, while lacking coverage of the many positive African-American, male figures in American culture. Speakers also took conservative, white politicians to task for blaming urban black people for "domestic economic woes that threatened to produce record deficits, massive unemployment, and uncontrolled inflation."[154]

FIGURE 3.8: The Million Man March, Washington D.C., 1995

The March focused on the ways that African-American people, and African-American men specifically, continued to be vilified by mainstream media and politicians and how this denigration led to decreased funding for inner-city programs designed to help people living at or below the poverty line. Civil Rights activist Reverend Jesse Jackson noted that these cuts included $1.1 billion dollars from the nation's poorest public schools.[155] The March also highlighted the concern that more black men were in prison than were in college.[156] A theme emerged that urban black people were born with three-strikes against them:[157]

- Insufficient prenatal care
- Inferior educational opportunities
- Jobless parents

The U.S. government was viewed not as partnered with and concerned about the lives of African-American people, but as a force committed to the criminal prosecution of black men and women, and as a source of worthless welfare programs that did not address some of the root causes of poverty and educational inequality within African-American communities.

According to the *Washington Post*, one year after the march, two-thirds of African-American people believe the Million Man March had a positive influence on black communities as a whole, while only one-in-five stated that they noticed improvement in the way that black men treat women.[158] David Bositas, senior research associate at the Joint Center for Political and Economic Studies in Washington D.C., notes that 1.5 million African-Americans registered to vote in the wake of the March,[159] while Benjamin Chavis, executive director of the March reports that beyond the increase in registered voters, there were also "increased adoptions of black children, a decrease in black on black crime, increases in child support payments from black men and increased membership in the NAACP, churches, mosques and other organizations."[160]

Criticism of the March focus on the fact that African-American men, but not women, were the invitees to the March, which prompted the statement, "Organizers excluded women from the March to send a two-part message, that men need to improve their character and that women need to recognize their place 'in the home.'"[161] Others disagreed, noting that beyond the inclusion of Maya Angelou and Rosa Parks, Betty Shabazz, Tynnetta Muhammad, and Dorothy Height of the National Council for Negro Women were program speakers.[162] Also noted was the fact that Minister Farrakhan used the event to call for "an end to the disrespect of black women, a moratorium on use of the "b-word," the absolute end to domestic violence and the immediate cessation of any and all kinds of sexual abuse and exploitation of women and children."[163]

Promise Keepers and Faith-Based Men's Groups

Founded in 1990 by ex-NCAA football coach Bill McCartney, *Promise Keepers* is a Christian-based men's group organized "for training and teaching on what it means to be godly men." The core beliefs of Promise Keepers are outlined in seven promises taken from their understanding of scripture, although they insist that they do not adhere to any particular denominational view:

1. A Promise Keeper is committed to honoring Jesus Christ through worship, prayer and obedience to God's Word in the power of the Holy Spirit.
2. A Promise Keeper is committed to pursuing vital relationships with a few other men, understanding that he needs brothers to help him keep his promises.

3. A Promise Keeper is committed to practicing spiritual, moral, ethical and sexual purity.
4. A Promise Keeper is committed to building strong marriages and families through love, protection and Biblical values.
5. A Promise Keeper is committed to supporting the mission of his church by honoring and praying for his pastor and by actively giving his time and resources.
6. A Promise Keeper is committed to reaching beyond any racial and denominational barriers to demonstrate the power of Biblical unity.
7. A Promise Keeper is committed to influencing his world, being obedient to the Great Commandment (Mark 12:30–31) and the Great Commission (Matthew 28:19–20).

The organization became known for their rallies, the largest being at the National Mall in Washington D.C., where it was reported to be the largest gathering of men in American history.[164] Promise Keepers continues today and has expanded its work around the world, although others have noted that Promise Keepers has experienced a sharp decline in attendance and support; there are signs that the organization is attempting to revive its dwindling numbers by appealing to a more youth-based audience.[165] [166]

One criticism of the group and its practices comes from the National Organization for Women, where the views and actions of Promise Keepers (PK) are seen as an attempt to roll back the progressive changes accomplished by the women's movement.[167] The criticism claims that PK is a conservative attempt to reestablish patriarchy and male supremacy by teaching men that they are "head of household" and that women should be subordinate to male authority. As stated by media relations expert Ami Neiberger-Miller, "PK encourages men to discover a 'Christian' masculinity, replete with warrior imagery, protectionism, and chest pounding. PK's definition of Christian masculinity posits that men mediate the spiritual lives of families and churches because they are men."[168] Women's groups have insisted that Promise Keepers attempts to destroy the egalitarian partnership approach to marriage and relationships that has helped women establish themselves in the workplace and that has in many respects helped men by alleviating the pressure on men to be sole economic providers, while creating the acceptance for men to be more nurturing partners and fathers. Neiberger-Miller continues,

> PK says that women should submit to their husbands. In *Seven Promises of a Promise Keeper* Tony Evans admonishes men to "take back" the leadership of their homes from their wives, saying that "there can be no compromise" on this issue. Women are instructed to submit to their husbands, "for the sake of your family and the survival of our culture."[169]

Another faith-based men's group is the American Catholic group *King's Men*, which follows closely in the tradition of Promise Keepers, and touts the slogan, "Leader. Protector. Provider."[170] Explaining King's Men, Wake Forest professor of religion Stephen B. Boyd states,

> In some ways, it's difficult to understand what a man's supposed to be like these days. Increasing numbers of us are not the only primary breadwinners. Our jobs have changed so much that the superior physical strength that made it natural for us to be the breadwinner, well, it doesn't take that to sit in front of a computer. When things are up in the air, one clear option is to go "traditional."[171]

Like Mythopoetic Men, King's Men promotes "outdoor, experiential retreats" for men as part of reclaiming a "daily masculine archetype" that King's Men find missing from what they take to be today's soft, emasculated forms of masculinity.[172] The stated purpose of the retreats is to train men in "orienteering, topography, weaponry, self-defense, survival skills, outdoor construction, fishing, wild game food preparation, and more."[173] Criticism of King's Men is largely the same critique made of Promise Keepers, that the consequence of implementing the stated principles of King's Men is the subjugation of women into subordinate roles of support to men's leadership.

Pro-Feminist Men's Organizations

NOMAS (National Organization for Men against Sexism) and AMSA (American Men's Studies Association)

Starting in the early 1970s, loosely organized groups of men began to form in support of the Women's Movement and second-wave feminist objectives. In 1975, the First National Conference on Men and Masculinity was held in Knoxville, Tennessee. Over the next several years, momentum and membership grew until in 1983 the *National Organization for Changing Men* (NOCM) was formed. Throughout the 1980s NOCM encountered numerous problems that included in-fighting among members over direction. In the book *Uneasy Males: The American Men's Movement, 1970–2000*, author Edward Gambill details the friction and controversy that ensued over pro-feminist factions of the NOCM and those who believed the organization should be guided by what they termed "male-positive" interests.[174] In 1987, men's rights activists were invited to speak on the subject of domestic violence, which turned into a heated exchange between the MRA speakers and radical feminist attendees. This exchange, coupled with growing tensions about the future of the organization, led to a resolution to ban individuals who did not agree with the NOCM guiding principles from speaking at future conferences.[175] Further tensions mounted over the hierarchal structure of the NOCM, which to some resembled the patriarchal structures they initially set out to challenge.

In 1990, the NOCM became the *National Organization for Men against Sexism*, or NOMAS.[176] In its statement of principles, NOMAS describes itself as an advocate for

> a perspective that is pro-feminist, gay affirmative, anti-racist, dedicated to enhancing men's lives, and committed to justice on a broad range of social issues including class, age, religion, and physical abilities.[177]

Emphasizing their support for "the continuing struggle of women for full equality," calling for "an end to all forms of discrimination based on sexual-affectional orientation, and for the creation of a gay-affirmative society," and committing itself to "examine and challenge racism in our organizations, our communities, and ourselves," NOMAS distinguishes itself as an antidiscrimination movement that extends well beyond issues of gender. According to NOMAS, the fundamental problem that needs to be addressed across gender, race, class, sexual-orientation, religion, physical condition, and oppression of all kinds is the unequal distribution of power.

At around the same time that NOMAS was forming, the Men's Studies Task Group, which was composed by early men's studies pioneers Martin Acker, Shepherd Bliss, Harry Brod, Sam Femiano, Martin Fiebert, and Mike Messner, became the Men's Studies Association (MSA).[178] The MSA hosted a conference in Pittsburgh in 1989, Atlanta in 1990, and Tucson in 1991 as part of a series of conferences organized by Men and Masculinity (M&M), a group supportive of antisexist political and personal agendas.[179] However, in 1991, MSA leadership decided that it was time to become an independent organization offering its own conference agenda and a split between MSA and M&M

resulted. NOMAS leadership did not approve of the separation along with the creation of separate men's studies conferences and banned any further plans to create separate conferences. Believing this decision to be unwarranted, in May of 1992, MSA leadership decided to go forward with organizing what would be the first *American Men's Studies Association* (AMSA) conference.[180]

The split was acrimonious and AMSA leadership accused NOMAS leadership of claiming that AMSA had abandoned its longstanding feminist principles. AMSA responded with the publication of their guiding principles as:

> Encouraging the refinement of the parameters of men's studies [based on] an ethical perspective which eschews oppression in all forms (namely, sexism, racism, homophobia, anti-Semitism, classism, et al.).[181]

In the end, AMSA did admit that going forward, they would not be governed exclusively by feminist principles, but would be committed to "providing a forum of open and inclusive dialogue which involves a spirit of mutual respect for our common humanity."[182] AMSA now includes mythopoetic views as well as the intersection of men's issues and religion into its conference program.[183]

The White Ribbon Campaign

On December 6, 1989, a man walked onto the campus and into a classroom of L'Ecole Polytechnique, Montreal, armed with a semi-automatic rifle and a hunting knife. He ordered men and women to separate and claimed that he was on a mission, stating "I hate feminists." After making this declaration, he proceeded to shoot all nine of the women present, killing six of them. He then roamed the hallways and cafeteria of the university targeting women. In all, he killed 14 women, and injured another 10 women and 4 men. He then turned the gun on himself and took his own life. In a suicide note, he blamed feminism for having ruined his life.[184] This event is now memorialized in Canada as a National Day of Remembrance and Action on Violence Against Women.[185]

Out of this tragedy **The White Ribbon Campaign** was formed as "the world's largest movement of men and boys working to end violence against women and girls, promote gender equality, healthy relationships and a new vision of masculinity."[186] Starting in 1991, the White Ribbon Campaign asks men to wear white ribbons as a "pledge to never commit, condone, or remain silent about violence against women and girls."[187] The mission statement of the White Ribbon Campaign states,

> Through education, awareness-raising, outreach, technical assistance, capacity building, partnerships and creative campaigns, White Ribbon helps to create tools, strategies and models that challenge negative, outdated concepts of manhood and inspire men to understand and embrace the potential they have to be a part of positive change."[188]

Today, more than 60 countries have active chapters of the White Ribbon Campaign.

Some criticism has been raised that the massacre in Montreal was the savagery of one man and should not be made into a political movement about men's violence against women. Melissa Blaise of the University of Quebec strongly disagrees, stating,

> When I became a feminist, around the year 2000, I was puzzled to see that some were still reluctant to talk in political terms about the attack. It seemed as though the most efficient way to dismiss the feminist explanation was to reduce everything to the psychology of a single mad man ... I always felt those women died in my name. Some of them probably weren't even feminist, they just had the nerve to believe they were peers, not subordinates of their male classmates.[189]

FIGURE 3.9: White Ribbon Campaign

Blaise argues that the fact that these women died strictly because they were women, targeted by a man who openly declared war on feminism made this a political event. Yet, there are actually some who argue that feminism provokes violence against women and view the massacre as one man's frustration, while others, including those who call themselves "masculinists" actually view the shooter as a hero for standing up to feminism.[190] [191] [192] [193]

The men of the White Ribbon Campaign argue that it is the task of men to challenge other men about men's violence against women, and that this challenge involves a ban on all forms of violence against women including sexual violence and sexual harassment. In writing a piece for White Ribbon Campaign, Tom Meagher, whose wife was raped and murdered, stated that three elements conspire to keep men from feeling more outrage about men's violence against women, problems he terms "The Danger of the Monster Myth,"[194]

1. Perpetrators are rarely archetype villains out of comic books; rather, they are often men who seem 'normal' and relatable.
2. Most victims suffer in silence, so their stories are not told.
3. Most victims are victimized by someone they already know.

The myth is that perpetrators of violence are monsters who look and behave like monsters; whereas, the truth is that they look ordinary and have the outward appearance of living ordinary lives that most men relate to as being similar to their own. It is the goal of the White Ribbon Campaign to get men to feel outrage toward the violent acts of other men, even though the majority of men are not violent, in an effort to create more impassioned men against violence, while also educating boys and men about men's violence against women and how to interrupt the cycles of violence that exist.

Mentors in Violence Prevention (MVP)

Founded in 1993 by antiviolence educator Jackson Katz, *Mentors in Violence Prevention* (MVP) is a nonprofit organization committed to ending bullying, gender violence, and school violence in its various forms. The centerpiece of MVP is the "Bystander Program," which focuses on empowering nonviolent men to intervene against violent peers who perpetrate violence against women and men. It also focuses on empowering nonviolent women who may be able to disrupt violent peers from committing violence.[195] MVP defines a 'bystander' as "a family member, friend, classmate, teammate, coworker—anyone who is imbedded in a family, school, social, or professional relationship with someone who might in some way be abusive, or experiencing abuse."[196] The MVP approach refocuses efforts away from reproaching men as violent perpetrators onto men and women as partners who can assist in disrupting a potentially violent episode from taking place.

MVP accomplishes bystander empowerment by working with boys, girls, men, and women in classes and workshops to master techniques in real-life scenarios to learn how to intervene to prevent violence, without placing themselves at physical risk. Based on a "playbook" that offers a variety of options for forestalling potentially violent occurrences, bystanders learn how they can get safely involved. These training sessions take place with high school students, athletic programs including high school, college, and professional athletes, in the military, and with incarcerated men. The four main goals of MVP are to:[197]

FIGURE 3.10: Jackson Katz, Founder, MVP

- raise participant awareness of underlying issues and unique dynamics of all forms of men's violence against women;
- challenge participants to think critically and personally (empathize) about these issues;
- open dialogue amongst participants about the dynamics and context of all forms of men's violence against women;
- inspire participants to be proactive leaders around these issues by challenging them to develop concrete options for intervention in potentially dangerous situations involving peers.

To date, the MVP program has been adopted by universities and organizations around the world and continues to provide a model of anti-violent masculinity designed to inspire and empower men and women to prevent, interrupt, and respond to gender violence and sexist abuse.[198 199]

A CALL TO MEN

Founded by Tony Porter and Ted Bunch, A CALL TO MEN is a violence prevention organization that focuses on creating a "shift [in] social norms that negatively impact our culture and promote a healthier and a more respectful definition of manhood."[200] Dealing with physical and sexual violence against women is, according to A CALL TO MEN, primarily the responsibility of men, since the majority of violence against women is perpetrated by men. Like MVP, A CALL TO MEN invites men to be proactive players in creating a better world for everyone by combatting violence where it is found. In the slogan, "Our liberation as men is directly tied to the liberation of women," A CALL TO

FIGURE 3.11: Tony Porter, A CALL TO MEN

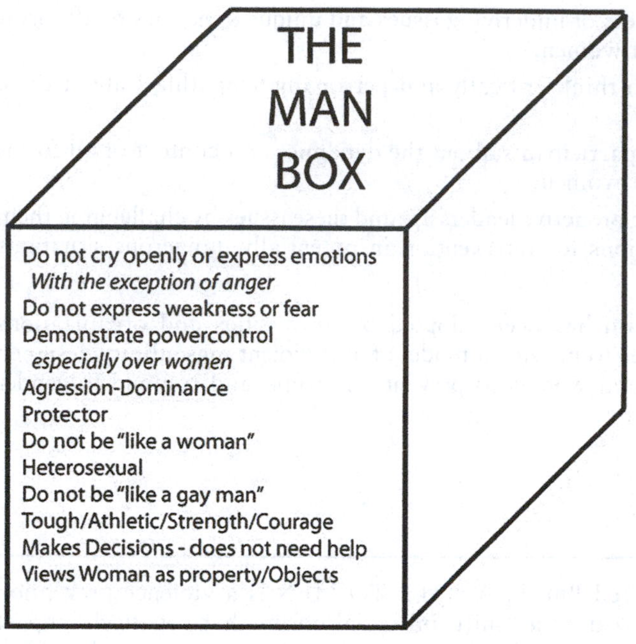

FIGURE 3.12: The Man Box

MEN encourages men to view girls and women in a respectful and loving way that is in many ways counter to the ways society instructs men to view women.[201]

In what Porter terms "The Man Box," men are instructed by society to live up to certain standards of behavior that are ultimately destructive to themselves and others (Figure 3.12).

Porter views contemporary male scripts as emphatically detrimental to boys and men by instructing them that showing fear or pain are signs of weakness. As a result, men are told to bottle up their emotions and keep their pain inside. This "man box" is a prison that informs men that weakness is equated with being or acting female, and if boys and men are taught from early ages that girls and women are weak and should be viewed primarily as sexual objects but never to be taken as credible equals, Porter asks, "How can there not be high rates of men's violence against women?"[202] The goal is to reconstruct the masculine paradigm into a caring, nurturing paradigm that values women, gay people, and all who identify themselves in nontraditional gendered ways. A CALL TO MEN asks men to view themselves as partners and authentic equals with women in the pursuit of becoming more liberated men.

Summary

Boys' and men's groups have been created and maintained for many centuries in the pursuit of a host of goals that are sometimes incompatible with one another. The most obvious distinction that can be made between men's groups is their alliance with or opposition to feminist principles. While many men's groups attempt to bridge the gaps that exist between men and women in ways that will promote equality, other men's groups appear devoted to a reclamation of men as dominant leaders of the family unit and society at large. Each progressive gain that women have made is viewed by these anti-feminist men's groups as an attack on men with the attending view that men are now the sex being oppressed. Pro-feminist men's groups respond that partnering with women in a genuinely egalitarian way promotes healthy relationships, decreases violence against women, and creates a healthier, sustainable society where oppression is reduced, empowerment is increased, and where the lives of both women and men are improved.

Notes

1 www.thecollegefix.com/post/24937/.
2 www.jsonline.com/news/opinion/a-open-letter-to-young-men-headed-off-to-college-b99566165z1-323275591.html.
3 www.msana.com/women.asp.
4 https://en.wikipedia.org/wiki/Freemasonry.
5 Ibid.
6 https://en.wikipedia.org/wiki/Masonic_lodge_officers.
7 www.npr.org/2009/09/16/112884584/secret-of-the-masons-its-not-so-secret.
8 https://en.wikipedia.org/wiki/Fraternities_and_sororities#Rushing_and_pledging_.28recruitment_and_new_member_periods.29.
9 "Books: Hawthorne's Line." *Time*, April 25, 1938.
10 https://en.wikipedia.org/wiki/Fraternities_and_sororities#Hazing.
11 https://en.wikipedia.org/wiki/Hazing.
12 www.bloomberg.com/news/articles/2013-07-24/mother-of-golf-prodigy-in-hazing-death-defied-by-fratpac.
13 www.rollingstone.com/culture/news/the-most-out-of-control-fraternities-in-america-20130828.
14 www.livescience.com/2528-hazing-young-men.html.
15 Ibid.
16 Ibid.
17 Ibid.
18 www.ibtimes.com/why-hazing-can-lead-positive-change-224185.
19 Ibid.
20 www.theguardian.com/commentisfree/2014/sep/24/rape-sexual-assault-ban-frats.
21 www.msnbc.com/krystal-clear/campus-sexual-assault-crisis-ban-fraternities.
22 www.cnn.com/2013/10/09/opinion/foubert-fraternities-rape/.
23 www.tandfonline.com/doi/abs/10.2202/1949-6605.1866?journalCode=uarp19.
24 Canan, Sasha N., Jozkowski, Kristen N., Crawford, Brandon L., "Sexual assault supportive attitudes, rape myth acceptance and token resistance in Greek and Non-Greek students from two university samples in the United States," *Journal of Interpersonal Violence*, March, 2016.
25 www.thehealingplace.info/what-are-rape-myths/.
26 Ibid.
27 Anderson, N. and Svrluga, S., "What a massive sexual assault survey found at 27 top U.S. universities," *The Washington Post, 15 September 2015.*
28 https://well.wvu.edu/articles/rape_myths_and_facts.
29 Schwartz, M.D. and Nograndy, C.A., "Fraternity membership, rape myths, and sexual aggression on a college campus," *Violence Against Women*, June, 1996.
30 Chapter 10, on men and violence, will take up a more expansive examination of rape and sexual crime, including sexual crimes committed by high school and college-aged young men.
31 https://rainn.org/get-information/sexual-assault-prevention/bystanders-can-help.
32 McMahon S., "Rape myth beliefs and bystander attitudes among incoming college students," *Journal of American College Health*, 59, 1 (2010), pp. 3–11. doi: 10.1080/07448481.2010.483715.
33 www.washingtonpost.com/local/education/beer-pong-body-shots-keg-stands-alcohol-central-to-college-and-assault/2015/06/14/7430e13c-04bb-11e5-a428-c984eb077d4e_story.html.
34 http://inewsource.org/2014/10/21/fraternity-culture-linked-to-college-sexual-assault-problem/.
35 Ibid.
36 https://en.wikipedia.org/wiki/The_Hunting_Ground.

37 http://fox5sandiego.com/2014/12/16/sdsu-fraternity-shut-down-amid-harassment-investigation/.
38 http://bigthink.com/focal-point/no-means-yes-yes-means-anal-frat-banned-from-yale.
39 http://jezebel.com/inside-the-student-activist-movement-tufts-university-1526094401.
40 www.huffingtonpost.com/soraya-chemaly/the-college-rape-problem-_b_6228844.html.
41 www.wsj.com/articles/SB10001424052748704658704576275152354071470.
42 Ibid.
43 Ibid.
44 http://finance.yahoo.com/news/eight-leading-national-fraternities-form-133500836.html.
45 Ibid.
46 http://thinkprogress.org/health/2014/09/24/3571363/fraternities-sexual-assault/.
47 www.campus-classics.com/top-5-reasons-to-join-a-fraternity-or-sorority/.
48 http://college.usatoday.com/2012/05/08/examining-the-benefits-of-greek-life/.
49 www.wsj.com/articles/greek-life-shown-to-be-linked-to-real-life-happiness-1401160205.
50 Ibid.
51 https://farm5.staticflickr.com/4076/4877473706_b9ef5e6d60_o_d.jpg.
52 www.theatlantic.com/education/archive/2014/03/the-hazing-problem-at-black-fraternities/284452/.
53 Ibid.
54 http://diverseeducation.com/article/8216/.
55 www.cnn.com/2015/03/10/opinions/sutter-oklahoma-fraternity-racist/.
56 www.slate.com/articles/life/inside_higher_ed/2015/03/behind_the_chant_discrimination_at_oklahoma_s_sae_chapter_goes_deeper_than.html.
57 http://college.usatoday.com/2014/12/08/clemson-fraternity-suspended-after-cripmas-party-backlash/.
58 www.slate.com/articles/life/inside_higher_ed/2015/03/behind_the_chant_discrimination_at_oklahoma_s_sae_chapter_goes_deeper_than.html.
59 Ibid.
60 Ibid.
61 www.huffingtonpost.com/2015/04/07/frats-shut-down-hazing_n_7001492.html.
62 Crouse, Karen, "Treasure of golf's sad past, black caddies vanish in era of riches," *New York Times*, April 2, 2012. www.nytimes.com/2012/04/03/sports/golf/from-a-symbol-of-segregation-to-a-victim-of-golfs-success.html?pagewanted=all&_r=0.
63 "Augusta National admits two women, including Condoleezza Rice," *USA Today*, August 20, 2012.
64 Boy Scouts of America, Fact Sheet. www.scouting.org/About/FactSheets/BSA_History.aspx.
65 Peterson, Robert, "Marching to a Different Drummer." *Scouting*, 2003. Boy Scouts of America.
66 Warren, A., 'Popular manliness: Baden-Powell, scouting and the development of manly character,' in *Manliness and Morality: Middle Class Masculinity in Britain and America 1800–1940*, ed. A. Mangan and J. Walvan (Manchester University Press, 1987), pp. 199–219 (203).
67 Barbey d'Aurevilly, "Du dandisme et de George Brummell" (1845), in *Oeuvres completes*, (Psychanalyse, 1925), pp. 87–92.
68 "In Regency England, Brummel's fashionable simplicity constituted in fact a criticism of the exuberant French fashions of the eighteenth century." See S. Schmid, "Byron and Wilde: The dandy in the public sphere," in *The Importance of Reinventing Oscar: Versions of Wilde During the Last 100 Years*, ed. J. Hibbard, et al., (Rodopi, 2002), p. 83.
69 Camus, Albert, *The Rebel: An Essay on Man in Revolt*, reissue (Vintage Press, 1992).
70 530 U.S. 640 (2000).
71 CNN, May 24, 2013, "Boy Scouts to allow gay youths to join." www.cnn.com/2013/05/23/us/boy-scouts-sexual-orientation/.
72 www.washingtontimes.com/news/2013/feb/4/the-boy-scouts-flirtation-with-dishonor-and-destru/?page=all.
73 www.scouting.org/scoutsource/BoyScouts.aspx.
74 www.cnn.com/2013/05/23/us/boy-scouts-sexual-orientation/.
75 Ibid.
76 www.hrc.org/blog/entry/boy-scouts-of-america-takes-historic-step-forward-for-gay-scouts-leaves-gay.
77 www.scouting.org/scoutsource/Media/mission.aspx.
78 www.girlscouts.org/who_we_are/history/.
79 www.girlscouts.org/who_we_are/advocacy/.

80 Tuttle, Kate, "Boy Scouts are from Mars, Girl Scouts are from Venus," *The Atlantic*, March 5, 2012.
81 Ibid.
82 Ibid.
83 www.ymca.net/sites/default/files/pdf/y-logo-history.pdf.
84 Frost, J. William, "Part V: Christianity and culture in America," *Christianity: A Social and Cultural History*, 2nd edition (Prentice Hall, 1998), p. 476.
85 http://en.wikipedia.org/wiki/Y.M.C.A._(song).
86 www.classicbands.com/village.html.
87 Ibid.
88 Campbell, Michael, *Popular Music in America: The Beat Goes On* (Cengage Learning, 2012).
89 www.ymca.net/about-us.
90 www.ymcatriangle.org/about-y/our-mission.
91 www.ywca.org/site/c.cuIRJ7NTKrLaG/b.7515807/k.2737/YWCA__Eliminating_Racism_Empowering_Women.htm.
92 www.ywca.org/site/pp.asp?c=mkI1L6MPJvE&b=6151095.
93 www.ywca.org/site/c.cuIRJ7NTKrLaG/b.9360119/k.7BA2/Our_Mission_in_Action.htm.
94 www.dailymail.co.uk/news/article-1344779/YWCA-drops-word-Christian-historic-Platform-51.html.
95 www.youngwomenstrust.org/about.
96 www.nytimes.com/2003/05/22/us/conservative-groups-oppose-new-leader-chosen-by-ywca.html.
97 Ibid.
98 Ibid.
99 Pleck, Joseph H. and Jack Sawyer, eds, *Men and Masculinity* (Prentice Hall, 1974).
100 Farrell, Warren, *The Liberated Man: Beyond Masculinity: Freeing Men and their Relationships with Women* (Random House, 1974).
101 Ibid.
102 http://en.wikipedia.org/wiki/Warren_Farrell.
103 Farrell, Warren, *The Myth of Male Power* (Berkley Trade, 1993).
104 Ibid.
105 www.brainyquote.com/quotes/quotes/t/thomaspain386293.html.
106 Bly, Robert, *Iron John: A Book about Men* (Addison-Wesley, 1990).
107 Ibid.
108 Bly, Robert, *The Sibling Society* (Addison-Wesley, 1996).
109 www.shsu.edu/piic/fall2006/scottbaker.html.
110 Messner, Michael, *Politics of Masculinities: Men in Movements* (Sage Publications, 1997).
111 Ibid., pp. 19–20.
112 Ibid., pp. 23–24.
113 http://mankindproject.org/about-mankind-project.
114 Ibid.
115 Vogel, Chris, "Naked Men: The ManKind Project and Michael Scinto," Houston Press, *Village Voice Media*, October 4, 2007.
116 http://masculineheart.blogspot.com/2010/05/digging-into-manking-projects.html.
117 Newton, J., *From Panthers to Promise Keepers: rethinking the men's movement* (Rowman & Littlefield, 2004).
118 www.mensdefense.org/RF_Doyle_Bio.htm.
119 Ashe, F., *The New Politics of Masculinity: Men, Power and Resistance* (Routledge, 2007).
120 http://ncfm.org/.
121 Ibid.
122 www.avoiceformen.com/policies/mission-statement/.
123 www.aei.org/scholar/christina-hoff-sommers/.
124 Hoff Sommers, Christina, *The War on Boys: How Misguided Feminism is Harming Our Boys* (Simon & Schuster, 2001).
125 www.theatlantic.com/magazine/archive/2000/05/the-war-against-boys/304659/.
126 The gendered education gap will be taken up more thoroughly in Chapter 4, which covers "The Boy Crisis."
127 www.huffingtonpost.com/2014/01/17/elisabeth-hasselbeck-feminism_n_4619669.html.
128 http://articles.orlandosentinel.com/2013-11-23/news/os-men-only-law-firms-20131113_1_divorce-cases-law-firms-alimony.
129 www.avoiceformen.com/policies/mission-statement/.
130 Kimmel, Michael, *Angry White Men* (Nation Books, 2013).
131 Fathers' rights groups will be taken up again and expanded upon in Chapter 5 on fatherhood.
132 www.fathersrights.org/.
133 Flood, Michael, "What's Wrong with Fathers' Rights?," in *Men Speak Out: Views*

on Gender, Sex, and Power, ed. Shira Tarrant, second edition (Routledge, 2013).
134 http://ncadv.org/learn-more/statistics.
135 www.avoiceformen.com/paul-elam/.
136 www.donotlink.com/framed?6470.
137 www.the-spearhead.com/2012/09/27/hows-that-women-in-the-military-thing-going-now/.
138 http://wehuntedthemammoth.com/2012/09/29/us-army-brig-general-charged-with-rape-whos-to-blame-according-to-the-spearhead-its-women/.
139 www.avoiceformen.com/mens-rights/false-rape-culture/challenging-the-etiology-of-rape/.
140 www.marieclaire.com/culture/a16688/mens-rights-activist/.
141 Ibid.
142 www.nationalcenterformen.org/page3.shtml.
143 Ibid.
144 Ibid.
145 http://boycottamericanwomen.blogspot.com/.
146 http://counterfem.blogspot.com/.
147 www.avoiceformalestudents.com/avfms-mega-post-10-reasons-false-rape-accusations-are-common/.
148 www.saveservices.org/.
149 www.returnofkings.com/63036/why-you-should-not-go-see-mad-max-feminist-road.
150 www.motherjones.com/politics/2015/01/warren-farrell-mens-rights-movement-feminism-misogyny-trolls.
151 Ibid.
152 www.msnbc.com/msnbc/mens-rights-conference-feminism.
153 Million Man March National Organizing Committee, "Million Man March Fact Sheet," in *Million Man March / Day of Absence; A Commemorative Anthology; Speeches, Commentary, Photography, Poetry, Illustrations, Documents*, ed. Haki R. Madhubuti, and Maulana Karenga (Third World Press, 1996), p. 152.
154 Nelson Jr., William E., "Black church politics and The Million Man March," in *Black Religious Leadership from the Slave Community to the Million Man March: Flames of Fire*, ed. Felton O. Best (The Edwin Mellen Press, 1998), p. 244.
155 Jackson, Sr., Reverend Jesse L., "Remarks Before One Million Men, Monday, October 16, 1995," in *Million Man March / Day of Absence*, 33.
156 Ibid.
157 Ibid.
158 www.washingtonpost.com/wp-srv/local/daily/oct/15/poll.htm.
159 www.finalcall.com/artman/publish/mmm-jamaica/article_101759.shtml.
160 Ibid.
161 Smith, Vern and Waldman, Steven, "Farrakhan On The March," *Newsweek* 126.15 (1995), 42.
162 www.finalcall.com/artman/publish/mmm-jamaica/article_101759.shtml.
163 Ibid.
164 Loose, Cindy, "Promise Keepers Headed for the Mall; Men's Christian Group Plans Oct. 4 Rally," *The Washington Post*.
165 http://hirr.hartsem.edu/research/religion_family_pksummary.html.
166 Ibid.
167 www.nytimes.com/1997/10/05/weekinreview/women-and-the-promise-keepers-good-for-the-gander-but-the-goose-isn-t-so-sure.html.
168 www.publiceye.org/ifas/fw/9609/promise.html.
169 Ibid.
170 http://thekingsmen.org/.
171 http://articles.philly.com/2010-10-18/news/24982333_1_retreat-faith-group-co-founder.
172 http://thekingsmen.org/tkm-retreats/into-the-wild-outdoor-experiential-retreat-for-men/.
173 Ibid.
174 Gambill, Edward L., *Uneasy Males: The American Men's Movement: 1970—2000* (i-universe, 2005).
175 Ibid.
176 www.nomas.org/history.
177 www.nomas.org/principles.
178 http://mensstudies.org/?page_id=5.
179 Ibid.
180 Ibid.
181 Ibid.
182 Ibid.
183 Ibid.
184 CBSDigitalArchives, www.cbc.ca/archives/categories/society/crime-justice/the-montreal-massacre/gunman-massacres-14-women.html.
185 http://en.wikipedia.org/wiki/National_Day_of_Remembrance_and_Action_on_Violence_Against_Women.
186 http://www.whiteribbon.ca/who-we-are/.
187 Ibid.
188 Ibid.
189 Blais, Melissa, *"I Hate Feminists!" December 6, 1989, and its aftermath* (Spinifex Press, 2014).

190 Conway, John Frederick, *The Canadian Family in Crisis* (James Lorimer and Company, 2003), 166.
191 Meyers, Helene, *Femicidal Fears: Narratives of the Female Gothic Experience* (State University of New York Press, 2001), 3–4.
192 Blais, Melissa, "Marc Lépine: heros ou martyr? Le masculinisme et la tuerie de l'École polytechnique," in *Le mouvement masculiniste au Québec*, ed. Mélissa Blais and Francis Dupuis-Déri (Les Éditions du remue-ménage, 2008), pp. 86–92.
193 Hanes, Alison, "Man threatens to repeat Montreal massacre," *Ottawa Citizen*, December 2, 2005, A9.
194 http://whiteribbonblog.com/2014/04/17/the-danger-of-the-monster-myth/.
195 www.jacksonkatz.com/mvp.html.
196 Ibid.
197 www.mvpnational.org/program-overview/mission-goals/.
198 Ibid.
199 The MVP program will be revisited in more detail in Chapter 9 on men and sports.
200 www.acalltomen.org/about-us/our-vision.
201 Ibid.
202 Keith, Thomas, *The Empathy Gap: Masculinity and the Courage to Change* (Media Education Foundation, 2015).

The Boy Crisis

"What is 5 + 4?"
"5 + 4?" asks the boy
"Yes, are you not paying attention?"
"Cindy, what is 5 + 4?"
"5 + 4 is 9."
Gus looks the boy in the eye and whispers, "God, you're dumb."
The boy's heart sinks. With tears dripping from his eyes, he mutters softly to himself, "I know I'm dumb. I'm really, really dumb."[1]

LEARNING OBJECTIVES

After reading this chapter, students should be able to respond to the following questions with an understanding of the terms and expressions employed:

- *What is Erik Erikson's* Psychosocial Development Theory, *and what has it to do with adolescent boys?* What are psycho-social stages of life *and what is it that Erikson terms an* identity crisis?
- *What are the salient features of what has been called* the boy crisis? *How does this crisis differ for boys of different backgrounds? What is the educational gender gap? What are the reasons why some believe boys are falling behind in education as compared to girls?*
- *To what extent do factors of race, ethnicity, or income background affect the rates of academic success for boys and young men, and what sorts of solutions have been suggested? When discussing the challenges for black, male adolescents, what does Howard C. Stevenson mean by* hypervulnerability, false images of manhood, *and* insecure masculinity? *What is* peer discrimination?
- *What are the rates of ADHD in boys as compared to girls? In what ways do ADHD affect boys? What are the criticisms of ADHD diagnoses and stimulant drug prescription?*
- *What are the arguments for and against single-sex classrooms? In what ways are single-sex classrooms considered by some to be good for boys? In what ways are single-sex classrooms thought to be detrimental to boys? What is*

Intergroup Contact Theory *and how does it conflict with single-sex education models?*

- *What are the rules of what William Pollack terms "the boy code"? What does Pollack mean by the expression "the mask of masculinity"? What is the* Sex Role Egalitarianism Scale *and the* Traditional Male Role Model Attitude Scale *and how did these tests show that boys today are both egalitarian and traditional in their views about gender?*
- *What are the central features of Michael Kimmel's* Guyland*? What does Kimmel mean by "a culture of entitlement," "a culture of silence," and "a culture of protection"? What are the central features of* The Bro Code*? In what ways do Hollywood films promote bro culture?*

For the past couple decades, many have noted that boys are not doing as well as girls in a host of areas, but particularly in terms of education. Girls are going to college and graduating at higher rates than boys. Boys are dropping out of high school at higher rates. Boys' GPAs are lower than girls. Boy are getting in trouble with law enforcement more often than girls. These problems have become so acute, according to some, that many are claiming there is a boy crisis that needs addressing with urgency. This chapter is going to take up these issues and examine what some believe to be solutions to "the boy crisis."

Throughout the middle-twentieth century, influenced by the work of Sigmund Freud, developmental psychologist Erik Erikson created a theory of personality development that included the notion that there are what he termed ***psychosocial stages of life*** as each individual collects a multitude of experiences through which a personal identity is ultimately constructed.[2] Child development became a central feature of Erikson's work, as he developed his views about personal identity. He insisted that the environment in which a child is raised plays a crucial role in establishing self-identity. It was Erikson, in fact, who coined the phrase "identity crisis," as a crisis whereby one is unsure who one is or how he or she fits into the world. As a result, an individual undergoes intense inner analysis marked by periods of personal trials, experimentation, and uncertainty.

During adolescence, a stage in life when ego identity and role confusion are most pronounced, Erikson argued that youths separate from parents and seek greater autonomy. During this time of life, adolescents are "sometimes morbidly preoccupied with what they appear to be in the eyes of others."[3] This means that adolescent peer interaction is elevated both in terms of time invested and influence. Erikson believed that by the time one reaches young adulthood, there is a stabilizing effect that accompanies a commitment to non-family, longer-term relationships.[4]

When considering the journey males take from early childhood to roughly the end of college, for those who attend college, there is no single masculine script that all boys and young men follow, although there are well-traveled paths that many take. With Erikson's views as theoretical background, this chapter is going to examine some of the more notable stages and stand-out moments in life when boys and young men seek to establish identity. Along the way, and in a similar vein as Erikson's "identity crisis," this chapter will take up what is being called a "crisis in masculinity," which begins as a "boy crisis." This crisis, if indeed it exists, is different for particular boys and men depending on factors such as age, race and ethnicity, socioeconomic background, sexual orientation, cultural or family expectations, biology, or any number of individual circumstances that can create challenges for boys and men. As we will see, researchers have been gathering evidence that document and purport to explain the boy crisis in terms of why boys are dropping out of school or failing at high rates, why boys are lacking in motivation and direction in life, whether and why young men are remaining in states of arrested development much longer than young men of previous generations, whether and to what extent higher rates of ADHD in boys is negatively affecting them, and ultimately what some believe can be done to turn these negative trends around.

The Education Gap

Contemporary literature on boys is replete with warnings that we are in the grip of a boy crisis, which includes concerns that boys are failing or dropping out of school at high rates, that boys are unmotivated slackers that are heading for disastrous adult lives, that boys are being outperformed by girls K through 12 and beyond. What are the facts? According to the National Center for Education Statistics (NCES), the high school dropout rates for boys has declined since 1990 when it stood at 12% as opposed to 2012 when it stood at 7%.[5] During the same time period, dropout rates for girls have gone from 12% to 6%.[6] In this sense, the boy crisis as applied to high school dropout rates might be interpreted as being blown out of proportion. But there are greater differences when turning to high school graduation rates, where girls are graduating at a rate of 84%, while boys are graduating at a rate of 77%.[7] This is often termed the educational gender gap.[8] [9] The National Honor Society reports that 64% of its members are girls.[10] Average graduating GPAs for girls is 3.10, while for boys, it is 2.90.[11] When turning to college and university admission rates, women outnumber men at a rate nearing 60% to 40%,[12] and since 1980, women have earned a whopping 10 million more college degrees than men,[13] even though men continue to earn more in salary than women, particularly by their mid-to-late 30s.[14] Sociologist Michael Kimmel argues that the educational gender gap should not be overstated noting that in 1960, 54% of boy and 38% of girls entered college directly out of high school, while today, 64% of boys and 70% of girls do so.[15] When turning to so-called elite colleges and universities, the gender gap does not materialize, with Harvard, Amherst, Princeton, Duke, U.C. Berkeley, M.I.T., Cal Tech, and the University of Chicago all maintaining over 50% and in some cases over 60% male enrollment.[16]

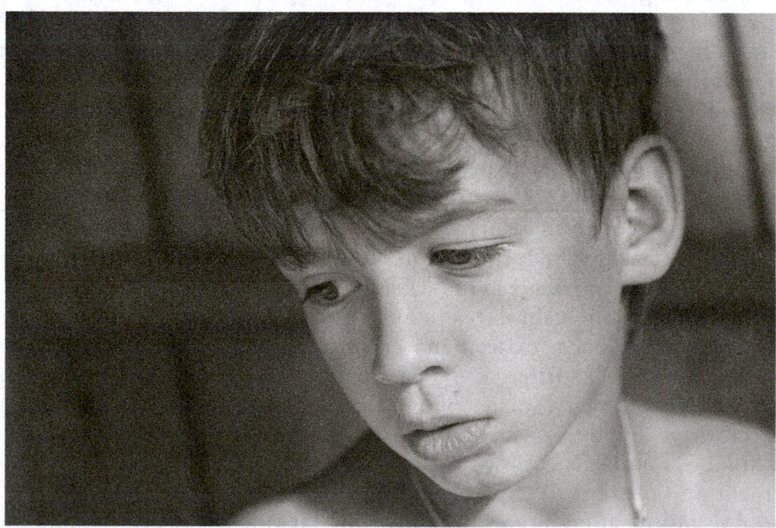

FIGURE 4.1: Of all animals, the boy is the most unmanageable. ~ Plato, *Laws* 808

Still, some researchers pin the educational component of the boy crisis to the problem of lower literacy skills in boys.[17] Part of the problem, according to Richard Whitmire, former President of the National Educational Writers Association, is that boys need phonics instruction more than do girls, while many teachers instruct "whole language" reading education, which emphasizes meaning and strategy instruction.[18] [19] In addition, Whitmire asserts that by the time boys enter middle school, the literacy gap widens, since by middle school the reading materials demand an improved command of the nuances of grammar and vocabulary, skills not attained during elementary school years.[20] A further problem is a lack of what Whitmire terms "boy books" as opposed to "girl books" in schools.[21] Boy books, Whitmire explains, are books centered on adventure, danger, and even material that girls might find disgusting in nature such as the *Captain Underpants* series of books, but that Whitmire calls "perfect boy books."[22] One of the reasons for this lack of "boy books" is that publishing companies publish more books aimed at girls than boys due to economics,[23] since males account for only 20% of the fiction market.[24] As a result, boys are given reading assignments on books that many boys view as being for girls, which, claims Whitmire, turns boys off reading.[25]

Others view the problem differently. Donald Gallo, English professor at Central Connecticut State University notes that even though "we're in a golden age of books for teenagers," boys gravitate more toward nonfiction.[26] Children's writer Jon Scieszka, however, argues that "boys don't feel comfortable exploring the emotions and feelings found in fiction, because the majority of adults reading [to them] are women [and so] boys might not see reading as a masculine activity."[27] Thomas Newkirk, author of *Misreading Masculinity: Boys, Literacy, and Popular Culture* argues that schools need to broaden their definition of what counts as literature, given that many boys enjoy reading fact books, graphic novels, sports magazines, science fiction, humor, and adventure fare.[28] University of Kent professor of sociology Frank Furedi goes further by claiming it is a myth to say that boys don't read or don't like to read.[29] According to Furedi, parents need to normalize reading in the home as part of an everyday activity. Boys also need to see adults reading, he argues, because it reinforces the idea that it is enjoyable and not simply an activity parents do with children.[30] When boys view reading as a grown-up activity that is fun and not simply practical, such as *having to* look through a game manual to learn how to play a game, and when adults take the lead in modeling reading as a pastime they choose over other pastimes, Furedi notes, boys will read.[31]

Socioeconomics and Boys of Color

Many researchers, however, have been skeptical about describing a boy crisis as a crisis that affects all boys in the same way without regard to identifiable differences between boys of distinct and divergent backgrounds. In their book *Adolescent Boys: Exploring Diverse Cultures of Boyhood*, Stanford University professor Judy Y. Chu and NYU professor Niobe Way argue that while most of the research into the lives of boys has focused on white, middle-class boys, African-American, Asian-American, and Latino-American boys must be understood on their own terms.[32] Writing for the *Washington Post*, social worker Carly Rivers and social scientist Rosalind Chait Barnett agree, noting,

> The alarming statistics on which the notion of a crisis is based are rarely broken out by race or class. When they are, the whole picture changes. It becomes clear that if there is a crisis, it's among inner-city and rural boys. White suburban boys aren't significantly touched by it.[33]

In the book *Adolescent Boys*, University of Pennsylvania professor of Urban Education and Africana Studies, Howard C. Stevenson, argues that black, male youths suffer from what he terms ***hypervulnerability***, which is "the internalization of negative images of black maleness," a psychological and physical exposure of one's feelings and actions to annihilation and dehumanization by one's family, friends, neighborhood, society, and the imagery social institutions manufacture and promulgate of black men.[34] Stevenson notes that black, male adolescents are aware of being racially profiled, followed in department stores, or when simply gathered in groups, and that they are overrepresented as those arrested, convicted, harassed by police, and incarcerated as compared to white, male youths. As a result of this awareness, young, black men will often adopt what Stevenson calls ***false images of manhood***,[35] resulting in ***insecure masculinity***, whereby one performs a set of behaviors "driven by fear to prove to the world that one's manhood isn't weak." The goal of these young men is to look tough regardless of one's internal reality. As mentioned in chapter seven on media, this performance is famously known as "the cool pose" as described in the work of Richard Majors and Janet Billson. Stevenson laments that this tough exterior robs black, male adolescents from completing childhood and substituting a script written by others for an authentic experience of being themselves. This is all the more inauthentic and subversive when one realizes that this *cool pose* is a script based on "white society's projected fears of Black manhood."[36] Even so, many white, suburban adolescent males also view this *cool pose* as a cool and therefore desirable pose, doing their best to emulate it, which, as Stevenson states, amounts to, "the blind leading the blind."[37]

FIGURE 4.2: Justin Bieber captured on camera 'flashing signs' in a demonstration of 'the cool pose'

THOUGHT BOX

Many have noted, as does Dr. Stevenson, that white, Latino, and Asian adolescent boys and young men will adopt what they view as being a cool, urban, black male persona. What precisely do you think makes this particular male performance so cool in the eyes of boys and men?

Ultimately, Stevenson argues,

> Black males must learn that they are not a lost generation. They deserve to be touched emotionally, physically, and intellectually and are capable of learning about and critically outmaneuvering the subtleties of American racism. They need what all boys need—care and compassion.[38]

In 2012, The U.S. Department of Education released its first-ever national data on graduation rates on a state-by-state basis.[39] This was the first time that states used a standardized and more rigorous means of measurement for both graduation rates and dropout rates.[40] Graduation rates became more transparent when broken down along lines of race and ethnicity. The report documented that "Asian students topped the graduation rates by demographic, with 79 percent of students finishing high school. White students followed with a 76 percent graduation rate, black students with 60 percent and Latino students with 58 percent."[41] Other reports show graduation rates for black and Latino males as being less than 50%, with graduation rates for New York City and Philadelphia hovering at 28%.[42] When turning strictly to black males, the NCES reported that in particular states, the graduation rates were especially poor, including Iowa, Nebraska, South Carolina, Florida, Delaware, Illinois, and the District of Columbia.[43] One report, however, noted that when looking at regions where resources are high and opportunities are equal, black males perform as well as their white, male counterparts, but that low-resource regions are especially vulnerable for poor performances by black, male students.[44] Other reports show that black, male students are slowly catching up to their white, male counterparts, but argue that it has taken black, male students nine years to close the graduation gap by three percentage points, leading John H. Jackson of The Schott Foundation for Public Education to note that at this rate, it will take black males 50 years to catch up completely to their white, male counterparts.[45]

If the educational gender gap is more pronounced for boys and young men of color, why and what can be done about it? Some studies report that African-American girls are graduating high school at a rate of approximately 58% compared to African-American boys at 48%.[46] Similarly, Hispanic girls are graduating high school at a rate of 58%, compared to Hispanic boys at a rate of 49%, and again, the numbers differ for different states.[47] These overall educational disparities compared to white and Asian students are often explained on the grounds of poverty and reduced resources.[48] One study, however,

FIGURE 4.3:

examined factors that went beyond issues of socioeconomics. Ronald Ferguson, director of Harvard University's "Achievement Gap Initiative," claims,

> There's accumulating evidence that there are racial differences in what kids experience before the first day of kindergarten. They have to do with a lot of sociological and historical forces. In order to address those, we have to be able to have conversations that people are unwilling to have.[49]

According to Ferguson, these unpopular conversations have to do, in part, with the ways parents raise their 2-, 3-, and 4-year-old children. The keys lie, states Ferguson, in "how much we talk to them, the ways we talk to them, the ways we enforce discipline, and the ways we encourage them to think and develop a sense of autonomy."[50] According to Ferguson, what needs to be done is to create a network of black and Latino mentors that work individually with at-risk students, along with assuring that these students receive "really good teaching."[51]

But education gaps drawn along lines of race and ethnicity do not tell us what to do about the gendered part of the educational gap. Ohio State University professor Terrell Strayhorn argues that for black men, talent and high school success are not enough to succeed at traditionally white colleges and universities. A third factor he identifies as "grit" is required. Strayhorn defines "grit" as "a dedication to pursuing and achieving a goal whatever the obstacles and failures along the way."[52] However, some universities such as Virginia Commonwealth University and the State University of New York, Albany, have been able to improve their graduation rates for black, male students by implementing cohort curriculum with specialized support services and mentoring programs designed specifically for black students taking STEM courses.[53]

Some have argued that male, African-American students enter college with low expectations by internalizing racist stereotypes, along with suffering from the burden of peer pressure for "acting white,"[54] to explain what has been termed "the achievement gap."[55] But other studies that conducted individual interviews with high-achieving African-American male students at six predominantly white universities found alternate explanations and solutions.[56] In interviews, high-achieving male, African-American students report that their success is due in part to "same-race peer mentoring."[57] University of Pennsylvania professor Shaun R. Harper argues that understanding black, male success in college needs to replace the emphasis on black, male underachievement or failure in college.[58] Other researchers agree with Harper,[59] arguing that mentors "impact students' decisions to attend, satisfaction with, and motivation to persist in postsecondary education," while also instilling a feeling of obligation in the student to show the mentor that the student is committed to success.[60] Strayhorn agrees in principle that success needs to be emphasized in the discussions of black, male college students, and that mentoring conveys benefit to the perceptions and lives of young, black men in college. However, Strayhorn also maintains that there is no single solution that will assure black, male success in college and that "merely increasing the number of supportive relationships available to Black men is unlikely to yield substantial gains in terms of their enrollment, retention, and eventual graduation."[61]

THOUGHT BOX

Discuss ideas for raising grades and retaining male students of color in high school and college. Are some of the ideas presented in this chapter worthwhile, or do you believe there are better ways to address dropout and failure rates, as well as elevating rates of success?

In one study, researchers speaking to African-American, Latino, and Asian adolescent males learned that while African-American and Latino boys spoke about discrimination by teachers, police, and shopkeepers and Latino teens would add concerns about language and immigration, Asian-American boys spoke about ***peer discrimination***, claiming that they were often harassed by African-American and Latino boys who believed that Asian students were being favored by teachers.[62] Other studies support similar findings, where Asian youths feel targeted within peer groups for allegedly receiving greater favor.[63] In addition, a study that specifically examined the experiences and perceptions of first and second generation Chinese-American adolescents found that these young people feel alienated both from their parents and their peers.[64] Alienation from parents typically comes about as a result of language barriers, parental work schedules, high parental educational expectations, and acclimated American enculturation.[65]

In addition to race and ethnicity, socioeconomic factors also play into the equation of staying in or dropping out of school. According to the NCES, only 59% of students who begin as freshmen at a four-year college or university receive their degree within six years.[66] Unsurprisingly, students who come from low-income backgrounds have, statistically, even less chance of college success.[67] Low-income students who score between 1200 and 1600 on their SAT's are half as likely to graduate college than their counterparts who come from the top 25% of income-backgrounds.[68] In 2013, the White House issued a report stating, "Low-income students face barriers to college success at every stage of the education pipeline, from elementary school through post-secondary education, sometimes in spite of their academic achievements," making clear that 'grit' as a psychological auger for low-income students, whether black or not, might not account for the very real, everyday obstacles low-income students face. The statistics suggest that being male and coming from a low-income background doubles the peril of failure, while being male, black, and coming from a low-income background places one at the highest risk of failure.[69]

In trying to account for why boys, regardless of race and class, are struggling to achieve academically in comparison to girls, there are numerous explanations. According to psychologist Michael Thompson,

> Girls outperform boys in elementary school, middle school, high school, college, and graduate school ... Girls are being told "go for it, you can do it;" they are getting an immense amount of support. Boys are hearing that the way to shine is athletically. And boys get a lot of mixed messages about what it means to be masculine and what it means to be a student. Does being a good student make you make you a real man? I don't think so ... it's not cool.[70]

Thompson, coauthor of the book *Raising Cain: Protecting the Emotional Life of Boys*, argues that along with normative, social scripts that instruct boys that education is not masculine or cool, another factor also challenges boys as a result of education practiced as a calm, structured environment: hyperactivity, or at least that boys, on average, are much more active than girls.[71] Thompson writes, "By school age, the average boy in a classroom is more active than about three-fourths of the girls."[72] These behavioral differences create reading-level differences, argues Thompson, which favor girls.[73] From early education, reading is prized as an assessment tool for judging learning abilities and learning disorders. Yet, success in reading usually takes calm, focused attention, a trait, claims Thompson, that boys do not possess at early ages. The predictable result is that girls achieve at higher rates, while boys struggle. In the end, Thompson argues that boys begin to see themselves as "losers or failures" at educational endeavors, which becomes a self-fulfilling prophecy for boys who cease putting forth an effort.[74]

FIGURE 4.4: Michael Thompson, author, *Raising Cain*

Thompson views the present educational system as unfairly favoring girls over boys by devaluing the natural, energetic traits boys possess and what he views as teachers mismanaging the classroom environment by attempting to retain a controlled setting designed to keep order. Teachers, according to Thompson, view boys' behaviors as unruly, disruptive, and basically negative, as behaviors that should be controlled or punished to conform to the 'girl-standards' of calm, scholarly repose. Thompson's solution is to rethink the way boys are educated by creating a learning environment that encourages verbalization and emotional energy, with an emphasis on praise and understanding rather than a steady stream of punitive measures designed to alter boys' natural, spirited propensities.[75] In general, Thompson asserts that boys need to feel cared-for and liked for who they are, rather than criticized and punished for not being who a teacher believes they should be.[76] Thompson also calls for more male teachers, arguing that boys need strong male role models in their lives and that men have a "calming effect" on boys.[77]

Sociologist Michael Kimmel agrees to an extent with Thompson that boys are subjected to a cultural account of masculinity that is toxic to their well-being, but he believes that the *Raising Cain* authors are continuing a "boys are radically different than girls" narrative that instead should be about inclusively building up children.[78] When informing educators and parents that boys want to be loved and given permission to indulge their emotions and high levels of physical activity, while being shown that empathy is a virtue, Thompson is calling for the very things feminists have been advocating for girls for decades.[79] However, the boisterousness that is often equated with boys' style of play Kimmel sees as privilege.[80] Once adolescence kicks in, Kimmel asserts, girls suppress ambition while boys inflate it.[81] It is not discrimination against boys that is causing problems, according to Kimmel, but an inflated sense of ability that keeps them in math and science courses they may be ill-equipped to handle. Boys are taught by a host of influential people in their lives that they are 'naturally' better at math and science than girls, and they begin to internalize those directives by pursuing STEM courses. Conversely, boys are told that girls are better at humanities and social sciences, such that courses in sociology, education, psychology, and literature are feminized in the minds of many boys, and then devalued for the same reasons boys are taught to devalue all that is feminine in nature, with the logical result of humanities and liberal arts courses populated in the majority by girls.

Kimmel notes that the "culture of cruelty" Kindlon and Thompson worry about in *Raising Cain* is the same culture that male pro-feminist writers have been concerned about for years, which is the concern that boys are instructed by peers and broader society to deny their feelings of empathy and compassion in the interest of being 'men' and that this denial does great harm throughout their lives. Kindlon and Thompson would like to see boys become more emotionally invested, to accept themselves as vulnerable without shame, to know that they are loved and accepted without having to perform the hypermasculine scripts that are issued to them by the surrounding culture, while also developing pride, confidence, and assertiveness without arrogance. As Kimmel notes, these are the very same goals feminists have had for girls for years so that the key today is to instill these character traits into both girls and boys without devaluing either of them.

Another resounding theme in the *Raising Cain* model is the "boys will be boys" determinism that draws from the idea that we must accept the aggressive, competitive, risk-taking behavior that is hard-wired into boys. Kimmel balks at this sort of reductionist determinism by asking of males, "We are also, after all, hard-wired toward compassion, nurturing, and love, aren't we?"[82] Kimmel's point is that some are choosing which "hard-wired traits" to accept and honor in boys and which to reject or downplay. Kindlon and Thompson might respond that they are not calling for downplaying the nurturing side that is a natural part of boys just as it is of girls, but that educators should be aware and encouraging of boys' more exuberant ways of expressing themselves. Kimmel worries that louder, raucous voices and behaviors can convert easily into arrogant, bullying voices and behaviors. If boys are validated in acting out in more dynamic and spirited ways, it is not unreasonable to expect some of this behavior to come in the form of talking over girls, interrupting girls and other boys, and indulging in behaviors that express entitlement over respect.

But beyond these apparent problems that make up the 'boy crisis,' Kimmel also asserts that 'the crisis' as taken up by most authors is one that ignores the complexities that exist for boys who are gay or transgender, or who come from backgrounds of poverty, or struggle with the effects of racism and other forms of discrimination. As stated earlier, the concerns about boys and education are different for boys of privileged backgrounds as compared to boys who come from low-income backgrounds. If there is a boy crisis, it cannot be seen as a crisis that affects all boys equally.

ADHD, ADD, and Single-Sex Education?

ADHD is a neurobehavioral disorder that involves the common symptomology of inattention, distractibility, impulsivity, and hyperactivity.[83] We have already seen that many researchers worry about neurological factors in boys that may inhibit or challenge their ability to compete on the academic playing field as it presently exists, and in study after study, rates of attention deficit disorder and hyperactivity that are commonly found to be behavioral culprits in academic underachievement are also found in rates that are higher in boys than in girls.[84] In fact, according to University of Miami professor of special education, Marjorie Montague, boys are diagnosed with ADHD (attention deficit hyperactivity disorder) three times more often than girls, although the research is unclear whether this disorder is inherent in boys at higher rates or whether teachers refer boys for examination more than they do girls.[85] What seems to be clear is that boys and girls who have been diagnosed with ADHD exhibit different symptoms from one another. In a study termed the Australian Twin ADHD Project, over 4,300 children diagnosed with ADHD were studied through questionnaires sent to parents and caregivers.[86] Researchers concluded that girls with ADHD exhibited higher rates of "separation anxiety disorder," while boys with ADHD exhibited higher rates of "oppositional defiant disorder" and "conduct disorder."[87]

When turning to how these higher rates of ADHD in boys affect educational outcomes, the research is complicated. Before a connection between ADHD and educational outcomes can be properly weighed, controls need to be in place to factor out other influences that may be coming into play. One study that attempted to do this by factoring in family income and level of parents' education found that children who exhibited symptoms of impulsiveness and restlessness scored significantly lower on math and reading tests, and had an increased probability of grade repetition, enrollment in special education, and delinquency, which included stealing, hitting people, and drug use.[88] These negative behaviors were not nearly as pronounced in boys that came from middle to high-income families or in families with well-educated parents.[89] When examining the results by sex, researchers were able to establish that boys and girls with moderate symptoms of ADHD were both similarly affected, but that when symptoms of ADHD are severe, the negative educational outcome for boys is much higher than for girls.[90]

A common way of dealing with symptoms of ADHD and ADD (attention deficit disorder) has been through the use of stimulant drugs. Advocates claim that the drugs work well in 70% to 80% of patients, are not habit-forming, and according to the National Institute of Health, have the mild side-effects of decreasing appetite and difficulties falling asleep, which, they claim, can be handled through lowered dosages.[91] Critics argue that stimulant drugs are over-prescribed, particularly for boys, and that the side-effects are more severe and potentially long-lasting. According to Duke University Professor Emeritus of medical psychology, Carmen Keith Conners, ADHD is over-diagnosed and stimulant drugs are being prescribed at unheard of, and dangerous levels.[92] Conners blames a two-decade campaign by pharmaceutical companies to publicize ADHD, followed by a promotional campaign to doctors to implement the drugs.[93] Estimates from IMS Health claim that profits from stimulant drugs in America hover at around $9 billion per year as of 2012 and that today, one in ten high school boys has a prescription for at least one of the stimulant drugs used to treat ADHD.[94]

Others view the rise in ADHD diagnoses and the increased prescription of stimulant drugs as part of a pattern that undermines boys. In the book *Boys Adrift: The Five Factors Driving the Growing Epidemic of Unmotivated Boys and Underachieving Men*,[95] physician and Ph.D. Leonard Sax spotlights five factors that he believes contribute to the boy crisis:

1. **Changes at School.** Here, Sax highlights three basic problems, as he sees it, with the ways boys are educated starting in kindergarten.
   a. Kindergarten has become about reading and writing before boys are ready for such tasks. Boys' brains, Sax argues, have not developed in key areas that perform these tasks well, whereas girls' brains have. If boys struggle early on in school, the likelihood is greater that boys will begin to hate school. Kindergarten should be about play and activities, not structured academics.
   b. Education has become focused on indoor-centered, reading, writing, computer-based models of learning, but boys need time outdoors to see, touch, smell, hear, and interact with their environments. Girls need this too, but girls are capable of succeeding at the "indoor model" of learning better than boys.
   c. Boys need competition. Under this category, Sax lists "traditional physical education" as important for boys, with an emphasis on activities that produce winners

and losers so that lessons are learned in both directions, along with the fact that competitive sports can instill the value of teamwork over individualism.

d. One suggestion Sax makes is to switch to single-sex classrooms, where boys are taught core values with the goal of creating gentlemen, while nurturing what Sax views as the natural liveliness that boys possess.[96] Like Thompson and Kindlon, Sax does not view current classroom dynamics as conducive to boys' more essential need for boisterous, tactile learning styles. Single-sex classrooms, Sax argues, would allow teachers to create environments more suitable for boys' and girls' different learning needs.

2. **Video Games.** While not applying to all boys, Sax argues that many boys enjoy the feeling of control and power that comes from being a powerful figure in a virtual world. Whatever losses are suffered within the context of the game are softened by the fact that the boy can restart the game and play over and over. Power and control are not traits many boys feel in real life, but in the virtual world, they can become figures of great power, control, respect, and danger.Yet one of the more problematic outcomes of chronic video-game play, as discussed in the chapter on media in this text and reiterated by Sax is that grades in school can suffer. Moreover, chronic video-game play has been shown to lead boys to be much more caring of their video game prowess, while disconnecting to the real world, even though it is the real world where high grades convert into acceptance into coveted spots in graduate school, and where professionals of various types are hired for lucrative careers. A further bit of fallout Sax sees for those boys who invest much of their time in video games is a recession of social interaction with friends, family, and people in general.

3. **Medications for ADHD.** As covered earlier, boys are diagnosed with ADHD at higher rates than girls, but a common concern Sax shares with other researchers is the over-prescription of medications that are given to boys, along with the notorious side-effects, in an attempt to help boys cope with their diagnosed condition. Specifically, stimulant-medications such as Ritalin, Adderall, Concerta, Focalin, Prozac, and Metadate are routinely prescribed by physicians for boys diagnosed with ADHD, ADD, depression, and even weight control at 30 times the prescription rate in 1987.[97]According to Sax, one of the most common reasons why doctors prescribe these drugs to boys involves the logic, "why not give it a try and see if it helps?" The problem is, according to some researchers, once the drugs are discontinued, particularly in adulthood, men become lazy and less motivated to action. It is believed that long-term exposure to some of the stimulant drugs listed above cause damage to the nucleus accumbens area of the brain, which has been linked to motivation and action.

4. **Endocrine Disruptors.** This category examines the view that plastic bottles are to blame for slowing the sexual development of boys, while flattening out gendered traits in boys and girls. According to Sax, the chemical compound *phthalates* that is used in the construction of plastic bottles has an estrogen-like effect on boys, lowering testosterone, and creates less masculine boys and less feminine girls.

5. **"Revenge of the Forsaken Gods"** This cryptic category refers to what Sax views as poor role models for boys today. Quoting author J.R. Moehringer, "to be a man, a boy must see a man," Sax argues that boys need to see and be around men who live with integrity, responsibility, courage, self-discipline, altruism, and empathy in order for boys to learn to integrate these traits into themselves. Manhood, argues Sax, is not something that simply happens to boys as they get older, but rather is an accomplishment that can easily go awry if older, male mentors are absent from their lives.[98] Instead, Sax argues, pop-culture offers the slacker, mid-twenties archetype found in

FIGURE 4.5: Psychologist Leonard Sax, author, *Boys Adrift*

the film *Failure to Launch* or the self-centered, materialistic, criminal mentalities found in many rap artists as cool characters that boys should emulate.[99]

Sax has his critics, many of them vocal critics of his notion that boys and girls require different styles of parenting and education. Perhaps the most barbed criticisms of Sax's views are that they promote sex stereotypes and are empirically ineffective. Diane F. Halpern, professor of psychology at Claremont McKenna College, states,

> A loud, cold classroom where you toss balls around, like Dr. Sax thinks boys should have, might be great for some boys, and for some girls, but for some boys, it would be living hell. It's simply not true that boys and girls learn differently. Advocates for single-sex education don't like the parallel with racial segregation, but the parallels are there. We used to believe that the races learned differently, too.[100]

Sax bristles at the comparison of same-sex classes with racially segregated schools, but Halpern adds that like past notions that white and black children learn differently as a justification for racially segregated schools, the same learning-differentiated justification is being used to promote single-sex schools, when there is no good science to back it up. For instance, a claim made by Sax is that girls "hear better than boys" so that quieter classrooms are appropriate for girls, while rowdier classrooms are appropriate for boys.[101] But University of Pennsylvania linguistics professor Mark Liberman refutes this notion, stating that there is no science to support the view that girls hear better than boys, and that, furthermore, Sax bases his view about sex-based hearing levels on a report that measured hearing differences in infants that instead of confirming the view that boys respond better to louder sounds, found that infant boys respond better than infant girls to softer sounds, the very opposite finding that Sax reports.[102] [103]

Hearing levels aside, the National Education Association published a report that seems to support the value of single-sex education, noting that "Studies suggest that when boys are in single-gender classrooms, they are more successful in school and more likely to pursue a wide range of interests and activities," and that "Girls who learn in all-girl environments are believed to be more comfortable responding to questions and sharing their opinions in class and more likely to explore more 'nontraditional' subjects such as math, science, and technology."[104] Ultimately, however, the NEA stops short of calling for single-sex classrooms advocating instead for additional research into the value and efficacy of single-sex education.[105]

On the concern that single-sex education promotes sex-stereotyping, essayist Margaret Talbot writing for *The New Yorker*, states,

> The presumptions behind [single-sex education] are fusty and often plain silly—girls thrive on team projects and collaboration; boys on bright lights, loud voices, and competition. Girls like reading; boys don't. Girls do calming exercises; boys run. I'll state the obvious: some boys do; some don't. The same goes for girls.[106]

Talbots's view is echoed by University of Texas psychologist Rebecca Bigler who argues,

> Schools play a larger role in children's lives beyond academic training—they prepare children for mixed-sex workplaces, families and citizenry. Institutionalizing gender-segregated classrooms limits children's opportunities to interact with members of the opposite sex and to develop the skills necessary for positive and cooperative interaction.[107]

Researchers from Arizona State University's School of Social and Family Dynamics agree, stating, "Positive and cooperative interaction with members of other groups is an effective method for improving intergroup relationships. Separating boys and girls in public school classrooms makes gender very salient, and this salience reinforces stereotypes and sexism."[108] [109]

Gender-integrated classrooms coincide with what is termed **intergroup contact theory**, which was developed by Gordon W. Allport, who hypothesized that interpersonal contact is the best way to reduce prejudice, stereotyping, and discrimination.[110] According to Allport, when people communicate and interact with others, they have the best chance of understanding and appreciating different points of view. Conversely, segregation hinders one's ability to understand the opinions, perspectives, and feelings of others. Applied to classroom environments, intergroup contact theory would support the idea of gender-integrated classes, with the inclusion of transgender and queer individuals, to promote understanding and acceptance. The idea is a simple one. It is difficult to understand and appreciate others if you have little contact with them and instead hear about others from those in your select group. Critics of single-sex education agree that boys talking about girls and girls talking about boys, but having little daily interaction with one another, is a breeding ground for stereotypical thinking where an "us versus them" mentality can begin to take place.

THOUGHT BOX

After reading the material on single-sex education, what do you believe is the best alternative? Are there advantages to single-sex education that make it a preferable model or does the lack of contact between boys and girls create more problems than solutions?

The Boy Code

In William Pollack's influential book *Real Boys: Rescuing Our Sons from the Myths of Boyhood*, Pollack introduces his reader to what he terms "the world of boys," where most boys live behind a ***mask of masculinity*** and adhere to the maxim that "everything's just fine" even if it is not.[111] In this world, boys learn to adopt a feigned sense of self-confidence and bravado to hide the shame of feeling powerless, vulnerable, and lonely. This mask is a performance that boys learn from men around them who in boyhood were also taught by men to solve their problems alone, rather than reaching out to others for help. This performance is part of what Pollack terms ***the boy code***.[112] When boys are unsure of themselves, they are taught to suck it up, keep up an appearance of resolute toughness, and remain silent in the face of pain. It is thought to be unacceptable and impermissible for boys who adhere to the boy code to show outward signs of fear or any other emotion that is viewed as a form of weakness. The boy code will not allow a boy to admit that he feels anything other than confident bravado and occasional anger, and infractions of this rule can yield castigation from peers in the form of name-calling, bullying, and social isolation.

By investing so much of their emotional energy in trying to show others that they are tough, autonomous, and resilient in the face of adversity, Pollack argues that boys begin to fall behind academically, since excelling in academics is yet another sign of male weakness as measured by the boy code. When coupled with the rule of remaining silent in the face of uncertainty, a classroom environment where raising one's hand when unsure is an important component to success poses a threat to the boy code's insistence that boys remain self-reliant. An obvious result is that boys fall behind academically by not seeking help when needed and that since much of education is accumulative, this

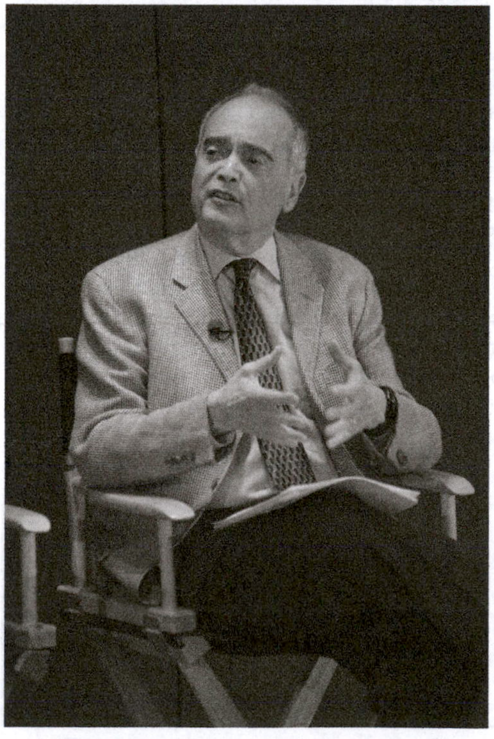

FIGURE 4.6: William S. Pollack, author *Real Boys*

falling behind takes on a snowball effect where minor unresolved ignorance in earlier lessons or in courses taken in the past convert into a major lack of understanding when confronting new concepts that rely on precedent knowledge.

Beyond these concerns about education, one of Pollack's more notable contributions to understanding boys is what he takes to be myths about boys and the truths behind these myths:[113]

Myth 1: Nature and testosterone win out over nurture.

Truth: A boy's behavior is shaped more by loved ones than by nature.

Myth 2: "Boys should be Boys," meaning that boys must be dominant and macho.

Truth: There are many successful ways to be a boy.

Myth 3: "Boys are toxic," meaning that boys are emotionally stoic and socially distant.

Truth: Boys are empathic, caring, and loving.

Pollack argues that because boys sometimes exhibit love differently than do girls, there is often a misdiagnosis of boys as being unloving. The main difference, as Pollack views it, is that boys will often show love through action rather than words. Boys will participate in play as a form of intimacy or by engaging in a helpful task for their parents or teacher. Boys also engage in action with friends as a form of bonding instead of verbal communication. Through the anecdotal stories from a variety of boys of different ages, Pollack discerns patterns of behavior that suggest boys yearn for closeness as much as do girls, but demonstrate this longing through a variety of actions, particularly when they do not feel judged by others or pressured to conform to the boy code.

For many boys, adolescence is a time of great change with associated feelings of confusion and anxiety.[114] According to Pollack, the source of this confusion and anxiety comes from two underlying psychological factors: society giving boys the mixed message that they need to be tough, manly, cool, confident, and strong, while also telling them to be sensitive, egalitarian, and open with their feelings.[115] Yet, it is challenging for boys to be both manly and empathic, cool and emotionally open, strong and vulnerable. Second, adolescent boys may not view manhood as being that attractive if they see it as being chained to a job they don't enjoy in order to support a family, or if they view manhood as the end of having fun in the name of being responsible. The result is that adolescent boys can feel ambivalence about becoming a man. On one side, manhood represents independence from mom and dad, which can be seen as excitingly liberating or numbingly frightening. But adulthood also represents for many boys a time when carefree amusements come to an end, especially if they see their father waking up at dawn and coming home in the evening exhausted and downtrodden.

Pollack also argues that the sexual bravado found among many adolescent boys is the result, in part, of anxiety boys feel about girls and the fact that girls mature physically, on average, earlier than boys. Pollack writes:

> Put a boy with a girl who physically matured several years earlier and you can only imagine how intimidated he will feel. Unfortunately, as we know, the more insecurity boys feel, the more compensatory bravado they'll exhibit. Hence, there is locker-room talk, reducing girls to objects, and bragging about conquests.[116]

Yet, Pollack continues, if girls want boys to be emotionally open and loving *before sex*, they will often be disappointed to discover that boys, who have been socialized around conflicting notions of emotional openness, cannot open up emotionally until *after sex*, which can lead girls to assume that boys don't care about them as persons. In reality, Pollack insists, boys are navigating the difficult waters of wanting connection while fearing rejection.[117] The desire to connect is real and even passionate in boys, but is tempered by a fear of repudiation, coupled with the socialized missive taught to boys that they should strive for emotional stoicism, which is a game of keeping feelings of love and tenderness out of public view. The result is that boys boast about sexual conquest to validate their masculine bona fides with peers, while insisting that love is a feminine emotion that should be shunned.

One of the more interesting findings of Pollack's research is the insight that boys today are both egalitarian and traditional.[118] What seems to be a prima facie contradiction is understood once we are able to see how society instructs boys to adopt both of these models instead of one over the other. To first document that boys are indeed adopting what appear to be contrasting approaches to being a man, Pollack administered the ***Sex Role Egalitarianism Scale*** test to 150 boys ages 12 to 18, drawing from boys living in urban locales. As Pollack predicted, the results of this test showed that the boys scored well within the range of scores that purport to show that the boys embrace an egalitarian ideal of gender roles. So, for instance, boys would agree with statements such as "Men and women should be given an equal chance for professional training" and "Courses in home management should be as acceptable for male students and for female students." Developed by Lynda and Daniel King, the test was designed to "measure attitudes toward the equality of men and women."[119] These same boys rejected statements like "The husband should be the head of the family" or "It is more appropriate for a mother rather than a father to change a baby's diapers."[120]

The results of this test might make it appear that attitudes in boys have shifted greatly from the patriarchal attitudes of the past, but Pollack was skeptical. So, he administered a second test developed by psychologist Joseph Pleck known as the ***Traditional Male Role Model Attitude Scale***. The statements in this test read, "I admire a guy who is totally sure of himself" and "It is essential for a guy to get respect from others" as well as "A man always deserves the respect of his wife and children," "It bothers me when a guy acts like a girl," and "Men are always ready for sex." As Pollack expected, the boys who scored well on the Egalitarian test also scored well on the Traditional test. This means, according to Pollack, that boys are conflicted about what it means to be a man. As society instructs boys to be caring and sensitive to the desires and needs of women, when questioned, they respond accordingly. But as society also instructs boys to be tough, autonomous, and in control, when questioned, they respond accordingly, perhaps without recognizing the apparent inconsistencies in their views.

Experiencing the boy code can be more challenging for boys who are gay or queer, or who sense that they might be gay.[121] While being socialized by the same paralyzing rules of the boy code, boys who discover they are gay can experience "profound feelings of isolation, fear, shame, and self-hatred."[122] Pollack also points out that boys can be confused about their sexual orientation, as attractions and feelings can wane or may not conform to peer expectations. The issue is compounded when a boy acts one way, but feels differently, as in the case where a boy is in a romantic relationship with a girl, but feels attraction to boys as well. Pollack argues that since our culture reinforces the traditional notion that one is either heterosexual or gay, as though sexuality is inescapably binary, boys can be confused about their sexual orientation when conflicting sexual feelings arise. Compounding this concern is the fear a boy may have about coming out to his family and friends, particularly if he has reason to believe that his family and friends will not receive the news favorably.

C.J. Pascoe on High-School Boyhood and the 'fag' Epithet

Anyone who has spent time around adolescent boys has been exposed to a prolific usage of homophobic slurs aimed at other boys and even objects. In her book, *Dude, You're a Fag: Masculinity and Sexuality in High School*, sociologist C.J. Pascoe investigates the use of homophobic slurs among high-school-aged boys to understand why so many boys of this age engage in this homophobic terminological display, a phenomenon not exhibited nearly as much in girls.[123] Examining the intersection between gender, sex, class, and ethnicity, Pascoe was able to discern identifiable patterns of homophobic slur usage by boys. According to the boys and girls interviewed, 'gay' was used as a synonym for 'stupid,' while 'fag' was reserved for unmasculine males. This meant that inanimate objects like shirts or backpacks could be viewed as 'gay,' but 'fag' was used only in connection to a person, in this case, certain males. What was surprising in the interview process was that many boys were emphatic that the use of the term 'fag' did not imply sexuality. Instead, they insisted, the term's use was designed to call someone an idiot. In fact, boys who used the term insisted that they would never aim the word 'fag' at an actual homosexual male.

The sort of things that received the 'fag' epithet, it turned out, was a host of different behaviors considered to be unmasculine, such as the way you cross your legs, caring too much about your clothes, dancing, or expressing interest, including platonic interest, in other boys. Interestingly, Pascoe learned that African-American boys were immune to the concerns about clothing and dancing, because, she was told, those items had to do with hip-hop culture, a culture that belonged to and was defined by African-American boys and men who in some respects stood as masculine icons to white, suburban-raised boys who could only approximate, but never fully embody, the cool style that African-American boys and men possessed.

Ultimately, the 'fag' epithet, like other homophobic slurs and slurs against women, is used by high school boys to reinforce heteronormativity. In general, Pascoe reports, high schools are "complex cultural arenas" that provide a context "in which boys and girls forge gendered and sexual identities."[124] Pascoe reports, "In time-honored high school rituals, masculinity and femininity were produced as opposites and unequal identities primarily through heterosexual practices, metaphors, and jokes."[125] By setting masculinity and femininity up as opposites and then devaluing feminine traits, heterosexual

FIGURE 4.7: C.J. Pascoe, author, *Dude, You're a Fag: Masculinity and Sexuality in High School*

masculinity becomes the default for normal and the preferable identity boys should adopt. Through the 'fag' designation, boys practice heteronormativity, while insisting they are not homophobic.

Psychologist Neill Korobov documents some of the same observations made by Pascoe, and argues that adolescent boys attempt to position themselves as being both normatively heterosexual and unprejudiced at the same time.[126] As American culture has gradually opened to accepting homosexuals and homosexual relationships, and this is true particularly among young people, adolescent boys find themselves in the double-bind of attempting to appear properly heteronormative to their peers, while not seeming to be homophobic, while ironically using homophobic slurs on occasion to validate the heteronormative aspect of their performance. This is why it is not unusual to hear adolescent boys and young men use homophobic slurs and then insist that they did not intend to, nor would they ever, aim those slurs at actual gay people. It is a high-wire, balancing act that attempts to please everyone.

THOUGHT BOX

Hazing rituals, as part of initiation into a college fraternity, appear to be disgusting, homophobic, yet ironically homoerotic. Discuss what you think might be some of the reasons for this.

An obvious problem, among many obvious problems with using homophobic slurs, is that name-calling is often used to bully others. Far from being an innocuous appellation, the 'fag' epithet has the dual effect of wounding boys who are at an age when their masculine identity is most fragile and vulnerable, creating hierarchies that privilege some boys over others, and maintaining a homophobic environment that keeps boys who are gay in the closet for fear of reprisal, while contributing to the high rates of suicide and suicide attempts by boys who identify as gay, queer, or transgender.

Cyber-bullying has been a particularly problematic area of adolescent bullying practices where homophobic, transphobic, and gendered slurs are commonly used as weapons. Studies have found that the combination of wider social acceptance of homophobia and transphobia along with the anonymity and detachment of an online setting create an ideal environment for bullying, unlike the face-to-face environment of classrooms and school hallways where homophobia has a better chance of being publicly shamed.[127] These same virtual environments invite bullying toward boys and girls who are disabled, immigrants, or those belonging to any marginalized group.[128] In one study that specifically examined the gender dynamics of cyber-bullies and cyber-bully victims, it was found that boys were more likely to cyber-bully others, but that girls were more likely to report the cyber-bullying to adults.[129] Another study that attempted to understand why boys and girls cyber-bully reported, through surveys, that many cyber-bullies claim to feel regret afterward, but also affirmed that cyber-bullying made them feel as though they were funny, popular, and powerful.[130]

Guyland and The Bro Code

In 2008, sociologist Michael Kimmel released the book *Guyland: The Perilous World Where Boys Become Men (Understanding the Critical Years between 16 and 26)*.[131] Kimmel describes Guyland as a heteronormative netherworld between childhood and adulthood that captures many young men with the promise of independence with few

FIGURE 4.8: Michael Kimmel, author *Guyland: The Perilous World Where Boys Become Men*

responsibilities. It places young men in arrested state of development where "almost men," to use Kimmel's expression, "have all the entitlement and none of the power."[132] It begins at the precipice of legal adulthood for many late-adolescent boys who, as Pollack noted, are concerned about what manhood is going to entail for them. Collectively, they are 'guys,' no longer 'kids' but not yet 'grown-ups' and according to the interviews conducted by Kimmel with hundreds of these 'guys,' they have a code, the guy-code, that emphasizes never showing emotion or admitting to weakness.[133]

Kimmel notes that the guy code is not the same everywhere and that differences can be found by class, race, age, and sexuality. But tying them together is the knowledge that they can be men when the circumstances call for behaving like men, as well as the security of also knowing that they can slip back into boyhood at a moment's notice. Kimmel parses guyland into three distinct but interacting cultures that drive the guy code, while insulating it from harm:[134]

> **A culture of entitlement:** even though 'guys' may not possess power in terms of wealth or other forms of abstract power, they feel that they have the power to do what they want, that the orthodox rules that apply to women do not apply to them. So, they *can if they so choose* curse loudly, revel in jokes about sex and rape, lash out in anger and violence if they feel wronged or disrespected, publicly make a spectacle of themselves, and when the time comes, nail down a good paying job with a secure future.
>
> **A culture of silence:** the guy code insists that 'guys' never rat out other 'guys,' so that the statute, "never speak in the face of other guys acting out in sexist, homophobic, bullying, or violent ways," is implicitly but forcefully maintained. If they witness bullying or harassment, the code entails that you remain a silent bystander.
>
> **A culture of protection:** 'guys' know that the community will protect them if they do wrong. From excusing men's violence as 'boys will be boys' or 'he's a fierce competitor' in the case of athletes who act out violently and shielding guys from responsibility by assuring that whistle-blowers are made aware of the consequences of tattling.

These "cultures" are at work when a news item breaks about a group of young men caught in an egregious case of hazing or when a group of young men are discovered to have gang-raped a girl or young woman. The sense of entitlement some men believe they have over women's bodies coupled with the belief that a network is in place to safeguard perpetrators from culpability provide conditions where sexual assault and rape are commonplace enough to cause President Obama to create a task force to understand how to successfully battle sexual assault and rape on college and university campuses.[135]

As Kimmel notes, much of 'guyland' is about validation. But the validation does not come from older men; it is a case of peers validating peers, as a sort of reality version of

Lord of the Flies.[136] The validation is clearly not based on integrity or moral responsibility, but the ability and willingness to view as positive, "drifting with the tide, going along with peer pressure even though you know it's both stupid and cruel, enabling or performing sometimes sadistic assaults against those who have entrusted their novice/initiative status into your hands."[137]

The humiliation, pain, and on occasion death that go hand-in-hand with hazing, which is considered to be a natural part of pledging a fraternity, is one of the more visible signs of young men going along to get along. As part of these rituals, a young woman or man may be subjected to sexual assault or rape, forced to binge drink or required to accept physical punishments of one kind or another. These are only some of the tools that codify the silence and loyalty that is at the heart of fraternal, guyland-bonding.

The obvious question is, if Kimmel is correct about the repugnant conditions of being an initiate into guyland, why do guys go along with it? The answers may be just as obvious: to fit in, to have friends, to be accepted, to be cool, to be aligned with alpha males who are popular, to have a shot at having sex with "hot girls," to have power without being responsible for your choices.[138] Guyland is the *Peter Pan syndrome* applied to adolescent boys and young men who would like to live in an environment of irresponsibility, while retaining the option of temporarily leaving their pornified, booze-driven *Neverland* to perform as adults when necessary.

In 2011, Media Education Foundation released educator Thomas Keith's film, *The Bro Code: How Contemporary Culture Creates Sexist Men*.[139] The Bro Code, one could argue, is the logical consequence of Pollack's boy code. Like Kimmel's *guyland*, the Bro Code is comprised of implicit and explicit rules for high school boys and college-aged men who wish to be accepted into bro-culture, which is a heteronormative, often vulgar, hypermasculine environment where boys and young men revel in politically incorrect words and actions, sexually objectify women, celebrate porn usage, find humor in rape, revile men who express traits they view as being feminine, repress emotional expression other than anger, use homophobic slurs, often drink alcohol in excess, and bond around sports, beer, cars, big trucks, womanizing, and sexist lifestyles. It is a place where boys who do not conform to bro-culture are in danger of being subjected to ridicule and bullying behaviors, and where women are in danger of verbal, physical, and sexual assault.

Bro-culture is the realm of "bros before ho's" such that boys and men elevate themselves in value over girls and women. It is a place where there is a war between the sexes and your value as a man is measured by "sexual conquest," as though sex for heterosexual men is a victory over women. For bros, the personhood and agency of girls and women is irrelevant if not an obstacle to overcome in the pursuit of "getting laid." Lying just beneath the surface of this sexual pursuit is often a feeling that women possess sexual power over men and that by receiving sex, or "tapping that ass" in bro-vernacular, men regain control and power over women, a power many bros believe is their birthright as men. Bros view women as "sexual teases" who dress provocatively and wear heavy makeup to tantalize them only to then instruct men not to stare, comment, or touch. Rape jokes are then used by bros to put women in their place, while also placing women on notice that their sexual teasing has limits that will be dealt with forcefully if necessary. When challenged, bros turn the tables by sarcastically insisting that "it was just a joke," as though anyone who challenges their sexism is a person lacking a sense of humor. These same men are quick to accept rape-myth narratives that rape allegations are mainly the result of women who were not raped, but used the allegation to retaliate against men they feel wronged them in some way. Like men's rights activists, bros often blame women when men are guilty of sexual harassment, sexual assault, or rape as a way of shirking responsibility and projecting culpability onto women.

With well-paying jobs in retreat and in the face of a challenging economy, we may wonder what the future of guyland, bro-culture, and the boy crisis will be. If many boys are stretching adolescence into their mid-to-late twenties and beyond, at the same time that women outnumber men in higher education, the future for bros may be bleak. Yet, the strong desire to belong to a group of popular young men will always be enticing to high school boys and young men entering college. Kimmel explains the motivation of boys who wish to take part in the guy code as:

> the desperate desire to feel worth, to feel powerful, to be validated as a man … Somehow, these almost-men seduce themselves into believing that these guys, a year older and so much cooler, hold the magical keys that will open the door to a feeling of confident manhood.[140]

In a desperate attempt to feel validated as alpha males, college-aged men will don diapers, swim through a kiddie-pool full of vomit, urine, and feces, eat omelets made of vomit, drink beer poured down fellow pledges' ass-cracks (these particular hazing rituals were exposed and reported by an actual fraternity member at prestigious Dartmouth University), or subject themselves to any number of disgusting and humiliating hazing rituals to prove to guys a year or two older that they have what it takes to be child-men.[141] The pornified, womanizing, binge-drinking, homophobic lifestyles that seduce many of these boys are sold as rites of passage into authentic bro-hood where the promise of women being sexually available to them at their beck and call, along with the respect of other almost-men, is secure (chapter three examines fraternity culture in more depth and detail).

THOUGHT BOX

What do you make of teen boys who use terms like 'gay' and 'fag' in derogatory ways, but profess not to have any homophobic intension behind their use? Is there a way to make sense of this disconnection or do you believe the boys are not being honest with others or themselves?

Media promote guyland and bro culture through a series of popular films that depict men acting as irresponsible and womanizing almost-men. That these films are comedies does not diminish their impact upon boys and young men who view the characters in these films as funny misfits whose lives are, in a strange way, adventurously attractive. Even though most of the men in these films are well beyond their adolescent years, they still live their lives as precocious, troublemaking teenagers whose booze and pot-filled antics are typically part of a larger strategy of obtaining sex. The boy-men of the film *Superbad* have been anointed in popular culture as the protégés of this guyland archetype where the character "McLovin'" (Christopher Mintz-Plasse) gets a fake ID in order to purchase alcohol with the ultimate goal of getting women drunk at an upcoming party to increase his chances of attaining sex. Along with his cohorts Evan (Michael Cera) and Seth (Jonah Hill), obtaining alcohol becomes a sign of maturity, they believe, since the three main characters are seniors in high school where one's ability to obtain alcohol is a sign of independence and adulthood.[142] But later films like *Hot Tub Time Machine* and *The Hangover* series of films depict much older men who continue living lives like the high school boys of *Superbad*, where partying, heavy drinking, and womanizing are normative patterns of older male behavior.

Of course, not every adolescent boy enters guyland or bro-culture. For many boys who avoid the trap of bro-culture, early fatherhood or other obligations that involve economic pressures may force them into a difficult job market without an education or

FIGURE 4.9: Christopher Mintz-Plasse, Jonah Hill, and Michael Cera in *Superbad*, 2007

FIGURE 4.10: Clark Duke, Rob Corddry, Craig Robinson in *Hot Tub Time Machine*, 2010

marketable job skills. While these men may still adopt sexist, womanizing views and behaviors, the lives of older bros in guyland are mainly reserved for those young men of privilege who have the economic means to survive while indulging their adolescent, womanizing fantasies. What happens as these same boys and young men eventually enter into their respective careers is a subject of speculation, but predictable speculation. Many of them will likely engage in sexually harassing behavior at work, while others may finally grow up and live lives of accountability. Fatherhood, for some, may or may not be a catalyst that creates the moment of clarity some men need to assess their beliefs and behaviors. In the next chapter, we will examine the subject of fatherhood, beginning with an investigation of adolescent boys and young men who become fathers along with the many challenges that face fathers today.

Summary

The boy crisis, as it is presently understood, is being examined and evaluated from many different perspectives. While some do not believe there is a boy crisis, for those who affirm the crisis, conflicting reasons are offered to explain it. In particular, many scholars note that the educational component of the crisis is mainly found in boys of color along with those who live in rural settings. Most scholars who research this crisis view it as highly problematic and as something that needs urgent attention. The problem is that researchers disagree on solutions. While some propose reinventing classroom experiences so that boys experience greater physically expressive play, others worry that treating boys differently than girls reinforces gender bifurcation that supports the false notion that boys are hard-wired for aggression, as well as implicitly granting permission for bullying behaviors. Critics also argue that it is a myth to assume that boys and girls learn differently from one another, noting that many boys respond favorably to quiet environments, while many girls respond favorably to more active and boisterous environments.

In response to what many view as a problem with boys, stimulant drugs have been prescribed to boys in record numbers, leading many experts to argue that these drugs are over-prescribed and often not based on accurate clinical diagnoses. As a result of this criticism, a host of alternatives to drug intervention have been sought to treat symptoms of ADHD and ADD, which are found in a higher number of boys than girls.

As boyhood gives way to adolescence, a number of scholars have found that increases in sexism and homophobia are common. From steady use of the 'fag' epithet to an adoption of sexist and womanizing views and behaviors, some boys enter young manhood in a state of arrested development and cling to a lifestyle of petulant inebriation and chauvinistic conduct as an attempt to avoid the responsibilities that attend adulthood, and to reinforce their desire to maintain an emotional distance from women by resisting commitment and love in favor of "sexual conquest." Many of these same boys simply want to fit in and find acceptance with their peers. For those who are successful at avoiding guyland and bro culture, some scholars contend that a more authentic and enriching life awaits them where emotional connectedness and the responsibilities of adulthood reside.

Notes

1 www.acadcom.com/acanews1/anmviewer.asp?a=53.

2 http://psychology.about.com/od/psychosocialtheories/a/psychosocial.htm.

3 Erikson, Erik, *Youth and Crisis* (W.W. Norton, 1968).

4 www.simplypsychology.org/Erik-Erikson.html.

5 http://nces.ed.gov/fastfacts/display.asp?id=16.
6 Ibid.
7 www.washingtonpost.com/local/education/high-school-graduation-rates-at-historic-high/2014/04/28/84eb0122-cee0-11e3-937f-d3026234b51c_story.html.
8 www.usnews.com/news/blogs/data-mine/2014/10/31/women-more-likely-to-graduate-college-but-still-earn-less-than-men.
9 It should be noted that other countries are experiencing similar gender gaps in education with girls outnumbering boys in college, and in many cases this gendered educational gap is much more pronounced than that found in the U.S.
10 www.nytimes.com/2010/03/28/opinion/28kristof.html?_r=0.
11 www.nationsreportcard.gov/hsts_2009/gender_gpa.aspx.
12 www.forbes.com/sites/ccap/2012/02/16/the-male-female-ratio-in-college/.
13 www.aei.org/publication/stunning-college-degree-gap-women-have-earned-almost-10-million-more-college-degrees-than-men-since-1982/.
14 www.forbes.com/sites/susanadams/2013/04/09/are-women-catching-up-in-pay/.
15 Kimmel, Michael, "A War Against Boys?" in *Men's Lives*, 9th edition (Pearson Education, 2013).
16 Ibid.
17 Whitmire, Richard, *Why Boys Fail: Saving Our Sons from an Educational System that's Leaving Them Behind* (AMACON Books, 2010).
18 Ibid., p. 41.
19 https://en.wikipedia.org/wiki/Whole_language.
20 Whitmire, *Why Boys Fail*, pp. 45–46.
21 Ibid., pp. 49–53.
22 Ibid., p. 50.
23 Ibid.,p. 51.
24 www.npr.org/templates/story/story.php?storyId=14175229.
25 Whitmire, *Why Boys Fail.*
26 www.nytimes.com/2011/08/21/books/review/boys-and-reading-is-there-any-hope.html.
27 Ibid.
28 www.huffingtonpost.com/charles-london/boys-dont-read-except-whe_b_859449.html.
29 www.telegraph.co.uk/education/educationopinion/11948122/Lets-scotch-the-myth-that-boys-dont-read.html.
30 Ibid.
31 Ibid.
32 Chu, Judy Y. and Way, Niobe, eds, *Adolescent boys: Exploring Diverse Cultures of Boyhood* (New York University Press, 2004).
33 www.washingtonpost.com/wp-dyn/content/article/2006/04/07/AR2006040702025.html.
34 Stevenson, Howard, C., "Boys in Men's Clothing: Racial Socialization and Neighborhood Safety as Buffers to Hypervulnerability in African American Adolescent Males," in *Adolescent Boys: Exploring Diverse Cultures of Boyhood*, Chu and Way, Chapter 3.
35 Ibid., p. 63.
36 Ibid., p. 64.
37 Ibid., p. 63.
38 Ibid., Chapter 3.
39 http://webcache.googleusercontent.com/search?q=cache:9_z78idwdtgJ:nces.ed.gov/pubs2014/2014391.pdf+&cd=1&hl=en&ct=clnk&gl=us.
40 www.huffingtonpost.com/2012/11/26/high-school-graduation-ra_n_2194378.html.
41 Ibid.
42 http://magazine.good.is/articles/is-public-education-failing-black-male-students.
43 http://blackboysreport.org/national-summary/black-male-graduation-rates.
44 Ibid.
45 www.huffingtonpost.com/2012/09/19/black-male-hs-graduation-_n_1896490.html.
46 www.manhattan-institute.org/html/cr_48.htm.
47 Ibid.
48 www.nytimes.com/2012/02/10/education/education-gap-grows-between-rich-and-poor-studies-show.html?pagewanted=all.
49 www.nytimes.com/2010/11/09/education/09gap.html.
50 Ibid.
51 Ibid.
52 www.huffingtonpost.com/2013/04/10/black-graduation-rates-grit-grades-study_n_3055051.html.
53 Ibid.
54 Fordham, Signithia and Ogbu, John, "Black students' school success: coping with the burden of 'acting white'," *Urban Review* 18 (1986).
55 Ford, Donna Y., Grantham, Tarek C., and Whiting, Gilman, W., "Another look at the achievement gap: Learning from the experiences of gifted black students," *Urban Education*, March, 2008.

56 Harper, Shaun R., "Peer support for African American male college achievement: Beyond internalized racism and the burden of 'acting white'," *The Journal of Men's Studies*, February, 2007.
57 Ibid.
58 Harper, Shaun R., *Black Male Student Success in Higher Education: A Report from the National Black Male College Achievement Study* (University of Pennsylvania, Center for the Study of Race and Equity in Education, 2012).
59 Stinson, David W., "African American male adolescents, schooling (and mathematics): Deficiency, rejection, and achievement," *Review of Educational Research*, Winter, 2008.
60 Wallace, Dawn., Abel, Ron., and Roper-Huilman, Becky, "Clearing a path for success: Deconstructing borders through undergraduate mentoring," *The Review of Higher Education*, 24, 1 (2000).
61 Strayhorn, Terrell L., "The role of supportive relationships in facilitating African American males' success in college," *NASPA Journal*, 45, 1 (2008).
62 Rosenbloom, Susan R. and Way, Niobe, "Experiences of discrimination among African American, Asian American, and Latino adolescents in an urban high school," *Youth & Society*, June, 2004.
63 Fisher, Celia B., Wallace, Scyatta A., and Fenton, Rose E., "Discrimination distress during adolescence," *Journal of Youth and Adolescence*, December, 2000.
64 Qin, Desiree B., Way, Niobe, and Mukherjee, Preetika, "The other side of the model minority story: The familial and peer challenges faced by Chinese American adolescents," *Youth & Society*, May, 2008.
65 Ibid.
66 http://nces.ed.gov/programs/digest/d13/tables/dt13_326.10.asp.
67 www.washingtonpost.com/news/storyline/wp/2014/10/20/why-poor-kids-dont-stay-in-college/.
68 Ibid.
69 www.aft.org/sites/default/files/periodicals/Wilson.pdf.
70 www.cbsnews.com/news/the-gender-gap-boys-lagging/.
71 Kindlon, Dan and Thompson, Michael, *Raising Cain: Protecting the Emotional Life of Boys* (Ballantine Books, 2000).
72 Ibid., p. 32.
73 Ibid., p. 33.
74 Ibid., p. 33.
75 Ibid., pp. 38–49.
76 Ibid., p. 49.
77 Ibid., p. 48.
78 Kimmel, Michael. "What about the boys?," in *Critical Social Issues in American Education: Democracy and Meaning in a Globalizing World*, ed. H. Vhi Shapiro and David E. Purpel (Routledge, 2004).
79 Ibid., p. 218.
80 Ibid., p. 218.
81 Ibid., p. 218.
82 Ibid., p. 222.
83 www.nytimes.com/health/guides/disease/attention-deficit-hyperactivity-disorder-adhd/print.html.
84 www.cdc.gov/ncbddd/adhd/data.html.
85 www.webmd.com/add-adhd/childhood-adhd/features/adhd-symptoms-in-girls-and-boys.
86 Levy, Florence, Hay, David A., Bennett, Kellie S., and McStephen, Michael, "Gender differences in ADHD subtype comorbidity," *Journal of the American Academy of Child & Adolescent Psychiatry*, April, 2005.
87 Ibid.
88 www.nber.org/bah/summer04/w10435.html.
89 Ibid.
90 Ibid.
91 www.nimh.nih.gov/health/publications/attention-deficit-hyperactivity-disorder/index.shtml.
92 www.nytimes.com/2013/12/15/health/the-selling-of-attention-deficit-disorder.html?pagewanted=all.
93 Ibid.
94 www.advisory.com/daily-briefing/2013/04/01/astronomical-rise-in-adhd-diagnoses-raises-questions.
95 Sax, Leonard, *Boys Adrift: The Five Factors Driving the Growing Epidemic of Unmotivated Boys and Underachieving Young Men* (Basic Books, 2009).
96 Ibid., pp. 163–166.
97 Ibid., p. 85.
98 Ibid., pp. 171–173.
99 Ibid., p. 171.
100 www.nytimes.com/2011/09/23/education/23single.html?_r=0.
101 Sax, Leonard, *Why Gender Matters: What Parents and Teachers Need to Know about the Emerging Science of Sex Differences* (Harmony Books, 2006).
102 http://languagelog.ldc.upenn.edu/nll/?p=171.

103 Sininger, Yvonne, Cone-Wessen, Barbara, and Abdala, Carolina. "Gender distinctions and lateral asymmetry in the low-level auditory brainstem response of the human neonate," *Hearing Research* 126 (1998), p. 58–66.
104 www.nea.org/tools/17061.htm.
105 Ibid.
106 www.newyorker.com/news/daily-comment/the-case-against-single-sex-classrooms.
107 www.utexas.edu/news/2011/10/03/bigler_coeducational_schooling/.
108 www.sciencedaily.com/releases/2011/09/110922141902.htm.
109 https://thesanfordschool.asu.edu/acces/evidence-based-answers-0.
110 http://en.wikipedia.org/wiki/Contact_hypothesis.
111 Pollack, William, *Real Boys: Rescuing Our Boys from the Myths of Boyhood* (Owl Books, 1999).
112 Ibid., p. 4–15.
113 Ibid., Chapter 3.
114 Ibid., Chapter 7.
115 Ibid., p. 146.
116 Ibid., p. 150.
117 Ibid., p. 151.
118 Ibid., pp. 165–167
119 www.sigmaassessmentsystems.com/assessments/sres.asp.
120 Pollack, *Real Boys*, p. 167.
121 Ibid., Chapter 9.
122 Ibid., p. 209.
123 Pascoe, C.J., *Dude, You're a Fag: Masculinity and Sexuality in High School* (University of California Press, 2011).
124 Ibid., p. 50.
125 Ibid., p. 50.
126 Korobov, Neill, "Inoculating against prejudice: A discursive approach to homophobia and sexism in adolescent male talk," *Psychology of Men & Masculinity*, July, 2004.
127 Pescitelli, Aynsley A., "MySpace or Yours?: Homophobic and transphobic bullying in cyberspace," Simon Frazer University Repository, August, 2013. http://summit.sfu.ca/item/13577.
128 Shariff, Shaheen, *Cyber-Bullying: Issues and Solutions for the School, the Classroom and the Home* (Routledge, 2008).
129 Li, Qing, "Cyberbullying in schools: A research of gender differences," *School Psychology International*, May, 2008.
130 Mishna, Fay, Cook, Charlene, Gadalla, Tahany, Daciuk, Joanne, and Soloman, Steven, "Cyber bullying behaviors among middle and high school students," *American Journal of Orthopsychiatry*, July, 2010.
131 Kimmel, Michael. *Guyland: The Perilous World Where Boys Become Men (Understanding the Critical Years Between 16 and 26)* (Harper-Collins, 2008).
132 Ibid., p. 43.
133 Ibid., p. 45.
134 Ibid., pp. 59–64.
135 www.notalone.gov/.
136 Kimmel, *Guyland*, p. 101.
137 Ibid., p. 102.
138 Ibid., pp. 115–116.
139 Keith, Thomas. *The Bro Code: How Contemporary Culture Creates Sexist Men* (Media Education Foundation, 2012).
140 Kimmel. *Guyland*, p. 116.
141 www.businessinsider.com/here-are-the-most-digusting-disturbing-things-we-read-in-rolling-stones-deep-dive-into-dartmouth-hazing-2012-3.
142 www.imdb.com/title/tt0829482/.

Fatherhood

I love being a father. I worry about [my family] all the time. That's the emotional bond and responsibility that sweeps over you when you have a family to look after. I care about them more than I care about myself, which I think is the real definition of love.

~Actor Brad Pitt[1]

LEARNING OBJECTIVES

After reading this chapter, students should be able to respond to the following questions with an understanding of the terms and expressions employed:

- *What is identity theory as it applies to fatherhood? What is "conscious fathering"? What is parental investment theory as it applies to fatherhood? What is the difference between* paternal investment *and* paternal involvement*? What does psychologist Louis Cozolino mean by the expression "social synapse"?*
- *What are some of the risk factors for adolescent boys who become fathers? What is "The Centerfold Syndrome" and what has it to do with adolescent fatherhood? What sorts of programs have been most effective in helping young fathers deal with the challenges they face?*
- *What are some of the challenges faced by single fathers? What are some of the common complaints made by single fathers?*
- *What are some of the unique challenges that face black fathers in America? How do scholars contend with the stereotype that black fathers tend to be absentee, dead-beat fathers? What challenges face Latino fathers? What are the differences between* machismo *and* caballerismo *with respect to Latino men and Latino culture? What are the stereotypes and realities of Asian-American fathers? What are some of the goals for Native American advocacy groups with respect to fathers?*
- *What have scholars learned about the father–daughter relationship? What are "purity balls" and what are the criticisms of these events?*

- *What have scholars learned about the father–son relationship? How important are fathers as role models to their sons? Are there differences between this relationship and the relationships between fathers and daughters?*
- *What is "the princess syndrome" and how can sons adopt problematic views about girls and women from parents, and particularly fathers, who reinforce this syndrome?*
- *What are the special challenges for gay fathers? What are the fears faced by gay and transgender sons and daughters who come out to their families? How do heterosexual fathers react upon learning that their son or daughter is gay or transgender?*
- *What are the central concerns of "Fathers' Rights Groups" and what are the critical responses to these groups? What is The National Fatherhood Initiative and what are their stated goals?*

One of the more common questions that arise about fatherhood is, "Is fathering fundamentally different from mothering?" It is almost impossible to respond to this question without also examining ideas about masculinity, femininity, and the cultural norms and expectations associated with being a father or mother. A longstanding, traditional view is that mothers are best in nurturing roles, while fathers are best in disciplinarian roles, along with being providers and protectors of the family. Neoconservative views of parenting continue to defend this traditional view of mothering and fathering. They argue that there are proper gender roles for mothers and fathers that create balance in a family and that help children define their own roles as boys and girls. Without these traditional structures in place, they argue, children can be confused in coming to their own gender identities and struggle to find their place in the world. Typically, these traditional views of parenting are attended by the belief that women and men are fundamentally different and that these differences need to be preserved and promoted in the raising of children. To this conservative stance, critics argue that traditional parenting models promote patriarchy, discourage girls from seeking leadership roles, lock boys and girls into rigidly assigned gender roles that often conflict with the child's unique gender identification, limit both women and men in their ability to access basic human traits that all people possess, deny fathers, in particular, the joy of nurturing their children in loving, tender ways, and is grounded in an untenable form of biological determinism that has long since been debunked. Against the background of this debate, two prominent theories of fatherhood have emerged: *Identity theory* and *parental investment theory*.

Theories of Fatherhood

Identity Theory

Identity theory is the view that a person's behavior is a function of his conception of identity, which derives from the positions he occupies in society and has been a leading theory in attempts to understand fatherhood. Like social and gender identity theories, approaches to parenting are thought by some to be a reflection of the ways people view the essence or normative role of parenting. Some view parenting as essentially authoritative, while others view parenting as being essentially about providing nurture and support.[2] One of the more noted theorists who developed identity theory as it applies to parenting is James Marcia, who argued that two factors inform one's identity as a father or mother: occupation and ideology. Grounded largely in Erik Erikson's views about identity and psychosocial development theory that were covered in the previous chapter, Marcia argued that identity is usually developed in adolescence, but can extend well past adolescence if the individual resists committing to any particular identity. A key to Marcia's concept of identity is whether the identity chosen is authentically autonomous or simply the passive product of adopting the identity modeled by one's parents. Marcia notes, "the individual about to become a Methodist, Republican farmer like his Methodist, Republican farmer father, with little or no thought in the matter, certainly cannot be said to have 'achieved' an identity, in spite of his commitment."[3] For some, then, fatherhood is a role taken through imitation, but Marcia also believes that others develop their identity as 'father' through an "internal locus of self-identification."[4] This 'self-identification' involves an active process of examination and evaluation as part of making a commitment to how a man views himself. For many men, 'father' is an integral part of their sense of self.

For the identity theorist, fatherhood is either a role passively adopted by individual men who are unconsciously responding to certain cultural or family norms or it is an active process of evaluation and self-discovery, where one consciously determines how one wants to approach fatherhood. Today, in what is termed "conscious fathering," classes have been created to assist new fathers in coming to an understanding about how they wish to be fathers. In one such program, new fathers are told,

> This class helps new fathers build a partnership with mom in helping care for and nurture their children from the very first day. Taught by men for men to allow for a unique experience related to skill development and building a frame for how you want to father.[5]

This individualized approach to fathering reflects a new, progressive way of viewing fatherhood, but also rebuffs the traditional notion of father-as-provider-protector-disciplinarian that permeates traditional accounts of fathering. For those in the tradition of Marcia, a consciously deliberated approach to fathering is vastly superior to a passive acceptance of one's cultural and family expectations of fathering.

Parental Investment Theory

Developed by evolutionary biologist Robert Trivers, parental investment theory explains time and effort provided by parents to their children as a feature of evolutionary dynamics that propel females, who have the most to lose, to invest more time and effort in raising and nurturing their children than males who are more aggressive in pursuing sex, but have less investment in nurturing offspring.[6] According to this theory, it makes "biological sense" that fathers invest less time and effort with their children, since nature has constructed men to spread their seed and can do so with greater frequency than females who can give birth only to one child every nine months or so. This theory does not provide justification but rather an explanation for why more fathers leave their families than do mothers, or why fathers, on average, devote less time to their children than do mothers.

In their book *Fatherhood: Evolution and Human Paternal Behavior*, anthropologists Peter B. Gray and Kermyt G. Anderson invite us to take an evolutionary view of fatherhood and begin by noting the variation that can be found across cultures when it comes to parental care. The Aka of the Congo Basin, for example, have developed fathering traits that are characterized by a close, nurturing relationship between fathers and their children that does not include negative forms of discipline such as physically striking their children.[7] This form of parenting, argue Gray and Anderson, is typical of hunter-gatherer cultures where cooperation is the key to survival.

Gray and Anderson distinguish between paternal *investment* and paternal *involvement*, the latter of which is taken up more by sociologists than evolutionary biologists. **Paternal investment** involves the allocation of resources such as time, food, or money that aid the child's long-term chances of health and survival, while **paternal involvement** consists of the activities of holding, feeding, changing diapers, and other *direct and indirect behaviors*[8] that attend to the child's physical and emotional needs.[9]

Anthropologists have documented that societies with greater male aggressiveness, greater rates of male–male competition, and men's participation in warfare are also societies where there is less direct paternal involvement.[10] In no society ever studied have men spent as much time as women in direct parental involvement.[11] Gray and Anderson conclude that "fathers face parenting with the evolved baggage of a male mammal, including weighing the optimal use of their time for mating versus parenting effort, and orienting with a male-specific physiology to parenting tasks."[12]

But cultures are subject to change over time. Sociologist Suzanne Bianchi reports that in the U.S. in 1956, men spent an average of .04 hours per day on direct childcare activities, a time amount that quintupled to one-full hour per day by 1996.[13] Personal care, including health-care related activities, between fathers and their children, in particular, increased from 14.8 minutes per day in 1971 to 44.9 minutes per day in 1998, and playtime between fathers and children doubled from 15.4 minutes per day to 32.3 minutes per day.[14]

At the same time, rates of paternal involvement can affect the ways sons view how they should conduct themselves within a particular cultural framework as they get older. Researchers have found that fathers who are largely absent from their sons' lives or who instill in them the view that life is competitive and risky tend to produce young men who more readily adopt a "live fast, die young" mentality as part of their reproductive strategy.[15] This research confirmed the view that early social experience has a direct bearing on children's behavior. When a baby is adopted into a family of different origin and culture than that of the birth parents, the child readily adopts the behavioral norms of the surrounding adoptive culture, an observation that debunks the notion that genes alone account for child and adolescent behaviors.[16] It was also shown that the crucial ages for paternal and parental involvement are the first five to seven years of life.[17] Psychologist Louis Cozolino, in fact, introduced the notion of a ***social synapse***, as a medium through which children are linked to families and cultures.[18] Cozolino argues that the brain itself is influenced by social interactions with others such that early cognitive development is a fluid process involving our relationships with parents and those who make up our broader social environment.[19]

THOUGHT BOX

Which of the two fathering theories presented here do you believe has the greatest merit? Are there ways to integrate the two theories together in a hybrid fashion, or are there negatives about one of these theories that discounts it in favor of the other?

In what follows, fathers of various backgrounds and circumstances are examined to better understand the associated traits, styles, and challenges that flow from being a dad in contemporary society. Many have noted a change in fathering styles today that are typified by more nurturing, hands-on fathering styles in contrast to what scholar Joseph H. Pleck termed the "father-as-distant-breadwinner" model of fathering that dominated the early nineteenth to mid-twentieth centuries.[20] Whether younger or older, residential or

FIGURE 5.1: Before I got married, I had six theories about raising children; now, I have six children and no theories. ~ seventeenth-century poet and satirist, John Wilmot[21]

nonresidential, whether cultural differences exist, whether a father with sons, daughters, or both, whether being a gay or heterosexual father, whether single or married, whether low or moderate income levels, this chapter explores the differing parenting styles and challenges that emerge for a variety of fathers today.

Teen Fathers

Teen birth rates are down over the past 25 years and this is true regardless of race or ethnicity of the birth mother (see Table 5.1).[22] Teen birth rates are also more or less prominent depending on state or region of the country (see Table 5.2).[23] Social scientists view this as very good news, but it does not mean that serious problems do not continue to exist. While teen pregnancy and the attendant struggles for girls who become mothers rightly receive a good deal of scholarly and pop cultural attention, less is said about boys who become fathers, and particularly low-income, teen fathers. The U.S. Department of Health and Human Services reports that approximately one in ten adolescent boys become fathers,[24] which, according to the Centers for Disease Control and Prevention, calculates to approximately 180,000 teen boys becoming fathers each year.[25] In a survey of 128 young fathers, 73% were unemployed, 60% were high-school dropouts, 40% had substance abuse problems, just under 30% had committed a felony, and less than half had declared paternity for their children.[26] This latter feature makes research into young fathers difficult and explains, in part, why the bulk of the research conducted on teen parents focuses on girls as teen mothers. But turning to the research at hand, what is known is that the majority of teen, male fathers do not want to receive counseling services and instead believe that employment will solve the majority of their problems.[27]

In interviews, young, unmarried fathers report that the level of involvement with their children is based on their relationship with and level of support from the mother of their children.[28] When asked, many teen fathers claim that they want more involvement in their children's lives; however, since few of them actually live with their children, they

TABLE 5.1 Teen birth rates for 15–19-year-olds by race/ethnicity, 2013

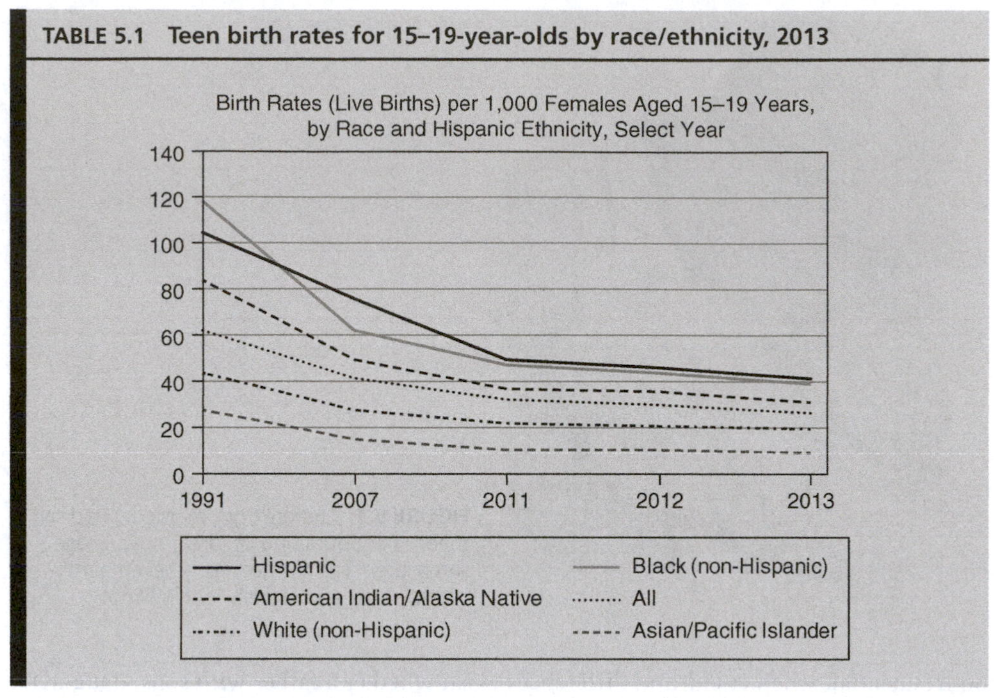

TABLE 5.2 Teen Birth Rates for 15–19-year-olds by state, 2014

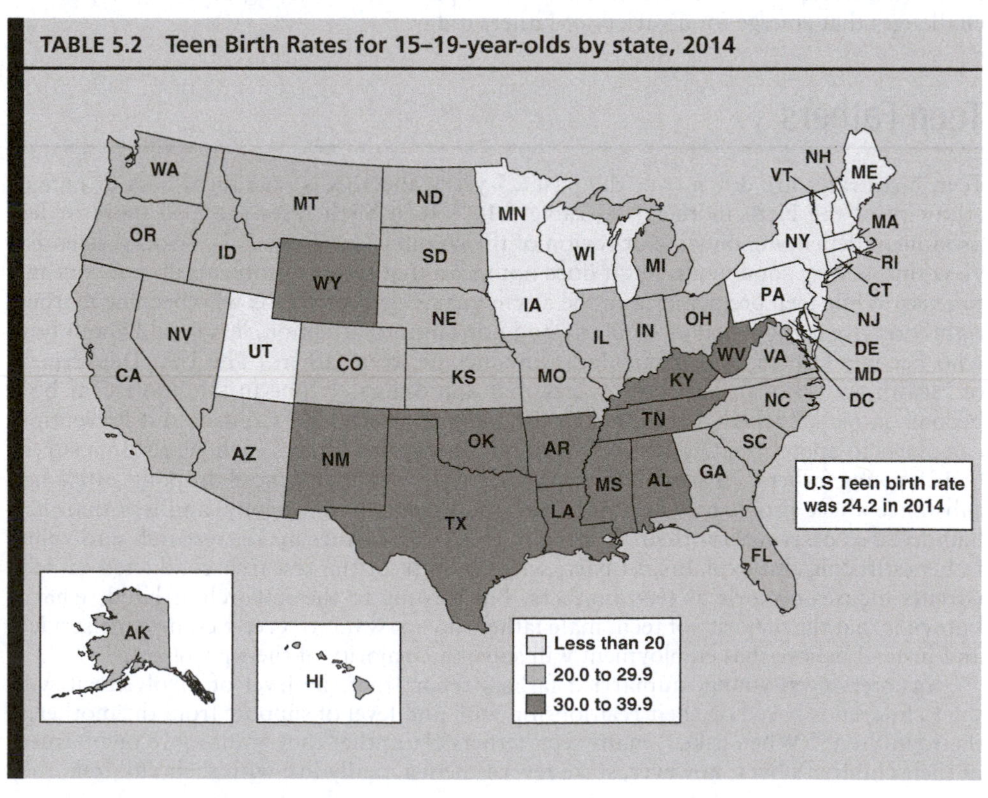

also claim to find it difficult to have the sort of emotional involvement they wish they could have with their children.[29] There are programs in place to help young fathers with counseling, food, diapers, free condoms, and help in finding work, but these programs are voluntary and require self-directed action.[30] It also turns out that many of these young fathers themselves grew up without a father and struggle to find adequate role models to help them understand what to do as new, young dads.[31] What is known is that children of nonresident, teen fathers experience a host of social disadvantages and developmental gaps including lower cognitive and behavioral scores on tests measuring these things than children living with residential fathers.[32]

In the book *When Boys Become Parents: Adolescent Fatherhood in America*, psychologist and counselor Mark S. Kiselica documents six salient factors that contribute to boys becoming teen fathers:[33]

- He is raised by a single parent.
- His mother had her first birth at an early age.
- One of his parents is suffering from depression.
- His family lacks social support.
- His parents do a poor job of monitoring his whereabouts.
- His family has gone through numerous transitions. (This is particularly true when a parent comes and goes within the family.)

For many of these adolescent boys, *guyland* and bro-culture (see chapter four) do not play a significant role in their daily lives, since college and fraternity life are not part of their experience. Instead, day-to-day existence revolves around finding work in the hope of being able to support their families. But it is this same economic imperative that often locks these boys and young men, just as it does girls and young women, into lives without higher education and the opportunity for more meaningful and lucrative careers.[34]

In addition to the six factors listed above, Kiselica spotlights several other elements that contribute to boys becoming fathers, beginning with the pressure many boys feel to have sex as part of validating their manhood.[35] Like the persistent cultural message to boys to act tough and not show signs of weakness, boys view having sex with girls as a rite of passage. Girls, notes Kiselica, are also pressured into having sex at young ages because in part, like boys, they are under the false impression that most people their age are having sex. In studies, 12-year-olds believe that 80% of people their age are having sex, when in fact, approximately 5% are sexually active.[36] Yet another factor in rates of teen sex is what psychologist Gary Brooks terms ***the centerfold syndrome***,[37] where boys receive certain messages about sex from media. Kiselica explains:

> Boys are socialized to view themselves as sexual pursuers and girls as sexual objects. Boys are also taught that they must demonstrate that they can have sex when they are young, even if their sexual experiences are devoid of emotional intimacy. In addition, boys are well aware of the dysfunctional norm that sex with girls involves a form of conquest through which the male must somehow get a female to submit to his will.[38]

In addition to peer pressure to conform to the masculine standard of "male as successful sexual pursuer of females," mass-media inform boys that "hot, sexy girls" are everywhere and want sex constantly. This means that boys who are unsuccessful in obtaining sexual contact with girls can be subject to ridicule by peers who may attack these boys as not being "man enough" to "score" with women if they believe that "women want it," but only with guys who are cool and have "game" or charm that women find attractive. So, for many adolescent boys, having sex equates to power and status within their peer groups so that some young men may be pushed into having sex before they feel they are ready.

A further problem that contributes to teen pregnancy and adolescent fatherhood is inaccurate and inadequate information about sex and contraception. When questioned, many young men believe that pregnancy cannot happen on the first sexual encounter or that virgins cannot get pregnant.[39] Those adolescent boys who have exclusive exposure to abstinence-only sex education in middle school or high school are particularly ignorant about the available contraceptive options for preventing pregnancy and do not have an adequate understanding on how to properly use condoms.[40] Other teens claim not to be concerned about pregnancy, stating that they either want a baby or view abortion as a form of birth control in the event of pregnancy.[41] Collecting these disparate considerations together, along with discoveries made about the mindset of many adolescent boys, Kiselica compiles a list of four main factors that contribute to adolescent, high-risk sex:

- Inconsistent condom use.
- Early sexual initiators.
- Multiple sex partners.
- Mixing sex with other high-risk behaviors such as drinking alcohol or drug use.

Boys who are early initiators of sex are found in higher number in inner-city communities and are more likely to coerce a partner into having sex, to contract STDs, and more regularly consume alcohol and illegal drugs.[42] [43] With respect to sex partners, one study reported that 54% of their survey population of adolescent boys claimed to be sexually active with multiple partners,[44] while 35% claimed to be intoxicated at the time of the sexual encounter.[45]

Kiselica notes that there are ways to help young fathers, beginning with outreach programs that build rapport and trust with adolescent fathers by taking the time to communicate with them and acknowledge their challenges.[46] Focusing on solution-based communication also helps to bridge gaps between adolescent fathers and case workers by asking positive-oriented questions such as:

- What do you want most for your child?
- What kind of relationship would you like with your baby?
- How would you like things to be between you and your partner?
- In what ways do you like to help your partner?
- What steps would you be willing to take to help you get a job?
- What are the conditions that would help you to return to school?
- What are your strengths or best qualities?

These sorts of questions create an environment of cooperation, but also set the stage for the kind of long-term involvement that adolescent fathers need to be successful parents. Adolescent fathers also need help with developing parenting skills and this is another focus of programs that attempt to aid young dads who are often receptive to older mentors who have been through what the young father is now experiencing.[47] Adolescent fathers may also need couples counseling and advice about peer and family relationships. The challenges for adolescent fathers can be multiple and ongoing such that programs and counseling require steady, long-term application and the flexibility to adapt to the unique concerns of individual teen fathers.

Some of the most effective programs that assist young dads are those that employ a "needs and resources assessment" to better understand what adolescent fathers feel are the most urgent obstacles to their success as fathers. When young fathers believe that their ideas are taken seriously, they are much more likely to accept assistance and are more likely to return for continued help. Kiselica notes that those programs that have the highest success rates in helping teen dads are those that provide a host of services structured to help young men, such as parenting classes, adult mentoring, educational and career counseling, educational instruction and GED classes, computer training, job training and placement, child-care services, substance abuse counseling, and many other helpful services that aid young parents.[48]

But challenges persist. Among the concerns about programs designed to help young parents is that child-welfare workers are primarily women who young men often claim do not understand or appreciate their needs as fathers. Cultural differences can also be a challenge, since many inner-city environments consist of considerable cultural diversity and this diversity itself is situated with differing views about fatherhood or responses toward teen fathers. Yet other challenges for programs that aid young parents involve language barriers and budgetary limitations, hours that do not include evenings and weekends, which tend to be times when day-workers can accommodate their schedules to attend the counseling and vocational services they need. As a remedy, Kiselica advises longer weekday and weekend hours of operation along with getting program managers to train staff specifically in father-based counseling and vocational training in addition to the aid they already provide to young mothers.[49] In addition, an active recruiting campaign to attract male case-workers may assist in creating greater long-term, teen father involvement in the services offered.

A further challenge for teen fathers is overcoming a pervasive generalization about teen dads: that they tend to be irresponsible, negligent trouble-makers. There is, in fact, a good deal of documented evidence, as cited above, that delinquent behavior often accompanies teenage fatherhood, but as the Medical Institute for Sexual Health states, there are numerous teen dads who want to be good fathers and who with greater support and encouragement, are capable of making healthy choices for themselves and their children.[50] Speaking about his experience on becoming a dad, teen father "David" writes,

> January 21st was the greatest day of my life. I was scared, but the doctor came out and I was excited to see my son. I can honestly say having a child is challenging but as a teen dad I can be responsible. I'm proud to call myself his dad.[51]

Most teen fathers do not plan or want to be fathers at such a young age, just as many teen mothers do not necessarily plan or want to be mothers at such a young age, but in the wake of pregnancy, child-birth, and ongoing child care, most experts are concerned more about how to help teen dads and moms than finding ways to denigrate them as reckless, irresponsible people. In fact, some of the best ways to disrupt the cycle of poverty found among young parents is, according to therapist and author Andrew Smiler, to lose the moral judgments, eliminate the deadbeat teen dad stereotype, help teen parents to find work and educational resources that gets them on the path to higher wages, teach young dads how to be emotionally-invested, nurturing fathers, help them to understand the importance of being flexible with their expectations about socialized gender roles so that young dads shift their ideas about time with their child from "babysitting" or "helping" to "parenting with your partner," and to assure that they have access to affordable birth control.[52]

Single Fathers

Single parents, in general, face a host of challenges that often include financial limitations, time allocation between work and childcare, visitation and custody concerns, the effects of continued conflict between parents, disruption in extended family relationships, child reactions to parents dating and establishing new relationships, and the effects of a breakup on their children's school performance and peer relations.[53]

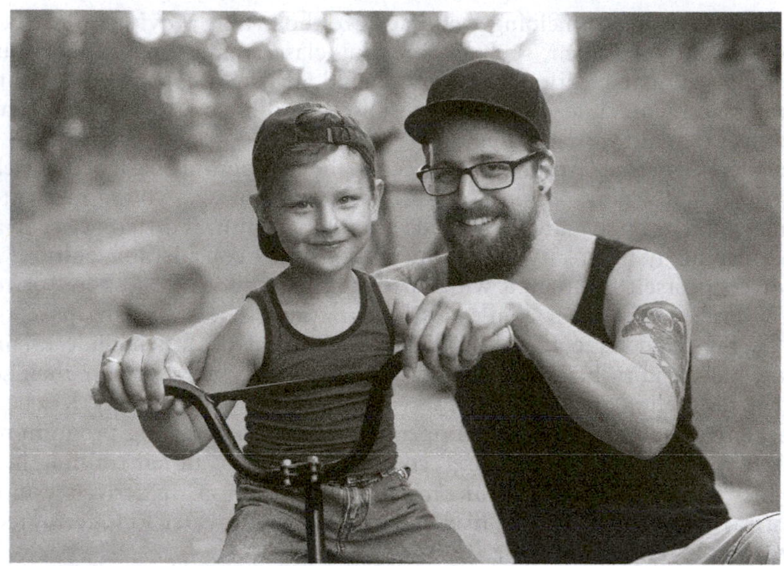

FIGURE 5.2: It is much easier to become a father than to be one. ~ American author Kent Nerburn[54]

In 1970, 85% of children under the age of 18 lived with two parents, but by 2006, this number had dropped to 66% and for those who were living with a single parent, 23% were living with their mother, while only 8% were living with their father,[55] although the number of single-father households has been rising steadily since the 1960s from approximately 300,000 to 2.6 million in 2011.[56] According to the Pew Institute, single fathers are more likely to have or be:[57]

- Higher incomes than single mothers.
- Less education than single mothers.
- Older.
- White.

Approximately half of all single fathers are separated, divorced, widowed, or never married and not living with a cohabiting partner.[58] Cohabiting single fathers, who make up the majority of the remaining half of single dads, tend to be disadvantaged in a variety of ways. They are younger, less educated, and more likely to be living at or near poverty levels than those single fathers who are not living with a spouse or cohabiting partner.[59]

There is a body of research that suggests children are in worse shape when their fathers are absent from the home and when little to no contact exists between fathers and children.[60] The oft-cited detriments include higher school dropout rates, less overall education, disruptive behaviors, higher substance abuse rates, poorer physical and mental health, less earnings as adults, and higher rates of non-marital births and divorce.[61] But critics argue that the degree to which these negative traits occur can be explained in part by self-selection.[62] For instance, parents in poor health or who are living near poverty levels may have a child who is then subject to the conditions of the parents, rather than falling into these categories exclusively due to a nonresidential father. It is also the case that simply because a father is not living with his children does not entail that he does not invest in his children. The level of investment is, of course, dependent on the father. Some nonresident fathers invest heavily in their children, while others do not. When levels of paternal investment and involvement are high, even though the father is nonresidential, research has found that teens have fewer behavioral problems.[63] Unsurprisingly, when nonresidential fathers are less distressed and have less inter-parental conflict, the well-being of children is coextensively higher.[64] This means that paternal residency may not be the pivotal factor in teen delinquency that many critics claim it to be and that the level of paternal involvement in their children's lives, whether residential or nonresidential, is far more important in predicting the long-term, well-being of children.

While some nonresidential single fathers complain that they do not receive enough time with their children, custodial single fathers also face challenges. These challenges are often the very same concerns faced by single custodial mothers, although some fathers who are raising girls will claim that they do not have the "girl experience" required to be in tune with the special needs of their daughters, a claim that single custodial moms sometimes make about raising sons.[65] But the common concerns of single, custodial fathers are identical with that of single, custodial mothers, which include the complaint that they do not get enough sleep or make enough money to adequately support the family on their own, or cannot juggle their schedules to be able to continue their educations, or that they struggle to explain to their children why their mother does not live with them or does not see them as often as the children wish.[66]

One complaint some single dads make is that as men, they were not raised to nurture others so that they feel unprepared to care for their children to the same degree as would a mother.[67] If in the past they accepted their paternal role as disciplinarian, they now feel forced to learn how to develop other parts of themselves. For some single fathers this development is a wonderful experience of self-discovery coupled with an increased feeling of connection with their children in ways never before experienced. As one single father advised,

> What I will share with any man who is stepping into this world of single parenting is to let go of your expectations. Parenting really isn't about tomorrow; it is about this very moment. Rules are good, but their little hearts, their expectations, their dreams are what it's all about.[68]

THOUGHT BOX

In the foregoing paragraph, you saw that some single dads complain that due to their socialization as men, they feel unprepared for the challenges of single fatherhood as opposed to single moms who they believe are prepared for the challenges of single motherhood. What do you make of this complaint, or how would you respond to the dads who make it?

Single father Neil Frewer, who lost his wife to breast cancer and raised his twin daughters on his own writes that although being a single parent is difficult, "the bond that exists between Kathryn, Natasha and me has grown because we are completely open, honest and supportive of each other."[69] Bob Greig, a single father from Denver, shares that after two years of being a single parent, he had a huge panic attack and collapsed, adding, "I gave up my consultancy business. I couldn't put the girls through the loss of another parent. My overriding thought was that it might help to speak to another dad in my position."[70] As a result of his experiences and challenges, Grieg established www.onlydads.org to support single parents and adds that "Contact with other men raising kids was empowering."[71] James Kidd, a custodial single father from Yellow Springs, Ohio, writes,

> It's not easy. Being someone who grew up without a father taught me how not to be. Nothing else matters to me except being there for my children. My greatest success would be that they grow into great adults and that they [are] happy regardless of what they do.[72]

African-American, Latino American, Asian American, and Native American Fathers

African-American Dads

When turning to African-American, Latino American, Asian American, and Native American fathers, the challenges and rewards of fatherhood are similar to those experienced by white fathers, but also include hurdles that many white fathers may rarely face. Within the family structures of African-American homes, for instance, according to a study that examined 162 two-parent African-American families, like that of white families, fathers were found to spend more time with their sons, while mothers were found to spend more time with their sons and daughters.[73] It was also found that mothers within African-American homes have a greater positive impact on their children's ethnic identities than do fathers.[74] However, fatherhood in African-American and Latino American cultures has not been researched nearly as much as scholars believe needs to be conducted to acquire more accurate and comprehensive data in order to better understanding the diverse needs and challenges that face these fathers. When research is conducted on African-American and Latino American fathers, a common concern is that an overrepresentation of low-income, struggling fathers creates negative stereotypes, while ignoring large populations of African-American and Latino American fathers that do not reflect the generalization. The predictable result is that overgeneralized, negative assumptions about black and Latino fathers are commonplace in both mainstream media and scholarly work.

Writing for The American Psychological Association, psychologist Shawna M. Cooper argues that far too much emphasis has been placed on negative attributes and stereotypes of black fathers and that it is long overdue to discuss the positive impact black fathers have on their children.[75] Research has shown that when compared with fathers of other ethnic groups, African-American fathers have greater or similar levels of engagement with their children, and this is particularly true between African-American

FIGURE 5.3: Committed fathers of color are everywhere throughout my life and they are virtually nowhere in the media. ~ journalist, Dori J. Maynard[76]

fathers and their sons.[77] Michigan State University professor of Family and Child Ecology, Harriette P. McAdoo concurs and adds that the stereotypical negative traits commonly associated with black fathers are actually traits found across ethnic and cultural lines and that factors tying them together are usually poverty, unemployment, and low-wage employment.[78] McAdoo argues that the "dead-beat dad" stereotype of black fathers is over-hyped by both laypersons and social scientists due in part to a media fixation on black fathers as absentee fathers.[79] For those black fathers who are away from their children, the most common reasons given are unemployment, imprisonment, and high death rates.[80] McAdoo argues that some unemployed black fathers separate from their families so that the mothers qualify for state aid.[81] But one of McAdoo's main concerns is that the negative stereotypes aimed at black fathers has a negative effect on the services, assistance, and support low-income, black families need.[82] That is, conservative pundits often use negative stereotypes about black fathers to argue that government aid should be cut from low-income families, believing that irresponsibility rather than unavoidable circumstances placed them in their current predicaments, for which they should not be "bailed out."

Anti-racism activist Tim Wise argues that conservative talk shows and news agencies routinely racialize welfare recipients to both demonize welfare as part of a larger social safety net and to gain white, working class approval.[83] Wise offers as one piece of evidence claims made by right-wing radio talk host Rush Limbaugh:

> the one thing the white, working class voters don't like is slothful welfare recipients. They don't like slackers. They don't like takers. They don't like people sitting on the couch, getting a welfare check, watching television, when they know they're paying for it.[84]

Limbaugh and other conservative apologists continue to make these sorts of claims despite the fact that according to U.S. Department of Commerce, the ratio of those on welfare is roughly even between white and black recipients.[85] But to appeal to "*white*, working class voters," instead of simply "working class voters" is to race-bait welfare as part of an overall appeal to white, racist sentiments. A narrative of this kind fits nicely with the stereotype that absentee black fathers are culpable for what conservative pundits believe to be unacceptably high rates of welfare.

In the piece, "Fatherhood in Contemporary Black America: Invisible but Present," psychologists Michael E. Connor and Joseph L. White argue that the stereotype of the absentee black father is inconsistent with structured interviews, community-based observations, and ethnography studies.[86] The results of this research support the notion that black fathers are united around certain fundamental traits and qualities anchored in African-American cultural values, which include "spirituality, improvisation, resilience, and connectedness to others through the extended family and the larger African-American community."[87] Connor and White note that there is a strong tradition in African-American culture to look up to powerful black men as role models and father figures, citing such notable men as Nat Turner, Congressman Adam Clayton Powell, Malcolm X, Jackie Robinson, Frederick Douglass, Reverend Martin Luther King, Jr., Richard Wright, and Ralph Ellison as longstanding role models for black men and the black community in general.[88] Beyond black men of historical acclaim, Connor and White also argue that leaders within the church are typically considered to be community leaders that influence younger men and help shape and reinforce a heritage of fatherhood with the African-American community.[89] With respect to black fathers in contemporary America, Connor and White contend that a challenging part of being a black man raising his children in America is to teach his children how to navigate being bicultural, meaning instilling in their children pride in being African descendants and part of contemporary African-American culture, while also teaching their children how to survive a white,

Euro-centered America that often denigrates being black and targets black males, in particular, as perpetrators of crime.[90] White fathers, by comparison, must strive to teach their children values that will help them succeed in life, but do not have to undo the damaging effects of a society that denigrates and targets whiteness as a detriment, nor do they have to reclaim cultural traditions that were systematically stripped from them through a legacy of slavery, imprisonment, segregation, and institutionalized racism.

University of Maryland sociologist Maria S. Johnson argues that the stereotype of African-American fathers as nonresidential, dead-beat dads is due in part to a disproportionate amount of research aimed at lower-income, nonresidential fathers who struggle to gain and retain employment in work environments that have not traditionally been amiable to African-American men.[91] As a result, there has been a proliferation of public representation of the black father as a dead-beat dad who does not financially support his family and who is uninvolved in raising his children. Writing for *The New York Times*, journalist Kenrya Rankin Naasel argues that these stereotypes are simply untrue. Citing research conducted by the Centers for Disease Control and Prevention, Naasel argues that whether the father is residential or nonresidential, black fathers are equally or more involved with their children than their white or Latino counterparts, including time feeding, dressing, reading to and playing with their children.[92] These findings were confirmed in reports issued by the National Center for Health Statistics and research conducted by the Pew Research Center, where senior researcher Gretchen Livingston stated about parenting and in particular fathering, "blacks look a lot like everyone else," such that the stereotype of African-American fathers as absentee, dead-beat dads is simply untrue.[93]

Latino Dads

With respect to Latino fathers, similar challenges arise. Latino dads try to instill pride in their children, while navigating biculturalism and the difficulties that young Latinos and Latinas face in a culture that denigrates and stereotypes people of color, and particularly those branded as undocumented workers. When scholarship is conducted on Latino fathers, it often overrepresents Latino fathers as struggling, low-income individuals and emphasizes their shared immigration experiences.[94] Another common area of research into Latino fatherhood is the representation of *machismo*, a strong, sometimes aggressive masculine pride, as central to the raising of sons.[95] By contrast, *caballerismo*, the positive image of a man who provides, respects, and cares for his family, is not a trait specifically passed from father to son, but an image of fatherhood that is commended and reinforced throughout Latino culture.[96] In fact, the characterization of Latino fathers as instilling a sense of *machismo* in their sons has been challenged with respect to the meaning of the concept.[97] Some claim that *machismo* is best interpreted as "exaggerated masculinity, physical prowess, and male chauvinism,"[98] [99] while others define *machismo* as best captured by traits of bravery, courage, stoicism, heroism, and ferocity.[100]

In Latino culture, fathers are central to the cohesion of the nuclear family. In the article, "Beyond the myths: Paternal values of Latino fathers," Michigan State University professor Francisco A. Villarruel and Southwest Texas State University professor Jaime Chahin argue that as the Latino population becomes the largest minority group in America, it is vital that the well-being of society is linked to the well-being of Latino and other minority groups.[101] Yet, they argue, little research has been conducted into fathering in Latino communities even though Latino families have been described in most literature as allocentric or collective in nature.[102] Latino culture is known for family relationships that extend beyond the nuclear family to the extended community, so that a *padrino* or *compadre* (godfather or mentor), along with grandparents and other family members, are involved in raising and nurturing children.[103] Villarruel argues that in many Latino families the role of father is central to the nuclear family as well as to the extended family network.[104] This means that the role of the father in Latino culture is sometimes misunderstood as being aloof from direct involvement in his children's lives. However, Villarruel argues that in Mexican culture, for instance, the father represents a man of honor and respect who teaches by example, and that this approach to fathering should not be interpreted as the father being emotionally distant from his children.[105] Professors Natasha Cabrera and Robert H. Bradley add that the fathering styles of Latino fathers differ greatly when factors of cultural values and beliefs, immigration experience, motivation to parent, and financial, social, and human capital are taken into account, such that there is no accurate way to describe Latino fathering in a generalized fashion without supporting stereotypes.[106]

Sociologist Veronica Terriquez notes that after controlling for other covariates, U.S.-born Latino fathers are found to participate in their children's school activities at the same rate as U.S.-born white fathers.[107] Parental involvement in their children's academic development can be all the more important in multicultural families where more than one language is spoken. In nuclear Latino families where Spanish is the primary language, critics have claimed that Latino children are disadvantaged in an American culture that has been resistant to bilingual education.[108] Proponents of bilingual education counter that it is American xenophobia and Anglocentrism that places Spanish-speaking youths at educational and occupational risk.[109] At the same time, the percentage of Hispanics in America who speak proficient English has risen from 59% in the 1980s to 68% today, which is affected by whether the person is U.S.-born (89%) or foreign-born (34%) respectively.[110] These language issues against wider American biases challenge Latino fathers and mothers who want their children to succeed, while trying to preserve the Spanish language, along with national or regional heritages, and cultural values in their children. The pressure to expose and reinforce Spanish in his children is expressed by Julio Ricardo Valera, founder of the website *Latino Rebels*, who, writing for the *Huffington Post*, states,

> My name is Julio and I am a failed Latino dad. I don't really know when I stopped talking to my two children (now both teenagers) exclusively in Spanish, but I think it was when I was traveling from Boston to California. The guilt has been with me ever since.[111]

The guilt expressed by Valero is felt by other Latino fathers who worry that without the Spanish language, a new generation of Latinos are being divorced from their heritage. Others are not so sure. Writing for the *Huffington Post*, John Paul Brammer argues that learning Spanish did not make him feel more Latino and that his Latino pride comes from his values and commitment to social justice for his community.[112]

Asian American Dads

Like African-American and Latino fathers, Asian American fathers struggle with stereotypes and negative representations proliferated in mainstream media and popular culture. But one of the more persistent views is that Asian American fathers and mothers are very strict and demand that their children achieve academically at very high levels. In fact, the expression "tiger mom" was created as a moniker for Chinese American parenting.[113] Scarlett Wang of New York University states that the *tiger mom* stereotype is exactly that, noting that most Chinese American parents do not subscribe to the model of pushing their children to the extreme in academics.[114] However, a number of studies have shown that Chinese parenting is either mostly or inherently authoritarian in nature, which, Wang argues, is rooted in the teachings of Confucius, who stressed the importance of social order.[115] Thus, strict disciplinary measures are sometimes undertaken to train children to behave in a socially acceptable manner. The goal of these measures is to raise children who are "good people" by contemporary, social standards of being a good person.[116] The challenging part for Chinese parents who are raising their children in America, like other first or even second generation American parents who hail from other cultures, is to raise their children in abidance with the values of both cultures. Interestingly, first generation children appear to do much better in life than second generation children, suggesting to Wang that immersion in American culture from birth creates a tension for parents and children. Since the more permissive American values run contrary to traditional Chinese values and codes of conduct, parents receive more defiance and resistance from their second generation children to the traditional authoritarian approach to parenting.[117] This same resistance and defiance is likely to be seen by children of parents who are navigating two or more cultures, where the values and practices of one culture are at variance with the values and practices of the other culture.

A complication of discussing characteristics of Asian American fathers, not unlike Latino American fathers, is that Asian American people hail from numerous cultures that admit a variety of traditions, attitudes, languages, and practices. In addition, first generation Americans, as noted above, do not necessarily hold or practice the views and customs of second generation or higher Americans. When turning strictly to Asian American parenting, there is no way to generalize about the parental practices of Chinese American, Japanese American, Korean American, Filipino American, Indonesian American, Pacific Islander American, and other Asian American cultures. Michigan State University scholars Desiree Baolian Qin and Tzu-Fen Chang state of Asian American fathers that while it is difficult to draw generalizations due to the many cultural differences and histories between varying Asian groups in America, traditional Asian societies are dominated by patriarchal traditions, which extend to parenting roles.[118] Fathers are considered head of the family, primary breadwinner, and are expected to distance themselves from domestic chores and childrearing responsibilities.[119] However, Qin and Chang found after examining multiple empirical studies that many contemporary Asian American fathers avoid traditional expectations and instead engage in more nurturing and affectionate contact with their children.[120] These findings, however, were mitigated by the observation that these same fathers became more authoritarian as their children reached adolescence and that this was especially true of the approach they took to their sons as opposed to their daughters.[121] Support for the stereotype of the Asian American father as demanding that their children achieve at high academic levels was borne out to some degree, but mainly with respect to low- and middle-class socioeconomic families.[122] Observed within these same socioeconomic conditions was an overall drop-off in paternal involvement with their children, since working very long hours constituted an employment pattern for many Asian American fathers who are striving to improve their family's socioeconomic position.[123]

THOUGHT BOX

For individuals who are members of more than one culture and whose primary language is other than English, how important do you feel it is for parents to teach or get tutoring in English for their children? Do you agree with Valero, above, that not teaching a native language to your children is to separate them from their native cultures, or do you believe Brammer is correct in claiming that learning or teaching native languages does not connect one more readily to one's native culture?

Native American Dads

Native Americans, including Alaskan Native people, in general, have not been well represented in research nor enjoy great visibility in mainstream media. But within this relative invisibility, Native people have struggled and in particular, Native men have experienced high rates of substance abuse and incarceration, which has had a profoundly negative effect on Native families.[124] [125] An organization that is fighting to change the lives of Native men for the better is the *Native American Fatherhood & Families Association* (NAFFA).[126] Started in 2002 and based in Arizona, NAFFA's purpose statement reads:

> NAFFA's approach was specifically designed to work with Native American men, who are among the hardest groups to work with. NAFFA takes the position that fathers are not the problem, but the solution and must take the lead in keeping families together.[127]

NAFFA is committed to engaging fathers to recognize the importance and what they term "the sacredness of fatherhood."[128] To achieve this goal, NAFFA hopes to restore "traditional, cultural American Indian family values," which in part means reuniting and reengaging Native fathers with their children.[129] Viewing incarceration as a serious problem for Native men, NAFFA institutes three important steps in what they term "reentry into Native America," involving the 3 R's of restorative justice:

- Redirect (finding alternatives to incarceration)
- Release (transitioning back into society after imprisonment)
- Reentry (connecting with resources and training to prevent recidivism)

In 2007, as part of the U.S. Department of Health & Human Services' Administration for Native Americans, *Native Prevention, Research, Intervention, Development, and Education* (PRIDE) was formed and headquartered in New Mexico "to develop and implement culture, strengths and spiritual based programs for Native people that inspire leadership, healing and wellness from colonization and multigenerational trauma."[130] PRIDE argues that Native men have been stripped of the connection to their heritage, and in response to a coerced acclimation to the European colonization of America, Native men are today one of the highest risk groups for substance abuse, violence including intimate partner violence, depression, and suicide.[131] In response to these devastating statistics, PRIDE developed "The Good Road of Life: Responsible Fatherhood" seminars as part of an outreach program to Native men in an effort to restore them to their Native cultural roots, traditions that honor family and help men regain a sense of their importance in the well-being of Native children and the health of their entire community.[132] To this end, PRIDE has worked closely with Native families to unify spouses, fathers and sons, fathers and daughters, and extended family members in a collective effort to promote positive male role models for their communities.[133]

In one specific region of the U.S., Sioux First Nations people of the Dakotas (also known as Lakota people of the Great Plains of North America) often encourage fathers to adopt *Akicita* standards of fathering, which is known as traditional warrior ways of life that involve policing, hunting, and upholding civil life within the community.[134] [135] Encouraging the passage of boyhood to manhood and fatherhood within Lakota tradition is an attempt to return men to pre-colonization and subjugation status, to return honor and respect to male influence in Lakota communities.[136] Bill Iron Moccasin, writing of *true Akicita* men and fathers, states:

> Anyone who accepts the identity of a warrior, we call *veterans*, should accept responsibilities. The single largest underutilized resource we have across Indian country are our veterans. We should be willing to sponsor youngsters, take them fishing, hunting, or camping. These were the roles of men in the old culture.[137]

At the same time, gang membership has been an ongoing problem for Native youths believed tied to substance abuse, discrimination, living without good male role models, and transitional living.[138] While gang life runs contrary to *Akicita* values, it is believed that adolescent boys are being recruited into gangs by appealing to an *Akicita* warrior myth, leading many within Native communities to emphasize the need for strong, positive male role models and fathers.[139]

In South Dakota, it is estimated that 46% of Native families are mother-only families.[140] A recurrent theme among many Dakota Native men is the concern that non-custodial fathers and children in fatherless homes have lost their spiritual center, that a reconnection with traditional spirituality is needed.[141] Beyond the worry about a loss of spiritualism, today, a majority of Native people continue to live in poverty and this predicament has contributed to what many view as a further emasculation of Native men.[142] Financial stress is listed by many Native families as the primary locus of family arguments and is a central predictor of divorce.[143] In fact, the median household income for Native American families is 70% that of all other racial and ethnic groups in the U.S.,[144] with the poorest communities found among those living in Native American reservations.[145] The federal government has initiated *Family Preservation* programs to address these high rates of poverty and insufficient resources for education and job skill training. What has been found is that predatory lending policies led many Native families to file bankruptcy and face foreclosure on their homes.[146] A strategy to help Native families recover has been to establish federal *Individual Development Accounts* (IDA) through which savings accounts are created with matching federal funds along with investment plans and financial literacy programs to assist Native families to manage their finances and build personal wealth.[147] While this sort of assistance is helping some, many Native families lack the resources to contribute to the IDAs, while others argue that any financial reparation should go through tribal leaders who are best equipped to work with community members.[148] Critics have noted that with many Native communities, there is a chain of command that must be acknowledged and respected if programs of these kind are to be successful.[149]

Dads and Daughters

Studies have shown that fathers, taking into account differing cultural and socioeconomic backgrounds, tend to socialize daughters differently than they do sons. In a survey of 426 fathers, sampled from white, Latino, and African-American fathers from low-income families, it was found that fathers of boys engage in more physical play, while fathers of girls engage in more literary play.[150] It was also found that these same fathers tend to channel their children's play-activities in what they take to be gender-appropriate roles before their children have a clear understanding of gender roles.[151] Marital status and the educational level of the father also play a role in child-play activities. For fathers who are married and have graduated from high school, the level of literary play is higher than those fathers who are unmarried or did not graduate high school.[152] Latino fathers were found to be overall less involved in play activities with their children than white or African-American fathers, but this difference attenuated when educational level was considered.[153]

FIGURE 5.4: There's something like a line of gold thread running through a man's words when he talks to his daughter, and gradually over the years it gets to be long enough for you to pick up in your hands and weave into a cloth that feels like love itself. ~American novelist, John Gregory Brown[154]

In a study where African-American daughters were asked about their relationships with their fathers, the majority reported high-quality relationships that endured over time, which had a profoundly positive influence on their lives.[155] Other studies have confirmed the importance of the father–daughter relationship in terms of the self-esteem and academic success of African-American girls.[156] Similar to the experiences of white and Latino girls, African-American girls report that the relationship with their fathers is most pronounced in sports activities, and felt that most of the contentious arguments with their fathers occur when the girls were adolescents and dealing with issues of boys and dating, suggesting that fathers are more protective of daughters than they are of sons.[157]

Much has been written about the relationship between fathers and sons and how this relationship impacts boys' views about what it is to be a man, but in general, less has been written about the relationship between dads and daughters. Psychologist Jennifer Kromberg notes that a girl's relationship with her father often shapes her conscious and unconscious expectations of what an acceptable romantic partner will be.[158] Kromberg writes:

> In my years of psychology practice, I've met very few women who did not unconsciously or consciously pick a romantic partner based on the characteristics of her father.[159]

Wake Forest University psychology professor Linda Nielsen agrees, stating:

> Women who grow up with meaningful, comfortable, conversational relationships with their dads make better choices in who they date, sleep with, and marry. If you have a good relationship with your dad, then you're not desperate for male approval.[160]

Unfortunately, adds Nielsen, the opposite is also true. If the relationship between a daughter and her father is strained or distant, a woman may wind up selecting partners who are combative or emotionally distant.[161] Coauthoring a study, M. Katherine Hutchinson of Boston College and Julie Cederbaum of USC add that "Paternal involvement is linked to positive social and psychological out-comes; an increased father–daughter communication can delay sexual debut and decrease frequency of engagement in intercourse."[162]

Conversely, in longitudinal studies of young women whose fathers were absent during their childhoods, there was a strong correlational association with early sexual activity and adolescent pregnancy.[163] In general, however, the more communication between parents and daughters about sex, the later sexual initiation takes place and the more consistent condoms and other forms of birth control are used, suggesting that attitudes about sex are not conveyed solely through contact with fathers.[164] Mothers who have developed an open and supportive relationship with their daughters have also had a measurable effect on delaying their daughters' initial sexual contact as well as their daughters' consistent use of birth control.[165] In cases of divorce, early sexual activity and teen pregnancy occur in greatest number when the divorce takes place during adolescence.[166] But as is the case with nonresidential fathers and children in general, the more involved a father is in his daughter's life, the less the daughter will internalize and externalize problems, including issues of sex, substance use, and low grades in school, and in many cases an overall boost in self-esteem and well-being has been witnessed and reported by parents.[167]

In a study of 447 women, researchers found that our culture's obsession with sexually objectifying women and the prolific media representations of women designed to please the male gaze lead many women to self-objectify and contribute to a host of negative outcomes, but that a positive father–daughter relationship can buffer these effects.[168] Interestingly, the study also found that high care–low overprotective fathers reported the lowest rates of negative eating attitudes and other negative behavioral outcomes, while high care–highly overprotective fathers reported much higher rates of negative eating

PURITY BALLS

Beginning in 1998 with Randy and Lisa Wilson in Colorado Springs, Colorado, purity balls were created, which are dances attended by fathers and daughters where daughters take a pledge to remain sexually abstinent until marriage. Fathers pledge to be men of integrity and responsibility, to be role models who act as the protector of the family. Fathers are also encouraged to praise their daughters' physical beauty in an attempt to build confidence in their daughters. Critics have been many. Eve Ensler, author of the *Vagina Monologues*, argues that purity balls reinforce the notion that men, in this case fathers, have the right to control the sexual lives of women, in this case their daughters.[1] A further criticism is that few young women who take the virginity pledge adhere to this pledge and are often uninformed about or unwilling to use birth control. Other opposition notes that purity balls are profoundly anti-feminist by attempting to control women's choices and by creating shame and guilt when women fail to observe the promises made. What is your opinion of "Purity Balls?" Do you believe they help strengthen the father–daughter bond? Do you instead believe critics are correct?

1 Jennifer Baumgardner, "Would you pledge your virginity to your father?," *Glamour*, January, 2007.

attitudes and self-objectification, leading researchers to conclude that "overprotective fathers may exacerbate the negative effects of body surveillance and shame."[169] Predictably, in interviews with women about their fathers, many women recount stories from their adolescence of their fathers using scare tactics to frighten them away from boys who were described as sex-crazed; or in other cases, they were criticized by their fathers for wearing revealing outfits that would allegedly trigger the "rape impulse" in boys and young men.[170]

What study after study confirms is that there is a great deal of importance in the father–daughter relationship that has lasting effects into adulthood. Some controversy over paternal approaches to daughters remains, but no one doubts that a father's involvement in his daughter's life has the ability to create positive or negative rippling effects throughout her life depending on the father's level of involvement and approach to fathering.

Dads and Sons

The interaction between fathers and sons spans, for many, 30 to 60 years, but most of the scholarship has focused on the first 18 years. Researchers are fairly united in maintaining the view that paternal involvement in their children's lives matters to the overall well-being of their children both in childhood and adulthood. Researchers have also confirmed what was suspected from hearing many anecdotal accounts: that younger fathers are showing a much more involved, nurturing approach to fatherhood than the paradigmatic model of fathering styles of the past.[171] [172] One researcher ties this new nurturing style to an attempt by some men to come to terms with the more distant relationship they experienced with their fathers.[173] Other researchers are not completely convinced that this new, nurturing father is undertaking a primary caregiver role. In one study,

FIGURE 5.5: No love is greater than that of a father for his son. ~author, Dan Brown

researchers determined that even in cases where fathers were self-identified "involved fathers," the primary parenting role fell to mothers and that the fathers in these cases were found to be in a part-time, secondary parenting role.[174] However, there is a good deal of subjectivity present. As predicted by identity theorists, fathers who consider the nurturing role central to their sense of self are found to be far more involved in their sons' and daughters' lives than those fathers who assess nurturing as having less importance to their identities as fathers.[175]

Writing for the *Huffington Post*, National Fatherhood Initiative (NFI) board member Roland Warren notes that dads often find their time taken by a host of activities that can leave a son feeling like he doesn't matter. Warren calls for men to manage their time in order to nurture their sons in a variety of ways that include hugging and kissing, but also engaging in activities with them such as cooking, playing, reading, and giving baths.[176] Sons, Warren argues, need to know that their fathers take an interest in the things the sons care about and that they are validated by knowing that their fathers take pride in them.[177] Psychologist Sylvia Rimm adds that dads can be the best of role models, but notes that even in the wake of long work hours and demanding schedules, good fathers need to find time for fun and laughter with their children, while being conscious of complaining about work too much in front of them, as kids need to view a strong work ethic and the accomplishments that result from hard work as an important and positive part of adulthood.[178] A study conducted by Penn State University's Department of Health and Human Development also found that sons and daughters who spend "increased time with dad" demonstrate higher rates of self-esteem and "social competence," a finding that did not yield the same correlational results with children who spent increased time solely with their mothers.[179]

THOUGHT BOX

Discuss whether you believe this more contemporary nurturing approach to fathering is a better approach to the traditional view of father as provider, protector, and disciplinarian. Do you believe there are positives and negatives to both styles of fathering?

When asked, many fathers view themselves as primary role model to their sons, particularly when they do not believe their own father was a particularly good role model.[180] Author and educator Geoffrey Canada adds,

> Men are extremely important in giving boys messages about being a man. Boys want to grow up to be like their male role models. And boys who grow up in homes with absent fathers search the hardest to figure out what it means to be male.[181]

But others note that fathers who model bad habits can be worse than absentee dads, since sons will often emulate their fathers' bad behaviors.[182] Negative modeling can include the bad habits of smoking and drinking to bouts of rage and violence.[183] Conversely, sons can learn from their fathers the virtues of patience, kindness, resilience, the ability and rewards of listening to others, owning mistakes, modeling a good work ethic, and respecting women.

On the subject of fathers as positive role models for their sons, the trait of teaching boys to respect girls and women has been gaining traction with authors and fathering organizations in the wake of increasing reports of men street-harassing women, sexual work-place harassment, sexual assault, rape, and victim-blaming.[184] [185] Many have noted that a father can be a profound influence on his son in terms of the way his son views women by instructing him, starting early in life, to respect women, but more importantly, modeling this form of manhood by example.[186] [187] Many feminists, however, argue that the trick is for fathers to teach sons to respect women, while also respecting women's autonomy, meaning not infantilizing women by teaching sons that men need to protect women as though they are children who cannot fend for themselves without men's assistance. Sons can learn this condescending lesson through a steady exposure to "***the princess syndrome***," a syndrome that was named after a theme drawn from the many animated Disney films that feature a girl or young woman who is rescued from her pitiful life by a charming and wealthy prince. The princess syndrome, according to child psychologist Jennifer L. Hardstein, "promotes the idea that if a girl is pretty enough and has fancy clothes and shoes, she will find love and popularity."[188] But beyond the potentially negative lesson this syndrome teaches girls, if boys are also taught that girls are fragile, but pretty princesses who need males to save and protect them, there exists a recipe for constructing men who view women as child-like dependents in need of male protection and guidance. Boys can also take away the message that women are attracted to men who possess wealth and power, a popular theme in contemporary music and film. Fathers have the potential to pass this instruction on to their sons in the way they treat and speak about women, but also in the way that they define the instruction "respect women" and what they mean when a father tells his son to "act like a gentleman."

THOUGHT BOX

What do you make of the princess syndrome in terms of its potential to influence the ways boys view girls? Is this a message sometimes reinforced by fathers in addition to media?

An insight from some researchers is that fathers tend to parent sons differently than daughters. Child development psychologist Kristin Berg Nordahl found that in the case of daughters, fathers and mothers were equally involved, but when the child is a boy, fathers tend to be more positively involved than the mother.[189] Positive paternal involvement includes initiating and sustaining play, signs of patience, holding, smiling, and communication of encouragement. Nordahl speculates that fathers may feel more comfortable with boys or it may be that fathers believe their presence as a role model in their sons' lives is more important than it is in their daughters' lives.[190] This may be especially true in cases where fathers believe that mothers are better suited to guide girls, while fathers are the better suited to guide boys, a view that is often found in faith-based and conservative approaches to parenting.

Gay Fathers

Certainly the love of father to son or daughter that was discussed in the previous sections applies every bit as much to the love fathers who are gay feel toward their children. Yet, even the concept of gay parenthood creates controversy in some quarters. Some critics argue that even though gay parents provide as much love as heterosexual parents, love is not enough.[191] They maintain the view that children need a married father and mother in order to create a proper balance of male–female perspective, arguing that mothers and

FIGURE 5.6: We're pioneers and not everyone is gonna embrace us for creating these types of families. But we're hoping that as interracial couples were discouraged from having children 20 years ago, 20 years from now, it will be no big deal that two men or two women are raising a family. ~ Will Halm, father[192]

fathers parent differently and that a child requires both styles of parenting in order "to be true to their gender designs" and to "develop into healthy adults."[193] According to conservative radio talk host Bryan Fischer,

> Children growing up in homosexual households have been shown to be more likely to experiment sexually, and as same-sex unions (as well as cohabitation) become the norm, this will only become more pronounced, producing more heartache, more children born out of wedlock, and more sexually transmitted diseases.[194]

Fischer later adds,

> It's almost impossible to overestimate the sexual confusion that young boys and girls will experience who grow up in these non-normative environments, a kind of confusion they will carry with them into the intimate relationships they pursue as adults, a confusion which will then be passed on to their children.[195]

While he is not a scholar, Fischer's views are echoed throughout much of the conservative cognoscenti of America. Same-sex marriage and same-sex parenting are viewed as dangerous social experiments that will leave children confused and vulnerable to sexual experimentation as well as, according to Fischer, "more [likelihood] to suffer from psychiatric disorders, abuse alcohol and drugs, attempt suicide, experience domestic violence and sexual assault, and increased risk for chronic diseases, AIDS, and shortened life spans."[196]

In 2012, sociologist Mark Regnerus claimed to have conducted a study that would expose "the myth" that gay parents were every bit as good as heterosexual parents. For conservative, anti-gay parenting groups, the Regnerus study became the "scholarship" they were hoping would emerge to support their claim that gay parenting was detrimental to children. Regnerus claimed to have examined 3,000 randomly selected American, young adults on what he terms "40 measures of social, emotional, and relationship outcomes."[197] According to Regnerus, adults raised by lesbian parents had negative outcomes in 24 of the 40 categories, while adults raised by gay fathers had negative outcomes in 19 out of the 40 categories.[198] In comparison to "married, biological parents," Regnerus claims that children of gay parents:[199]

- are *much* more likely to have received welfare (IBF 17%; LM 69%; GF 57%);
- have lower educational attainment;
- report less safety and security in their family of origin;
- report more ongoing "negative impact" from their family of origin;
- are more likely to suffer from depression;
- have been arrested more often;
- if female, have had more sexual partners—both male *and* female.

In addition, Regnerus claimed that children of gay fathers are three times more likely to become gay themselves than those raised by heterosexual couples and were at greater risk of being sexually molested by their parents or adult caregivers.[200]

However, in the wake of the Regnerus study, hundreds of social science scholars have challenged the methods and instruments used by Regnerus in reaching his conclusions. They noted that Regnerus himself admitted that "for those respondents who indicated that a parent had a 'same-sex relationship,' these categories were collapsed to boost sample size."[201] Critics went on to state:

> Specifically, this paper fails to distinguish family structure and family instability. Thus, it fails to distinguish, for children whose parents ever had a same-sex relationship experience, the associations due to family structure from the associations due to family stability.[202]

More problems emerged when critics also revealed that:

> Respondents were asked whether their parents had ever had a same-sex relationship. The author then identifies mothers and fathers as "lesbian" or "gay" without any substantiation of parental sexual orientation. It is inappropriate and factually incorrect for him to refer to these parents as "gay" or "lesbian" throughout the paper.[203]

In the end, social scientists of various specialty disciplines condemned the study as lacking academic integrity. So strong was the condemnation of the study by scholars that a federal judge in Michigan struck down Michigan's ban on same-sex marriage after stating, "The Court finds Regnerus's testimony entirely unbelievable and not worthy of serious consideration," adding that "the research was hastily conducted at the behest of a third-party funder."[204] The third-party funder was revealed to be conservative-based Witherspoon Institute.[205] Regnerus eventually admitted that, as a person of faith, he was "not a fan of same-sex marriage" before conducting his research.[206] In 2014, anti-same-sex-marriage supporters in Utah dropped the Regnerus study from their legal brief, although the study continues to be cited by the conservative organization Heritage Foundation and by FOX News even though Regnerus's own department of sociology at the University of Texas, Austin, rebuked his study as being "fundamentally flawed" and "inappropriately cited."[207 208 209 210]

In defense of gay parenting, researchers found that "Children from same-sex families scored about 6 percent higher on general health and family cohesion, even when controlling for socio-demographic factors such as parents' education and household income," writes Simon Crouch of the University of Melbourne. However, on most health measures, including emotional behavior and physical functioning, there was no difference compared with children hailing from heterosexual families.[211] One study found that same-sex parents tend to distribute household work in a more egalitarian manner so that children learn to work together in partnered ways, sharing responsibilities more equally.[212]

With respect to gay fathers, research has shown that the children of gay fathers benefit by learning first-hand the insidious nature of homophobic and heterosexist attitudes in society.[213] These lessons teach sons and daughters of gay fathers the importance of tolerance and respecting differences in others.[214] It has also been found that gay men who become fathers "report greater closeness with their families of origin and heightened self-esteem as a result of becoming parents and raising children."[215] This does not mean, of course, that gay fathers do not face special challenges. As one gay dad writing for the *Huffington Post* states, "being a gay dad is especially hard: there are so few of us and we have very few peers and role models."[216] Still, the numbers of gay dads have risen over the past few decades and is predicted by many to rise further over the next few decades.[217]

It has been suggested by some that children of gay parents carry a higher risk of being bullied and this concern has even been raised by some psychologists, but interestingly, within families with gay and lesbian parents the issue is not considered to be as great a problem.[218] Yet, this concern remains as one central reason critics give against gay parenting.[219] Others note that this same reason was given in the 1950s and 1960s to retain a ban on interracial marriage and continues to be a common harangue made by racists against interracial coupling and marriage today.[220] At the same time, while biracial and multiracial children are more likely to be bullied and victimized than children who identify with a single race,[221] very few argue that anti-miscegenation laws should make a return. Ultimately, advocates of gay parenting argue that it is our culture's bigoted attitudes about gay men and women that need to change, not the fact that gay men and women are now raising children in higher numbers than ever before.

Gay and Trans Sons and Daughters Coming Out to their Heterosexual Fathers

In an emotional video posted to YouTube and viewed by more than 17 million people, gay twin brothers, Austin and Aaron Rhodes, came out to their father.[222] Upon learning the sexual orientation of his sons, their father stated, "It's the way things are, you know? You're grown people. You grew up in a lot different generation than me. I just don't really know what to say—you know I love you both and that'll never change."[223] The experience of coming out to one's father who is heterosexual can be an extremely frightening experience for a gay son or daughter who is unsure how his or her father is going to react. Many heterosexual fathers harbor strong homophobic views and, for them, the thought that their son might be gay is considered to be one of the worst developments possible. In worst-case scenarios, gay sons can be physically assaulted or "disowned" by parents.[224] [225] Yet, as expected, the ways that heterosexual fathers react to learning about their sons or daughters being gay is widely divergent, and it is this unpredictability that also makes it scary to come out to parents.

In one study conducted with college students who were asked to imagine having a child come out to them as gay, in line with predictions, the more convinced the student

FIGURE 5.7: I just don't want you not to love us anymore. ~ Austin Rhodes to his father[226]

was that homosexuality is a choice, the more negative the reaction.[227] The fear for gay and transgender sons and daughters to come out to parents is particularly acute when parents are conservative and religious. At the website www.Christianity.com, parents are instructed to ask their son who has informed them he is gay, "Do you think it's wrong and are you seeking help to change and be delivered?"[228] Parents are then told,

> if he says that he believes homosexuality to be okay and he's decided to pursue it, then while assuring him of your continued love and care, you must lovingly warn him of the spiritual and physical dangers of homosexuality.[229]

When conservative, religious parents discover their son or daughter is gay or transgender, they will sometimes seek out "therapeutic options" in the belief that their child has a problem that needs to be fixed. Some Christian groups have gone as far as to blame parents, and specifically "weak fathers," for their children turning out gay.[230] Psychologist and former president of the National Association for Research and Therapy of Homosexuality (NARTH) Joseph Nicolosi writes,

> There is no such thing as a 'gay child' or a 'gay teen.' We are all designed to be heterosexual. Confusion about gender is primarily a psychological condition, and to some extent, it can be modified.[231]

In his book *A Parent's Guide to Preventing Homosexuality*, writing about those he terms "pre-homosexual boys," Nicolosi adds,

> At the heart of the homosexual condition is a distortion of the fundamental concept of gender. In boys, there can be a "gender wound"—a kind of emotional injury—in early childhood that leads the boy to see himself as "different."[232]

He then states of the majority of fathers of gay sons that they are "soft, weak and placid, with a characteristic emotional inadequacy."[233] When you connect the dots of Nicolosi's position, it is difficult to know the extent of fear the gay son of a father who subscribes to Nicolosi's views must feel. In fact, and unsurprisingly given the religious views many conservative fathers hold, many gay men who were raised in conservative households report that coming out to their father was more difficult than coming out to their mother, and that their relationships with their mothers were closer and more positive than with their fathers both before and after coming out.[234]

Transgender girls and boys coming out to heterosexual fathers who hold traditional views about gender are also often met with shock, resistance, and even hostility. Although many parents already know that their son or daughter is transgender through their child's choice of clothing, hair, and other external indicators, many other parents meet the news that their child is transgender with surprise and react negatively upon being informed. In one study, transgender youth reported that 54% of mothers and 63% of fathers reacted negatively.[235] It is also the case that the greater the gender nonconformity of the youth, the more negative the reaction of the parent.[236]

Yet, contemporary culture is changing, even if slowly, in overall attitudes about gay, lesbian, bisexual, transgender, and queer-gender people. For many young people, coming out to their mothers, and especially fathers, is an experience of great joy and relief when they realize that their parents love and accept them as they are without also hoping to change them. As psychotherapist and social worker Michael C. LaSala notes from his work with gay teens who have come out to their parents,

> For the youth in my book, coming out to their parents (who were not rejecting) gave them a sense of relief and helped solidify their identities as gay men and lesbian women—and some parents found that a son or daughter's coming out actually made their families closer and stronger.[237]

But interestingly, Dr. LaSala also advises that it is best for some teens to stay in the closet if they know that their parents are highly homophobic, the parent has threatened the child with violence, the teen is economically dependent on the parent, or if the teen knows that rejection would be devastating to him or her.[238] LaSala argues that a child's welfare is more important than the parents' need to know their child's sexual orientation of gender identity.

Father's Rights Groups

In the wake of a divorce, paternal custody and joint-custody have increased in the U.S. over the past several decades.[239] Paternal custody hovers at around 10% of child-custody cases, while joint-custody has risen from 5% in 1988 to 27% in 2008.[240] According to the Pew Research Institute, approximately 22% of divorced fathers see their children more than once a week, 29% of divorced fathers see their children one to four times per month, and 27% of divorced fathers do not see their children at all.[241] In cases of joint custody, both parents are considered custodial parents, which means that children reside at both the mother's and father's residence, while both the mother and father share associated costs and care of the children. In noncustodial cases, one parent does not have physical custody, although child-support may be ordered by the court as payment the noncustodial parent pays to the custodial parent in order to care for the children. As covered in chapter three, fathers' rights groups have sprung up around the nation challenging both custodial issues and child support. Attorneys have, in fact, created practices that attend solely to fathers who believe they have been wronged by a system that they believe unfairly shows preference to mothers in determining child custody, and by attaching child-support payments to the father in amounts they believe to be excessive or that they claim leave them little ability to pay their own bills or possess any discretionary income, which, they argue, could be used in the time they spend with their children.

While claiming no political affiliation, the majority of father's rights activists are white, heterosexual, and politically conservative.[242 243] A theme of fathers' rights groups is the view that family court is gender-biased against men. Political science professor Stephen Baskerville is a leading fathers' rights activist who has compiled a long list of allegations against family court that include:[244]

- mass incarcerations without trial;
- children forcibly separated from parents who are under no suspicion of wrong-doing;
- forced labor facilities created specifically for parents;
- children abused and killed with the backing of government officials;
- children forced by governmental officials to act as informants against their parents;
- children instructed to hate their parents with the backing of government officials.

The strong anti-government rhetoric, emblematic of ultra-conservative political movements, is a focal point of Baskerville's indignation. In what he terms *the divorce industry*, family court is responsible, he believes, for a government-led demonizing of men, where fathers are unjustly accused and criminalized. He claims that the few attorneys who have spoken out on behalf of aggrieved fathers about these allegations have been suspended or disbarred.[245]

Against this tirade, sociologist Michael Flood responds to fathers' rights activists that while some men are disadvantaged and some women are privileged, many divorced fathers pay little to no child-support.[246] But most importantly, Flood cites three ways that fathers' rights advocates have had a damaging effect on violence against women, children, and even other men.[247]

1. **Fathers' rights groups have placed a father's contact with his children above the concern for the safety of the children.**

   Flood notes that in Australia, fathers' rights groups have been successful in getting the "right to contact" principle instituted in the courts, which has placed children in danger in those cases where the father has a history of violence.

2. **Fathers' rights groups have undertaken a systematic discrediting of women and children who have experienced violence at the hands of their respective husband or father.**

   Here, fathers' rights activists assert that women routinely fabricate allegations of domestic violence in order to gain leverage in family court. These allegations contribute to both victim-blaming and to victims being unwilling to come forward in the belief that they will not be taken seriously, which assures that cases of violence will go unpunished and that the likelihood of continued violence is high.

3. **By attempting to modify public responses to victims and perpetrators of violence, fathers' rights groups harm female and male victims alike. They do this by trying to erode the protections in place for victims of domestic violence and by enhancing the freedoms and rights of alleged perpetrators.**

   With respect to families going through divorce, fathers' rights groups call for keeping families together at least in terms of continued bi-parental contact with their children, regardless of the violent history of the father or mother. By blaming victims of violence and maintaining the view that most allegations of violence are cases of false reporting, fathers' rights groups open the door for recidivist violence, regardless of the gender of the victim. In fact, since fathers' rights groups, like men's rights groups in general, insist that women perpetrate violence as much as do men, by their own reasoning they place men in danger of being victimized by contending that allegations of domestic violence are routinely false reports made by parents who are attempting to gain leverage in family court.

Not all father's rights, conservative, or faith-based fathering groups are as angry and indignant as Baskerville, although many tend to view the family courts with skepticism and lament that there are more resources for single mothers than there are for single fathers. One organization that promotes "responsible fatherhood" and attempts to increase the involvement of "committed fathers" with their children is the faith-based organization The National Fatherhood Initiative (NFI).[248] Founded in 1994 by author and former deputy director of the White House Office of Faith-Based and Community Initiatives under President George W. Bush, Don Eberly, NFI goals include decreasing absentee fathers, and in their own words, "to improve the well-being of children by increasing the proportion of children growing up with involved, responsible, and committed fathers."[249] The NFI claims that there is a "father crisis" in America today as a result of high divorce rates, absentee fathers, and fewer involved fathers in their children's lives.[250] As a result, they claim that fathers missing from their children's lives contribute to higher rates of poverty, delinquent behaviors in children, higher rates of youth crime and incarceration rates, higher rates of teen pregnancy and STD transmission, higher rates of drug and alcohol usage, higher rates of childhood obesity, and, conversely, that having the biological father involved in his children's lives lessens their risk of physical and sexual abuse, while elevating their chances of success in school and preparing them for happier and healthier adult lives.[251]

THOUGHT BOX

What do you make of the arguments made by fathers' rights groups? Do you believe the criticisms of Michael Flood have merit?

Summary

There are a host of challenges that exist for fathers today. Many of these challenges are shared by both mothers and fathers, while other challenges are more prevalent for fathers or more prevalent for mothers as the case may be. This chapter focused on the challenges and rewards of fatherhood across age, culture, socioeconomic status, and sexual orientation, which includes the challenges for gay fathers as well as the challenges gay, bisexual, transgender, and queer-gender children face in coming out to their heterosexual fathers.

While there are traits found to be common for most fathers, the research is clear that generalizations about fathering styles and fatherhood in general are difficult to support. Teen fathers who lack the resources to care for themselves or their families possess challenges not as present for older fathers and particularly those fathers who enjoy greater resources. But single fathers also face challenges not as present for married or cohabiting fathers, who benefit from the parenting contributions of a spouse or partner, although there are often stark differences between the challenges for fathers who are married versus fathers who are cohabiting with a partner. Beyond marital status and partnerships, cultural backgrounds greatly influence parenting styles and condition the way some men view their parental roles.

For fathers within some cultures, negative stereotypes continue to abound, generalizations combatted by cultural scholars who argue that the stereotypes, often racist in nature, harm men and families.

Many men are forced to navigate parenthood while contending with the pressures and challenges of dual or more cultural influences. Native American fathers represent a group, for instance, who have had to confront the tensions between traditional Native beliefs and values and the contemporary American beliefs and values that have infiltrated Native communities, which, many argue, have harmed Native people and made parenting a strenuous and difficult matter, while creating incarceration rates for Native men that have profoundly undermined the family structure.

But across many cultures, fathers have been found to spend more time with sons than daughters or engaged in more physical play with their children, while mothers have been found to engage in more literary play. At the same time, younger American fathers have been found to be more affectionate and involved in their children's lives than those of the past. Yet it still appears that the majority of fathers do not assist their wives or partners with so-called domestic chores that much so that many argue an egalitarian structure to parenting has not yet been achieved. Throughout most cultures, fathers tend to police gender roles with their children more so than do mothers. Boys are directed toward traditional toys, clothing, and activities the fathers feel are male-appropriate, while directing their daughters toward what they believe are more suitable female toys, clothing, and activities. There are certainly plenty of counterexamples to this traditional form of paternal gender-monitoring of children, but trends continue to support tradition over innovation. With younger generations departing from some of the more traditional notions of parenting and gender role identities, the future of parenting, and of fathering more specifically, may be in for much greater change going forward.

Notes

1 www.today.com/parents/brad-pitt-says-fatherhood-has-made-him-richest-man-alive-2D80186760.
2 Schwartz, Seth J., Luyckx, Koen, and Vignoles, Vivian L., *Handbook of Identity Theory and Research* (Springer Science & Business Media, 2011).
3 Marcia, James E., "Ego-Identity Status," in Michael Argyle, *Social Encounters* (Penguin, 1973), p. 340.
4 Ibid., p. 350.
5 www.parenttrust.org/index.php?page=class-conscious-fathering.
6 https://hampedia.org/wiki/Key_Terms_in_Evolutionary_Biology_of_Sex,_Gender,_and_Sexuality:_Parental_investment_theory.
7 Gray, Peter B. and Anderson, Kermyt G., *Fatherhood: Evolution and Human Paternal Behavior* (Harvard University Press, 2010).
8 *Direct behaviors* are typically identified as those involving physical interaction, while *indirect behaviors* are identified as those such as financial investment for a child's future where care-giving is met at a distance.
9 Ibid., pp. 32–33.
10 Ibid., pp. 37–38.
11 Ibid., p. 38.
12 Ibid., p. 39.
13 Bianchi, Suzanne, "Maternal employment and the time with children: Dramatic change or surprising continuity?," in *Demography* (Springer-Verlag, 2000), pp. 401–414.
14 Gauthier, Anne H., Smeeding, Timothy M., and Furstenberg, Frank F., "Are parents investing less time in children? Trends in selected industrialized countries," *Population and Development Review*, December, 2004.
15 Belsky, Jay, Steinberg, Laurence, and Draper, Patricia, "Childhood experience, personal development, and reproductive strategy: An evolutionary theory of socialization," *Child Development*, August, 1991.
16 Richerson, Peter J. and Boyd, Robert, *Not By Genes Alone: How Culture*

Transformed Human Evolution (University of Chicago Press, 2005).
17 Belsky, Steinberg, and Draper, "Childhood Experience."
18 Cozolino, Louis, *The Neuroscience of Human Relationships: Attachment and the Developing Social Brain* (W.W. Norton, 2006).
19 Ibid.
20 Pleck, Joseph H., "American fathering in historical perspective," in *Families in the U.S.: Kinship and Domestic Politics*, ed. Karen V. Hansen and Anita Ilta Garey (Temple University Press, 1998), p. 353.
21 www.goodreads.com/quotes/56543-before-i-got-married-i-had-six-theories-about-raising.
22 www.hhs.gov/ash/oah/adolescent-health-topics/reproductive-health/teen-pregnancy/trends.html.
23 Ibid.
24 www.hhs.gov/ash/oah/news/e-updates/eupdate-3.html.
25 www.cdc.gov/nchs/data/nhsr/nhsr051.pdf.
26 Weinman, Maxine L., Smith, Peggy B., and Buzi, Ruth, S., "Young fathers: An analysis of risk behaviors and service needs," *Child and Adolescent Social Work Journal*, December, 2002.
27 Ibid.
28 Devault, Annie, Milcent, Marie-Pierre, Ouellet, Francine, Laurin, Isabelle, Jauron, Manika, and Lachanrite, Carl, "Life stories of young fathers in contexts of vulnerability," *Fathering: A Journal of Theory, Research, and Practice about Men as Fathers*, Fall, 2008.
29 Ibid.
30 http://articles.latimes.com/2013/jul/13/local/la-me-la-fathers-20130714.
31 Ibid.
32 Mollborn, Stephanie and Lovegrove, Peter J., "How teenage fathers matter for children: Evidence from the ECLS-B," *Journal on Family Issues*, 32, 1 (2011), pp. 3–30.
33 Ibid., p. 47.
34 Ibid., p. 17.
35 Rodetti, M., "Urban teen parents," in *Children in the Urban Environment: Linking Social Policy and Clinical Practice*, ed. Norma Phillips and Shulamith Straussner (Charles C. Thomas Publishing, 2006).
36 Brooks, Gary R., *The Centerfold Syndrome: How Men can Overcome Objectification and Achieve Intimacy with Women* (Jossey-Bass Publishing, 1995).
37 Kiselica, Mark S., *When Boys Become Parents: Adolescent Fatherhood in America* (Rutgers University Press, 2008), p. 19.
38 Ibid., p. 20.
39 Ibid.
40 Ibid., p. 26.
41 Kaestle, C.E., Halpern, C.T., Miller, W.C., and Ford, C.A., "Young age at first sexual intercourse and sexually transmitted infections in adolescents and young adults," *American Journal of Epidemiology* 161, 8 (2005).
42 O'Donnell, L., O'Donnell, C.R., and Stueve, A., "Early sexual initiation and subsequent sex-related risks among urban minority youth: The Reach for Health Study," *Family Planning Perspectives* 33, 6 (2001).
43 Ibid., p. 268–275.
44 Turner, C.F., Ku, L., Rogers, S.M., Lindberg, L.D., Pleck, J.H., and Sonenstein, F.L., "Adolescent sexual behavior, drug use, and violence: increased reporting with computer survey technology," *Science*, May, 1998.
45 Ibid.
46 Kiselica, *When Boys Become Parents*, p. 91.
47 Ibid., p. 105.
48 Ibid., p. 111.
49 Ibid., p. 162.
50 www.medinstitute.org/2011/07/teen-fathers-the-forgotten-partner/?doing_wp_cron=1454882309.4930870532989501953125.
51 www.washingteenhelp.org/pregnancy/david-story.
52 www.rolereboot.org/culture-and-politics/details/2014–11-breaking-cycle-poverty-helping-teen-fathers/.
53 https://childdevelopmentinfo.com/family-living/single-parenting-challenges-rewards/.
54 http://heavy.com/social/2015/06/single-father-dad-best-inspirational-quotes-sayings/.
55 www.pewsocialtrends.org/2013/07/02/the-rise-of-single-fathers/.
56 Ibid.
57 Ibid.
58 Sigle-Ruston, W. and McLanahan, S., "Father absence and child well-being: A critical review," Center for Research on Child Development, Princeton University, 2002.
59 Ibid.
60 www.fathers.com/statistics-and-research/the-consequences-of-fatherlessness/.
61 Ibid.
62 King, Valerie and Sobolewski, Juliana M., "Nonresident fathers' contributions to

adolescent well-being," *Journal of Marriage and Family*, August, 2006.
63 Ibid.
64 Fine, Mark and Harper, Scott, "The effects of involved nonresidential fathers' distress, parenting behaviors, inter-parental conflict, and the quality of father–child relationships on children's well-being," *Fathering, A Journal of Theory, Research, and Practice about Men as Fathers*, 2006.
65 http://singleparents.about.com/u/ua/resourcesforsingledads/challenges_single_dads_face.htm.
66 Ibid.
67 www.fatherhood.org/fatherhood/the-challenge-of-becoming-a-single-father.
68 Ibid.
69 www.express.co.uk/expressyourself/150521/Single-parent-fathers-Raising-our-girls-alone-is-a-joy-and-a-challenge.
70 Ibid.
71 Ibid.
72 www.daytondailynews.com/news/lifestyles/relationships-special-occasions/single-dads-reflect-on-greatest-success-biggest-ch/nYKjz/.
73 McHale, Susan M., Crouter, Ann C., Kim, Ji-Yeon, Burton, Linda M., Davis, Kelly D., Dotterer, Aryn M., and Swanson, Dena P., "Mothers' and fathers' racial socialization in African American families: Implications for youth," *Child Development*, September, 2006.
74 Ibid.
75 www.apa.org/pi/families/resources/newsletter/2015/08/african-american-fathers.aspx.
76 www.insidebayarea.com/opinion/ci_12655378.
77 Ibid.
78 http://quod.lib.umich.edu/m/mfr/4919087.0003.102?rgn=main;view=fulltext.
79 Ibid.
80 Ibid.
81 Ibid.
82 Ibid.
83 www.timwise.org/2012/08/were-gonna-scapegoat-like-its-1995-welfare-and-the-never-ending-lies-of-the-american-right/.
84 Ibid.
85 www.statisticbrain.com/welfare-statistics/.
86 Connor, Michael E. and White, Joseph, L. "Fatherhood in contemporary black America: Invisible but present," in *Black Fathers: An Invisible Presence in America* (Routledge, 2005).
87 Ibid.
88 Ibid.
89 Ibid.
90 Ibid.
91 Johnson, Maria S. "THROUGH A DAUGHTER'S EYES: Understanding the Influence of Black Fathers on Their Daughters' Conceptualizations of Fatherhood and Womanhood," Ph.D. diss., University of Michigan, 2010. https://deepblue.lib.umich.edu/bitstream/handle/2027.42/78827/johnmar_1.pdf?sequence=1&isAllowed=y.
92 www.nytimes.com/roomfordebate/2014/03/12/the-assumptions-behind-obamas-initiative/its-a-myth-that-black-fathers-are-absent.
93 http://articles.latimes.com/2013/dec/20/local/la-me-black-dads-20131221.
94 Cabrera, Natasha J., Aldoney, Daniela, and Tamis-LeMonda, Catherine S., "Latino fathers," in *Handbook of Father Involvement: Multidisciplinary Perspectives*, 2nd edition (Routledge, 2013).
95 Glass, Jon and Owen, Jesse, "Latino fathers: the relationship among machismo, acculturation, ethnic identity, and paternal involvement," *Psychology of Men & Masculinity* 11, 4 (2010), pp. 251–261.
96 Ibid.
97 Taylor, Brent and Behnke, Andrew, "Fathering across the border: Latino fathers in Mexico and the U.S.," *Fathering* 3, 2 (2005).
98 Sociologist Maxine Baca Zinn argues that this sense of *machismo* is not unique to Latino culture, but is often ascribed to Latino culture by Anglo society.
99 Dececco, John and Girman, Chris, *Macho Men: Seduction, Desire, and Homoerotic Lives of Latin Men* (Routledge, 2013).
100 Mirande, Alfredo, *Hombres Y Machos: Masculinity and Latino Culture* (Westview Press, 1997).
101 Villarruel, Francisco A. and Chahin, Jaime, "Beyond the myths: Paternal values of Latino fathers," *Michigan Family Review*, Winter, 1997.
102 Ibid.
103 Ibid.
104 Ibid.
105 Ibid.
106 Cabrera, Natasha and Bradley, Robert H., "Latino fathers and their children," *Child Development Perspectives* 6, 3 (2012).
107 Terriquez, Veronica. "Latino fathers' involvement in their children's schools," *Family Relations: Interdisciplinary Journal of Applied Family Studies*, August, 2013.

108 www.hoover.org/research/bilingual-education-critique.
109 Ibid.
110 www.pewhispanic.org/2015/05/12/english-proficiency-on-the-rise-among-latinos/.
111 www.huffingtonpost.com/entry/confession-latino_dad_us_56068385e4b0af3706dc76cc?utm_hp_ref=mostpopular.
112 www.huffingtonpost.com/john-paul-brammer/to-the-latinos-who-cant-s_b_8127434.html.
113 http://steinhardt.nyu.edu/appsych/opus/issues/2013/spring/wang.
114 Ibid.
115 Ibid.
116 Ibid.
117 Ibid.
118 Baolian Qin, Desiree and Chang, Tzu-Fen, "Asian American fathers," in *Handbook of Father Involvement: Multidisciplinary Perspectives*, 2nd edition, ed. Natasha J. Cabrera, Catherine S. Tamis-LeMonda (Routledge, 2013).
119 Ibid.
120 Ibid., p. 267.
121 Ibid., p. 267.
122 Ibid., p. 269.
123 Ibid., p. 271.
124 http://qz.com/392342/native-americans-are-the-unseen-victims-of-a-broken-us-justice-system/.
125 Feldstein, Sarah W., Venner, Kamilla L., and May, Philip A. "American Indian/Alaska Native Alcohol-Related Incarceration and Treatment," *American Indian and Alaska Native Mental Health Research* 13, 3 (2006), pp. 1–22.
126 http://nativeamericanfathers.org/.
127 http://nativeamericanfathers.org/about/.
128 http://indiancountrytodaymedianetwork.com/2011/11/22/engaging-dads-recognizing-sacredness-fatherhood-63965.
129 Ibid.
130 www.acf.hhs.gov/programs/ana/success-story/native-nonprofit-teaches-the-good-road-of-life.
131 Ibid.
132 Ibid.
133 Ibid.
134 www.newworldencyclopedia.org/entry/Sioux.
135 White, Joseph M., Godfrey, Joyzelle, and Moccasin, Bill Iron, "American Indian fathering in the Dakota Nation: Use of Akicita as a fatherhood standard," *Fathering* 4, 1 (2006).
136 Ibid.
137 Simonelli, R., "Lessons from the Old Culture: An interview with Bill Iron Moccasin," *Wellbriety* 4, 2 (2003).
138 White, Godfrey, and Moccasin, "American Indian Fathering."
139 Ibid.
140 Ibid.
141 Ibid.
142 Ibid.
143 www.acf.hhs.gov/sites/default/files/ana/reference_guide_for_native_american_family_preservation_programs.pdf.
144 The Harvard Project on Native American Economic Development for the Annie E. Casey Foundation, "The Context and Meaning of Family Strengthening in Indian America." August, 2004. From the Annie E. Casey Foundation web site: http://www.aecf.org/upload/PublicationFiles/fs_indian_america.pdf.
145 Ibid.
146 Ibid.
147 Ibid.
148 Ibid.
149 Ibid.
150 Smith-Leavell, Ashley, Tamis-LeMonda, Catherine S., Ruble, Diane N., Zosuls, Kristina M., and Cabrera, Natasha J., "African American, White and Latino fathers' activities with their sons and daughters in early childhood," *Sex Roles*, October, 2011.
151 Ibid.
152 Ibid.
153 Ibid.
154 http://thoughtcatalog.com/lorenzo-jensen-iii/2015/08/30-sweet-tear-jerking-quotes-about-fathers-daughters/.
155 Cochran, Donna L., "African American Father–Daughter Relationships: The Impact on the Daughters' Perception of and Interaction with Men," Ph.D. diss., University of Michigan, 1992.
156 Cooper, Shauna M., "Associations between father–daughter relationship quality and the academic engagement of African American adolescent girls: Self-esteem as a mediator?" *Journal of Black Psychology*, August, 2009.
157 Belgrave, Faye Z., *African American Girls: Reframing Perceptions and Changing Experiences* (Springer Science & Business Media, 2009), p. 42.
158 www.psychologytoday.com/blog/inside-out/201307/how-dads-shape-daughters-relationships.

159 Ibid.
160 www.telegraph.co.uk/women/womens-life/10895290/How-our-fathers-influence-the-partners-we-choose.html.
161 Ibid.
162 Hutchinson, M. Katherine and Cederbaum, Julie A., "Talking to daddy's little girl about sex: Daughters' reports of sexual communication and support from fathers," *Journal of Family Issues*, September, 2010.
163 Ellis, Bruce J., Dodge, Kenneth A., Fergusson, David M., Horwood, L. John., Pettit, Gregory S., and Woodward, Leeann, "Does father absence place daughters at special risk for early sexual activity and teenage pregnancy?" *Child Development*, May, 2003.
164 Hutchinson, M. Katherine, "The influence of sexual risk communication between parents and daughters on sexual risk behaviors," *Family Relations*, February, 2004.
165 Inazu, Judith K. and Fox, Greer L. "Maternal influence on the sexual behavior of teen-age daughters," *Journal of Family Issues*, March, 1980.
166 Quinlan, Robert J. "Father absence, parental care, and female reproductive development," *Evolution and Human Behavior*, June, 2003.
167 Mitchell, Katherine S., Booth, Alan, and King, Valarie, "Adolescents with nonresidential fathers: Are daughters more disadvantaged than sons?" *Journal of Marriage and Family*, August 2009.
168 Miles-McLean, H., Liss, M., and Erchull, M.J. "Fathers, daughters, and self-objectification: Does bonding style matter?" *Body Image*, September, 2014.
169 Ibid.
170 Firestone, Robert, Firestone, Lisa A., and Catlett, Joyce. *The Self Under Siege: A Therapeutic Model for Differentiation* (Routledge, 2013), p. 102.
171 Miller, Eric D., "Why the father wound matters: Consequences for male mental health and the father–son relationship," *Child Abuse Review*, September, 2012.
172 Pruett, Kyle D., "Role of the father," *Pediatrics*, September, 1998.
173 Ibid.
174 Wall, Glenda and Arnold, Stephanie, "How involved is involved fathering? An exploration of the contemporary culture of fatherhood," *Gender & Society*, August, 2007.
175 Rane, Thomas R. and McBride, Brent A., "Identity Theory as a guide to understanding fathers' involvement with their children," *Journal of Family Issues*, April, 2000.
176 www.huffingtonpost.com/2013/05/01/father-son-relationships-dad-raising-boy_n_3186191.html.
177 Ibid.
178 www.sylviarimm.com/article_amazboys.html.
179 www.cnn.com/2012/08/24/living/dads-and-self-esteem/.
180 Daly, Kerry, "Reshaping fatherhood: Finding the models," *Journal of Family Issues*, December, 1993.
181 www.pbs.org/parents/raisingboys/masculinity02.html.
182 Stephens, Karen. "Parents are Powerful Role Models for Children," *Parenting Exchange*, www.easternflorida.edu/community-resources/child-development-centers/parent-resource-library/documents/parents-powerful-role-models.pdf.
183 www.huffingtonpost.com/louise-pennington/bad-father-definition_b_3588558.html.
184 http://fatherhood.about.com/od/sonsanddads/a/Teaching-Our-Sons-To-Respect-Women.htm.
185 www.huffingtonpost.com/carina-kolodny/the-conversation-you-must-have-with-your-sons_b_3764489.html.
186 http://michiganradio.org/post/dads-need-teach-sons-respect-women-example-blogger-says.
187 www.fathers.com/s7-hot-topics/c42-your-marriage/how-dads-can-teach-sons-to-respect-women/.
188 www.dailymail.co.uk/femail/article-2077635/Princess-Syndrome-Disney-heroines-teach-trade-looks-value-material-things.html.
189 www.huffingtonpost.com/2013/05/01/father-son-relationships-dad-raising-boy_n_3186191.html.
190 Ibid.
191 Hansen, Trayce, "Same-Sex Marriage Is Harmful to Children," in *Gay Marriage*, ed. Debra A. Miller (Greenhaven Press, 2012). At Issue. Rpt. from "Same-Sex Marriage: Not in the Best Interest of Children," *The Therapist* (2009). *Opposing Viewpoints in Context*. http://ic.galegroup.com/ic/ovic/ViewpointsDetailsPage/DocumentToolsPortletWindow?displayGroupName=Viewpoints&jsid=0a4f51743413fd17

8feec681daf55caf&action=2&catId=&documentId=GALE%7CEJ3010014234&u=viva2_tcc&zid=a9764475de34e422c34761f9631ce865.

192 http://andilipman.com/educ330/quotes.html.

193 www.cfcidaho.org/why-children-need-male-and-female-parent.

194 www.renewamerica.com/columns/fischer/080707.

195 Ibid.

196 Hansen, "Same-Sex Marriage Is Harmful to Children."

197 www.washingtontimes.com/news/2012/jun/10/study-children-fare-better-traditional-mom-dad-fam/?page=all.

198 Ibid.

199 www.frc.org/issuebrief/new-study-on-homosexual-parents-tops-all-previous-research.

200 Ibid.

201 https://familyinequality.wordpress.com/2012/06/29/200-researchers-respond-to-regnerus-paper/.

202 Ibid.

203 Ibid.

204 www.slate.com/blogs/outward/2014/03/21/michigan_same_sex_marriage_ban_struck_down_along_with_fake_regnerus_research.html.

205 www.scribd.com/doc/129660276/Mark-Regners-and-Witherspoon-Institute-Collaboration-Report.

206 www.slate.com/blogs/outward/2014/03/21/michigan_same_sex_marriage_ban_struck_down_along_with_fake_regnerus_research.html.

207 www.slate.com/blogs/outward/2014/04/10/utah_gay_marriage_opponents_drop_mark_regnerus_debunked_study.html.

208 www.heritage.org/research/commentary/2012/06/dad-mom-and-gay-parenting.

209 www.foxnews.com/opinion/2012/06/12/study-finds-host-challenges-for-kids-gay-parents/.

210 http://thinkprogress.org/lgbt/2014/03/04/3357631/regnerus-department-flawed/.

211 www.washingtonpost.com/news/morning-mix/wp/2014/07/07/children-of-same-sex-couples-are happier-and-healthier-than-peers-research-shows/.

212 Ibid.

213 Bigner, Jerry J., "Gay men as fathers," *Journal of Gay & Lesbian Social Services*, October, 2008.

214 Ibid.

215 Bergman, Kim, Rubio, Ritchie J., Green, Robert-Jay, and Padron, Elena. "Gay men who become fathers via surrogacy: The transition to parenthood," *Journal of GLBT Family Studies*, April, 2010.

216 www.huffingtonpost.com/alex-davidson/the-challenges-of-being-a_1_b_6095350.html.

217 http://williamsinstitute.law.ucla.edu/press/press-releases/as-overall-percentage-of-same-sex-couples-raising-children-declines-those-adopting-almost-doubles-significant-diversity-among-lesbian-and-gay-families/.

218 Clarke, Victoria, Kitzinger, Celia, and Potter, Jonathan, "'Kids are just cruel anyway': Lesbian and gay parents' talk about homophobic bullying," *British Journal of Social Psychology*, December, 2010.

219 Ibid.

220 www.huffingtonpost.com/grace-buchele/8-questions-interracial-couples-are-tired-of-hearing_b_4415858.html.

221 www.nveee.org/statistics/.

222 www.huffingtonpost.com/2015/01/14/gay-twins-come-out_n_6474068.html.

223 Ibid.

224 www.huffingtonpost.com/2014/08/28/family-son-coming-out-gay-video_n_5731462.html.

225 www.thegailygrind.com/2014/08/28/christian-parents-caught-tape-beating-gay-son-moments-disowning/.

226 http://time.com/3669675/twin-brothers-come-out-to-dad/.

227 Arnesto, Jorge C. and Weisman, Amy G., "Attributions and emotional reactions to the identity disclosure ('coming out') of a homosexual child," *Family Process*, May, 2004.

228 www.christianity.com/christian-life/marriage-and-family/mom-dad-i-m-gay-a-christian-parent-s-response.html?p=0.

229 Ibid.

230 www.christianpost.com/news/do-parents-cause-homosexuality-50784/.

231 www.breakpoint.org/bpcommentaries/entry/13/17196.

232 Nicolosi, Joseph, *A Parent's Guide to Preventing Homosexuality* (IVP Books, 2002).

233 http://josephnicolosi.com/fathers-of-male-homosexuals/.

234 Cramer, David W. and Roach, Arthur J., "Coming out to mom and dad: A study of gay males and their relationships with their parents," *Journal of Homosexuality* 15, 3–4 (1988).

235 Grossman, Arnold H., D'Augelli, Anthony R., Jarrett-Howell, Tamika, and Hubbard, Steven, "Parent' Reactions to Transgender Youth' Gender Nonconforming Expression and Identity," *Journal of Gay & Lesbian Social Services*, October, 2008.
236 Ibid.
237 www.psychologytoday.com/blog/gay-and-lesbian-well-being/201103/should-you-come-out-your-parents.
238 Ibid.
239 http://time.com/109460/divorce-shared-custody-of-kids-is-on-the-rise/.
240 Ibid.
241 www.pewsocialtrends.org/2011/06/15/a-tale-of-two-fathers/.
242 Gavanas, A., Kimmel M.S., and Aronson A., eds, *Men and Masculinities* (ABC-CLIO, 2004), 289–291.
243 Crowley, Jocelyn E., *Defiant Dads: Fathers' Rights Activists in America* (Cornell University Press, 2008).
244 www.stephenbaskerville.net/default/.
245 Ibid.
246 http://ncadv.org/learn-more/statistics.
247 Flood, Michael, "What's wrong with fathers' rights?" *Men Speak Out: Views on Gender, Sex, and Power*, 2nd edition (Routledge, 2013).
248 http://en.wikipedia.org/wiki/National_Fatherhood_Initiative.
249 www.guidestar.org/organizations/23–2745763/national-fatherhood-initiative.aspx#mission.
250 www.fatherhood.org/father-absence-statistics.
251 Ibid.

Chapter

6

Media and Masculine Representation I: The Construction of 'Normal'

In point of fact, what is interesting about people is the mask that each one of them wears, not the reality that lies behind the mask ... Life imitates art far more than art imitates life ... A great artist invents a type, and Life tries to copy it, to reproduce it in a popular form.

~ Oscar Wilde in *The Decay of Lying*[1]

LEARNING OBJECTIVES

After reading this chapter, students should be able to respond to the following questions with an understanding of the terms and expressions employed:

- *How has media historically represented men of color, or gay and trans-men? By contrast, how have white, heterosexual men been traditionally represented in media? What are the disparities between men and women in the TV and film industries? Why do critics believe gender and race equality in the entertainment industry is important?*
- *What is cultivation theory? What is the "mean-world syndrome"? How do these things potentially pertain to beliefs about gender and men in particular? What is "mainstreaming"? What is "otherness" and what has it to do with media consumption?*
- *What is the "Jersey-Shore Effect" with respect to media and young men?*
- *In what ways do media sell normalcy? How do media sell normative ideas about masculinity and manhood?*
- *Does violent media consumption affect boys' and men's views and actions? What does social learning theory predict about the above question, and why?*

- *What does antiviolence educator Jackson Katz mean by the "tough guise"? In what ways have media "upped the ante" with respect to male representation and violence? How is comedy sold to boys and young men? How is "Jackass-styled" risk taking a version of the tough guise?*
- *Do males, in general, have a different sense of humor than females or is there another way of accounting for gendered interests in differing comedy styles? How is "tough-guise" masculinity bound up in Jackass-styled humor? How do comedians defend sexist humor, and what are the criticisms of these defenses? How does comedy affect men's views about masculinity and women?*
- *How do video games, including interactive games, influence the boys and men who play them? How do male gamers react to criticism? What do these reactions tell us about gamer culture?*

Media Misrepresentation

The complexity and diversity of contemporary media make it one of the more challenging areas of academic research. The depiction of men, in particular, has blossomed into a multifaceted and diverse mosaic of masculine expression and identities. In the past, however, male representation in television and film was more limited, narrow, and stereotypical in nature. While media generalizations about men and masculine expression remain prevalent, there was a time, for instance, when gay, male characters were nonexistent, or when the suggestion that a male character might be gay was presented overwhelmingly in tones of either suspicion or comedy. Men in drag were a routine part

FIGURE 6.1: Flip Wilson (right) circa early 1970s

FIGURE 6.2: Michael Caine in *Dressed to Kill*, 1980

of television comedy shtick, which no doubt had an alienating effect on transgender women who were essentially mocked or feared, while emphasizing to boys and men the notion that exploring any feminine part of yourself was completely out-of-bounds and subject to derision.

Black, male characters in television and film were usually depicted in subservient positions to white men and overwhelmingly portrayed as uneducated, criminal, or hypersexual in early film and TV shows. From D.W. Griffith's 1915 iconic film *Birth of a Nation*, which was used by the Ku Klux Klan as a recruiting tool,[2] to the *Blaxploitation* films of the 1970s, to John Amos's hard-working, but under-educated-for-better-paying-work James Evans Sr. in *Good Times*, African-American men in TV and film were famous for being poor, unschooled, attendants of one kind or another. Media historian J. Fred MacDonald notes that, in 1970, there were 19 different shows that featured black actors in prominent roles that also employed scripts that addressed relevant social issues of the time, but that by 1971, all except *The Flip Wilson Show*

FIGURE 6.3: Stepin Fetchit (left) in *Bend of the River*, 1952

were cancelled, as network executives believed that viewers wanted escapism rather than thought-provoking shows during prime-time viewing hours.[3] Only the CBS hit *All in the Family* remained as a half-hour situation comedy that broached issues of race and racism in America, but did not feature an African-American actor in a regular, meaningful role. In 1984, Bill Cosby created *The Cosby Show*, which challenged media stereotypes about black men and black families of the past, but was not without its own controversy as black scholars criticized Cosby for ignoring the social strife and institutional barriers that existed for black people in the 1980s.[4] Georgetown University professor Michael Eric Dyson argues, for instance, that Cosby did not seem to appreciate the struggle of the African-American experience such that *The Cosby Show* portrayed a black family as being untouched by racism and in fact compounded the problem by catering to the politically conservative message that black people just need to work hard and stop making excuses in order to pull themselves out of poverty and become successful members of mainstream American society.[5]

Native American men, when depicted at all, were often played by white actors in makeup, donning traditional Native American clothing, and commonly found in roles as savages and warriors in an assortment of Western films that were popular throughout the early to mid-twentieth century. Today, it is rare to see Native men and women in media at all. Latino men, like African-American men, were typically cast as poor or working class gangsters and other criminals in urban barrios, a stereotype that stubbornly persists today in many films.

Asian men, an often collective identity in media, while rarely depicted in past media, were either martial artists capable of great violence, or cast in supportive asexual roles to white characters. Today, the theme of Asian men as dangerous and invincible martial arts experts or asexual lab technicians whose characters are on-screen only in scenes calling for their technical expertise and who otherwise do not exist are still prevalent stereotypes.[6]

White men, on the other hand, have been and continue to be overrepresented in media and are traditionally cast in roles of being "American," heroic, sexual, brave, noble, wealthy, and usually as protagonists in positions of power and authority.[7]

FIGURE 6.4: White actor cast as Native American in *The Searchers,* 1956

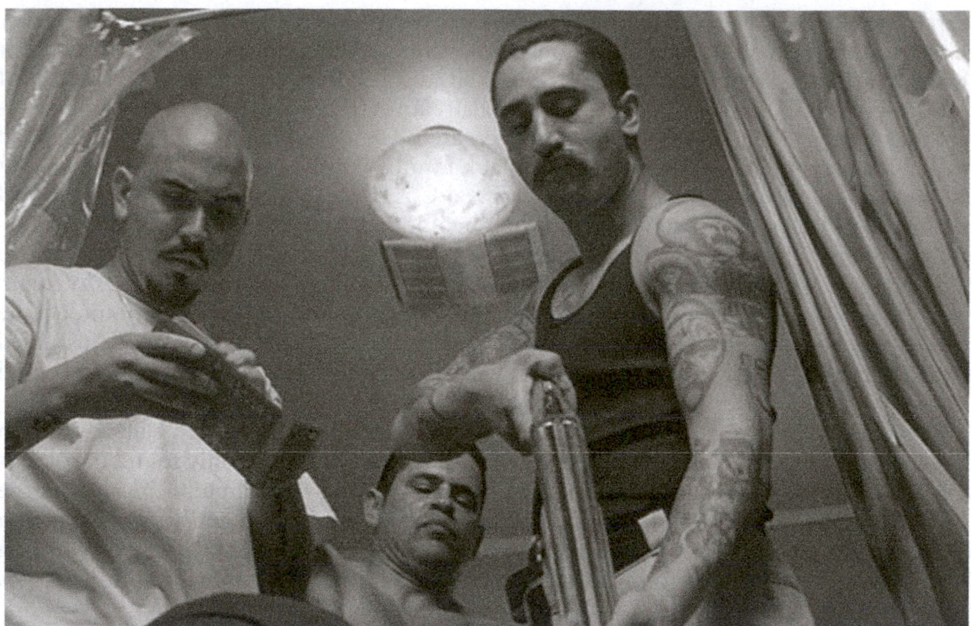

FIGURE 6.5: Noel Gugliemi, Raymond Cruz, Cliff Curtis in *Training Day,* 2001

FIGURE 6.6: Mickey Rooney in *Breakfast at Tiffany's*, 1961

Dr. Darnell Hunt, director of the Ralph J. Bunche Center for African American Studies at UCLA, reports that in what is considered to be the most comprehensive study of the entertainment industry ever conducted, it was found that while ethnic minorities make up nearly 40% of the overall U.S. population, they make up 16% of broadcast scripted show creators, and 30% of writers.[8] When turning to film studio heads, 94% are male and 100% are white.[9] Television network and studio heads are 71% male and 96%

FIGURE 6.7: Actor B.D. Wong in *Jurassic World*, 2015

FIGURE 6.8: Actor Chris Evans as Captain America, 2011–Present

white.[10] Hunt concludes, "The report paints a picture of an industry that is woefully out of touch with an emerging America that is becoming more diverse by the day."[11] Predictably, when white executives, writers, directors, and producers dominate the television and film industries, a lack of diversity follows.

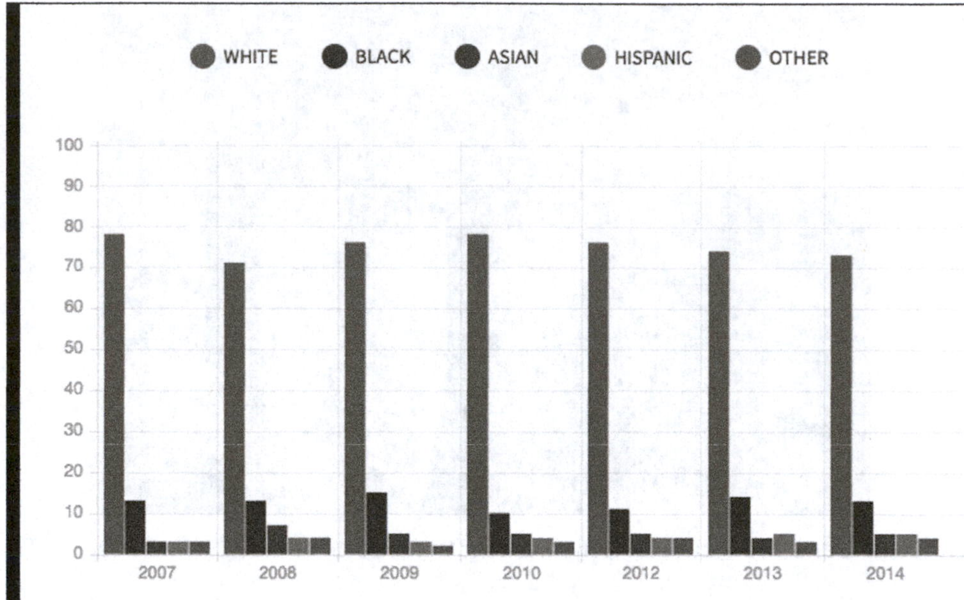

FIGURE 6.9: Percentage of characters by race/ethnicity in top-grossing films: 2007–2014

Today, media caricatures, while being challenged far more than in the past, continue to propagate U.S. media entertainment. Consider the depiction of African-American men in film. In 2016, several high-profile African-American stars boycotted the Academy Awards, including Will Smith, Jada Pinkett-Smith, and Spike Lee, after no black actors were nominated for awards for the second straight year.[12] Beyond the underrepresentation of African-American characters in film, another concern lies in the roles written for black characters. Writing for the *New York Times*, Brandon K. Thorp argues that Hollywood values "black performances" that fit certain narratives. For instance, writes Thorp, of the ten black women who have ever been nominated for an Academy Award, nine of them played characters who were either homeless or soon to be homeless.[13] Of the 20 black men who have ever been nominated for best actor, 13 of them involved characters who were arrested or incarcerated.[14] In 15 of the 20 films, the actor's character is violent or involved in criminal behavior.[15] Seven of these same characters abuse or mistreat women.[16] To be fair, argues Thorp, many of the films that feature black men and women as the central protagonist center around people who face "intolerable oppression with unimaginable resolve," but this still does not address the underrepresentation of people of color in Hollywood films nor the fact that the vast majority of films that feature a black actor in major roles are notable only in their relationship to the white characters in the film, such as Morgan Freeman's role in the film *The Shawshank Redemption* or Denzel Washington's role in the film *Philadelphia*. If a film is made about the lives of ordinary black people, states Thorp, the film is labeled a "black film" and receives far less attention from the 6,028 voting members of the Academy during nomination season.[17]

The lack of diversity is equally pronounced when looking at the ratio of men to women who enjoy positions of decision-making power in the television and film industries. While women make up more than half of all people in the U.S., they are woefully underrepresented in the television and film industries, and this is particularly true when turning to positions of executive power. Directors, for instance, are responsible for controlling the artistic and dramatic aspects of a television show or film, which often includes

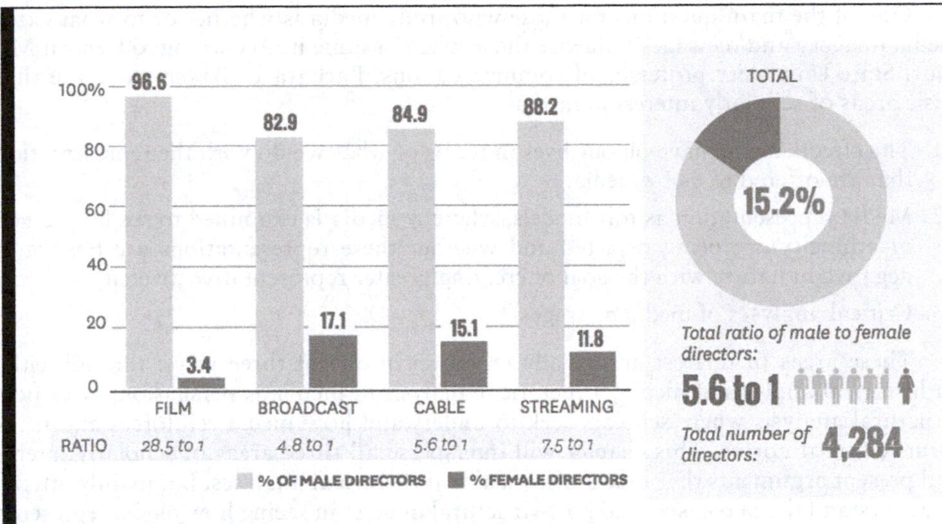

FIGURE 6.10: Director gender by media platform

input on casting the actors. When turning to directors, the ratio of men to women is approximately 5.6 to 1. Those who are responsible for screenwriting, which include creating the characters who appear in television shows and films, the ratio of men to women is approximately 2.5 to 1.

This means, of course, that the vast majority of entertainment media we consume is created by men, and overwhelmingly, white men. Writer Nneka Samuel, in explaining why diversity in film matters, writes that the character development in film for female characters or characters of color is dependent on the writer's ability to "know the struggle personally" in order to translate that struggle into the script, and that when this does not happen, the result is usually a "watered-down, generic" version of the character and the story.[18]

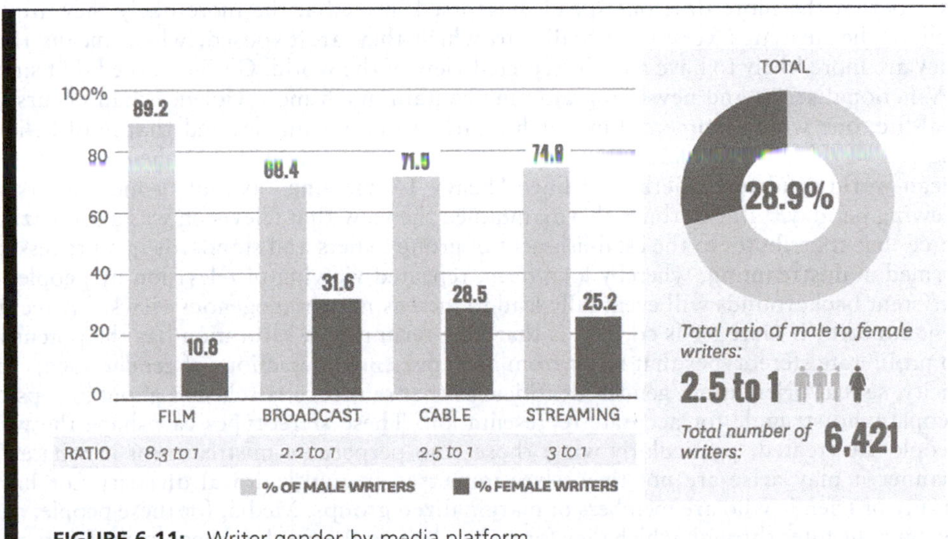

FIGURE 6.11: Writer gender by media platform

One of the main questions for those who study media is whether or to what extent media imagery and messages influence those who consume it. According to Central Missouri State University professor of communications, Barbara L. Baker, there are three basic areas of scholarly interest in media:

1. The effects media have on our lives in terms of what we do with the representations that are offered to us by media.
2. Media representation as role models, whereby media is examined to see how gender or ethnicity are being depicted and whether these representations are positive or negative in nature with the goal of creating greater representative diversity.
3. Critical analyses of media messages.[19]

These areas of interest are usually taken up in one of three ways: through either an historical analysis of media, a rhetorical analysis of media as persuasion, or as post-structural analysis where scholars seek to understand how media reinforces and transforms cultural norms. This chapter will intersperse all three areas of scholarly interest and present arguments that reflect historical and rhetorical analyses, but mainly attempt to understand the persuasive and post-structural interest in seeing how media representation, and the attending messages, influence and even alter cultural standards of masculinity and manhood. An essential part of understanding media narratives and imagery, whether as part of deconstructing regulative masculine standards or any other media-constructed prescription, is to discern and comprehend the normative elements embedded in those narratives and images.

Cultivation Theory

Whoever controls the media, controls the culture.

~ Poet and author, Allen Ginsberg

Developed by professor of communications George Gerbner, cultivation theory asserts that the more time one spends engrossed in media, the more likely they are to believe the mediated version of reality to which they are exposed, which means that they are more likely to have a misinterpreted view of the world. Gerbner noted that since TV fictional series and news programming contain much more violence than occurs in real-life, one who is immersed in watching television has an elevated chance of believing the world is much more violent than it is.[20] Gerbner termed this phenomenon, **the mean-world syndrome**. Gerbner defined "heavy TV viewing" as four or more hours of viewing per day.[21] But Gerbner also maintained the view that television was a socializing force that contributes to the establishment of group beliefs and standards in a process he termed **mainstreaming**, whereby long-term, repeated viewing of television by people of different backgrounds will eventually lead to increasingly homogenous views.[22] A recurrent concern, if Gerbner is correct, is that long-term media saturation has the potential to proliferate stereotypes that result from misrepresented depictions of gender, race, ethnicity, sexual orientation, gender identities, or that reinforce falsehoods about groups of people who struggle for accurate representation. These stereotypes can shape the way people are treated, particularly when those who perpetuate mistreatment in whatever manner it may arise are not themselves immersed in multicultural diversity nor have family or friends who are members of marginalized groups. Media, for these people, can become the filter through which they form their beliefs about what phenomenologists and

FIGURE 6.12: George Gerbner (1919–2005)

many sociologists term ***otherness***, the notion that there is a gulf between self and other such that others are opposed to self, meaning in contemporary terms that difference is viewed as threatening or less valuable, which is often witnessed in the ways that members of marginalized social groups are treated by members of dominant social groups.

One of the more common contemporary criticisms of cultivation theory is that today's media is a conglomeration of very different kinds of media representation so that the homogenization effect of mainstreaming may not be as uniform today as it may have been during Gerbner's time. Often, however, a particular network is devoted to attracting a particular market. A&E Network's *Lifetime* channel, for instance, has long been considered to be a channel designed to appeal to women, while ESPN programming is thought to have a much more male-centric viewership.[23] And so one response to critics is that those with common interests will likely gravitate toward similar media, reinforcing certain narratives to members of niche groups. Then again, the groups attracted to similar media could number in the millions, as in the case of men around the world who patronize pornography. For these groups, the mainstreaming effect Gerbner outlined could be very real.

The implications of cultivation theory to gender, and in this case masculinity, are fairly obvious. If men are being depicted by media in unrealistic ways, perhaps in terms of muscularity, sensuality, intellect, or success, it is likely that these depictions will have an effect on some men's beliefs, including undermining the self-esteem of those men who feel they do not or cannot live up to the mediated depictions they consume. Men might also attempt to modify their appearance or behaviors based on what they see as an attractive mediated masculine archetype. If, on the other hand, women are being depicted by media in one-dimensional, hypersexual ways, men who consume these media representations may develop unrealistic ideas about women's interest in sex or how to attenuate their behavior toward women in circumstances where sexual interest may arise.

FIGURE 6.13: Pauly D of MTV's *Jersey Shore*

Consider, for example, the 2009 through 2012 MTV hit reality show, *Jersey Shore*, where young men and women shared a house on the waterfront of New Jersey, while film crews documented their exploits of binge drinking, bar fighting, and anonymous sex. Jersey Shore became the all-time, highest-rated show for MTV.[24]

The male cast of *Jersey Shore* offered viewers salon-tanned, muscle-bound, tough guy posturing, who spent hours each day in the gym pumping weights, while filling their nights drinking at local bars, trolling for women with whom to have sex. The men of *Jersey Shore* were in many ways a throw-back to traditional, tough-exterior, womanizing masculinity. As might be predicted by cultivation theory, throughout schools, malls, beaches, and party environments around America, boys and young men could be seen emulating the muscular, tanned, tattooed tough guys.

We might call this form of imitation **the Jersey Shore effect** (boys and men consciously imitating the masculine representations found in media), which provides visual support to the claims of cultivation theory that people will emulate the media they consume, when saturated with common media scripts. This monkey-see, monkey-do, **homosocial** phenomenon was visibly ubiquitous with young men trying to out-tough one another in displays of hypermasculinity designed to achieve credibility with other men and sexual interest from women. Jersey Shore ran its course at the end of 2012, but powerfully reinforced the point that media can and often do have a profound influence on shaping the normative, masculine script that many boys and men follow. This same form of media imitation can be seen over different eras, as when boys and young men imitated the styles and attitudes of popular bands of the 1960s and 1970s.

From young men who imitated the mop-top look of The Beatles, to folk hippies who rallied around "free love," folk music, cannabis, and protesting the war in Vietnam, to many styles, trends, and attitudes seen today, personal identities for men and women, independent of gender or sexual identities, can be the result of group influences that are found in surrounding popular culture and the media that constructs or documents these styles and identities.

Much of what follows in this chapter assumes that cultivation theory applies to media consumption for many people today, with the acknowledgement that media have grown and diversified, while continuing to influence the views that men and women hold about themselves and one another. Even if media are more diverse, groups of boys or men who share common interests are more likely to also share the consumption of common media, which will predictably convert into identifiable patterns of behavior. These patterns can become common enough to produce a normalizing effect that ripples throughout the culture, creating boundary conditions for gendered behaviors and hierarchies that form through compliance or resistance to these norms.

Media and the Construction of 'Normal'

> Everyone knows that when you look at a television ad, you do not expect to get information. You expect to see delusion and imagery.
>
> ~ Noam Chomsky[25]

Author and media analyst Jean Kilbourne has spent the majority of her professional life examining and explaining the ways that media and advertising sell more than products, that they sell normative ideas about beauty, sensuality, femininity, masculinity, and happiness.[26]

On advertising, Kilbourne writes:

> Ads sell more than products. They sell values, they sell images, they sell concepts of love and sexuality, of success, and perhaps most important, of normalcy.[27]

But ads and broader media also commonly gender their messages to appeal to a particular target audience they hope to attract, given whatever products and ideas they hope to sell. Media normalcy is by its very nature a crafted, mediated set of images and narratives designed by individuals who are motivated to raise ratings or increase profit to the company for which they have been hired. This does not mean, of course, that media

FIGURE 6.14: Jean Kilbourne

FIGURE 6.15: Dodge "Ram" truck ad

normalcy in terms of gender depiction is one, united representation, since different markets require different strategies. But it does mean that there are people behind the scenes who are formulating the images and messages in ways that might have nothing to do with reality in an attempt to shape opinion or influence purchasing habits. If they are successful, consumers will view certain representations of masculinity and femininity as being *normal* and desirable.

Imagine, for example, being an ad agency that has been given a contract by the Chrysler Group to increase sales to Dodge trucks. If you want to assure that those customers who would be most interested in purchasing a Dodge truck are exposed to your ad, you would begin by conducting demographic research to determine who the typical Dodge truck driver is. If the research reveals that the typical Dodge truck driver is male, age 25–45, working class, and heterosexual, the next step would be to discover which TV shows, films, radio programs, magazines, and other media draw the most individuals matching that particular demographic audience. For print advertisement, your ad might wind up looking something like Figure 6.15.

Here, you have an ad boasting its sponsorship of the "American tradesman," featuring a man working street construction who is probably going to require a vehicle that is capable of hauling various sorts of construction materials. For TV ads, the marketing agent must figure out which shows this typical Dodge truck driver will view. This search may reveal that your best marketing vehicle is sports programming. So, you purchase advertising time during an assortment of NFL, NBA, MLB, NHL, and NCAA televised games over the course of a year. For print ads, you might also purchase space in *Sports Illustrated*, *ESPN the Magazine*, *Sporting News*, and other magazines that are directed toward sports fans. You would then want to develop a slogan that appeals to your target market. Figure 6.16 shows one of the actual slogans advertisers created to appeal to this imaginary Dodge-truck driving man.

The slogan "Guts, Glory, Ram" would then be voted on by committee to be appropriately masculine and heteronormative to appeal to the particular demographic the ad agency hopes to reach. Potential clients, it would be argued in meetings, will feel good knowing that Dodge "Ram" truck drivers are tough, rugged, have "guts" and seek "glory," which becomes a normative template for working class masculinity. It informs men who might belong to the target audience that "weak, wimpy men do not drive our trucks, but tough, no nonsense, badass 'real men,' like you, do."

There are an endless number of ads like these that imply to men that there is a particular way to be a man if you wish to be respected by other men, adored by women, or

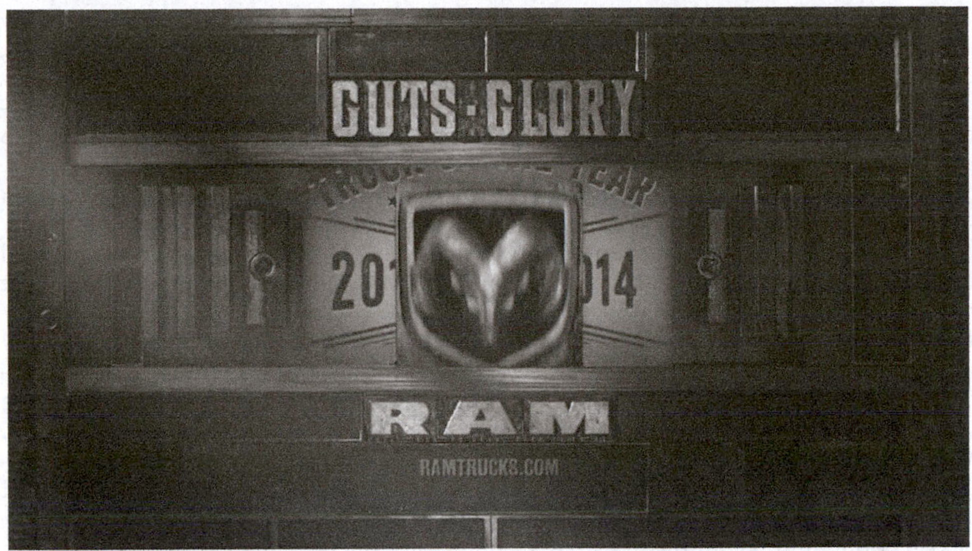

FIGURE 6.16: Dodge "Ram" Truck ad slogan, "Guts – Glory – Ram"

viewed as successful. The ad by Mercedes Benz in Figure 6.17 takes a different approach to masculinity than the Dodge ad.

Here, the target demographic is clearly different than the working class appeal of the Dodge ad. The normative script includes the idea that financially successful men who wish to exude the sort of debonair style and sophistication of George Clooney will want to drive a Mercedes Benz, which touts the slogan, "the best or nothing."

FIGURE 6.17: Mercedes Benz ad featuring George Clooney

The "Ram-tough" working class hero and the suave George Clooney man of worldly sophistication represent different socioeconomic versions of the so-called *alpha male*, each of whom is in firm control of his respective domains. Media have found a way to appeal to both models without scrapping the notion of there being an alpha prototype, albeit a plurality of prototypes depending on the audience one is attempting to persuade.

The socioeconomic and gendered narratives found in advertising are only one media venue through which gender, and in this case masculine normalcy, is produced. Many media critics have been more concerned about media violence and whether repeated exposure to mediated violence has an influence on young people who consume violent media content. In particular, criticism of media violence has been aimed at movies, TV shows, and video games that media analysts view as glamorizing violence to a largely young, male audience. The concern is that boys and young men who saturate their entertainment lives viewing and interacting with violent media become desensitized to real-life violence and place themselves at risk for being more aggressive, antisocial, and violent. While this argument is contentious, short-term and longitudinal studies have been conducted to determine the extent to which media consumption influences the choices and actions boys and men will commonly take who interact with violent media.[28] [29] [30] The next section will take up this research, examine the conclusions that have been drawn, the criticism that has followed, and the responses to these critical concerns.

THOUGHT BOX

Examine several television shows or advertisements that feature men and women, or boys and girls. Who is the target audience they are trying to attract? What normative messages about masculinity and femininity can you discern? Do you notice any stereotypical narratives in place about men or women? Do you believe there are harms emanating from these normative narratives?

Boys, Men, and Violent Media

> I'm not responsible for what some person does after they see a movie.
>
> ~ Quentin Tarantino[31]

American children between the ages of eight and 18 spend, on average, six hours and 21 minutes per day consuming entertainment media.[32] By age 18, the average young person will have viewed an estimated 200,000 acts of media violence.[33] Protagonists in American media overwhelmingly employ violence to resolve conflict than the use of any other technique.[34] The American Academy of Pediatrics reports,

> Exposure to violence in media, including television, movies, music, and video games, represents a significant risk to the health of children and adolescents. Extensive research evidence indicates that media violence can contribute to aggressive behavior, desensitization to violence, nightmares, and fear of being harmed.[35]

For years, pronouncements have been made about the negative effects associated with young people who consume violent media, but many of these claims have drawn skepticism. Some of this criticism stresses the complications of causation over correlation, while other critics argue that much of the early research was conducted under laboratory conditions yielding the results unreliable since the findings did not account for the numerous variables beyond media consumption that contribute to violent, antisocial behavior. These variables include exposure to violence in the home, at school, or in the community. Other factors include substance usage or issues involving brain chemistry and mental disorders.

Psychologist Albert Bandura, famous for **social learning theory** (discussed in chapter two), was one of the more notable researchers in the 1960s and 1970s to link consumption of violent media to aggressive behavior. Bandura constructed the now famous Bobo doll experiments, where children witnessed an adult interact aggressively with the doll by striking it with a mallet while yelling phrases "hit him" or "kick him," after which the adult would receive either a reward, a punishment, or no consequence at all.[36] Bandura found that children who witnessed the aggressive behavior aimed at the doll were more likely to behave aggressively than those children who did not witness the aggressive behavior. He also noted that boys acted more aggressively in greater numbers than did girls. Three distinct criticisms of Bandura's doll experiment followed:

1. That selection bias was present since the children used in the experiment were drawn exclusively from the nursery of Stanford University. This meant that the children used were white children of privilege so that the study did not account for potential differences in children of different backgrounds.
2. That generalizations were made about media and aggression without accounting for the differences in history of the children. As stated above, one might expect differences in outcome depending on differences of home or community environment.
3. That ambiguities existed in temporal sequencing. This means that the age of the children used were at a stage of brain development when they might have less ease discerning fantasy from reality. Older children, it was thought, may be better equipped to make this discernment, thereby yielding different results.

But research continued. In the 1980s, psychologists L. Rowell Huesmann and Leonard Eron found that children who watch a great deal of violent television programming are more prone to showing higher rates of aggression when they become teenagers.[37] Huesmann and Eron based their results on having continued to follow the lives of the children into adulthood to see whether they were eventually charged with and convicted of violent crimes. As in the case of the Bandura research, criticism immediately ensued that any number of factors could have contributed to violent behaviors in adulthood that had little or nothing to do with television viewing habits in childhood.

Iowa State University psychologist Craig A. Anderson has been compiling research for over two decades on the connections between violent media consumption and aggressive and violent behavior, focusing on two questions:

1. Is there a significant association between exposure to media violence and aggressive behavior?
2. Is this association causal? That is, can we say that violent television, video games, and other media are directly causing aggressive behavior in kids?[38]

Anderson argues that employing experimental, cross-sectional, and longitudinal studies across visual media (television, film, video games), have established a significant relationship between exposure to violent media and physically aggressive behavior.[39] Anderson defines physical aggression as "behavior that is intended to harm another person physically, such as hitting with a fist or some object."[40] Anderson argues that particularly in the case of boys,

> Each time people play violent video games, they rehearse aggressive scripts that teach and reinforce vigilance for enemies (i.e., hostile perception bias), aggressive action against

> others, expectations that others will behave aggressively, positive attitudes toward use of violence, and beliefs that violent solutions are effective and appropriate.[41]

Anderson adds that as young people become more and more immersed in violent media culture, "interactions with teachers, parents, and nonaggressive peers are likely to degenerate, whereas interactions with other 'deviant' peers may well increase."[42]

Critics have argued that the connections that have been shown to exist between exposure to violent media and physical aggression are flawed. Among the more common objections are:

- While violent media consumption has increased, violent crime rates have dropped in most U.S. cities.[43]
- The links found between violent media consumption and actual violence are based on flimsy evidence and correlational data.[44]
- Factors other than media are responsible for violence and antisocial behavior.[45]
- The frequent anecdotal report by gamers, "I play violent video games and I'm not violent."[46]

Anderson responds to some of the more conspicuous objections by noting:

- Correlational relationships are relevant. The saying, "correlation is not causation," is an over-simplification that downplays the importance of high correlational data of the kind used in astronomy and biology. Correlational data is also capable of falsification, an important requirement for scientific research.
- High levels of repeated violent media consumption have been linked by correlation to higher rates of delinquency that includes fighting at school and arrests for violent crime.
- Variables known to influence real-life aggression and violence have the same effects on laboratory measures of aggression.
- Even non-aggressive individuals have been shown to behave aggressively after short exposures to violent media.
- Even as violent crime rates have dropped in some regions of the U.S. over the past two decades, youth violence has not.[47] In addition, rates of violence can decrease for a number of reasons that have nothing to do with media usage, such as the establishment of strict three-strike laws or an improved economy.
- Anecdotal evidence cannot be used to reliably support a generalization.

Anderson acknowledges that predicting violence is not a matter of isolating one risk factor and that other factors, such as poverty, exposure to family or community violence, substance use, and mental disorders certainly contribute to overall rates of violence, but that repeated exposure to media violence must be considered part of the tapestry of elements that produce aggressive and violent behavior. Anderson states, "I think it's clear that violent media is one factor; it's not the largest factor, but it's also not the smallest."[48]

Research psychologist Paul Boxer of Rutgers University agrees with Anderson, adding that even when other factors are considered, such as academic performance, encounters with family and community violence, and emotional problems, "childhood and adolescent violent media preferences contributed significantly to the prediction of violence and general aggression."[49] For their study, Boxer and his colleagues interviewed 820 Michigan adolescents on questions of media consumption. An analysis of the data revealed that integrating "violent media exposure scores" into cumulative risk totals "added significantly to the prediction of both violence and general aggression."[50] This sort of finding does not reveal whether violent individuals are drawn to violent media or whether violent media produces violent individuals, but in either case, Boxer, Anderson, and other researchers who study the connections between media and violence conclude that exposure to violent media has a sum negative effect to children, adolescents, and adults, particularly in males.

Two meta-analyses (correlational and experimental) were also made across cultures where both American and Japanese children were tested to see whether aggressive behaviors that included hitting, shoving, and kicking increased in those children who played violent games as opposed to those who did not. In looking at the behaviors of 1,595 total children, which included reports from teachers, each group of children who played violent video games demonstrated elevated levels of physical aggression as compared to those children who did not play the violent games, and this was true even after documenting aggression levels in the children before exposure to the games.[51]

Not everyone is convinced. Christopher J. Ferguson of Texas A&M University does not believe the data proves as much as scholars like Anderson think it does.[52] Ferguson goes so far as to suggest that playing violent video games should be used in therapy to relieve stress,[53] arguing that "violent games reduce depression and hostile feelings in players through mood management."[54] Other researchers are more cautious. Psychiatrist Paul Weigle of the Natchaug Hospital who specializes in child and adolescent psychiatric medicine suggests that there is a sub-population of children who are more vulnerable to violent media, arguing, "there are multiple studies showing that boys who are less empathetic or rate themselves as aggressive prefer violent video games. They self-select."[55] Weigle's assessment helps make sense of the fact that most adolescent males who indulge in violent media do not act out violently, while a smaller proportion of these same boys engage in patterns of aggression, hostility, and violence. If one who already suffers from increased levels of aggression and violence plays violent video games and immerses himself in violent media, Weigle suggests that the combination is like pouring gasoline on an already existing fire.

In an attempt to narrow the focus of research to at-risk youths, Iowa State University psychologist Douglas Gentile who runs the Media Research Lab reports that knowing three things about a test subject is the best predictor of violence in adolescents:

- Has the subject gotten into a fight in the last year?
- Does the subject consume a lot of violent media?
- Is the subject a boy?[56]

If the answer to each of these questions is 'yes,' Gentile claims that with an 80% level of accuracy in prediction, the boy will engage in bullying behavior.[57] Gentile also points out that even if it turns out that violent media consumption and usage is not the most important trait of the three in predicting violence, it is the trait that is most easily controlled, so that it makes little sense not to moderate the media boys regularly consume.[58]

THOUGHT BOX

After reading arguments both for and against the idea that repetitive violent media consumption contributes to aggressive, sometimes violent behavior and to the desensitization of actual violence, which side do you believe made the more compelling case?

The Tough Guise: Jackson Katz on Male Representation in Media

God-damn, I'm the stuff men are made of.

~ John Wayne[59]

In 1999, antiviolence educator Jackson Katz released the film *Tough Guise: Violence, Media and the Crisis in Masculinity* and in 2013 Katz created an updated version of the film entitled, *Tough Guise 2: Violence, Manhood and American Culture.*[60] In each of these films, Katz points to the fact that the vast majority of violence in America is perpetrated by males and investigates the forensic question, why? The preponderance of scholars who research violence admit that the problem is multifaceted, and Katz agrees, but notes that the majority of those researching violence ignore, for the most part, that it is males who are perpetrating the bulk of violence in America.[61] Those who do acknowledge that boys and men are responsible for the majority of violence in America and around the world often defuse the analysis by chalking it up to biological inherencies resistant or impervious to environmental intervention. But Katz challenges this notion, in part, by evaluating the normative scripts found in media produced for boys and men as a factor alongside other environmental influences that shape the ways that boys view themselves and others. Like Kilbourne, Katz asks us to take media seriously as an influential source in the lives of boys and men, a feature of male socialization that reinforces certain identifiable narratives about what a man *should* be.

Katz is not making the argument that violent media consumption in the absence of any other risk factor causes otherwise docile males to commit acts of violence, but that a media system is in place to encourage and glamorize violence to generations of boys and men, many of whom possess other risk factors for violence. From TV shows to films to video games to music, media construct images and narratives that reinforce the notion that boys and men should meet conflict and the desire for gratification with aggression

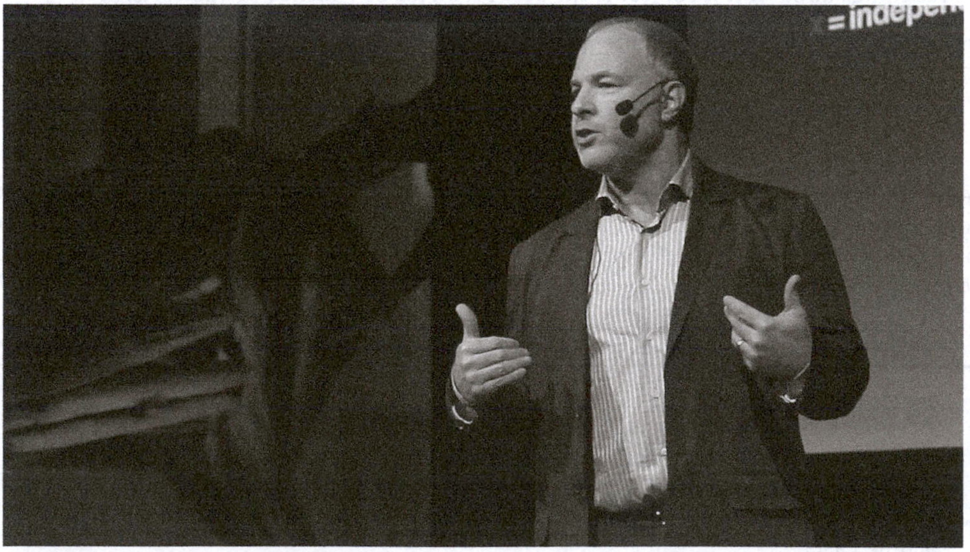

FIGURE 6.18: Antiviolence educator, Jackson Katz

FIGURE 6.19: John Wayne (1907–1979)

and violence, while encouraging these same boys and men to remain emotionally stoic under most other circumstances. Katz notes that the aggressive-stoic masculine archetype has an important media history that includes the larger than life, iconic image of John Wayne (Figure 6.19).

In a storied career that spanned six decades, Wayne personified the gun-slinging, tough guy, loner that became emblematic of mid-twentieth-century hegemonic masculinity. Wayne's many on-screen characters were decisive men of action who routinely employed violence to achieve goals, while carefully avoiding any signs of what producers of his time would view as emotional weaknesses such as looking to others for help, signs of grief, or peaceful, verbal negotiation tactics when physical force was available.

One of the more interesting things Jackson Katz uncovers about John Wayne is the extent to which Wayne's on-screen persona was an act or performance that did not correspond neatly with his life away from the camera. His real life and reel life, one might say, were fairly incongruent. John Wayne's real name was Marion Morrison, a name Fox Studio executive Raoul Walsh believed to be too feminine for the masculine persona he wished to construct, and so 'John Wayne' was born.[62] Biographer Scott Eyman notes that Wayne himself, in discussing his characterization of the gun-toting defender of what he believed to be unquestionable American values, claimed that his on-screen persona was a construction of "the kind of man I'd like to have been."[63]

On camera, Wayne was a larger-than-life gun-fighting, tough guy who rode broncin' bucks into town to confront an assortment of villains, while in reality, son Michael Wayne reveals that his father did not particularly like horses and rode them for film roles only when necessary.[64] Off camera, Wayne was a formidable chess-player and fan

FIGURE 6.20: John Wayne in *The Longest Day*

of Shakespeare who favored tailored suits over jeans and cowboy boots. Wayne was also famous for his depiction of the rough and fearless soldier or military commander who heroically led troops to victory against the odds, while in reality, Wayne never served in the military even though many of his acting colleagues, including Henry Fonda (who won the Bronze Star) and Jimmy Stewart (who flew a B-24 into Nazi-occupied Europe, twice received the Distinguished Flying Cross, and rose from the rank of private to colonel in four years of service) returned to their acting careers as war heroes. Wayne suffered from some physical ailments that initially prevented him from military service, but was reclassified 1-A (draft eligible) by the U.S. military in 1944.[65] Wayne, however, remained in Hollywood to pursue his acting career.

The point Katz is making is that John "The Duke" Wayne was a media construction, sold to an audience that valued no-nonsense, tough-talking, gun-blazing men as the archetype for American masculinity. Increasingly, as films were viewed as influential and motivating sources for a host of ends, they were used as propaganda tools to recruit men into the military and to sell audiences on purchasing an assortment of products touted by bankable, matinee stars.[66] To these ends, image was everything. At the end of World War II and with the rise of the Soviet Union, John Wayne could now be called upon to play U.S. House Un-American Activities Committee investigator "Big Jim McLain" who breaks up a ring of Communist Party organizers who are up to no good.[67] Hollywood producers were no longer simply selling entertainment; they were crafting and marketing image, in this case a masculine image, to American audiences that viewed actors like Wayne as templates for manhood and role models for male youth.

But Katz notes that Wayne's hypermasculine image was tame by comparison to the tough-guy archetypes looming on the Hollywood horizon. Filmmakers did not take long to determine that if violence sells, hyper-violence will sell even better. Enter Clint Eastwood as Dirty Harry.

Eastwood's "Dirty Harry" was a cynical, angry, no nonsense man of few words who "did not play by the rules," a theme that would be replicated many times over by male action stars for decades to come. While other officers in Harry Callahan's fictional San Francisco police unit worried about civil rights or seeking negotiated resolutions to tense situations, Harry let his 44-caliber Smith and Wesson do the talking. While other men talked, Harry acted. The "silent man of action" paradigm has also been lionized by conservative pundits on television talk shows as representing the way men *should* be, while arguing that feminism has created *soft, feminine* men who are afraid to take action.[68] Conservative pundits have essentially pointed to fiction to describe what should

FIGURE 6.21: Clint Eastwood as "Dirty Harry," 1971, 1973, 1976, 1983, 1988

be reflected in reality, a view of manhood as tough, silent, unemotional (other than anger), able to physically intimidate and dominate others, and perpetually ready to wield violence.

However, even the silent, deadly Harry Callahan was not the pinnacle of tough-guy machismo on the silver screen. A cascade of male action stars would rise in the 1980s that challenged Dirty Harry's throne of tough, silent, deadly man of action. One of the more prominent action stars was Arnold Schwarzenegger, who, in *The Terminator* series of films, became a cyborg killing machine without rival.

Schwarzenegger's terminating cyborg reduced talking points to comic-book styled slogans before killing someone or as dramatic threats of future violence. The terminator's "I'll be back" or "hasta la vista, baby" became pop cultural memes that reinforced the point that men need little in the way of words to be respected men of action. The terminating automaton didn't think, feel, consider, reflect, negotiate, discuss, consult, debate, or compromise. Arnold's terminator killed, period.

At around the same time, Al Pacino starred in one of the most iconic films for masculine violence in the history of filmmaking, a remake of the 1932 classic about the rise and fall of a gangster, a film that continues to be held by many young men as the most influential film of all time, *Scarface* (Figure 6.22).

Pacino's depiction of Cuban-born gangster Tony Montana, nicknamed 'Scarface,' has become perhaps the most treasured character in motion picture history to young men who view and praise him as the toughest, most ruthless figure in film history. In almost idolatrous terms, rapper Snoop Dogg states of *Scarface*, "It's one of the most important movies of all time ... this cat is just like me."[69] Music entrepreneur and record executive Kevin Liles states, "Everybody could relate to the struggle that Tony went through and when you do it that way, you always end up in jail or dead."[70] The life-lesson "violence begets violence" may have resonated with some, but violence as a vehicle for upward mobility has been one of the more prominent take-away points from *Scarface* for many young men who view life on the streets as a matter of, as rapper 50 cent's 2003 release put it, "Get Rich or Die Tryin'." As with most action films that feature a male protagonist, Montana's violence, including murder, is a routine activity portrayed as an unemotional necessity in the service of dealing with conflict, or simply as a means to get what you want.

FIGURE 6.22: Al Pacino as "Scarface" 1983

UPPING THE ANTE

Antiviolence educator Jackson Katz exposes a trend in media, and in this case film media, to construct more hyper-masculine, violent imagery over the past several decades. The following collage of film clips documents what Katz terms a "ratcheting up" of violent masculinity from the days of Humphrey Bogart's depiction of nightclub owner Rick Blaine in 1942's *Casablanca* to John Wayne's Rooster Cogburn to Clint Eastwood's Dirty Harry to Sylvester Stallone's John Rambo to Arnold Schwarzenegger's Terminator as a robotic killing machine:

FIGURE 6.23:

FIGURE 6.24:

FIGURE 6.25:

Continued

FIGURE 6.26:

What it means to be a tough, male lead in action-adventure motion pictures has gone from what many would consider to be tepid characterizations of men who use violence to serve a greater good in films of the early to middle twentieth century to more contemporary sociopathic automatons and vicious killers for whom torture and violence are a way of life.

FIGURE 6.27:

Today, it is probably impossible to understand the relationship between violent media and boys and men without also considering the work of filmmaker Quentin Tarantino. For fans of violent, action films, few filmmakers can compete with Tarantino's graphic depictions of blood, torture, and mayhem. Tarantino's films have received an enormous amount of attention from film scholars who debate his use of sadistic violence, the specter of racism, and whether his depiction of women is sexist. Also notable is his love for revenge as the central motivation for violent reprisal, which serves as an attempt to bring moral justification into what would otherwise be psychopathic mayhem. It is beyond debate that Tarantino's films are wildly popular and critically acclaimed, but these are also films overwhelmingly embraced by men even if it is true that according to some of his admirers, Tarantino's female characters are often strong women placed at the center of the story.[71]

Media analyst Rich Jepson notes that men have been attracted to violent films, including films featuring organized crime figures, for decades.[72] The specter of power and control has been a particularly successful combination in drawing men to TV shows such as *The Sopranos* or films such as Martin Scorsese's epic feature, *Goodfellas*. Protagonists in films of this genre are often men who command respect from other men, while exuding sexual appeal to women. Jepson explains that men desire these traits in their own lives so that characters such as Tony Soprano, Tony Montoya, Don Corleone, and in Tarantino films an assortment of male characters who command respect and fear, are templates of masculinity. When these characters also command the sexual attention of women, either through authentic sensual attraction or simply as purchased sexual commodities, the allure these characters have to many men could not be higher.

However, Tarantino rejects the notion that his films have any effect on rates of real-life violence, pointing instead to the societal problems of mental illness and a lack of gun control.[73] Yet, Tarantino also insists that violence is the best form of cinematic entertainment, stating, "I'm a big fan of action and violence in cinema," continuing, "That's why Thomas Edison created the motion picture camera—because violence is so good."[74] Tarantino believes that fantasy and reality are utterly separate realms such that mediated violence has no effect on the actions and thinking of actual boys and men. In 11 total releases, Tarantino films have a collective box office draw of just under $1,500,000,000,[75] forcefully making the point that whether or not violence in cinema is good, it is clearly profitable.

Jackson Katz notes that it is a common ploy for filmmakers and media producers to point to gun lobbies and mental health problems as the main factors that create societal violence, while gun lobbies point to violent entertainment as the problem, without either of them acknowledging that violence is an issue of masculinity. Katz notes that women also have access to guns and suffer from mental illness at roughly the same rate as men, but commit far less violence.[76] For Katz, men's violence is not an either–or issue of gun access versus media violence or mental health versus media violence, but instead a pervasive problem bound up in the ways that men are socialized to think of themselves as men. Media, which saturate the male view with glorified acts of gun violence, coupled with the proliferation of guns in America, work together to construct one of the more visible normative scripts for navigating masculinity, while contributing to men's ideas that hostility, aggression, and violence are acceptable, and even preferable, ways to deal with conflict.

THOUGHT BOX

Quentin Tarantino marches out a defense of violent media that is very common: fictional media is fantasy, not reality. Boys and men do not act out violently because of the media they consume. Other factors create violence. Many media critics disagree, as seen in the material covered in this chapter. Do you think Tarantino is correct or is he neglecting the findings of contrary research?

Katz's "tough guise" does not apply only to young men. Contemporary action stars include Vin Diesel, Dwayne (The Rock) Johnson, and Jason Statham, but older actors such as Bruce Willis, Sylvester Stallone, Will Smith, Tom Cruise, Harrison Ford, Nicolas Cage, Liam Neeson, Robert Downey Jr., Denzel Washington and other bankable action-film stars attempt to hold on to their youth through accepting films roles that depict men of exceptional physical strength who possess the ability to negotiate violence, often coupled with a love interest who is more than 20 years younger, which no doubt appeals to older men in society who struggle with aging and the feeling that they are becoming irrelevant and impotent.

One of the most lucrative series in contemporary action film history has been the *Fast & Furious* franchise, which features another key aspect of the *tough guise*: dangerous risk-taking behaviors. Starring Vin Diesel and featuring high-action, illegal street racing, the *Fast & Furious* films have earned over $2.5 billion,[77] garnering millions of world-wide fans, and helped escalate dangerous street racing on the streets of America.[78] One of the stars of *Fast & Furious*, Paul Walker, actually died while driving with fellow race-car enthusiast Roger Rodas in a speed-related accident in Los Angeles that has been investigated as involving a street race with another vehicle.[79] An *International Business Report* article reports:

THE BECHDEL TEST

Many observe that the film industry in Hollywood is an industry dominated by men at the executive levels of power.[1] [2] Predictably, critics argue, films reflect this male dominance by possessing male protagonists in the vast majority of film releases each year. Additionally, roles for women are notably sparse or one-dimensional in nature.[3] The stereotype of women as sexual seductresses, the trope of eyeglasses obscuring a woman's "true beauty," the directive of women looking for love and in need of protection, the convention of black women as having "attitude," the Latina as "exotic, hypersexual, and seductive,"[4] and then, conversely, older women as asexual, matronly, domestic, and often bad-tempered when in positions

Continued

of authority, led American cartoonist Alison Bechdel to create a test that could be used to judge gender inequality in films and other media.[5] The test assesses fictional media on the basis of whether there are at least two women in a scene who talk to one another about a subject other than a man or love. Sometimes an addition to the test requires that the female characters have names. When judged by these criteria, only about half of all films produced pass the test. According to NPR reporter Neda Ulaby, the test continues to resonate because, "it articulates something often missing in popular culture: not the number of women we see on screen, but the depth of their stories, and the range of their concerns."[6] Many have pointed out that a film may pass the test and still possess sexist content. Perhaps the most visible star in Hollywood who has addressed the ongoing problem of quality roles for women in Hollywood is Academy-Award winning actor Geena Davis, whose *Geena Davis Institute on Gender in Media* researches, educates, and advocates for creating gender equality in media, including media content created for children.[7]

1 http://abcnews.go.com/US/men-dominate-film-industry-study/story?id=13439590.
2 http://www.nytimes.com/2014/12/28/movies/in-hollywood-its-a-mens-mens-mens-world.html?_r=0.
3 http://www.huffingtonpost.com/2014/12/16/snl-hollywood-female-character_n_6333530.html.
4 http://thestripesblog.com/2014/02/12/the-misrepresented-and-hypersexualized-latina/.
5 https://en.wikipedia.org/wiki/Bechdel_test.
6 Ibid.
7 http://seejane.org/.

> The National Highway Traffic Safety Administration (NHTSA) said that in the year following the release of the first Fast & Furious film, street-racing fatalities skyrocketed. At least 135 people died in accidents from possible races, according to HHTSA—almost twice as many as the year before.[80]

But as Jackson Katz argues, media reports often de-gender the language when reporting a story that involves violence, particularly youth violence, and the same is true with street-racing fatalities. The use of terms such as 'people' or 'youth' disguises the gendered nature of these dangerous activities. The fact is that the overwhelming number of street racing arrests, injuries, and fatalities involve young men.[81] [82] Once again, cultivation theory predicts that men who are interested in street racing will be drawn to films like *Fast & Furious*, which glamorize street racing and stoke interest and desire in those same men. Risk-taking has long been a sizable part of masculine socialization, but is not limited to more obvious examples such as street-racing. In the next section, we will investigate how risk-taking, along with sexist and homophobic anecdotes, are a big part of the comedy men consume.

Guy Humor? Boys, Men, and Comedy

If no meant no, then every man would die a virgin.

~ Comedian, Daniel Tosh

Risk-taking misadventures by boys and young men were reported in the wake of the success of the 2000–2002, MTV series *Jackass* and subsequent films based on the TV show. The show was billed as a comedy featuring the exploits of young, white men who would engage in dignity-defying and often dangerous stunts to get laughs. Often dismissed as being "guy humor," stunts included jumping off of a building holding only an umbrella, stuffing raw chicken into their underwear (wearing only underwear) and then walking a tightrope over a pond filled with alligators, or placing a toy truck inside the rectum of one of the young men before going to medical facilities to get x-rayed to film the technician's reaction. It did not take long for boys and young men to begin emulating the pranks of the *Jackass* crew, resulting in broken bones, hospital trips, and eventually, death.[83]

Even though the cast of *Jackass* did not perform the traditional *tough guise* found in male stars of violent actions films, the tough guise was present in the form of a dare: *are you crazy enough to do this?* It became a testing ground for manhood to be willing to do things either dangerous or humiliating. In his article, "Better to die than cry: A longitudinal and constructionist study of masculinity and the health risk behavior of young American men," psychologist William Courtenay reports that in a survey of 1,880 males ages 15–19, it was found that the more traditional their views about masculinity and manhood, the more likely they were to engage in risk-taking behavior.[84] Courtenay notes that the findings of this research supports,

> the feminist and constructionist theory of men's health proposed in the study ... that when men are denied access to the resources necessary for constructing normative or hegemonic masculinity, they must seek other accessible resources, such as traditional beliefs or health risk behaviors, in order to validate their masculinity.[85]

Many boys and young men are not part of a socially favored male hierarchy, yet long for the validation that comes from being a popular athlete, man of wealth, or young man who receives validation through gang affiliation or being attractive to women. For these non-alpha boys and men, risk-taking in the form of being willing to do things others would consider crazy becomes the avenue for showing other boys and men that they are tough.

Since certain comedies are aimed mainly at young, male audiences through the conscious construction of higher rates of vulgarity, risk-taking, humiliation, sexual innuendo, sarcasm, and demonstrable cynicism, many have wondered whether it is fair to say that there exists "guy humor" that is detectably distinguishable from humor enjoyed by most women, and, if so, why these forms of comedy appeal to males. Comedian Adam Carolla has created a career through the use of sexist jokes, and goes further than most by claiming that not only is there "guy humor," but that "guy humor" is funnier than "girl humor":

> The reason why you know more funny dudes than funny chicks is that dudes are funnier than chicks. If my daughter has a mediocre sense of humor, I'll tell her, "Be a staff writer for a sitcom. They'll have to hire you and you don't have to produce that much."[86]

Carolla's condescending assessment of women assumes that because certain forms of comedy are funny to him or funny to many men, they are by nature funnier than comedy that appeals to girls and women. Like Carolla, comedy legend Jerry Lewis stated in 1998 that he did not find women to be particularly funny,[87] and the late author, polemicist Christopher Hitchens echoed similar sentiments in 2007.[88] Comedian Tina Fey, creator of the syndicated comedy *Thirty Rock* responded to the view that women aren't funny by stating, "It is an impressively arrogant move to conclude that just because you don't like something, it is empirically not good."[89]

The success of the *Jackass* franchise with boys and young men was coupled by the launch of TV shows such as *Family Guy* and big-screen box-office hits like *The Hangover* trilogy, which feature crude and often sexist, homophobic humor as the antithesis of romantic comedies often labeled "chick-flicks." Targeting adolescent males, *Family Guy* is an animated show created by media jack-of-all-trades Seth MacFarlane as a crude imitation of the long-running Fox hit *The Simpsons*. MacFarlane's *Family Guy* stars the Griffin family featuring married couple Peter and Lois, their three children Meg, Chris, and Stewie, dog Brian, and a womanizing sex-predator in the character of "Quagmire," who casually introduces rape jokes, lewd sexual content, homophobic and transphobic badinage, and jokes about domestic violence.[90 91]

In a partial list of *Family Guy* rape jokes, a waiter asks Quagmire if he would like his usual drink with a roofie for his date. In episode 21 of season 2, Quagmire attempts to rape a woman and is immune to the mace she sprays in his eyes, as a joke implying that he is a serial rapist. In episode 7 of season 4, Quagmire attempts to drag character Brooke's body off of the set and stops only when he realizes he is being filmed. In episode 5 of season 9, Quagmire is seen dragging away an unconscious woman after she had been defeated in a boxing match.[92]

Macfarlane's defense of rape jokes is the ploy that the audience is not laughing at rape or rapists, but at the character's stupidity,[93] assuming that his young male audience knows at whom and at what they are supposed to be laughing. MacFarlane's critics argue that he irresponsibly introduces rape jokes that perpetuate rape culture by minimizing violent sexual assault in comedic terms to a largely young, male audience at a time when

FIGURE 6.28: Scene from *Family Guy* with character Quagmire

sexual assault is rampant enough within the targeted age demographic of the show, high school and college for President Obama to call for a White House task force to investigate it, and in light of the fact that the vast majority of sexual crime is committed by boys and men.[94 95]

On the heels of the success of *Family* Guy, cable TV shows with similar content infiltrated youth media with shows such as Comedy Central's *Tosh.0* featuring middle-aged, white, male, presumably heterosexual, comedian Daniel Tosh, whose sexist, homophobic-homoerotic-transphobic, rape-joke-laden, racist brand of humor targets adolescent boys and college-aged young men. Tosh has become an icon in male-youth culture and among college fraternity men for his controversial humor that is often aimed at sexual activities, women, rape, homosexuals, transgender people, people with disabilities, people of color, and people from various cultures.

Like *Family Guy*, Tosh taps into a young, mainly white, heterosexual, male audience that views humor aimed at topics like rape as "politically incorrect," an expression that attempts to both vindicate fans of Tosh, while condemning critics by assuming that they don't understand comedy or are simply lacking a healthy sense of humor. It is this connection to being outside of the mainstream and into "dangerous, politically-incorrect" subject matters where women, people of color, gay people, and people with disabilities are mocked that attracts many young males. Defenders of Tosh's style of humor argue that "he zings everyone" so that no particular group is targeted and that he is self-deprecating so that even he is not immune from attack.[96]

In 2012, in a well-publicized rant at a comedy club, Daniel Tosh responded to a female patron who criticized his use of rape jokes by stating, as recounted by the female patron, "Wouldn't it be funny if that girl got raped by like 5 guys right now? Like right now? What if a bunch of guys just raped her?"[97 98] Long-time comedian Gilbert Gottfried defended Tosh's "edgy jokes" by instructing critics not to listen if they are offended,[99] while critics note that the narratives that are part of a comedian's material seep into popular culture so that "not listening" does not mean that one is immune from the behaviors of those who are listening.

THOUGHT BOX

Famed comedian George Carlin once stated, "I think it's the duty of the comedian to find out where the line is drawn and cross it deliberately."[1] What do you think? Do you agree? Are there lines that should not be crossed in comedy? What about rape jokes? What would you say to someone who claimed, "It's just a joke; don't take it so seriously!"

1 www.goodreads.com/quotes/133108-i-think-it-s-the-duty-of-the-comedian-to-find.

Today, one of the most successful comedians in the comedy business is Kevin Hart. About skin color, Hart mused, "Light-skinned women usually have better credit than a dark-skinned woman ... Broke ass dark hoes ... Lol."[100] When challenged, Hart asked dark-skinned women to stop being so sensitive and to remember that he is a comedian. The "it's just a joke" excuse has been the mantra of most comedians when challenged about content that is racist, sexist, homophobic, or negatively aimed at members of any traditionally oppressed group. Critics respond that comedy is tricky, because sarcasm is a tool used often by bullies, while satire has also been used effectively as a tool for social and political commentary. But since men have historically enjoyed power over women, the concern is that comedy can be used as a weapon to deride women, while maintaining male privilege. This is particularly true of rape jokes. Comedian Sarah Silverman satirically noted in a comedy sketch the problems with rape jokes:

> Needless to say, rape, the most heinous crime imaginable. Seems it's a comic's dream, though. ... Who's going to complain about a rape joke? Rape victims? They don't even report rape. That's right, let's take them down a notch! They've had it too good for too long, am I right?[101]

Some have criticized Sarah Silverman for employing what they view as "guy humor" with higher levels of vulgarity,[102] but others praise Silverman for using comedy as a vehicle for shedding light on a problem within comedy that aims its jokes at those who are oppressed or disadvantaged.[103]

Often walking a thin line, but offering a very different version of male comedy, comedian Louis C.K. has carved out a self-deprecating niche in comedy, while avoiding clichéd sexist jokes. Questioning why women continue to go out with men, he wonders:

> How do women still go out with guys when you consider the fact that there is no greater threat to women than men? Globally and historically, we're the number one cause of injury and mayhem to women. You know what our number one threat is? Heart disease![104]

But this is the exception to the rule. A number of high-profile, contemporary, male comedians continue to offer up sexist and often vulgarly sexist jokes to get laughs:[105]

- *Give that pussy up and stop this bullshit*

  ~ Tracy Morgan
- *Now they fine CBS $1 million for Janet Jackson's nipple. Think what they could get for Hillary Clinton's cunt.*

  ~ Bill Maher
- *There are a lot less female comics who are authentic. I see a lot of female comics who to please an audience will act like men.*

  ~ Eddie Brill
- *My girlfriend bought a cook book the other day called 'Cheap and easy vegetarian cooking.' Which is perfect for her, because not only is she vegetarian, she is cheap and easy.*

  ~Jimmy Carr
- *The closest I came to making love to a black woman was I masturbated to a picture of Aunt Jemima on a pancake box.*

  ~ Howard Stern

THOUGHT BOX

Is it worse when male comedians use sexist material aimed at women, rather than when women make fun of men? Does the power dynamic between men and women matter to the humor of the joke? Comedian Louis C.K. claimed on *The Daily Show* that comedians and feminists are 'natural enemies' because "stereotypically speaking, feminists can't take a joke and comedians can't take criticism."[1] (He later stated that due to criticism he received about this quote, he has since reconsidered his view on this.) What do you think?

1 www.thedailybeast.com/articles/2012/07/18/daniel-tosh-rape-joke-are-comedy-and-feminism-enemies.html.

Boys, Men, and Video Game Culture

In a 2006 study of college-aged gamers, it was found that although women are now playing video games at higher rates than ever before, men were twice as likely to admit that gaming occupied two or more hours a day of their time and that the accumulated time playing games interrupted both sleep and class preparation.[106] The appeal video games have on youth culture, and particularly teen boys and young men, cannot be overestimated. According to Forbes Magazine, Grand Theft Auto 5 by itself has garnered just under $2 billion in sales worldwide.[107] Yet, video games like Grand Theft Auto have come under a great deal of scrutiny. Many scholars who have examined and evaluated contemporary video games note that traditional and exaggerated binary gender roles are common for the avatars that players use when playing, or as characters embedded in the game. Male avatars are typically muscular and violent, while female avatars are hypersexual and compliant. In one study, it was determined that male characters in games are four times more likely to be portrayed on the covers of M-rated games and that those female characters who are depicted on covers are overwhelmingly cast in sexually provocative roles.[108] The representation of female characters in video games has remained at a fairly constant rate of 15%,[109] so that men are greatly overrepresented. More importantly, in a survey of teen gamers, both boys and girls who play M-rated games are much more likely to view men as aggressive and women as sexual in real life.[110] In further surveys of male gamers, it was found that "long-term exposure to video game violence is correlated with greater tolerance of sexual harassment and greater rape myth acceptance."[111]

In a 2012 study, researchers confirmed that male gamers, but not female gamers, were much more likely to accept rape-myth narratives.[112] **Rape myth**[113] includes the view that rape occurs much less frequently than reported by women or by statistical gathering agencies such as the U.S. Department of Justice. Rape myth advocates also argue that women often falsely accuse men of rape as a means of retaliation when women are angry. They claim that consensual sex will often be reported as non-consensual sex if a woman believes that the man is not interested in a romantic relationship with her. Thus, again,

FIGURE 6.29: Grand Theft Auto V characters

rape myth advocates believe that rape is used as a tool by vindictive women to get even with men they feel have wronged them in some way.

Another aspect of the rape myth narrative is the view that when it comes to sex, women like it rough. Social psychologist Karen E. Dill notes that this particular feature is a theme in games like Grand Theft Auto, where gamers, through their avatar, can walk up to a woman who is depicted as a prostitute, physically assault her, and then hear from the female character, "I like it rough."[114] The mixture of sex and violence has been one of the more concerning aspects of violent video games for those media critics who examine them. In a 2010 study, researchers M.Z. Yao, Chad Mahood, and Daniel Linz investigated the link between playing violent video games with sexualized themes and actual inappropriate sexual behavior from college-aged men.[115] The men in the study who play sexually-themed, violent video games self-reported that they often behave inappropriately toward women in social settings to the point of crossing the line into sexual harassment.[116]

In 2012, after launching her Kickstarter campaign for *Tropes versus Women in Video Games* video series, media critic Anita Sarkeesian was verbally attacked and threatened with rape and murder for criticizing the ways that women are depicted in games like Grand Theft Auto. Rage-filled gamers created a game entitled "Beat Up Anita Sarkeesian," where players could inflict virtual physical assault to her image.[117] Others sent Sarkeesian illustrations of sexual assault being perpetrated to her. In an interview with *Mother Jones*, Sarkeesian responded,

> Some male gamers with a deep sense of entitlement are terrified of change. They believe games should continue to cater exclusively to young heterosexual men with ever more extreme virtual power fantasies. So this group is violently resisting any movement in the direction of a more inclusive gaming space.[118]

The threats became so intense that Sarkeesian cancelled a speaking appearance she was scheduled to make at Utah State University over concern about her personal safety.[119]

FIGURE 6.30: Media analyst, Anita Sarkeesian

Many have decried the vulgar, sexist, and violent comments found in the virtual world in general, but the comments found in gaming circles have been found to be particularly misogynistic. Concordia University professor Mia Consalvo notes that

> Each event taken in isolation is troubling enough, but chaining them together into a timeline demonstrates how the individual links are not actually isolated incidents at all but illustrate a pattern of a misogynistic gamer culture and patriarchal privilege attempting to (re)assert its position.[120]

Writer Leigh Alexander agrees, adding,

> Game websites with huge community hubs whose fans are often associated with blunt Twitter hate mobs sort of shrug [and] say things like 'we delete the really bad stuff, what else can we do' and 'those people don't represent our community' – but actually, that's what your community is known for.[121]

Mixing pre-existing misogyny with the safety of anonymity found in virtual comment spaces, gamer culture is free to mass-produce hatred, bigotry, and violent threats to anyone who appears to question the sanctity of their masculine domain.

Veteran game developer Ralph Koster opines that some of the rage that emits from male gamers is due to their sense of marginalization from the rest of society so that they feel exhilarated when they can get people to pay attention to them.[122] By being outrageous and making claims that are socially unacceptable, gamers are able to receive a heightened sense of power that they never receive in real life. Erasmus University professor Jeroen Jansz argues that adolescent boys are attracted to the autonomy violent video games provide to them at a time in their lives when teen boys are constructing an identity. The safety of the gaming environment allows boys to explore emotions that are unsuitable for civilized society.[123] If autonomy is the attraction, it would make sense that many male gamers feel threatened by feminist critiques of their hallowed, sexist space. For boys and young men, violent and sexist video games are the equivalent of a virtual man-cave, where they can indulge their taboo, misogynistic sides with impunity, and heaven help anyone who challenges their male privilege.

THOUGHT BOX

Why do you think virtual comment spaces are such hostile environments toward women, and particularly feminists?

To see whether there is a connection between playing violent video games and actual aggression in boys, a number of empirical studies have been conducted. In one of the more cited studies, groups of boys were split into two groups; one group played violent video games, while the other group played non-violent video games. The researchers wanted to see how the boys would behave during free-play time between exposures to gaming.[124] Researchers reported that those boys who played violent video games exhibited significantly more object-aggression and interpersonal aggression than did the boys who played non-violent games.[125] These results were confirmed by sociologist Craig A. Anderson in experimental studies that showed a connection between violent video game play and aggressive behavior coupled with a decrease in "helpful behavior" and overall empathy for others.[126] [127] In fact, researchers have also found that the more time boys invest in playing violent video games, the higher the predictive success of aggressive behavior.[128] There have, however, been other studies that purport to show that a causal or correlative link has not been established between violent video game play and aggressive or violent behavior.[129] Villanova University professor Patrick Markey notes that behavioral scientists are often called upon to offer evidence that violent video game play is connected to violence in the wake of a school shooting or some other similar violent episode involving a young, male perpetrator.[130] But Markey warns that scientists, like himself, need to be cautious about reporting results of video game studies that do not have sound, empirical support, since pinning violence to video game play may undermine efforts to discover other, more direct causes of violence.[131] Critics of naysayers like Markey make the point that studies which purport to disconnect violent video game play to aggressive behaviors often show only that a positive correlation between violent video game play and violent assault and homicide cannot be made, but that this is a far cry from discrediting links between violent video game play and aggressive or antisocial behaviors.

In related studies, researchers were able to link what they termed "pathological gaming" to lower social competence, higher rates of impulsivity, lower school performance, and higher rates of depression, particularly in adolescent boys.[132] Other studies have warned of the potential for video game addiction in some adolescent boys,[133] although another study tied excessive game play to other underlying personality problems rather than to alleged inherent addictive properties of games.[134] Still, much of the research into violent video game play, especially in boys, has found correlative links between repeated violent game play and a range of negative attitudes and behaviors. All sides agree that much more research needs to be done, since interactive gaming along with the graphic realism of the associated violence is a new and emerging phenomenon in the lives of boys and young men.

Summary

Cultivation theory argues that people will begin to view reality through a tainted media lens if they immerse themselves in media. But since media are diverse, the reality warp will conform to the types of media one regularly and repeatedly consumes. The ramification to men and norms of masculinity is that the media men consume may have an important impact on the way men view themselves. It may also taint the way men view women. It may make some men feel powerful and other men feel weak. It may influence men to draw normative conclusions about masculinity and femininity. Yet, this chapter only scratches the surface of media representation of men and masculinity and since media have become so rich and diverse, the next chapter will continue to take up advertising aimed at men, media as it relates to gay and trans masculinity, depictions of men of color, the so-called 'metrosexual' version of masculinity, and the conservative backlash that has formed in response to what is believed to be a more feminized masculinity in media. The chapter ends with an examination of media literacy, which supporters believe is needed in children's and adolescents' lives to help them become more responsible, critical consumers of media.

Notes

1 http://virgil.org/dswo/courses/novel/wilde-lying.pdf.

2 "A Birth of a Nation essays." Megaessays.com.

3 http://jfredmacdonald.com/bawtv/bawtv13.htm.
4 Dyson, Michael Eric, *Is Cosby Right? Or has the Black Middle Class Lost Its Mind?* (Basic Civitas Books, 2005).
5 Ibid.
6 http://sitemaker.umich.edu/psy457_tizzle/the_model_minority.
7 http://townhall.com/tipsheet/cortneyo-brien/2014/03/01/white-men-everyone-else-womens-media-centers-sexist-report-n1801539.
8 www.bunchecenter.ucla.edu/wp-content/uploads/2015/02/2015-Hollywood-Diversity-Report-2–25–15.pdf.
9 Ibid.
10 Ibid.
11 www.dailymail.co.uk/news/article-2563561/Hollywood-place-white-men-New-study-finds-women-minorities-dramatically-underrepresented-films-television.html.
12 http://dailycaller.com/2016/01/22/academy-struggles-to-find-big-name-black-presents-ahead-of-oscars/.
13 www.nytimes.com/2016/02/21/movies/what-does-the-academy-value-in-a-black-performance.html?smid=tw-share.
14 Ibid.
15 Ibid.
16 Ibid.
17 Ibid.
18 http://madamenoire.com/615551/race-movie-jesse-owens/.
19 Baker, Barbara L., "Sexism in media," www.academia.edu/1667813/Sexism_in_Media.
20 Gerbner, George, "Cultivation theory," in *A First Look at Communication Theory*, ed. E. Griffin, 8th edition (McGraw Hill, 2012), pp. 366–377.
21 Ibid.
22 Gerbner, G., Gross, L., Morgan, M., and Signorielli, N., "Growing up with television: The cultivation perspective," in M. Morgan, ed. *Against the Mainstream: The Selected Works of George Gerbner* (Peter Lang, 2002), pp. 193–213.
23 www.businessweek.com/stories/2001-12-23/television-for-women-no-ones-laughing-now.
24 http://latimesblogs.latimes.com/showtracker/2010/01/jersey-shore-finale-breaks-ratings-records-for-mtv.html.
25 www.brainyquote.com/quotes/authors/n/noam_chomsky_3.html.
26 Kilbourne, Jean, "Beauty … and the beast of advertising," Center for Media Literacy, www.medialit.org/reading-room/beautyand-beast-advertising.
27 Kilbourne, Jean. *Killing Us Softly 4: Advertising's Image of Women* (Media Education Foundation, 2010).
28 www.aacap.org/aacap/Medical_Students_and_Residents/Mentorship_Matters/DevelopMentor/The_Impact_of_Media_Violence_on_Children_and_Adolescents_Opportunities_for_Clinical_Interventions.aspx.
29 www.princeton.edu/futureofchildren/publications/journals/article/index.xml?journalid=32&articleid=60§ionid=291.
30 www.apa.org/action/resources/research-in-action/protect.aspx.
31 www.thewire.com/entertainment/2013/01/quentin-tarantino-violence-quotes/60900/.
32 Roberts, D.F., Foehr, U.G., and Rideout, V., *Generation M: Media in the Lives of 8–18 Year-Olds* (Henry J. Kaiser Family Foundation, 2005).
33 Huston, A.C., Donnerstein, E., Fairchild, H,, et al., *Big World, Small Screen: The Role of Television in American Society* (University of Nebraska Press, 1992).
34 Webb, T., Jenkins, L., Browne, N., Afifi, A.A., Kraus, J., "Violent entertainment pitched to adolescents: An analysis of PG-13 films," *Pediatrics* 119, 6 (2007).
35 American Academy of Pediatrics, "Media violence," Council on Communications and Media,2001,http://pediatrics.aappublications.org/content/124/5/1495.full#ref-24.
36 Bandura, A. "Influence of models' reinforcement contingencies on the acquisition of imitative responses," *Journal of Personality and Social Psychology* 1, 6 (1965), pp. 589–595.
37 Huesmann, L.R. and Eron, L.D. *Television and the Aggressive Child: A Cross-National Comparison* (Erlbaum, 1986).
38 Anderson,C.A.,Berkowitz,L.,Donnerstein,E., Huesmann, L.R., Johnson, J., Linz, D., Malamuth, N., and Wartella, E., "The influence of media violence on youth." *Psychological Science in the Public Interest*, 4 (2003), pp. 81–110.
39 www.psychology.iastate.edu/faculty/caa/Video_Game_FAQs.html.
40 Ibid.
41 Anderson, Craig A. and Dill, Karen E., "Video games and aggressive thoughts, feelings, and behavior in the laboratory and in life," *Journal of Personality and Social Psychology* 78, 4 (2000), pp. 772–790.

42 Ibid.
43 http://mediacoalition.org/only-a-game/.
44 http://mediasmarts.ca/violence/what-do-we-know-about-media-violence.
45 Ibid.
46 www.greatschools.org/students/media-kids/1567-violent-media-and-aggressive-kids.gs.
47 Anderson, Craig A., "Violent video games: Myths, facts, and unanswered questions," American Psychological Association, 2003. www.apa.org/science/about/psa/2003/10/anderson.aspx.
48 *New York Times*, February 11, 2013. www.nytimes.com/2013/02/12/science/studying-the-effects-of-playing-violent-video-games.html?_r=0.
49 http://psychcentral.com/news/2008/11/20/media-violence-linked-to-aggression/3379.html.
50 Ibid.
51 www.cnn.com/2008/HEALTH/family/11/03/healthmag.violent.video.kids/.
52 www.nytimes.com/2013/02/12/science/studying-the-effects-of-playing-violent-video-games.html?_r=0.
53 http://kristenjtsetsi.com/2013/05/16/video-games-violence/.
54 Ibid.
55 Ibid.
56 www.news.iastate.edu/news/2012/07/09/bullying.
57 Ibid.
58 Ibid.
59 http://johnwayne.com/life-legacy/quotes/.
60 www.mediaed.org/cgi-bin/commerce.cgi?preadd=action&key=237.
61 The chapter on men and violence documents and categorizes rates of violence by gender.
62 Eyman, Scott, *John Wayne: The Life and Legend* (Simon & Schuster, 2014).
63 Ibid.
64 Wills, Gary, *John Wayne's America* (Simon & Schuster, 1998).
65 Gagliasso, Dan, "John Wayne, World War II, and the draft," Breitbart, February, 2010. www.breitbart.com/Big-Hollywood/2010/02/28/John-Wayne--World-War-II-and-the-Draft.
66 Cones, John W., "A study in motion picture propaganda." www.filmreform.org/study.htm.
67 See Big Jim McLain at http://gb.imdb.com/title/tt0044418/.
68 "Fox News says feminism is 'feminizing' American men," *Chicago Tribune*, January 21, 2014. http://articles.chicagotribune.com/2014-01-21/news/ct-talk-huppke-feminism-20140121_1_u-s-census-bureau-fox-news-feminine-men.
69 *New York Times*, Archives, September 23, 2003. www.nytimes.com/2003/09/23/movies/foul-mouth-with-following-20-years-later-pacino-s-scarface-resonates-with-young.html.
70 "'Scarface' echoes mightily with hip-hop artists," *USA Today*, September 18, 2003. http://usatoday30.usatoday.com/life/movies/news/2003-09-17-scarface_x.htm.
71 *Bitch Flicks*, November 25, 2013. www.btchflcks.com/2013/11/revenge-of-the-pussycats-an-ode-to-tarantino-and-his-women.html#.U9_0E9_n_rc.
72 www.richjepson.com/why-we-love-gangsters/.
73 *NY Daily News*, January 11, 2013. www.nydailynews.com/entertainment/tv-movies/quentin-tarantino-interviewer-shutting-yur-butt-article-1.1238179.
74 *The Telegraph*, January 12, 2010. http://www.telegraph.co.uk/culture/film/film-news/6975563/Quentin-Tarantino-violence-is-the-best-way-to-control-an-audience.html.
75 www.the-numbers.com/person/140200401-Quentin-Tarantino#tab=summary.
76 "Gender and women's mental health." World Health Organization, www.who.int/mental_health/prevention/genderwomen/en/
77 www.theguardian.com/film/2001/jun/26/news.
78 Ibid.
79 www.ibtimes.com/paul-walkers-death-fast-furious-stars-fatal-accident-highlights-dark-side-street-racing-1493178.
80 Ibid.
81 www.thestate.com/2014/07/14/3563726/horry-county-police-charge-nine.html.
82 www.popcenter.org/problems/street_racing/.
83 www.newser.com/story/153599/jackass-stunt-kills-german.html.
84 Courtenay, William Henry, "Better to die than cry? A longitudinal and constructionist study of masculinity and the health risk behavior of young American men," *Humanities and Social Sciences* 59, 8-A, (1999), p. 3207.
85 Ibid.
86 www.crushable.com/2014/03/12/entertainment/sexism-in-comedy-misogyny/.

87 www.huffingtonpost.com/2013/05/23/jerry-lewis-female-comedians-not-funny_n_3326623.html.
88 www.vanityfair.com/culture/features/2007/01/hitchens200701.
89 www.beamsandstruts.com/bits-a-pieces/item/768-tinyfey.
90 Di Fino, Nando, "Funny or die? Family Guy's domestic abuse episode raises questions of taste and appropriateness." *Mediaite.* http://www.mediaite.com/tv/funny-or-die-family-guys-domestic-abuse-plot-line-raises-questions-of-taste-and-appropriateness/.
91 Jefferson, Whitney, "Family Guy hits horrible new low with domestic abuse episode." *Jezebel.*
92 www.change.org/petitions/stop-rape-jokes-on-family-guy.
93 Interview with Seth MacFarlane. www.nytimes.com/2009/09/13/magazine/13FOB-Q4-t.html?_r=0.
94 www.huffingtonpost.com/madeline-wahl/how-rape-jokes-contribute_b_5240592.html.
95 "Understanding the Perpetrator," University of Michigan Sexual Assault Prevention & Awareness Center. http://sapac.umich.edu/article/196.
96 www.tv.com/news/breaking-down-tosh0s-off-color-humor-25183/.
97 www.usmagazine.com/celebrity-news/news/daniel-toshs-rape-joke-defended-by-comedians-2012127.
98 http://jezebel.com/5924937/daniel-tosh-is-sorry-he-told-a-female-audience-member-that-she-should-get-hilariously-raped.
99 www.cnn.com/2012/07/16/opinion/gottfried-tosh-joke/.
100 www.theroot.com/blogs/the_grapevine/2014/06/kevin_hart_claps_back_against_allegations_of_hating_dark_skinned_women.html.
101 Ibid.
102 http://variety.com/2013/tv/columns/sarah-silvermans-bad-career-move-being-as-dirty-as-the-guys-1200834142/.
103 www.huffingtonpost.com/gina-barreca/post_4924_b_3396205.html.
104 http://en.wikiquote.org/wiki/Louis_C.K.
105 www.crushable.com/2014/03/12/entertainment/sexism-in-comedy-misogyny/.
106 Ogletree, Shirley Matile and Drake, Ryan, "College students' video game participation and perceptions: Gender differences and implications," *Sex Roles* 56, I. 7–8 (2007), pp. 537–542.
107 www.forbes.com/sites/davidthier/2014/05/13/grand-theft-auto-5-has-sold-nearly-2-billion-at-retail/.
108 Burgess, Melinda C.R., Stermer, Steven Paul., and Burgess, Stephen R., "Sex, lies, and video games: The portrayal of male and female characters on video game covers," *Sex Roles*, June, 2007.
109 www.bbc.com/news/technology-27824701.
110 Dill, Karen E. and Thill, Kathryn P. "Video game characters and the socialization of gender roles: Young people's perceptions mirror sexist media depictions," *Sex Roles*, December, 2007.
111 Dill, Karen E., Brown, Brian P., and Collins, Michael A., "Effects of exposure to sex-stereotyped video game characters on tolerance of sexual harassment," *Journal of Experimental Social Psychology*, September, 2008.
112 Simpson-Beck, Victoria, Boys, Stephanie, Rose, Christopher, and Beck, Eric, "Violence against women in video games: A prequel or sequel to rape myth acceptance?" *Journal of Interpersonal Violence*, April, 2012.
113 Rape myth is defined and discussed in several places in the text when material covers attitudes about rape and sexual assault in the event that readers do not cover each chapter in detail.
114 Dill, Karen E. "Violent video games, rape myth acceptance, and negative attitudes toward women," *Violence Against Women in Families and Relationships*, 4 (2009), pp. 125–140.
115 Yao, M.Z., Mahood, C., and Linz, D. "Sexual priming, gender stereotyping, and likelihood to sexually harass: Examining the cognitive effects of playing a sexually-explicit video game." *Sex Roles*, January, 2010.
116 Ibid.
117 www.washingtonpost.com/news/morning-mix/wp/2014/08/29/gaming-vlogger-anita-sarkeesian-is-forced-from-home-after-receiving-harrowing-death-threats/.
118 www.motherjones.com/media/2014/05/pop-culture-anita-sarkeesian-video-games-sexism-tropes-online-harassement-feminist.
119 www.huffingtonpost.com/2014/10/15/anita-sarkeesian-utah-state-university-firearms_n_5989310.html.
120 http://adanewmedia.org/2012/11/issue1-consalvo/.

121 www.gamasutra.com/view/news/224400/Gamers_dont_have_to_be_your_audience_Gamers_are_over.php.
122 http://learning.blogs.nytimes.com/2014/10/17/how-sexist-is-the-gaming-world/?_r=0.
123 Jansz, Jeroen, "The emotional appeal of violent video games on adolescent males," *Communication Theory*, 15, 3 (2005), pp. 213–241.
124 Irwin, Roland A. and Gross, Alan M., "Cognitive tempo, violent video games, and aggressive behavior in young boys," *Journal of Family Violence*, September, 1995.
125 Ibid.
126 Anderson, Craig A., "An update on the effects of playing violent video games," *Journal of Adolescence*, February, 2004.
127 Anderson, Craig A., Shibuya, Akiko, Ihori, Nobuko, Swing, Edward L., Bushman, Brad J., Sakamoto, Akira, Rothstein, Hannah R., and Saleem, Muniba, "Violent video game effects on aggression, empathy, and prosocial behavior in Eastern and Western countries: A meta-analytic review," *Psychological Bulletin*, March, 2010.
128 Lemmons, Jeroen S., Valkenburg, Patti M., and Peter, Jochen, "The effects of pathological gaming on aggressive behavior," *Journal of Youth and Adolescence*, January, 2011.
129 Markey, Patrick M., Markey, Charlotte N., and French, Juliana E. "Violent video games and real-world violence: Rhetoric versus data," *Psychology of Popular Media Culture*, August, 2014.
130 www.usnews.com/opinion/articles/2013/04/29/no-link-between-violent-video-games-effects-and-school-shootings.
131 Ibid.
132 Gentile, Douglas A., Choo, Hyekyung, Liau, Albert, Sim, Timothy, Li, Dongdong, Fung, Daniel, and Khoo, Angeline, "Pathological video game use among youths: A two-year longitudinal study," *Pediatrics*, February, 2011.
132 Gentile, Douglas, "Pathological video-game use among youth ages 8 to 18: A national study," *Psychological Science*, May, 2008.
133 Grusser, S.M., Thalemann, R., and Griffiths, M.D., "Excessive computer game playing: Evidence for addiction and aggression?" *Cyber-Psychology & Behavior*, May, 2007.
134 Wood, Richard T.A., "Problems with the concept of video game 'addiction': some case study examples," *International Journal of Mental Health and Addiction*, October, 2007.

Chapter

7

Media and Masculine Representation II: Advertising, Heteronormativity, and the Construction of Male Insecurity

The lack of substantial LGBT characters in mainstream film, in addition to the outdated humor and stereotypes, suggests large Hollywood studios may be doing more harm than good when it comes to worldwide understanding of the LGBT community.

~ Sarah Kate Ellis, CEO, GLAAD[1]

LEARNING OBJECTIVES

After reading this chapter, students should be able to respond to the following questions with an understanding of the terms and expressions employed:

- *What does media analyst Douglas Rushkoff mean by a "feedback loop?" How does this loop influence the way advertisers market products to boys and men? What is "anti-marketing marketing"?*
- *How do media imagery of women influence boys' and men's views of women? What is the Freudian "Madonna–whore complex" and it what are its implications for contemporary men? With respect to media that eroticizes violence toward women, what is meant by "attitude polarization"? What have researchers learned about eroticized violence and its effect on men and women?*
- *What is meant by 'medicalized masculinity?' What is 'subvertising'? What are some of the more common male insecurities that ad agencies exploit to motivate men to buy products?*
- *What is "metrosexual" masculine representation? What is the history of gay and trans-male media representation? How are these media representations*

portrayed today? What are the criticisms of such representations? What is the meaning of the expression, "cis-gendered"? How has subvertising helped expose sexist double standards in media?

- *What is meant by the "Duck Dynasty Backlash"? In what ways are certain reality-based programs considered to be conservative reactions to gender diversity, particularly in relation to male representation?*
- *What is media literacy and why do media critics advocate for it? What are the five concepts and five core questions of media literacy?*

Advertising: Framing Men's Perception of Women and Profiting on Creating Male Insecurity

In discussing the ways that advertising and broader media is successful in gaining viewership and product allegiance, media analyst Douglas Rushkoff argues that the products that are produced for youth culture and the ads that are created to attract young people are the result of a **feedback loop**, whereby kids watch media to figure out how to be cool and fit in with their peer groups, while media watches kids to determine the best strategies to employ to get young people to commit to brand loyalty, whether products or TV shows.[2] The broader concept involves a strategy known as **anti-marketing marketing** or sometimes **guerrilla marketing**, where marketers target their advertising to particular groups without appearing to advertise. One thing contemporary marketers have determined about youth culture is that it is a culture that will turn away from traditional advertising campaigns that simply and directly ask consumers to "buy our product." So, they attempt to seamlessly associate their products with music, concepts, or celebrities that young people have branded "cool" in the belief that this coolness will rub off on their products. This approach, in fact, was the technique used by soft drink maker Sprite to rise from lower sales figures in the early 1990s to ultimately rival Coke and Pepsi in several larger market regions of the U.S.[3] Sprite attempted to get young people to connect hip-hop culture with Sprite and the attempt was successful. It wasn't long before many other ad agencies jumped on the anti-marketing marketing bandwagon to maximize sales to youth culture.

But product makers and marketing firms also use this technique to target gendered markets. One of the more successful gendered marketing campaigns has come from fast-food giant CKE Restaurants, parent company of Carl's Jr. and Hardee's restaurants. The fast food ad campaigns gained notoriety in 2005 by running TV ads depicting "celebutant" Paris Hilton washing her Bentley in a bikini while eating a Carl's Jr. burger:

Identifying what restaurant industry analyst Dean Haskell called Carl's Jr.'s target audience, Haskell states, "Their customers are generally 18 to 34-year-old males. And 18 to 34-year-old males tend to have only one thing on their minds. Sex sells, and they've seen an increase in traffic." But criticism from a number of watchdog groups poured in and CKE decided to change course, hiring new ad agency *David and Goliath*. However, after a one-year partnership, CKE fired *David and Goliath* after sluggish sales were blamed on toned-down sexualized ads. New agency *72andSunny* was hired to bring the sexualized ads back, which they have done with gusto, signing Paris Hilton to join *Sports Illustrated* model Hannah Ferguson in what has been described as one of the raciest and most sexualized ad campaigns to date.

CKE, while drawing criticism for its racy ads, is certainly not the only company to employ scantily-clad women to sell products. Similar sorts of ads have been produced by Budweiser, Miller Lite, Go Daddy, Pepsi, Axe Body Wash, Google, American Apparel,

FIGURE 7.1: Paris Hilton, Carl's Jr. ad, 2005

FIGURE 7.2: Paris Hilton and Hannah Ferguson, Carl's Jr., 2015

Radio Shack, and Ford Motor Company.[4] At the same time, forces have mounted to combat ads of this kind. Boycotts have been organized to get the attention of advertisers and product makers in an attempt to get them to change course.[5] Other strategies to fight sexist ads come in the form of **subvertising**, where parody ads are created to make a point about the sexist marketing practices of some agencies.

FIGURE 7.3: An example of subvertising

That heterosexual, adolescent boys and young men are the target market for most ads that hypersexualize and one-dimensionalize women is explicitly acknowledged by the agencies that produce them. Highly sexualized ads that feature women who are offered as examples of idealized, feminine beauty have been roundly criticized as having negative overall effects on girls and women who struggle with body image and self-esteem, not to mention the fact that the sexual objectification of women leads to an overall one-dimensionalizing, devaluing of women who are routinely sexually harassed at work and must fight to be taken seriously in their professional lives. Less examined are the ways that these ads affect boys and men.

THE MADONNA–WHORE COMPLEX

First identified by Freud, the Madonna–whore complex is an alleged pathology that develops in men who are unable to remain in committed, stable, loving relationships.[1] Freud phrased it this way: "Where such men love they have no desire and where they desire they cannot love."[2] Psychoanalytic traditions view this complex as stemming from overprotective mothers such that men who are raised by such mothers will seek out maternal women for loving relationships desiring what their mother did not provide, but also long for sexual satisfaction that cannot be directed at one's surrogate mother. In more contemporary, non-psychoanalytic versions of the complex, boys and young men are awash in imagery of hypersexual women on a daily basis through media representation, but also through contact with the many young women who have internalized the sense of power that comes through sexuality. At the same time, these men desire emotional intimacy. As children, many boys are taught to respect their mothers, but to view with lust instead of respect these "other women" who adorn themselves in sexual displays. Some argue that

FIGURE 7.4: Sigmund Freud

parsing women into binary categories creates the same effect that Freud discovered was present in many men who live lives of deception and discontentment trying to satisfy parts of themselves they believe cannot be fulfilled through one relationship.

1 https://en.wikipedia.org/wiki/Madonna%E2%80%93whore_complex.

2 Freud, Sigmund, "*Über die allgemeinste Erniedrigung des Liebeslebens" [The most prevalent form of degradation in erotic life]. Jahrbuch für psychoanalytische und psychopathologische Forschungen* 4 (1912), pp. 40–50.

University of North Carolina, Chapel Hill professor Julia T. Wood explains that one of several pervasive gendered scripts in media that polarize gender is the trope of men as aggressor and sexual subject, women as victim and sex object.[6] Wood notes that the very traits women are encouraged to develop (physical beauty, sexiness, demure passivity) contribute to their victimization, while the traits men are encouraged to develop (aggressiveness, dominance, sexual prowess, and physical strength) are those linked to the abuse of women. Wood's view is that if women are instructed to develop and emphasize physical appearance and sexuality as their primary source of value, while men are instructed to develop and emphasize physical strength, aggressiveness, and sexual prowess, an unequal balance of power is established. Media instruct men that women are one-dimensional sex-objects, while men are praised for possessing a multitude of empowering traits. Even though many of these traits are less than perspicuous (physical strength, intelligence, ambition, assertiveness, knowledge, logical thinking, scientific acumen, dignity, respect, ingenuity, tenacity, success that is independent of sensual appeal) they elevate in the minds of many men their status, power, and importance over women.

Through the lens of media, sex is treated as a game of pursuit. Men are the pursuers, while women are the pursued. In this game, it is the responsibility of women to look seductive, while it is the goal of men to receive sex from these seductive women. But for men, receiving sex comes with complications. In media, women appear to constantly crave sex as though it is the single most important thing on their minds, even though men quickly discover in real life that this is far from the truth. So, men must figure out how to work around any barriers a woman puts in place to prevent sex. Media critic Jean Kilbourne argues that this media script, albeit unrealistic, is a script that paves the way for violence, in this case sexual violence, against women.[7] This may also explain why some men become furious or sarcastically condescending when women challenge their opinions. If men view women as not being their intellectual equals, it explains why men not only discount women's voices, but become enraged and violent on one end of the scale or patronizing on the other when women appear to question what some men believe is their natural authority as men.

Wood, like Kilbourne, notes that when mediated sexual scripts include the conflation of sex and violence, or when violent behavior is made to look sexy, as in the 2005 film *Mr. and Mrs. Smith*, the most toxic mediated messages are produced (Figure 7.5).

In media, violence and dominance are often portrayed as a natural part of healthy, sexual desire that erupts from time to time in the heat of passion. Some men who have linked together the mediated scripts of sex and violence view sexual dominance, including physically and verbally aggressive behaviors toward women, as normal expressions of sexual desire. In a study where men were exposed to films depicting violence against women, and particularly sexualized violence against women, a normalizing effect was measured in men who were less likely to have negative emotional reactions to scenes where women are brutalized, and when surveyed later, considered these films as not being degrading toward women.[8]

Similar results have been documented in studies dating back to the early 1980s, where ***attitude polarization*** was found to exist between men and women who view the same films.[9] After viewing films that sexualize violence, men and women were given a "sexual attitude survey" several days later without being told that there was any relationship between the survey and watching the films.[10] Results of the surveys indicated that men who had viewed films that depicted sexualized violence toward women had an increased level of acceptance of eroticized intimate partner violence, while women who were surveyed had the opposite reaction.[11] These results are part of what has been called the ***desensitization of violence against women*** based on the reports by men after repeated exposure to media that sensationalizes or eroticizes men's violence against women.

FIGURE 7.5: Angelina Jolie and Brad Pitt as Mr. and Mrs. Smith, 2005

In related work, researchers from Washington State University reported that men who read *Maxim*, *Playboy*, and other so-called men's magazines, where sexualized images of women are commonplace, are less likely to seek a woman's consent before initiating sexual contact and are more likely not to respect sexual boundaries.[12] Similarly, researchers from the University of Surrey and Middlesex University in Great Britain gave groups of men and women descriptions of women for evaluation, some taken from "men's magazines" and others from convicted rapists.[13] Not knowing the sources of the descriptions, both men and women who took part in the study were unable to reliably recognize which descriptions were taken from men's magazines and which descriptions were submitted by convicted rapists. When asked to rate the descriptions as being more or less derogatory, the consensus from test subjects was that the quotes taken from the magazines were more derogatory. Here is a sample of descriptions given of women, sources omitted:

- There's a certain way you can tell that a girl wants to have sex ... The way they dress, they flaunt themselves.
- Some girls walk around in short-shorts ... showing their body off . . . It just starts a man thinking that if he gets something like that, what can he do with it?
- You'll find most girls will be reluctant about going to bed with somebody or crawling in the back seat of a car ... But you can usually seduce them, and they'll do it willingly.
- Girls ask for it by wearing these mini-skirts and hot pants ... they're just displaying their body ... Whether they realize it or not they're saying, 'Hey, I've got a beautiful body, and it's yours if you want it.'
- Some women are domineering, but I think it's more or less the man who should put his foot down. The man is supposed to be the man. If he acts the man, the woman won't be domineering.
- When girls dress in those short skirts and things like that, they're just asking for it.
- Girls love being tied up ... it gives them the chance to be the helpless victim.
- A girl may like anal sex because it makes her feel incredibly naughty and she likes feeling like a dirty slut. If this is the case, you can try all sorts of humiliating acts to help live out her filthy fantasy.

In chapter six, we saw that *cultivation theory* predicts that this sort of *mainstreaming* effect is a product of an identifiable group of men who consume similar media, in this case media that generalizes the notion that women crave sex, including aggressive, violent, or humiliating sex, even when women claim otherwise.

As part of the larger mechanism of socialization, the messages embedded in advertising, media analyst Jean Kilbourne notes, send normative instructions to men just as they do to women. Advertisers, for instance, recommend that men "man up!" instead of adopting any styles that could be interpreted as being feminine in nature. In a series of Miller Lite commercials, males are ridiculed for saying or doing something that others in the ad view as girlish or feminine.[14] The ads play on men's insecurities that they will be viewed as being soft or weak in the eyes of their male friends or in the eyes of women.

In other attempts to play on men's insecurities, a host of television ads have been launched by the makers of Viagra, Cialis, and Levitra that play on the notion that men can regain confidence through taking pills for erectile disorder. In what has been termed ***medicalized masculinities***, sociologist Meika Loe argues that "The Viagra Body" is part of what can be called a masculine boost.[15] For many men, notes Loe, "the project of restoring 'normal functioning' cannot be divorced from achieving normal masculinity."[16] For men who attach a great deal of importance to sexual competence, 'normal masculinity' is tied to sexual performance so that any problems or perceived problems with

FIGURE 7.6: Miller Lite "Man Up!" ad

achieving and maintaining an erection is directly associated with masculine identity and self-worth. The ads themselves use suggestive language such as "don't let erectile dysfunction let you down," or anxiety-building lines such as "when the time is right, will you be ready?"[17] Sociologist Michael Kimmel adds:

> Male sexual socialization informs men that sexuality is the proving ground of adequate gender identity and provides the script that men will adopt, with individual modification, as the foundation for sexual activity.[18]

Ads that attempt to exploit men's nervousness about sexual performance assure that the era of the little blue pill remains firmly in place as part of *normal* masculine functioning. As long as a strong association between sexual performance and normative

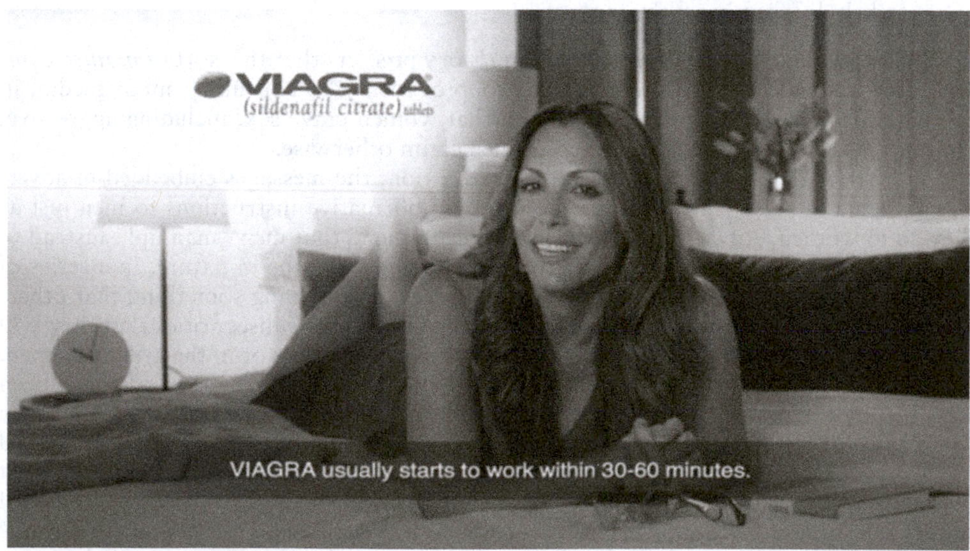

FIGURE 7.7: Viagra ad

masculine identity continues to reign, companies will attempt to exploit that connection. (Erectile dysfunction drugs will be covered in more detail in Chapter 12, 'Men, Health, Aging'.)

A similar ad campaign targeting men involves enticing men to get "penis enlargement therapy." Sociologists Sarah Jane Brubaker and Jennifer A. Johnson argue that "erectile enhancement internet ads create a text of masculinity through constructing a crisis of masculinity and selling the solution."[19] These ads prey on the male insecurity that men are losing control and power in an increasingly feminized world, and hence a "crisis of masculinity" is both created and resolved through medication. By placing greater importance on body image in the shaping of normative, masculine identity, men can regain a sense of power and control they feel they have lost by enlarging the size of their penises.

Brubaker and Johnson also point out that ads of these kind "reassert hegemonic ideals, i.e. the *othering* of and domination over women and phallocentrism."[20] Penis enlargement ads attempt to get men to associate power with physicality and sexual prowess, while reassuring men that control, and particularly sexual control over women, is within their grasp through the assistance of pharmaceutical supplements (Figure 7.8).

Beyond exploiting men's insecurities that they are losing or have lost power and sexual appeal, the harms that befall men from media and advertising are some of the same harms that befall women such as body dysmorphic disorder, whereby one scrutinizes and finds fault with one's body leading to lowered self-esteem, depression, and sometimes eating disorders. The difference is that with men, media portray ideal masculine bodies as muscular and powerful, rather than as thin and waif. Men will often go to gyms to bulk up rather than slim down in pursuit of bodies they see in films and magazines as desirable. Some men will go to extremes by taking supplements, including dangerous and illegal substances, to try to attain an ideal that has been sold to them in media.

Other ads aimed at men attempt to promote gender segregation or exploit men's fear that anything they do could be interpreted as being feminine. In the Dove shampoo ad in Figure 7.10, the man is seen rushing home to wash out the "female shampoo" he has been using with Dove Men + Care shampoo to regain his masculinity.[21] Other ads that attempt to exploit the masculine instruction "do not do anything considered to be feminine" include the Jim Beam whiskey ad that states in the copy, "'The men rode into the saloon' is never followed by 'and ordered Merlot.'"[22] The embedded insult in ads of these kind is not only aimed at women and gay men, but any man who does not conform

FIGURE 7.8: Penis Enlargement ad

FIGURE 7.9: Dr. Pepper ad

FIGURE 7.10: Dove Men's Shampoo ad

to the heteronormative, hypermasculine archetype reinforced in much of contemporary society.[23]

In one of the more vivid attempts to expose the extreme gender polarity of ads aimed at men versus ads aimed at women, some clever subvertising has been created that reverses traditional gender roles to make a point (Figure 7.11).

These role-reversed ads are intended to evoke laughter, but the laughter itself indicates that what has been normalized for female bodies in ads is found to be ridiculous when the

FIGURE 7.11: Gendered role reversal subvertising

same poses and sexual innuendo is applied to male bodies. This exposed double-standard makes the point that women are expected to be sexualized and posed in positions of sexual availability in ways that are beneath the dignity of men. We are then supposed to find humor in images of men being posed in these same hypersexual postures.

But not all media attempt to attract men through hypermasculine, heteronormative appeals to sexual prowess or to exaggerated muscularity or to anxieties about not appearing feminine or gay. Media have become more diverse by offering an assortment of non-conforming masculine representations alongside an increased presence of gay, bisexual, transgender, and queer-gender characters in film and TV. In the next section, we see that this diversity has been met with a mixture of praise, condemnation, and critical analysis.

The Metrosexual, Gay Male Representation, and the Heteronormative Backlash

In chapter six, we examined some of the stereotypes that existed in early television's portrayal of feminine men or men thought to be gay as a common punch line of a joke in a comedian's routine. The specter of men who possessed a feminine demeanor was material for comedy, innuendo, and suspicion. But media representations of masculinity today have become much more diverse from the time that John Wayne and an assortment of tough guys graced the male landscape of motion pictures. From Tobey Maguire's "Peter Parker" in the *Spiderman* trilogy to the male cast of *The Big Bang Theory* to *Academy Award* nominated films such as *Birdman* and *The Imitation Game*, to a number of high-profile cable TV shows that feature gay, male characters, a more vulnerable masculine persona has emerged in TV and film that has made generalizations about media and masculinity more difficult to draw. It is not that a sensitive or cerebral male lead has taken over the hypermasculine "man's man" archetype found in most action films, but that masculine space has opened for more diverse male expression.

The advance of untraditional masculine representation in media spawned the term 'metrosexual' by British writer Mark Simpson who informs us,

> The typical metrosexual is a young man with money to spend, living in or within easy reach of a metropolis. He might be officially gay, straight or bisexual, but this is utterly immaterial because he has taken himself as his own love object and pleasure as his sexual preference.[24]

Simpson views British soccer star David Beckham as the prototype metrosexual, who is wealthy and meticulous in his appearance, while in America, actors George Clooney, Brad Pitt, and Hugh Jackman are often seen as fitting the prototype. In television, *American Idol* host Ryan Seacrest is considered to fit the bill. These are not men lacking in self-confidence or social acuity like the characters in *The Big Bang Theory*, but they also do not conform to the over-the-top tough-guy archetypes found in action films. The metrosexual represents an intermediate position between the rugged posturing of hyper-masculine, media tough guys and the refinement of male fashion models. For ad agencies, the metrosexual is sexually ambiguous enough to serve as a model aimed at both male heterosexual and homosexual target audiences. In this respect, he is a marketing dream.

The metrosexual is a man designed to be marketed to, as a refined and articulate gentleman who takes great interest in the accoutrements of couture and personal grooming, while retaining enough of the manly characteristics found in his hypermasculine alter ego to appeal to a wide range of men. Media have actually been fond of the metrosexual before the term 'metrosexual' was devised. In the 007 series of films, for instance, British agent James Bond is the debonair man of mystery who is worldly wise, intelligent, charming, particularly to younger women, and adept at violent physical confrontation while always managing to appear suave and well-groomed.

In addition to metrosexual masculine expression, TV and film have unveiled a host of gay and trans male and female characters that conform to stereotypes of the past. The hackneyed convention of the gay, male character as flamboyant, hyper-emotional, or single-mindedly sexual continues to be a common media trope. From the campy

FIGURE 7.12: David Beckham

performance of Chris Tucker's 'Ruby Rhod' in *The Fifth Element* (1997) to Nathan Lane's highly emotional 'Albert Goldman' in contrast to Robin Williams's reserved 'Armond Goldman' in *The Birdcage* (1996), to Sasha Baron-Cohen's satirical performance in 'Bruno' (2009), gay male representation has been typified in many films as hypersexual, hyper-emotional, and almost always comedic in nature. On the other hand, the depiction of gay and trans characters is slowly changing in the direction of more diversity and authenticity. From 1998 through 2006, NBC produced the hit show *Will & Grace* to mixed reviews despite its winning 16 Emmys and receiving 83 nominations.[25]

FIGURE 7.13: Nathan Lane and Robin Williams, *The Birdcage*

FIGURE 7.14: Sacha Baron Cohen as 'Bruno'

The show centered on the relationship between gay, male attorney Will Truman and his best friend Grace Adler along with characters Karen Walker, who works for Grace, and Jack McFarland, a struggling actor who is gay and flamboyant. Criticism from many within gay communities ensued, arguing that the show's portrayal of gay men fell back on gay stereotypes when it could have broken the mold to create new, more complex representations of gay masculinity. Some praised the show, arguing that greater visibility leads to greater acceptance. However, others argued that, particularly in the comedy genre, shows like *Will & Grace* actually reinforce heterosexism and heteronormativity by continuously comparing gay masculinity to heterosexual masculinity; that is, by depicting gay masculinity as embodying a lack of traditional masculinity.[26] University of Utah professor Helene Shugart argues, in fact, that given the heteronormative sensibilities of the target audience for shows like *Will & Grace*, homosexuality is normalized through the lens of heterosexual, male privilege and in so doing, gay, male identity is measured against the standard of heteronormative masculinity, ultimately reinforcing the hegemonic nature of heteronormativity.[27]

In addition to *Will & Grace*, there have been a number of TV shows over the last decade or so that featured or feature LGBTQ characters, including *Oz* (HBO), *Modern Family* (ABC), *Glee* (Fox), *The Ellen DeGeneres Show* (NBC), *RuPaul's Drag Race* (MTV), *The L-Word* (Showtime), *Queer Eye for the Straight Guy* (Bravo), *Angels in America* (HBO), and perhaps most notably, the Showtime production *Queer as Folk*, which followed the lives of a group of gay men and women living in Pittsburgh. Story lines explored areas that mainstream network television would normally not touch such as coming out, ex-gay ministries, drug use and abuse, gay-bashing, discrimination in the workplace based on sexual orientation, active gay Catholic priests, internet pornography, and "bug chasers" (HIV-negative individuals who actively seek to become HIV-positive).[28] The *New York Times* called *Queer as Folk* "a more honest *Sex and the City* about gay men,"[29] and was embraced by many within gay communities for its "authenticity,"[30] although others insist that queer lives cannot be captured in TV shows where diversity is not the norm and stereotypes continue to rule the airwaves.[31]

THOUGHT BOX

As we have seen, some argue that film and TV shows depicting gay and transgender characters are good because exposure leads to acceptance, while others argue that misrepresentations, stereotypes, and one-dimensional portrayals of gay and trans men and women do more harm than good. What do you think?

In the theater, director Ang Lee brought writer Annie Proulx's short story *Brokeback Mountain* to the silver screen, exposing the struggle of closeted gay men who are living double lives. Set in the hills, mountains, and valleys of Wyoming, *Brokeback Mountain* (2005) tells the story of Ennis and Jack, two cowboys/ranchers who meet in the summer of 1963 and develop a complex romantic and sexual relationship even though each of them is married with children and living publicly as a heterosexual man. *Brokeback Mountain* was viewed by many as a breakthrough film where gay men were no longer depicted in one-dimensionally flamboyant or comedic ways. Reviewers, however, interpreted the film in one of two ways: emphasizing the theme of past and present rural homophobia, or as a traditional love story.[32] The concern for some is that this latter way of interpreting the film undermined the challenge to homophobia that was the crux of Proulx's story line.[33]

In broader culture, *Brokeback Mountain* also served as a vehicle for exposing the homophobia of many heterosexual men, particularly those employed in traditional male-centered careers. ESPN talk-show personalities and other sports analysts, for instance, sprinkled their shows with jokes about *Brokeback Mountain*, as in any case where one of their male colleagues stated on-air something remotely friendly, sparking the common rejoinder, "Don't go Brokeback on me!" The pinnacle of the homophobic jokes surrounding *Brokeback Mountain* may have come when singer Willie Nelson recorded the song, "Ain't Going Down on Brokeback Mountain" in 2009 with the refrain, "I ain't going down on Brokeback Mountain; that shit ain't right."[34]

THOUGHT BOX

After viewing the film *Brokeback Mountain*, discuss the messages you believe were central to the film. What does *Brokeback Mountain* say about homophobia and heteronormativity in America?

Media representations of nonconforming or queer-gender men have been especially thorny. As discussed at the beginning of chapter six, male comedians in television in the 1960s and 1970s often performed in drag as part of a comedy sketch, behaving in over-the-top, campy ways in an attempt to get laughs from studio audiences. The concept of transgenderism was not yet before the consciousness of most Americans and comedians assured that transgender men and women would not be accepted by mainstream America for some time by turning transgenderism into a joke. The notion of campy, unbalanced transgender women and men was codified by Tim Curry's character, a self-proclaimed 'transvestite' from "Transsexual, Transylvania," in the *Rocky Horror Picture Show* (1975). The other stereotype that permeated the image of transgender men and women was one of dangerous pathology. Transgender women, in particular, were depicted as having a psychological illness in films like Alfred Hitchcock's *Psycho* (1960) where Anthony Perkins's character dons a wig and his dead mother's clothing to murder those women his male identity feels an attraction toward, or *Dressed to Kill* (1980), where Michael Caine plays a psychologist who suffers from mental illness and kills women he is attracted to while wearing a wig and women's clothing. The Academy Awards were virtually swept by the film *Silence of the Lambs* (1991), where a psychotic killer known as 'Buffalo Bill' is skinning victims as part of his attempt to transition from male to female. Refuting these stereotypes has been a long, arduous, and ongoing process for transgender women and men today.

With a mixture of praise and criticism, the film *TransAmerica* (2005) features Felicity Huffman as a pre-operative male-to-female trans-person who learns that she is a parent. In *Boys Don't Cry* (1999), based on the true story of Brandon Teena, Hilary Swank plays Brandon, a young transman who finds love in a rural Nebraska setting only to be brutally beaten, raped, and murdered by former friends upon learning that Brandon is biologically female. *The Crying Game* (1992) is a psychological thriller that features actor Jaye Davidson as a transgender woman. The film generally received praise, although there were mixed reviews about the writing of the transgender character in the film.[35] In one of the more controversial performances, Jared Leto plays 'Rayon,' a transgender woman who has contracted AIDS in *Dallas Buyers Club* (2013). The controversy surrounding many of the performances of transgender men and women is most pronounced in those cases where the actor is not himself or herself transgender. Like the concerns raised by Native Americans who criticized Western movies where white actors were hired to play

Native American characters in early film and TV, transgender people argue that media representations of trans-people need to come from actors who are actually transgender, and that misrepresentations by well-intentioned **cis-gender** (identifying one's gender with the sex one was assigned at birth) actors serve to distort the complexities found in the transgender community. Members of the transgender community would also like to see writers who are transgender author the roles for transgender characters so that greater insight into the nuances and complexities of transgender individuals might be rendered into characters regardless of the gender identity of the actor.[36]

An aspect of mediated depictions of transwomen in TV and film is the impact it has on men. Because a transwoman is biologically male, unless or until she has undergone sex reassignment surgery, the distorted misrepresentation of transwomen by media is yet another reinforcing factor that demonizes men who embrace feminine identities or identify as women. Because media has depicted transwomen as unbalanced or even dangerous, a normative trope flows into mainstream culture that men who identify in a feminine way have psychological disorders that make them threatening, particularly toward children. We have witnessed this concern in the warnings issued by some that transwomen in women's restrooms pose a threat to girls and women.[37] The presence of transwomen in women's restrooms has in fact set off a debate in contemporary feminist circles about safe spaces for women.[38] Critics counter that feminism was built upon an anti-essentialist platform such that those who condemn transwomen for invading women's spaces are adopting an essentialist definition of gender that has, as a consequence, the reinforcement of transphobia in American culture.[39] [40]

THOUGHT BOX

How important do you think it is for gay, bisexual, and transgender characters to be played by gay, bisexual, and transgender actors? What concerns do you have, if any, about cases where these characters are played by heterosexual or cis-gendered actors? How important do you think it is for transgender writers to be writing the roles for transgender characters?

The Duck Dynasty Backlash

In what could credibly be described as a heteronormative backlash to the rise of the suave metrosexual and the emergence of gay, male representation in media has come a wave of television reality shows that celebrate a rugged, rustic masculine identity. In 2010, *The History Channel* created the show *Swamp People*, featuring men killing alligators in the swamps of Louisiana, and at the top of the ratings came *A&E Network*'s reality show *Duck Dynasty* that follows the lives of the Robertson family who generated a fortune with their production of duck calls. Self-identified "rednecks," the eldest Robertson son declares, "I was born this way. You ain't a redneck unless you're off the road and in the swamps."[41] In a perhaps not so veiled allusion to the view that homosexual men and women are "born this way," the Robertson men represent a blustery declaration of heteronormative masculinity that is untainted by the socialized effect of contemporary culture. Donning camouflage attire and bandanas, and sporting long hair and beards (this latter feature, interestingly, has been replicated by a number of white, major league baseball players), *Duck Dynasty* stands as the willful and celebratory antithesis to the evolving masculine diversity found on TV and media in general.

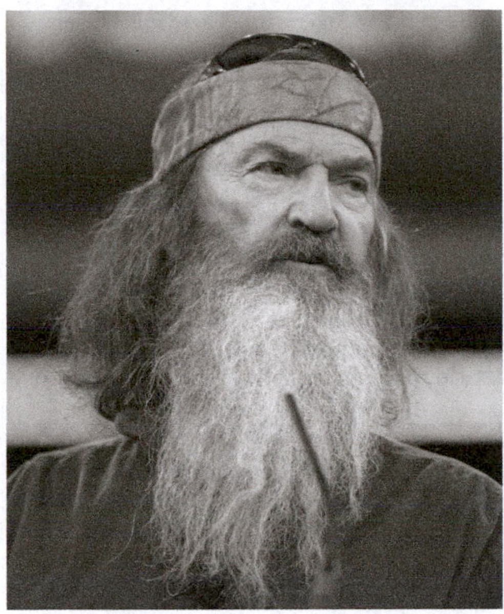

FIGURE 7.15: Phil Robertson of *Duck Dynasty*

The Robertson men captured American audiences with their hypermasculine representation of Southern masculinity, a no-nonsense approach to manhood, "family values," and allusion to conservative, Christian beliefs through nightly prayer along with Phil Robertson's anti-gay comments in a 2013 *GQ* magazine interview.[42]

University of North Carolina, Charlotte professor Karen Cox argues that while shows like *Duck Dynasty* purport to provide insight into Southern masculinity, they actually reinforce stereotypes about Southern men as belonging to "a mythically rural, white, poorly educated, and thickly accented region that has yet to join the 21st century."[43] University of San Francisco professor of law, Luke Boso adds,

> Another important reason to draw attention to rural masculinities is because they have symbolic significance for all men, and they affect how society at large thinks about manhood. In the collective American imagination, rural men are paragons of real men. Contemporary political dialogue reflects this idea when it classifies small town America as real America. Pop culture feeds this notion too: one only need turn to the History Channel or A&E, where hit shows like Swamp People, Ax Men, Mountain Men, Ice Road Truckers, and Duck Dynasty deliver lessons on how to be a real man. These representations cast rural men as rough, tough, independent, and in control of themselves and their surroundings. To many, these men are heroes because they represent the American ideal and embody qualities most prized in masculinity. The rural man's unrivaled status in his community, the real and imagined dirtiness of his jobs, and the lore associated with the recreation of rugged outdoorsmen make dominant rural masculinities symbolic of the most authentic masculinity—for rural and urban men alike. The cultural salience of rural men in the construction of all masculinities helps explain why certain men everywhere are targets for ridicule and abuse.[44]

Boso highlights the hegemonic dimension of reality shows like *Duck Dynasty* that purport to capture authentic manhood against which non-traditional masculinities can be judged. Historian Jarret Ruminski agrees and adds,

> The Robertson men's beards alone do not a successful show make. But their beards do symbolize and invoke a long history of cultural construction based around generic

Southern American values served up hot and ready to many Americans. These folks want a little something simpler in their lives to combat what they see as a host of uncomfortable modern social changes.[45]

U.S. Senator Ted Cruz (R-Texas) agrees with this analysis of *Duck Dynasty* but spins the analysis in a positive light, offering the defense, "This is a show about a god-fearing family of successful entrepreneurs who love guns, who love to hunt, and who believe in the American Dream."[46] For many conservative Americans, *Duck Dynasty* is the perfect remedy to the shift in masculine media representation over the past couple decades, a shift critics view as soft, weak, and profoundly unmanly. *Duck Dynasty* and shows like it have been a hit with conservatives who feel that what many FOX News pundits have termed the "wussification of America" has caused contemporary men to become feminized and vulnerable to an increasingly hostile world that wishes to see America dethroned from its seat of power and privilege.[47]

Media Literacy

Many who examine and evaluate media professionally have called for courses in media literacy in schools at the youngest possible ages to help provide the tools young people need to think critically about the media they consume. They point out that smart, profit-motivated people are employed to entice kids to purchase, or get their parents to purchase, a host of products and to view or interact with certain TV programs, games, music, and other sorts of media. It is easy to manipulate groups of boys, teens, and even young adults who are trying to figure out how to fit into their peer groups, particularly, as we saw earlier in the chapter, if advertisers and media producers can successfully get young people to view the products they are selling or the programs they are promoting as being cool. Media literacy in its most general sense can be described as critical thinking applied to media.

FIGURE 7.16: Tessa Jolls, President, Center for Media Literacy

TABLE 7.1

	Core Concept	Core Question
Authorship	All media messages are constructed.	*Who created this message?*
Format	Media messages are constructed using a creative language with its own rules.	*What creative techniques are used to attract my attention?*
Audience	Different people experience the same media message differently.	*How might different people understand this message differently from me?*
Content	Media have embedded values and points of views.	*What lifestyles, values, and points of view are represented in, or omitted from, this message?*
Purpose	Most media are organized to gain profit and/or power.	*Why is this message being sent?*

Center for Media Literacy president Tessa Jolls lists five core concepts and five core questions for media shown in Table 7.1.[48]

As examined in chapter six, media messages are often targeted to specific audiences in order to achieve the greatest potential for success. These targets can be parsed out by age, class, and in many cases, gender. When men are the target audience for media product, the content is often an appeal to men's sense of authentic manliness, which usually involves physicality, sexual prowess, economic power, control, and respect from other men. Other times, scare tactics are used to appeal to men's insecurities. When media targets elementary, middle-school, and high school aged boys, an appeal to being cool and fitting in is usually at the core of the message. By asking critical questions about media, and discussing the various responses to those questions, consumers of media can begin to understand underlying assumptions, normative prescriptions, and the manipulating styles used by media to become more astute consumers. Media literacy offers tools for boys and men of various ages to critically sift through the many hegemonic, masculine scripts being offered as templates for masculinity, while also helping to reveal the hyperbolic or outright dishonest sexual scripts about women. Media literacy can also function as a filter through which stereotypes about gender and sexual orientation are revealed and challenged. Media, in its entirety, is a powerful vehicle for instruction and proponents of media literacy argue that power of that magnitude requires appropriate investigative and evaluative tools to provide girls, boys, women, and men with the ability to more thoroughly understand the narratives that are being sold to them.

THOUGHT BOX

If you were to design a media literacy course, what specific points would you want to emphasize about media aimed at boys and men?

Summary

When we think about the potential harms of advertising, we normally think about the effects upon women, and in particular the one-dimensional, hypersexual representations, the undermining of women's self-esteem by profiting from making women self-conscious of their bodies, the scrutiny of women's looks in general, eroticizing violence in a culture where women are abused and battered at very high rates, and a contributing force to a host of eating disorders that plague women in much higher numbers than men. But this is not to say that men are not influenced in harmful ways by the toxic effects of advertising—quite the reverse. When boys and men are bombarded with hypersexual imagery of women as one-dimensional sex objects, it reinforces a longstanding meme in the minds of men that women's value is dependent on their looks, and this can affect the ways boys and men think about and treat girls and women.[49]

But beyond the various ways media create sexist stereotypes that help shape the ways men view women, media also contribute to the ways men view themselves. Media are awash in narratives that men should be hypermasculine, denying and rejecting any versions of masculinity that even remotely appear feminine in nature. One of the consequences of such media content is that gay and gender nonconforming men will continue to be singled out for ridicule and abuse. It also has the effect of keeping boys and men in rigidly defined parameters of masculine expression out of fear of being bullied or socially alienated. At a time when American culture is slowly opening up to more diverse forms of masculinity, media, including fictionalized, reality-based, and advertising media, ironically serves as being both on the cutting edge of expanded masculine expression and as a regressive and repressive source of limiting and constraining hegemonic forms of masculinity.

Notes

1 www.theguardian.com/film/2014/jul/23/hollywood-criticised-lgbt-gay-characters-glaad.
2 Rushkoff, Douglas, *The Merchants of Cool* (PBS Frontline, 2000).
3 Ibid.
4 www.adweek.com/adfreak/10-most-sexist-ads-2013-154550#radioshack-knows-you-want-its-hot-phallus-1.
5 http://breakupwithgodaddy.com/, http://mic.com/articles/14366/boycott-axe-deodorant-the-latest-ad-campaign-proves-that-sexism-sells.
6 Wood, Julia T., *Gendered Lives: Communication, Gender, and Culture*, 10th edition (Wadsworth Cengage Learning, 2009), pp. 276–279.
7 Kilbourne, Jean, *Killing Us Softly 4: Advertising's Image of Women* (Media Education Foundation. 2010).
8 Linz, Daniel, Donnerstein, Edward, and Penrod, Steven, "The effects of multiple exposures to filmed violence against women," *Journal of Communication*, September, 1984.
9 Malamuth, Neil M. and Check, James V., "The effects of mass media exposure on acceptance of violence against women: A field experiment," *Journal of Research in Personality*, December, 1981.
10 Ibid.
11 Ibid.
12 https://news.wsu.edu/2014/05/27/study-links-mens-magazine-readers-unwanted-sexual-behaviors/#.VF6E09EtAaI.
13 www.surrey.ac.uk/mediacentre/press/2011/69535_are_sex_offenders_and_lads_mags_using_the_same_language.htm.
14 http://mensstudies.org/?p=2577.
15 Loe, Meika, "The Viagra blues: Embracing or resisting the Viagra body," in *Medicalized Masculinities*, ed. Dana Rosenfield and Christopher Faircloth (Temple University Press, 2009).
16 Ibid., p. 31.
17 www.boston.com/news/globe/editorial_opinion/oped/articles/2005/07/17/life_vs_lifestyle/.
18 Kimmel, Michael S., *The Gender of Desire: Essays on Male Sexuality* (SUNY Press, 2005), p. 143.
19 Brubaker, Sarah Jane and Johnson, Jennifer A., "'Pack a more powerful punch' and 'lay the pipe': Erectile enhancement discourse as a body project for masculinity," *Journal of Gender Studies*, October, 2007.
20 Ibid.
21 www.huffingtonpost.com/2013/03/20/dove-shampoo-ad-man-hair_n_2914549.html.

22 https://s-media-cache-ak0.pinimg.com/736x/13/58/2a/13582a8e7891551e83f6368be30a143f.jpg.
23 In Chapter 12 ads will be taken up again as normative instructions to shape men's views about themselves that are part of a systematic cultural narrative about men fitting into a tightly defined sense of manhood.
24 Simpson, Mark. "Here come the mirror men: Why the future is metrosexual." marksimpson.com.
25 www.emmys.com/shows/will-grace.
26 Battles, Kathleen and Hilton-Morrow, Wendy. "Gay characters in conventional spaces: Will and Grace and the situation comedy genre," *Critical Studies in Media Communication* 19, 1 (2002), pp. 87–105.
27 Shugart, Helene A., "Reinventing privilege: The new (gay) man in contemporary popular media," *Critical Studies in Media Communication*, 20, 1 (2003).
28 www.mirror.co.uk/news/uk-news/bug-chasing-men-deliberately-trying-2033433.
29 www.nytimes.com/2005/08/06/arts/television/06mart.html?_r=0.
30 http://tvcriticism2013.blogspot.com/2013/11/queer-as-folk-and-homosexual.html.
31 *Film Commune*, December, 2006. http://filmcommune.blogspot.com/2006/12/queer-as-folk-double-edged-sword-of.html.
32 Cooper, Brenda and Pease, Edward C., "Framing *Brokeback Mountain*: How the popular press corralled the 'Gay Cowboy Movie,'" *Critical Studies in Media Communication* 25, 3 (2008).
33 Ibid.
34 http://lyrics.wikia.com/Willie_Nelson:Ain't_Goin'_Down_On_Brokeback_Mountain.
35 Halberstam, J., *In a Queer Time & Place: Transgender Bodies, Subcultural Lives* (New York University Press, 2005), p. 81.
36 www.huffingtonpost.com/jules-horowitz/why-trans-people-need-to_b_7865840.html.
37 www.nj.com/opinion/index.ssf/2016/04/transgender_publoc_restrooms_pose_a_threat_to_wome.html.
38 www.newyorker.com/magazine/2014/08/04/woman-2.
39 https://politicalaspects.wordpress.com/2015/04/04/trans-in-the-toilet-the-ethics-of-womens-spaces/.
40 https://bitchmedia.org/post/the-long-history-of-transgender-exclusion-from-feminism.
41 Hernandez, Leandra H., "I was born this way: The performance and production of southern masculinity in A&E's *Duck Dynasty*," in *Reality Television: Oddities of Culture*, ed. A.F. Slade, A.J. Narro, and B.P. Buchanan (Lexington Books, 2014).
42 Magary, Drew, "What the Duck?" *GQ*, January 2014, p. 1/3.
43 Hernandez, "I was born this way."
44 Boso, Luke A., "Policing masculinity in small-town America," *Temple Political & Civil Rights Law Review*, October, 2014.
45 www.salon.com/2013/10/20/the_secret_conservative_message_of_the_duck_dynasty_beards/.
46 http://prospect.org/article/why-duck-dynasty-became-latest-conservative-cultural-touchstone.
47 www.slate.com/blogs/xx_factor/2013/12/26/fox_news_duck_dynasty_pajama_boy_why_is_conservative_media_so_worried_about.html.
48 www.medialit.org/reading-room/five-key-questions-form-foundation-media-inquiry.
49 https://en.wikipedia.org/wiki/Madonna%E2%80%93whore_complex.

Chapter

8

Masculinity and Music

My deepest motivation comes out of the house that I grew up in and the circumstances that were set up there ... my father struggled to find work. I saw that was deeply painful and created a crisis of masculinity.

~ Bruce Springsteen[1] [2]

LEARNING OBJECTIVES

After reading this chapter, students should be able to respond to the following questions with an understanding of the terms and expressions employed:

- *Trace the ways that masculine expression has evolved over the past 60 or so years in music and through the masculine representations of music artists.*
- *Who were the "crooners" and what was typified in this version of masculine style?*
- *In what ways did The Beatles, along with other artists from the 1960s, disrupt longstanding masculine archetypes?*
- *In what ways were the 1970s a gendered expansion of the 1960s? In what ways did artist David Bowie challenge the boundary conditions of traditional masculinity?*
- *At the same time that traditional gender and sexual expression was being challenged by white 1970s music artists, what sorts of themes were being produced by black music artists?*
- *In what ways were 1980s music stars both an extension and reversal of 1970s masculine identities?*
- *What is it that Bruce Springsteen and others have termed* a crisis of masculinity?
- *Describe the gender evolution of male music stars in the twentieth century. What do Richard Majors and Janet Billson mean by "the cool pose"? Why does "respect" matter so much to men who identify with hip hop culture? What, according to Yale sociologist Elijah Anderson, is* The Code of the Street?

- *What are the more salient lyrical themes of male country music artists? In what ways does country music mirror the masculine reclamation found in* Duck Dynasty *characters? What is "bro-country," and what is the criticism of this subgenre of country music?*
- *What are the reasons given by fans of metal bands in defense of the misogynistic and sexist lyrics found with some artists? How do critics respond?*

When James Brown wailed this classic line in 1966, he wasn't far from the truth. Although the women's movement was well underway, challenging and breaking through the doors of longstanding male domination was still in the distant future and many would rightly argue continues to be an ongoing challenge. In the 1960s, men were very much in charge of almost every dimension of societal power, which was also true of the music industry, an industry overwhelmingly controlled by men.

Under-examined in much of the scholarly work on masculinities is music and musical artists, even though over many generations, music artists have had a profound influence on youth culture. From the time that crooners surged onto the musical landscape in the 1940s and 1950s to the present day hip hop, pop, country, and rock music artists, those who become pop-cultural sensations, including music stars, have an immense impact on masculine identity and performance. One thing that is astounding about popular music and popular culture is the speed with which musical and visual styles change. With the advent of MTV and today social media, the visual representations of music artists and the images they create are every bit as important as the music they perform.

In fact, popular music, in particular, is and has been an interconnected blend of visual, musical, lyrical, and live performance art that has captivated fans for generations. With so many songs about love, romance, and sex, issues of gender, power, and sexuality are constantly on display in music in one of the more perspicuous ways possible. With respect to men and masculinities, the styles and demeanors of male, singing stars, like that of film stars, have had a visible influence on the ways that boys and men dress, speak, and behave. From Frank Sinatra's swinging, guy-about-town to Elvis Presley's country-bred, courteous, pretty-boy good looks, to the feminized glam bands of the 1970s, to today's street-wise hip hop artists, male music stars and various musical groups have influenced boys and men in countless ways. An interesting question

> It's a man's world.
>
> ~ James Brown

FIGURE 8.1: James Brown

FIGURE 8.2: Frank Sinatra

FIGURE 8.3: Elvis Presley

is whether the changes in musical and visual styles of music artists serve as a catalyst for certain gendered societal changes witnessed over different eras or whether societal changes are a catalyst for musical and visual changes in music artists. Documenting the many gendered changes that have occurred and continue to occur in popular music, this chapter will take a chronological approach to investigating the intersection between music and masculinities.

In their day, Frank Sinatra and Elvis Presley weren't just singers, they were male templates of emulation for millions of young men who wanted the magnetically cool personas of these stars to rub off on them. As male singers became known as **crooners** and heartthrobs, women swooned and men jumped on the bandwagon to imitate these singing stars. But the specter of the crooner as archetypal hetero-male that helped define manliness for several decades in the persons of Bing Crosby, Perry Como, Nat King Cole, Dean Martin, Frank Sinatra, and later Elvis Presley, shifted drastically when in 1960, a band of four British musicians from Liverpool, England changed music history forever, and in a sense, challenged what it meant to be a man. Hated by the male music establishment that came before them, The Beatles took the world by storm. Suddenly, the "fab-four, mop-tops" were being imitated far and wide by boys and men who grew their hair longer and adopted a more feminized masculine style. The 1960s, in general, were a time of sexual and gender exploration that stretched the edges of traditional gender boundaries, and The Beatles were instrumental as one of the catalysts of that change. The images of The Beatles are certainly not revolutionary by today's standards, but in the early 1960s, they were considered radical and subversive. In his book, *Men, Masculinity and the Beatles*, British sociologist Martin King argues that The Beatles signaled a male revolt that predated much of second-wave feminism.[3] The Beatles were an early prototype of non-conformity to a male culture that had been raised on traditional masculine standards of emotional stoicism, psychological control, physical strength, and a repugnance to being perceived as possessing any trait considered to be feminine in nature.

Author John Whitehead concedes that the masculine challenge posed by The Beatles may not have been intentional, because there was also a traditional masculine underpinning

FIGURE 8.4: The Beatles

to their appeal, but notes that The Beatles' music also represented a challenge to traditional masculine, musical territory by focusing on the subject of love in novel ways.[4] For instance, John Lennon's "In My Life" was a notable antithesis to The Rolling Stones' "Street Fighting Man," and light years removed from the more traditional love songs that spoke to an intimate romantic relationship between a man and woman. The transition from Elvis Presley's "Love Me Tender" (1956) to John Lennon's iconic anthem "All You Need Is Love" (1967) is a progression from a heteronormative, first-person torch song to an expansive notion of love that reaches out to humanity as a global community. One of the reasons for this dramatic shift in lyrical content from the 1950s to the 1960s was the fact that many music stars went from being singers to artists who wrote their own songs and this change brought about far more introspective and socially conscious lyrics to popular music that for past decades was recognized for feel-good messages that had mass appeal. The 1960s were also famously a time of social upheaval in the wake of protests against the war in Vietnam and an increasing sense of self-examination that included challenges to traditional sexual and gender identities. In line with 1967's "summer of love" ethos, Lennon's masculine expression was in stark contrast to the masculine mindset embedded in the 1967 film *The Dirty Dozen*, where Lee Marvin leads a band of misfits turned Army commandos on an apparent suicide mission into Nazi-occupied territory. Reviewer Bosley Crowther described the film as "a studied indulgence of sadism that is morbid and disgusting beyond words."[5] So, even though 1967 is remembered as the year of "flower power," it is inaccurate to assume that a universal shift in masculine identity had taken place simply because a hippie generation captured headlines. Still, a social revolution had taken place that included challenges to the traditions of masculinity and manhood in America.

MASCULINITY AND THE BLUES

Many of the 1960s and 1970s white rock bands and artists including Elvis Presley, Jerry Lee Lewis, The Rolling Stones, The Beatles, Led Zeppelin, The Allman Brothers, Eric Clapton, and others, appropriated and innovated the music of black, blues-guitarists such as Blind Lemon Jefferson, Muddy Waters, Robert Johnson, Paul Butterfield, John Lee Hooker, T-Bone Walker, Willie Dixon, Albert King, Buddy Guy, Howlin' Wolf, Jimmy Reed, and B.B. King, to name a few of the more notable blues guitarists of the twentieth century. Jimmy Page, guitarist for Led Zeppelin, admitted that he plagiarized blues artists, but adds, "I always made sure to come up with some variation, in most cases it's hard to tell the original source."[1] Blues is a genre of music that originated from poor and working class African-Americans in areas of the deep South and the delta regions of America from St. Louis to Chicago.[2]

The lyrics speak of hardship, lost love, longing, racist oppression, and an overall melancholy that came with growing up poor and black in Jim Crow segregated America.[3] But the black musicians who created the blues rarely profited from it. White artists began to do their own versions of the songs written by black blues artists or wrote their own songs borrowing heavily from the blues, while profiting enormously. In terms of masculinity, the original blues came from a place of dejected and oppressed manhood, but in the hands of wealthy white artists, the masculine performance was one of confidence bordering on cockiness. The influence of the blues can be heard today in the work of many music artists ranging from soul singer Sam Smith to pop and R&B superstar Bruno Mars.

Continued

FIGURE 8.5: Howlin' Wolf

FIGURE 8.6: Muddy Waters

FIGURE 8.7: T-Bone Walker

FIGURE 8.8: B.B. King

1 http://hubpages.com/entertainment/The-White-Appropriation-of-Rhythm-and-Blues.
2 https://en.wikipedia.org/wiki/Blues.
3 Ibid.

As transformative as the 1960s were, looming on the musical horizon was a much more radical shift in masculine expression. The sexual revolution of the 1960s became commodified by 1970s music artists as gender-bending went from being shocking to profitable. Male pop and rock music stars in the early 1970s brought about a seismic gender transformation with the emergence of glam-bands and the more androgynous and sexually ambiguous persona of David Bowie. While Alice Cooper, the New York Dolls, The Sweet, and T. Rex were groups composed of heterosexual men donning feminine personas, David Bowie revealed his sexual orientation as gay and then revised it to bisexual,[6] while eclipsing the fame of the other artists. From the 1940s and 1950s when Sinatra topped the music charts to the early 1970s when David Bowie became a cultural icon, an enormous shift in masculine identity had taken place. Of course, not all or even most men adopted these new, masculine styles, but the fact that "masculine-cool" was changing and becoming more diverse and feminized was visibly taking hold of popular culture. As the writer who coined the expression 'metrosexual' Mark Simpson states of Bowie, he is "both masculine and feminine, and neither."[7] The concept of gender itself was a constricting notion that Bowie consciously worked to transcend. With the New York City art community heralding Andy Warhol as a visionary pop-artist as background, David Bowie ascended to rock music superstardom and helped open the door to diverse masculine expression and new dialogues about what it is to be a man. Of Bowie, McGill University professor Will Straw notes,

> I think in terms of the mainstreaming of cross- and transgender personalities, [Bowie] is extremely important, more so than any other figure in popular music.[8]

In the wake of David Bowie's death in 2016, writer Lisa Perrott adds,

> Bowie fell to earth and thrust himself into this cycle of mimicry at a prescient moment in the seismic landscape of gender politics. Never content to just mimic the costume and bodily gestures of other performers, Bowie has been a cultural alchemist. He transgresses the boundaries of normalised gendered behaviour.[9]

FIGURE 8.9: Alice Cooper

FIGURE 8.10: David Bowie

The legacy of David Bowie to the world of gender and sexuality will be written by generations to come, but his impact on issues of gender and masculinity alone speaks to the power of music stars to influence culture far beyond the boundaries of music.

So pronounced was the gender blurring of 1970s music artists that older artists often followed suit in imitating the androgynous styles created by the now successful careers of Bowie, Alice Cooper, and Elton John. Among the more notable rock luminaries of the 1970s, Mick Jagger, Rod Stewart, and Robert Plant embodied a particular hegemonic masculine archetype of their time that incorporated the swagger and cockiness of a more traditional masculine variety, but that also, at least in terms of physical presentation, disavowed a traditional masculine appearance. Against this background of hegemonic masculine expression, albeit with androgynous overtones, were female music stars who were challenging male supremacy and authority, such as Helen Reddy, whose iconic 1971 song "I Am Woman" captured and memorialized the passion of the women's movement. Reddy's anthem both united and polarized women and men who were grappling with a new gendered reality of women reclaiming their agency and pushing an American culture to rethink gendered restrictions and boundaries. At the same time, artists such as Joni Mitchell, Aretha Franklin, Carole King, Diana Ross, Tina Turner, and Linda Ronstadt commandingly documented the emerging power of female artists and paved the way for future stars Madonna, Annie Lennox, Whitney Houston, and, today, Beyoncé, Lady Gaga, Katy Perry, Rihanna, and Taylor Swift.

MILES DAVIS

Like the blues, rock, and hip hop, a genre of music considered to be authentically American in origin is jazz. Of the many jazz luminaries past and present, one of the most iconic figures is Miles Davis. Noted as a virtuoso trumpet player who transformed jazz into an esoteric and experimental art form, Miles Davis is a jazz legend. Along with John Coltrane, Charlie Parker, Dizzy Gillespie, Charles Mingus, Thelonious Monk, Oscar Peterson, Bill Evans, and Art Tatum, Davis revolutionized jazz and widened the audience beyond traditional jazz aficionados. But in some respects, Miles Davis transcended jazz itself. American cultural critic Gerald Early writes, "Miles Davis achieved fame as a jazz musician and cultural icon in the 1950s and 1960s—the era of the civil rights movement. Against this backdrop, Davis appeared as a bona fide leader of men in a field of endeavor dominated by men: modern jazz."[1]

Davis has been called "an uncompromising representation of black manhood."[2] Like Muhammad Ali in boxing, Miles Davis was an image of defiance against white supremacy; and for this defiance, he stood out as a black man who would not accept a subordinate position in racist America. At the same time, Davis battered women, a fact he admitted to in his memoirs.[3] Like many black men of his time, he rightly viewed racism with disgust and contempt, but did not feel the same about sexism and misogyny. Men like this are often called 'complex'. But it could be said that Davis's race–gender double standard served as a progenitor to the many artists who have denounced racism in the most passionate ways possible, while referring to women as 'sluts', 'bitches', and 'whores'. It places women of color in a double-bind: the struggle of dealing with racism while also dealing with sexism and violence aimed at them from men who believe women

Continued

should know their place. Yet Miles Davis continues to be viewed as a masculine template, a black man who did not cower in the face of white supremacist policies and racist violence, but who instead stood as an icon of strong, defiant black masculinity.

1 Early, Gerald, "On Miles Davis, Vince Lombardi, & the crisis of masculinity in mid-century America," *Daedalus*, 131, 1 (2002).
2 Early, Gerald, *Miles Davis and American Culture* (Missouri Historical Society Press, 2001).
3 Davis, Miles. *Miles, The Autobiography* (Simon & Shuster, 1990).

THOUGHT BOX

Make a list (perhaps a top ten list) of male artists that you feel have had a big influence on gender and particularly masculine standards in popular culture. Discuss what it was about them, coupled with the era in which they were prominent, that caused them to be so influential.

Yet, as unconventional masculine expression and an increased female presence reigned in rock, black male artists described a different reality. Stevie Wonder took up where Marvin Gaye, Curtis Mayfield, Jackie Wilson, and Sam Cooke left off, writing and performing music that testified to the struggle that came with growing up in tough, urban environments. Wonder's "Living for the City," for instance, was an anthem to growing up black and poor in 1970s America. The stark realities of Wonder's vision of Black America was far removed from the eccentricities of Bowie's *Ziggy Stardust*, and represented a masculine contrast to the androgyny celebrated by a host of white music stars. In many respects, the social commentary made by Wonder, Mayfield, and Gaye in the 1970s foreshadowed the

FIGURE 8.11: Stevie Wonder, circa early 1970s

LATIN AMERICAN MUSIC: A DIVERSE MUSICAL FUSION

In the 1960s and 1970s, as American popular music was being divided between rock artists, who were overwhelmingly white, and R&B artists, who were predominantly black, Latino artists emerged with a unique, hybrid musical sound that integrated elements of Mariachi and other traditional Latin music styles with the familiar American pop and R&B styles of the times. Starting with Richie Havens' classic "La Bamba," to the bands El Chicano and Malo to the superstardom of Carlos Santana, Latino artists carved out a diverse fusion of musical styles that helped to define the blend of Latino cultures with mainstream American traditions in music.

Mexican-American and other forms of Latin-pop, rock, and R&B continue to proliferate American music. These styles represent a cross-over blend of music and messages that define Latino masculinity in widely divergent ways. From the multicultural street toughness of War's "Slippin' Into Darkness" and "The World is a Ghetto" to Tierra's "Together," which speaks to a more romantic, family-centric portrayal of masculine identity, Latino music stars are today found in R&B, hip-hop, and rap music in growing numbers.[1]

1 www.mtv.com/news/1951232/18-most-influential-latino-rappers/.

more militant social critiques looming on the horizon by groups like N.W.A and Public Enemy in the late 1980s and early 1990s. From Sam Cooke's "A Change is Gonna Come" (1964), which powerfully captured the growing feeling in the 1960s of profound social change on the cultural horizon to Gil Scott-Heron's "The Revolution Will Not Be Televised" (1971), black music was on the cutting edge of exposing American racism and the social unrest that resulted from centuries of racist violence and exclusion.

Particularly in response to the Jim Crow segregation laws that were being challenged across the nation and the overt racist practices found in housing, employment, and education, black music stars placed a spotlight on racial inequality in America. White musicians like Bob Dylan and John Lennon may have hinted at political hypocrisy and needed social reform, but they could not compete with the social urgency of black artists like James Brown, who in 1968 roared, "Say it loud; I'm black and I'm proud."[10] One way of interpreting the differences between white and black popular music in the late twentieth century is to note that white male artists enjoyed a luxury to explore more esoteric sides of themselves, while black male artists had two basic paths they could take: romantic love songs, which were embraced by white and black audiences alike as safe, nonthreatening subjects that make people feel good, or songs about survival and protest against white supremacy, which were not embraced by white audiences for the obvious reason that the protests were responses to institutional policies that held African-American people back from obtaining the wealth and authority white people took for granted.

However, the 1970s ended with a cocaine-driven, disco thud. The 1980s ushered in a new generation of music fans who were finished with the excesses and what were viewed as the superficialities of the 1970s, while MTV, launched in 1980, created the need for artists to visually promote their music. At the same time, the sexual and gender explorations of the 1970s were now being reined in by a more conservative temperament that was part of the Reagan presidential years and masculine expression followed suit. Other than the notable exceptions of Britain's Boy George of Culture Club, Robert Smith of The Cure, and American superstars Prince and Michael Jackson, a throw-back to more

PUNK ROCK AND MASCULINE ENMITY

The late 1970s witnessed a transformation in music and masculine performance, as punk rock emerged as a response to the disco era of commercialized music and feminized masculinity. British groups such as Sex Pistols and The Clash led the way to a more stripped down, angry, hetero-tough masculinity.

Sensitive and introspective male music artists such as Jackson Browne, Dan Fogelberg, James Taylor, and Paul Simon, while remaining very popular, were being usurped in youth culture by a male-centric, angry, socio-political musical force ready to revolutionize popular music and target political angst at what they took to be convention, tradition, and institutional power. By the early 1980s much of this raw power and rage was harnessed and commercialized by newer British artists U2, The Police, Joe Jackson, and Elvis Costello. While still powerful and political, the new-wave British invasion represented a more refined, traditional masculinity that resonated with young men living in the suburbs as much as it did the boys and men living in inner cities.

FIGURE 8.12: Sex Pistols

masculine-traditional artists like The Police, U2, John Mellencamp, Van Halen, Bruce Springsteen, Bon Jovi and heartthrob boy-band Duran Duran emerged as neo-classical versions of conventional masculinity.

Like Bowie in the 1970s, some music artists of the 1980s addressed issues specific to gender and perhaps more than any other eighties artist, Bruce Springsteen's music celebrates the struggles of the working class man, a man who is overworked, downtrodden, and largely invisible to the power brokers of American capitalism. Speaking to reporters, Springsteen stated,

FIGURE 8.13: Prince

> [My] deepest motivation comes out of the house that I grew up in and the circumstances that were set up there, which is mirrored around the United States with the level of unemployment we have right now.[11]

In the biography, *Bruce Springsteen and the Promise of Rock 'n' Roll*, Springsteen goes on to state, "My father struggled to find work. I saw that was deeply painful [and] created a crisis of masculinity."[12] Author Hanna Rosin describes this crisis of masculinity as a feeling of loss of identity, writing, "Man has been the dominant sex since, well, the dawn of mankind. However, this is no longer the case. The very notion of patriarchy has been challenged in the wake of the economic recessions of the 1990s and early 2000s."[13] If men have been told that their principal societal role is to be provider and protector of the family, economic recession triggers a challenge to that role. Springsteen is one of many artists who weds his music to larger social issues to raise awareness, and in this case, to make visible an ongoing crisis felt by working class men around the nation. He raised this same sense of awareness about veterans returning from Vietnam in his iconic song "Born in the U.S.A.," of which Springsteen states, "'Born in the U.S.A.' is about a working class man in the midst of a spiritual crisis. He's isolated from the government, isolated from his family, to the point where nothing makes sense."[14]

By the late 1980s, music was typified by a stark split between commercial "big-hair" rock bands, and the emergence of what some have termed "the golden era of hip hop." The big-hair bands can be described as a celebration of sexist, womanizing, party-centered rock-and-roll with Motley Crue, Bon Jovi, and Poison leading the way. The parroted message of many big-hair, hard rock bands was one of personal indulgence and excess, whether in terms of sex, substances, or both. At approximately the same time, a diversity of black, male expression rose initially from The Bronx and eventually to inner-cities and suburbs throughout America. From Run D.M.C., Public Enemy, Big Daddy Kane, and De La Soul to A Tribe Called Quest and Jungle Brothers, hip hop flourished as DJs and rappers combined to create new musical expression that reflected the issues and views of African-American and Latino people living in urban environments.

But controversy surrounded a number of rap and hip hop artists, as critics associated the music with militancy, street violence, and misogyny. The militancy was directed at institutions and social forces that created and perpetuated conditions of poverty in the inner city, while also maintaining what rappers believed to be racism directed toward the black community by police forces around the nation. As rage toward social conditions heightened, a collection of artists became synonymous with what became known as 'gangsta rap', a genre of hip hop that rhymed about gang life, confrontation with the police, and life on the streets in urban America. Rappers Ice-T and N.W.A were emblematic of artists who hailed from a hard, street-wise culture that used guns and violence to obtain ends, while harshly criticizing the LAPD for race-profiling and racist behaviors toward black youths. Gangsta rap adopted one of the most hypermasculine and violent male performances in the history of popular music, a persona imitated by both inner-city boys and men and white, middle-class, suburban boys and men who hoped to glom onto the hypermasculine, street credibility believed to make these rappers cool. This cultural appropriation sometimes continues to be seen by white artists who believe their association with urban black culture will make them seem cool to their fans. But much of the criticism aimed at the artists who rhymed about street violence and sex was based on the perception that the artists glamorized and promoted gang life, killing, and sexually objectifying women as attractive lifestyle choices, rather than as simple journalistic reports of life on the streets. Against the background of homicide being the number one cause of death for black males between the ages of 15 and 34,[15] many challenged what was considered to be a pandering of black death for profit by certain rap and hip hop artists.[16]

THE GOLDEN AGE OF HIP HOP

Hip hop has enjoyed a decades-old legacy that until very recently has been a male-dominated form of music that resonates to a generation of young people who connect to the beats and rhymes that document street wisdom and attitudes. Considered to revolve around the late 1980s and early 1990s, the golden age of hip hop included artists LL Cool J, Run-D.M.C., Public Enemy, KRS-One, Eric B. & Rakim, De La Soul, A Tribe Called Quest, Slick Rick, and Jungle Brothers among others.

The golden age of hip hop is sometimes referred to as an era of diverse black, male expression to distinguish this period from later periods of hip hop when artists' rhymes homogenized around themes of gang life, drug sales, sexual dominance over women, and displays of wealth.[1] At the same time, the diversity found in hip hop was on display, as early versions of gangsta rap in artists such as Ice-T, Geto Boys, and N.W.A coexisted with the sex and party rhymes of 2 Live Crew, Too Short, Kid 'n Play, and MC Hammer. Of the era, author and educator Jelani Cobb states,

> what made the era they inaugurated worthy of the term golden was the sheer number of stylistic innovations that came into existence ... in these golden years, a critical mass of mic prodigies were literally creating themselves and their art form at the same time.[2]

Continued

FIGURE 8.14: Chuck D of Public Enemy

1 Hurt, Byron. *Beyond Beats and Rhymes* (Media Education Foundation, 2006).
2 Cobb, Jelani William, *To the Break of Dawn* (New York University Press, 2007), p. 47.

The flip-side to hip hop's and rap's anger and social consciousness came from groups that branched into misogyny with rhymes about women and sex. 2 Live Crew's "We Want Some Pussy," "Me So Horny," "Face Down Ass Up," "Dick Almighty," and "Pop That Pussy" blasted out of club speakers, while album sales went double-platinum.[17] Georgetown University sociologist and cultural analyst Michael Eric Dyson writes,

> While 2 Live Crew's right to express its artistic worldview should be protected, that artistic worldview must be strongly and vociferously criticized ... on the basis of a civilly responsible resistance to their rap narratives, which glorify malicious sexual machismo and eroticize violent and vengeful sexual behavior.[18]

Dyson, while supporting artistic freedom, views rhymes that sexually denigrate women as part of larger social ills that intertwine race, class, gender, and age.[19] Author and social activist bell hooks rejoins critics by arguing that the misogyny found in certain genres of rap is simply part of a "sexist continuum, necessary for the maintenance of patriarchal social order." hooks argues that, in actuality, the criticism of 'gangsta rap' involves the vilification of young, black men who are targeted for derision when the misogyny in their rhymes is actually nothing more than an extension of the "white supremacist, capitalist, patriarchy" that has guided American culture for generations.[20]

In fact, in support of hooks's assessment that black men are being singled out for criticism, the same sort of womanizing, sexist lyrics fueled many white rock bands' narratives throughout the 1980s, but to far less criticism. In Motley Crue's "Ten Seconds to Love," similar, if somewhat less vulgar, sexual themes as those of 2 Live Crew are found with women described as "ten minute pets" who exist to "shine my pistol" until the male

KURT COBAIN

At the same time that "big hair" rock bands disappeared and the golden age of hip hop was in full swing, a Seattle-based band named Nirvana was led by a singer/songwriter who became one of the most iconic figures in rock history, Kurt Cobain. In what can credibly be viewed as a backlash to the excesses of the 1980s, "grunge" bands broke onto the musical landscape, effectively ending the tenure of most big-haired, glam bands and ushering in a postmodern anarchist form of masculine expression that eschewed commercialism, even though the grunge artists prospered commercially. It was a study in contradiction, but spoke to a generation of young people who wanted a new musical and social direction from the bands and artists patronized by their older siblings. Of Cobain, gender scholar Cortney Alexander writes,

> Kurt Cobain looked at masculinity from a stance of marginality. He offered, through his music and art, such striking insights into masculinity's dysfunctions. Cobain constructed an image that was highly suspicious of normative, hegemonic gender while desperately trying to find a comfortable relationship within socially acceptable gender roles.[1]

1 http://www.genderacrossborders.com/2011/05/31/kurt-cobain-and-masculinity/.

protagonist of the song "cums" in sexual satisfaction. The metaphor of penis as 'pistol' or 'gun' should not go unnoticed. It is a common metaphor in lyrics to refer to a man's penis as a weapon. By analogy, the woman becomes the target of the weapon, and this against the background of incredibly high rates of intimate-partner, physical and sexual violence in America. While insisting that artists, black and white, should be held accountable for the sexist anecdotes they construct and market to young, male audiences, hooks would view the lack of criticism of Motley Crue and the denigration of 2 Live Crew as more evidence that in America, "what better group to labor on this 'plantation' than young, black men?"[21] Still, young men around the nation of various ethnic and socioeconomic backgrounds rally around the narratives of money, sex, and power that are intoxicatingly attractive to a generation of men who long for identity, status, power, and control, particularly if these same men lack these things in their own lives.

During the 1990s, artists Tupac Shakur and the Notorious B.I.G. (Biggie Smalls) were the focal points of an alleged rivalry between east coast and west coast rappers that many believe led to their deaths.[22] The angry posturing, public insults, and nightclub brawls were the high-profile backdrop for what many young men in gangs believed was descriptive of life on the streets. To the young men living in urban environments, police officers were the enemy and the goal in life was to get respect, which largely came through violence or the threat of violence. In interviews with gang-affiliated, incarcerated men, University of Colorado, Denver, professor Paul Stretesky found that for young men living in inner-cities, gun possession became a tool to wield power and get respect that came only with having a tough, violent reputation.[23]

The music of artists like Tupac Shakur fell right in line with this urban, street tough mentality. University of Maryland psychologist Derek Iwamoto deconstructs Shakur's music with greater emphasis on masculinity, beginning with the lyrics in Shakur's song, "Hit 'Em Up," where Shakur rhymes about gang life and killing other men with indifference to the pain and violence of the streets. Iwamoto observes that while a superficial analysis of lyrics like these will lead some to view rappers like Shakur as socially deviant, a more astute reading of Shakur's lyrics reveals that:

> The most significant and often overlooked factor that perpetuates and reinforces extremely violent and competitive behavior is the way that the American culture defines and lionizes masculinity ... understandably, young men of color often enter into hypermasculine behaviors to combat the degrading effects of racism on their self-esteem.[24]

Young men growing up in tough, urban environments attempt to get respect in a world they see as hostile to them. So, they adopt what authors Richard Majors and Janet Billson term ***the cool pose***, which is a dilemma for black men in America.[25] As young, black American men discovered that saving money and persevering were not pursuits that brought them the success white men enjoyed, due largely to institutional obstacles and racist policies, whether overt or hidden, many black men became angry, frustrated, and felt alienated from the promise of the American dream. As a result, men of color adopted a tough exterior, a pose that kept feelings of pain inside, while demonstrating to the outside world that they are tough enough to take whatever is thrown at them, including the indignity of struggling and often failing to protect and provide for their families, qualities held as normative, masculine traits for American men.

But much like other hip hop artists, Shakur was complex, revealing different sides of himself and his art. In the rhyme, "Dear Mama," Shakur writes passionately about his love and respect for his mother. In his book, *The Education of Kevin Powell: A Boy's Journey into Manhood*, author Kevin Powell, who worked as a writer for *Vibe Magazine* at the time, interviewed Tupac Shakur on a number of occasions and writes of a sensitive young man after interviewing him at Riker's Island while Shakur was incarcerated on charges of sexual assault.[26] Of that 1994 interview, Powell writes that Shakur insisted he would no longer smoke weed, was not a gangsta, and that "thug life was dead."[27] The following year, Powell interviewed Shakur again, now out of prison, smoking weed, angry and defiant. Writing about the parallels between his life and Shakur's life, and by extension the lives of many young, black men, Powell continues, "Tupac was me, and I was him, ghetto children from birth, living until it was our turn to die."[28] In 1996, Tupac Shakur was killed in a drive-by shooting in Las Vegas, Nevada, while driving with music mogul Sug Knight.[29] To date, no one has been charged with the crime. The very next year, rapper "The Notorious B.I.G." (Biggie Smalls) was shot and killed in a drive-by shooting in Los Angeles, California and, as with Shakur, no arrests have been made.[30]

This notion of getting respect is one of the most salient elements found in hip hop and inner-city culture. Explaining this desire for respect, Yale University sociologist Elijah Anderson exposes what he terms ***the code of the streets***,[31] writing:

> At the heart of the code is the issue of respect—loosely defined as being treated "right," or granted the deference one deserves. However, in the troublesome public environment of the inner city, as people increasingly feel buffeted by forces beyond their control, what one deserves in the way of respect becomes more and more problematic and uncertain ... In street culture, especially among young people, respect is viewed as almost an external entity that is hard won, but easily lost, and so must constantly be guarded ... Many of the forms that dissing can take might seem petty to middle-class people, but to those invested in the street code, these actions become serious indications of the other person's intentions.[32]

For many young men in hip hop culture, which is an extension of the code of the streets, respect is the available currency in the absence of economic capital. As Anderson states, this may be a foreign concept to middle-class boys and men who possess tangible assets, but to young men who cannot relate to a life of economic privilege that includes a legacy of inherited wealth, education, and career, respect becomes an immediate surrogate for traditional forms of success.

At the same time that street-wise hip hop dominated the listening habits of young, music fans from diverse racial, ethnic, and socioeconomic backgrounds, a softer, more romantic retro-masculine performance hit the airwaves in artists that included Boyz II Men, Babyface, Backstreet Boys, N'SYNC, R. Kelly, Bobby Brown, and Brian McKnight. This was also a time when female artists exploded onto the music scene with Janet Jackson, Mary J. Blige, Mariah Carey, Whitney Houston, TLC, En Vogue, and Destiny's Child, from which contemporary superstar Beyoncé emerged. Never before had so many female artists surged to the top of the music charts and sold out stadiums that were usually reserved for male artists. But for men, the 1990s can be viewed as an interesting time that bifurcated masculine expression into hard, tough street styles and softer, sentimental masculine performance. This contrast of masculine styles gave way to a much more violent, misogynistic set of artists who took rap and hip hop by storm.

From the 1990s through the 2000s, multiplatinum artists emerged on the musical landscape such as Dr. Dre (originally from N.W.A), Snoop Dogg, Eminem, and 50 cent, who connected with a largely young, male audience that transcended race and class. While continuing to display the cool pose and rhyming about violence, these artists also emphasized the message of women as sexual playthings. From Dr. Dre's "Bitches Ain't Shit" to Eminem's rhyme "Bagpipes from Baghdad" where he calls singing star Mariah Carey a "cunt" and "fucking whore"[33] and his rhymes where he boasts about killing women[34] to 50 cent's "Candy Shop," women were a central target of anger and sexual violence for artists of this era. These artists were marketed as sexual icons who possess power over women and who demand that women serve them sexually when called upon to do so. As a measurement that these sexist messages resonated with young men across the country, record sales for gangsta rap surged. While Public Enemy's "Fear of a Black Planet" sold a very respectable 1.5 million copies,[35] white rapper Eminem's "The Marshall Mathers LP" sold 23 million copies worldwide.[36] In the film *Generation M: Misogyny in Media and Culture* (2008), antiviolence educator Jackson Katz makes the point that Eminem has publicly pronounced that he will not use the N-word in his rhymes because he understands the ability of words to cause harm, but liberally uses the B-word, H-word, and

FIGURE 8.15: Dr. Dre

FIGURE 8.16: Eminem

C-word to refer to women in an incredible display of hypocrisy.[37] In filmmaker Byron Hurt's 2006 documentary film *Hip Hop: Beyond Beats and Rhymes*, rapper Jadakiss reveals that once the sales of a hip hop album passes 700,000, "it's all white people buying it,"[38] making the point that the violence and misogynistic content appeals to a broad, male consumer base that transcends those living in tough, inner-city conditions. Much like Tarantino films, misogynistic gangsta rap captivated boys and men living at very different ends of the American socioeconomic spectrum.

THOUGHT BOX

In the film *The Merchants of Cool* (2000) Interscope Records co-founder and chairman Jimmy Iovine claims that when a new style of music begins to take off, "there's no stopping that train,"[1] as though it is simply an organic movement that springs from youth culture that is beyond the control of the music industry. Yet in the film *Beyond Beats & Rhymes* (2006), ex-Def Jam Records president Carmen Ashurst-Watson claims that when major record labels bought up the indie labels that were producing the biggest hip hop artists of the time, the lyrical content changed dramatically and that was not a coincidence.[2] In the same film, Chuck D of Public Enemy agrees and claims that content manipulation occurs in the music industry to drive sales. If Ashurst-Watson and Chuck D are correct, what does it say about record labels and male consumers that highly misogynistic lyrics became so profitable?

1 http://www.pbs.org/wgbh/pages/frontline/shows/cool/.
2 http://www.pbs.org/independentlens/hiphop/.

Other critics of certain forms of hip hop claim that masculine ego is a prominent feature of some of the most notable hip hop artists past and present.[39] University of Connecticut Professor William Jelani Cobb argues in *Beyond Beats and Rhymes* that the braggadocio prominently found among many hip hop artists is part of a "psychic armor" that black men adopt to deal with conditions in the city.[40] Young men in urban environments are challenged daily on their toughness by other young men. Street credibility becomes a badge of authenticity in a young man's life on the streets when other traditional resources are difficult to obtain. When young men grow up in environments where good-paying jobs are scarce, yet are told that a *real man* is one who possesses money and power, it makes sense to see music entrepreneurs like P. Diddy (Sean Combs), Jay Z, and other successful rappers and producers flaunt a materialistic lifestyle as a display of having overcome hostile conditions to become recipients of the American dream, not unlike the conspicuous luxury that men like Donald Trump enjoy. Today, rappers like Wiz Khalifa and Rick Ross take up where those before them left off. Khalifa rhymes mainly about money, sex, and smoking weed, while Ross takes up the well-worn territory of hyper-wealth and sex. But it would not be fair to hip hop and hip hop culture to exclude the rappers who defy these hyper-materialistic, sexist themes. Rappers Talib Kweli, Mos Def, Common, Lupe Fiasco, Immortal Technique, Dead Prez among others stand as testimony to the diversity within rap and hip hop culture, and their collective work ventures far outside the mainstream of hip hop narratives about violence, sex, and money to confront contemporary social issues.

In fact, one of the more celebrated rappers today is Kendrick Lamar whose work has been called "socially conscious," a label Lamar does not embrace, but rather insists, "I want people to recognize me as just a human being, period. I talk about whatever I feel and whatever I go through."[41] Lamar points to Tupac Shakur as the artist having the most influence on his music. On socially conscious rhymes, Shakur himself stated, "If we really are saying rap is an art form, then we got to be true to it and be more responsible for our lyrics."[42] Yet some have questioned whether being socially conscious is a label rappers want to have, and whether "rhymes of wisdom" have commercial appeal. In 2003,

FIGURE 8.17: Kendrick Lamar

rap-mogul Jay Z stated explicitly in "Moment of Clarity" that he wishes he could create rhymes that are more like the socially conscious work of artist Common, but that since becoming incredibly wealthy without creating socially conscious rhymes, he no longer has that dream.[43]

THOUGHT BOX

What do you think about the claim that socially conscious rap and hip hop is not commercially viable? Is this claim true or mistaken? If true, does that say something about hip hop culture, or masculinity within hip hop culture? Why do you believe certain artists snub the label "socially conscious?" Does the label imply a masculine softness in a culture that rewards street-tough masculine archetypes?

HIP HOP, RAP, AND HOMOPHOBIA

In the film *Hip Hop: Beyond Beats & Rhymes* (2006), filmmaker Byron Hurt interviews hip hop star Busta Rhymes and asks Rhymes whether hip hop is ready for a gay rapper?[1] Rhymes states that he won't take that conversation on, adding, "you talking about that homo shit?"[2] Rhymes explains that his culture does not accept homosexuality and refuses to talk any further about it. For some time, certain artists in hip hop and rap have been fairly vocal about their homophobia, including artist Eminem who uses the slur 'fag' and 'faggot' in many of his rhymes. Although he defends his use of these slurs by claiming that they are not aimed at gay people, in tracks like "Rap God" Eminem brags about breaking a table over the back of a couple 'faggots' and goes on to sarcastically shame a male as a "little gay boy" who he believes to be "so gay" he cannot say it with a "straight face."[3] Eminem's fans have long defended his use of homophobic slurs by claiming he is being ironic by using language in sophisticated ways that do not intend harm. Eminem himself claims that, growing up, the term "fag" was used interchangeably with derisive insults "bitch," "punk," or "asshole" as an explanation why his use of "fag" is not intended in a bad way.[4]

But like the rest of American culture, hip hop and rap have been undergoing their own transformations. Rap star Wale recently stated, "I think 2015 is another world, as compared to 1995. It used to be taboo to be a part of the gay community, now it's taboo to speak bad on the gay community."[5] In 2012, singer-rapper Frank Ocean came out and stated afterward, "I feel like a free man."[6] Other prominent rappers who have come out in the past few years are Deadlee, Cazwell, Solomon, Le1f, Angel Haze, Zebra Katz, and Tori Fixx, while transgender artists Mykki Blanco and Katastrophe also enjoy success in hip hop and rap. When you add the many pop, rock, and R&B artists who are openly gay, including classic artists Elton John, Barry Manilow, George Michael, Freddie Mercury, Michael Stipe, Culture Club's Boy George, Judas Priest singer Rob Halford, and newer artists Sam Smith, Adam Lambert, and Ricky Martin, music culture can be seen as undergoing a renaissance in attitude toward homosexuality. Yet it is also a measurement of

Continued

society's homophobia that many artists have struggled with coming out in the fear that validation of their sexual orientation may not be accepted well by fans and may ultimately hurt their careers. However, music culture, like much of American culture in general, is changing and challenging homophobia so that many present and future music stars will likely struggle far less with the decision to come out publicly.[7]

---

1 Hurt, Byron. *Hip Hop: Beyond Beats & Rhymes* (Independent Lens, Media Education Foundation, 2006).
2 Ibid.
3 www.azlyrics.com/lyrics/eminem/rapgod.html.
4 www.thedailybeast.com/articles/2013/11/04/eminem-responds-to-anti-gay-criticism-with-same-excuses.html.
5 www.huffingtonpost.com/2015/04/09/wale-gay-rapper_n_7029092.html.
6 http://pitchfork.com/news/47067-frank-ocean-opens-up-about-his-sexuality/.
7 www.newnownext.com/afterelton\coms-top-50-gay-male-musicians/02/2011/.

THOUGHT BOX

Do you think male representation in music is a reflection of prevailing cultural standards at particular historical eras, or do you believe male representation in music influences masculine expression in larger culture? Could it be instead that influence flows in both directions? For instance, music artists in the 1960s reflected the more liberal, anti-establishment sentiments of their time, while many rap artists in the 2000s reflected the more hyper-capitalistic sentiments of their time. Is commercial appeal tied to social and economic sensibilities of particular eras?

Country

While hip hop continues to be at the core of youth culture, other music genres have contributed to shaping masculine standards. A genre of music that is under-examined academically is country-western music, which has evolved over the past two decades to appeal to younger audiences. Alongside a handful of notable female artists that include Faith Hill, Carrie Underwood, and crossover artist Taylor Swift, country music is dominated by white male artists. Tim McGraw, Kenny Chesney, and Luke Bryan are some of the male stars who top the country charts as heteronormative masculine icons for largely white, young men who identify with a host of anthems that include working class conservatism and traditional gender roles for men and women. Through the lens of country music, men are hard-working breadwinners who sometimes indulge and struggle with alcohol, celebrate sexually liberated, but ultimately submissive women, laud traditional family values, deeply love the woman in their life, cope with heartbreak, drive trucks, and cherish their freedom. Another important aspect of manhood in country music is the man as heroic figure who perseveres despite the odds.

Taken together, these themes speak to a generation of men who view contemporary society as a poisonous prescription for taming and domesticating men. Much like the masculine performances in *Duck Dynasty*, the throw-back to conventional patriarchal

FIGURE 8.18: Tim McGraw

masculinity in country music can be viewed as a rebellion against the cultural forces that are considered to be weakening the unbridled, untamed masculine spirit. Country music culture is thus, for men who identify with it, an unapologetic reclamation of masculine pride from the clutches of postmodern masculine deconstruction with the interesting caveat that many contemporary male country music stars have songs in their catalog that chronicle their emotional vulnerability, a narrative that went largely missing during Waylon Jennings's and Willie Nelson's outlaw era.

At the same time, even though country music is famous for more traditional gender characterizations, country music is experiencing a degree of gender scrutiny as more female artists are challenging the stereotype of women in lyrics and videos as passive, sexually objectified eye candy. In 2014, artists Maddie & Tae, made up of Madison Marlow and Taylor Dye, released "Girl in a Country Song" as a critical response to the ways that male country music stars depict women in their songs.[44] Specifically, "Girl in a Country Song" was a response to a string of songs that have been labeled "bro-country" that include "Get me Some of That," by Thomas Rhett, "Aw Naw," by Chris Young, "Redneck Crazy," by Tyler Farr, "My Kinda Party," "Dirt Road Anthem," and "Take a Little Ride," by Jason Aldean, "Boys 'Round Here," by Blake Shelton, and "Get Your Shine On," by Florida Georgia Line.[45] **Bro-Country** is generally defined as a subgenre of country music that centers around the sexual objectification of young women, the consumption of alcohol, partying, and pickup trucks.[46] Older, more established country artists such as Willie Nelson Alan Jackson, Kenny Chesney, Travis Tritt, Brad Paisley and others have criticized bro-country as a poor representation and stereotype of country music and country music culture. Kenny Chesney, on the portrayal of women in bro-country claimed, "Over the last several years, it seems like anytime anybody sings about a woman, she's in cutoff jeans, drinking and on a tailgate ... they objectify the hell out of them."[47] Blake Shelton responded that younger fans didn't care about "the old farts who complain about their songs," but later apologized when country legend Ray Price reminded Shelton of the legacy he was slandering that opened the doors for contemporary country artists like Shelton. Others have not been apologetic. In response to critics, country artist Jason Aldean flippantly stated that "nobody gives a shit" about the opinions of critics.[48] Still, as testimony that a critical analysis of sexism in country music is underway and gaining support, on December 20, 2014, "Girl in a Country Song" reached number one on the Country Airplay chart.[49]

THOUGHT BOX

Musical styles have been, and in many ways continue to be, racially segregated. That is, with very few exceptions, rock and country music have witnessed an overwhelming presence of white artists and a white fan base, while R&B, hip hop, and rap have had an overwhelming number of black artists, and pop music is probably the only mainstream style that has seen much more racial integration. Why do you think this is the case? The interesting caveat, of course, is that fans of hip hop and rap are racially integrated more so than that of rock and particularly country. In what ways might gender, socioeconomic class, and political alliance effect the race and gender of artists and their fan base? We see, for instance, that with metal music (covered below) the fan base is overwhelmingly male. To say that the themes found in metal appeal to males more than females is to push the question to another question "why?"

Metal

An odd but tenacious genre of music that attracts males as its overwhelming support demographic is metal. Arguably, beginning with the rise of the band Black Sabbath in the early 1970s, metal has been a category of music that is filled with sub-categories. But central to the genre is the predominance of males, and more specifically white males, as both band and audience members. With themes of death, hell, Satan, pain, torture, rape, murder, rotting corpses, violence, and sometimes even politics, metal continues to flourish. The iconography of most metal bands is embedded in fantasy with themes that one finds most often in horror films. Will Straw views the predominance of males in metal culture as a connection based on knowledge.[50] Pride is taken in possessing intimate knowledge of the various metal genres as well as knowledge of styles of musicianship and guttural screaming. This is not the sort of math-science book knowledge commonly associated with "nerd" culture, but rather a niche culture knowledge that demonstrates to other metal-heads that you possess an authenticity in your relation to metal music. At the same time, boys and men who consider themselves metal-heads have in common with nerd culture a conscious separation from mainstream music and popular culture. It is a badge of honor in metal culture that one does not participate in interests found most commonly in jock culture or the commercial music produced for the masses. That metal, in all its various forms, is a category that is largely composed of an underground, untraditional community in the U.S. makes it all the more attractive to boys and men who consume it.

Critics have noted, however, that extreme sexual violent content has found its way into the lyrics of some metal artists' work with all the concerns that attend eroticized violence in other media. The band Cannibal Corpse boasts the song, "Stripped, Raped, and Strangled" that celebrates the rape and murder of a young woman and goes on in graphic detail to describe the torture, rape, and strangulation of seven female victims in all. In the same vein, the band Devourment employ lyrics that include stripping women, smashing fists into women's faces, and stabbing women in the guts so that "the fucking [can] begin."[51] Fans point out that the luridly violent and misogynistic lyrics are created for purposes of fantasy in the same way that horror films are produced to evoke mediated fear and fantasy, but not to cause actual harm.[52] Critics argue, however, that lyrics of brutal rape and murder cannot simply be dismissed on grounds of fantasy. Music critic Jill Mikkelson asks, "Would we tolerate an epic glorification of lynching? No. So, why is

FIGURE 8.19: Cannibal Corpse

sexual violence shrugged off?"[53] Mikkelson goes on to state that when artists are challenged about lyrics of this kind, they become defensive and avoid the conversation.[54] Writing for Houston Press, Kristy Loye states, "Metal is long overdue for an overhaul ... its exclusion of women and rampant sexual aggression needs a serious reckoning," adding that metal is quickly becoming an embarrassing subclass of musical racism and sexism.[55] Shawna Potter, lead vocalist for the feminist punk band War on Women notes, "When men in bands write misogynistic or sexist lyrics, they're just writing what they know. Society has shaped us to believe that women are second-class citizens, here on Earth for men's pleasure and that men are entitled to women's bodies."[56]

> **THOUGHT BOX**
>
> Artists and record company executives will often argue that violent lyrics, including sexually violent lyrics like those discussed here, are only meant to be taken in a fictional sense similar to the way that horror films are taken to be fictional entertainment. What do you think of this argument?

Summary

It is hard to accurately quantify the impact masculine identity in music has had on boys and young men over eras, but there is little doubt that for generations, male music stars have represented masculine archetypes to young men who are looking for identities that they believe offer them status among other males and sexual credibility in the eyes of women. At the same time, contemporary popular music, like American culture at large, is opening to LGBTQ artists and taking seriously LGBTQ issues, and this direction will almost certainly continue to grow. With respect to masculinities, while music styles and music artists will continue to evolve, like the question of the chicken or the egg, we are left to wonder whether music stars influence masculine identity in larger culture or whether there are elements within culture that influence the masculine identities of male, music stars. In all likelihood, the transaction between masculine styles in music and larger culture is a fluid exchange of ideas and archetypes that will continue to reflect the evolving nature of masculine identities within society with boys and men looking to music culture and music culture looking at boys and men to construct new, masculine archetypes.

Notes

1 www.cnn.com/2012/06/18/showbiz/bruce-springsteen-wrecking-ball-working-man/.
2 Dolan, Marc, *Bruce Springsteen and the Promise of Rock 'n' Roll* (W.W. Norton, 2012).
3 King, Martin, *Men, Masculinity and the Beatles* (Ashgate Publishing, 2013).
4 Whitehead, John W., "How the Beatles changed the world," The Rutherford Institute, November 30, 2005. www.rutherford.org/publications_resources/oldspeak/how_the_beatles_changed_the_world_an_interview_with_steven_d_stark.
5 www.nytimes.com/movie/review?res=EE05E7DF173DE267BC4E52DFB066838C679EDE.
6 www.theguardian.com/music/2006/jan/22/popandrock.davidbowie.
7 www.high50.com/us/culture/the-first-metrosexual.
8 www.cbc.ca/news/arts/david-bowie-lgbt-1.3399216.
9 www.cnn.com/2016/01/11/fashion/david-bowie-gender-drag/.
10 https://en.wikipedia.org/wiki/Say_It_Loud_%E2%80%93_I'm_Black_and_I'm_Proud.
11 www.cnn.com/2012/06/18/showbiz/bruce-springsteen-wrecking-ball-working-man/.
12 Dolan, *Bruce Springsteen and the Promise of Rock 'n' Roll*.
13 Rosin, Hanna. *The End of Men and the Rise of Women* (Riverhead Books, 2013).
14 www.neatorama.com/2012/11/13/The-Most-Misunderstand-Political-Campaign-Song-in-History/.
15 www.politifact.com/punditfact/statements/2014/aug/24/juan-williams/juan-williams-no-1-cause-death-african-americans-1/.
16 www.seattlepi.com/ae/tv/article/On-TV-Film-is-tough-viewing-for-hip-hop-heads-1229203.php.
17 https://en.wikipedia.org/wiki/As_Nasty_As_They_Wanna_Be.
18 Dyson, Michael Eric, *Reflecting Black: African-American Cultural Criticism* (University of Minnesota Press, 1993), p. 173.
19 Ibid., p. 174.
20 hooks, bell. "Who Takes the Rap?" February, 1994. http://race.eserver.org/misogyny.html.
21 Ibid.
22 www.theguardian.com/music/2011/jun/13/tupac-biggie-deaths.
23 Stretesky, Paul and Pogrebin, Mark R., "Gang related gun violence: Socialization, identity, and self," *Journal of Contemporary Ethnography*, February, 2007.
24 Iwamoto, Derek, "Tupac Shakur: Understanding the identity formation of hypermasculinity of a popular hip-hop artist," *The Black Scholar*, 33, 2, Black Identity, Black Perspectives (2003), pp. 44–49.
25 Majors, Richard and Billson, Janet, *Cool Pose: The Dilemma of Black Manhood in America* (Touchstone, 1991).
26 Powell, Kevin, *The Education of Kevin Powell: A Boy's Journey into Manhood* (Atria Books, 2015).
27 Ibid., p. 224.
28 Ibid., p. 225.
29 https://en.wikipedia.org/wiki/Tupac_Shakur.
30 https://en.wikipedia.org/wiki/The_Notorious_B.I.G.
31 www.theatlantic.com/magazine/archive/1994/05/the-code-of-the-streets/306601/.
32 Ibid.
33 www.nydailynews.com/entertainment/music/5-eminem-brutal-lyrics-aimed-women-article-1.2318164.

34 Ibid.
35 http://en.wikipedia.org/wiki/Fear_of_a_Black_Planet.
36 http://en.wikipedia.org/wiki/The_Marshall_Mathers_LP.
37 Keith, Thomas, *Generation M: Misogyny in Media and Culture* (Media Education Foundation, 2008).
38 http://webcache.googleusercontent.com/search?q=cache:ts99NlyrOAEJ:www.mediaed.org/assets/products/233/transcript_233.pdf+&cd=1&hl=en&ct=clnk&gl=us.
39 Rose, Tricia, *The Hip Hop Wars: What We Talk About When We Talk About Hip Hop—And Why It Matters* (Basic Civitas Books, 2013).
40 Hurt, Byron, *Beyond Beats and Rhymes* (Independent Lens, Media Education Foundation, 2006).
41 http://hiphopdx.com/news/id.21561/title.kendrick-lamar-addresses-being-labeled-as-a-conscious-rapper.
42 Ibid.
43 www.vibe.com/2014/01/opinion-conscious-rap-dead/.
44 https://en.wikipedia.org/wiki/Girl_in_a_Country_Song.
45 Ibid.
46 https://en.wikipedia.org/wiki/Bro-country.
47 Ibid.
48 Ibid.
49 https://en.wikipedia.org/wiki/Girl_in_a_Country_Song.
50 Straw, Will, "Characterizing rock music cultures: The case of heavy metal." *Canadian University Music Review* 5 (1984), pp. 104–122.
51 http://noisey.vice.com/blog/death-metal-misogyny.
52 http://www.thestar.com.my/news/nation/2006/01/05/fans-defend-black-metal/.
53 http://noisey.vice.com/blog/death-metal-misogyny.
54 ibid.
55 www.houstonpress.com/music/metals-problem-with-women-is-not-going-away-anytime-soon-7858411.
56 Ibid.

Chapter 9

Boys, Men, and Sports

Football is the last bastion of hope for toughness in American men

~ Head Football Coach Jim Harbaugh[1]

I've always known I liked guys. I never really liked sports, but I really have no choice. I was pushed into sports by my dad because he wanted his son to grow up to be a real man … high school football is all about manliness and toughness. It's a true hell on earth for me, and the homophobia is unbelievable. My coaches try to motivate us to hit harder, crunch more, or throw farther by calling us fags all the time. And if you can't do something, or mess it up, you get called a fag. My teammates call all the guys fags, but I think that if they really knew I was, I'd get beaten up. So I just go about trying to prove I'm straight by dating women and talking about girls all the time.

~ Dale, from Eric Anderson's book, *In the Game: Gay Athletes and the Cult of Masculinity.*[2]

LEARNING OBJECTIVES

After reading this chapter, students should be able to respond to the following questions with an understanding of the terms and expressions employed:

- *What common positive traits are associated with sports in the lives of boys and men? What three beneficial traits can a young person who participates in sports possess, according to psychologist Marilyn Price-Mitchell? What is the homosocial aspect of sports?*
- *In what ways have sports been successful in making strides in race-relations in America? In what ways do sports reinforce racial stereotypes?*
- *In what ways do coaches have an influence on boys and men beyond wins and losses?*
- *Are there identifiable signs when a man's devotion to sports has become an obsession? What is meant by "borrowed glory"? What does sociologist Michael Messner mean by "covert intimacy" in regard to men and sports-talk? What is the connection between male sports fans and alcohol consumption? With respect to sports fans, what is meant by the term "blasting"?*

- *What is CTE and how might it be associated with traditional views of masculinity? What is the connection between performance enhancing drugs and masculinity?*
- *In what ways do locker-room environments promote sexist and homophobic attitudes? What do group-pressure conformity studies reveal about male, locker-room chatter?*
- *With respect to high-profile, wealthy, male athletes going bankrupt, what is "the superman syndrome"?*
- *What conflicting opinions exist with respect to professional cheerleaders? What influence upon sports fans do cheerleaders have?*
- *How are professional sports dealing with players who abuse their girlfriends, wives, or acquaintances? What does the answer to this question tell us about gender norms, and particularly masculine norms, in America?*
- *What are the criticisms of university administrators and pro sports officials when it comes to handling athletes who have committed sexual assault and rape? What is the bystander effect?*
- *What are the* Not Alone *and* 1 is 2 Many *programs?*

For many boys and men, sports are an integral part of their lives. From little league to pop warner football to soccer to basketball and hockey, many boys place sports, and usually team-sports, as an important centerpiece in their lives. The positives for boys active in sports are often listed as learning to work within the context of a team, cooperation with others to achieve common goals, learning to win and lose with dignity, the development of a strong work ethic, improved physical health, learning to channel aggression in constructive ways, and higher levels of self-esteem. In non-team sports such as golf and tennis, boys also learn the importance of self-discipline, hard-work, focused attention, and personal achievement. Boys also learn to work with a coaching staff, which can have a powerful mentoring effect in boys' lives, and particularly those boys who may lack positive male role models in their lives. For young men, sports can continue to reinforce these positive attributes and at its best, instill an ongoing sense of cooperation and team work. As men get older, sports are often included in their lives as either a part-time hobby or weekend pursuit, as fans of college and professional teams, or as coaches and mentors in their sons' and daughters' lives. Sports, therefore, has the ability of being a strong bonding experience between fathers, mothers, and children, while also being a force of continual contact with virtues of personal and group achievement. On the other hand, sports culture can reinforce negative ideals such as sexism, homophobia, transphobia, hypermasculinity, over-aggression, bullying, certain health problems, and sports obsessions to the detriment of other important aspects of a boy's or man's life. This chapter will examine a host of issues involving the effect of sports on boys' and men's lives from the valuable to the adverse.

Positive Aspects of Sports in Boys' and Men's Lives

As listed in the introduction to this chapter, sports have been associated with a number of positive traits in the lives of boys and men. The University of Missouri Women's and Children's Hospital cites several beneficial things that come about through a child's contact with sports:[3]

- Learning: many athletes do better at school due to the reinforcement in sports of a skillset that is important to athletes: memorization, repetition, and learning.
- Teamwork: through learning to cooperate and communicate well with others, sports can teach young people the importance and ability to work with others toward the achievement of common goals.
- Health benefits: sports promote fitness and help achieve weight goals, but can also discourage smoking and drinking alcohol, since success in sports often requires strong lungs and a sharp, unobstructed mind.
- Self-esteem: through hard work comes success, and as boys and young men are able to achieve their athletic goals, confidence is a natural side-effect.
- Stress relief and collegiality: athletics allows young people to release stress in healthy, constructive ways, while also forming friendships that transcend the athletic court or playing field.

With childhood obesity rates climbing, researchers note that young people who engage in sports have a better chance of avoiding obesity and the health risks associated with what some experts are calling a national epidemic of childhood obesity.[4] The teamwork aspect of sports participation also reinforces friendships between boys who might not otherwise meet. Boyhood alliances of this kind can be beneficial for boys who are shy or who feel socially awkward. The cooperation between teammates working toward common goals can be a natural starting point for bonding between boys who can extend this sense of cooperation to other relationships in their lives. In many cases, teamwork is an integral part of professional life in business, education, government, science, and a host of pursuits and activities where people interact. Involvement in sports also provides boys and men the working skills of tenacity, courage, and determination that can translate to many other areas of life.

Learning to forge positive relationships with others is also an important element of building self-esteem and inner strength. As reported by the *American Academy of Child & Adolescent Psychiatry*, athletic involvement in team sports can help children develop friendships, have fun, learn to play fair, improve self-esteem, and learn to navigate both winning and losing in constructive and respectful ways.[5] Athletics provide opportunities for teachable moments about life in cases when passion within the context of athletic competition turns into boastfulness, anger, or disrespect toward opponents or officials. In what sport-psychologist Jim Taylor terms "team culture," boys can learn acceptable behaviors that extend to the ways that boys face conflict.[6] If players accept normative rules of conduct within a team environment, positive behaviors will be reinforced between teammates that will be accepted more readily than in environments where this team culture is not in place.

A further benefit for boys who are involved in athletics is that sport becomes a vehicle for family involvement. Parents and siblings often support a boy's or girl's participation in sports, and this can be an amalgamating force for families in general. Furthermore, sporting events are often places where families interact with other families, which benefits overall community involvement. In an age of greater social isolation due to increasing levels of youth involvement in electronic forms of entertainment and social media, sports distinguish themselves as real-time, socially integrated environments where young people interact and bond with one another to pursue common goals.

On the other hand, there have been numerous reports of parents behaving poorly at their children's sporting events. Parental "over-involvement" has led to interference with coaching decisions, which undermines both the authority of the coach and the respect which he or she receives from players. Parents can also behave disrespectfully toward officials on the court or field, which has the effect of teaching boys that authority should be undermined in displays of rage or sarcastic incredulity when a ruling goes against them. Parents can also hyper-criticize their child's play or obsess about winning, undermining the many positive lessons found in youth sports.

But ideally, psychologist Marilyn Price-Mitchell points to three aspects of sports participation that can be positive for boys and youth in general: intensity, continuity, and balance.[7] Taking each in order, "intensity" is a feature of greater time investment in sports participation that yields a superior knowledge of tactics and strategy. According to Price-Mitchell, intensity creates the development of strategic thinking, a skill that can help young people when they enter the job market along with the mastery that follows from repetitively implementing these skills. By "continuity," Price-Mitchell argues that making a commitment to one's participation in sports trains young people to persevere in the wake of setbacks, a trait that will help young people in life when they are faced with obstacles that everyone faces from time to time. By "balance" Price-Mitchell refers to young athletes' ability to time-manage their lives in order to successfully excel at sports, while also learning to achieve in other aspects of their lives such as school performance and other extracurricular commitments they have undertaken. Learning to balance one's life so as to be successful in more than one pursuit, argues Price-Mitchell, is one of the most important aspect of the lessons taught when one is involved in sports. Of course, these traits are ideals. Some athletes may spend an inordinate amount of time pursuing sports to the detriment of other pursuits, but with proper guidance and involvement, many experts argue that sports provide more positives than negatives.

Beyond the benefits to boys, many have noted that sports are often bonding activities for men. This bonding experience is known as **homosociality**. Young men bond around socio-sexual themes in male–male friendships that can sometimes take precedence over their relationships with women. Sociologist Michael Flood writes that much like the behaviors witnessed in military academies, homosocial interactions will shape the normative prescriptions of men's sexual and social relations.[8] The storytelling feature of male bonding around sports can be sexist and homophobic, but, according to sociologist Douglas Hartmann, understanding male sports culture is a key to understanding masculinity in contemporary American culture.[9] Heteronormativity itself is on display most transparently in the ways that males interact and bond with one another around sports, particularly team sports, and much of this heteronormative instruction is reinforced by sports media aimed at men.[10]

When sports journalists speak or write about sports, there is a sense of both tradition and beauty they see in the games they cover that accounts for the widespread popularity of sports. With team sports, there is an exhilaration, aesthetics, and an elegance to athletics, writes literary theorist Hans Gumbrecht, that includes strategic elements, which generates spectator participation.[11] The battle of strategy and will within regulative constraints creates a human drama that pulls the fan into the contest. There are individual competitions within the larger framework of team dynamics that keep interest high throughout the athletic event. Pitchers battle hitters in Major League Baseball. Receivers battle defensive backs in the NFL. There is a game within a game that keeps sports fans plugged into a contest even when the outcome of the game is a foregone conclusion.

In fact, entire cities can galvanize around their sports teams. Arguments have been made that sports are vital to cities both economically and in fostering a spirit of civic pride.[12] An example of civic pride can be seen in the way that the people of Cleveland, Ohio, reacted to news that NBA star LeBron James was leaving the Cleveland Cavaliers to join the Miami Heat, only to return to the Cavaliers four years later.[13] Upon James leaving Cleveland, fans burned his jerseys and tossed James memorabilia into trash cans. Cleveland sports fans were despondent, as their native son, who was considered by many to be the best player in the NBA and the hope for Cleveland to finally win a championship, left to pursue success elsewhere. When James announced that he was returning to

Cleveland to pursue another championship, the collective Cleveland sports fan base was elated and filled with renewed hope. As other NBA stars joined James in Cleveland on his quest to bring a championship to the city, an enthusiasm and confidence replaced the pessimism held by many Cleveland residents who until then had been resigned to mediocrity and watching from the sidelines as other cities raised championship flags. For better or worse, community inhabitants acquire a collective identity in the ups and downs of their city's NCAA and professional sports teams.

Sports can also be viewed as the ultimate meritocracy, where talent mixed with hard work pay off in lucrative contracts and championship rings. The meritocratic aspect of sports is seen by many as a template for civic fairness and diversity. In fact, a notion of egalitarianism also exists in the attitudes of sports fans, as when a very wealthy owner fields a team of superstars in the absence of salary caps or concern over luxury taxes. In these cases, fans in other cities will sometimes form a bond in their mutual dislike of the Goliath team that was purchased through unequal spending. A sense of fairness is a fairly common regulating assumption that fans hold in the belief that the playing field should start out as equal, although others enjoy the idea of a Goliath team that might succumb to loss at the hands of a less financially subsidized team. Ideally, teams are constructed from a pool of talented players without regard to race or ethnic background. The common goal of team owners, managers, coaches, and players is to win, and winning is pinned to fielding the best available players. Yet, the diversity aspect of sports is a relatively new phenomenon, as the history of team sports in America has been one of discrimination and bigotry. For decades, professional team sports were played exclusively by white male players. Women's sports were unheard of and frowned upon, except in certain individual, non-contact sports like ice-skating, or as exceptions to the rule such as the women's baseball league during World War II, when men had gone off to war.[14] For generations, team sports have been dominated until very recently by men, and to this day, media coverage of sports focuses overwhelmingly on male sports. For many, there is a palpable link between sports and masculinity.

The Intersection between Sports, Race, Politics, and Masculinity

One of the more notable points sports historians will sometimes make about the positive influence of sports on society is the contributions sports has made to challenging racism in America. This judgment is controversial for a number of reasons. In surveys, most Americans claim that professional sports have been successful in mollifying racism in American culture.[15] Scholars, however, warn that this contention about sports mitigating racism is fraught with complications. Sports and cultural scholar Grant Jarvie notes that there are tensions when listing the connections between sports and racism that include:[16]

- Sports are a possible instrument for integration, which can then mitigate racism more generally.
- Sports contribute to the unique political struggles of people of color.
- Sports create stereotypes about people of color.
- Sports make statements about masculinity, which can then convert to racist judgments about men of color.

From the entry of Fritz Pollard and Bobby Marshall into what is now the NFL in 1920, to Jackie Robinson entering Major League Baseball in 1947, to Earl Lloyd entering

FIGURE 9.1: Jackie Robinson, Brooklyn Dodgers (1947–1956)

the NBA in 1950, professional sports have gone from all-white leagues to leagues dominated by people of color. From the jeers of early racist fans who did not want professional sports to racially integrate to cheers from contemporary fans who simply want their favorite teams to win, sports have transformed into leagues and teams that draw from players who hail from different parts of the world. This transformation has led some to claim that the integration of sports has opened minds that were once closed to racial integration in other areas of public life such as schools, housing, and jobs.

However, others argue that sports foster stereotypes. Critics contend that one of the more pervasive and tenacious stereotypes is the longstanding one that African-American men are naturally athletic, while Caucasian men are naturally more intelligent.[17] Perhaps one of the most visible places in sports where this racist dichotomy continues to flourish is in conversations about black quarterbacks in the NFL. Long considered to be a position that requires more than innate athletic ability, great quarterbacks are said to require quick thinking and accurate decision-making abilities, while under intense, time-constrained pressure. In an unguarded moment, the once Vice President of Player Personnel for the Los Angeles Dodgers, Al Campanis, stated, and was fired for stating, that he believed of African-American men that "[they] may not have some of the necessities to be a field manager or perhaps general manager,"[18] an oft-heard racist stereotype among fans and insiders who believe that people of color are not smart enough to be given positions of decision-making leadership in sports. High-profile conservative pundit Rush Limbaugh contributed to this racist convention by stating that "The media has been very desirous that a black quarterback do well," as part of his criticism of then Philadelphia Eagles' quarterback Donovan McNabb, who responded by stating, "It's sad that you've got to go to skin color. I thought we were through with that whole deal."[19] But Limbaugh was not through with racist comments, as he then stated in 2007 that "the NFL all too often looks like a game between the *Bloods* and the *Crips* without any weapons" and later claimed, in the belief that clarifying his disdain for racism would set the record straight, "Slavery—indentured servitude, whatever you want to call it—is abominable, *particularly in a free country*," blithely assuming that slavery is not as bad in countries that do not tout the importance individual freedoms.[20]

RACIST LOGOS AND MASCOTS IN SPORTS

One of the more visible forms of racism in sports is found in the controversy surrounding the name of the NFL team Washington Redskins. A coalition of 100 Native American and social justice groups sent a letter to television and radio broadcasters in every city with an NFL team asking them not to utter the Washington Redskins name.[1] The NAACP joined in denouncing the name 'Washington "Redskins"' stating, "What affects one of us, affects us all."

Washington "Redskins" owner Daniel Snyder argues that the team name is meant as a "badge of honor," but Jacqueline Johnson Pata, executive director of the National Congress of American Indians responds by arguing that the use of Native Americans as mascots is demeaning and harmful, adding, "By recognizing the ongoing disparagement of American Indians and Alaska Natives and asking the NFL to change the name of the D.C. franchise, the Leadership Conference reconfirms its commitment to fighting for equal rights for Native peoples."[2] Other allegations of racist logos and mascots include the logos from the Cleveland "Indians" and the Atlanta "Braves." Native Americans have longed maintained the view that

FIGURE 9.2: Washington "Redskins" logo

FIGURE 9.3: Cleveland "Indians" logo

Continued

FIGURE 9.4: Florida State University "Seminoles" logo

racist logos and mascots create negative stereotypes about Native American men as "savages" and "warriors" that had to be tamed by white men of European descent.

Universities also promote these same racist symbols with stereotyped imagery of Native Americans as primitive, savage warriors. The Florida State University "Seminoles" and the North Dakota "Fighting Sioux" are among the more notable examples of this sort of thing. In each of these cases, Native men are used as mascots for a sports team.

The National Congress of American Indians posts on its website, "rather than honoring Native peoples, these caricatures and stereotypes are harmful, perpetrate negative stereotypes of America's first peoples, and contribute to disregard for the personhood of Native peoples."[3] Yet there are those who continue to defend the practice of using Native people, and more precisely Native men, as sports mascots, claiming it is meant as a measure of respect.[4] [5] Others argue that the names and imagery of Native men as mascots is simply a matter of tradition.[6] But then, slavery and racism has a long tradition in American culture without too many defending it. Can you imagine an NCAA or professional sports team calling themselves "The Blackskins" and using racist iconography of a black man as a mascot or logo, and then defending it by claiming that it is tradition or that it is used out of respect for black people?

FIGURE 9.5: Imagine NBA or NCAA team "the Blackskins" and their above logo

Continued

If you believe there is a difference between the two that makes one racist and the other not racist, what is that difference?

1 www.washingtonpost.com/local/native-american-coalition-urging-broadcasters-not-to-use-redskins-name/2014/09/03/1a33cce4-337e-11e4-9e92-0899b306bbea_story.html.
2 www.washingtonpost.com/local/civil-rights-groups-coalition-calls-for-washington-redskins-to-change-name/2013/12/12/14ee6248-635a-11e3-aa81-e1dab1360323_story.html.
3 www.ncai.org/proudtobe.
4 http://ftw.usatoday.com/2014/08/redskins-video.
5 http://conservativetribune.com/redskins-is-not-racist/.
6 www.huffingtonpost.com/rev-emily-c-heath/redskins-and-respect-a-li_b_4178743.html.

In 2014, NBA players joined the national discussion about racism in America by wearing tee-shirts that read "I Can't Breathe" in response to the death of Michael Brown in Ferguson, Missouri and Eric Gardner in Staten Island, New York at the hands of police officers.[21] Eric Gardner was an African-American man who was killed by being held in a choke-hold by police officer Daniel Pantaleo in New York—a maneuver that is prohibited—even though he was not resisting and instead stating desperately that he couldn't breathe.[22] A grand jury in New York did not indict Mr. Pantaleo and this set off a wave of protests across America.[23] FOX News pundit Geraldo Rivera criticized athletes who wore the tee-shirts suggesting that athletes should use their influence to spread "more urgent messages to the black community such as 'Be a better father' or 'Raise your children.'"[24] In similar fashion, members of the St. Louis Rams entered the field on game day with their hands in the air as a symbol of solidarity with those who were protesting police brutality against African-American people.[25] On sports talk radio, many white fans around the country were angry that players had taken this stand, commenting that players were "ruining the game" and "abusing their privilege of being professional athletes" by "making sports political."[26]

Sports journalist and author Dave Zirin makes the point that professional sports, and particularly the NFL, have been and continue to be political, using examples such as the public funding of stadiums, displays of nationalism and militarism at sports arenas, war planes flying overhead during the national anthem, or having military commanders flip the coin at the opening of games.[27] Zirin is not claiming that supporting troops is wrong, rather his point is that it is a myth to view sports as apolitical. More specifically, Zirin argues that the politics of sports is decidedly conservative in orientation with examples including ex-NFL player Tim Tebow's endorsement of *Focus on the Family*, a conservative organization that condemns homosexuality and views being gay as "repairable," or the militarist-friendly FOX News talking point that criticism of the war in Iraq meant that the critic is not patriotic or that the critic is an actual traitor to America.[28] As the military has been politicized by journalists and politicians, the inclusion of a military presence during sporting events creates a de facto politicization of sports that, at a minimum, debunks the claim of critics that some players have politicized what is otherwise apolitical. Zirin notes that criticism almost always ensues after a player publicly adopts what is taken to be a politically liberal position such as NBA all-star Steve Nash's position against war in general.[29] At the same time, conservative political affiliation is not met with the same controversy in sports. Understanding that the NFL has a large base of conservative fans and that media and teams have exploited this fact to promote games and network programming by associating NFL product with military pageantry,

FIGURE 9.6: Author, sports journalist, Dave Zirin

conservative group "Americans for Prosperity" set up booths outside of NFL stadiums on game days to hand out free tee-shirts to fans who are willing to provide personal contact information in order to receive materials from the conservative organization.[30]

Other scholars have noted that media representations of athletes of color have often been stereotypes.[31] Some of the ways that these racist stereotypes are framed is when a sportscaster refers to white players' work ethic versus the 'natural athletic talent' of African-American athletes. Yet another way these stereotypes are reinforced is by suggesting that white players have leadership qualities or greater composure under pressure, while African-American and Latino players are physically talented and passionate. One example of racist stereotypes has been the media treatment of Japanese players in Major League Baseball, where players like Hideo Nomo, Hideki Irabu, Hisashi Iwakuma, and Ichiro Suzuki are often depicted in idealized ways as being respectful and humble players who allegedly fit well into American society, as opposed to some African-American and Latino players who are sometimes depicted as arrogant, aggressive, and often rude in media interviews.

A specific example of racist stereotypes in sports can be seen in the treatment of NBA point guard Jeremy Lin. While playing for the New York Knicks, Lin, who was born in Los Angeles, attended Harvard University, and is of Taiwanese descent, came off of the bench in the wake of an injury to starting guard Iman Shumpert in 2012.[32] Lin's performance was so impressive that a global following ensued under the banner "Linsanity." At the same time, Lin's emergence was met with several racist misadventures including Ben & Jerry's introduction of "Taste the Lin-Sanity" frozen yogurt, which included fortune cookies, or the MSG image that featured Lin's head popping out of a fortune cookie that read, "The Knicks' Good Fortune."[33] Jokes about Asians also followed in the wake of Lin's success in the NBA, as one ESPN commentator used the occasion of a Knicks loss to state that there was a "chink in the armor" of the Knicks.[34]

Sports, race, and masculinity are features often united in the ways that athletes are depicted and considered. Athletic prowess itself has generally been regarded as a measurement of masculine aptitude. Those boys and men who are not athletically interested or inclined are common targets for bullying and ridiculed as being males who do not measure up to the masculine standards posed by contemporary culture. But as athleticism and masculinity are enmeshed at the same time that men of color have excelled in sports, the paradigm of masculinity becomes, for some, the association of hegemonic masculinity with alleged black masculine, athletic superiority. Males are then sometimes judged against a stereotype that stratifies masculinity by race and ethnicity. Being athletically talented, muscular, physically strong and capable, highly competitive, and aggressive becomes not only a stereotype about black masculinity, but a hegemonic masculine template against which all men are judged and against which some men judge themselves. Against this background, a jock–nerd duality has longed been part of male culture, where more athletically inclined men are usually considered to be superior not only in terms of coordination and physical strength, but in terms of their alleged superior social aptitude and ability to attract women.

If male sports is a religion for some men, ESPN can plausibly be viewed as their church. Founded in 1979 and owned by Disney, ESPN generates more revenue for Disney than all of its other properties combined.[35] The vast majority of ESPN coverage of sports is men's sports whether television or radio coverage or sports-talk formatted programming. Male athletes are lionized and revered for their enormous athletic talent, while sports media profits from covering everything from dazzling plays on the field to scandals that erupt off of the playing field. One problem with sports-celebrity media coverage is that some of the good things players do off of the playing field or basketball court are not given much media attention, while arrests and strip club wrongdoings are fodder for weeks of ratings-motivated coverage. Seattle Seahawks all-star Richard Sherman made this point powerfully and exposed racist assumptions when asked by a sports journalist why "all of you football guys go to strip clubs to rain down money on strippers?" Sherman responded, "Well, I've never gone into a strip club and thrown money, so I couldn't tell you."[36] The feeding frenzy of sports media to uncover the most salacious story about star athletes has sometimes made it look more like tabloid journalism than anything approaching respectable news gathering and has assisted in proliferating negative stereotypes, including racist stereotypes, about athletes.

THOUGHT BOX

To what extent do you believe the so-called "jock–nerd polarity" continues to be an element of school-aged children, bullying, and masculine culture in general? Is there a problem, in your opinion, with the amount of praise and attention given to athletes as opposed to men and boys who excel in other pursuits?

The Problematic Intersection of Boxing and Men of Color

For decades, the world of boxing was dominated by white boxers. Historian Will Cooley of Walsh University notes that boxing has been a traditional domain where "white-ethnic" boxers were heralded as "symbolic affirmations of collective masculinity."[37] From Irish-American boxing legend Jack Dempsey to Italian-American boxers, sometimes branded "Italian Stallions," Rocky Graziano and Jake LaMotta, about whom the film *Raging Bull* (1980) starring Robert DeNiro was made, boxing has been a realm where working class men proved their toughness, but where racial and ethnic divides were also on display. Boxing fans would split down racial and ethnic lines to root for the boxer who vicariously represented the men who hailed from Irish, Italian, or Jewish neighborhoods,

FIGURE 9.7: Jack Johnson (left) and Jim Flynn (right) prepare to box, 1912

as the case may be. As African-American boxers emerged, most notably Jack Johnson, who in 1908 defeated Tommy Burns to capture the heavyweight championship of the world, a search began to find what was termed, "the great white hope."[38]

In a capitalist, patriarchal culture such as American culture, manhood has long been measured by either economic wealth or physical strength. For those men who came from lower socioeconomic backgrounds and neighborhoods, personal wealth seemed unattainable leaving physical strength and fighting ability as the default measurement for masculine credibility. But given the racist nature of American culture, the fact that black boxers were beginning to dominate boxing in the twentieth century posed a challenge to those who believed fighting ability to be at the central core of masculinity and manhood. If black men consistently defeated white men in the boxing ring, white men were stuck with a conundrum: either view black men as more masculine than white men, or reinvent masculine credibility as having to do with something other than physical prowess and fighting ability. Contemporary boxer Floyd Mayweather Jr. recognized this very fact when he stated in an interview,

> In boxing, we know who's dominating. Black fighters and Hispanic fighters [are] dominating in this sport. And this is not a racial statement but there's no white fighters in boxing that's dominating, so they had to go to something else and start something new.[39]

The most notable and polarizing figure in American boxing history was the figure of Muhammad Ali. Born "Cassius Clay" in Louisville, Kentucky, Ali converted to Islam in 1965, vocally opposed the war in Vietnam, was known for his flamboyant style in the ring, and perhaps most memorably for his caustic statements that didn't shy away from the subject of race. About his refusal to be inducted into the armed forces, Ali stated, "no Vietcong ever called me nigger."[40] Emphasizing both race and socioeconomics, Ali claimed of fans of his opponent Joe Frazier, "The only people rooting for Joe Frazier are

FIGURE 9.8: Muhammad Ali, 1966

white people in suits, Alabama sheriffs, and members of the Ku Klux Klan. I'm fighting for the little man in the ghetto."[41]

Even though headline boxing events today are multimillion dollar spectacles that take place in the splashy surroundings of Las Vegas and other exotic cities, there is still a working class, masculine identity shaping the sport. Present-day boxing is dominated by Latino boxers, while the presence of African-American boxers continues, but in a less prevailing way. In the book *Boxing and Masculinity*, Gregory Rodriquez, director of Arizona State University's Center for Social Cohesion, writes,

> In the first half of the twentieth century, Los Angeles boxing contributed to a sense of ethnic belonging among Mexican-descent people in much the ways flags, anthems, religious icons, geographical boundaries, commonality of language, political structures, and the ideas of shared culture did. In the second half of the century, movements for Mexican American self-determination in the United States heightened awareness of group differences; nationalistic and ethnic expressions in boxing permitted the blurring of differences and helped to unite a people behind a single sporting ideal.[42]

As boxing both solidifies and blurs ethnic identities, a common factor for many young men who enter the boxing profession is the lure of wealth and recognition. In line with American capitalistic masculinity, many young men who grow up in poverty or near poverty view sports, and in this case boxing, as an avenue out of poverty and into lives of prosperity and fame.

The fighting styles of Latino boxers has been described as *Latinidad*, which has come to mean in boxing circles, a very aggressive form of fighting that has been contrasted by the more stylized fighting approaches of white and African-American boxers, although authors David J. Leonard and Carmen R. Lugo-Lugo view this designation as being more a stereotype that corresponds to the more common generalization of Mexican men as "macho, self-sacrificing individuals who are willing to sacrifice their safety and well-being for their families or personal goals."[43] [44] Still, others view boxing, along with other contact sports considered aggressive or violent in nature, as promoting racial stereotypes or at least that media coverage of these sports support racial stereotypes, the most common being that African-American and Latino men are, by nature, more aggressive and violent than white and Asian men.[45]

THOUGHT BOX

Until recently, boxing and MMA fighting have been male-centric sports. Both have drawn criticism for their violence and celebration of violence. But they have also been criticized for promoting racial stereotypes. What are your thoughts about this?

Homophobia in Sports

In the book, *In The Game: Gay Athletes and the Cult of Masculinity*, sociologist and former NCAA coach Eric Anderson details the link between sports and homophobia.[46] Despite the recent emergence of gay athletes in professional sports, Anderson argues that sports culture continues to support a deeply homophobic environment where homosexuality is synonymous with "weakness and emotional frailty," such that the term *gay athlete* "remains an oxymoron."[47] The institution of organized sports is itself, reports Anderson, predicated on "an orthodox form of masculinity that is rigid and exclusive for many types of men and most women."[48] Yet gay men are attracted to sports, Anderson speculates, in part because competitive athletics continue to be one of the most gender-segregated institutions in Western culture.[49] At the same time, sports beams with "young, toned, sexualized, and highly masculinized bodies," which serve as homoerotic enticement for gay boys and men.[50]

OPENLY GAY ATHLETES IN PROFESSIONAL TEAM SPORTS

In 2013, Jason Collins was first openly gay player to play in the NBA; In 2014, Michael Sam became the first openly gay player to be drafted by an NFL team, although he did not play in an NFL game; Glenn Burke who played for the Los Angeles Dodgers and Oakland A's from 1976 to 1979 made no secret of his sexual orientation to the front office or teammates, came out to the rest of the world in a 1982 article for *Inside Sports* and later in an appearance on *The Today Show* with Bryant Gumbel.[1]

FIGURE 9.9: Michael Sam

1 www.theatlantic.com/entertainment/archive/2013/05/actually-jason-collins-isnt-the-first-openly-gay-man-in-a-major-pro-sport/275523/.

Yet with all of the outward signs of homophobia in sports, Anderson also notes that attitudes toward homosexuality are rapidly changing in the U.S. and among American athletes. In a 2014 ESPN survey of 51 NFL players, 85% claimed that a teammate's sexual orientation didn't matter to them.[51] A 2015 survey of sports fans reported that 73% supported the signing of gay or lesbian players to professional sports teams.[52] This is not to say that there are no longer issues that need to be addressed. Former NFL player Wade Davis claims that there still exists a culture in the NFL that is okay with casual homophobia and sexist language.[53] With the emergence of gay athletes coming out in professional sports, Davis continues, there will be more accountability. Many of today's players are under the assumption that no one is offended by the homophobic slurs because many pro athletes are convinced that there are no gay players on their team. But with players coming out, Davis notes, that assumption can no longer be held. Jason Collins, who is credited as being the first openly gay player to play in the NBA adds,

> When we get to the point where a gay pro athlete is no longer forced to live in fear that he'll be shunned by teammates or outed by tabloids, when he's not compelled to hide his true self, then coming out won't be a big deal. We're not there yet.[54]

With respect to the changing attitudes toward homosexuality and homosexual relationships, Anderson adds,

> If masculinity is predicated on homophobia, and homophobia is the chief policing agent against behaviors coded as feminine, then the reduction of cultural homophobia would lead to a significant change to the manner in which masculinity is both constructed and maintained.[55]

If Anderson is correct, sports culture may be at a crossroads. He writes, "if everything changes round sport, sport will either have to change or it will lose its social significance and be viewed as a vestige of an archaic model of masculinity."[56] Cultural institutions like sports have been forced to adapt to social change as did Major League Baseball with the entry of Jackie Robinson in 1947 and the eventual emergence of international players or avoid diversity at their own peril.

FIGURE 9.10: Sociologist, Eric Anderson

THOUGHT BOX

Do you agree with Eric Anderson that sports must adapt to the increasing acceptance of homosexuality or risk being seen as archaic and outmoded? Discuss the specific ways you believe sports need to change. Are there policies that need changing or is this transformation more a product of individual attitudes that must keep up with societal change? A bit further into the chapter, we examine coaching. What can coaches do to facilitate changes in attitude within sports with respect to sexism and homophobia?

Intersex Athletes

Beyond the many instances of homophobia in sports, intersex athletes face discrimination that reinforce the gender binary conventions of greater society. As sociologist Erving Goffman notes in his oft-cited article, "The Arrangement Between the Sexes,"

> The functioning of sex-differentiated organs is involved, but there is nothing in this functioning that biologically recommends segregation; that arrangement is totally a cultural matter.[57]

Goffman's work is most famous for his insight into the gendered nature of advertising, but it also deftly reveals how popular culture is grounded in maintaining a firm, dual gender identification. Individuals who do not conform to this duality are treated with suspicion and conjecture. This ill treatment can be notably seen in the treatment of intersex athletes. *Intersex* describes a person who possesses variation in sex characteristics, whether chromosomal or genital. These variations can take the form of genital ambiguity, a nonconventional genotype or sexual phenotype. Like all individuals, intersex people can have various gender identities, which include traditional or nontraditional gender identities.

With respect to sports, members of the intersex community have faced judgment and disqualification as officials attempt to enforce strict binary sex and gender regulations in their respective sports. One of more persistent concerns is that intersex athletes have an unfair advantage when participating in women's competitions. The charge is that intersex athletes possess more testosterone than most women, giving them a biological edge over the competition. This charge, however, has been debunked.[58] Most conspicuously, experts have noted that there is no evidence that elevated serum-testosterone levels bring about heightened athletic performance.[59] The view that elevated Serum-T levels enhance athletic performance finds some evidence only when massive amounts of testosterone are introduced to the system and is found to enhance only very specific types of athletic activity such as weight lifting where muscle mass is important.[60] For runners in track and field events, increased muscle mass can actually be a detriment.

More controversial are the actions that have been taken to "confirm gender" in sports, and most notably in the Olympics and world sporting events. Beginning in 1950, female athletes competing in world athletic events were subjected to *gender verification testing* by the IAAF (International Association of Athletics Federations).[61] [62] Political scientist Maren Behrensen argues that gender testing is unethical and pointless, and asks, "Do we need gender police in professional sports?"[63] Behrensen condemns the practice of targeting certain athletes and subjecting them to the indignity and humiliation of a procedure that has no bearing on athletic ability and that further violates privacy in the service of accommodating interphobia.[64] Stanford bioethicist Katrina Karkazis concurs and adds, "the fact that sport is divided into male and female categories is the real background problem here."[65]

CASTER SEMENYA

In 2009, South African middle distance runner Caster Semenya won silver and gold medals in 800-meter distance events at World Championship events. It was announced that the International Association of Athletics Federations (IAAF) subjected her to gender testing after her victories.[1]

Semenya's coach, Wilfred Daniels, resigned in the wake of the IAAF ruling that forced her to undergo gender testing, claiming that he failed to protect her. In an interview, Semanya stated, "God made me the way I am and I accept myself."[2]

FIGURE 9.11: South African middle distance runner, world champion, Caster Semenya

1 https://en.wikipedia.org/wiki/Caster_Semenya.
2 Ibid.

Writer and intersex activist Hilda Viloria calls out the Olympics by arguing that gender verification and the discrimination it supports contradicts the Olympics' own charter, which reads in part, "Every individual must have the possibility of practicing sport, without discrimination of any kind."[66] Viloria argues that the issues involved with intersex athletes are not really about sex, but about perceptions of gender and class.[67] Dr. Payoshni Mitra who is an advisor for Sports Authority of India, notes that if people are really concerned about fairness, then factors such as the greater access first-world athletes have to training resources ought to be taken into account.[68] Viloria agrees and adds,

> What infuriates me is that intersex women of color from Third World nations, who escaped harmful medical practices as infants, are still being hurt if they're "found out"

> as adults. Their healthy bodies and successful careers are being ripped away because of some people's irrational fear of their difference.[69]

An even greater indignity and discriminatory judgment lurks in the view that intersex is a condition that needs to be corrected, a judgment made of homosexuality in the past.[70] Elizabeth Reis of the University of Oregon argues that we should question the ethics of any who promote the view that intersex individuals have a pathology that requires therapeutic intervention, a view actually sponsored by some on the International Olympics Committee (IOC).[71] The issue, argues Reis, is not one of concern for unfair athletic advantage, but one of discrimination that is grounded in the view that *gender normality* must be maintained.

Coaches

As mentioned above, for many boys and young men, coaches become surrogate father figures who command great respect and serve as role models for behavior. As with other aspects of sports, the influence a coach has on boys and young men can be enormously positive. Former UCLA and NBA basketball star Jamaal Wilkes stated the following about his legendary coach at UCLA, John Wooden:

> What he taught us transcended basketball and related to life. It stuck with all of us. The things he said were simple, yet profound. He was highly efficient and a genius when it came to teaching.[72]

Coach Wooden was famous for his "pyramid of success," which was a 15-step initiative meant to be applied to "the game of life" every bit as much as the game of basketball. Wooden's pyramid was built upon 15 steps with a theme of being the best that you can be rather than being concerned about competition,[73] as captured in his statement, "As long as you try your best, you are never a failure."[74] Wooden also emphasized the importance of the team over any one individual's accomplishments and argued that success in teamwork is achieved when no one cares about who gets credit.[75]

FIGURE 9.12: Duke University's Men's Head Basketball Coach Mike Krzyzewski

The praise bestowed upon Coach Wooden has been echoed over time by many players who worked under coaches who promoted values and life-lessons. About the late Coach Dean Smith of the University of North Carolina, former player Al Wood states,

> He used to tell us, "there's 10 million people in China who don't know we played a ballgame tonight." That's putting the game of basketball into perspective. We would give it all that we have when we're on the court, but it's not life and death, and that's perspective.[76]

It is not uncommon for players to lionize their coaches and remember life-lesson talks more than the sports-related talks. One of the more cited quotes by a coach comes from legendary basketball coach Jim Valvano, who died of cancer in 1993 at age 47, but is remembered for his courage, determination, and wisdom in statements like, "Cancer can take away all of my physical abilities. It cannot touch my mind, it cannot touch my heart, it cannot touch my soul," and his iconic quote that was meant to transcend both basketball and cancer, "Don't give up. Don't ever give up."[77]

On the other hand, coaches who practice poor behaviors can also influence their players in negative ways. In April, 2013, Rutgers University fired men's basketball coach Mike Rice after a video was released showing Rice verbally and physically abusing players.[78] In the video, Rice can be seen throwing basketballs at players, while berating them with verbal attacks calling them "faggots" during a team practice session. Sports journalist Andrew Sharp writing for SB Nation argues that the Rice scandal at Rutgers University is simply the tip of an iceberg, that many NCAA coaches behave in similar ways when cameras are not capturing their exploits.[79] In 2014, the College of Charleston fired its men's head basketball coach, Doug Wojcik, after allegations of verbal abuse against players and staff led to an investigation.[80] In 2015, Vanderbilt University's men's basketball coach Kevin Stallings was captured on film yelling at a player, "I'll fucking kill you."[81] Legendary NCAA basketball coach Bob Knight was famous for courtside tirades that would include blistering levels of profanity aimed at referees, throwing chairs across the court in displays of rage and immaturity aimed at a referee decision; he once stated in an interview with NBC correspondent Connie Chung, "if rape is inevitable, relax and enjoy it."[82] The number of young men who played under Knight and who looked up to him then and now is enormous in size.

While coaches hold tremendous sway over boys and young men, the problem of coaches who abuse their power and who reinforce sexist and homophobic messages to players has risen to the point that Spike TV created the reality show *Coaching Bad*, featuring ex-NFL player Ray Lewis and anger management specialist Dr. Christian Conte, to investigate and seek solutions to this growing problem.[83] Of the show, executive producer John Irwin states,

> I think it's an eye-opening experience to see what could be happening out there if you have a child who's involved in sports. It gives you a sense that if your kid tells you something's going on, parents will know what to watch out for overall.[84]

In Florida, the issue of out-of-control coaches in youth sports led lawmakers to draft a bill that would require coaches who are thrown out of a game by officials to be banned for the season.[85] Speaking about the bill, state senator Jeremy Ring noted, "youth coaches also serve as teachers, and schools wouldn't allow similar behavior in classrooms."[86] In addition to poor behaviors by coaches, many people have witnessed the reprehensible behavior of parents who, while attending their son's or daughter's athletic event, release a torrent of foul language and threatening behavior in the wake of a referee, umpire, or coaching decision that they believe adversely affected their child, while children look on.

Writing for NFL Player Engagement in a piece entitled "A Call to Coaches," Tony Porter, Director of men's leadership organization *A CALL TO MEN* writes,

> Envision a football coach at the end of a practice surrounded by forty boys all on one knee looking up at him. What a wonderful time to have a conversation with our boys and young men about being men of integrity, substance, and character.[87]

Knowing how important coaches are in the lives of boys and men, non-profit organization *Positive Coaching Alliance* (PCA) was founded by Jim Thompson in 1998 within Stanford University's athletic department and has assembled a who's who of sports figures on the advisory board to promote the idea that the "win-at-all-costs" mentality found in much of youth sports needs to be replaced with a model of coaching that creates a positive, character-building experience for boys and young male athletes.[88] PCA emphasizes three main points: (1) the double-goal of winning while also promoting the more important goal of teaching life lessons, (2) assuring that coaches train athletes to play with honor and respect of rules, opponents, officials, teammates, and self, and (3) fostering a kind of positive-coaching style that will come to dominate coaching approaches around the nation.[89] Many agree that coaching is in need of a revolution that emphasizes honor and respect within the framework of athletic competition that all too often is more about winning at any cost. As the controversial owner of the Oakland Raiders, Al Davis, once infamously stated, "Just win, baby!" This acquisitive proclamation today serves as the hallmark of NCAA and professional sports, as coaches' careers are determined by their records of wins and losses. Many, both in and outside of the sports world, believe it is time to adopt a different model.

THOUGHT BOX

Do you agree with State Senator Ring that coaches are teachers and so must be held accountable for hostile outbursts or do you believe coaching is different from classroom teaching? Explain your answer. What, in your opinion, is the best way of handling overzealous and unruly parents who attend sporting events that feature their child? If the answer is to force them to leave the game, who will or should reinforce such a directive?

The Sports Fan: Pastime or Male Religion?

For many men, contact with sports is an ongoing pastime well beyond their years of playing sports. This can be a positive thing for many men who find comradery with other men and women who share their love for sports and who cheer on a team together, or who enjoy debating with one another over a variety of sports-related minutiae. For others, the 'fanatic' part of 'sports-fan' comes to define their involvement in and allegiance to sports. For these men, sports are a quasi-religion that commands much of their time and emotional energy. Some of these fans approach their passion for sports with a similar intensity found in coaches and the players themselves.

Sports psychologists have in the past believed that sports fans are alienated and lonely, but research from the University of Kansas suggests the very opposite.[90] According to researchers, sports fans experience fewer bouts of depression than non-sports fans.[91] Robert Cialdini of Arizona State University argues that the fan today identifies himself with the athlete and becomes centrally involved in the wins and losses of his favorite team.[92] Cialdini notes that the sports fan is able to gain self-esteem and respect through participating in the glory of his team's success independent of the lack of any personal

FIGURE 9.13: Oakland Raiders fan

success he himself has achieved. This sense of **borrowed glory** is reflected in the language used by fans in the wake of a victory: "we won."[93] The connection between fans and team success or failure can be all the more intense when a fan internalizes the elation or sorrow associated with wins and losses.

But other research has revealed problems. In one study, fans of college sports were found to engage in higher levels of binge and heavy alcohol consumption than non-sports fans.[94] Another study noted that one in 12 sports fans leaves a game intoxicated with a blood-alcohol level of .08 or higher.[95] When you consider that an average NFL game packs in 67,500 fans,[96] that equates to 5,625 legally drunk fans who leave each NFL stadium each week during football season. Collectively, that brings the total number of legally drunk fans hitting the road after NFL games to 90,000.[97] Many of them are probably not driving, but many are. According to The Harvard School of Public Health, 53% of sports fans binge drink when drinking alcohol, with a statistical edge going to men over women.[98] According to the Harvard study, because of their heavier drinking, sports fans are more likely to experience problems that include higher rates of run-ins with the law, sexual violence, and for those who are students, overall problems with their schoolwork.[99] One of the authors of the study, Henry Weschler, blames, in part, the alcohol industry's long-time connection of its product with sports, along with liquor stores', bars', and supermarkets' promotional alcohol specials that are tied into certain athletic events like the Super Bowl, World Series, NBA Championship, NCAA Basketball Tournament, or NFL Monday Night Football.[100]

In the book *Professional Marketing and Advertising Essays and Assignments*, author Tony Ma notes that advertisements for beer specifically target men with a surplus of sexually objectified women as props to reel in the male gaze.[101] Likewise, in *Sport, Beer, and Gender: Promotional Culture and Contemporary Social Life*,[102] professors Lawrence Wenner and Steven Jackson argue that because men consume more than twice as much beer in America than women, breweries place more than 70% of their marketing budget into appealing to men.[103] Beer consumption, as part of a male-bonding, sports-related ritual becomes commodified by advertisers the way that poems, flowers, and chocolate are commodified parts of Valentine's Day. Fortunately for advertisers, unlike Valentine's Day and other festive holidays, sports-related male bonding around the consumption of beer occurs almost every day of the year. There is no day during the year when a moratorium on sporting events is observed. In a similar vein, advertisers of whiskey and tequila promote hard liquor as a "man's drink" during televised sporting events that feature celebrities who shame those men who drink what are considered to be feminine alcoholic beverages.

Beyond the problem of excess alcohol consumption, in the book *Masculinities, Gender Relations, and Sports*, Jim McKay, Michael Messner, and Donald Sabo take up the relationship between male sports fans and aggression.[104] One aspect of this research notes that male sports reinforce a particular variety of hegemonic masculinity that is a prominent feature of sports media and is considered to be a factor in the valorization and naturalizing of men's capacity for violence.[105] Similar to the hegemonic masculine bonding found among college fraternity members, researchers have found that a patriarchal hierarchy is often discovered within groups of men who are avid sports fans. These zealous male sports fans emphasize physical competition and male-dominance through physical prowess, and support "violent performative masculine styles."[106] This means, of course, that those men who do not measure up to these validated masculine styles are vulnerable to ridicule and bullying by men who define masculine acceptability through the lens of athletic physicality and a competitive dominance model of masculinity on display throughout sports culture.

In his book *Beer, Babes, and Balls: Masculinity and Sports Talk Radio*, sociologist David Nylund borrows from Michael Messner's notion of ***covert intimacy*** to explain the bonding of men around the traditional masculine themes found in sports-talk radio as a way to avoid investigating their "inner lives," while also serving as a "refuge from women."[107] Messner explains *covert intimacy* as a practice of men "doing together" rather than talking about issues or feelings they may have.[108] Male bonding around sports allows men to indulge in hours of sports-talk with other men without having to engage in what many men view as the uncomfortable introspective analysis found in some daytime

FIGURE 9.14: Sociologist, researcher, and author Michael Messner

television talk shows that target female audiences. In this way, sports talk is a masculine buffer that permits men to avoid having to confront more troubling things about themselves including whatever problems they may be experiencing in their domestic, professional, and personal lives.

Researchers have also found that NCAA male athletes commit a disproportionate amount of violence against women when compared against NCAA male non-athletes.[109] In one famous study, researchers Crosset, Benedict, and McDonald found that even though NCAA division I male athletes make up 3.3% of the total NCAA student population, they commit 19% of the sexual assaults.[110] In follow up studies, researchers investigating male sports subcultures found that sexually exploiting women was often a common practice, which included higher levels of ridicule aimed at women, casual sex, sharing sexual partners, and actual rape.[111] In connecting the dots, studies linked male, NCAA team-sport athletes with higher rates of chauvinist attitudes, predatory sexual attitudes about women, acceptance of rape myth narratives, greater use of sexist and homophobic slurs, and an overall lack of accountability for transgressions. Many male fans of team-sports were also found to engage in higher rates of aggression-related behavior in the wake of wins or losses of their favorite teams, instead of the cathartic effect some believe occurs as a result of released aggressive behavior during the playing or viewing of a game.[112] This effect was not found in the same degree with female fans.[113] In fact, male fan enjoyment was correlated with viewing higher levels of violent sports play.[114] This result has led some researchers to speculate that team sports such as football are more likely to produce aggressive behavior in male fans than non-team sports such as golf or tennis.[115] Fans viewing baseball, because incidents of violence are far less than that found in football, also registered less aggressive behaviors. McKay, Messner, and McDonald conclude that some male fans construct their identities around their sports teams with some of these fans exhibiting behaviors termed ***blasting*** or aiming homophobic and sexist insults at members of "out-groups," which can be players and fans of other teams, as permissible and even expected fan behaviors.[116]

CTE (Chronic Traumatic Encephalopathy) and Masculinity

In 2013, *Frontline PBS* created a documentary film series that investigated concussions and the onset of CTE (Chronic Traumatic Encephalopathy) among NFL players, entitled *League of Denial: The NFL's Concussion Crisis*.[117] The series investigates the long-term effects of repeated hits to the heads of players that include depression, early onset dementia, and other traumatic-brain-injury-related illnesses. In autopsies, 76 of 79 of deceased NFL players were found to have degenerative brain disease.[118] Physicians have now examined the brains of 128 living football players and found that 101 of them test positive for CTE.[119]

Boxing, Mixed Martial Arts (MMA) fighting, and professional wrestling are also sports that have come under scrutiny for their contributing to brain injuries. In 2007, professional wrestler Chris Benoit killed his wife, his seven-year-old son, and himself. Speculation about steroid use and CTE followed. Neurosurgeon Julian Bailes, the head of neurosurgery at West Virginia University, examined the brain of Benoit and concluded that Benoit's brain had incurred injury consistent with what might be expected of an 85-year-old Alzheimer's patient.[120] Yet none of this has had an impact on ticket sales or the policies of boxing, MMA, professional wrestling, or the NFL other than a 15-yard penalty attached to helmet-to-helmet hits. If anything, the CTE findings and subsequent discussions about how to best handle the problem has turned into a debate about masculinity. While some studies have been conducted to investigate better ways to protect players,[121] [122] some conservative FOX News pundits including FOX contributor Glenn Beck, have suggested that concern over head injuries is simply another example of how contemporary culture "wussifies" men and weakens sports.[123] [124] [125] This is yet another way that politically conservative messages find their way into organized team sports. So-called "real men" are supposed to be able to take a hit, while wussified men whine, cry, and seek better protection for players. In 2013, former NFL all-star Junior Seau committed suicide, after which an autopsy revealed that he was suffering from CTE.[126] In the aftermath of Seau's suicide, in a written statement, NFL spokesman Greg Aiello announced,

> The [Seau] finding underscores the recognized need for additional research to accelerate a fuller understanding of CTE. The NFL is committed to supporting a wide range of independent medical and scientific research that will both address CTE and promote the long-term health and safety of athletes at all levels.[127]

At the same time, in what sociologist Eric Anderson terms "a crack in the hegemonic system of American football," NFL quarterback Aaron Rodgers pulled himself from a game after suffering a hit to the head.[128] In a male culture that often approaches injury in a "suck-it-up-walk-it-off" manner, Anderson views Rodgers's self-withdrawal coupled with sports-media's approval of his action a case of "major sport media beginning to support the notion of health over a masculine warrior narrative."[129] In 2015, 24-year-old Chris Borland, linebacker for the San Francisco 49ers, quit the NFL due to concerns about contracting CTE.[130] Writing for *The Nation*, Dave Zirin adds, "Science is not the NFL's friend. The more people know about the effects of tackle football, the more you're going to see parents withhold their kids from playing and the more you're going to see players make the kind of choice that Chris Borland is making. Because a rising star like Borland was sure to receive a lucrative contract, he's actually sacrificing something for the principle of his own health and that makes it a political act."[131]

Meanwhile, the NFL has refused to cooperate and collaborate with the producers of *League of Denial: The NFL's Concussion Crisis* and insisted that all NFL logos be removed from the show, prompting filmmaker Michael Kirk to state, "They obviously don't want to talk about it and it's too bad, because it's a huge, huge problem."[132] [133] In 2013, ex-NFL players, which included Hall of Fame players Tony Dorsett and Jim McMahon, filed a class-action lawsuit against the NFL, claiming that the NFL concealed information about the dangers of brain injury.[134] In all, over 4,500 ex-players entered into the lawsuit. The players were seeking compensation for past, current, and future medical care they have or will incur due to head hits. In August of 2013, the NFL agreed to pay players, collectively, $765 million after court-ordered mediation.[135] Currently, the NFL searches for better ways to protect players from head injuries, while negotiating the delicate balance of continuing to profit from the image of professional football players as gladiators and warriors who risk life and limb on the gridiron each Sunday morning and Monday night during the long NFL season.[136] [137]

THOUGHT BOX

To what extent do you believe the culture of men's sports helps shape hegemonic masculinity in America? Describe the ways that mediated sports influence the ways male sports fans view themselves.

Performance Enhancing Drugs and Masculinity

With multi-year, multi-million dollar contracts on the line, Major League Baseball (MLB) athletes in the 1990s and 2000s began using performance-enhancing drugs in an attempt to improve statistics that would aid their agents in contract negotiations with owners. Suddenly, home run records that had stood a long test of time were not only challenged, but obliterated. Power pitchers were now throwing in the mid-to-upper 90 mile-an-hour range into their late thirties. Fans were selling out stadiums across the country and management was happy.

But in 2005, former MLB power-hitter Jose Conseco published the book *Juiced: Wild Times, Rampant 'Roids, Smash Hits & How Baseball Got Big* documenting the widespread use of steroids and performance-enhancing drugs in MLB that allegedly accounted for the skyrocketing home run and strike out statistics.[138] Canseco's book was initially met with skepticism and scorn. But as player after player began to admit to steroid usage, Canseco's claims no longer seemed implausible to baseball fans, sports journalists, and the MLB community at large. Increasingly, accusations and angry denials became commonplace with some resulting in lawsuits. Many fans were disillusioned, and MLB commissioner Bud Selig called for an independent investigation headed by former U.S. Senator George Mitchell to discover the extent to which MLB players were using performance enhancing drugs.[139] The resulting conclusions drawn by the Mitchell report read like an indictment with some of the biggest names in baseball implicated in steroid and human growth hormone usage, prompting commissioner Selig to vow that actions would be taken.[140]

While greed along with the concern that younger players might be brought up from the minor leagues to replace older players who were making huge amounts of money no doubt pushed many MLB players to use performance-enhancing drugs, masculinity was

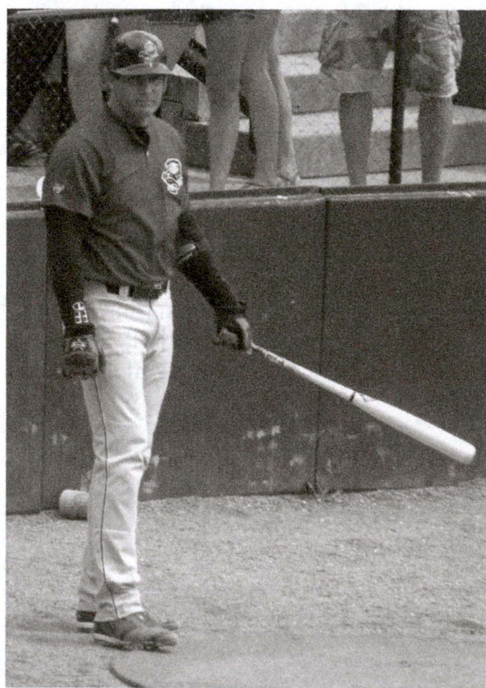

FIGURE 9.15: Ex-MLB Star Jose Canseco, author of *Juiced: Wild Times, Rampant 'Roids, Smash Hits & How Baseball Got Big*

another factor in steroid usage. A bigger, more muscular look began to be emulated by wrestlers, MMA fighters, and other athletes. There was also a feeling that baseball was now a more masculine game than once considered by some pre-steroid era sports fans. Hitting 480-foot home runs was now a sign of masculine power reserved for big, tough men, while hitting 98 or even 100 miles per hour on a radar gun designated certain pitchers as strong, manly men in a profession that used to be viewed as being more genteel in nature as compared to other team sports. Relief pitchers entered games from the bullpen to AC/DC music blaring over the loudspeakers as opposed to the polite and almost carnival-like organ music of the past. Baseball was no longer a gentle pastime to while away hot summer days and nights. It was now a man's game where bench-clearing brawls might highlight an otherwise slow-paced game of strategy and skill.

But along with increased athletic performance, many were beginning to blame steroid use for episodes of violence. Dr. Gary Wadler of New York University's School of Medicine cites several negative side-effects of steroid usage that include depression, extreme irritability, feelings of invincibility, and episodes of rage and aggression that came to be termed "'roid rage" by members of the media.[141] Suddenly, sports analysts were wondering out loud whether steroid use had contributed to acts of violence committed by some athletes, such as Benoit's murder of his family.[142] In an interview with CBS News, Dr. Wadler reported that steroid use was associated with a loss of impulse control and that it could easily be implicated in acts of violence.[143] Not everyone was convinced. A study conducted in Sweden questioned the causal connection between steroid use and violence noting that those who had committed acts of violence while taking steroids were also linked to the taking of poly-substances over the course of their lifetimes.[144] Still, the National Institute on Drug Abuse reports that men who take anabolic steroids can experience extreme mood swings that run the gamut from euphoria to paranoid feelings of jealousy to manic bursts of anger and violence.[145]

Steroid usage has increasingly become a men's issue, since it is now used by men of different backgrounds to achieve a more muscular appearance. Body builders, in particular, have been known to ingest a steroid regimen, along with synthetic forms of testosterone, to increase muscle mass.[146] But men coming from different walks of life who regularly work out in gyms have also taken to steroid usage as a way to maximize the muscular effect of weightlifting to achieve a particular physical appearance. This quest for visible upper-body muscularity is not uncommon in adolescent males and young men who connect muscularity to masculinity.[147] In a study of young male football players who regularly worked out with weights, researchers found that muscularity was considered foundational to masculine prowess and gaining the attention of young women.[148] Researchers of the study concluded that athleticism and following certain traditional masculine norms that include risk-taking, being in control of one's emotions, and physical competency were primary to the masculine identity of the majority of college football players interviewed.[149] Being a man who commands respect and the adoration of women were also high on the list of desired traits by young men who conform to traditional masculine norms and who acknowledge the social benefits of appearing to be physically strong and visibly muscular.[150] Steroid usage is often viewed by these young men as a metabolic shortcut to attaining their desired goals.

Locker Rooms as Citadels of Sexism and Homophobia?

It is probably correct to state that sports do not cause sexism and homophobia, rather that sexism and homophobia are symptoms of larger societal problems. In the chapter on boyhood, we saw that many experts view peer pressure as a major influence on boys' behaviors. Within sports culture, locker rooms have garnered a reputation for being environments of male peer pressure unlike many others. Until recently, locker rooms were spaces unwelcome to women, where men could say and behave as they wished with little to no scrutiny. From hypermasculine displays of bravado to sexist and homophobic slurs and comments, athletes felt immune from the criticism that would befall them if these same behaviors and conversations were made public.

KNBR-San Francisco radio talk host Damon Bruce stated on-air of men's locker rooms, "This is guy stuff. This is men's stuff. Women, ladies, sensitive guys, we're not changing it for you. It's the last place where guys get away with locker room talk. That's how you have fun, that's how you bond." Of locker room culture, Ohio State University sociologist Timothy Jon Curry writes,

BULLYING IN THE NFL

In 2014, scandal hit the Miami Dolphins as text messages revealed a pattern of bullying that had been ongoing between lineman Richie Incognito and Jonathan Martin. An inquiry into the matter revealed examples of harassment, bullying, racism, and homophobia. NFL Commissioner Roger Goodell launched an investigation that led to a 148-page report that detailed a Miami Dolphins locker room that was replete with bullying and harassment.[1] Martin eventually left the team claiming that he could no longer put up with the relentless trash-talking and bullying that permeated the locker room and field of the Miami Dolphins.

In one of the texts sent by Incognito to Martin, Incognito threatened Martin's sister, stating,

> We are going to run train on your sister. I'm going to fuck her without a condom and cum in her cunt. I'm going to bang the shit out of her and treat her like shit. Hear your sister has a wolf-puss. A fat, hairy pussy.[2]

The violently worded, misogynistic, racist, and homophobic nature of the texts rocked NFL sports-writers who cover the NFL,[3] while Incognito attempted to defend the texts as "coming from a place of love.",[4] It was later revealed that Martin was routinely called a "bitch," "pussy," "cunt," and "faggot" by Incognito and other Miami Dolphins.[5] The Miami Dolphins subsequently suspended Incognito with pay. In 2015, the Buffalo Bills signed Incognito to a one-year, $2.25 million contract.[6]

1 www.washingtonpost.com/sports/redskins/nfl-commissioned-report-finds-culture-of-intolerance-in-miami-dolphins-locker-room/2014/02/14/5d10bf3c-95a8-11e3-afce-3e7c922ef31e_story.html.

2 www.sbnation.com/nfl/2014/2/14/5411608/worst-of-the-richie-incognito-jonathan-martin-report-miami-dolphins.

3 www.salon.com/2014/02/14/nfl_releases_shocking_report_detailing_richie_incognitos_racist_and_homophobic_abuse/.

4 www.cnn.com/2013/11/10/us/richie-incognito-interview/.

5 Ibid.

6 http://espn.go.com/nfl/story/_/id/12292322/richie-incognito-buffalo-bills-close-deal.

> The men's locker room is enshrined in sports mythology as a bastion of privilege and a center of fraternal bonding. Peer group dynamics encourage antisocial talk and behavior, much of which is directed at the athletes themselves. To avoid being targeted for put-downs, the men engage in conversations that affirm a traditional masculinity. As a result, their locker room talk generally treats women as objects, encourages sexist attitudes toward women and promotes rape culture.[151]

NFL all-star running back Adrien Peterson stated of locker-room talk, "You are in a locker room with 60 alpha males. There's so much that's said in the locker room that people would go crazy if they knew half of the things we say."[152] Lewis & Clark College professor of education, Brandon Sternod writes,

> For men and boys, the locker room and playing field are prime locations for learning and/or performing heterosexual masculinity. Even at an early age, boys and young men are performing heterosexual masculinity by competitively bantering with teammates about sex and their sexual exploits with females. In these very public discussions, male athletes are expected to express not only their sexual desire for females but, more importantly, their dominance over them (and hence the dominance of all things "masculine" over all things "feminine"). Failure to do so or failure to do it in a correct way often results in ridicule.[153]

USC sociologist Michael Messner adds, "The pressure to be seen by one's peers as "a man"—indeed, the pressure to see oneself as "a man"—makes most young males play along with the homophobic and sexist locker room banter."[154] The insolated locker room environment plays out one of the more common observations about boys and men: that males will often behave much differently in groups than they will one-on-one. In the book *Sex Differences in Social Behavior: A Social-Role Interpretation*, psychologist Alice H. Eagly writes:

> In relation to group-pressure conformity studies, gender roles should be salient because group members provide one another with an audience, which should heighten self-presentational concerns. Moreover, in this research, group members generally interact without well-defined specific roles that would make competing role expectation salient.[155]

Male locker rooms are one of the most noticeable environments for peer-culturally accepted behaviors within male, team-athletic culture. The privacy athletes feel, along with the exclusion of women and others who may be viewed as "outsiders," creates a setting that is ripe for otherwise inappropriate and socially unacceptable language and behavior that pivot around sexist, homophobic, and often racist jesting as part of a contest for masculine credentials within the group. Eagly notes that locker rooms create audiences for which young men can perform and receive validation and adulation. It becomes a self-reinforcing environment where violating societal rules is commended and encouraged. It is not surprising, then, that if sexism and homophobia have become disparaged positions in contemporary society, male locker rooms are replete with such banter.

Writing for *The Business Journal*, ex-NFL player Jack Brewer argues that the locker-room culture of sexism and homophobia is not going to change any time soon due to three main factors:

- NFL players are hired for their size and playing abilities, not for their sensitivity.
- Locker rooms are sacred environments for athletes where players bond. This means that players will not challenge other players over their use of sexist or homophobic language.
- Playing in the NFL is a short-term career for most so that they are not interested in rocking the boat and challenging the status quo.[156]

Brewer's point is that professional sports cannot be compared to corporate America, where certain behavioral protocol is expected and maintained. The locker room, in particular, is an environment where the men who do not use sexist and homophobic slurs are expected to mind their own business and not disturb the flow of male bonding at the expense of women, gay, trans, and queer people. A longstanding rule of male culture in general is that guys are supposed to abide by the unspoken but understood oath not to disclose, denounce, or disrupt the bad behaviors of other men. The sexism, homophobia, and hypermasculine bravado found in locker-room environments will change only if a perspective change toward inclusivity occurs within male culture in general so that sexism, homophobia, and transphobia are treated more like racism, which, although persistently practiced, does not enjoy the widespread approval that other problematic "isms" enjoy in sports due mainly to the racial integration of sports culture.

Sexism in Sports Journalism

Exactly who the very first female sportscaster or sports journalist happened to be is debatable, but the pioneers of female sports journalism are considered to be Jane Chastain, Donna De Varona, and Jeannie Morris.[157] Until very recently, sports and sports journalism has been dominated by men. When women were allowed entry into this historically male profession, as Leandra Reilly, first woman to do play-by-play of an NBA game, states, "The networks used to pick women for their looks."[158] Gayle Gardner, who was the first female sports anchor to appear on a weekly network sports program, adds, "For women especially, this profession will never stop being a struggle with constant blows which must be taken."[159] Erin Andrews, the host of sports talk-show *Fox College Saturday*, recalls her days of sideline interviews and being called "sideline Barbie" or "sideline princess" by sports bloggers; she was routinely scrutinized for what she was wearing or asked questions like "How she would look eating a hot dog?"[160] [161] Boston sports radio host Kirk Minihane called Andrews "a gutless bitch" and after dispensing with an empty apology a week later, stated of Andrews, "If she weighed 15 pounds more she'd be a waitress."[162]

Sports journalist Lesley Vissers, the only woman to be enshrined in the Pro Football Hall of Fame, states of being a woman covering sports, "We all have scar tissue. I always tell the young women coming up, 'You can have a long career, but you better have a tough skin'.'"[163] Writing for ESPN, former sportswriter and former assistant dean of Harvard University, Robin Herman, recalls her "fan mail" after crossing the gender barrier by covering male athletes in locker rooms. She recalls herself and others who dared to cross this line being called "whores, prostitutes and worse."[164] Today, Herman views with disdain the way female sports journalists are treated when covering men's sports, observing:

> She is on the sideline, and the men are up in the anchor booth. "On the sidelines" is a common expression in the English language; it means out of the action, out of the decision-making. Someone on the sidelines is a bystander, an observer, a person who has no agency.[165]

In response, critics who argue that the booth is reserved for ex-professional athletes whose insight into the game is more astute than sports reporters, many legendary booth analysts, play-by-play anchors, and sports-talk hosts never played the game, including Marv Albert[166] (who was convicted of assaulting a woman in Virginia), Mike Tirico[167] (who was suspended by ESPN for multiple incidents of sexual assault, solicitation, and stalking female co-workers), Chris Berman, Michael Wilbon, Stephen A. Smith, Tony

Kornheiser, Brett Musburger, Mike Greenberg, Max Kellerman, Jim Rome, and many others. Today, while women make up 46.9% of the overall workforce in America, they make up 7% of sports reporters.[168] These percentages exist in the face of the fact that many women have now had successful careers in the WNBA or as highly touted NCAA or Olympic athletes. Reinforcing Herman's indignation, Anne Doyle, writing for *Forbes* magazine, writes that it is time for sports broadcasting to stop relegating women to sideline eye candy, referring to the fact that the majority of female sideline sports reporters are considered to be on the sidelines for their looks, a view unwittingly reinforced by longtime sportscaster Brett Musberger who, speaking of female sports-reporter Holly Rowe, stated that she "was really smokin' tonight."[169]

MEDIA COVERAGE OF MALE VERSUS FEMALE SPORTS

ESPN dominates sports coverage in America. However, it does not do so in gender-equal ways. Consider the sports of basketball and tennis. In the case of basketball, it is a team sport with a high degree of physical contact. With tennis, it is mainly an individual sport (except in doubles play) and requires no physical contact with your opponent. When *ESPN* covers basketball, men's basketball dominates coverage. The star players of the NBA, as a result, are almost household names. Stars of the WNBA, no matter how talented, toil away in relative anonymity. Predictably, the league minimum annual salary in the NBA is $490,180,[1] compared to WNBA rookie salaries of $34,500.[2]

FIGURE 9.16: Stephen Curry, NBA star

FIGURE 9.17: Maya Moore, WNBA star

Continued

FIGURE 9.18: Serena Williams

FIGURE 9.19: John Isner

Yet, turning to the sport of tennis, the stars of tennis, whether women or men, often have the same level of visibility, with female stars today enjoying perhaps greater visibility. It is common for people to defend this gendered inequality by claiming that male athletes have greater physical strength or that sports media is simply giving people what they want, but is it true that sports fans want much more male sports coverage than female sports coverage, and if so why? Why is it that tennis seems to be an exception to the rule? Is it the case that high-contact team sports draw a different kind of fan than sports where aggressive, high-levels of physical contact is not the rule?

1 https://sports.vice.com/en_us/article/basketballs-gender-wage-gap-is-even-worse-than-you-think.
2 http://www.altiusdirectory.com/Sports/wnba-salaries.php.

In terms of gender equality in officiating, the NBA currently has two full-time female referees,[170] while no female umpires exist in major league baseball[171] and there have only been six total female umpires in the history of minor league baseball.[172] In 2015, the NFL hired its first full-time female official in the person of Sarah Thomas, who happens to also be the first woman to officiate an NCAA football game.[173] But critics have called the introduction of women officiating professional men's sports "a publicity stunt" or an attempt at political correctness in an age when diversity is being emphasized in professions across the board.[174] NFL player Sen'Derrick Marks stated, "For the league, it's great publicity. The NFL is all about monopolizing every opportunity."[175]

In 2006, ex-MLB player Keith Hernandez stated on-air, "I won't say that women belong in the kitchen, but they don't belong in the dugout."[176] This claim was in response to trainer Kelly Calabrese's presence in the San Diego Padres' dugout during a game. The Padres' then manager Bruce Bochy voiced surprise at Hernandez's comment and stated in response, "I didn't think gender was even an issue anymore."[177] Like the criticism of female journalists who interview male athletes in the locker room, some male athletes and fans alike view sports as a woman-free zone where "men can be men" without worrying about being checked for sexism, racism, or homophobia. Professional athletes, in particular, are part of a culture that unapologetically celebrates male privilege often at the expense of women and gay people.

At the same time, high-profile NCAA and professional athletes, like all celebrities, are followed by media everywhere they go; their words and actions are often documented through the lens of a camera and a microphone. This has been the case all the more in the wake of 24-hour sports news coverage on radio and television. The attention bestowed upon young men who succeed in sports is unrivaled except perhaps by those who become music or acting stars. Those who rise to the level of sports star often go from backgrounds of economic struggle and relative anonymity to lives of instant opulence and name recognition. Some of these stars learn to navigate their sudden wealth and fame within healthy boundaries and are able to successfully create a sense of balance in their lives, while other sports stars, not unlike other celebrities, experience public melt-downs that involve drugs, sex, violence, and eventual bankruptcy. One report noted that 78% of NFL players and 60% of NBA players are broke within five years of retirement despite earning more in one year than many people earn over a lifetime.[178] [179] Director of ESPN's 30 for 30 documentary film *Broke*, Billy Corben, speculates that this phenomenon is due to what he terms **the superman syndrome**, whereby professional athletes have been told almost all of their lives that they are special and elite, which can get them to believe that they are expert and elite at anything they do including financial investing.[180] [181] In response to this ongoing problem, some leagues have created financial literacy education programs in the hope of curtailing the common economic downfall of so many ex-pro athletes.[182]

Sex, Beer, and Violence: Professional Sports as Heteronormative Male Fantasy

Many have commented that professional sports, and particularly the NBA and NFL, are a perfect storm of the stereotypical male fantasy trio of sports, beer, and pornified women. Writing for the *New York Times*, sports columnist William C. Rhoden writes:

> While cheerleading at the high school and collegiate levels has become competitive and athletic, today's N.F.L. cheerleaders are little more than props that reinforce objectified

FIGURE 9.20: Washington "Redskins" Cheerleaders

> sex roles. The professional cheerleader has become feminized and eroticized ... team owners should consider jettisoning the eye-candy culture of cheerleaders.[183]

There are currently six NFL teams that do not have an official cheerleading squad.[184] One of those teams is the New York Giants (although they do employ the "Gotham City Cheerleaders" for home games), whose owner John Mara recently stated, "Philosophically, we have always had issues with sending scantily clad women out on the field to entertain our fans. It's just not part of our philosophy."[185] The New York Giants are joined by the Pittsburgh Steelers, Detroit Lions, Green Bay Packers, Chicago Bears, and Cleveland Browns.[186] Sports journalist Smriti Sinha writes that it is time for the NFL to ban cheerleaders, adding,

> The league [created] a committee of domestic violence experts to send the message: we're going to improve the lot of women with any ties to our league. It is ridiculous that they are putting on this veneer of caring about women while objectifying and dehumanizing their most visible female employees.[187]

In her book, *Go! Fight! Win!: Cheerleading in American Culture*, professor of American studies at the University of New Mexico, Mary Ellen Hanson, writes of the tensions between the role and significance of contemporary cheerleaders:

> The cheerleader is an instantly recognized symbol of youthful prestige, wholesome attractiveness, peer leadership and popularity. Equally recognized is the cheerleader as symbol of mindless enthusiasm, shallow boosterism, objectified sexuality, and promiscuous availability.[188]

Hanson views cheerleading in American sports as a phenomenon that has been evolving since the 1960s. She argues that it is almost comical to view the transition from cheerleaders leading a crowd in cheers as part of team spirit in the 1960s to the scantily clad, sexually provocative cheerleaders of today's NBA and NFL cheerleading troops. She notes that some of the dance routines undertaken by professional cheerleaders come directly from videos that teach pole dancing and stripping. Sandy Hingston, writing for the magazine *Philadelphia*, agrees with Sinha that cheerleading should be banned by the NFL, stating of her concern about talking to her daughter, "How, exactly, do you tell a seven-year-old, 'They're there to get men sexually aroused and inspire pornographic fantasies?'"[189] Hingston continues, "[cheerleaders are teaching] seven-year-olds that a woman's place in life is to stand on the sidelines looking pretty while men get things done."[190]

Not everyone agrees with the criticism. The majority of NFL cheerleaders claim to love their jobs, even though they are paid very little for the work they do.[191] When listing the positives of being an NFL cheerleader, one of the most cited reasons is that as NFL cheerleaders, they are able to have exciting experiences and meet influential people who are able to open doors of opportunity for them they might not otherwise have.[192] Through this lens, professional cheerleading is a career decision that can help young women create success in their fields of interest. Other cheerleaders disagree. As one NFL cheerleader put it, "It's degrading. It's embarrassing to even talk about."[193] Part of that degradation and embarrassment is having to go through "jiggle tests" to assess how firm each part of their bodies are, along with being told how to style their hair, manicure their fingernails, and how to properly wash intimate areas.[194] Missy Mooty, who is a member of the Minnesota Vikings cheerleading squad, disagrees, stating,

> We take a lot of pride in our uniforms and we like to use them to represent the team. I feel that if we offer a classy and poised portrayal, then hopefully that is the way that it is received. Like anything, it's in the eye of the beholder.[195]

Ex-president of the Association for Women in Sports Media, Joanne Gerstner, responds that if cheerleading is simply about team spirit, why don't we see the same thing at women's sporting events?

THOUGHT BOX

What is your view of cheerleading today, particularly the style and role of cheerleaders in professional sports? Do you find legitimate purposes in their roles or do you side with Rhoden and Hanson in stating that cheerleading has become sexist by sexually objectifying women strictly for the male gaze? Do you agree with Sinha and Gerstner who argue that cheerleading should be banned by the NFL? Why or why not?

Athletes, Intimate Partner Violence, Sexual Assault, and Rape

While the subject of men and violence will be taken up in the next chapter, a chapter on men and sports would be remiss if it ignored the highly publicized cases of athletes and intimate partner violence, along with league responses to such violence. In 2014, NFL Pro Bowl player Ray Rice was caught on film striking his fiancé in an elevator, knocking her unconscious in what became one of the biggest scandals in professional sports. But those journalists who cover sports were quick to point out that Rice's intimate partner violence was part of a long legacy in sports that until very recently has gone almost completely ignored.[196] [197] In fact, until waves of protest rolled into NFL league offices, Commissioner Roger Goodell initially set the penalty to Rice at a two-game suspension.[198]

In the wake of the Ray Rice scandal, Major League Baseball Commissioner Bud Selig boasted that that sort of thing rarely happens in baseball, stating, "We haven't had any cases I'm happy to say for a long, long time. I can't remember when the last time was."[199] While "a long, long time" is unclear, in 2006, then-Philadelphia Phillies pitcher Brett Myers, who is 6'4" and 240 pounds was seen by multiple witnesses beating up his wife 'Kim' who is 5'4" and 120 pounds in front of the Hynes Convention Center in Boston.[200] Witnesses who called 911 described the assault as particularly vicious and overheard Kim Myers state, "I'm not going to let you do this to me anymore," suggesting that the assault was not the first time it had happened.[201] Writing for SB Nation, sports journalist Mike Bates states that Major League Baseball's record on domestic violence is actually worse than that found in the NFL, citing cases that involved multiple players including Chuck Knoblauch, Kirby Puckett, John Leuke, Jose Canseco, Daryl Strawberry, Albert Belle, Pedro Astacio (who pleaded guilty for punching his pregnant wife, yet started the season for the Colorado Rockies), Milton Bradley, Francisco Rodriguez (assaulting his girlfriend and on another occasion assaulting his girlfriend's father), Julio Lugo (twice arrested for striking his wife and threatening to kill her in front of police), Hall of Fame coach Bobby Cox, and recently, Colorado Rockies' shortstop Jose Reyes, New York Yankees relief pitcher Aroldis Chapman, and Los Angeles Dodgers' outfielder Yasiel Puig.[202] [203] In over 25 years, no player incurred any commissioner-led sanction due to intimate partner violence until 2016 when Aroldis Chapman received a 29-game suspension and Jose Reyes was suspended for 51-games for violating MLB's new domestic violence policies.[204]

One of the more regrettable reactions to a male athlete's violence against a woman came in ESPN analyst Stephen A. Smith's warning to women not to "provoke wrong action" in the wake of the TMZ release of the notorious Ray Rice video.[205] Once again, men's violence against women took a backseat to victim-blaming as it is not uncommon for athletes, coaches and managers, team presidents, owners, agents, player's unions, and sports journalists to rally around male athletes as an initial reaction to off-field violence.[206] In other cases, a player's criminal past is rarely a deterrent against selecting that player in the draft if a team is convinced that his athletic prowess can convert into team wins.[207] Another form of athlete-involved violence against women occurs when players commit sexual assault or rape. The many accounts of athlete-involved rape and sexual assault have taken center-stage in the news of late and continue to be discussed as a major problem in high school, college, and professional sports.[208]

Consider the actions or lack of action taken by league officials in the wake of an assault by high-profile athletes. Ben Roethlisberger, long-time quarterback for the Pittsburgh Steelers, was twice suspended by the NFL for a 2008 incident in Nevada and a 2010 incident in Georgia where allegations of sexual assault were made.[209] Even though charges were dropped in each case, the victim in the Georgia incident testified to investigators that Roethlisberger escorted her to a VIP area of the club they were attending and pulled out his penis, to which she firmly stated that she did not want any sexual contact with him.[210] She proceeded to exit the VIP room and entered the bathroom believing it to be a safe place, but Roethlisberger followed her into the women's bathroom where he proceeded to rape her to her continued pleas for him to stop.[211] An eyewitness at the club reported seeing Roethlisberger's bodyguard drag the victim to the backroom and noted that the victim was extremely intoxicated and seemed unaware of what was happening.[212] The NFL suspended Roethlisberger for six games for violating its personal conduct policy, but he served only a four-game suspension after the NFL commissioner Roger Goodell reduced the suspension by two games.[213]

For those who argue that Roethlisberger should not have had any sanctions against him since the charges were dropped, much of what happened that evening was corroborated by witnesses, and rape is the single-most difficult violent crime to prosecute for a host of reasons that have nothing to do with the perpetrator's innocence.[214] [215] [216]

Prosecutions, let alone convictions, are even harder to get when charges are leveled against a celebrity who has the resources to hire top-notch defense attorneys.[217] In addition, police officers are often skeptical of reports of rape and charges are seldom filed.[218] In one study, police officers revealed that departments have to decide the extent of resources they want to expend to pursuing cases of sexual assault and weigh that figure against their wariness that the charges could be false.[219] In surveys, some officers actually claimed that if a woman reporting rape does not seem to be "distraught enough," she will be viewed as less credible.[220] One officer in the study stated bluntly, "If there is no physical evidence and you said you got raped, did you get raped? ... No."[221]

THOUGHT BOX

NHL Hall of Fame goalie Ken Dryden states, "It's really a sense of power that comes from specialness ... anyone who finds himself at the center of the world [he's] in has a sense of impunity."[1] With respect to high-profile athletes, do you think Dryden is correct? Does the special treatment many athletes receive over the course of their lives contribute to the reasons why there are a great number of cases of sexual-based offenses committed by athletes?

1 www.cnn.com/2010/CRIME/04/16/roethlisberger.incident/.

Some of the fault, argue critics, is that institutions, including league officials or university officials in the case of student athletes who commit rape or sexual assault, will impede investigations and cover-up reports for the sake of the reputation of the school, league, or to retain the millions of dollars pouring into sports programs. The Penn State University scandal is perhaps the most infamous of these cases. In 2011, the news story broke that assistant football coach Jerry Sandusky was being charged for multiple counts of sexual abuse of children.[222] But the Sandusky scandal turned out to be the tip of an iceberg as several Penn State officials were also questioned about the ethical and legal obligations they may have violated by not reporting the crimes when it became clear that they had knowledge the molestations were taking place. Emails surfaced that legendary head football coach Joe Paterno along with university president Graham B. Spanier and athletic director Tim Curley had conversations about what to do in the wake of learning about Sandusky's offenses.[223] In the end, Paterno, Spanier, and Curley decided to keep quiet and discipline Sandusky by barring him from taking any more children onto campus and encouraging him to seek professional help.[224]

The Sandusky scandal at Penn State is a high-profile instance of many sexual assault and rape investigations across NCAA and professional sports. In 2014, three University of Oregon male athletes were charged with gang rape.[225] One of the accused, Brandon Austin, had been accused of raping a woman while at Providence College in Rhode Island, but was still able to transfer to the University of Oregon.[266] Psychology professor Jennifer Freyd of the University of Oregon filed a Clery complaint[227] when she believed the university was not taking appropriate action.[228]

Challenging and empowering friends, family, colleagues, teammates, and other peers who have knowledge of violence, but who choose not to get involved has been at the center of the work conducted by antiviolence educator Jackson Katz whose leadership program ***Mentors in Violence Prevention*** (MVP) trains men and women who are known peers how to intervene to disrupt violence, but more importantly how to transform the present culture of violent masculinity by implementing the many important insights of feminist and social justice activism. Working with women and men from diverse racial, ethnic, and cultural backgrounds, the MVP program has collaborated with high schools, universities, college and professional athletes, and the U.S. military in bringing what they term *the bystander approach* to gender violence prevention, which encourages people "to speak out in the face of abusive behavior before, during, or after an incident ... to create a peer culture where sexist abuse is seen as uncool and unacceptable. For men in particular, this abuse comes to be seen as a transgression against—rather than an enactment of—the social norms of masculinity."[229]

While MVP works with both women and men, an emphasis is placed on encouraging men – in sports culture and everywhere else – to interrupt and challenge other men's sexist attitudes, which condition and license physical, emotional, and sexual abuse. [230] The ultimate goal of MVP is nothing less than a complete transformation of the prevailing acceptance of violent masculinity, which is typified by aggression, intimidation, controlling and coercive behaviors, and violence as acceptable and preferred masculine traits. MVP works to reinvent normative masculinity so that abuse of others is seen as contrary to what it means to be a man. There are other programs that offer violence intervention training, but often depoliticize and degender conversations about violence in the belief that such straightforward talk will discourage men from participating and taking seriously the message. But MVP has found that in nurturing environments, men display great valor in confronting the realities about men's aggression and violence and demonstrate a willingness to challenge themselves and others in bringing about these requisite changes. The MVP program is built on the notion that violence will not end without changing a culture of violent masculinity that permeates contemporary society at its very core, and that accomplishing this enormous task will take the willingness of men to take an honest look at themselves and commit to becoming proactive partners with women in bringing about a new and progressive, nonviolent template for masculinity.

In 2009, the *Center for Court Innovation* submitted to the U.S. Department of Education an evaluation of the *mentors in violence prevention program* as applied at Syracuse University in New York.[231] The study noted that students rated the program as being excellent, although there were challenges which included staff turnover and burnout related to the amount of time commitment required to train and maintain the program.[232] Some central conclusions drawn by the report was that MVP training can work with proper funding that could sustain a pool of staff trainers who would be responsible for recruitment, particularly in creating diversity of participants, and mandatory programming.[233] Anyone who has worked in the field of sexual harassment and sexual violence prevention knows that perpetrators, including most bystanders, are rarely interested in learning about and changing their behaviors. The report concludes that resistant participants would require prolonged, mandatory engagement in the program in order to have a chance at success.[234]

In response to the many high-profile cases of intimate partner and sexual violence committed by athletes, many athletes themselves have participated in public-service announcements that urge an end to men's violence against women. Organizations have formed that combat domestic violence with support from some major sports stars. Two of those organizations are ***1 is 2 Many*** and ***Not Alone*** formed by The White House Task Force as a proactive part of the reauthorization of the Violence Against Women Act introduced originally by then Senator Joseph Biden and signed into law by President Bill Clinton in 1994.[235] [236] [237] *1 is 2 Many* has created a series of awareness-raising PSAs that feature both professional athletes and TV and film stars to lend their support to combat men's violence against women.

Some NCAA athletes have also joined the voices in the fight against men's violence against women. Mississippi State University football player D.J. Looney states:

> This is like cancer. The difference is, nobody wants to talk about it. We, as athletes, hold ourselves to higher standards and so does the media. If something happens, the whole world hears about it. We need to decide if we want to fix the problem or be a part of the problem.[238]

But many are quick to note that until the NCAA takes more seriously responses to intimate partner violence, things are not going to change. One of many cases involved University of Oregon running back LaMichael James, who was arrested and charged with assaulting his girlfriend, for which he sat out one game.[239] Or, UNLV's Tre'Von Willis, who was charged with felony domestic battery by strangulation and was suspended from play for only three games, two of which were exhibition games.[240] NCAA president Mark Emmert stated in the wake of these lenient sanctions, "At the national level we have to have serious conversations to see if we can find a way to send an unequivocal message that this will not be tolerated."[241]

THOUGHT BOX

Given the resistance to change by some institutions and many men, discuss approaches to successfully combat sex discrimination, sexual harassment, and sexual violence. What ideas do you have that you feel might get through to men who are currently apathetic or even hostile to the notion of ending sexual harassment and sexual violence? Do you believe recruiting athletes to these causes helps? If so, what does this say about contemporary masculinity?

Summary

Sports create opportunity, but opportunity for both growth and empowerment or regression and oppression. While boys and young men benefit in a host of ways by participating in sports, too many times sports culture has been a bastion of sexism, homophobia, racism, and breeding ground for bullying. Sports culture sometimes reinforces a male hierarchy where men who are athletic stand as archetypes against whom non-athletic men are judged and mistreated. The stratification of boys and men into athlete and non-athlete comes to be a measurement of *superior* and *inferior* starting in elementary school and then passed along throughout middle school, high school, and sometimes college. Media reinforce the notion that athletes are gifted and special by bestowing a considerable amount of adulation on them from the time they reach collegiate sports. Professional athletes are often treated with the same idol worship as conferred upon television, film, and music stars. Like television, film, and music stars, some professional athletes handle fame and prestige well, while others do not. But whether high-profile athletes behave well or not, it is uncontroversial that they have an enormous role model effect on boys and young men.

Sports also carry with it a double-edged sword when it comes to issues of race and racism. While many believe that the racial integration of American team sports has helped bring about greater tolerance and acceptance, others point out that racism and ethnic intolerance continues to be problem for sports, a problem exacerbated by the persistent use of racist logos and mascots in both NCAA and professional sports that use effigies of Native Americans to promote a model of warrior-savage masculinity. But the treatment and depiction of black, Latino, and Asian athletes also continues to be a problem, particularly for violent contact sports where athletes of color are commonly judged as being physically gifted and passionate, while white athletes are often portrayed as being intelligent and poised.

As sports has become a multi-billion-dollar industry, winning above all else has been an unfortunate model that often supplants the concern for the well-being of men, women, and fans alike. Performance enhancing drugs have tarnished the reputation of many star athletes and seduced lesser-known athletes to use banned substances in the interest of furthering their careers. At the same time, sports injuries, including CTE, have been down-played by the NFL, boxing commissions, and MMA fighting organizations so as not to disrupt the flow of revenue into league coffers. Coaching has witnessed a plague of abusive coaches who personally attack players through the use of homophobic and sexist slurs designed to motivate them to play harder. The profitability of sports has also led universities and professional athletic conferences to overlook and downplay physical and sexual assaults committed by players, and particularly those allegations leveled toward star players.

Against this unfortunate background, players, coaches, and some league officials are trying to clean up sports and create policy designed to instill greater accountability for infractions. Sports culture is having to meet the challenge of a more diverse society that has come a long way in accepting gay, bisexual, and transgender individuals. Sports culture must also confront its history with respect to the physical and sexual assault of women by athletes and coaches instead of mollifying the subject by aligning with breast cancer awareness in an attempt to appear female-friendly. Critics believe sports culture has a long road ahead of itself to enact the sort of change that would count as having a lasting and meaningful impact toward restoring nobility to sports many feel is currently lacking.

Notes

1 www.detroitnews.com/story/sports/2015/04/19/hbo-jim-harbaugh-reveals-um-love-real-sports/26042201/.

2 Anderson, Eric, *In the Game: Gay Athletes and the Cult of Masculinity* (State University of New York Press, 2005).

3 www.muhealth.org/services/pediatrics/conditions/adolescent-medicine/benefits-of-sports//.

4 www.medpagetoday.com/Pediatrics/Obesity/33750/.

5 www.aacap.org/AACAP/Families_and_Youth/Facts_for_Families/Facts_for_Families_Pages/Children_And_Sports_61.aspx/.

6 www.psychologytoday.com/blog/the-power-prime/201307/build-positive-and-high-performing-sports-team-culture/.

7 Price-Mitchell, Marilyn, "The psychology of youth sports: When playing the game fosters positive outcomes for kids," *Psychology Today*, January, 2012.

8 Flood, Michael, "Men, sex, and homosociality: How bonds between men shape their sexual relations with women," *Men and Masculinities*, May, 2007.

9 Hartmann, Douglas, "The sanctity of Sunday football: Why men love sports," *Journal of Sport and Social Issues*," August, 2003.

10 Messner, Michael, *Taking the Field: Women, Men, and Sports* (University of Minnesota Press, 2002).

11 Gumbrecht, Hans Ulrich, "Epiphany of form: On the beauty of team sports," *New Literary History* 30, 2 (1999), pp. 351–372.

12 *Professional Sports: The Challenges Facing the Future of the Industry: Hearing Before the Committee on the Judiciary U.S. Senate* (Diane Publishing, 1998).

13 www.usatoday.com/story/sports/nba/cavaliers/2014/07/11/lebron-james-return-cleveland-cavaliers-contract-miami-heat/12444643/.

14 www.aagpbl.org/index.cfm/pages/league/12/league-history.

15 www.rasmussenreports.com/public_content/lifestyle/general_lifestyle/april_2013/53_say_pro_sports_have_helped_race_relations_in_u_s.

16 Jarvie, G., and Reid, I., "Race relations, sociology of sport and the new politics of race and racism," Department of Sports Studies, University of Stirling, 2002.
17 Gane-McCalla, Casey, "Athletic blacks vs smart whites: Why sports stereotypes are wrong," *The Huffington Post*, May 25, 2011. www.huffingtonpost.com/casey-ganemccalla/athletic-blacks-vs-smart_b_187386.html.
18 http://articles.latimes.com/1987–04–09/news/mn-366_1_black-leaders.
19 http://sports.espn.go.com/nfl/news/story?id=1627887.
20 www.wnd.com/2009/10/112839/.
21 http://espn.go.com/nba/story/_/id/12001456/lebron-james-kyrie-irving-cleveland-cavaliers-kevin-garnett-deron-williams-brooklyn-nets-wear-breathe-shirt-reference-eric-garner.
22 http://en.wikipedia.org/wiki/Death_of_Eric_Garner.
23 www.wsj.com/articles/new-york-city-police-officer-wont-face-criminal-charges-in-eric-garner-death-1417635275.
24 www.washingtonpost.com/blogs/early-lead/wp/2014/12/11/geraldo-riveras-message-to-lebron-james-wear-be-a-better-father-shirt-not-i-cant-breathe/.
25 www.huffingtonpost.com/2014/11/30/rams-ferguson-hands-up_n_6245294.html.
26 www.sportingnews.com/nba/story/2014–12–12/eli-manning-lebron-james-eric-garner-michael-brown-nfl-nba-activist-athletes-new-york-giants-cleveland-cavaliers-george-town-hoyas.
27 www.thenation.com/blog/176171/dave-zirin-collision-sports-and-politics#.
28 www.thenation.com/blog/163592/dave-zirin-tim-tebow-and-nfls-political-hypocrisy.
29 http://sports.espn.go.com/nba/columns/story?id=1527038.
30 www.npr.org/blogs/itsallpolitics/2012/09/17/161272851/football-and-conservative-politics-do-mix-for-some-nfl-fans.
31 www.academia.edu/977429/Stereotypes_of_race_and_nationality_Sport_magazine_coverage_of_MLB_players_from_2000_to_2007.
32 http://en.wikipedia.org/wiki/Jeremy_Lin.
33 http://espn.go.com/new-york/nba/story/_/id/7617213/new-york-knicks-jeremy-lin-ben-jerry-apologizes-lin-sanity-flavor.
34 www.sbnation.com/nba/2012/2/18/2807696/espn-chink-in-the-armor-headline-jeremy-lin.
35 http://en.wikipedia.org/wiki/ESPN.
36 http://ftw.usatoday.com/2014/01/richard-sherman-strip-clubs-media-day-super-bowl.
37 Cooley, Will, "'Vanilla Thrillas': Modern boxing and white-ethnic masculinity," *Journal of Sports & Social Issues*, September, 2010.
38 www.pbs.org/wgbh/amex/fight/peopleevents/e_race.html.
39 www.cagepotato.com/floyd-mayweather-jr-expertly-brings-race-boxing-vs-mma-debate/.
40 https://en.wikipedia.org/wiki/Muhammad_Ali.
41 Ibid.
42 Rodriguez, Gregory, "Boxing and masculinity: The history and (her)story of Oscar de la Hoya," in *Latino/a Popular Culture*, ed. Michelle Habell-Pallan and Mary Romero (New York University Press, 2002).
43 Heiskanen, Benita. *The Urban Geography of Boxing: Race, Class, and Gender in the Ring* (Routledge, 2012), p. 86.
44 Leonard, David J. and Lugo-Lugo, Carmen R. *Latino History and Culture: An Encyclopedia* (Routledge, 2015), p. 78.
45 www.encyclopedia.com/article-1G2–2831200077/boxing.html.
46 Anderson, *In the Game.*
47 Ibid., p. 13.
48 Ibid.
49 Ibid.
50 Ibid.
51 http://espn.go.com/nfl/story/_/id/10468830/forty-four-51-nfl-players-surveyed-say-teammates-sexual-orientation-matter.
52 http://thinkprogress.org/sports/2015/01/29/3616510/three-fourths-americans-support-openly-gay-athletes-pro-sports/.
53 http://thinkprogress.org/sports/2014/11/21/3595024/how-jason-collins-coming-out-changed-sports-forever/.
54 Ibid.
55 Anderson, *In the Game.*
56 Ibid., p. 16
57 Goffman, Erving, "The arrangement between the sexes," *Theory and Society* 4, 3 (1977).
58 http://press.endocrine.org/doi/pdf/10.1210/jc.2014–1391.
59 Ibid.
60 www.nytimes.com/2006/08/10/fashion/10Fitness.html?_r=2&.
61 https://en.wikipedia.org/wiki/Gender_verification_in_sports.

62 https://en.wikipedia.org/wiki/International_Association_of_Athletics_Federations.
63 www.iwm.at/publications/5-junior-visiting-fellows-conferences/vol-xxix/maren-behrensen-2/.
64 Ibid.
65 www.advocate.com/commentary/2014/09/18/op.-ed-stop-freaking-out-about-female-intersex-athletes.
66 Ibid.
67 Ibid.
68 Ibid.
69 Ibid.
70 https://en.wikipedia.org/wiki/Homosexuality_and_psychology.
71 www.womensbioethics.org/index.php?s=355.
72 www.nola.com/sports/index.ssf/2010/06/former_ucla_players_note_john.html.
73 www.uclabruins.com/ViewArticle.dbml?ATCLID=208274583.
74 Ibid.
75 Ibid.
76 www.foxsports.com/carolinas/story/former-unc-players-remember-dean-smith-as-greater-man-than-coach-020815.
77 https://en.wikipedia.org/wiki/Jim_Valvano.
78 www.nj.com/rutgersbasketball/index.ssf/2013/04/mike_rice_fired_at_rutgers_aft.html.
79 www.sbnation.com/college-basketball/2013/4/3/4178392/mike-rice-fired-abuse.
80 www.usatoday.com/story/sports/ncaab/2014/08/05/college-of-charleston-fires-doug-wojcik-after-verbal-abuse-allegations/13635155/.
81 http://observer.com/2015/03/coaching-bad-executive-producer-discusses-his-eye-opening-look-into-athlete-abuse/.
82 www.nytimes.com/1988/04/27/sports/knight-is-criticized-over-rape-remark.html.
83 www.spike.com/shows/coaching-bad.
84 http://observer.com/2015/03/coaching-bad-executive-producer-discusses-his-eye-opening-look-into-athlete-abuse/.
85 www.wtsp.com/story/news/politics/florida/2015/03/31/bad-coaches-bill-moves-through-senate-committee/70718626/.
86 Ibid.
87 www.nflplayerengagement.com/prep/articles/call-to-coaches/.
88 http://en.wikipedia.org/wiki/Positive_Coaching_Alliance.
89 Ibid.
90 www.nytimes.com/2000/08/11/sports/sports-psychology-it-isn-t-just-a-game-clues-to-avid-rooting.html.
91 www.breitbart.com/sports/2013/03/19/sports-fans-less-prone-to-depression/.
92 Ibid.
93 Ibid.
94 Nelson, Toben F. and Wechsler, Henry, "School spirits: Alcohol and collegiate sports fans," *Addictive Behaviors*, January, 2003.
95 www.myfoxtwincities.com/story/17617739/8-percent-of-sports-fans-legally-drunk-after-game.
96 https://en.wikipedia.org/wiki/List_of_National_Football_League_attendance_figures.
97 The figure of 90,000 is the result of multiplying 5,625 cases of legally drunk fans leaving NFL stadiums times 16 weekly games, not including bye weeks.
98 www.cbsnews.com/news/alcohol-ignites-sports-fans/.
99 Ibid.
100 Ibid.
101 Ma, Tony, *Professional Marketing and Advertising Essays and Assignments* (Tony Ma Publishing, 2014).
102 Wenner, Lawrence A. and Jackson, Steven J., *Sport, Beer, and Gender: Promotional Culture and Contemporary Social Life (Popular Culture and Everyday Life)*, 2nd edition (Peter Lang, 2008).
103 Ibid.
104 McKay, Jim, Messner, Michael, Sabo, Donald. *Masculinities, Gender Relations, and Sports* (Sage Publications, 2000).
105 Ibid.
106 Ibid.
107 Nylund, David. *Beer, Babes, and Balls: Masculinity and Sports Talk Radio*, SUNY Series on Sport, Culture, and Social Relations (SUNY, 2007).
108 McKay Jim, Messner, Michael, and Sabo, Donald, *Masculinities, Gender Relations, and Sport* (Sage, 2000), p. 90.
109 www.humankinetics.com/excerpts/excerpts/does-on-field-violent-behavior-lead-to-off-field-violence.
110 Crosset, Todd, Benedict, Jeffrey R, McDonald, Mark A. "Male student-athletes reported for sexual assault: A survey of campus police departments and judicial affairs offices," *Journal of Sports & Social Issues*, May, 1995.
111 McKay, Messner, and Sabo, *Masculinities, Gender Relations, and Sports.*

112 Ibid.
113 Ibid.
114 Ibid.
115 Flood, Michael and Dyson, Sue, "Sports, athletes, and violence against women," *NTV Journal* 4, 3 (2007).
116 McKay, Messner, and Sabo, *Masculinities, Gender Relations, and Sports.*
117 www.pbs.org/wgbh/pages/frontline/league-of-denial/.
118 www.pbs.org/wgbh/pages/frontline/sports/concussion-watch/76-of-79-deceased-nfl-players-found-to-have-brain-disease/.
119 Ibid.
120 "Benoit's brain showed severe damage from multiple concussions, doctor and dad say," ABC News, September 5, 2007.
121 http://espn.go.com/nfl/story/_/id/8061129/nfl-10-steps-make-game-safer.
122 http://time.com/3686040/super-bowl-nfl-helmets/.
123 http://insider.foxnews.com/2013/10/24/us-sports-being-wussified-fox-and-friends-asks-john-mcenroe.
124 www.foxsports.com/collegefootball/story/helmet-safety-rules-not-making-players-wimps-wussball-092212.
125 www.glennbeck.com/2013/12/12/the-wussification-of-america-mlb-to-ban-home-plate-collisions/.
126 http://articles.latimes.com/2013/jan/10/sports/la-sp-sn-junior-seau-brain-20130110.
127 Ibid.
128 Anderson, Eric and Kian, Edward M., "Examining media contestation of masculinity and head trauma in the national football league," *Men and Masculinities*, June, 2012.
129 Ibid.
130 http://espn.go.com/espn/otl/story/_/id/12496480/san-francisco-49ers-linebacker-chris-borland-retires-head-injury-concerns.
131 www.thenation.com/blog/201713/dave-zirin-science-not-nfls-friend.
132 www.sbnation.com/2013/8/22/4648936/espn-frontline-documentary-nfl-concussions.
133 www.pbs.org/wgbh/pages/frontline/sports/league-of-denial/a-note-from-frontline-espn-and-league-of-denial/.
134 http://espn.go.com/nfl/story/_/id/11232366/former-nfl-players-christian-ballard-gregory-westbrooks-sue-union-head-injuries.
135 www.nfl.com/news/story/0ap1000000235494/article/nfl-explayers-agree-to-765m-settlement-in-concussions-suit.
136 www.nfl.com/news/story/09000d5d81990bdf/article/new-nfl-rules-designed-to-limit-head-injuries.
137 http://chicago.cbslocal.com/2012/10/10/bernstein-nfl-players-are-gladiators-like-it-or-not/.
138 http://en.wikipedia.org/wiki/Juiced:_WildTimes,_Rampant_%27Roids,_Smash_Hits_%26_How_Baseball_Got_Big.
139 http://en.wikipedia.org/wiki/Mitchell_Report.
140 Ibid.
141 https://espn.go.com/special/s/drugsandsports/steroids.html.
142 www.cbsnews.com/news/facts-and-myths-about-roid-rage/.
143 Ibid.
144 http://blogs.discovermagazine.com/neuroskeptic/2014/08/30/myth-roid-rage/.
145 www.drugabuse.gov/publications/drugfacts/anabolic-steroids.
146 www.bodybuilding.com/fun/drobson221.htm.
147 www.currentpsychiatry.com/home/article/bodybuildings-dark-side-clues-to-anabolic-steroid-use/75b1b27512a90b3fae41d8cf8433d184.html.
148 Steinfeldt, Jesse A., Gilchrist, Garret A., Halterman, Aaron W., Gomory, Alexander, Steinfeldt, Matthew Clint, "Drive for muscularity and conformity to masculine norms among college football players," *Psychology of Men & Masculinity*, February, 2011.
149 Ibid.
150 Ibid.
151 Curry, Timothy Jon, "Fraternal bonding in the locker room: A Profeminist analysis of talk about competition and women," *Sociology of Sport Journal*, 8, 2 (1991).
152 www.foxsports.com/nfl/story/adrian-peterson-on-locker-room-culture-people-say-crazier-things-than-just-the-n-word-112113.
153 Sternod, Brandon, "Come out and play: Confronting homophobia in sports," in *Learning Culture Through Sports: Perspectives on Society and Organized Sports*, ed. S. Prettyman and B. Lampman (Rowman & Littlefield, 2010), p. 94.
154 Messner, Michael and Sabo, Donald. *Sex, Violence, & Power in Sports: Rethinking Masculinity* (Crossing Press, 1994).
155 Eagly, Alice A., *Sex Differences in Social Behavior: A Social-Role Interpretation* (Lawrence Eribaum, 1987), p. 109.

156 www.bizjournals.com/bizjournals/how-to/human-resources/2013/11/political-correctness-nfl-miami-dolphins.html?page=all.
157 www.americansportscastersonline.com/womeninsportscasting.html.
158 Ibid.
159 Ibid.
160 www.hollywoodreporter.com/news/erin-andrews-hannah-storm-rampant-604915.
161 www.huffingtonpost.com/2013/08/15/erin-andrews-female-sports-reporter-sexism_n_3761035.html?.
162 www.mediaite.com/online/boston-morning-radio-host-calls-erin-andrews-a-gutless-bitch/.
163 www.hollywoodreporter.com/news/erin-andrews-hannah-storm-rampant-604915.
164 www.huffingtonpost.com/robin-herman/let-them-wear-towels_b_3596663.html.
165 http:/espn.go.com/espnw/w-in-action/nine-for-ix/article/9481107/espnw-how-far-female-journalists-really-come.
166 www.nytimes.com/1997/09/26/us/marv-albert-pleads-guilty-and-is-dismissed-by-nbc.html.
167 www.thedailybeast.com/articles/2014/07/01/world-cup-anchor-mike-tirico-s-bizarre-history-reports-of-stalking-and-sexual-harassment.html.
168 http://thewalkon.org/females-in-sportscasting/.
169 www.forbes.com/sites/annedoyle/2013/01/21/its-time-for-sports-broadcasting-to-stop-relegating-women-to-sideline-eye-candy/.
170 www.newsday.com/sports/columnists/barbara-barker/violet-palmer-paved-the-way-for-female-nba-referees-1.9915072.
171 http:/espn.go.com/espnw/news/article/6837609/calling-shots-women-striking-mlb.
172 Ibid.
173 www.nfl.com/news/story/0ap3000000484343/article/sarah-thomas-blazes-trail-as-nfls-first-fulltime-female-official.
174 http://ftw.usatoday.com/2015/04/sarah-thomas-nfl-official.
175 www.washingtonpost.com/news/morning-mix/wp/2015/04/09/how-sarah-thomas-became-the-nfls-first-full-time-female-referee/.
176 http://sports.espn.go.com/mlb/news/story?id=2419291.
177 Ibid.
178 http://blog.mint.com/how-to/from-stoked-to-broke-why-are-so-many-professional-athletes-going-bankrupt-0213/.
179 www.si.com/vault/2009/03/23/105789480/how-and-why-athletes-go-broke.
180 www.npr.org/2015/01/27/381724445/how-do-some-highly-paid-athletes-go-bankrupt-theyre-risk-takers.
181 http://espn.go.com/30for30/film?page=broke.
182 www.npr.org/2015/01/27/381724445/how-do-some-highly-paid-athletes-go-bankrupt-theyre-risk-takers.
183 www.nytimes.com/2010/10/17/sports/football/17rhoden.html.
184 http://en.wikipedia.org/wiki/National_Football_League_Cheerleading.
185 www.nytimes.com/2010/10/17/sports/football/17rhoden.html.
186 www.mlive.com/lions/index.ssf/2014/03/detroit_lions_proud_to_be_1_of.html.
187 https://sports.vice.com/en_us/article/its-time-for-the-nfl-to-ban-cheerleaders.
188 Hanson, Mary Ellen, *Go! Fight! Win!: Cheerleading in American Culture* (Popular Press, 1995).
189 www.phillymag.com/news/2011/02/04/shake-it-baby/.
190 Ibid.
191 www.sportingnews.com/nfl/story/2014–09–11/nfl-cheerleaders-treatment-pay-salary-lawsuits-jills-raiderettes-minimum-wage-women.
192 http://america.aljazeera.com/articles/2014/1/31/cheerleaders-admitwork-doesntpaythebillsbutlovethejob.html.
193 http://nypost.com/2014/04/27/my-life-as-a-buffalo-jill/.
194 Ibid.
195 www.cnn.com/2013/10/25/sport/nfl-cheerleaders-minnesota-vikings-mvc/.
196 Withers, Bethany P., "The integrity of the game: Professional athletes and domestic violence," *Harvard Journal of Sports and Entertainment Law* 1, 1 (2010), pp. 146–179.
197 http://groupthink.jezebel.com/a-culture-of-apathy-professional-sports-domestic-vio-1634626258.
198 http://espn.go.com/nfl/story/_/id/11257692/ray-rice-baltimore-ravens-suspended-2-games.
199 http://hardballtalk.nbcsports.com/2014/09/12/bud-selig-cant-remember-the-last-domestic-violence-incident-in-major-league-baseball/.
200 http://articles.philly.com/2006–08–14/sports/25397025_1_boston-police-transcript-brett-myers.

201 Ibid.
202 www.cbssports.com/mlb/eye-on-baseball/25406495/puig-reyes-chapman-under-mlb-investigation-for-domestic-violence.
203 www.sbnation.com/mlb/2014/7/28/5936835/ray-rice-chuck-knoblauch-minnesota-twins-mlb-domestic-abuse-violence.
204 Ibid.
205 http://thedailybanter.com/2014/07/espn-commentator-says-women-shouldnt-provoke-men-domestic-violence/.
206 http://articles.philly.com/2006–06–29/sports/25402799_1_boston-street-corner-myers-case-brett-myers.
207 www.nytimes.com/2015/01/31/sports/football/no-1-debate-in-tampa-whether-to-draft-jameis-winston.html.
208 http://pact5.org/resources/prevention-and-readiness/athletes-and-sexual-assault/.
209 www.salon.com/2015/08/26/its_not_just_michael_vick_the_steelers_still_have_a_rape_culture_problem_too/.
210 www.cnn.com/2010/CRIME/04/16/roethlisberger.incident/.
211 Ibid.
212 Ibid.
213 http://usatoday30.usatoday.com/sports/football/nfl/steelers/story/2012–01–20/ben-roethlisberger-settles-lawsuit/52702798/1.
214 www.nydailynews.com/opinion/convictions-sex-crimes-cases-hard-article-1.1053819.
215 www.uic.edu/orgs/cwluherstory/CWLU-Archive/saysorry.html.
216 www.theguardian.com/society/2007/feb/01/penal.genderissues.
217 www.scu.edu/ethics/focus-areas/more/resources/equal-justice-under-law/.
218 www.slate.com/blogs/xx_factor/2014/11/18/how_cops_respond_to_rape_a_new_study_f_officers_at_one_police_department.html.
219 Ibid.
220 Ibid.
221 Ibid.
222 https://en.wikipedia.org/wiki/Penn_State_child_sex_abuse_scandal.
223 www.nytimes.com/2012/07/01/sports/ncaafootball/paterno-may-have-influenced-decision-not-to-report-sandusky-e-mails-indicate.html?_r=0.
224 Ibid.
225 www.huffingtonpost.com/2014/05/15/university-of-oregon-complaint-rape_n_5331120.html.
226 Ibid.
227 Chapter 10 will cover The Clery Act and Clery complaints on NCAA campuses.
228 www.huffingtonpost.com/2014/05/15/university-of-oregon-complaint-rape_n_5331120.html.
229 http://www.mvpstrat.com/the-bystander-approach/.
230 Ibid.
231 www.courtinnovation.org/sites/default/files/MVP_evaluation.pdf.
232 Ibid.
233 Ibid.
234 Ibid.
235 http://en.wikipedia.org/wiki/Violence_Against_Women_Act.
236 www.whitehouse.gov/1is2many.
237 www.notalone.gov/.
238 http://sports.espn.go.com/ncaa/columns/story?columnist=oneil_dana&id=5680182.
239 Ibid.
240 Ibid.
241 Ibid.

Chapter

10

Men, Anger, Violence, and Crime

The terror he caused was such that, if I felt I could have succeeded, I would have killed him. My childish instinct was to protect my mother, but the man hurting her was my father, whom I respected, admired and feared.

~ Actor Patrick Stewart discussing his father's violence against his mother[1]

Learning Objectives

After reading this chapter, students should be able to respond to the following questions with an understanding of the terms and expressions employed:

- *What is criminologist Candice Batton's theory of male violence?*
- *What have anger-management specialists learned about anger and men? What does psychologist Robert F. Levant mean by the expression 'normative male alexithymia' with respect to men and anger? How have therapists rebranded therapy to make it more desirable to men?*
- *What is the Power–Control Theory of delinquency? What are the criticisms of this theory? What conclusions are drawn by proponents of P–C theory with respect to patriarchal families versus egalitarian families?*
- *In what ways do hegemonic masculinities and violence intersect? How is hegemonic masculinity associated with sexual assault and rape?*
- *What is* The Campus Safety Act *and how do critics argue that it hurts the victims of rape and sexual assault? What is the* Campus Sexual Violence Elimination Act? *What is* rape culture? *What is* re-traumatization? *Why does antiviolence educator Jackson Katz call rape "a men's issue"?*
- *What are* The Clery Act *and* Title IX *as they pertain to campus violence?*
- *With respect to sexual violence in the military, what is* The Military Justice Improvement Act?

- *What is Messerschmidt's Masculinity Hypothesis? In what ways have gang affiliation and the behaviors that flow from gang life been termed 'doing masculinity'? What is the* machismo syndrome *as described by some scholars? What are 'marginalized masculinities'?*
- *What are thought to be some of the factors that drive boys and young men into joining gangs?*
- *In relation to men's violence, what is meant by "restorative justice" and how does it differ from "retributive justice"?*
- *What are the incarceration rates for black men as compared to white men, and what sorts of factors are believed to account for these disparities?*
- *What is the* Prison Rape Elimination Act of 2003 *and what are the ongoing concerns with respect to prison rape? What are the goals of the organization* Black and Pink?
- *What are considered to be the most accurate predictors of men's violence? What connections have been found between alcohol usage and men's violence?*
- *With respect to violence against men, who are the primary perpetrators? What is the "Conflict Tactics Scale" (CTS) and how is it used to document intimate partner violence? How do the criteria of the CTS affect intimate partner violence statistics with respect to gender?*

In considering the intersection of men, anger, violence, and crime, this chapter will address men's perpetrated violence and crime, including violence directed toward boys and men. As covered in the chapter on biology, some believe that males are prone to violence through hormonal influences not found in the same degree in females. If this explanation is correct, combatting male violence becomes much more difficult, since it would involve either biological intervention or finding ways to socialize boys that might disrupt biological impulses. However, as exposed in the chapter on biology, much of the research conducted on the alleged connection between testosterone levels in males and heightened states of aggression and violence has not panned out as expected. When serum-testosterone levels have been increased in both males and females, increased levels of competition have sometimes been discovered, but increased levels of aggression and violence have not been witnessed. Yet, men are incarcerated for violent crimes at rates much higher than that of females. According to the Bureau of Justice Statistics, one out of nine cases of male crime is violent in nature, while one in 56 cases of female crime is violent in nature.[2] According to the FBI, males are responsible for the vast majority of violence in America with male offender percentages as follows:

- 98% of forcible rape
- 91% of murder
- 85% of robbery
- 80% of family violence
- 78% of aggravated assault

In one example of male perpetrated violence, of 63 out of 64 mass-shootings at schools in the past two decades, boys were the perpetrators[3] and 98% of mass shooters in general are male.[4] It also turns out that the overwhelming majority of school and mass shooters are white.[5]

Everything from gun proliferation to substance abuse to mental disorders to problems of dysfunctional home environments to violent media to environmental influences have been blamed for the levels of violence in America, but often missing from the analysis is the fact that boys and men commit the vast majority of violent acts, even though girls and women live in the same environments, suffer from mental illness at roughly similar rates to boys and men, abuse substances at similar rates, also come from dysfunctional homes, play violent video games, and live in a culture of gun proliferation.

In earlier chapters, we examined *social learning theory*, which has been one of the central theories thought to explain violence. According to social learning theory, violence is a learned behavior through childhood exposure to witnessed or experienced violence where there were no negative consequences to the perpetrator of the violence. In simpler terms, children learn to be violent by observing violence modeled in the home. There are limitations to social learning theory, such as the correlational factors of poverty, the influence of media, socialized notions of male supremacy, which include societal expectations of men as breadwinner and protector, and individual factors that may place a person at risk for violence.[6] So, while social learning theory continues to be considered a worthy area of research, it is considered by many to be incomplete as an explanatory thesis for violence.

When men who perpetrate violence are captured, prosecuted, convicted, and incarcerated, the problems of men's violence do not end. Within the confines of prisons and detention centers, men's violence continues to be a serious problem. The victimization of incarcerated men by other inmates and institutional staff is a well-documented problem across the country. The dangers are all the worse for men who are gay, bisexual, or transgender in a criminal justice system that has been unresponsive to their needs and in some cases make things worse by misunderstanding the nature of prison violence. Regulations, programs, and treatment intervention plans have been proposed to mitigate violence in penitentiary environments, but those who work in this area agree that much more needs to be done if violence within incarcerated environments is to be stopped.

Why men perpetrate violence at much higher rates than women is a subject of continued debate, but **Candice Batton** of the University of Nebraska argues,

> Some research supports the idea that males are much more likely than females to develop negative attributions of blame that are external in nature, that is, "The cause of my problems is someone else or some force outside of me."

This external blame translates into anger and hostility toward others. Women, on the other hand, are more likely to develop negative attributions of blame that are internal in nature, that is, "The cause of my problems is some failing of my own: I didn't try hard enough, I'm not good enough."[7] If Batton is correct, the gendered nature of violence can be seen as a product of the different ways boys and girls are socialized to view themselves and their relationship to others with respect to accepting responsibility for their actions. If boys believe others are responsible for the negative circumstances they are experiencing, they are more likely to lash out against others as retribution for what they perceive as the wrong done to them. If, on the other hand, boys are taught to take greater responsibility for their actions, Batton's theory would predict that a greater number of men will be less violent.

Men and Anger Management

Part of the connection between men and violence is found in how boys are socialized to deal with conflict as opposed to ways that girls are taught to deal with conflict.

Anger management specialists regularly see this gendered response to conflict in therapeutic settings. Psychotherapist Ron Potter-Efron, having logged over 25,000 hours of therapy, characterizes the majority of his male clients as "highly reluctant" participants who in most cases are in therapy as the result of an ultimatum made by their wives or girlfriends or as the result of a court order.[8] One persistent problem with men who experience trouble with anger-control, reports Potter-Efron, is that these men are "untrained in experiencing and communicating other emotions."[9] That men are 'untrained' in dealing with their emotions speaks to the pervasive way that boys are raised to avoid emotions other than anger, and this is particularly true in the face of conflict.

Anger management specialist Steven Stosny holds a "boot camp" for couples and in treating over 1,200 men, Stosny finds that "Most male anger comes from feeling like a failure as a protector, provider, and sexual-lover."[10] At the same time, Stosny writes, many men project their feelings of inadequacy onto their wives so that they can adopt the role of victim in the relationship:

> Victimhood gives [men] a temporary sense of self-righteousness, along with a retaliation impulse, which stimulates anger ... He gets caught on a roller-coaster of resentment-anger-depression-resentment-anger-depression. Chronic blame keeps him mired in victim-identity, which continually reignites the cycle.[11]

Getting men to disrupt and replace this cycle with healthier habits of communication is the aim of relationship counseling and anger management, argues Stosny, which speaks to men's ongoing difficulties with communication, particularly when feeling hurt or inadequate in some way. But again, it is rarely a man's idea to seek out counseling even in the presence of severe emotional problems. Psychologist Robert F. Devant coined the expression ***normative male alexithymia*** which means, "without words for emotion," to describe a common pathology present in men who require counseling for issues of anger.[12] Devant argues that many men learn as boys to suppress their feelings and particularly those feelings they view as exposing vulnerability such as caring, empathy, compassion, sadness, and love.[13] Psychologist and masculinity researcher James Mahalik agrees and adds,

> To benefit from counseling, a man must admit that he needs help, must rely on the counselor and must openly discuss and express emotion. These requirements conflict with traditional ideals of what it means to be male: toughness, independence and emotional control.[14]

Interestingly, when searching for strategies to get more men to seek out counseling, psychologist John Robertson found that changing the language in brochures was effective in getting men to view counseling in a positive light.[15] For instance, by swapping out the term 'therapy' with 'consultation' and emphasizing self-help and personal achievement rather than 'assistance,' more men were willing to initiate counseling to address their emotional issues.[16] The thinking behind the change in terminology was that language of self-reliance over language of requiring help from others would lend itself better to men's traditional socialization toward independence and autonomy.

Another strategy some therapists will use to get men to open up about their feelings is self-disclosure.[17] While not all counselors are comfortable with this technique, it has been shown that men, and particularly men who are reluctant to disclose their feelings, are more willing to discuss their feelings after a therapist discloses his or her own anxieties.[18] Counselors have also been effective with men by informing them that certain feelings are quite common. When men feel embarrassed and anxious about engaging a stranger in an emotionally vulnerable conversation, counselors have found it useful to explain to male clients that fears associated with marriage, career, fathering, and many other emotionally challenging issues are prevalent and that there are steps men can take to regain control of what they can control: their reactions to upsetting circumstances.[19] Given many men's desire for being in control, some counselors have found it to be advantageous to exploit this inclination by positioning the counseling process as a process that allows a man to control some problematic way that he is reacting to circumstances outside of his control.[20] The thinking of many counselors who work with men is that therapy will not be able to undo a lifetime of socialized beliefs about manhood, but may be successful in using those beliefs to assist men in creating healthier ways to deal with stress and upsetting circumstances.

THOUGHT BOX

After reading about some of the ways that counselors assist men who struggle with anger and other emotional issues, do these techniques seem to you to be the best way to go about it? Can you think of other, perhaps better, ways of getting men to have a positive attitude about counseling?

The Power–Control Theory of Delinquency

The power–control theory of delinquency purports to explain why trouble-making behavior is more pronounced in boys than it is in girls. Developed by John Hagan, A.R. Gillis, and John Simpson of the University of Toronto, the power–control theory speculates that the amount of freedom juveniles are given, coupled with a tolerance of male misbehavior by some parents, leads to higher rates of delinquency in boys.[21] The key to this theory is family structure, the amount of supervision in place over children, and the strict or permissive attitudes of the parents involved. The power–control theory also investigates the rates of delinquency between patriarchal families where the father exerts control and discipline and egalitarian families where both the father and mother share in rule-making and disciplinary measures. Patriarchal families were thought to spring from the acceptance of traditional gender roles of parenting coupled with power differentials in the workforce.

Power–control theories of criminology sprung out of feminist theories of crime, where it was predicted that egalitarian families would produce less violent offspring and overall less delinquency than patriarchal families. The idea was that patriarchal families will exert more control over daughters than sons due to an ideological orientation of parents who, it was assumed, would give sons more freedom to explore, experience, and sometimes err in the world as part of a male's expected role as breadwinner and protector of the family. The expectation was that parents in patriarchal family settings encourage their sons to be more competitive, which involves greater risk-taking, while daughters are groomed for supportive roles in adult life. Conversely, an egalitarian family, it was thought, would exert less control on daughters in the expectation that they would enter the workforce along with sons and assume roles traditionally reserved for men. In sum, an egalitarian approach to parenting was supposed to decrease the gender stratification of delinquency.

THOUGHT BOX

To what extent do you believe Hagan and University of Toronto scholars have made the case for egalitarian parenting as a tonic for male, adolescent delinquency? Do you instead think that the critics (below) have successfully dislodged the power–control account of delinquency in favor of alternative theories, or do you believe there are take-away points from both sides that can work together to form a viable explanation and mitigation of increased male adolescent delinquency?

Criticism of the power–control theory of delinquency comes from researchers Simon Singer and Murray Levine who observe that mothers in egalitarian households were more protective of their daughters than those from patriarchal households, a finding that ran contrary to the prediction made by power–control theorists.[22] Further criticism came from those who argued that power–control models of delinquency focus almost entirely on traditional family structures, which include intact, two-parent families and single mothers.[23] When extending power–control theory beyond dyadic, biological parents and single-mother households to single-father households and step-family households, researchers discovered a host of complications that impact the initial conclusions of the power–control model. Other critics note that family structure is but one factor that may influence delinquency. Power and class dynamics within society as a whole can have an influence on delinquency rates.[24] Further criticism appeals to the fact that minor delinquent episodes in adolescence are not good predictors of chronic criminal behavior in adulthood. But the main criticism of the power–control theory of delinquency comes from those who insist that gendered patterns of delinquent behavior, like gendered patterns of violence in general, are due to structural, neurological differences between boys and girls so that upbringing and family structure have little to do with delinquency, and particularly acts of aggression and violence.[25]

Hegemonic Masculinity and Violence

The connection between masculinity and violence has been at the center of research by gender scholars R.W. Connell and James Messerschmidt, who argue that male-perpetrated violence, and particularly sexual violence, is often the result of men who feel inadequately masculine against the background of a hegemonic, masculine culture.[26] The key to understanding the concept of hegemonic masculinity is power. It is the construction of the hegemonic element of masculinity, argue Messerschmidt and Connell, that creates a feeling of deficiency and incompetency in some men and also creates a hierarchy of masculine expression within cultural and niche communities.[27]

The notion of hegemonic masculinity began with field studies at Australian high schools, where male hierarchies had formed.[28] The observed hierarchies were structured around both gender and class. But, as research continued, the notion of hegemonic masculinity evolved into a growing recognition of there being a plurality of masculinities, that there was not one sense of hegemonic masculinity that applied to all environments where hierarchies form. One thing that became clear in the research is that hegemonic masculinities involve actions based on perceived differences in power.[29] This means that hegemonic masculinity becomes a normative ideal

FIGURE 10.1: R.W. Connell, University of Sydney

not necessarily available to the majority of men, but that codifies men's dominance over women. Connell writes, "Hegemony does not mean violence, although it could be supported by force; it means ascendancy achieved through culture, institutions, and persuasion."[30] Power differentials are crucial to the concept of hegemonic masculinities; they define who is rewarded and who is punished by members of the target community.

Although Connell does not equate hegemony with violence, it is common for force, bullying, verbal abuse, and coercion of various types to attend hegemonic masculinities as consequences for women and those men who do not enjoy the privileges of hegemonic masculine status. As mentioned earlier in the text, criticism has focused on what ideal hegemonic masculinity actually looks like, since there are prototypes for different social groups. While a muscular, athletic man might be the hegemonic archetype in some social networks, the man of wealth who does not possess a muscular physique might be a hegemonic archetype in other social networks. In prison culture, for example, where physical might usually determines the masculine pecking order, having a large, muscular physique coupled with a reputation for violence and intimidation is viewed as the hegemonic archetype within most incarcerated environments. Other cultures may have very different notions of what counts as ideal masculinity, but hierarchical structures define the concept of hegemonic masculinity regardless of the variance found in individual instances.

But as Connell, Messerschmidt, and others have emphasized, hegemonic masculinity has had, and continues to have, enormous consequences for women. If boys are raised to believe that men have an elevated value over women, or worse, that women can be considered property in the context of relationships, then some men will act out with contempt, aggression, and sometimes violence when challenged, or believed to be challenged, by women. The adherence to this gendered hierarchy by men can have particular consequences in the case of sexual consent. If some men believe in their superiority to women and view sexual encounters with women as entitlements, this perceived hierarchy creates an environment ripe for sexual coercion, sexual assault, and rape.

JESSE PRINZ ON THE WARRIOR HYPOTHESIS

The City of New York University philosophy professor Jesse Prinz, in an issue of *Psychology Today*, evaluates the evolutionary psychological theory that men are violent by nature. In what has been termed the *Male Warrior Hypothesis*, evolutionary psychologists argue that men's increased levels of violence compared to women is the result of prehistoric conditions where men formed violent coalitions in order to "capture women, collect resources, that make men more attractive to women."[1] Prinz rejects this idea, responding to three objections:

Objection 1: Intergroup aggression predates agriculture, so agriculture cannot be the cause of male violence. The archeological evidence dates back 30,000 years.

Response: (i) Agriculture and farming handed men a monopoly on power. As property owners, men were able to control wage-earning power, (ii) archeological evidence for violence dates far into our history so that the capacity to kill may have evolved for hunting but does not clearly explain intergroup violence, and (iii) conclusions based on the behaviors of other species (see van Vugt and Ahuja on chimpanzee coalitional violence[2]) is dubious. In fact, bonobos, which are closer genetically to humans than chimpanzees, do not form coalitions for purposes of violence.

Objection 2: Evolution affects psychology. Men and women have evolved to have different psychological traits.

Response: While evolution affects psychology, there is no evidence that there is a gendered difference in the psychological dispositions of men and women. In fact, this evolutionary explanation was long used to explain why women were not capable of excelling in universities, a notion long ago debunked. In many social experiments, gendered differences have been linked to what parents (and researchers) expected and urged in boys and girls so that the results they garnered were biased.

Objection 3: Culture is a product of biology because cultural learning is innate.

Response: There is a difference between male upper-body physical strength and male violence. Furthermore, while social learning is responsible for culture, it does

FIGURE 10.2: Jesse Prinz

Continued

not follow that biology produces culture. "Saying that culture is a product of biology is like saying that Shakespeare's genes wrote *Hamlet*."

So, what is Prinz's explanation of violence? Prinz argues that power dynamics probably account for most historical and contemporary violence. He states, "Violence is a complex problem, which no simple biological approach can diagnose or remedy. Factors such as political instability, population density, and income inequality are associated with massive differences in violence across cultures, and these differences are observed while gender ratios remain constant. Of course, men still hold most of the power in the world, and it is no surprise, then, that they perpetrate most of the violence. But that too is a historical fact, not a biological given. If we focus on biology instead of economic and historical variables, we will miss out on opportunities for progress."[3] If Prinz is correct, if social and economic power dynamics were gender-reversed, women would probably be more violent than men.

---

1 www.psychologytoday.com/blog/experiments-in-philosophy/201202/sex-and-violence -male-warriors-revisited.
2 Van Vugt, Mark and Ahuja, Anjana, *Naturally Selected: The Evolutionary Science of Leadership* (Harper Business, 2011).
3 www.psychologytoday.com/blog/experiments-in-philosophy/201202/why-are-men-so-violent.

Men's Sexual Violence in High School and College

One of the most visible topics today related to men's violence is the rate of sexual assault and rape among high school students and on college campuses. In chapter three, we examined the issue of college fraternity men who engage in or are bystanders in cases of sexual assault and rape as part of organizational complicity. There is a large body of research that reveals cases of rape and sexual assault are greatly underreported, but when victims do report an assault, it is often the case that schools do not take appropriate action.[31] Some of this was considered in chapter nine where the *Clery Act* was introduced in the context of student athlete perpetrated sexual assault. But high school rates of sexual assault have risen, and concerned groups everywhere are struggling to understand how to best address the enormity of this issue. Two concerned high school seniors, Alexandra Kudatsky and Melissa Morgan, writing for the *Huffington Post*, decided to ask their principal about addressing rape and sexual assault on high school campuses after reading health textbooks that were completely silent on the issue.[32] To their surprise, although to no one's surprise who has worked in this field, instead of supporting the students, their principal warned that any actions taken by the school could result in angry phone calls from parents and retaliation from peers.[33] When the two students hung posters around their school that read "Steps to avoid rape: 1. Don't Rape!" the posters were torn down and the two were told that "rape doesn't happen in high school; why are you doing this?"[34] Finally, the students made a video modeled after the White House initiative "It's On Us," which was played at their school as part of a "Week of Action," during which public service announcements were aired to raise awareness about rape and sexual assault in high school.[35] The week ended with student Katie Koestner's presentation to underclassmen and upperclassmen on her personal experience with rape to a standing ovation.[36]

Koestner's story, and those of her classmates, attempt to raise student and administrative awareness about rape and sexual assault, spotlighting a problem that has echoed around the country. Many students meet stories of rape and sexual assault with skepticism, and institutions are often more concerned with risk management, damage control, and institutional reputations than with becoming proactive partners with rape victims to stop rape on their campuses.[37] In some cases, conservative legislators have introduced measures that will make it more difficult for rape survivors.[38] For instance, Rep. Matt Salmon (R-Ariz.) introduced ***The Campus Safety Act*** that restricts colleges from investigating cases of rape and sexual assault unless police agencies are involved,[39] which is actually in violation of Title IX.[40] Unsurprisingly, many fraternities support *The Campus Safety Act* with the National Panhellenic Conference and the North American Interfraternity Conference spending $210,000 lobbying for the institution of the Act by colleges around the nation.[41]

THE CLERY ACT AND TITLE IX

The Clery Act was signed into law in 1990 and requires all colleges and universities that participate in federal financial aid programs to disclose information about crime on and near their campuses.[1] The Clery Act was a legal response to Lehigh University's 38 violent crimes in three years that went unreported to the campus community. The Clerys argued that if this information were made known, their daughter Jeanne would never have attended the university.[2] Jeanne Clery was raped and murdered at Lehigh University on April 5, 1986. The Clerys were awarded $2 million in damages. It is now the law that campus officials are required to inform the public of all crimes committed on their campus. Many universities have come under scrutiny by the Department of Education for violations, including Eastern Michigan University, Penn State University, and Virginia Tech for failing to issue warnings in a timely manner to assist students, faculty, and parents of prospective students.

Title IX is a portion of the United States Education Amendments of 1972, which reads, "No person in the United States shall, on the basis of sex, be excluded from participation in, be denied the benefits of, or be subjected to discrimination under any education program or activity receiving federal financial assistance."[3] Under Title IX, sex discrimination in education is prohibited. It specifically prohibits sexual violence, which includes rape or sexual assault, sexual harassment, stalking, voyeurism, exhibitionism, verbal or physical sexually-based threats or abuse, and intimate partner violence.[4] As a result of Title IX, schools must have in place an established procedure for handling complaints of sex discrimination, sexual harassment, and sexual violence. In such cases, an institution must take immediate action to ensure that victims can continue their education free of any retaliatory harassment or behaviors. This means that institutions must insure that accused students are unable to approach or interact with victims. During disciplinary hearings concern over perpetrators' attempts to intimidate and silence victims and witnesses is handled by barring the accused from questioning or challenging victims.[5]

1 https://en.wikipedia.org/wiki/Clery_Act.
2 Ibid.
3 https://en.wikipedia.org/wiki/Title_IX.
4 http://knowyourix.org/title-ix/title-ix-the-basics/.
5 Ibid.

In 2012, students at 29 universities brought legal action against their institutions on charges of negligence in the handling of sexual assault reports and being in violation of Title IX.[42] Their combined efforts resulted in the adoption of the ***Campus Sexual Violence Elimination Act (SaVE)***, introduced by U.S. Senator Bob Casey Jr. (D-PA) and House Representative Caroline Maloney (D-NY), which mandates institutions to create policies on the handling of rape and sexual assault reports that build around four themes: transparency, accountability, education, and collaboration.[43] In 2014, Vice President Joseph Biden introduced new administration guidelines and policy recommendations to deal with sexual assault on college campuses that included "a tool kit for conducting anonymous surveys, a checklist for developing sexual misconduct policy, templates for agreements between colleges, local law enforcement, and rape crisis centers."[44] Many colleges and universities reacted with ambivalence, as they expressed the view that they did not want the government telling them what to do.[45] One concern raised by victim advocates is that victims may not report sexual assaults if they believe their reaching out for health services would automatically trigger an investigation.[46] New guidelines were issued that allowed health care specialists and women's center counselors to keep reports confidential.[47] Only the Title IX coordinator and certain designated employees are compelled by law to report cases of victim reports.[48]

But an ongoing roadblock to getting victims to report sexual assault is the specter of what will happen to them when they declare their victimization to others. In many cases, a victim is afraid she or he will be blamed for the assault. The term ***rape culture*** was invented to describe a set of pervasive behaviors and instructions that help facilitate rape, including blaming victims, trivializing sexual assault often through jokes, inflating false rape report statistics, scrutinizing a victim's choice of clothing, mental state, level of intoxication, motives, and sexual history, and teaching women to avoid being raped rather than stressing the importance to boys and men not to rape.[49] Victim-blaming, in particular, creates a two-pronged danger: it casts culpability away from perpetrators so that perpetrators are free to continue assaulting others, and it has a silencing effect on victims who worry that they will be targeted for shame and reprisal. This latter form of victim-blaming has been termed ***re-traumatization***, since the victim is now being attacked a second time.[50]

Rape and sexual assault are commonly framed as "women's issues," but antiviolence educator Jackson Katz argues that campus rape, and rape in general, is a men's issue due to the fact that 99% of all rapists are men.[51] [52] [53] Katz claims that changing rape culture requires changing the attitudes of men. Placing the burden on women to protect themselves from being raped in no way affects the beliefs and practices of men as long as men continue to trivialize rape and view women as sexual opportunities. But men are a stubborn demographic in this regard, since many men are either apathetic to the problem of rape or openly hostile to the judgment that men need to change. Men's apathy to rape and rape victims no doubt springs from a general view among men that men are not themselves going to be raped, coupled with the assurance that they, personally, are not rapists. Yet, between 85% to 90% of rape victims know their attacker,[54] and about half of all rapes occur on a date.[55] This means that the view of rapists as being shadowy figures hiding in parking lots or behind shrubs or bushes is simply false. The vast majority of men who rape women and who rape other men do so in the context of knowing the victim and usually in a romantic, quasi-romantic, friendship, or acquaintance context. Other men who may have knowledge of a rape or sexual assault taking place are encouraged in male culture to remain silent. If Katz is correct, the apathy and resistance of men to take rape and sexual assault seriously is a central ingredient in keeping the crimes of rape and sexual assault as pervasive as they are.

RAPE STATISTICS AND THE VIOLENCE AGAINST WOMEN ACT OF 2013

While men's rights activists and other rape myth supporters continue to deny rates of rape in America, the White House Council on Women and Girls notes:

> In calculating the prevalence of rape, The Centers for Disease Control and Prevention (CDC) counts completed forced penetration, or alcohol/drug facilitated completed penetration. Like other researchers, the CDC considers attempted forced penetration to fall within the definition of "rape" because that crime can be just as traumatizing for victims.[1]

The CDC goes on to note that the most common form of rape victimization experienced by women is completed forced penetration, with the following percentages: 12.3% of women in the United States are victims of completed forced penetration, 8% are victims of alcohol/drug facilitated completed penetration, and 5.2% are victims of attempted forced penetration. Many of these victims experience multiple forms of these subtypes of rape in their lifetimes.[2] Statistics gathered by the National Institute of Justice, Bureau of Justice Statistics, include:

- An estimated 20–25% of college women will experience rape or attempted rape during her college career.
- 12.8% of completed rapes, 35% of attempted rapes, and 22.9% of threatened rapes occurred during a date with the perpetrator.
- 22% of victims were victims of multiple rapes.
- Less than 5% of completed or attempted rapes were reported to law enforcement.

Research has also uncovered that 63% of college men who rape women are serial offenders, with repeat offenders admitting that they committed an average of six rapes each.[3] [4] The report also revealed that almost 11% of college men report committing at least one rape from the time they were 14-years-old until the end of college.[5] Another study reported that 15% of women raped while at college were incapacitated by alcohol or drugs, the majority of victims being college freshmen.[6] In 80% of cases of rape, the victim knows the perpetrator.[7] The U.S. Department of Justice reports that approximately 16% of cases of rape are reported to authorities, that among college women, approximately 12% of cases of rape are reported, and that each year, approximately 300,000 college women are raped or sexually assaulted.[8] Contrary to what rape myth supporters state, false reporting of rape is estimated by Department of Justice to occur in approximately two to five percent of cases.[9] Beyond the unbelievable suffering of victims, rape costs the U.S. government $127 billion each year, which is more than any other crime.[10]

On February 12, 2013, the U.S. Senate passed the reauthorization of the **Violence Against Women Act** (VAWA), which among the highlights includes within the definition of sexual assault situations in which the victim lacks the capacity to consent, increases funding to address rape kit backlogs, creates Inspector General audits of rape and sexual assault evidence in the custody of state or local

Continued

government agencies, and requires the National Institute of Justice to develop protocols and practices for the effective collecting and processing of DNA evidence in rape cases.

1 www.whitehouse.gov/sites/default/files/docs/sexual_assault_report_1-21-14.pdf.
2 Ibid.
3 Lisak, David and Miller, Paul M., "Repeat rape and multiple offending among undetected rapists," *Violence and Victims*, 17, 1 (2002).
4 www.eab.com/daily-briefing/2015/07/20/jama-most-campus-rapes-not-committed-by-serial-offenders.
5 Ibid.
6 http://health.usnews.com/health-news/articles/2015/11/18/1-in-6-female-college-freshmen-raped-while-incapacitated-study.
7 www.bjs.gov/index.cfm?ty=pbdetail&iid=5176.
8 www.nsopw.gov/en-US/Education/FactsStatistics?AspxAutoDetectCookieSupport=1.
9 www.nsvrc.org/sites/default/files/publications_nsvrc_factsheet_media-packet_statistics-about-sexual-violence_0.pdf.
10 Ibid.

Rape in the U.S. Military

Women make up approximately 14.5% of active military personnel, which makes the U.S. military one of the most male-centric occupations in the nation.[56] One particular area of research into hegemonic masculinity and sexual violence is military culture, which adopts a traditional masculine socialization in training men to be soldiers. In the Academy Award nominated documentary film, *The Invisible War*, filmmakers Kirby Dick, Amy Ziering, and Tanner King Barklow expose the epidemic rates of rape within the U.S. military, the cover-ups of its existence, the negligible investigations in the wake of a report, the lack of institutional support for victims, and its profound personal consequences to victims and families of victims.[57] It is estimated that over a half million women and men have been sexually assaulted and raped while serving in the U.S. military.[58] In the wake of reports to commanding officers, rape victims have been threatened with loss of rank and accused of false reporting, investigations have been dropped with little explanation, counseling has been difficult to obtain, and victims are sometimes policed by the very individuals perpetuating the sexual assaults.[59] Of the thousands of reports of sexual assault and rape of military personnel each year, it has been estimated that 16% lead to court-martial charges, and it is often the commanding officer who ends an investigation before charges can be filed by claiming that the charges were unfounded, case closed.[60] Leading the charge to create change in the military with respect to rates of rape and sexual assault, U.S. Senator Kirsten Gillibrand (D-New York) states, "We have to create a climate where these cases, number one, are reported, number two, are prosecuted, and number three, are convicted."[61] In response to the thousands of complaints by victims, Senator Gillibrand sponsored the ***Military Justice Improvement Act*** (MJIA) to protect victims against retaliation upon reporting a sexual assault.[62] According to the supporting literature, "This reform moves the decision whether to prosecute serious crimes to independent, trained, professional military prosecutors while leaving military crimes to the chain of command."[63] The MJIA was inspired by the film *The Invisible War* along with the acknowledgment from the Department of Defense that the military's zero-tolerance policy toward rape and sexual assault had failed.[64] Gillibrand's analysis of

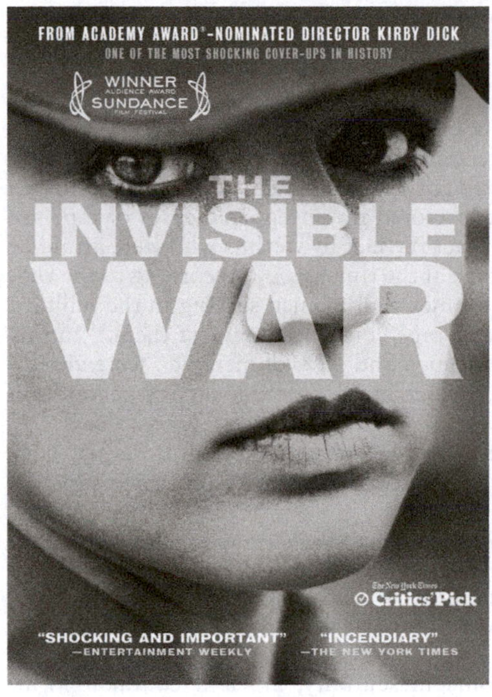

FIGURE 10.3: *The Invisible War* (2012)

The Department of Defense's Annual Report on Sexual Assault for the year 2014, revealed that,

> 75% of the men and women in uniform who have been sexually assaulted lack the confidence in the military justice system to report the crimes committed against them ... [that] supervisors were responsible for sexual harassment and gender discrimination in 60% of cases demonstrates a system deeply in need of reform.[65]

Conservative senators James Inhofe (R-OK) and Lindsey Graham (R-SC) led a filibuster blocking a senate vote on the MJIA, leaving it in judicial limbo for the time being.[66]

Critics argue that military justice is different than civilian justice and should be given preferential treatment in the specialized environment of the military. Writing for the Heritage Foundation, Charles Stimson argues, "our military justice system exists in order to help the military to succeed in its mission: to defend the nation ... Ultimately, it is structured to fight and win wars."[67] While not advocating for allowing sexual assault to continue unabated in the military, Stimson continues,

> Commanding officers in the military have a wide range of tools available to enforce good order and discipline. Taking that power away from commanding officers eliminates an indispensable authority that cannot be transferred to another if we are to demand accountability from commanders for prosecuting and preventing sexual assaults.[68]

Part of this argument holds that military officials are tougher than judge advocates such that cases of sexual assault, it is believed, will be handled more severely by the military than by civilian prosecutors. But former Air Force chief prosecutor, Col. Don Christiansen, responds, "While it is a common refrain that commanders are tougher than judge advocates, there appears to be no evidence of convening authorities sending cases to trial contrary to their legal advice."[69] Christiansen adds of the MJIA,

> The act, if passed, only affects the ability to refer felony-level, non-military offenses to trial ... retaliation rates show commanders are failing to protect victims now. Recent Human Rights Watch reports prove the retaliation is severe and pervasive.[70]

In 2014, U.S. Secretary of Defense, Chuck Hagel, reported that sexual assault in the military had risen 8% from 2013 to the record high of 5,983 cases, and this number was provided with the caveat that it accounted for less than one-fourth of actual rates of sexual assault when unreported cases were factored in (unreported cases of rape are approximations based on surveys made years after the fact by victims who were afraid or felt shame to come forward and report the attack at the time).[71] [72] [73] According to the U.S. Department of Defense, approximately 12% of men and women serving in the military report at least one instance of sexual assault or rape committed against them.[74] In this same report it was noted that one-half of the women and 35% of men who were victimized experienced "penetrative sexual assaults," which include forcible rape or penetration with an object.[75]

In the piece, "Rape, War, and the Socialization of Masculinity: Why our Refusal to Give up War Ensures that Rape cannot be Eradicated," psychologist Eileen Zurbriggen argues:

> Particular elements of traditional masculinity that are implicated [in rape] include status and achievement; toughness and aggression; restricted emotionality; and power, dominance, and control. It is argued that society's need for effective soldiers is the root cause of traditional masculine socialization; this socialization ensures that rape will be prevalent.[76]

This is one particular form of hegemonic masculinity, albeit a common form, that, if Zurbriggen is correct, ensures that men in the military will continue to commit rape and sexual assault at high rates without some form of institutional intervention. Researcher Chang-Hun Lee adds of American military personnel serving overseas, "the isomorphism with hegemonic masculinity is achieved and maintained through culturalization and institutionalization among male soldiers, [which] explains higher rates of rape incidents committed by United States Army personnel stationed in South Korea."[77] The common thread in these arguments is that socialized and institutionalized power and control is inculcated into the minds of many military men from the start of basic

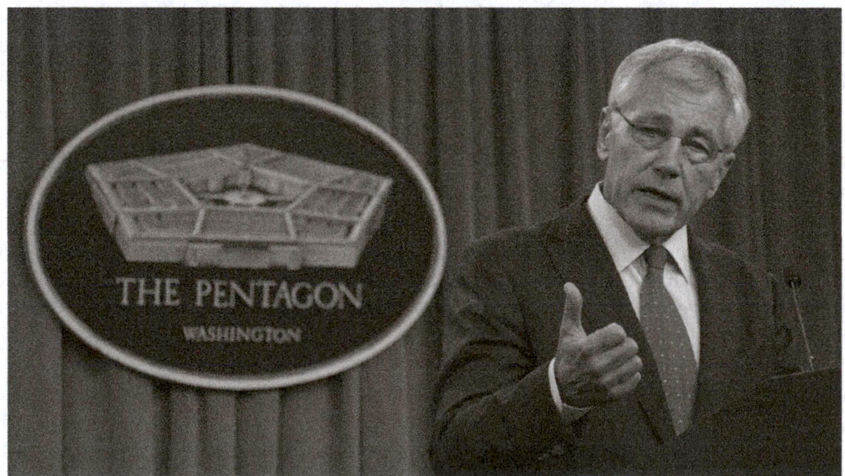

FIGURE 10.4: U.S. Secretary of Defense, Chuck Hagel, responding to questions about rates of rape in the military

training throughout their tenure of service, and that the sexual hierarchy found in the more common military form of hegemonic masculinity contributes to increased rates of rape and sexual assault perpetrated by military men, particularly when coupled with reports of skeptical responses by commanding officers empowered to investigate and report instances of rape to military judicial personnel for probable cause hearings.[78]

Political scientist and author Michael Kaufman notes that masculinities are social constructs that define power relationships between men and between women and men.[79] Writing of masculinities, Kaufman states,

> Especially in their hegemonic versions, they are a set of stereotyped assumptions about what it means to be a man. By prescribing and proscribing certain behaviors, having definitions of gender limit us as human beings to a code that supposedly comes with our biological sex.[80]

The prescription and proscription Kaufman writes of can be viewed most notably in environments such as athletics or the military, where a strong sense of hypermasculine and hypofeminine attitudes and behaviors are expected in male recruits. At the same time, if gender performance is policed such that traditional feminine traits are devalued at approximately the same rate that traditional masculine traits are over-valued in these environments, a precedent is established that creates greater worth in men than women. For men who rape women and other men, sex is viewed as power-over-another, as acquisition, and as therefore validating the sexual hierarchy of men over women and less masculine men. This same hegemonic, masculine template also accounts for the longstanding resistance to gay and transgender men and women serving in the military as well as those in civilian life, an attitude that has only recently been challenged.

THOUGHT BOX

Some scholars claim that the military training techniques that attempt to convert young, civilian men into soldiers are a template for constructing men who are prone to commit higher rates of sexual assault and rape than men in civilian populations. At the same time, critics argue that soldiering requires tough, aggressive men who must be prepared if called upon to go into battle. Is this a paradox or are there solutions available that you believe can resolve what appears to be a dilemma?

Men, Gangs, and Incarceration

A particular type of criminal organization that is unique to men is organized crime and membership in gangs. Women often take part in gangs, and a substantial amount of scholarship has emerged that examines female gangs and female involvement in gangs, but gangs in America are overwhelmingly founded, run, enforced, and populated by boys and men.[81] Scholars have been researching gangs for close to a century, with the work of Frederic Thrasher claiming in 1927 that gangs were the result of immigrant boys coming to America wanting to distance themselves from their parents and the heritage of being from a culture with which they no longer identified.[82] In the 1950s, novelist Albert Cohen viewed gangs as a result of a working class rebellion against the feminizing effects of contemporary culture.[83] Other scholars have focused on poor and working class men and their struggle to acclimate to a limited job market in difficult economies.[84]

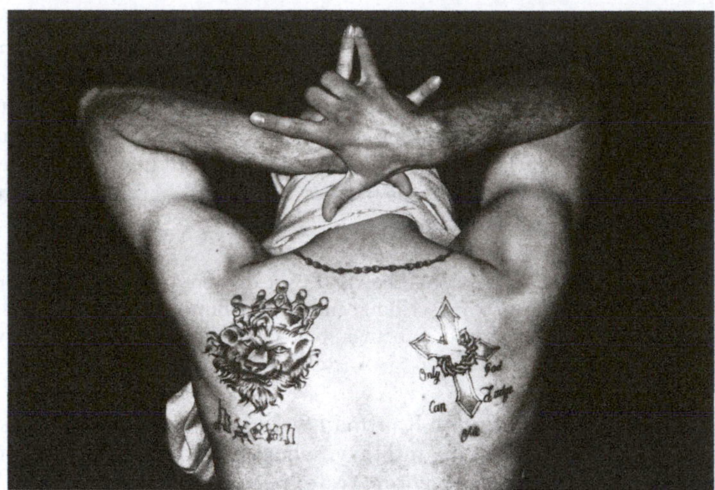

FIGURE 10.5: Latin Kings, flashing sign

But it wasn't until the work of sociologist James Messerschmidt of the University of Southern Maine that gang affiliation was viewed as involving issues of masculinity in concert with class and race.[85] Messerschmidt focused on turf-protection, toughness, dominance, and the willingness to act out violently when conflicts arise. This became known as ***Messerschmidt's Masculinity Hypothesis***, which states that "violent incidents are more likely to include highly masculine men who have few traditional outlets to assert their masculinity."[86]

By "traditional outlets to assert their masculinity," Illinois State University researcher Jessie L. Krienert refers to satisfaction in job and monetary earnings, experiencing a happy marriage, successful parenting, and enjoying satisfying sexual performance.[87] Krienert recognizes that other traits may contribute to men's violence and that much more research is required, but a survey of men who are serving time in prison reveals a multitude of men who fit very well the Messerschmidt profile for violence.

But gangs also carry a practical significance to members by serving as protection and support of an extended family. In the book *Gang Life in Two Cities: An Insider's Journey*, former gang member turned scholar, Robert J. Duran argues that gang life is, in part, a reaction to the racial oppression created by the colonization of parts of America.[88] Duran recounts his initiation into gang life:

> *It is late on a Saturday night in 1993 at the home of a Mexican-American gang member in West Ogden, Utah. I am 16 years old. The occasion is a party following that night's successful attack on members of a rival group. At the request of a young woman, the gang has gone to the house of an enemy group and beaten up the occupants—a fight I participated in, though I am not a member of the gang. The mood is celebratory as people recount the bravery, loyalty, and fighting skills they displayed during the attack. There is a discussion about whether it was a mistake to shout the gang's name at the victims of the beat-down, and talk turns to the question of whether anyone will snitch on the gang.*
>
> *Suddenly attention is focused on me: I am the only person in the house who is not a member. A tall man walks in my direction and confronts me. Do I want to join? The room becomes silent. Angry glances are thrown in my direction, while my friend Rudy protests that I am not a threat to the gang. I have only two options: I can fight and be accepted into the gang, or I can be attacked while attempting to leave. Either way I get roughed up, but if I leave I make enemies instead of friends and I will be seen as a coward.*

> *After a brief delay I walk into the center of the room, set down my quart of beer, throw up my hands, and say, "Let's go!" Everyone in the room becomes excited about another opportunity to fight. The house owner says, "Let's take it outside so we don't get blood all over." We walk outside and the gang leaders surround me. I look at the person in front of me and begin throwing punches. A barrage of fists and feet come at me from all angles, and everything turns into a chaotic blur. After what seems like an eternity, someone says, "Okay, okay, that is good."*
>
> *I feel like I stepped out of the eye of a tornado. Someone tells me I can go inside and wash my face off. I walk inside and look into the mirror. My face and body are beaten and bruised. I cup my hands as I pour water over my face and smile happily when I realize that I did not lose any teeth. I came out okay. When I step outside I am greeted welcomingly. The mood is once again celebratory as I am told about some of the gang's rules and hand signs. I am now a member.*[89]

The violence of initiation belies the welcoming embrace of membership. For these men, they are now part of an extended family sworn to protect one another. The most famous quote of gang affiliation is "blood in, blood out," which usually means that one must kill someone to get in, or at least shed blood, and can never leave the gang except through death. There is a strong sense of loyalty that goes with this commitment that not only guarantees solidarity and mutual defense, but maintains a strict pledge never to cooperate with law enforcement, particularly in the investigation of fellow gang members.

Masculinities play an integral role in the violence of gang life. The notion of "doing masculinity," a concept borrowed from West and Zimmerman, who coined the expression "doing gender," is considered to be crucial to the violent actions that accompany gang activities.[90] For instance, writing of Chicano gang masculinity, researchers Edward Orozco Flores and Pierrette Hondagneu-Sotelo argue that in the wake of poverty, joblessness, and institutional barriers to success in mainstream society, Chicano men who gravitate to gangs practice a marginalized form of masculinity, which include aggressive behaviors, physical force, controlling behaviors over women, and displays of dominance as part of what has been termed by some scholars, ***the machismo syndrome***.[91] [92] In particular, of Chicano gangs in Los Angeles, Flores and Hondagneu-Sotelo write that a common masculine performance includes what is called *locura*, which means "a type of craziness or wildness" and "the appearance of a lack of impulse control."[93] These behaviors, coupled with heavy drug and alcohol use, support a culture of street violence and territoriality that has been commonly associated with Chicano gang life.[94] But researchers note that many of these sorts of behaviors are viewed across many **marginalized masculinities**, where men belonging to groups that have had limited access to employment and vocational success due to institutionalized barriers and other factors, assume a tough, street-hard masculine style as a way of receiving the respect they do not receive through conventional social means.

John Hagedorn of the University of Illinois, Chicago, writes of gang life, "Male gang members typically display an aggressive masculinity expressing values of respect and honor and condoning violence as a means to settle disputes."[95] Respect is perhaps the most cherished value in gang life, both in and out of prison. Getting respect from others is viewed as having achieved status and power. It is thought to be a form of social capital in environments where actual monetary capital is limited. In article after article, authors identify *respect* as that which is at the top of the list of importance for men.[96] [97] [98] Writing for the *Christian Science Monitor*, International Studies scholar Jane Lampman argues that feeling disrespected may be at the root of men's violence.[99] New York University's James Gilligan agrees, arguing that shame, humiliation, and disrespect "constitutes the basic psychological motive, or cause, of violent behavior."[100] In working with violent offenders, Gilligan writes,

> I was surprised to discover that I kept getting the same answer when I asked one man after another why he had assaulted or even killed someone: "Because he disrespected me."[101] [102]

This repetitive response by incarcerated men who commit violent offenses is found to be at the etiological root of some of the most violent acts.[103] In searching for solutions to men's violence, Gilligan notes that in his research, "we found one program and only one that was 100% successful in preventing recidivism. And that was the prisoner getting a college degree while in prison."[104] Without an education in hand, prisoners upon release reoffend and return to prison in 65% of cases, while those who receive an education while in prison reoffend and return to prison in 1% of cases.[105] Globally, Gilligan asserts,

> The main social and economic causes of violence—and I'll add political causes—are those that divide the population into the superior and the inferior, the strong and the weak, the rich and the poor. The more highly unequal a society is, the higher its rates of violence. For example, the most powerful predictor of homicide rates throughout the world—and this has been repeated in dozens of studies—is the size of the gap between the rich and the poor. The greater the degree of economic inequality in a society, the higher the murder rate, the lower the inequality, the lower the murder rate.[106]

There is little doubt by scholars that economic inequality drives a great deal of violence, and particularly gang violence where part of the attraction to joining a gang includes the acquisition of quick money that avoids the standard labor of long hours and slow acclimation of capital.

But like a good deal of negative media representation of men of color, gangs in America are often racialized so that black and Latino men are overrepresented, with coverage of Crips, Bloods, Latin Kings, and the Mexican Mafia on shows like *Gangland* (*The History Channel*)[107] that document the lives of street and prison gangs around America. Less covered are the biker gangs across America that consist mainly of white and Latino men, who often hail from backgrounds that are not steeped in poverty. Many of these biker gangs exclude black men from riding with them.[108] Part of the reason that biker gangs evade media coverage is that they consciously keep a low profile until an event exposes their exploits such as the melee in Waco, Texas in 2015, where nine bikers were killed and 177 arrested, and 480 weapons were seized.[109] Among the more prominent outlaw motorcycle gangs (OMG) today are the Cossacks, Bandidos, Mongols, Pagans, Outlaws, Sons of Silence, Warlocks, Vagos, and most famously, Hells Angels, who have gained notoriety for their criminal exploits that include drug trafficking, theft, and organizing prostitution rings.[110] Many of these bikers wear a patch that announces them as "1%ers," which is meant to denote that 99% of bikers are "God-fearing, family oriented, upstanding citizens," while 1% are bikers notably and proudly "hard-riding, hard partying, outside-the-mainstream" of society.[111] These 1%ers became known as outlaws, even though biker gangs publicly insist that they are not criminal organizations.[112]

With respect to masculinity, biker gangs have been found to be gender-segregated by role and level of authority, whereby men are in power positions that include negotiation, regulation authors and enforcers, and arbiters of conflict. They tend to be politically conservative in matters of gendered division of labor and have garnered reputations for treating the women in their ranks as property.[113] [114] Some have argued that the scholarship into these groups is imprecise and not well documented due to the covert nature of their activities, while others have insisted that many of the women associated with biker gangs are proud and willing participants who have chosen the lives they live.[115] But under the pretense of personal liberty, many OMGs institute a strict hierarchy that includes officers, chapter presidents, and a male-dominated echelon that embraces an

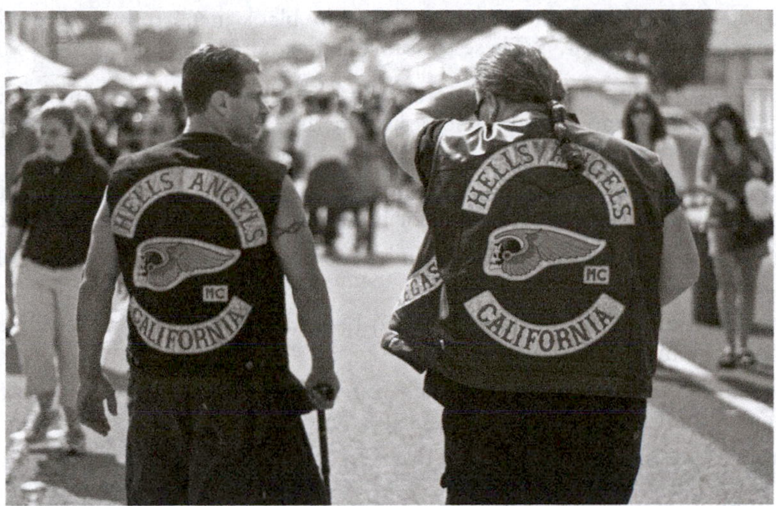

FIGURE 10.6: Hells Angels

authoritative hegemonic masculine culture where women are not allowed to hold positions of leadership.[116] In many respects, the men who participate in OMGs hold values that mirror the conservative and traditional masculine ideals of the *Duck Dynasty* men albeit more extreme countercultural versions of the patriarchal masculinity on display in TV shows that feature throw-back, reactionary masculinities.[117]

Researcher Adam Baird found that a difference in family support and training contributes to those who choose gang affiliation from those who do not. Baird argues that boys whose families strongly support them and instill a "moral rejection" of gangs have a much better chance of avoiding gang life compared to those who do not receive this moral training of gangs.[118] In addition, those who affiliate with gangs often admire older gang members and perceive the gang as "an attractive pathway to manhood."[119] In fact, the initiation ritual described by Robert Duran above can be viewed as an initiation into manhood and not simply as an inauguration into gang life. Rituals marking the entry of boys into manhood have been a central cultural observance for many generations. From Bar Mitzvahs to Confirmation, rituals mark a transition in a young man's life in many divergent cultures. Entry into gang life is no different. For many boys who join gangs, the "jump in" is a rite of passage that is facilitated to show gang members that the initiate has the toughness it takes to be a member. Some members are "blessed in," which means that their admission is the result of being related to current or past gang members, but all gang membership is given only at the approval of gang leaders.[120]

With respect to imprisonment, men are incarcerated at approximately 13 times higher rate than women.[121] According to the NAACP, African-Americans make up one million of the 2.3 million incarcerated inmates in America,[122] and one in six black men have been incarcerated in their lifetimes.[123] The majority of these arrests and convictions are drug-related offenses.[124] The Pew Research Center confirms the numbers provided by the NAACP and adds that black men are six times more likely to be arrested, convicted, and incarcerated than white men, while wage gaps have increased between black and white households over the past two decades.[125] Many have argued that the racial disparity rates for incarceration are based on racial profiling techniques employed by police officers, but other factors are also believed to account for the disparity. David Cole, professor of law at Georgetown University, along with a number of other researchers, writes that there are documented factors that explain why black men are incarcerated at much higher rates than white men.[126] These factors include:

- Open-air marketplaces where more black people purchase, sell, and use drugs are easier to police than suburban homes where the majority of white people purchase, sell, and use drugs.
- Open-air marketplaces have been correlated to low socioeconomic neighborhoods that are populated by people of color in higher percentages than white occupants.
- A much greater number of black and Latino people are pulled over by police officers than white people.
- Black men are 12 times more likely to be sent to prison for drug-related crimes than white men.
- Black and Latino men are more likely to receive longer sentences for same or lesser offenses than white men for same or greater offenses.[127]
- Penalties are increased for selling drugs in school zones.

This final point affects people of color more than white people due to the fact that a greater density of people of color live in inner-city environments, which makes it more likely that drug sales in inner-city neighborhoods qualify as drug sales within school zones. At the same time, studies have shown that white people purchase and use drugs at roughly the same rates as people of color.[128] When identical crimes are prosecuted resulting in a conviction, research has shown that black and Latino men are more likely to receive longer prison sentences than their white, male counterparts, which supports the claims of those who argue that racism is present in the criminal justice system.[129] [130] [131] When gender is considered, men of all racial and ethnic backgrounds exceed women in drug use by approximately 40%.[132]

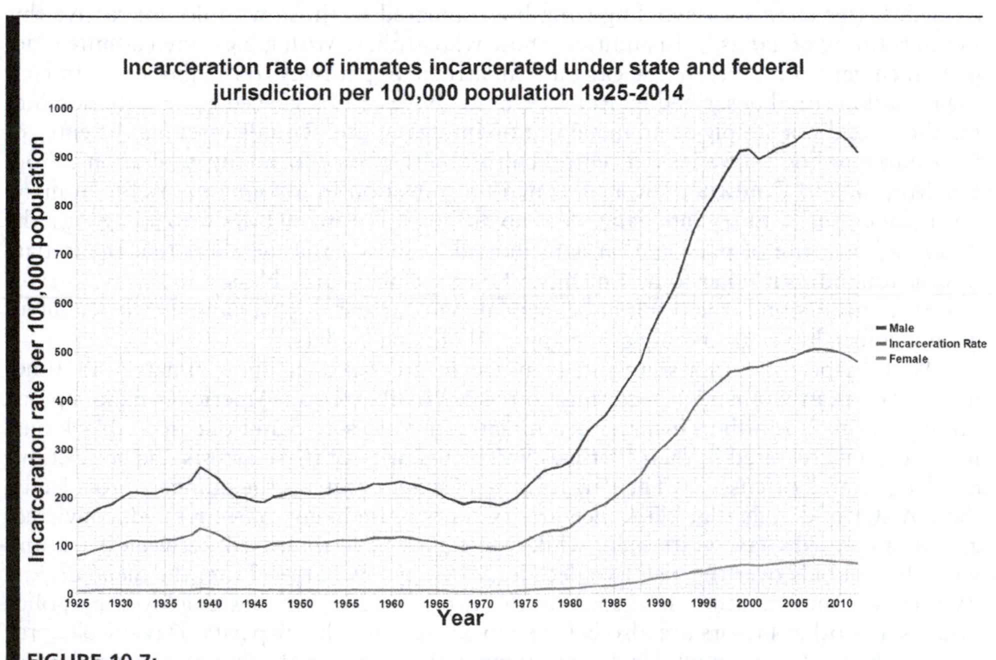

FIGURE 10.7:

When crimes are coded "violent," including murder, manslaughter, simple and aggravated assault, rape, torture, kidnapping, carjacking, bank robbery, and the use of a gun in the commission of a crime, men are the perpetrators at a rate of 83% over women, which also accounts for men's much higher rates of incarceration, since these crimes yield longer prison terms than do non-violent crimes.[133] At the same time, law professor Sonja Starr of the University of Michigan found that men are given longer sentences than women when convicted of the same crimes in federal court.[134] In fact, Starr's research documents that females arrested for a crime are twice as likely than men to avoid incarceration if convicted.[135] One theory for the gender disparity in incarceration rates is that judges are more sensitive to women's increased roles in the caretaking of children.[136]

Men's prisons are infamously organized by gangs and stratified by race, which reinforce through intimidation and violence a code of behavior among inmates. The general population within prison walls is a mixture of men who have been convicted for a variety of crimes and whose sentences run from several years to life behind bars without the possibility of parole. These are environments where a violent form of hegemonic masculinity is viewed by inmates as fundamental for survival. A daily routine of working out with weights, building muscle mass, gang affiliation, and receiving tattoos over the course of one's incarceration are considered normative parts of prison life.

Prison Rape

Sexual contact in prison is the result of coercion, "grooming," forcible rape, or consensual partnering, but is not considered by many inmates to make one homosexual.[137] Prison rape is a common practice. As survivors of prison rape have noted, once a prisoner is raped, he is then "marked as a victim for repeated sexual assault for as long as he remains locked up."[138] It is estimated that 60,000 cases of prison rape occur each year in both juvenile and adult facilities, although concrete, documented numbers are impossible to know since reporting rape in prison can lead to even more attacks upon the victim.[139] The Federal Bureau of Prisons reports that between 9% and 20% of inmates are sexually assaulted.[140] While reports of rape and sexual assault in prison have increased substantially in the past two decades, it is thought to be more a product of increased counseling services and the threat of AIDS that has resulted in more reports.[141] Juveniles incarcerated with adults are five times more likely to report being victims of sexual assault than juveniles incarcerated in juvenile facilities.[142] Suicide rates for juveniles locked up in adult facilities are 7.7 times higher than that found in juvenile facilities.[143] It is estimated that 10,000 juveniles are locked up in adult facilities at any given time, and there are measures to stop this practice.[144] Twenty-one states have no minimum age for trying children as adults,[145] [146] and all but Nebraska, New Mexico, and New York have provisions whereby a juvenile court judge may waive jurisdiction and transfer a case over to adult criminal court.[147] Prosecutors in many cases also have discretion over whether to file a case in juvenile or adult criminal court.[148]

As part of American University's Washington College of Law, "The Project of Addressing Prison Rape" was formed to implement the *Prison Rape Elimination Act of 2003 (PREA)*, and to provide training, technical assistance, and legal guidance for correctional agencies, advocates, and survivors who want to effectively prevent, respond to, and eliminate sexual abuse in custodial settings.[149] Congress has responded to *PREA* by recommending a multi-pronged approach to understanding and eliminating prison rape, which includes,

- A comprehensive statistical review by BJS of the incidence and effects of prison rape.
- The creation of a DOJ review panel to conduct hearings, with subpoena power over officials who run the three facilities with the highest incidence and the two facilities with the lowest incidence of prison rape.
- The requirement that the National Institute of Corrections (NIC) provide training and technical assistance and serve as a national information clearinghouse.
- The award of grants—developed and administered by the Bureau of Justice Assistance (BJA)—to assist States in implementing *PREA*'s requirements.
- The award of research grants by the National Institute of Justice (NIJ) to address issues exclusive of the prevalence or extent of the problem of prison rape, which the U.S. Congress put on BJA's agenda.
- The creation of a Federal commission to develop national standards for the detection, prevention, reduction, and punishment of prison rape, with the caveat that the commission would not be able to recommend standards that would add costs to prison administration.[150]

However, many have noted that there has been a refusal by states to comply to the *PREA* standards, with only New Hampshire and New Jersey having certified compliance.[151] In fact, Texas, which received $3.7 million in federal aid to combat prison rape and which has one of the worst records of sexual violence within incarcerated environments, refuses to implement *PREA* standards.[152] Ex-Texas Governor Rick Perry stated of *PREA* that it is "a counterproductive and unnecessarily cumbersome and costly regulatory mess."[153] To date, all states have either complied with *PREA* standards or are promising to work toward that goal except Utah, Arkansas, and Alaska.[154]

Gay and Transgender Men in Prison

Many gay men serving time in prison seek segregation rather than having to deal with the sexual abuse that gay men endure when in general population. Writing for the *Huffington Post*, Rodney Smith, who is openly gay and serving an eight-year sentence in a Louisiana prison recounts his experiences as "pure hell."[155] Smith reports that openly gay men are targeted for abuse and told that reporting the abuse would be a death sentence.[156] At 23 and self-described as "scrawny," Smith recounts being sold between inmates and raped repeatedly.[157] He fears and grieves for the many LGBT people currently incarcerated and faced with rape on a daily basis both by other inmates and prison staff.[158] Because gay prisoners and other vulnerable groups in prison are targets for violence, many prisons have instituted a "sensitive-needs yard," which segregates these vulnerable members of the prison population from the general population.[159] This provision is part of a larger protective custody arrangement for inmates considered to be at risk from the larger inmate community. These same provisions are now provided to transgender men and women, although critics argue that much more needs to be done to protect vulnerable populations in prison.[160]

One of the central problems is that those men who rape other men in prison are often defined by prison officials as 'homosexual,' such that prison officials will view victimization as proof of homosexuality and thereby conclude that sex between inmates is consensual in nature.[161] [162] Gay inmates, in fact, while commonly targeted for attack, are not likely to be perpetrators of sexual abuse.[163] In response to the violence perpetrated against LGBT people in American prisons, the Boston-based organization *Black and Pink* was formed as a self-described feminist, antiracist, queer liberation group organized to address "the specific violence of the prison industrial complex against LGBTQ people."[164] *Black and Pink* responds to LGBTQ needs in incarcerated environments through advocacy programs, education, direct services, and organized efforts that include aid and support to prisoners who are gay, bisexual, transgender, queer-gender, asexual, and intersex.[165] Realizing that LGBTQ inmates may feel isolated and scared, *Black and Pink* created pen-pal correspondence program through which people may befriend LGBTQ inmates, reportedly reaching over 10,000 LGBTQ inmates as of January 2016.[166]

> **THOUGHT BOX**
>
> Given that prison rape and the mistreatment of LGBTQ inmates are enormous problems, what provisions, laws, and regulations do you believe should be instituted to address these ongoing problems?

Retributive and Restorative Justice

With respect to men's violence, some direct the solution to incarceration while others believe a more rehabilitative and victim-sensitive approach is needed in what is termed a restorative approach to men's violence.[167] **Restorative Justice** is a broad-spectrum set of practices designed to meet the needs of victims, families, communities, and offenders in the wake of violence.[168] There are three central practices associated with restorative justice:

- *Victim–offender mediation*: mediated, face-to-face dialogues between victim and perpetrator designed to empower victims, to agree upon reparations, and to get offenders to humanize the victim, thereby creating empathy that otherwise does not exist.[169]
- *Family group conferencing*: trained facilitators converse with family members, friends, justice officials, and service providers to work out amends made by perpetrators, while fully holding perpetrators accountable for their actions.
- *Peace-making circle*: dialogues between victims and offenders may be the result of previous dialogues by community leaders, family members, and justice officials in determining the conditions of the meeting and the goals hoped for by the victim–offender dialogue.

Mediation between victim and offender is viewed as therapeutic for both the victim and the offender. Victims are able to ask questions of the offender that may have been simmering for years, and the resulting contact may allow victims some measure of closure. For offenders, contact with the victim allows offenders to humanize the person they victimized along with affected family members and this leads some offenders to accept greater responsibility for their actions.

However, a common response to crime, and particularly violent crime, is increased incarceration, longer sentences, and diverting tax dollars toward hiring more law enforcement personnel, building more prisons, and viewing punishment as a punitive measure designed to hold an individual responsible for his actions, while deterring future crime. This approach is known as **retributive justice**. Here, the inmate is paying a debt to society for inflicting harm on others and breaking the laws that proscribe such conduct. There may be a rehabilitative goal collateral to the primary objective of punishment for past wrongdoing, although this would not be the case for the death penalty or life without the possibility of parole. Men who are serving life sentences often state that they have nothing to lose other than the more languishing torment of isolation in a tiny cell, or what is termed "solitary confinement," often termed "the hole."[170] Critics of the retribution model of punishment include James Gilligan, who argues,

> We need to recognize the difference between punishment and restraint. When people are dangerous to themselves or others, we restrain them—whether they are children or adults. But that is altogether different from gratuitously inflicting pain on them for the sake of revenge or to "teach them a lesson"—for the only lesson learned is to inflict pain on others.[171]

Gilligan views prison life as a place not designed for rehabilitation, but an environment where violent masculinity is reinforced, only to be unleashed at some point after the prisoner is granted parole. He writes,

> The assumption here is that when somebody's done something bad, the only way we can teach them not to keep doing that bad thing is to punish them and that will teach them. The fact is, we know that that is exactly the opposite of the truth. We have abundant evidence, many different lines of evidence showing that punishment does not inhibit or prevent violence. On the contrary, punishment is the most powerful stimulant of violence we've discovered yet.[172]

THOUGHT BOX

With respect to crime and punishment, does retributive or restorative forms of justice make more sense to you? Is there a combination of the two that creates a better model of justice? What do you say to those who claim that restorative justice coddles violent prisoners and does not deter them from recommitting violent offenses? On the other hand, what do you say to those who claim that retributive justice creates ever-more violent men who are prone to reoffend? In essence, what do we do about the cycle of incarceration in which many men find themselves?

Alcohol and Men's Violence

Anecdotal testimony has, for generations, led to the widespread belief that alcohol usage contributes to higher rates of violence, but it has only been more recently that studies have corroborated this connection. The results of research have been fairly predictable. In one study, a high degree of correlation was found between those men who had risk factors of neglect or abuse in childhood, coupled with rates of alcohol consumption and spousal abuse.[173] More specifically, childhood neglect was the largest predictor of physical spousal abuse, while witnessing or experiencing violence in childhood was a bigger predictor of spousal psychological abuse.[174] In both cases, alcohol was found to exacerbate these behaviors. Other studies have corroborated the link between alcohol use by men and intimate partner violence (IPV), while surprisingly, little correlation has been found between drug use by men and IPV.[175] High-severity

FIGURE 10.8:

intimate partner violence, as opposed to low or moderate severity IPV, was also found in higher rates when coupled with male alcohol usage in high-unemployment neighborhoods.[176] One study was able to show that men who are diagnosed as being alcoholic have rates of IPV four-times that of sample populations.[177] This finding gained support when it was shown that violence decreased significantly after men completed alcohol-treatment programs.[178]

In a fairly remarkable study, a positive correlation was made between alcohol use, violence, and what researchers termed "low intelligence."[179] Intelligence was measured using the Ammons Quick test, which measures 'verbal intelligence' and the Trial Making test, which measures 'visual-motor intelligence.'[180] The Ammons Quick test has been used since the 1960s as one of the standard IQ tests, now primarily taken online, and evaluates passive picture-vocabulary abilities, while the Trial Making test measures visual attention and task switching such as connecting dots as quickly as possible. Low scores on these two tests were used to identify "low-intelligent" males as compared to moderate or high-intelligent males. These intelligence identifications were then cross-checked with levels of alcohol consumption. Researchers found that "the prevalence of violence increases significantly at low intelligence and high alcohol consumption levels," concluding that, particularly in the case of young men, "The combination of heavy drinking and lower intelligence is associated with a synergistic surge of violent behavior."[181]

Psychologist Adrienne Heinz notes that very few people actually become violent when drinking, while physician David Caldicott adds that personality is a central factor in determining who becomes aggressive and who does not.[182] But the personalities of those who act out violently when drunk are those who also demonstrate aggressive tendencies when sober, and in both cases men have been shown to behave more aggressively when sober or drunk than women.[183] Neuroscientists argue that alcohol abates the executive functioning of the brain so that one who drinks will have less control over the part of the brain that keeps impulsiveness in check.[184] [185] If boys and men are more impulsive on average than girls and women, alcohol use would serve as a catalyst for even higher levels of male-impulsiveness, which would account for higher levels of dare-devil and fight-inducing behaviors in males. This may also explain why men are found to drive while intoxicated at higher rates than women.[186] [187] According to the Centers for Disease Control and Prevention, men binge drink alcohol at twice the rate of women, and commit suicide under the influence of alcohol at higher rates than women.[188] Unfortunately, men are also less likely than women to seek treatment when suffering from alcoholism and alcohol abuse, creating a prescription for higher rates of violence including self-violence.[189]

Violence Against Men (Is Intimate Partner Violence Gender-Symmetrical?)

With a great deal of emphasis today on men's violence against women, some argue that men as victims of violence is less acknowledged, examined, and evaluated. In fact, men are victims of homicide at a higher percentage than women (76.8%), although women are victims of homicides as a result of domestic violence (63.7%) and are victims of sex-related homicides at much higher rates (81.7%).[190] Since men commit homicide at vastly higher rates than women (89–91% depending on source),[191] [192] the majority of men who are murdered are murdered by other men. When homicide is drug-related, 90% of victims are men, and when gang-related, 94.6% of victims are men.[193] But again, in these cases, men are also overwhelmingly the perpetrators of such homicides.[194]

Men's rights activists often claim that violence against men is much higher than reported and rarely considered when discussions about intimate partner violence arise, and certainly, intimate partner violence against men does occur. Writing for *The Guardian*, Nicola Graham-Kevan notes that 7% of domestic violence convictions are those perpetrated by women against men.[195] Yet, other studies suggest that rates of intimate partner violence are gender symmetrical.[196] Or, depending on which study one uses, the rate of male victims by female perpetrators is 25%, 35%, or 50%, with other studies

FIGURE 10.9:

suggesting that an accurate percentage of male victimhood is simply unknown.[197] When violence is sexual in nature, studies agree that males perpetrate the vast majority of the violence, while females make up the vast majority of the victims.[198] In terms of victimology, one in six women and one in 33 men report experiencing an attempted or completed rape at some time in their lives.[199] But when men's rights activists suggest that non-sexual, intimate partner violence is gender symmetrical, sociologist Michael Kimmel argues that the statistical-gathering procedures are flawed, while other important factors are ignored entirely. Kimmel begins by asking,

> Does gender symmetry mean that women hit men as often as men hit women? Or that an equal number of men and women hit each other? Does symmetry refer to men's and women's motivations for such violence, or does it mean that the consequences of it are symmetrical?[200]

To answer these questions, Kimmel first notes that the vast majority of reports claiming that intimate partner violence is roughly gender equivalent are based entirely on the **Conflict Tactics Scale (CTS)**, which has come under great scrutiny. The CTS simply counts the cases of violence without taking account of the circumstances surrounding each case. So, for instance, if a woman is severely beaten and defends herself by pushing back against the male perpetrator, the CTS scores one "conflict tactic" for both the male and the female involved.[201] If a woman punches or pushes her husband or boyfriend in an attempt to stop the man from assaulting a child or from sexually assaulting her, the CTS counts this as one "conflict tactic" on the part of the woman, but none on the part of the man. The CTS also ignores the question, "who initiated the violence?," which may inform us who the aggressor and defender were, which speaks to offensive and defensive conflict tactics. Another problem with the CTS, Kimmel notes, is that it does not account for the severity of the injuries sustained nor the differences in the reported violent episodes. In the majority of cases where men report an incident of intimate partner violence against them, they describe pushing, shoving, grabbing, and slapping, while women at a rate of ten times that of men describe the episode as their having been "beaten up."[202] The consequences in terms of severity of injury tells the story. About one-third of all cases of female homicide is due to intimate partner violence, while only 4% of male homicide victims result from intimate partner violence.[203]

When men's rights activists claim that intimate partner violence is gender symmetrical, their claims carry some weight only at the lower end of violence, meaning at the level of pushing and shoving, but not in cases where the injuries sustained require medical attention or hospitalization. According to the CDC, in 2010, 241 men were murdered by their partners, while 1,095 women were murdered by their partners.[204] These gendered differences in degree of violence bear out year after year.[205] Approximately 1.3 million cases of rape take place each year with one in five women being raped in their lifetime versus one in 71 men being raped in their lifetime.[206] Critics point out that because our culture places greater levels of shame on male victims of rape, fewer men will report being raped or seek out counseling in the wake of being raped. The cultural pressure placed on men to be strong, powerful, and independent causes many men to resist reporting the assault to authorities and decreases the likelihood that they will reach out for emotional support as well, which likely accounts for some of the lower levels of statistical documentation on men who are victims of sexual violence.

Intimate partner harassment and intimidation is another form of IPV where researchers report that somewhere between 75% and 80% of the stalking of a partner or ex-partner is committed by men.[207] Stalking includes appearing at one's workplace, home, or school without invitation as part of an ongoing pattern of surveillance or through phone, text, mail, and social network forms of intimidation or threat. Stalkers are also known to send flowers, candy, and love-letters in an attempt to win-back an ex, but become stalking behaviors when the recipient does not respond or has responded that the gifts are unwelcome.[208] In research headed by University of Mississippi criminologist Eric Lambert, it was found that men and women view stalking differently.[209] The women surveyed viewed stalking as being more dangerous than did the men, who were more prone to view stalking as involving strangers and who commonly blamed victims for the stalking behaviors.[210] When men are the ones being stalked, in 60% of the cases, it is other men stalking them, whether an ex-partner or the ex-boyfriend or ex-husband of a woman who is now following the man she is currently dating.[211] All 50 states have laws in place making stalking a crime.[212]

What is known about intimate partner abuse is that there is a well-established cycle that constitutes a pattern of intimate partner violence behavior. First noticed by psychologist Lenore Walker in 1979, the cycle appears in four parts, as shown in Figure 10.10.

While this famous cycle does not apply in every case of intimate partner violence, since many report a constant siege of assault by their partners, it is common enough to use as a red-flag indicator of a pattern of abuse.[213] During the tension phase, arguments turn into verbal abuse often over common domestic issues such as money, jobs, jealousy, or children. During the abusive stage, physical violence is perpetrated upon the victim by the perpetrator. The timing of the physical abuse can be unpredictable and seemingly out-of-the-blue, while other cases of violence come at the peak of the tension stage. The violence then ends and a stage begins where the perpetrator feels guilt and expresses remorse. During this stage, the perpetrator will often exhibit kind, loving behaviors attended by apologies, generosity, and helpfulness. The contrite behaviors of the perpetrator often assure the victim that the abusive behaviors will not be repeated and that the relationship can be salvaged. But since this cycle is a pattern, the abuse is usually mollified for a brief period of time, after which a phase of tension begins again.

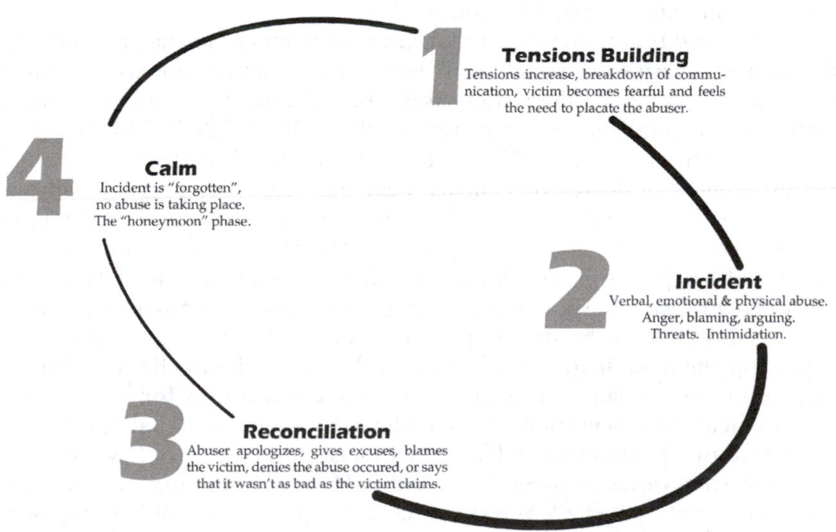
Cycle of Abuse
1
Tensions Building
Tensions increase, breakdown of communication, victim becomes fearful and feels the need to placate the abuser.
2
Incident
Verbal, emotional & physical abuse. Anger, blaming, arguing. Threats. Intimidation.
3
Reconciliation
Abuser apologizes, gives excuses, blames the victim, denies the abuse occured, or says that it wasn't as bad as the victim claims.
4
Calm
Incident is "forgotten", no abuse is taking place. The "honeymoon" phase.

FIGURE 10.10: The cycle of domestic violence

Summary

As we have witnessed in this chapter and others, there are many theories that purport to explain why violence is committed much more often by men than by women and part of that analysis also attempts to determine what can be done to decrease men's violence. Solutions run the gamut. From biological intervention in the case of theories that support an endemic source of men's violence to parenting styles in the case of theories that support a developmental source of men's violence with an emphasis on childhood experiences, theorists attempt to solve the problem of men's violence depending on their theoretical commitments. Others raise concerns about poverty, the repetitive use of violent media, the proliferation of guns in American culture, to a pervasive hegemonic script that supports a patriarchal culture that encourages men to be tough and not back down in the face of conflict. Answers no doubt lie in a complex interaction of these factors in varying degrees and with individual circumstances affecting some men more than others.

But this chapter also reviewed the problems of sexual violence in the military, within incarcerated environments, and models of justice supported in the wake of men's violence. No one considers the solutions to men's violence to be simple or quickly achievable. But sexual violence in the military as well as violence both inside institutional detention centers and within society at large are urgent problems that almost everyone acknowledges require serious and immediate attention. Some of the more acute patterns of men's violence are witnessed in the context of relationships. Whether between friends, acquaintances, dates, romantic relationships, or marriage and cohabiting contexts, there are palpably high levels of physical and sexual violence occurring within the very homes where victims live. Some of this violence is so structured, it has been documented by scholars as constituting a pattern or recurring cycle. Understanding men's violence and the most effective ways to mitigate and eradicate it is one of the most urgent challenges of the twenty-first century.

Notes

1 www.theguardian.com/society/2009/nov/27/patrick-stewart-domestic-violence.
2 www.bjs.gov/content/pub/pdf/wo.pdf.
3 www.cnn.com/2a015/06/27/us/mass-shootings/.
4 http://time.com/114128/elliott-rodgers-ucsb-santa-barbara-shooter/.
5 https://davinasquirrel.wordpress.com/2012/04/13/school-shootings/.
6 www.appsychology.com/IB%20Psych/IBcontent/Options/HumanRelationships/Rel9.htm.
7 http://time.com/114128/elliott-rodgers-ucsb-santa-barbara-shooter/.
8 www.alternet.org/personal-health/angry-brain-how-help-men-uncontrollable-tempers.
9 Ibid.
10 www.psychologytoday.com/blog/anger-in-the-age-entitlement/201004/anger-men-and-love.
11 Ibid.
12 www.apa.org/monitor/jun05/helping.aspx.
13 Ibid.
14 Ibid.
15 Ibid.
16 Ibid.
17 www.ncbi.nlm.nih.gov/books/NBK 144290/.
18 Ibid.
19 http://cognitivetherapy.cc/anger-management-for-men.
20 Ibid.
21 Hagan, John, Gillis, A.R., Simpson, John, "Clarifying and extending power-control theory," *The American Journal of Sociology*, January, 1990.
22 Singer, Simon I., and Levine, Murray, "Power-Control Theory, gender and delinquency: A partial replication with additional evidence on the effects of peers," *Criminology* 4 (1988), pp. 289–302.
23 Bates, Kristin A., Bader, Christopher D. and Mencken, F. Carson, "Family structure, power-control theory, and deviance:

Extending power-control theory to include alternate family forms," *Western Criminology Review* 2003.
24 Ball, R., Cullen, F., and Lilly, R, *Criminological Theory: Context and Consequences*, 5th edition (Sage, 2011).
25 Regoli, Robert, Hewitt, John D., and DeLisi, Matt, *Delinquency in Society*, 8th edition (Jones & Bartlett , 2009).
26 Messerschmidt, James W., "Becoming "Real Men," Adolescent Masculinity Challenges and Sexual Violence," *Men and Masculinities*, January, 2000.
27 Connell, R.W. and Messerschmidt, James W., "Hegemonic masculinity: Rethinking the concept," *Gender & Society* 19, 6 (2005), pp. 829–859.
28 Ibid.
29 Ibid.
30 Ibid.
31 www.usnews.com/news/articles/2015/03/05/high-schools-and-middle-schools-are-failing-victims-of-sexual-assault.
32 www.huffingtonpost.com/alexandra-kudatzky/how-we-started-a-conversa_b_7191934.html.
33 Ibid.
34 Ibid.
35 Ibid.
36 Ibid.
37 http://prospect.org/article/sex-lies-and-justice.
38 www.huffingtonpost.com/entry/congress-safe-campus-act_us_56378d46e4b0631799130302.
39 Ibid.
40 Ibid.
41 Ibid.
42 http://scar.gmu.edu/newsletter-article/what-you-need-know-about-sexual-assault-college-campuses.
43 Ibid.
44 www.insidehighered.com/news/2014/04/30/white-house-calls-colleges-do-more-combat-sexual-assault.
45 Ibid.
46 Ibid.
47 Ibid.
48 Ibid.
49 www.southernct.edu/sexual-misconduct/facts.html.
50 https://en.wikipedia.org/wiki/Victim_blaming.
51 www.ted.com/talks/jackson_katz_violence_against_women_it_s_a_men_s_issue/transcript?language=en.
52 https://sapac.umich.edu/article/196.
53 http://bjs.gov/content/pub/pdf/SOO.PDF.
54 www.nij.gov/topics/crime/rape-sexual-violence/campus/pages/know-attacker.aspx.
55 Ibid.
56 www.cnn.com/2013/01/24/us/military-women-glance/.
57 http://invisiblewarmovie.com/.
58 The Invisible War press kit. http://invisiblewarmovie.com/images/The-InvisibleWarPressKit.pdf.
59 Ibid.
60 http://mic.com/articles/29935/sexual-assault-in-the-military-97–5-of-all-military-rapes-aren-t-punished.
61 Ibid.
62 www.gillibrand.senate.gov/mjia.
63 Ibid.
64 Department of Defense Annual Report on Sexual Assault in the Military, Fiscal Year 2014.
65 www.gillibrand.senate.gov/mjia.
66 http://rhrealitycheck.org/article/2014/12/11/vote-blocked-gillibrands-military-sexual-assault-bill/.
67 www.heritage.org/research/reports/2013/11/sexual-assault-in-the-military-understanding-the-problem-and-how-to-fix-it/.
68 Ibid.
69 www.huffingtonpost.com/don-christensen/the-military-justice-improvement-act-ensures-justice_b_7596940.html.
70 Ibid.
71 See The National Research Center on Domestic Violence to better understand statistics-gathering methods on unreported cases of rape. www.vawnet.org/research/print-document.php?doc_id=2103&find_type=web_desc_AR.
72 www.militarytimes.com/story/military/pentagon/2014/12/04/pentagon-rand-sexual-assault-reports/19883155/.
73 www.vawnet.org/research/print-document.php?doc_id=2103&find_type=web_desc_AR.
74 Ibid.
75 Ibid.
76 Zurbriggen, Eileen L., "Rape, war, and the socialization of masculinity: Why our refusal to give up war ensures that rape cannot be eradicated," *Psychology of Women Quarterly*, December, 2010.

77 Lee, Chang-Hun. "Institutionalized hegemonic masculinity and rape by United States Army personnel in South Korea: A perspective on military subculture," *Asian Journal of Criminology*, June, 2010.
78 www.nolo.com/legal-encyclopedia/military-court-martial-trial-procedures.html.
79 www.michaelkaufman.com/2012/what-is-healthy-masculinity/.
80 Ibid.
81 Miller, Jody and Brunson, Rod K., "Gender dynamics in youth gangs: A comparison of males' and females' accounts," *Justice Quarterly*, August, 2006.
82 Thrasher, Frederic, *The Gang: A Study of 1,313 Gangs in Chicago* (University of Chicago Press, 1927; 1929).
83 Cohen, Albert K., *Delinquent Boys: The Culture of the Gang* (The Free Press, 1955).
84 Kyriacou, D.N., Hutson, H.R., Anglin, D., Peek-Asa, C., and Kraus, J.F., "The relationship between socioeconomic factors and gang violence in the City of Los Angeles," *The Journal of Trauma*, February, 1999.
85 Messerschmidt, James, *Masculinities and Crime* (Rowman & Littlefield, 1993).
86 Ibid.
87 Ibid.
88 Duran, Robert J., *Gang Life in Two Cities: An Insider's Journey* (Columbia University Press, 2013).
89 Ibid., Introduction.
90 West, Candace and Zimmerman, Don H., "Doing Gender," *Gender & Society*, June, 1987.
91 Flores, Edward O. and Hondagneu-Sotelo, Pierrette, "Chicano gang members in recovery: The public talk of negotiating Chicano masculinities," *Social Problems* 60 (2013). https://ucconsortiumssl.files.wordpress.com/2015/08/flores-flores-and-hondagneu-sotelo-2013.pdf.
92 Yablonski, L., *Gangsters: 50 Years of Madness, Drugs, and Death on the Streets of America* (New York University Press, 1997).
93 Flores and Hondagneu-Sotelo, "Chicano gang members in recovery."
94 Ibid.
95 Hagedorn, John M. "Gang," *Encyclopedia of Masculinities* (Sage, 2003).
96 www.psychologytoday.com/blog/the-joint-adventures-well-educated-couples/201210/women-need-love-and-men-need-respect.
97 http://thealbanyjournal.com/2010/10/men-want-respect/.
98 www.meetyoursweet.com/women/blog/the-one-thing-men-want-more-than-your-love.
99 www.csmonitor.com/2006/0223/p14s01-lire.html.
100 Ibid.
101 http://powderclegg.blogspot.com/2012/12/james-gilligans-preventing-violence.html.
102 Gilligan, James, *Preventing Violence (Prospects for Tomorrow)* (Thames and Hudson, 2001).
103 Gilligan, James, *Violence: Reflections on a National Epidemic* (Vintage Books, 1997).
104 www.psychalive.org/a-new-approach-to-violence-treatment-an-interview-with-dr-james-gilligan/.
105 Ibid.
106 Ibid.
107 https://en.wikipedia.org/wiki/Gangland_(TV_series).
108 Barker, Thomas, *Biker Gangs and Organized Crime* (Routledge, 2010).
109 www.cnn.com/2015/10/29/us/texas-biker-shootout-new-details/.
110 http://listverse.com/2009/08/18/top-10-notorious-american-biker-gangs/.
111 www.outlawsmcworld.com/onepercenter.htm.
112 Dulaney, William L., "A brief history of 'outlaw' motorcycle clubs," *International Journal of Motorcycle Studies*, November, 2005.
113 Carlie, Mike, *Into the Abyss: A Personal Journey into the World of Street Gangs* (M. Carlie, 2002).
114 Hopper, C.B. and Moore, J., "Women in outlaw motorcycle gangs," *Journal of Contemporary Ethnography* 18 (1990).
115 Rappaport, J. "Community narratives: Tales of terror and joy," *American Journal of Community Psychology* 28, 1 (2000), pp. 1–24.
116 Librett, Mitch, "Wild pigs and outlaws: The kindred worlds of policing outlaw bikers," *Crime Media Culture: An International Journal*, 4 (2008).
117 Danner, Terry A. and Silverman, Ira J., "Characteristics of incarcerated outlaw bikers as compared to non-biker inmates," *Journal of Crime and Justice* 9 (1986).
118 Baird, Adam, "The violent gang and the construction of masculinity amongst socially excluded young men," *Safer Communities* 11 (2012).
119 Ibid.

120 http://people.missouristate.edu/michael-carlie/what_i_learned_about/gangs/join_a_gang.htm.
121 http://webcache.googleusercontent.com/search?q=cache:1ijoPJwJ_KcJ:www.bjs.gov/content/pub/pdf/p11.pdf+&cd=1&hl=en&ct=clnk&gl=us.
122 www.naacp.org/pages/criminal-justice-fact-sheet.
123 Ibid.
124 Ibid.
125 www.pewresearch.org/fact-tank/2014/07/18/chart-of-the-week-the-black-white-gap-in-incarceration-rates/.
126 www.washingtontimes.com/news/2013/nov/14/cole-and-mauer-reducing-crime-by-reducing-incarcer/. www.huffingtonpost.com/keith-rushing/the-reasons-why-so-many-b_b_883310.html.
127 Warren, Patricia, Chiricos, Ted and Bales, William, "The imprisonment penalty for young black and Hispanic males: A crime specific analysis," *Journal of Research in Crime & Delinquency*, May, 2011.
128 www.pbs.org/wgbh/pages/frontline/shows/drugs/buyers/whoare.html.
129 www.kansas.com/news/nation-world/national/article1027661.html.
130 www.usnews.com/news/blogs/data-mine/2014/12/11/no-justice-is-not-colorblind.
131 www.huffingtonpost.com/bill-quigley/fourteen-examples-of-raci_b_658947.html.
132 www.pbs.org/wgbh/pages/frontline/shows/drugs/buyers/whoare.html.
133 Krienert, Jessie L., "Masculinity and crime: A quantitative exploration of Messerschmidt's hypothesis," *Electronic Journal of Sociology*, 2003.
134 Starr, Sonja B., "Estimating gender disparities in federal criminal cases," *University of Michigan Law and Economics Research Paper*, No. 12–018, August, 2012.
135 Ibid.
136 Ibid.
137 www.queerty.com/hunger-for-touch-the-real-truth-behind-gay-sex-in-prison-may-shock-you-20140925.
138 https://malesurvivor.org/ArchivedPages/rts.html.
139 Ibid.
140 https://en.wikipedia.org/wiki/Prison_rape_in_the_United_States#cite_note-8.
141 Ibid.
142 Frost, Martin, et al., "Youth prisons and training schools: Perceptions and consequences of the treatment–custody dichotomy," *Juvenile and Family Court*, February, 1989.
143 http://web.archive.org/web/20080426040919/http://www.spr.org/en/factsheets/basics.asp.
144 www.eji.org/childrenprison.
145 Ibid.
146 www.ojjdp.gov/ojstatbb/structure_process/qa04105.asp?qaDate=2009.
147 www.ncjrs.gov/html/ojjdp/9912_2/juv5.html.
148 Ibid.
149 www.wcl.american.edu/endsilence/.
150 www.nij.gov/journals/259/pages/prison-rape.aspx.
151 www.hrw.org/news/2014/05/30/dispatches-us-states-lag-addressing-prison-rape.
152 Ibid.
153 Ibid.
154 http://bigstory.ap.org/article/69e449692755437c99575412123e2c24/idaho-finally-agrees-comply-federal-prison-rape-law.
155 www.huffingtonpost.com/rodney-smith/prison-rape-gay-rights_b_4504331.html.
156 Ibid.
157 Ibid.
158 Ibid.
159 http://articles.latimes.com/2005/sep/16/local/me-prison16.
160 www.nytimes.com/2011/04/07/opinion/07thu2.html?_r=0.
161 Ibid.
162 www.hrw.org/legacy/reports/2001/prison/report4.html.
163 Ibid.
164 www.blackandpink.org/purpose-analysis/.
165 Ibid.
166 http://elwilsondesign.sexy/pen-pals/.
167 Morris, Allison and Gelsthorpe, Loraine, "Re-visioning men's violence against female partners," *The Howard Journal of Criminal Justice*, November, 2000.
168 Ptacek, James and Frederick, Loretta, "Restorative justice and intimate partner violence," National Resource Center on Domestic Violence, www.vawnet.org/domestic-violence/print-document.php?doc_id=1656&find_type=web_desc_AR.
169 Ibid.
170 https://en.wikipedia.org/wiki/Solitary_confinement.
171 www.nytimes.com/roomfordebate/2012/12/18/prison-could-be-productive/

punishment-fails-rehabilitation-works.

172 www.psychalive.org/a-new-approach-to-violence-treatment-an-interview-with-dr-james-gilligan/.

173 Bevan, Emma and Higgins, Daryl J., "Is domestic violence learned? The contribution of five forms of child maltreatment to men's violence and adjustment," *Journal of Family Violence*, September, 2002.

174 Ibid.

175 Cunradi, Carol B., Caetano, Raul, and Schafer, John, "Alcohol-related problems, drug use, and male intimate partner violence severity among US couples," *Alcoholism: Clinical and Experimental Research*, April, 2002.

176 Ibid.

177 O'Farrell, Timothy J., Fals-Stewart, William, Murphy, Marie, and Murphy, Christopher M., "Partner violence before and after individually based alcoholism treatment for male alcoholic patients," *Journal of Consulting and Clinical Psychology*, February, 2003.

178 Ibid.

179 Welte, J.W. and Wieczorek, W.F., "Alcohol, intelligence and violent crime in young males," *Journal of Substance Abuse*, 1998. www.ncbi.nlm.nih.gov/pubmed/10689662.

180 Ibid.

181 Ibid.

182 www.abc.net.au/health/thepulse/stories/2014/01/30/3934877.htm.

183 Ibid.

184 http://pubs.niaaa.nih.gov/publications/aa63/aa63.htm.

185 http://sciencenetlinks.com/student-teacher-sheets/alcohol-and-your-brain/.

186 www.psychologytoday.com/blog/the-imprinted-brain/201205/sex-differences-driven-impulse.

187 www.cdc.gov/alcohol/fact-sheets/mens-health.htm.

188 Ibid.

189 Green, Carla A., "Gender and use of substance abuse treatment services," National Institute on Alcohol Abuse and Alcoholism. http://pubs.niaaa.nih.gov/publications/arh291/55–62.htm.

190 United States Department of Justice, "Homicide Trends in the United States," Alexia Cooper & Erica L. Smith, BJS Statisticians, November, 2011.

191 www.fbi.gov/about-us/cjis/ucr/crime-in-the-u.s/2011/crime-in-the-u.s.-2011/offenses-known-to-law-enforcement/expanded/expanded-homicide-data.

192 The FBI reports that perpetrators of murder are men in 89.3% of cases of homicide when the gender of the perpetrator is known. www.fbi.gov/about-us/cjis/ucr/crime-in-the-u.s/2011/crime-in-the-u.s.-2011/offenses-known-to-law-enforcement/expanded/expanded-homicide-data.

193 Ibid.

194 Ibid.

195 www.theguardian.com/commentisfree/2011/jun/07/feminism-domestic-violence-men.

196 Ibid.

197 Ibid.

198 National Institute of Justice. http://www.nij.gov/topics/crime/rape-sexual-violence/pages/victims-perpetrators.aspx.

199 Ibid.

200 Kimmel, Michael, "Gender symmetry in domestic violence: A substantive and methodological research review," *Violence Against Women*, November, 2002.

201 Ibid.

202 Ibid.

203 Ibid.

204 www.cdc.gov/violenceprevention/intimatepartnerviolence/consequences.html.

205 www.cdc.gov/violenceprevention/sexualviolence/datasources.html.

206 Ibid.

207 https://sapac.umich.edu/article/65.

208 Ibid.

209 Lambert, E.G., Smith, B., Geistman, J., Cluse-Tolar, T., and Jiang, S., "Do men and women differ in their perceptions of stalking: an exploratory study among college students," *Violence and Victims* 28, 2 (2013), pp. 195–209.

210 Ibid.

211 www.uh.edu/wgrc/safety-and-violence-prevention/stalking%20/.

212 https://victimsofcrime.org/our-programs/stalking-resource-center/stalking-laws/criminal-stalking-laws-by-state.

213 www.domesticviolenceroundtable.org/domestic-violence-cycle.html.

Chapter

11

Men, Sex, and Pornography

I remember when I first discovered internet porn—I was 17 years old. Fascinated by this world of unleashed sexual expression and fantasy, I couldn't get enough of it. As I grew up and began exploring my own sexuality, I discovered just how different watching pixels on a screen was compared to the intimacy of making love with another human being. I thought I'd outgrow my porn habit over time. But I never did. I didn't know it then, but porn had become an addiction. And, like most addictions, it was a behavior that I was ashamed to talk about or even admit was a problem. "Yeah, everybody watches porn," I remember hearing. It seemed so pervasive and culturally accepted that having an actual conversation about it was a total non-starter. So I kept it to myself. I thought I had my habit under control. I thought I could quit porn whenever I felt like it. I even tried to quit a few times and then rationalized my eventual return to the addiction. I always felt like a hypocrite watching porn. Here I was, a man who is striving to be an ally to women, perpetuating the very culture of violence and misogyny that I was ostensibly trying to fight. The reality was that most of the videos I found online had titles that included words like "bitch" or "slut" and showcased controlling behaviors that were rooted in a culture of subjugation and objectification, where women are nothing more than sexual bodies to be exploited and dominated by men. Last February, after a decade of use, I decided to quit watching porn for 1 year. I did this, both for the challenge of seeing if I could do it, and for the chance to see how life might be different. Now this may not seem like a big deal, but it was actually a radical commitment to uphold. Today marks my 1-year anniversary of life without porn. It hasn't been easy, particularly as a single guy, but what I've learned about myself through this experience has transformed my life forever.

~ Dan Mahle,[1] writer for the *Good Men Project*

LEARNING OBJECTIVES

After reading this chapter, students should be able to respond to the following questions with an understanding of the terms and expressions employed:

- *What is erotica and how is it often distinguished from pornography? What are some of the theories for why men prefer pornography over erotica?*
- *What was* the playboy philosophy? *In response to the playboy philosophy, theologian Henry Cox published "Playboy's Doctrine of the Male." What, according to Cox, were the central points of this "doctrine"?*

- *What was "the Meese Report" and what were its findings about pornography? In what ways did pornography change after the Meese Report?*
- *What is gonzo porn? What have surveys taught researchers about men's porn usage versus women's porn usage? What is bukkake porn and what are the theories as to why men enjoy this form of pornography?*
- *How is some pornography racist in nature? What is "the brute" stereotype?*
- *How has amateur porn influenced the porn market and what effects has it had on the content of pornography? What is* revenge porn *and what are the gendered consequences and legal ramifications of this form of pornography?*
- *With respect to repetitive porn usage, what is the* availability error? *How might Gerbner's "mean-world syndrome" relate to porn usage?*
- *What is acceptance and commitment therapy and in what ways is it thought to help those who struggle with porn usage?*
- *According to UCLA research psychologist Rory Reid, what are the two most reported patterns of behavior found in men who have developed porn obsessions? What is meant by 'natural addictions'?*
- *What is the "catharsis defense" of pornography?*
- *What are the major debate points between pro-porn feminists and anti-porn feminists?*
- *What has research discovered about couples who habitually bring porn into their relationships?*
- *What points are made in favor of, and in opposition to, gay male pornography? What is "gay for pay" pornography and what debate surrounds it?*

Over the last few decades, men's sexuality has been at the forefront of ad campaigns whether in terms of male enhancement, erectile dysfunction, ads that attempt to sexually stimulate men, or ads that sexually objectify men. At the same time, pornography, which has long been produced by men for men has gone through a number of dramatic changes due to internet access, increased competition, and content revision specifically designed to attract male consumers. Although much of the discussion surrounding pornography focuses on how pornography affects women, the influence of pornography on men almost always has to do with the ways that men who habitually use porn treat women. Some of the concerns about men who consume porn while in a relationship is that they may coerce their partners to perform sexual acts, based on the pornographic scenes they watch, that their partners are uncomfortable or unwilling to perform, or that porn usage diminishes their capacity and desire for intimacy with their partners.

One of the more contentious parts of a discussion about porn is whether or not pornography use can turn into an addiction similar to that of alcohol and substance addiction. The debate surrounding this particular aspect of porn use splits experts but also highlights a further debate about whether porn usage harms, helps, or has a negligible effect on men and men's sexual lives. This feature of the porn examination brings in the work of neuroscience, but also the behavioral effects of habitual pornography usage.

Feminist analyses of porn, which is split into pro-pornography and anti-pornography feminism, often calibrates around porn's alleged influence on men's mistreatment of women versus women's sexual freedom. That is, part of the concern about male porn consumption is that pornography plays an instrumental role in one-dimensionalizing women as sexually subordinated and commodified beings who exist for the sexual objectification and gratification of men. If these analyses are correct, pornography is an instrument of patriarchy that reinforces the role of men as subject and women as object. Others draw a direct line between male porn usage and physical, sexual, and emotional abuse to women. At the same time, there are feminists who defend porn as being sexually liberating for women. These self-titled "pro-sex feminists" argue that it is patronizing to challenge the choices women make, including those choices to view or participate in pornography. They view critics as prudish and out of step with the notion of women as sexual beings who wish to embrace their sexuality.

This chapter will also investigate the argued differences of gay male pornography and mainstream heterosexual pornography. Many have argued that the critiques of heterosexual porn simply do not apply to gay male pornography. The argument is that with heterosexual porn there is a traceable history of men subordinating women that informs the role of most women in porn, while there is no similar traceable pattern of gay men subordinating other gay men. This point is, of course, debatable. One notable and common observation about porn designed for heterosexual men is the heterosexist normalizing of lesbian porn as product made for the heterosexual, male gaze, and how the heterosexist fetishizing of lesbianism affects actual lesbians.

However, those who criticize pornography also point out that we live in a media culture that continues to depict men as sexual aggressors, or that furthers the idea that men should be sexually aggressive with women in order to measure up to cultural expectations placed on men. Pornography, they argue, fits right in with the patriarchal notion that men should dominate women sexually and in almost every other aspect of life. This chapter will explore the variety of ways that men's and women's sexuality is and has been affected by pornography, beginning with the conventional division between erotica and pornography and continuing with the magazines and adult materials that have been marketed to men for decades.

Erotica

Erotica is sometimes distinguished from pornography by telling a story that involves sexual themes rather than through sexually explicit scenes.[2] Forms of erotica have been found throughout the world dating back thousands of years and across various cultures. Paintings, drawings, and sculptures, both heterosexual and homosexual in nature, were created with decidedly sexual themes. By the early twentieth century, erotica was typified by nude or partially nude women in various scenes of displaying or caressing themselves, either alone or with other women. Erotica has been and continues to be found in literary pieces as well. Today, erotica enjoys a great deal of success, with female consumers.[3] Several examples of erotic literature include *Delta of Venus* by Anais Nin, *Tropic of Cancer* by Henry Miller, and *Fear of Flying* by Erica Jong. While many men enjoy erotica and many women enjoy pornography, contemporary erotica is considered by many to appeal more to women than men.[4]

Reasons why more men enjoy pornography than erotica range from theories about the alleged visual emphasis in men's brains to the view that pornography celebrates men's dominance over women, a trope that many men enjoy. In "Feminism, Moralism, and Pornography," activist/writer Ellen Willis argues that erotica embraces a gender-mutual experience of pleasure, while pornography often depicts men's sexual power over women.[5] Willis notes that the etymology of the word 'pornography' supports this gender unequal interpretation, since the origin of the word 'pornography' comes from the Greek word 'porne' meaning 'prostitute,' *pornography* then meaning "writings about prostitutes."[6] [7]

Gahyun Youn of the Korean Association of Sexology found in his study of 215 college undergraduates that while both genders experience erotic fantasies throughout a typical day, men tend to have more explicit and visual imagery in their sexual fantasies, while women enjoy more romantic, emotional, and erotic imagery.[8] Citing a number of previous studies, Youn explains that sexual feelings and fantasies are often mitigated for women due to dimorphic sexual socialization.[9] This would serve as yet another explanation for women's increased usage of erotic materials and men's increased usage of pornography. As a society reduces or eliminates sexual double-standards, it is thought that women would enjoy pornography at roughly similar rates as men. However, Youn also notes that, for men, a pornographic video clip offers a quicker journey from initial arousal to sexual release than does erotic guided fantasy.[10] In fact, Youn's study concluded that men were significantly more sexually aroused by short pornographic video clips, while erotic guided fantasy had little effect on men, but a pronounced effect on women.[11] Youn admits that self-reporting can be an inaccurate tool for arousal rates, since cultural factors may influence some, and mainly women, not to report arousal even in the presence of arousal, and different target demographics may respond differently to the materials. But Youn argues that even with these factors considered, and with the acknowledgement that more research is required, women are aroused by the sorts of erotic fantasies embedded in erotica materials more than are men, while men's sexual arousal is tied much more to short exposures of visual pornography where sexually explicit materials are employed. These gendered differences to arousal do not change whether the subjects are heterosexual or homosexual.[12]

Hugh Hefner, *Playboy,* and the Emergence of Pornographic Magazines

It is difficult to overestimate the contribution to porn culture of Playboy Enterprises founder Hugh Hefner. In 1952, Hefner quit his job as a copywriter at *Esquire* magazine and by 1953 launched *Playboy* magazine. Today, Playboy Enterprises is estimated to be worth more than $200 million.[13] Along with the magazine and the nightclubs that carried the *Playboy* title and logo in the 1960s and 1970s, Hefner created what became known as ***the Playboy philosophy***, which he touted as a mission of free speech and sexual liberty against what he viewed as the repressive forces of society and government that sought to censor sexual expression and limit sexual choice.

In 1961, theologian Harvey Cox published an article entitled, "**Playboy's Doctrine of the Male,**" in which Cox set about to interpret the belief system of Hefner's fledgling magazine and lifestyle.[14] In determining what was causing the explosion of popularity of *Playboy*, Cox argued that the notoriety went beyond the exposure of nude women, and concluded,

> *Playboy* appeals to a highly mobile, increasingly affluent group of young readers, mostly between eighteen and thirty, who want much more from their drugstore reading than bosoms and thighs. They need a total image of what it means to be a man.[15]

A central part of *the Playboy philosophy*, argued Cox, was to view males as consumers and females as commodities, but this was particularly marketed to men as a sign of prestige and affluence. Cox argued that *Playboy* instructs men to swagger with confidence, which they are told causes women to swoon with desire. Sex itself becomes a leisure activity and women become an indispensable *Playboy* accessory.[16] Another prominent aspect of the "Playboy Doctrine" is the instruction to men that they should not emotionally commit themselves to women and that a cardinal male sin is betrothing oneself

FIGURE 11.1: Hugh Hefner

in matrimony. The women of *Playboy*, in contrast to women in the real world who demand respect and equality, are non-threatening, opinion-less seductresses "who make no demands on [men] except sex."[17] As Cox viewed it, *Playboy* was an escape from maturity, responsibility, and gender equality. The sexual choices Hefner defended were mainly found in men having a variety of women at their disposal. Pictures of Hugh Hefner in the press reinforced this notion, as the majority of images taken of the adult-magazine publisher were comprised of Hefner surrounded by a collection of young, scantily-clad women. The gender-converse of this formula (a woman surrounded by young, scantily-clad men) was a rarity.

In the wake of the success of *Playboy Enterprises*, two other men's magazines found great success in American culture: Bob Guccione's *Penthouse* magazine, which, founded in the U.S. in 1969, became the main competitor to *Playboy*, and Larry Flynt's *Hustler* magazine, founded in 1974, considered by many to be a more raunchy, sexually graphic, lowbrow version of *Playboy*.[18] Many, in fact, view *Hustler* as marking the onset of an ongoing competition between pornographers for male patronage with more sexually provocative, graphic, and crude depictions of sex. Living up to its reputation for crudeness and tastelessness, *Hustler* regularly featured a cartoon character named "Chester the Molester" and a steady litany of rape jokes, that included jokes about child rape. In one cartoon, an underage girl is viewed looking at a middle-aged man with the caption, "You call THAT being molested?" The cartoonist who created "Chester the Molester," Dwaine B. Tinsley, and who worked for Hustler Magazine throughout the 1970s was convicted in 1984 for sexually molesting his 13-year-old daughter.[19]

At its peak in the late 1970s, *Hustler* magazine enjoyed a membership subscription of 3 million, which today has dropped to approximately 500,000.[20] Flynt has been sued a number of times, but attempts to defend his brand of pornography on a First Amendment, freedom of speech basis.[21] While standing before the Supreme Court of the United States, Flynt yelled, "Fuck this court!" and referred to the justices as "nothing but eight assholes and a token cunt," referring to Justice Sandra Day O'Connor.[22] In March of 1978, a gunman shot Flynt and his lawyer outside of a Georgia courthouse, causing permanent paralysis to Flynt's legs.[23]

FIGURE 11.2: Larry Flynt

Today, so-called men's magazines that feature scantily-clad or nude women posed in provocative positions have been effectively replaced with internet pornography. Along with the more graphic sexual scenes, internet porn has allowed boys and men to stream and download videos on their home computers and smart phones. The proliferation and ease of access to pornography has fueled a good deal of research to investigate the effects of prolonged, habitual use of pornography on men, women, and relationships with arguments running both in support of and in opposition to porn. The central concern of those who criticize porn has to do with how men who habitually use porn treat women, but there are further concerns about whether porn has a negative overall effect on society's treatment of women, men's sexual and emotional health, and relationships.

The Meese Report and the Emergence of Internet Pornography

To discuss pornography is to discuss a multitude of images and narratives that can be very different from one another; but until very recently, the porn industry has been an industry made by men for men. Typical of the early era of filmed pornography, pornographic scenes were staged and scripted to emulate mainstream, feature films, but of course with the inclusion of sexually explicit scenes. The 1970s were a decade when pornography became more publicly visible, with theaters created specifically for adult films. Theaters of this type became known for their seedy reputations and mainly male clientele. This was also a time when the first "porn stars" emerged on the American pop cultural landscape in figures like John Holmes, Harry Reems, and Ron Jeremy.[24] The women in pornography were equally if not more famous. Seka, Marilyn Chambers, and Linda Lovelace, whose film *Deep Throat* (1972) was mentioned by television host Johnny Carson, were almost household names.[25] The pornographic film *The Devil in Miss Jones* (1973) was reviewed favorably by celebrated film critic Roger Ebert,[26] and for a while it seemed as though pornography was being accepted by many as fitting in with the 1970s sexual liberation movement.

"May the bluenoses leave it lay for the pleasure of those whose taste it is.

STANDS PHOTOGRAPHICALLY HEAD AND SHOULDERS ABOVE 'THROAT'...AND MORE VARIED! THE FIRST TEN MINUTES ACHIEVE MODIGLIANI TONES. THE CAST IS ENTHUSIASTIC...GEORGINA SPEVLIN MAKES A MARK ON YOUR EMOTIONS!"

Judith Crist, *NEW YORK MAGAZINE*

"The Most Interesting Film of its Kind to Date!

BECAUSE IT DISSOLVES THE DISTINCTION BETWEEN SEX FILMS AND ART FILMS. GEORGINA SPEVLIN'S PERFORMANCE WAS REMARKABLY PERSUASIVE!"

Charles Michener/*NEWSWEEK*

"The 'Devil in Miss Jones' is Unique, Surprising, Provocative!

EXCEPTIONALLY WELL FILMED AND ACTED—AS WELL AS LUSTILY PERFORMED, AND GOES ANOTHER BIG STEP TOWARD BRIDGING THE GAP BETWEEN SERIOUS ART FILMS AND THOSE PREVIOUSLY LABELED SEXPLOITATION."

Bruce Williamson/*PLAYBOY*

"The Picture is a Sensation!

A BREATHTAKING EROTIC ODYSSEY, THE LIKES OF WHICH HAS NEVER BEEN SO STRONGLY DEPICTED ON THE SCREEN. IF MARLON BRANDO CAN BE PRAISED FOR GIVING HIS ALMOST-ALL IN 'LAST TANGO IN PARIS,' ONE WONDERS WHAT THE REACTION WILL BE TO MISS JONES' LEAD, GEORGINA SPEVLIN, WHOSE PERFORMANCE IS SO NAKED, IT SEEMS TO BE A MASSIVE INVASION OF PRIVACY. THE FINALE TAKES JEAN-PAUL SARTRE'S 'NO EXIT' TO A LOGICAL, AND SURPRISINGLY MORALISTIC EXTREME."

Addison Verrill/*VARIETY*

FIGURE 11.3: *The Devil in Miss Jones*, 1973

In the 1980s, President Ronald Reagan ordered Attorney General Edwin Meese to investigate pornography and the porn industry.[27] As a result of this investigation, what came to be known as "the Meese Report" was issued, a report that roundly criticized pornography as unequivocally harmful and in need of regulation. In the wake of the Meese Report, Surgeon General C. Everett Koop formed a weekend workshop of "recognized authorities" to discuss and draw conclusions about pornography.[28] A consensus was formed around the following conclusions by those who attended the workshop:

1. Children and adolescents who participate in the production of pornography experience adverse, enduring effects.
2. Prolonged use of pornography increases beliefs that less common sexual practices are more common.
3. Pornography that portrays sexual aggression as pleasurable for the victim increases the acceptance of the use of coercion in sexual relations.
4. Acceptance of coercive sexuality appears to be related to sexual aggression.
5. In laboratory studies measuring short-term effects, exposure to violent pornography increases punitive behavior toward women.[29]

Recommendations stemming from the Meese Report and C. Everett Koop's workshop included stricter state and federal regulations governing the production and distribution of porn. But the Meese Report did not have much effect on the porn industry, as the 1980s ushered in VHS and eventually DVD sales that introduced profits unknown during the tenure of adult theaters. Pornography was now available for home viewing, which took away the shame some felt in walking to the ticket booth of an adult theater; and as a result, the porn industry flourished.

In the 1990s internet pornography launched what is now a multi-billion dollars per year industry worldwide with males making up the vast majority of porn clientele.[30] Porn actors and actresses make anywhere from $50 to $1,000 per scene depending on the activities required and women usually make more money than their male counterparts.[31] Ironically, the onset of internet pornography created competition that was unheard of when pornography was produced largely by of a handful of companies working out of Southern California's San Fernando Valley. This competition resulted in greatly lowered profits for the porn production companies that flourished in the 1980s and early 1990s.[32] Suddenly, the focus of the porn market was website memberships, including live-streaming options and real-time, interactive sessions with paid performers. These latter features continue to be a thriving part of the contemporary porn market. This newfound competition also ushered in fetish and niche porn websites to appeal to more narrow markets, but also the emergence of gonzo porn and other more extreme forms of pornography in order to attract clientele through shock value and word-of-mouth. **Gonzo porn** is usually defined by more graphic sex scenes where the cameraman is often a participant in the sex act. Gonzo scenes are typified by long, close-up sex acts with no surrounding scripts or set-up scenes. Self-described founder of gonzo porn, John Stagliano, is considered by many to have initiated the genre through his "Buttman" series of films.[33] But gonzo porn also brought about more aggressive content, in which women are dominated and humiliated, along with being physically and verbally abused by the man or men in the scene and is often defended as consensual "rough sex."[34]

With the success of gonzo porn, pornographer John Thompson created the American Bukkake series of films, which spun off of the bukkake porn that was being produced in Japan.[35] In **bukkake porn**, women are often filmed kneeling in front of groups of men who urinate and ejaculate on them.[36] Today, pornography studios in Germany and Japan produce most of this genre of porn overwhelmingly for male consumption, although American pornographers also continue to produce this style of porn along with other degrading forms of pornography. One theory for the success of bukkake is that "The viewer identifies with the ejaculating men, experiencing a sense of vicarious pleasure."[37] However, feminist scholar Gail Dines views the attraction of men to bukkake porn as the desire to degrade women and to treat women as property that can be used in any vile way a man sees fit.[38] In her book *Pornland: How Porn has Hijacked Our Sexuality*, Dines quotes pornographer Bill Margold as stating,

> I'd like to really show what I believe the men want to see: violence against women. I firmly believe that we serve a purpose by showing that. The most violent we can get is the cum shot in the face. Men get off behind that because they get even with the women they can't have.[39]

Dines views bukkake porn as representing the pinnacle of men's anger and resentment toward women. Writing for *The Guardian*, Dines states,

> The fantasy of porn is that [a woman] is an object who exists to be penetrated, dehumanised and then disposed of. She has no bodily integrity, limits or dignity. She is not someone to worry about, care for or protect from physical harm.[40]

For more than two decades, University of Texas, Austin, professor Robert Jensen has also criticized pornography and the porn industry. In explaining why so many men enjoy pornography and particularly the hard-core, gonzo porn that proliferates the internet today, Jensen writes:

> Because I'm a man, women sometimes assume I can also provide a simple answer to their question, "Why does he want to do that to me?" There is a simple, though not pleasant, answer rooted in feminism: In patriarchy, men are socialized to understand sex in the context of men's domination and women's submission. The majority of the pornography that saturates our hyper-mediated lives presents not images of "just sex," but sex in the context of male dominance. And over the past two decades, as pornography has become more easily accessible online and the sexual acts in pornography have become more extreme, women increasingly report that men ask them to participate in sex acts that come directly from the conventional male-supremacist pornographic script, with little recognition by men of the potential for pain, discomfort, or distress in their partners.[41]

Jensen goes on to describe how pornography usage by men leads to a diminished ability to feel empathy toward women:

> The most challenging question [I receive from women] is: "Why can't he understand why I don't want that?" The strength of sexual desire plays a role, but here the answer is really about the absence of empathy, the lack of an ability to imagine what another human being might be feeling. Pornography has always presented women as objectified bodies for male sexual pleasure, but each year pornography does that with more overt cruelty toward women. The "gonzo" genre of pornography, where the industry pushes the culture's limits with the most intense sexual degradation, encourages men to see women as vehicles for their sexual pleasure, even depicting women as eager to participate in their own degradation. After more than two decades of work on this subject, I have no doubt of one truth about contemporary pornography: It is one way that men's capacity for empathy can be dramatically diminished.[42]

One of the most common criticisms of pornography is that it sexually objectifies women, and to sexual objectify a person is to dehumanize that person. Empathy is the ability to feel what another is feeling, even if through imagination. If one sees a parent grieving over the loss of their child and hears their story, one can feel empathy with them even if one has not lost one's child. But one cannot empathize with objects such as tables and chairs. With pornography, Jensen is arguing that women are reduced strictly to beings of sexual utility, things, and vessels for a man's or men's sexual release. In these instances, intimacy or any feelings of caring are absent and hence empathy is not possible.

At the same time, many couples believe that pornography can help them explore sexually, spice up their sex life together, and strengthen their relationship. Three studies were conducted to put those views to the test. Spencer B. Olmstead and his colleagues at the University of Tennessee found that men and women in relationships perceive the consequences of porn-viewing differently. Men mainly view porn usage in positive terms, while women are more concerned with whether their partner is watching and using pornography as a surrogate for sex with them.[43] [44] Psychologist Nathaniel Lambert found that more women than men who are in relationships view porn as a threat to the stability of their relationship.[45] [46] Psychologist Amanda Shaw and her research team found that those couples who do not bring pornography into their relationship report having lower levels of negative communication, higher levels of commitment to their partners, and higher levels of overall sexual satisfaction in their relationships.[47] In yet another study conducted by Andrea M. Guinn, Nathaniel Lambert, and other researchers, it was found that those couples who repeatedly use pornography have higher rates of infidelity.[48] Surprisingly, this discovery was found to exist even with those couples who reported sexual satisfaction within their relationship.[49]

Research scholar Gail Dines states of men's usage of porn,

> the earlier men use porn, the more likely they are to have trouble developing close, intimate relationships with real women. Some of these men prefer porn to sex with an actual human being. They are bewildered, even angry, when real women don't want or enjoy porn sex.[50]

Dines concludes after research into the viewership of types of porn that,

> The most popular acts depicted in internet porn include vaginal, oral and anal penetration by three or more men at the same time; double anal; double vaginal; a female gagging from having a penis thrust into her throat; and ejaculation in a woman's face, eyes and mouth.[51]

Dines continues,

> To think that so many men hate women to the degree that they can get aroused by such vile images is quite profound. Pornography is the perfect propaganda piece for patriarchy. In nothing else is their hatred of us quite as clear.[52]

But if Dines's analysis is correct, porn usage by men is not mitigated by scenes of degradation and instead establishes the sexual dominance and debasement of women by men as natural:

> The more porn sexualises violence against women, the more it normalises and legitimises sexually abusive behaviour. Men learn about sex from porn, and in porn nothing is too painful or degrading for women.[53]

In fact, in pornography the word 'no' is almost never heard, and if heard, does not lead the man or men in the scene to cease sexually assaulting the woman or women in the scene. If anything, resistance is often part of a scripted plot development to elicit arousal or as part of a sexual game being played between the participants.

Writing specifically to men about men's choices to masturbate to pornography, Jensen states:

> I assume that many men reading this [article] masturbate, or have masturbated, to pornography. That makes us johns. I don't mean that most men have necessarily bought a woman from a pimp in prostitution, though no doubt some of us have. I'm talking, instead, about the far more common experience of pornography ... In pornography, the pimp is called a publisher or a video producer, and the john is called a fan or a pornography consumer. But that doesn't change the nature of the relationship: It involves one person (usually a man) selling another person (usually a woman) to a third person (usually a man). When you masturbate to pornography, you are buying sexual pleasure. You are buying a woman. The fact that there are technologies of film or video between you and the pimp doesn't change the equation. Legally, it's not prostitution and legally, you're not in trouble. But you are still a john.[54]

The arguments that apply to prostitution, that women are turned strictly into sexual commodities, which in turn creates a supply–demand equation where the majority of prostitution involves men *purchasing* women, argues Jensen, apply equally to pornography. The supply would not exist without the demand so that as long as men desire to engage in sex with women as a non-intimate, non-committal business exchange, pimps and pornographers will exploit that desire for profit.

In an article co-authored by Robert Jensen and Gail Dines, pornography is seen as the quintessential commodification of women. It is the invasion and extension of capitalism into our most intimate domain. Jensen and Dines write:

> [In pornography], what is being commodified is crucial to our sense of self. Whatever a person's views on sexuality, virtually everyone agrees it is an important aspect of our identity. In pornography, and in the sex industry more generally, sexuality is one more product to be packaged and sold.[55]

FIGURE 11.4: Anti-porn author Robert Jensen

Jensen and Dines also argue that it is impossible to disconnect the commodification of women's bodies in pornography with patriarchy. As covered in chapter one, any society where men dominate positions in government, create public policy, while also holding the majority of economic wealth is a patriarchal society. Patriarchy is built on the notion of hierarchies that are themselves defined by an inequality of power. Pornography documents this inequality on film, particularly in the genres of gonzo, bukkake, dramatized rape, time-stop, and other forms of porn that graphically depict the subordination of women by men, in some cases in demeaning and violent ways. In **time-stop pornography**, for example, one type of scene involves a man arguing with a woman or women often in a business or office setting. The man then pushes a button that freezes time so that the women are frozen like mannequins while the man is free to move about. The man in the scene subsequently rapes the women, leaves their clothing off of them after the rape, and returns time to normal so that the women become aware of what has happened, are shocked and humiliated.

Dines also exposes an element of porn that is less frequently discussed: the open racism that is often found in mainstream pornography. Mainstream media, while still struggling with a multitude of racist generalizations and the absence or underrepresentation of individuals belonging to certain racial or ethnic groups, has been forced to be cautious about its representation of people of color or face public reprisal. No such caution or fear of reprisal exists for pornography. Titles from mainstream pornography include, "Oh no! There's a negro in my mom!" "Slant eye for the straight guy," "Anal with Oriental slant," "Bang that Black bitch white boy," "Bangkok Suckee Fuckee: 98 Hot Thai chicks suckee and fuckee huge white dicks!"[56] In other porn videos, men wearing Ku Klux Klan costumes, sporting the sheets and pointy head-wear, rape black women. Dines writes:

> Not satisfied to call her the usual gonzo terms of slut/whore/cum-dumpster, [black women are] often referred to as "black ghetto hoes" with mouthy attitude who need to be taught a lesson. This stereotype of black women as promiscuous, overbearing and in need of control is one that continues.[57]

FIGURE 11.5: Michael Eric Dyson

Sex therapist Marty Kline strongly disagrees, writing:

> If you want to see racial stereotypes in porn, you'll find them: white women rammed with huge black erections. Black women thrilled to blow white musclemen. Considering that all these portrayals are sexual fantasy, anyone who calls those racial stereotypes needs to look at their own racism, not the viewers'.[58]

The defense of porn as fantasy is one of the more common defenses made, but certainly not a defense that would be made about mainstream fictional TV shows and movies if racist caricatures or themes were present. But apparently Kline does not view films entitled "I Can't Believe you sucked a Negro, 7" (there are 10 installments in all) with the added caption, "Now with more dark-skinned Negroes in every box," as promoting racist stereotypes or as simply being racist in nature.[59] Many African-American scholars point out that a central theme in D.W. Griffith's film *Birth of a Nation* (1915) was the depiction of black men as being sexually insatiable, particularly in their desire for white women.[60] [61] Georgetown University professor Michael Eric Dyson states:

> Few images have caused more anxiety in the American sexual psyche than the black male embodiment of phallic prowess. A sordid range of stereotype, jealousies, and fears have been developed around black men wielding their sexuality in ways that are perceived as untoward, unruly, or uncontrolled.[62]

While Dyson is not specifically referring to pornography, the longstanding racist stereotype about black, male sexuality is a stereotype that is exploited throughout porn-marketing of black men as out-of-control "Negroes" who are not just hypersexual, but aggressively so. In the award-winning documentary film *Hip-Hop: Beyond Beats & Rhymes*, Dyson points out that racist stereotypes harm both black men and black women.[63] When any group has to fight to correct ignorant generalizations, the struggle to achieve dignity, respect, and occupational success can be all the more difficult. With respect to black men and women in America, Dyson argues:

> From the very beginning of the black presence on American soil, stereotypes have distorted relations between the races, including those involving sex. Black females were the nurturing Mammy, the sarcastic sapphire, the promiscuous Jezebel, and now, in our day, the welfare queen, and the hoochie mama.[64]

FIGURE 11.6: Anti-porn feminist Gail Dines

The racist caricature of black men as sex-crazed rapists was known for generation as "the brute" archetype, which characterized black men as "savage, violent male predators who target helpless victims, especially white women."[65] Much of porn today exploits this very caricature in the name of sexual fantasy, as though this explanation redeems the racist content, while other racist caricatures involving Asian, Latino, and Middle Eastern people go largely ignored or critics themselves are denounced as being racist for pointing out the racist content.

THOUGHT BOX

Why do you think pornography has been able to "get away with" openly racist content? Why hasn't public condemnation been as pronounced as it would be if mainstream films featured content of this kind? Is it simply a matter of not enough people knowing about the racism in porn, since porn does not compete with the sales of mainstream films, or is there something more going on? Does the racism in porn turn some people on? Is there a sexual power-dynamic at play that makes racist porn attractive to some consumers? Is it just that porn consumers are seldom social critics? Or do you agree with Kline that the porn described above is not racist in nature?

Amateur Porn

In the 1980s, with increased access to what were called camcorders (early video cameras for home use), people began videotaping their sexual activities. Most of these videos were used by the couples who filmed them or were sold at local video rental stores in the amateur adult section. Later that decade, Homegrown Video was launched by Greg Swaim as a venture that distributed homemade sex videos.[66] Homegrown was eventually sold to adult film performer Farrell Timlake (aka Tim Lake in porn videos) who turned amateur porn into a lucrative industry.[67] Many of the better-selling amateur videos created porn stars, including Stephanie Swift, Melissa Hill, Rayveness, and Meggan Mallone.[68] By 1998, Homegrown hired Spike Goldberg who, with Timlake, created New Destiny Internet Group. In 2013, Goldberg was named CEO of Homegrown Video.[69]

Today, amateur porn has taken a huge chunk of the internet pornography market. In 2008, *ABC News* covered the story of several amateur pornographers who started their own pornographic websites to make extra money.[70] Increasingly, people began uploading their home videos to sites such as XTube.com, a video sharing site that charges clients to view short, homemade films. The challenge for many pornographers is to make a profit in a market where free porn proliferates the internet. XTube.com uses the hook of allowing audiences to get to know the models, form relationships, and play a role in directing the sex acts filmmakers produce.[71] Justin Arilan, sales and support manager for XTube.com, claims that his site earns between $140,000 and $160,000 per month.[72] While internet porn is estimated to generate $14 billion per year, the amateur market has cut into the profits enjoyed by the professional porn companies and continues to be a major presence in the online porn world.[73]

Some who have researched amateur porn argue that it tends to be more egalitarian in content than professionally produced pornography, due in part because the couple or couples in the videos are married or in a relationship.[74] Another common notion is that more egalitarian content in amateur porn is a result of democratizing porn such that a normalizing effect on the content of porn is produced as couples making porn view other amateur porn to get ideas on how to shape content.[75] Other researchers argue that scholars are able to "use amateur porn as a lens through which to examine cultural production and consumption, labor and sexual commodities, and may yield further insights on its individual, social, and economic impact."[76] In essence, amateur porn is viewed by some as a visual laboratory into the sexual interests and fantasies of ordinary working and middle class people, and they claim that the sexual interests of ordinary people are fairly egalitarian.

Not everyone agrees. Writing for *Feminist Current*, self-described anti-pornography activist writer Jonah Mix begins by quoting the abstract of a Canadian study that concluded porn users hold egalitarian views about sex:

> Composite variables were used to test the hypothesis that pornography users would hold attitudes that were more supportive of gender non-egalitarianism than nonusers of pornography. Results [showed that] pornography users held more egalitarian attitudes—toward women in positions of power, toward abortion—than nonusers of pornography.[77]

Mix notes that the study defines a porn user as "anyone who has viewed an X-rated film in the preceding year," and that this designation yields vacuous the definition of porn users, while also dates itself since the expression "X-rated films" no longer applies. He states, "It's an unacceptably broad standard for declaring people porn users. Under this metric, someone who masturbates to *Facial Abuse* twice a day is counted as equal with a dude who clicked a sidebar ad for *Girls Gone Wild* nine months ago." Beyond this problem, Mix adds that those who conducted the surveys for the study defined 'sexism' as to make only the most "cartoonish patriarchs" capable of sexism and misogyny. Mix's point is that one can believe women should have a right to abortion, should not be judged negatively for having careers outside of the home, and still hold sexist and misogynist views. Heterosexual amateur porn, like heterosexual professional commercial porn, is based overwhelmingly on a male-centric script. In fact, in a 2014 study of pornographic content, researchers found that amateur porn actually contained more gender inequality at the expense of women than did professional pornography.[78] One example of the male-centricity of mainstream heterosexual pornography is the ratio of fellatio to cunnilingus, where 84% of clips depict a woman performing oral sex on a man while only 37% of clips depict a woman receiving oral sex from either a man or woman.[79] For male porn users, they may feel that there is no inconsistency in their belief that women have the right to careers and that they should cum on women's faces as part of what they believe to be an egalitarian sex fantasy.

Amateur porn also spawned in the late 2000s what became known as ***revenge porn***, which are sex clips released online, through cell phones, text messages, email, and social media without the consent of those in the clip, usually in response to a relationship breakup in an attempt to humiliate an ex-partner.[80] Sociologist and criminologist Michael Salter argues that much of revenge porn is gender-biased against women by playing on historical sexual double-standards for men and women.[81] Salter maintains that revenge porn is part of a larger pattern of sexual violence to "contest women's parity of participation in the public sphere and the cultural excuse and victim blaming that facilitates this."[82] In fact, estimates have placed women as victims of revenge porn in more than 95% of reported cases.[83] The non-consensual nature of revenge porn and the shame that it is aimed at generating is the key to understanding how contemporary cultures reinforce a "pejorative view of women who engage in sexual behaviour that is considered immodest or unfeminine and even an implicit endorsement of their punishment by others."[84] In the United States, tort, privacy, and copyright laws have been invoked as legal remedies against people who release revenge porn, and slightly more than half of all U.S. states now have laws expressly applicable to revenge porn, including some laws that prohibit the distribution of sexually explicit photographs and films by any person "knowing that he is not licensed or privileged to do so and without the subjects' consent."[85] As a result of legislation in some states, a number of revenge porn sites have been taken down from the internet, and criminal convictions have been upheld and prison terms administered for violators.[86]

Gendered Porn Usage, Sexual Violence, and the "Pornification" of America

In a survey of 4,000 women and 4,000 men conducted by *Cosmopolitan Magazine*, researchers published the following findings with respect to pornography usage among men and women (93% of respondents were heterosexual).[87] On the question, "How often do you watch porn?" respondents reported:

TABLE 11.1

	Daily	Once every few days	Not that often
Men:	32.5%	56.5%	11.0%
Women:	3.8%	25.0%	71.2%

The survey also revealed the most popular traits men look for in the women in porn scenes in descending order:

- Youth
- Large Breasts
- Skinny
- Large Butt
- "Milf" (mom I would like to fuck)

Two-thirds of the men in the survey also reported that they orgasm faster from watching porn than they do from real-life sex, and 85% of the surveyed men also claimed that they would ask a partner to do something they saw in porn.[88] Researchers concluded that many women are not as put off by pornography as initially expected, but that viewing habits and post-viewing expectations were fairly different between women and men.[89] What is impossible to answer with such a simple consumption-based set of questions is the extent to which porn usage infiltrates the behaviors of those who consume it on a regular basis. However, the survey does confirm one common view about porn consumers: men greatly outnumber women in their consumption of porn and particularly in terms of the regularity of usage.

The question of whether or to what extent porn usage affects men's views about sex and women can be difficult to answer. These questions have been around for a long time and have been taken up by the courts. Justices Black's and Douglas's dissent to the

Supreme Court decision in *Roth v. United States* (1957) summarizes one of the main criticisms made by those who defend pornography:

> To allow the state to step in and punish mere speech or publication that the judge or jury thinks has an undesirable impact on thoughts but that is not shown to be part of unlawful action is drastically to curtail the First Amendment.[90]

While this dissenting opinion has to do with constitutional protections, the intent expresses the same concern when someone argues that there is no evidence that watching porn leads men to sexually assault or rape women. The complication is that if one is looking for causal connections, the search is probably hopeless. But if one is softening the claim to say that porn usage *contributes* to men's sexual violence against women, the question now falls on what we mean by 'contributes'? There can be a plurality of contributing factors that bring a man to commit a sexual offense and in this case, it can be nearly impossible to weigh each of the contributing factors for degree of influence. Other factors may be altogether *post hoc* in nature, meaning "thought to be causal or contributing factors when in fact they are not," although in the case of men using pornography to masturbate on a regular basis, a prima facie observation can be made that men's views may be skewed in favor of the perspective that women want sex most or all of the time, and that resistance by women is a form of flirting, a common theme in pornography. In critical thinking courses, a common influence to belief-formation is known as ***the availability error***, which states that perception can be influenced when one immerses oneself in a particular type of media.[91] For instance, one who immerses himself in news media may adopt the view that the incidence of violence in society is much higher than it actually is due to his saturated viewing of media that reports violence. Media analyst George Gerbner famously termed this phenomenon ***the mean-world syndrome***, which occurs when a person saturates himself in mass media and draws the conclusion that the world is much more dangerous than it is.[92] Apply this concept to repetitive porn usage and we might be able to label a parallel phenomenon, ***the porn world syndrome***.

University of Michigan law professor and noted feminist scholar Catharine MacKinnon argues that pornography is more than words and images: "We are talking about acts of discrimination: sex-based coercion, force, assault, and trafficking in sexual subordination."[93] MacKinnon contends that depictions of subordination contribute to actual subordination, which influences the ways that women are treated at home and in the workplace. The *Antipornography Civil Rights Ordinance*, coauthored by MacKinnon and feminist writer Andrea Dworkin, proposed to identify pornography as a violation of women's civil rights and opened the door to lawsuits against producers of pornography. In adjudicating MacKinnon's and Dworkin's ordinance, the Seventh Circuit Court ruled in *American Booksellers v. Hudnut* (1985) that,

> [P]ornography is central in creating and maintaining sex as a basis of discrimination. Pornography is a systematic practice of exploitation and subordination based on sex which differentially harms women. The bigotry and contempt it produces, with the acts of aggression it fosters, harm women's opportunity for equality and rights [of all kinds.][94]

MacKinnon clarifies, writing, "Our argument is not that ideas and actions are causally connected, although they no doubt are. It is that pornography is factually connected in many ways to a whole array of tangible human injuries."[95]

Others maintain that there is not enough evidence to support the claim that porn contributes to men's sexual violence against women. Journalist Michael Castleman argues that if pornography causes harm to women, we should have seen increases in rates of rape and sexual assault starting in the late 1990s when internet porn made pornography more

FIGURE 11.7: Catharine MacKinnon

readily available to consumers. Instead, he argues, since 1995, rates of rape have fallen by 44% and ends his piece by stating:

> The evidence clearly shows that from a social welfare perspective, porn causes no measurable harm. In fact, as porn viewing has soared, rates of syphilis, gonorrhea, teen sex, teen births, divorce, and rape have all substantially declined. Perhaps mental health professionals should *encourage* men to view it.[96]

Some of the down-trend in STD transmission rates and teen pregnancy may be explained as the result of improved sex education courses in middle school and high school in many school districts around the nation, even though abstinence-only sex education continues to be found in more conservative regions of America. In addition, instances of sexual assault and rape are notoriously difficult to document with any degree of accuracy since it is now widely recognized that rape is greatly underreported.[97] [98] Some have speculated that rates of sex-based crime have diminished in the wake of increased incarceration, including the implementation of three-strike laws, with Texas showing the greatest downturn in crime in the wake of rising incarceration rates.[99] Others, however, point out that there are numerous factors that influence rates of crime and that rates of incarceration do not account, solely or even primarily, for the downturn in crime witnessed over the past two decades.[100] Still, Castleman's objection that sex crimes lessened at a time that porn usage rose is one that is widely used in an attempt to debunk there being a connection between porn viewing and sexual assault.

A similar and abiding idea from those who defend pornography is that porn usage by men is cathartic, that pornography can reduce sexual assault by giving men a release for their pent-up sexual desires. Sexologist Milton Diamond of the University of Hawaii sees a positive side to porn usage by men, stating, "Usually after somebody masturbates and they have their orgasm, they're not as interested in sex as they were 10 minutes before, so I think it dissipates the interest to go out and do anything illegal."[101] Diamond claims that research into sexual violence supports this view, arguing, "Rates of sexual violence [usually] go down after pornography becomes more prevalent."[102] In "Pornography, Public Acceptance and Sex Related Crime: A Review," Diamond argues that wherever pornography has increased in availability, sex crimes have either decreased or not increased.[103] In fact, Diamond notes, according to FBI and Department of Justice statistics, the incidence of rape declined markedly from 1975 to 1995, the very decades in which porn transitioned from theater and video tape access to internet access.[104] Diamond admits that porn, like any freedom such as the freedom to bear arms, can be misused, but that causal connections have not been established and that the misuse by some should not restrict the access of the many.[105]

Psychologist Christopher Ferguson of Texas A&M University agrees with Diamond, noting the drop in rates of rape since the 1960s and that between 1980 and 2000, the states within the U.S. that had the least access to the internet, and so the least access to pornography, experienced a 53% increase in rape incidence, while states with the most internet access experienced a 27% drop in the number of reported rapes.[106] Other researchers have attempted to disconnect the idea that porn usage causes harm to the viewer. In 2009, psychologist Michael P. Twohig of Utah State University conducted a study of 299 undergraduate students and found that a key to understanding whether young people considered their porn usage to be problematic had to do with their moral or religious upbringing rather than there being anything wrong with their mental states.[107] Twohig argues that for those who develop problematic internet pornography viewing behaviors or attitudes, the problems result more from an internal struggle with their urges to view porn than from viewing porn itself.[108] In these cases, Twohig recommends what is termed **acceptance and commitment therapy**, where subjects are encouraged to allow thoughts to come and go without struggling with them, to be more "in the moment" and receptive to what is important to oneself in those moments, and setting goals that are carried out responsibly.[109] The view is that learning to release socialized reactions to pornography will help users absolve themselves from guilt and shame that are at the root of self-reported harms.

Other scholars argue that porn defenders like Castleman and Diamond greatly oversimplify the consequences of habitual porn usage, that sexual violence is only one type of harm that ensues from repetitive porn usage. University of Alabama professors of law Richard Delgado and Jean Stefancic argue, "Like racial depiction, which is deeply embedded in culture, the harm of pornography is rendered invisible and makes depiction of female subjugation resistant to regulation."[110] The tangible effects of embedding pornographic missives into mainstream, popular culture may be found both in the ways that men speak about and treat women, and the ways in which many women treat themselves. In what actress and author Rashida Jones termed *the pornification of everything*,[111] critics argue that pornography creates a mainstream culture of sexually objectifying women where women gain value primarily through what Gail Dines terms "their fuckability."[112] This, argues Dines, creates a dilemma for women; they can either cave into the pressure of a pornified culture to do whatever is in their power to be "fuckable" in the eyes of men, or they can choose to be invisible.[113]

In addition to the pressure placed on women to look sexually appealing and sexually available to men, others argue that a culture of pornography conditions some men to view women as having worth only in terms of their sexuality, which contributes to some of the glass ceilings women have experienced when trying to advance in professional careers. Texas Christian University professor Ryan J. Burns reports that through the administration of surveys, men who admitted to habitual porn usage also admit to viewing women in stereotypical feminine gender roles, while persistently describing women in sexual terms.[114] By accepting stereotypical feminine gender roles, men commonly attribute as *natural*, supportive roles to women and leadership roles to men. If it turns out that men dominate the decision-making process of hiring and professional advancement in certain professions, and if some proportion of these men are habitual porn users, the fact that they will view women in traditional feminine, supportive roles, as Burns notes, creates a prima facie case for the idea that porn usage by these men reinforces glass ceilings in male-dominated professions.

Men and Porn Addiction?

One of the concerns about habitual porn usage by men is the worry that some men form a porn addiction much like some people become alcoholics. The analogy between porn viewing and alcohol consumption maintains that for some people it does not become a problem, while for others, it controls and hampers their ability to lead productive lives. Whether porn usage leads to addiction in some, however, is hotly debated. On the view that for some men porn addiction is a very real problem, UCLA research psychologist and author Rory Reid clarifies the problem that some men have with pornography:

> A lot of times people misconstrue pornography problems in the sense that they cast pornography problems as somebody is horny or has a sensational sexual appetite. Although pornography involves sex and sexual behavior, in my experience clinically, pornography problems are no more about sex than an eating disorder is about food.[115]

For those men who develop a problem with pornography, states Reid, **two different patterns emerge:**

> One pattern is they actually start to engage in a lot of hyper sexual behavior with their romantic partners. They start to demand additional types of sexual behaviors ... Another pattern is that they have a diminished sexual appetite. That happens for a couple of reasons. One is because of the variety of pornography on the Internet, they become desensitized to the sexual arousal in general. They are masturbating, they are satisfied, they don't really feel the craving, the urge, the desire to be close and intimate with their spouses in a sexual way. There tends to be a withdrawal and disconnect from people in general, especially on an emotional level.[116]

The argument goes that for many porn users, quick sexual gratification becomes a substitute for intimacy. The repetition of this practice of porn-fueled masturbation creates a habit of behavior that is difficult for some men to break. A result that follows from this habit of behavior is that sexual interest and the desire for emotional intimacy shift away from a partner onto the mediated images of pornography. In counseling sessions, those who identified as compulsive porn users reported that they developed problems experiencing intimacy with their partners and spent more time cruising internet porn sites searching for clips that matched their sexual fantasies.[117]

FIGURE 11.8: Rory Reid

While not terming problematic porn usage an addiction, further research corroborated a theme of intimacy issues with men, with research subjects reporting two central and reoccurring problems (1) that habitual porn users felt "smothered" by their partners, and, (2) that these same individuals neglected "common relationship maintenance."[118] Kinsey Institute research fellow Heather Rupp argues that, "men prefer novelty, while women are more interested in stable dynamics," about which University of Indiana professor Paul Wright states, "Men still have instinctual preferences today because those preferences served a reproductive purpose for their ancestors. Men's modern environment has changed dramatically, but their evolved sexual preferences have not."[119] This evolved desire for sexual variety in men, according to evolutionary psychologists, explains why men enjoy viewing porn: men can sexually connect in virtual reality with hundreds of different women without committing emotionally to any of them.[120] This explanation does not account for millions of men who do not appear to desire sexual variety, but research psychologist Scott A. McGreal argues that those men who prefer "unrestricted women who do not demand sexual exclusivity" also tend to find the women on internet pornography websites more sexually attractive than their wives.[121] The fact that these men married in the first place may have more to do with cultural or family expectations than an authentic desire to marry. Evolutionary psychologists sometimes point to gendered sexual fantasies as lending support to the notion that males and females are looking for different things in partners. In one study of 307 college students (182 female, 125 male), in what they termed *sexual psychologies*, researchers discovered predictable contrasts in sexual fantasy responses along gendered lines.[122] Men were more sexually responsive to visual images and partner variety, while women were more interested in character traits.[123] It is important to note that women were not disinterested in men's physical appearances, but that more women expressed a sexual or romantic interest beyond visual representation that was often lacking in men's responses. These gendered sexual psychologies allegedly explain why sexual intimacy with men is less common than with women, and why some men will prefer emotionally unattached sexual relationships via pornographic surrogacy.

But at what point does porn usage become a problem? The Kinsey Institute reports from a study that 9% of porn users who tried to stop viewing and using porn were unsuccessful in doing so.[124] This seems to be a small number, but according to the National Institute on Alcohol Abuse and Alcoholism, approximately 9% of men who drink alcohol have what they term an Alcohol Use Disorder (AUD).[125] In fact, men meet the criteria for alcohol dependency adopted by the Centers for Disease Control at more than twice the rate of women.[126] It is also the case that men form what the National Institutes of Health term *pathological gambling behaviors* at more than twice the rate of women.[127] These gendered differences in addiction and obsession rates may be due to any number of factors, but one theory is that men's brains are wired for addiction in greater number than for women.[128] If this is so, it makes sense that a product made mainly by men for men that has a measurable influence on the pleasure centers of the brain would create more compulsive use in men than women. What counts as pathological behavior is not universally recognized, but is often connected to one's ability to function adequately in society. A common list of pathology indicators includes suffering, danger to self, lack of control, unpredictable behavior, inability to hold down a job, inability to interact with others, and violations of commonly held social standards of behavior.[129] A person can obviously view and use porn without crossing these lines, but this does not mean that everyone who views and uses porn avoids crossing these lines, just as not everyone who consumes alcohol is able to avoid crossing the lines into alcoholism.

Reid reports that for many of the men who experience difficulties in their lives due to porn usage, seeking help is often a result of an ultimatum from a girlfriend or a romantic partner.[130] Not unlike an intervention orchestrated by family members and loved ones in the case of substance abuse, the person struggling with porn use can be highly resistant to treatment. At the University of Texas, Dallas, the student counseling center cites indicators that one has developed a psychological dependency on porn that include:

- The use of pornography consumes your thinking. When you are not using pornography, you think about it frequently and anticipate when you will use it again. You spend increasing amounts of time using pornography.
- Your use of pornography has negative consequences in your life. For example, you may neglect responsibilities or become less effective in your job or in academics. You might spend too much money on pornography or put yourself in dangerous situations you would not normally be in due to the pornography or sexual addiction. You may have been caught using pornography in inappropriate places such as work or a campus computer lab.
- Your use of pornography causes problems in your intimate relationships, such as creating emotional distance between people you love or causing those in a relationship with you to feel neglected. You may lose relationships due to the pornography.[131]

Like other dependencies, pathology is often gauged, as noted above, by the negative effects exposure and repeated usage have in the lives of consumers, and these effects are commonly revealed through self-reports or partner reports.

Part of the controversy over porn addiction is whether neuroscience confirms or refutes it. In the case of a physical substance like alcohol, biochemical reactions can be traced in the brain in what are termed neuroadaptations and neural deficits that commonly accompany alcohol dependence.[132] There are also common behavioral indicators associated with alcohol addiction that include a compulsive preoccupation with obtaining alcohol, loss of control over functioning, the development of tolerance, and impaired social and occupational functioning.[133] Like other addictive disorders, alcoholism is also characterized by a "chronic vulnerability to relapse after cessation of drinking."[134] Neurologists often use functional magnetic resonance imaging (fMRI) to map blood flow to certain parts of the brain to better understand specific cognitive tasks performed under the influence of alcohol or other substances.[135] A central question for those who claim porn addiction is real is whether similar neuro-mapping and behavioral indicators are found in the person who appears to have developed a porn-dependency. Neuropsychiatrist Valerie Voon argues that porn use creates similar brain patterns found in alcoholics, observing that the ventral striatum is a structure of the brain that processes reward, motivation, and pleasure.[136] Of this brain structure, Voon states,

> When an alcoholic sees an ad for a drink, their brain will light up in a certain way and they will be stimulated in a certain way. We are seeing this same kind of activity in users of pornography.[137]

Neuroscientist Eric Nestler agrees, writing,

> evidence indicates that the VTA-NAc pathway mediates, at least in part, the acute positive emotional effects of natural rewards, such as food, sex and social interactions. [This] region has also been implicated in so-called '**natural addictions**' (that is, compulsive consumption for natural rewards) such as sexual addictions.[138]

Nora Volkow, head of the National Institute on Drug Abuse (NIDA), in agreement with Nestler, adds that pornography addiction should be subsumed under a group of addictions known as **natural addictions**, which include gambling and food addictions.[139] What makes some addictions "natural" is that the addictive behavior is created by the release of chemicals already existing in the brain such as dopamine, opioid peptides, glutamate, and serotonin.[140]

Neuroscientist William Struthers of Wheaton College argues that the brain "under the influence of porn" behaves much like the brain under the influence of other substances, writing,

> The brain has natural pathways which are involved in reinforcement and pleasure which are activated through natural drivers like eating, drinking and sex. Neurologically, porn hijacks this natural system in the same way that drugs do, by tricking the brain into thinking that it is getting food, drink or sex.[141]

In the case of eating, for example, the ingestion of sugar can cause signs of addiction through binge-eating, which creates a 10% sucrose solution repeatedly releasing dopamine in the nucleus accumbens of the brain.[142] What happens in this case is that the feeling of appetite satiety is postponed, creating a cycle of excessive eating.[143] The argument for porn addiction runs on parallel points. During sexual activity, or simply sexual arousal, the amygdala, nucleus accumbens, ventral tegmental area (VTA), cerebellum, and pituitary gland is stimulated by a surge of brain chemistry.[144]

Neurosurgeons Donald L. Hilton and Clark Watts argue that in the case of addiction, a well-documented cerebral dysfunction takes place, whereby there is damage to the "braking system" of the brain.[145] This damage to the braking systems are termed *hypofrontal syndromes* and work as a progressive atrophy of the frontal lobes of the brain as seen in fMRI scans over time.[146] Hypofrontal syndromes are found in those suffering from compulsive overeating, but are also found in the brains of those who suffer from compulsive sex disorder.[147] Hilton and Watts argue that critics do not deny the existence of compulsive eating disorders because the effects of overeating can be seen in the obese person, but that critics abound when neuroscientists make claims of compulsive sex disorders, since the effects are not visible to the naked eye.[148] Hilton and Watts continue by arguing that compulsive internet pornography use has been found to create similar hypofrontal syndromes and has been documented in a recent Mayo Clinic report as showing improvement through naltrexone treatment based on

> cellular adaptations in the (pornography) addict's PFC result in increased salience of drug-associated stimuli, decreased salience of non-drug stimuli, and decreased interest in pursuing goal-directed activities central to survival. [149]

Hilton and Watts claim that the majority of porn addiction skeptics dismiss the alleged addiction by claiming it is trumped up by religious and moralistic zealots, but that the neuroscientific evidence is rapidly amassing in support of porn addiction. They write, "Just as we consider food addiction as having a biologic basis, with no moral overlay or value-laden terminology, it is time we looked at pornography and other forms of sexual addiction with the same objective eye."[150]

Health systems consultant Rick Nauert rejects the notion of porn addiction, stating, "Describing someone as a porn addict may make for catchy headlines, but in reality, there is no strong scientific research that shows such addictions actually exist."[151] Psychologist David Ley agrees and adds that labeling porn viewing as a pathology ignores the benefits that may flow from porn usage:

> Viewing pornography can improve attitudes towards sexuality, increase the quality of life and variety of sexual behaviors, and increase pleasure in long-term relationships. It provides an outlet for sexual behaviors or desires, and its consumption or availability has been associated with a decrease in sex offenses, especially child molestation.[152]

This is the familiar **catharsis defense** that suggests masturbating to porn will alleviate one's desire to rape women and sexually molest children. According to this defense, allowing pedophiles to view and masturbate to porn should reduce cases of child sexual abuse. In addition, Ley argues that viewing porn, like having sex itself, increases pleasure and since, he claims, there is nothing wrong with pleasure, de facto, there is nothing wrong with porn.

Sex therapist Robert Weiss responds that Ley's work ignores a great deal of scientific evidence that supports both sex addiction and porn obsession, while willfully overlooking the suffering that many experience who enter counseling to come to terms with their porn usage.[153] Weiss claims that one of Ley's biggest problems is his rigid insistence that orgasm is always good, therefore anything that leads to orgasm is necessarily good.[154] What Ley does not understand, argues Weiss, is that sex addiction is not about gaining orgasms just as gambling obsessions are not simply about winning or losing. Like drug use, Weiss claims, the addict seeks to ward off a host of problems that might include loneliness, low self-esteem, anxiety, depression, and other triggers that the individual is battling. Weiss argues that viewing compulsive porn use as a healthy desire for pleasure is to greatly oversimplify a much more complicated psychology underlying those who suffer from obsessive porn disorders.

As mentioned above, psychologist Michael Twohig raises another common concern about claims of porn addiction when he argues that those who believe porn use can lead to porn addition are fueled by sex-hang-ups brought on by religious and moral socialization. If one is socialized to connect sexual activity and morality as necessary partners, one is more inclined to view sex as being problematic and in need of restraint and regulation. Evolutionary psychologist Michael Ruse agrees and notes that a conservative religious upbringing is more likely to produce moral judgments about sex, and particularly toward sexual acts that do not or cannot lead to procreation.[155] Presumably, porn viewing revolves around the goal of masturbation, which cannot lead to procreation and so becomes a prime candidate for moralizing.

Ley believes there is a further problem in labeling certain men 'porn addicts,' stating, "We need better methods to help people who struggle with the high frequency use of visual sexual stimuli, without pathologizing them or their use thereof."[156] Ley appears to acknowledge the fact that some porn consumers "struggle" with "high frequency use of visual sexual stimuli," or habitual porn usage, but insists that we should refrain from labeling this struggle a problem. Yet it is unclear why these individuals would seek help for something that is not considered to be a problem. Furthermore, if compulsive porn usage is not considered to be a problem, it may be more difficult to generate funding for the research into something that is not considered pathological.

Cambridge University conducted a study to see whether porn addiction mirrors drug addiction in the brain with the added interest of seeing whether or to what extent compulsive porn usage was negatively affecting the lives of users.[157] A core finding of the study was that the brain activity of compulsive porn users differs very little from the brain activity found in drug addicts.[158] But lead researcher Valerie Voon also argued, "There is no question these people are suffering. Their behavior is having a negative impact on multiple levels of function, especially social function; they are unable to control their behaviors."[159] Still, some consider porn addiction to be better addressed as a compulsion. The distinction between the two is normally considered to be a matter of dependency. A compulsion is considered to be a strong urge to do something as part of a larger part of the addictive process, while an addiction is an indulgence considered to be required by the victim to cope with life.[160] If this definition of addiction is correct, with plenty of disagreement, problematic porn usage would probably not be considered an addiction and instead would be classified as a compulsion.

In 2016, Utah governor Gary Herbert signed a resolution declaring porn usage to be a public health crisis.[161] The resolution identifies several individual, public, and societal health harms resulting from porn usage including,

- low self-esteem and body image in adolescents
- the hypersexualization of teens and prepubescent children
- the normalization of violence, abuse, and rape
- an increased demand for sex trafficking, prostitution, and child pornography
- the sexual objectification of women, which "teaches girls they are to be used and teaches boys to be users"
- impacts on brain development and functioning, including "deviant sexual arousal" and difficulty forming relationships[162]

The resolution draws the conclusion that porn usage is linked to a lessening of desire in young men to marry, a dissatisfaction in men who are married, and increased rates of infidelity, as well as claiming that the dependency some men develop toward porn usage is so intense, professional help is required to get these men away from their porn usage.[163] Critics of the resolution have argued that the science is not reliable enough to draw the generalized claims being made by supporters of the resolution.[164] Beyond the concern about science, critics also note that anti-porn pundits refuse to provide proper sex education to offset whatever harms may come about through repetitive porn usage so that boys and young men are filling this void with pornography.[165]

THOUGHT BOX

After reading some of the arguments for and against the existence of porn addiction, what are your views? Conduct some additional research and see who you believe is making the better argument. Do you feel that the analogy to alcoholism and other substance addictions is appropriate? If you don't believe 'addiction' is the correct identification, do you believe there is a point where habitual porn usage may cause harm to a person's life, and, if so, what sorts of circumstances would qualify as porn usage becoming a problem for someone?

The Feminist Porn Debate

Covering the feminist debate surrounding pornography is not to divert the focus away from men and pornography; rather, in many respects it highlights this connection by reinvigorating the debate about porn usage, free will, fantasy, what counts as sexual liberation versus sexual exploitation, the gender dynamics found in most mainstream porn, the intersection of patriarchy and porn, and men's attempts to control and define women's sexuality.

At the same time, the subject of pornography splits feminist writers, some of whom laud porn as part of a libertarian view about sex, women's bodies, and women's choices, calling themselves *sex-positive feminists*, while others criticize porn for the many reasons cited in earlier sections.[168] Today, a pronounced split between anti-porn and pro-porn feminists remains. Both sides emphasize that they are pro-sex, but disagree about the

FIGURE 11.9: Pornography is the theory; rape is the practice. ~Feminist author Robin Morgan[166]

FIGURE 11.10: Pornography benefits women, both personally and politically. ~Feminist author Wendy McElroy[167]

production, usage, and consequences of pornography. The pro-porn feminist group *Our Porn Ourselves* composed a manifesto that reads:

- Anti-porn feminists do not represent the women of Our Porn Ourselves.
- Anti-porn feminists do not represent all feminists.
- It is wrong to tell a woman how to enjoy her sexuality, to do so is to deny a woman's right over her sexuality.

- For a woman to try to control another woman's sexuality is to create a world that is harmful to women.
- The women of Our Porn Ourselves enjoy pornography.
- Women and men should not be judged for watching and enjoying pornography.
- Pornography is simply a sex aid enjoyed by women and men whether heterosexual or homosexual; those who watch pornography are not sick, and porn does not cause men to abuse their wives, rape, or become pedophiles.
- Women are adults who can make up their own minds about whether to watch and enjoy porn or not.
- The women of Our Porn Ourselves need to be heard.[169]

The pro-pornography feminist position usually revolves around several main points: that scolding women who enjoy porn is a patronizing attitude toward women that does not respect women's agency. In addition, the point is often made that pornography has not been shown to lead to harm against women, and, as we read above, may produce a cathartic effect for some men. Finally, porn defenders generally view porn critics as prudish moralizers who consider those who enjoy porn to be sexual deviants.

One of the more prominent pro-porn feminists is self-described individualist, anarchist Wendy McElroy who states, "Pro-sex feminists retain a consistent interpretation of the principle 'a woman's body, a woman's right' and insist that every peaceful choice a woman makes with her own body must be accorded full legal protection, if not respect."[170] McElroy views the successes of the anti-pornography movement as wins for censorship that often carry negative consequences for women:

> When the Canadian Supreme Court decided (1992) to protect women by restricting the importation of pornography, one of the first victims was a lesbian/gay bookstore ... among the books seized by Canadian customs were two books by Andrea Dworkin, *Pornography: Men Possessing Women* and *Women Hating*.[171]

When confronting the specific points anti-pornography feminists make regarding porn's degradation and harm to women, McElroy argues that concepts like 'degrading' are subjective and that the research into alleged links between porn usage and sexual violence is unreliable.[172] Instead, McElroy insists that pornography benefits women in the following ways:[173]

- It provides sexual information to women about possibilities, including those sexual possibilities that women have been told are taboo most of their lives.
- It allows women to indulge their sexual fantasies, including rape fantasies.
- It allows women to enjoy what they have been told should be shameful to them throughout their lives.
- It can be therapeutic, particularly for those who do not have a partner.
- It promotes sexual freedom to women, a demographic that men have attempted to control sexually throughout history.
- It may have a cathartic effect on men who have violent urges toward women.
- It helps legitimize female sex-workers who are stigmatized by society, often find work conditions unsafe, and find it difficult to obtain legal remedies to work-related disputes.

A key to McElroy's defense of pornography is the view that porn helps women gain autonomy from the patriarchal structures that throughout history have bound women to men. The feminist side of the 1960s sexual revolution involved the reclamation of female sexuality away from the control of men. Those women who were viewed as sexually uninhibited were inevitably labeled 'sluts' and 'harlots' as part of the larger practice of controlling women's sexuality, a practice that can be seen throughout time and particularly within the regulations of Western religions. McElroy views porn as women's opportunity to break away from male tyranny to discover and celebrate their own sexual lives.

Anti-porn feminist Maya Shlayan responds, "Porn is not compatible with feminism," adding, Lies about anti-porn feminists—that we're in bed with the religious Right (we aren't), that we snub our noses at the women in pornography (we don't), or that we support censorship (also not)—have painted the feminist anti-porn movement as something rigid, outdated, and anti-sex.[174] Shlayan views as ridiculous the claim that porn offers women a daring, adventurous form of freedom and quotes porn-industry veteran Vanessa Belmond, "I never met any woman that had a professional career and left it to go into porn just for fun. Many got into it because of financial desperation."[175] Shlayan's criticism attempts to disrupt the defense that going into pornography is for many women a free and authentic choice. There are often a host of background circumstances that draw women to the porn industry, just as there are a host of circumstances that account for why many people accept jobs they hate, which is usually due to financial need. Still, this is not to say that all women in the porn industry hate their work or feel trapped in a degrading career from which they are unable to free themselves. In fact, some female porn performers claim to enjoy their work, including porn star Asa Akira who states, "I'm an exhibitionist; I'm hypersexual," and views her work as "the perfect job."[176]

A key to understanding anti-pornography feminist responses to pro-porn feminists is found in the insistence that it is a myth to suggest that in order to be sex-positive, you must be pro-pornography. Robert Jensen, in the film *The Bro Code: How Contemporary Culture Creates Sexist Men*, argues that pornography constrains sexual liberty by offering very narrow, formulaic sexual scripts that have the effect of creating a normative range of behaviors that instruct the viewer what "good sex" is supposed to look like, while overwhelmingly placing men in positions of sexual dominance over women.[177] While there are forms of pornography that place women in the role of having sexual dominance over men, these forms do not compete economically with the more common themes of a man blackmailing a woman into having sex, a professor having sex with a student, a man forcing a woman to pay a debt through having sex with him, and other scripts where the man exerts power over a woman in the scene by coercing her into having sex.[178] The fact that these forms of pornography are commercially profitable speaks to some men's sexual desires to exert power over women. Rape-fantasy porn, for instance, which is another popular genre of porn, is often excused as courting women's fantasies, rather than the notion that men desire to see women raped.[179] The context often hinges on whom is in the position of dominance and whom is in the position of submission and how these depictions influence those viewing pornography.

THOUGHT BOX

After examining the disparate views of pro-pornography and anti-pornography feminists, which side do you believe makes the better case, and why?

Gay Male Pornography

An interesting question arises almost immediately when considering the potential harms of gay male pornography: do the criticisms of heterosexual pornography extend to gay pornography as well? The prima facie response would be 'no', since in the case of gay male pornography there is no well-defined subordinated group who have endured millennia of sexual mistreatment at the hands of an oppressor group. Another way of saying this is that since the sexual participants in gay male porn are men, there is no clear history of one group of gay men subordinating another group of gay men. No doubt individual gay men have been subordinated and mistreated by other individual gay men and, of course, gay men in general have been marginalized and mistreated by mainstream heterosexual culture, but gay porn does not exploit this mistreatment in the way critics of heterosexual porn argue that women are subordinated by men in mainstream heterosexual pornography. So, does gay male porn escape criticism? It depends on whom you ask.

The anecdotal testimonies of many gay men online recount positive experiences with pornography. In surveys, gay men tend to view porn as a masturbatory aid and not as having much influence on gay men's attitudes and behaviors.[180] What critical analysis can be found has to do with gay male representation in the majority of gay male pornography. Researcher John Mercer writes:

> My analysis concerns itself with the homosexual prototypes in the texts of American gay pornographic videos. I am referring here to the recurrent deployment of an idealized, generic, muscular, male performer typified by what Richard Dyer has described as the "Californian ideal sort of clean anonymity."[181]

Concern about the normative aspect of there being a generic, white, muscular, athletic gay prototype is echoed in the work of many writers who focus on gay male representation in media. Middlebury College sociologist C. Winter Han writes that within gay male communities there are unspoken, and sometimes spoken, gay, masculine archetypes that are placed on pedestals to serve as regulating templates for how attractive gay masculinity should look. Han writes that within gay male culture, "Asian men are not masculine enough, black men are too masculine—The narrow range of acceptable masculinity is reserved for white men—gay or straight—because, ultimately, it benefits them."[182] Many gay men of color, argues Han, are marginalized and then jump through compensating hoops in an attempt to achieve what he terms "the mythical masculine norm":

> We spend hours at the gym toning our bodies and building our muscles to fit with the gay masculine norm. Some of us disguise our speech, alter our style, and we watch our steps in an effort to appear more straight to the untrained eye.[183]

Han is not laying blame for these normative gay archetypes onto pornography, per se, but the iconography of gay masculinity that Mercer discusses is certainly on display in much of the pornography produced for gay men.

Mercer adds that a problem that has plagued academic discussions about porn is that the analysis usually leads to the dichotomy of claiming "pornography is irreducibly bad or that pornography is good in a rather unquestioning fashion."[184] In recounting the benefits that flow from gay male pornography, Todd G. Morrison lists the fact that masturbating to porn is a form of safe sex that also validates, for many young, gay men, their sexual orientation.[185] That is, in a culture that can demonize homosexuality, gay pornography can reinforce the idea that "being homosexual is acceptable and even desirable."[186] For gay boys and men, the romantic and sexually imagery they are exposed to from mainstream media is almost exclusively heterosexual in orientation. A further point made by Morrison is that gay pornography has the effect of reversing patriarchal notions that only women can be sexually objectified. Morrison writes:

> [Heterosexual men] seem to operate from the assumption that the power (indeed, the right) to scrutinize others in aesthetic terms is theirs alone. Gay pornography reveals that those in positions of power can be denied subjectivity—that they can be treated as objects.[187]

John Mercer adds that "gay pornography is at the heart of anything approaching a gay culture. The primary thing that gay men have in common is a shared sexuality ... a facile observation but the cultural articulation of that form of sexuality is extremely important."[188] Speaking specifically to the differences between heterosexual porn and gay male porn, psychologist Bertram J. Cohler writes:

> In contrast to heterosexual porn, gay porn is a more differentiated genre. Rather than an instrument of repression, it is an instrument of liberation, portraying the variety of means possible for realizing sexual satisfaction. While heterosexual pornography subjugates women to men, gay porn reflects shared fantasies about men.[189]

Cohler's perspective resonates among many gay men that pornography is a shared experience among equals, rather than a medium that subordinates one group to another.

However, in his book *Gay Male Pornography: An Issue of Sex Discrimination*, Christopher N. Kendall defends the view that gay male porn reinforces misogyny and heterosexism.[190] Kendall, quoting feminist scholar John Stoltenberg, writes, "As artefacts of a heterosexist culture that is rigidly polarized by gender, gay male sex films exhibit the apotheosis of male sexual functioning as imagined by men, who, not unlike straight men, dread the taint of feminization."[191] Kendall provides an example of the heterosexism found in gay male pornography with an excerpt of gay male erotica published by *Manscape Magazine*:

> I pushed his pecs together [and] started tit-fucking him like a chick. Of all the things I did to him, I think he hated that the most. It made him feel like a girl. I said, "Oh, my bitch got such pretty titties! ... made to serve a man's dick."[192]

Kendall, claiming that this scene is "neither extreme nor atypical," goes on to state of gay male porn that "it encourages those who use it to become more valued, more "male," less "female."[193] The dominant and submissive sexual roles, like much of heterosexual porn, are gendered to place men in positions of power and women in positions of subordination to men. Kendall also attacks gay male porn as embodying the opposite qualities of sexual liberation:

> While some gay men may "choose" to be objects of eroticized violence, degradation, beatings, and verbal abuse, as presented in gay male pornography (and one should query why), not everyone wants this "choice." Any liberation theory that embraces dehumanization as a means of ensuring equality is frightening and politically questionable.[194]

Kendall concludes by stating that gay male porn instructs gay men that "we should find validation in submission laced with humiliation."[195]

On the other hand, the type of porn Kendall cites above does not exhaust the available genres of gay male pornography. In what is termed "twink porn," a softer, more feminine male archetype is the focus of attraction. The term 'twink' is slang within gay male culture used to describe a young man who is usually slim to average in build, lacking body or facial hair, and appearing younger than his chronological age.[196] Twink porn is considered to promote femininity rather than denigrating it, and shows that like heterosexual porn, gay male pornography cannot be overly generalized in content or character.

One final thing to mention about gay pornography and men is the hetero-normalizing and fetishizing of lesbian porn. While there are porn sites dedicated purely to lesbian sex, heterosexual porn uses as a common trope the imagery of lesbian sex as arousal impressions for heterosexual men. In one of the more discussed sexual double-standards, heterosexual men are socialized to view lesbian sex as highly erotic and gay male sex as repulsive, with the caveat that the women having sex with one another are conventionally cis-attractive to men, which usually means being conventionally alluring to men while also wearing the makeup and lingerie men are used to seeing in heterosexual porn. If the women having sex are "butch" or what Jack Halberstam terms *female masculine*, heterosexual men are conditioned to view the women and by extension the sex as unattractive.[197] Once again, heteronormativity and heterosexism creep into media, even in those cases where the media has nothing ostensibly to do with heterosexual men.

THOUGHT BOX

After considering the various points made in favor of and in opposition to gay, male pornography, which do you believe are the better points being made? Do you think the view that claims, "participants in gay, male pornography are all men, which takes away concerns about sexual exploitation and subordination" is a good point? Are there further points about gay, male pornography, positive or negative, not considered here?

Gay for Pay

One of the more discussed aspects of gay male pornography today is the phenomenon of "gay for pay" porn actors who are self-identified heterosexual men, but who engage in sex with other men for money. At a forum organized by the University of Southern California as part of their "bisexuality awareness week," actor Wolf Hudson, who identifies as heterosexual, stated, "the performance itself is totally non-sexual ... It's always very mechanical."[198] Porn actor Reese Rideout added that even though he is heterosexual, he prefers acting in gay porn because, "It's actually a more comfortable setting. You're treated more like an actor and less like a prop."[199] These sorts of comments fuel an ongoing debate about bisexuality in men. Some argue that like heterosexuality and homosexuality, bisexuality is a sexual orientation, while others do not classify it as an orientation.[200] [201] But the majority of men who identify as heterosexual and who perform sexual acts in gay pornography do not view themselves as bisexual.

After being characterized as gay or bisexual by family members, gay-for-pay actor Paul Cannon writes of labels,

> I guess I would be considered bisexual, [but] the reason I don't like labels like that is bisexuality has this negative connotation of being confused, and I'm definitely not confused. I definitely find women attractive, but there's certain aspects of men that I find attractive. I don't think that's confusion.[202]

In 2015, MTV launched the reality-based show *True Life*, which follows the lives of two heterosexual men who make their living performing in gay, male pornography.[203] One of the two men has a girlfriend who for some time did not know his profession, and was very upset upon learning what he did for a living. The other man is married to a woman, has children, and impassively explains that his decision to work in gay pornography is strictly a matter of providing for his family.[204]

Writing for the *Huffington Post*, gay social media authority Brad Hammer claims that he has worked with 25 gay-for-pay actors and found that the notion of men being entirely heterosexual or entirely homosexual is a myth.[205] On the other hand, cultural critic and author Jeffrey Escoffier explains,

> All sexual conduct in the video porn industry is an example of situational sexuality inasmuch as the performers are often required to engage in sexual acts for monetary compensation that they would not otherwise choose to perform and with partners for whom they feel no desire.[206]

The mechanistic nature of the sexual performance in porn, whether gay or heterosexual, purports to provide an explanation for how presumably heterosexual men can perform sexually in gay pornography. But it also speaks to the detachment of sexual acts from intimacy in porn. At the same time, defenders of porn will often claim that the purpose of pornography is to create a fantasy purely for sexual arousal and not as a template for navigating the complexities of a relationship.

Writing of his experience in gay male pornography while being heterosexual, Ned Mayhem (a stage name) claims it was a liberating feeling, adding,

> For me, porn was a first step toward genuinely not caring what people think about my identity. I had been trying for years to overcome the internalized shame our culture heaps onto any expression of sexuality outside of a rigidly defined patriarchal structure.[207]

Mayhem views his transition into gay male porn as transformative without altering his identity. But he also claims that "gay for pay" actors are not looked upon kindly by gay male porn performers because they take work away from genuinely gay performers.[208] Mayhem also notes that a problem he finds with porn in general, whether gay or heterosexual, is that there is a prescriptive form of masculinity on display that he believes to be greatly limiting and ultimately harmful. He noticed that in casting calls for gay male porn or heterosexual porn, there was an explicit proscription "no femmes" and demands that the actor "must be masculine," which he views as draconian and harmful to the many versions of masculinity that abound outside the world of porn.

THOUGHT BOX

After reading the arguments for and against pornography, where do you stand and why? Do you believe pornography is, on average, helpful or hurtful to women? Do you believe, on average, pornography is helpful or hurtful to men? Do you believe, on average, pornography is helpful or hurtful to relationships? What are your views about heterosexual men working in gay, male pornography?

Summary

Men's sexuality is not, of course, dependent on or defined by pornography. But the connections between pornography use and male sexuality have been, and continue to be, researched and debated due to the fact that so much of the pornography consumer market is male. As such, investigations into the consequences of long-term, habitual porn usage by men will continue. With internet porn sites in fevered competition with one another, many predict that the content of pornography will become more extreme and degrading to women, rather than there being any progressive movement toward egalitarian reform. Similarly, the debate between feminists about pornography and its effects on men, women, and relationships is bound to continue as pornography-inspired content continues to gain greater visibility in mainstream culture.

One thing that has certainly changed from past generations is that masturbation is no longer demonized, and the mainstreaming of porn is considered to be one of the conduits for this reversal. Pornography advocates, in fact, argue that the greater visibility of pornography has created a less sexually repressive culture, although others maintain that America is loosely composed of two conflicting cultural forces: those who push for more liberatory and autonomous sexual lives and those who wish to restrain and subjugate sexual liberty. The problem is that among those who defend sexual liberty, some view pornography as an instrumental part of that liberty, while others view pornography as an impediment to that liberty. The arguments in this chapter exposed much of that debate, while focusing more narrowly on men's use of porn and the complications that extend beyond claims of agency, fantasy, and sexual liberty.

Notes

1 http://changefromwithin.org/2014/02/12/one-mans-journey-how-i-stopped-watching-porn-for-1-year-and-why-im-not-going-back/.
2 https://en.wikipedia.org/wiki/Erotica.
3 www.everydayhealth.com/columns/dr-laura-berman-on-love-and-sex/men-and-women-differ-in-their-tastes-for-erotica/.
4 Juffer, Jane, "Excessive practices: Aesthetics, erotica, and cultural studies," in *The Aesthetics of Cultural Studies*, ed. Michael Berube (John Wiley & Sons, 2008).
5 Willis, Ellen, "Feminism, moralism, and pornography," *New York Law School Review*, 1993.
6 Ibid.
7 www.etymonline.com/index.php?term=pornography.
8 Youn, Gahyun, "Subjective sexual arousal in response to erotica: Effects of gender, guided fantasy, erotic stimulus, and duration of exposure," *Sexual Behavior*, February, 2006.
9 Ibid.
10 Ibid., p. 95.
11 Ibid., p. 96.
12 www.psychologytoday.com/blog/evolution-the-self/201206/gay-or-straight-male-is-male-is-male.
13 www.forbes.com/sites/jeffbercovici/2011/01/10/playboy-goes-private-in-207-million-deal/.
14 http://theologyandthecity.com/2013/09/07/15-august-13-the-playboy-doctrine-of-male/.
15 Ibid.
16 Ibid.
17 Ibid.
18 https://en.wikipedia.org/wiki/Hustler.
19 https://en.wikipedia.org/wiki/Chester_the_Molester.
20 Ibid.
21 https://en.wikipedia.org/wiki/Larry_Flynt.
22 Ibid.
23 www.biography.com/people/larry-flynt-9542114#hustler-controversy.
24 https://en.wikipedia.org/wiki/Golden_Age_of_Porn.

25 Ibid.
26 www.rogerebert.com/reviews/the-devil-in-miss-jones-1973.
27 https://en.wikipedia.org/wiki/Meese_Report.
28 https://en.wikipedia.org/wiki/Anti-pornography_movement_in_the_United_States.
29 Ibid.
30 http://techcrunch.com/2007/05/12/internet-pornography-stats/.
31 http://howtodoporn.blogspot.com/.
32 http://articles.latimes.com/2009/aug/10/business/fi-ct-porn10.
33 Weasels, P., "The quick and dirty guide to Gonzo." GameLink.com.
34 www.alternet.org/sex-amp-relationships/gonzo-porn.
35 https://en.wikipedia.org/wiki/John_Thompson_Productions.
36 https://en.wikipedia.org/wiki/Bukkake.
37 Kick, Russ, ed., *Everything You Know About Sex is Wrong: The Disinformation Guide to the Extremes of Human Sexuality (and Everything in Between)* (The Disinformation Company, 2005), p. 98.
38 www.theguardian.com/commentisfree/2012/aug/28/porn-syphilis-money-shot-condoms.
39 Dines, Gail, *Pornland: How Porn Has Hijacked Our Sexuality* (Beacon Press, 2010).
40 www.theguardian.com/commentisfree/2012/aug/28/porn-syphilis-money-shot-condoms.
41 http://goodmenproject.com/featured-content/pornography-is-what-the-end-of-the-world-looks-like/.
42 Ibid.
43 Olmstead, Spencer B., Negash, Sesen N., Pasley, Kay, and Fincham, Frank D., "Emerging adults' expectations for pornography use in the context of future committed romantic relationships: A qualitative study," *Archives of Sexual Behavior* 42 (2013), pp. 625–635.
44 www.psychologytoday.com/blog/tech-support/201407/what-porn-does-intimacy.
45 Lambert, Nathaniel M., Negash, Sesen, Stillman, Tyler F., Olmstead, Spencer B., and Fincham, Frank D. "A love that doesn't last: Pornography consumption and weakened commitment to one's romantic partner," *Journal of Social and Clinical Psychology* 31, 4 (2012), pp. 410–438.
46 Ibid.
47 www.psychologytoday.com/blog/tech-support/201407/what-porn-does-intimacy.
48 Gwinn, Andrea Mariea, Lambert, Nathaniel M., Fincham, Frank D., and Maner, Jon K., "Pornography, relationship alternatives, and intimate extradyadic behavior," *Social Psychological and Personality Science*, 4, 6 (2013), pp. 699–704.
49 Ibid.
50 www.theguardian.com/lifeandstyle/2010/jul/02/gail-dines-pornography.
51 Ibid.
52 Ibid.
53 Ibid.
54 Jensen, Robert, "Just a John?: Pornography and men's choices," in *Men Speak Out: Views on Gender, Sex, and Power*, ed. Shira Tarrant, 2nd edition (Routledge, 2013).
55 http://uts.cc.utexas.edu/~rjensen/freelance/pornographyisaleftissue.htm.
56 www.ebaumsworld.com/pictures/view/831793/.
57 http://msmagazine.com/blog/2010/08/27/yes-pornography-is-racist/.
58 www.psychologytoday.com/blog/sexual-intelligence/201102/the-myth-racist-pornography.
59 www.antipornography.org/racism-in-porn-industry-harsh-reality-exposed.html.
60 www.bbc.com/culture/story/20150206-the-most-racist-movie-ever-made.
61 https://pdjeliclark.wordpress.com/2015/02/08/a-terrorizing-mythology-on-the-100th-anniversary-of-birth-of-a-nation/.
62 Dyson, Michael Eric, *Reflecting Black: African-American Cultural Criticism* (University of Minnesota Press, 1993), pp. 169–171.
63 http://www.mediaed.org/discussion-guides/Hip-Hop-Discussion-Guide.pdf.
64 Dyson, Michael Eric, *The Michael Eric Dyson Reader* (Basic Books, 2013).
65 www.authentichistory.com/diversity/african/4-brute/.
66 https://en.wikipedia.org/wiki/Homegrown_Video.
67 Ibid.
68 https://en.wikipedia.org/wiki/Amateur_pornography.
69 https://en.wikipedia.org/wiki/Homegrown_Video.
70 http://abcnews.go.com/Business/SmallBiz/story?id=4151592&page=1.
71 Ibid.

72 Ibid.
73 Ibid.
74 Attwood, Feona, ed., *Porn.com: Making Sense of Online Pornography* (Peter Lang, 2010). www.peterlang.com/download/datasheet/53750/datasheet_310207.pdf.
75 Attwood, *Porn.com*.
76 DeLamater, John and Plante, Rebecca F., eds, *Handbook of the Sociology of Sexualities* (Springer, 2015).
77 www.feministcurrent.com/2015/09/22/new-study-says-porn-users-have-egalitarian-attitudes-so-what/.
78 Klaassen, Marleen J.E. and Peter, Jochen, "Gender inequality in internet pornography: A content analysis of popular pornographic internet videos," *The Journal of Sex Research*, 52, 7 (2015).
79 Gorman, Stacy, Monk-Turner, Elizabeth, and Fish, Jennifer N., "Free adult internet websites: How prevalent are degrading acts?" *Gender Issues*, December, 2010.
80 www.academia.edu/4585975/Responding_to_revenge_porn_Gender_justice_and_online_legal_impunity.
81 Ibid.
82 Ibid.
83 www.huffingtonpost.com/soraya-chemaly/a-primer-on-online-misogyny-revenge-porn-is-only-one-dimension_b_7691900.html.
84 www.academia.edu/4585975/Responding_to_revenge_porn_Gender_justice_and_online_legal_impunity.
85 https://en.wikipedia.org/wiki/Revenge_porn.
86 Ibid.
87 www.cosmopolitan.com/lifestyle/videos/a20835/how-you-watch-porn-survey/.
88 Ibid.
89 Ibid.
90 *Roth v. United States*, 354 U.S. 476 (1957).
91 Vaughn, Lewis, *The Power of Critical Thinking: Effective Reasoning about Ordinary and Extraordinary Claims*, 4th edition (Oxford University Press, 2013).
92 https://en.wikipedia.org/wiki/Mean_world_syndrome.
93 www.nybooks.com/articles/archives/1994/mar/03/pornography-an-exchange/.
94 *American Booksellers v. Hudnut*, 771 F.2d 323 (7th Cir. 1985).
95 www.nybooks.com/articles/archives/1994/mar/03/pornography-an-exchange/.
96 www.psychologytoday.com/blog/all-about-sex/200904/does-pornography-cause-social-harm.
97 https://rainn.org/get-information/statistics/reporting-rates.
98 www.huffingtonpost.com/2013/11/21/rape-study-report-america-us_n_4310765.html.
99 http://abcnews.go.com/US/story?id=95580&page=1.
100 www.theatlantic.com/politics/archive/2015/02/the-many-causes-of-americas-decline-in-crime/385364/.
101 www.livescience.com/19251-pornography-effects-santorum.html.
102 Ibid.
103 www.hawaii.edu/PCSS/biblio/articles/2005to2009/2009-pornography-acceptance-crime.html.
104 www.the-scientist.com/?articles.view/articleNo/28803/title/Porn--Good-for-us-/.
105 Ibid.
106 www.scientificamerican.com/article/the-sunny-side-of-smut/.
107 Ibid.
108 www.huffingtonpost.com/steven-c-hayes-phd/watching-porn-the-problem_b_719149.html.
109 https://en.wikipedia.org/wiki/Acceptance_and_commitment_therapy.
110 Delgado, Richard and Stefancic, Jean, "Pornography and harm to women: 'No empirical evidence?'" *Ohio State Law Journal*, 53 (1992).
111 www.glamour.com/entertainment/2013/12/rashida-jones-major-dont-the-pornification-of-everything.
112 http://gaildines.com/2010/07/ms-magazine/.
113 Ibid.
114 https://shareok.org/handle/11244/336.
115 www.pornaddicthubby.com/ConfrontingYourSpousesPornographyProblem.html.
116 Ibid.
117 Philaretou, Adreas G., Mahfouz, Ahmed Y., and Allen, Katherine R., "Use of internet pornography and men's well-being," *International Journal of Men's Health*, June, 2005.
118 Hertlein, Katherine M. and Stevenson, Armeda, "The seven 'as' contributing to internet-related intimacy problems: A literature review," *Journal of Psychosocial Research on Cyberspace*, 2010. www.cyberpsychology.eu/view.php?cisloclanku=2010050202.
119 www.menshealth.com/sex-women/porn-debate.

120 www.psychologytoday.com/blog/unique-everybody-else/201212/porn-stars-and-evolutionary-psychology.
121 Ibid.
122 Ellis, Bruce J. and Symons, Donald, "Sex differences in sexual fantasy: An evolutionary psychological approach," *The Journal of Sex Research* 27, 4 (1990).
123 Ibid.
124 www.apa.org/monitor/2014/04/pornography.aspx.
125 www.niaaa.nih.gov/alcohol-health/overview-alcohol-consumption/alcohol-facts-and-statistics.
126 www.nytimes.com/health/guides/disease/alcoholism/risk-factors.html.
127 www.ncbi.nlm.nih.gov/pubmed/12716271.
128 www.rehabformen.com/recovery-blog/researchers-think-male-brains-may-be-hard-wired-for-addiction.
129 www.simplypsychology.org/abnormal-psychology.html.
130 www.pornaddicthubby.com/ConfrontingYourSpousesPornographyProblem.html.
131 www.utdallas.edu/counseling/pornaddiction/.
132 http://pubs.niaaa.nih.gov/publications/arh313/185–195.pdf.
133 www.jneurosci.org/content/22/9/3332.full.
134 Ibid.
135 www.psychologytoday.com/blog/where-science-meets-the-steps/201407/mapping-aa-the-neuroscience-addiction.
136 www.deseretnews.com/article/865587003/New-UK-study-finds-porn-affects-brain-like-drugs-alcohol.html?pg=all.
137 Ibid.
138 www.ncbi.nlm.nih.gov/pmc/articles/PMC3050060/.
139 Ibid.
140 Ibid.
141 http://guiltypleasure.org/how-is-porn-addiction-similar-to-drug-addiction/.
142 www.ncbi.nlm.nih.gov/pubmed/21768998.
143 Ibid.
144 www.medicaldaily.com/brain-sex-how-brain-functions-during-orgasm-274052.
145 www.ncbi.nlm.nih.gov/pmc/articles/PMC3050060/.
146 Ibid.
147 Ibid.
148 Ibid.
149 Bostwick, J.M. and Bucci, J.A., "Internet sex addiction treated with naltrexone," *Mayo Clinic Proceedings* 83, 2 (2008), pp. 226–230.
150 http://www.ncbi.nlm.nih.gov/pmc/articles/PMC3050060/.
151 http://psychcentral.com/news/2014/02/13/exploding-the-myth-of-porn-addiction/65835.html.
152 Ibid.
153 http://blogs.psychcentral.com/sex/2012/04/debunking-david-j-ley%E2%80%99s-the-myth-of-sex-addiction/.
154 Ibid.
155 Ruse, Michael, "Is homosexuality bad sexuality?" in *Philosophical Perspectives on Sex & Love*, ed. Robert Stewart (Oxford University Press, 1995).
156 www.aic.gov.au/media_library/publications/proceedings/20/goldsmith.pdf.
157 Voon, Valerie, et al., "Neural correlates of sexual cue reactivity in individuals with and without complusive sexual behaviours," *PLos One*, July, 2014.
158 Ibid.
159 Ibid.
160 http://addictions.about.com/od/howaddictionhappens/a/addcompulsion.htm.
161 www.washingtonpost.com/news/the-fix/wp/2016/04/22/anti-porn-advocates-are-changing-the-game-and-it-starts-with-utah-declaring-it-a-public-health-crisis/.
162 www.npr.org/sections/thetwo-way/2016/04/20/474943913/utah-declares-porn-a-public-health-hazard.
163 Ibid.
164 www.nytimes.com/2016/04/22/us/utah-declares-pornography-public-health-crisis.html.
165 Ibid.
166 https://en.wikiquote.org/wiki/Robin_Morgan.
167 www.wendymcelroy.com/freeinqu.htm.
168 Duggan, Lisa and Hunter, Nan D., *Sex Wars: Sexual Dissent and Political Culture* (Routledge, 1995).
169 www.examiner.com/article/our-porn-ourselves-a-feminist-pro-porn-manifesto-response-to-the-feminist-anti-porn-movement.
170 www.wendymcelroy.com/freeinqu.htm.
171 Ibid.
172 Ibid.
173 Ibid.

174 www.fairobserver.com/region/north_america/whose-porn-whose-femnism/.
175 Ibid.
176 www.theglobeandmail.com/life/relationships/im-an-exhibitionist-im-hypersexual-porn-star-asa-akira-on-why-she-loves-her-job/article18826704/.
177 Keith, Thomas, *The Bro Code: How Contemporary Culture Creates Sexist Men* (Media Education Foundation, 2011).
178 http://healthland.time.com/2011/05/19/mind-reading-the-researchers-who-analyzed-all-the-porn-on-the-internet/.
179 Ibid.
180 Morrison, Todd G., "'He was treating me like trash, and I was loving it …': Perspectives on gay male pornography," *Journal of Homosexuality*, 47, 3–4 (2004).
181 Mercer, John, "Homosexual prototypes: Repetition and the construction of the generic in the iconography of gay pornography," *Paragraph* 26, 1–2 (2003).
182 Han, C. Winter, "Darker shades of Queer: Race and sexuality at the margins," in *Men Speak Out: Views on Gender, Sex, and Power*, ed. Shira Tarrant, 2nd edition (Routledge, 2013).
183 Ibid.
184 Mercer, John, *Eclectic Views on Gay Male Pornography: Pornucopia* (Routledge, 2013), p. 209.
185 Ibid.
186 Ibid.
187 Ibid.
188 Ibid.
189 Ibid.
190 Kendall, Christopher N., *Gay Male Pornography: An Issue of Sex Discrimination* (University of British Columbia Press, 2004).
191 Ibid., 115.
192 Kendall, Christopher N., "Gay Male Liberation Post *Oncale*: Since When Is Sexualized Violence Our Path to Liberation?," in *Directions in Sexual Harassment Law*, ed. Catherine MacKinnon and Reva B. Siegel (Yale University Press, 2004), p. 230.
193 Ibid.
194 Ibid.
195 Ibid.
196 https://en.wikipedia.org/wiki/Twink_(gay_slang).
197 Halberstam, J., "The Good, the Bad, and the Ugly: Men, women, and masculinity," in *Masculinity Studies & Feminist Theory: New Directions*, ed. Judith Kegan Gardiner (Columbia University Press, 2002).
198 http://dailytrojan.com/2010/02/10/adult-film-actors-give-insight-to-gay-porn/.
199 Ibid.
200 www.huffingtonpost.com/2013/11/06/bisexuality-straight-men-study-_n_4226065.html.
201 www.csun.edu/~psy453/bisex_n.htm.
202 www.queerty.com/sit-down-with-a-gay-for-pay-porn-model-his-family-and-their-thoughts-on-sexuality-20140822.
203 www.cosmopolitan.com/entertainment/tv/news/a50587/mtv-true-life-gay-for-pay-porn/.
204 www.gaystarnews.com/article/mtvs-true-life-docuseries-features-gay-for-pay-porn-actors/#gs.=ledQyA.
205 www.huffingtonpost.com/brad-hammer/gay-for-pay_b_4473285.html.
206 Escoffier, Jeffrey, "Gay-for-Pay: Straight men and the making of gay pornography," *Qualitative Sociology*, December, 2003.
207 Mayhem, Ned, "Male and Queer in the porn industry," in *Men Speak Out: Views on Gender, Sex, and Power*, 2nd edition, ed. Shira Tarrant (Routledge, 2013).
208 Ibid., p. 83.

Chapter 12

Men, Health, and Aging

(James Ryan addressing Capt. Miller's grave) *I tried to live my life the best I could ... I hope I've earned what all of you have done for me.*
(Ryan's Wife) *James?*
(Ryan) *Tell me I have led a good life?*
(Ryan's wife) *What?*
(Ryan) *Tell me I'm a good man.*
(Ryan's wife) *You are.*

~*Saving Private Ryan*, 1998[1]

LEARNING OBJECTIVES

After reading this chapter, students should be able to respond to the following questions with an understanding of the terms and expressions employed:

- *What are some of the more pervasive ways that men are told to define success? What, according to sociologist Robert Morgan, is a "class agent," and what has it to do with men?*
- *What is meant by Type A personalities and Hardy men? In what ways was the Type A personality criticized by Hardy-men advocates?*
- *What did researchers learn about the intersection of race and poverty? How did researchers establish that racial bias is present in hiring practices across America? Why is homelessness thought to plague men in greater number than women?*
- *What is "The Forbes Facelift"? and what has it to do with men? How has the "beauty industry" marketed grooming products, including lines of makeup, to men? What do these marketing campaigns tell us about men?*
- *What sorts of traits typify the syndrome* mascupathy *as identified by psychotherapists Charlie Donaldson and Randy Flood? What is* Normative Male Alexithymia *as described by psychologist Ronald Levant?*
- *With respect to the high rates of suicide in men, what explanations and treatment options are offered? In researching men and depression, what typical traits are found in men who suffer from depression?*

- *What reasons do men give for putting off going to doctors for physical ailments?*
- *What are some of the explanations offered for the unusually high rates of suicide in the military?*
- *What is known about the connection between depression and testosterone levels in men?*
- *What are the common fears men have about aging? What are some of the factors thought to contribute to a "mid-life crisis" and why does this crisis appear to affect men more noticeably than women?*

Capitalism existed before the European insurgence into North America.[2] But America has become synonymous with the rise of hyper-capitalism, a fierce allegiance to free-market enterprise that has created multiple class hierarchies and more billionaires than any other nation on Earth by a wide margin.[3] For generations, many American men have been taught that success as a man means to be provider and protector of the family. This instruction suffuses throughout a man's life and becomes for many men the goal that creates meaning and purpose in life. In America, this capitalist mindset also shapes the boundary conditions for success and failure. Men are often judged on the basis of their income or lack thereof. Increasingly, success as a man in contemporary American culture has been marketed to men as possessing wealth rather than to simply provide family sustenance, and to then flaunt that wealth in the presence of others. At the same time, the pressure that capitalistic success creates for men is attended by men's resistance to seek help and counseling when pressures weigh too heavily. Instead of balancing various aspects of life, men have been instructed to work longer hours and try harder to achieve this capitalistic version of success. The unfortunate, but predictable, consequence is that men, and increasingly women, suffer from a variety of stress-related illnesses, which contribute to men committing suicide at higher rates than women. As men continue to age, a growing fear of irrelevance grips many men who realize that their economically productive years are behind them and the search for new relevancy begins. This chapter traces the proposed causes, effects, and suggestions for men's health, the pursuit of youth, worries about aging, high rates of suicide, and, for some, a crisis in relevancy and purpose.

Masculinity and Capitalism: Work, Stress, and Male Versions of Success

Capitalism has played a central role in normative, American masculinity over many generations. Men have been judged by the amount of money they earn and the trappings of material success they place on display. The drive for materialistic success creates economic hierarchies, but also a playing field for masculine performance where competition between men is measured by affluence coupled with an emotional stoicism that rebukes sentiment. The specter of the cool-tempered executive who wields power over others is a dominant figure in male lore and the protagonist in many Hollywood films. Whether Michael Douglas's portrayal of "greed is good" stock-guru Gordon Gekko in the film *Wall Street* or Christian Bale as billionaire playboy Bruce Wayne who secretly keeps Gotham City safe as Batman in *The Dark Knight* or Robert Downey Jr. as genius, billionaire, playboy Tony Stark who through his technological innovations, morphs into Iron Man to keep America safe from a host of villains, the hyper-successful, corporate entrepreneur who embodies many of the masculine traits that boys are taught to desire

FIGURE 12.1: "The beauty of me is that I am very rich." ~real estate billionaire, Donald Trump

and pursue in their quest for respect has been mythologized in dozens of films and cultural anecdotes. In one of the more quoted moments in the quintessential male-friendly 1983 film *Scarface*, Al Pacino as Tony Montana states to his friend and business partner as a lesson in American culture, "In this country, first you get the money, then you get the power, then you get the women."[4]

On the influence the hyper-tough, contentious, cash-rich masculine archetype has on boys, psychologist James Gabarino asserts, "too many boys succumb to the cultural stereotypes of a socially toxic society that defines manhood in terms of aggression, power, and material acquisition."[5] Sociologist Michael Kimmel concurs and describes the normative masculine script that most boys receive as "an ideology of masculinity that we inherited from our fathers, and their fathers before them, an ideology that promises unparalleled acquisition coupled with a tragically impoverished emotional intelligence."[6] From reporting the salary arrangements for professional athletes on ESPN to the conspicuous consumption of wealth by music stars to the constant boasting of his enormous wealth by real estate mogul Donald Trump, the connection between wealth and manhood is constantly made throughout popular culture to generations of boys and young men who are searching for their own masculine identities.

In a study conducted by Lorraine Dyke and Steven Murphy of Carleton University, women and men were asked for their definition of success.[7] Women in the survey placed more emphasis on balancing work and relationships, while men placed greater emphasis on personal wealth.[8] These findings confirm a generalization that many expect to hear about women and men when gendered discrepancies about success are revealed, but they also represent a stereotype. The career paths that individual men and women pursue will influence the level of importance they place on material success. So, a man who seeks a career in teaching will probably have less interest in economic success than a woman who pursues a Wall Street career. Still, even among many working class men, material wealth is considered to be the benchmark of male success despite the fact that the opportunities for opulent lifestyles are unavailable to most men.

In some respect, the "working class hero" of countless media depictions has transformed into a suburban wealth wannabe, who surrounds himself with the material trappings of success to the best of his economic abilities. Expensive cars, trucks, homes, electronics, watches, and other jewelry place material success on display to whomever the individual hopes to impress. One of the ways that working class men and women try to meet the demands of material success is to take on extra jobs, work longer hours, and amass credit card debt that perpetuates a cycle of liability and wealth-appearance, ultimately creating a perpetual cycle of financial crisis. So while women are instructed in popular culture to compete with one another in terms of beauty and sex appeal, men are instructed to compete with one another for the respect, envy, and power that comes with affluence.

Sociologist David Morgan, in his piece "Class and Masculinity," argues that class is one social hierarchy that has always been implied as a strong identifier with men and masculinity.[9] With respect to status, Morgan notes that economics has long been considered a measurement of "the social distribution of honor or prestige."[10] In patriarchal cultures such as American culture, men hold the vast majority of wealth and are thus the arbiters of class or what Morgan terms **class agents.**[11] A lineage of male power plays a significant role in determining successive generations of men enjoying economic privilege over women. One of the main factors in the continuation of this gendered class inequality is ownership of land and other possessions. Morgan reports that in the case of property, we find a long history of different kinds of property inheritance running through male lineage.[12] In another sense of inheritance, occupational lineage has historically been handed down by father to son so that generations of bankers or doctors or coal miners pass through male genealogy along with the status or lack of status each of these occupations carry with them. To take Donald Trump as an example, Trump's father Fred Trump was a real estate investor who built and operated apartment complexes throughout New York City in the 1960s and 1970s.[13] His son Donald joined the company at age 22, and by 28 he was named president of Trump Management.[14]

Of the various economic classes found in American society, it is the wealthiest classes or "power elite" that Morgan highlights as having a strong influence on constructing hegemonic masculinity.[15] The "Trumps" of American culture are seen as wielding great power over the lives of others, as having their every desire met, and as attracting willing sexual partners who would otherwise have little to do with them. American capitalism instructs men from early ages that money equals power and that acquisition is a measurement of male power in particular. In fact, a recent Bloomberg Business feature explained that heavy recruiting from college fraternities is one reason why Wall Street investment firms, brokerage houses, and banks and lending institutions continue to be bastions of male-domination and privilege.[16] An insider culture of wealth and masculinity led some to blame the 2008 financial crisis on the greed encouraged by a longstanding, take-no-prisoners male management approach to wealth acquisition.[17] When asked why more women are not well represented on Wall Street, one billionaire alumnus of Sigma Alpha Epsilon explained that "mothers can't be focused traders because children are emotional distractions from the moment they latch onto their mothers' bosoms."[18]

At the same time, the physical and emotional fallout of men who internalize the notion of material wealth as masculine power has been documented by researchers far and wide. A study from the University of Michigan found substantial stress increases in men who transition from communist societies to capitalist societies.[19] Researcher Daniel Kruger reports that in 14 post-Soviet countries, homicide and suicide rates doubled and that the transition negatively affected men more than women, as mortality rates for men climbed 9.3% higher for men than women and that this impact was especially pronounced for men in their "economically prime years."[20] Some of these upward trends in homicide and suicide rates may be attributed to the growing pains of new and therefore unstable market-based economies where crime flourishes, but the fact that men outnumber women in accounting for these rates can be seen as part of masculine template that is part of any capitalist patriarchy.

The attempt to attain the masculine ideal of wealth by pushing oneself to work harder and longer hours has also been linked to a host of health problems. Working overtime is positively correlated to higher rates of depression.[21] Sleep deprivation is also a common problem for people who work long hours. The documented health problems that accompany sleep deprivation include higher rates of automotive and workplace accidents, higher rates of heart disease, high blood pressure, stroke, diabetes, and irritability, and decreased sex drive.[22] According to a 2014 Gallup poll, the average American full-time worker spends 47 hours per week on the job and 40% of workers report that they log over 50 hours per week at work.[23] Between trying to pay down debt, residing in high cost-of-living regions of the U.S., working in low-wage occupations, and attempting to generate personal wealth, many Americans work far more than the touted eight-hour work day and often work more than five days per week. For many, work does not stop when they return home in the evening. Teachers have to create lesson plans and grade assignments, business reports have deadlines, and many American workers create home-based businesses to supplement their incomes.[24] [25] In 2015, the Department of Labor introduced new guidelines for overtime that promote overtime pay for hourly and salaried employees,[26] with a net result of lower income earners applying for more overtime and suffering more of the negative effects associated with working long hours. Many are praising the new overtime guidelines as a win for women, since many women working in clerical and receptionist roles were salaried before the new guidelines, while being pushed to work long hours. Under the new guidelines, salaried workers will also qualify for overtime pay.[27] This means that employers will not be able to create a loophole by manipulating employee job titles in order to pay workers on the basis of salaries and thereby less than they would make as hourly employees. But it also means that the concerns of working longer hours to make more money will be more acute going forward.

THOUGHT BOX

Examine ads that promote wealthy lifestyles, for goods like high end real estate, stock market investing, expensive cars, watches, and other jewelry. What percentage of the ads feature male actors/models versus female actors/models in positions of power and wealth? Who do you believe is the target audience? What conclusions do you draw after viewing and considering these ads?

Books have been written and studies conducted in attempts to understand and explain the relationship between stress and coronary heart disease (CHD); and for over six decades the search has focused on personality types that have been thought until recently to be typical of men who push themselves to overachieve in order to obtain the American dream of personal wealth.[28] The overachiever type was dubbed "Type A" and was considered to be one of the main causes of stress and other health concerns in men. In particular, it was thought that men were encouraged to adopt Type A personalities as an extroverted, normative approach to business success.[29] In fact, it was two cardiologists who coined the expression "Type A personality" based on observations they made about heart patients' behaviors.[30] But Type A personalities were also supposed to denote a kind of person who was ambitious, driven, and dedicated to socially upward mobility.

As Elianne Riska notes in her book *Masculinity and Men's Health: Coronary Heart Disease in Medical and Public Discourse*, identifying oneself as a Type A became a marker for "positioning oneself in the moral order and in the social hierarchy of work."[31] It became a badge of honor among those who sought to distinguish themselves from other personality types they believed to be lazy, servile, and complacent.

By the late 1970s and early 1980s, authors Salvador Maddi and Suzanne Kobasa supplanted what they considered to be the negative associations of a Type A personality into what they argued was a healthier and more successful male archetype termed ***the hardy man***, a man typified by hard work, commitment, and self-control.[32] Being able to multitask, cope with ongoing change, and successfully wear the hats of businessman, husband, and father, while keeping everything under control was the hallmark of the emerging hardy executive. In the words of Salvador Maddi,

> When you can navigate professional and personal changes in a way that furthers your and your employer's goals, strengthens your ability to turn adversity to advantage and deepens professional and personal meaning, you succeed as an employee and as a person. That's the Way of Hardiness!"[33]

Where the Type A man was characterized by impulsive behavior and poor interpersonal skills due to his obsessive drive to achieve at any cost, the hardy man remains in control under the most stressful circumstances, succeeds professionally, while being told that his responsibility, self-control, and adaptability will prevent him from enduring the poor health consequences of the Type A man.

Critics have argued that hardiness does not buffer stress for men and has been associated with neuroticism.[34] Moreover, it is thought that the stoic model of masculine stress management is precisely what leads many men to internalize their problems and sink into depression. Other critics, such as Riska, have argued that hardiness is an attempt to validate and legitimize traditional masculinity, while implicitly denying the efficacy of business approaches that are considered by some to be feminine in character.[35] [36] For instance, some argue that men are taught in business settings to be confrontational when challenged, while women are instructed to avoid confrontation and instead to seek resolution through negotiation and consensus building.[37] Also considered to be a male-centered administrative approach to business is the preference of a top-down management style where executives create policy that is then handed down to subordinates to carry out, while a female-centered approach is considered to be a cooperative management environment where ideas and policy matters are created through the collaborative efforts of executive management and non-executive employees. One of the speculative advantages of adopting this cooperative management style is that employees will be more personally involved and committed to a company that values their opinions. Conversely, employees may not be as committed to a company that seems dictatorial in nature.[38] If hardiness lines up better with traditional male styles of management, it may be considered biased against women if executive management also buys into the traditional notion that men are better at creating decisive policy. Proponents of hardiness counter that further research has found that the traits of control and commitment have been positively correlated to successful stress and health management, while lack of control and lack of commitment have consistently been found to bear a direct negative effect on health because they are psychologically stressful.[39] Critics, however, insist that a cooperative approach to business management has nothing to do with being out of control or lacking commitment. Still, while the term 'hardiness' is not used with great frequency in today's business world, the concepts underlying hardiness are still very much employed as a preferred management model for executives.

Men and Economic Disparity in America

America is both the wealthiest nation in the world and the most economically unequal nation in the world.[40] With $63 trillion in total private wealth, America towers above all other nations, while there is little support in America for redistribution of that wealth.[41] America also has many pockets of poverty and urban blight. When capitalism defines a nation's ethos and wealth defines masculine power, and wealth is unequally distributed, there is a recipe in place for many men feeling the need to compensate for their lack of wealth in other ways to preserve their pride and identity. It is rare for a very wealthy man to be muscle-bound and physically intimidating, unless his wealth is in part the product of his muscular physique as in the case of actors Arnold Schwarzenegger or Dwayne Johnson, better known to his fans as *The Rock*. For men who do not enjoy economic power, physicality can be used as a surrogate for power. In the article, "Acting Tough in a Tough World: An Examination of Fear among Urban African American Adolescents," University of Pennsylvania scholars Diane M. Hall, Elaine F. Cassidy, and Howard C. Stevenson argue that young African-American men living in lower socio-economic environments adopt a tough, "anger expression" in response to fears of "lethal calamitous events."[42] Inner-city environments are rife with dangers, and young men living in these conditions, regardless of their race or ethnicity, will more readily adopt a hypermasculine exterior to deal with these dangers. This is part of *the cool pose* described by Richard Majors discussed in the media chapters, but is often misinterpreted as an attitude of defiance, when in fact, argues Majors, it is a way for black youths to maintain a sense of integrity and esteem in response to economic inequality, to deal with black male homicide and incarceration rates, and preserve an appearance of remaining cool despite the many dangers of living in violent surroundings.[43] Majors claims that this cool pose is a form of psychological armor that often prevents young, black men living in urban environments from opening themselves up emotionally to others, which itself perpetuates a cycle of frustration and pain.[44]

FIGURE 12.2:

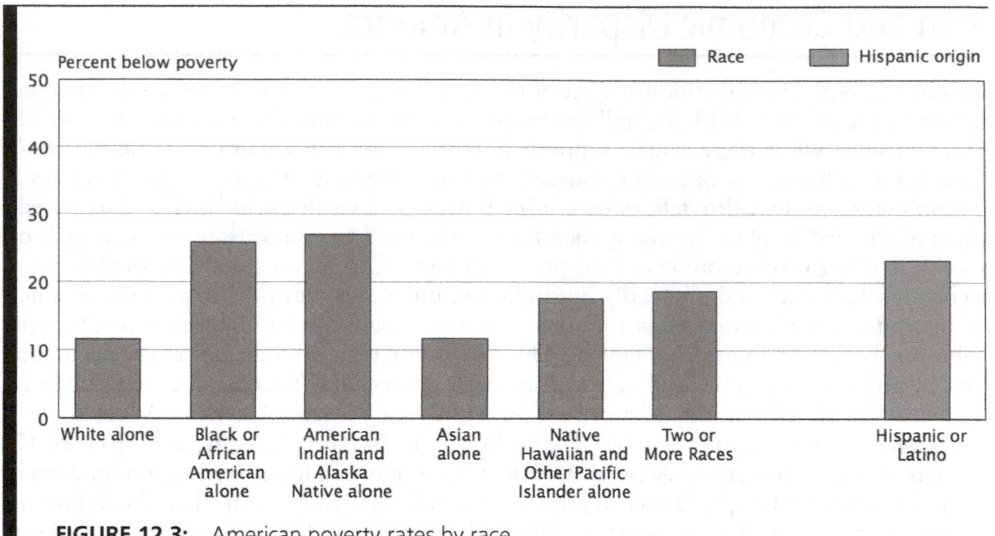

FIGURE 12.3: American poverty rates by race

According to the U.S. Department of Commerce, black, Latino, and Native American men outnumber white men living below the poverty line at a rate of more than two to one (see Figure 12.3). A consequence of living at or below the poverty line is decreased overall health.[45] [46] The National Institutes of Health reports that the stress of living in poverty has been positively correlated to impaired learning abilities in children.[47] In addition, research has shown that living in poverty increases one's chances of depression, unhealthy diets, obesity, diabetes, high blood pressure, heart disease, and lowered access to quality health care.[48] Given the racial disparity of poverty in America, this means that, collectively, men of color will suffer from these problems at much higher rates than white men. According to research conducted by the National Poverty Center, racial disparities in poverty create collateral negative consequences for people of color such as lower language and vocabulary skills, and higher arrest and felony conviction rates, the latter of which result in bans on voting, jury service, and receiving federal college loans and grants.[49] A two-city audit also revealed that employers are more likely to hire a white applicant over an equally qualified black applicant for the same job at a rate of two-to-one.[50] Writing for *Fortune Magazine*, Brett Arends notes that the racial bias in hiring is often fueled by the fear employers have that customers prefer white contacts over contacts with people of color.[51] Researchers from the University of Wisconsin working with economics professors from the University of Pennsylvania and Auburn University submitted 9,400 fake resumes of nonexistent recent college graduates to online job applications for positions based in Atlanta, Baltimore, Portland, Los Angeles, Boston, and Minneapolis.[52] To designate ethnicity, half of the fake candidates were given names considered to be "typically white" such as Cody Baker, Jake Kelly, Claire Kruger, and Amy Rasmussen. The other half of fake applicants were given names considered to be "typically black" such as DeShawn Jefferson, DeAndre Washington, Ebony Booker, and Aaliyah Jackson. The results of the experiment revealed that those with "typical African-American names" were 16% less likely to be called for interviews than those with "typical white-sounding names," demonstrating that employment opportunities are greater for white candidates than they are for people of color, dispelling the myth that equal qualification means equal opportunity.[53]

At the same time, a pervasive American ethos of rugged individualism and race-neutral meritocracy has eroded support for antipoverty programs.[54] In surveys, Americans today are more likely to believe in the possibility of upward mobility than they were 20 years ago, even as the economy has been sluggish, particularly in areas of manufacturing and other working class occupations.[55] The notion of personal responsibility pervades American values despite many circumstances beyond the control of people living in poverty that include psychological disorders, especially for at-risk populations such as veterans returning from war.[56] In fact, according to the U.S. Department of Housing and Urban Development, on any given night, approximately 48,000 veterans are homeless.[57] As expected, people of color are overrepresented among the homeless population of America, including among homeless veterans.[58] [59] The rate of homeless African-American people in America seeking out the refuge of homeless shelters is one out of every 141 black families, a rate seven times higher than that found in white families.[60] Coupled with racial disparities in the amount of intergenerational transfer of wealth and the many structural obstacles noted above, poverty and homelessness are a racialized phenomenon in America that does not appear to be changing any time soon. When looking strictly at homelessness and gender, of the 3.5 million homeless people in America, the U.S. Department of Housing and Urban Development reports that 67% are male,[61] of which the majority are single men,[62] and 39% are children under the age of 18.[63] Among the reasons given why men greatly outnumber women among the homeless population are men's higher likelihood of being veterans, men's tendency not to seek treatment for mental illness and substance abuse, men's higher rates of alcohol and drug use as compared with women's use of substances, and men's socialized imperative not to seek help when jobless or financially destitute.[64] This is not to say that women do not suffer immeasurably from homelessness and in fact may be living on the streets as a result of being violently victimized by a husband or boyfriend and forced to remove their children from a dangerous home environment, but statistically, men are living without homes in greater numbers than women. Interestingly, this fact is not a problem unique to America. A report by the University of Sheffield, England, states that of those homeless people who died on the streets in the U.K. between 2001 and 2009, 90% were men.[65]

Men and the Pursuit of Youth and Beauty

Elective cosmetic surgery has grown immensely over the past several decades, but has until very recently been dominated by female clients. The American Society for Aesthetic Plastic Surgery reports that there has been a 43% increase in surgical and nonsurgical procedures on men over the past five years, and that since 1997 there has been a 273% increase in overall procedures performed on men.[66] Dr. Douglas Steinbrech, a prominent cosmetic surgeon, explains that many men in positions of corporate power view their looks as important to their careers, and so request what Steinbrech terms the ***Forbes Facelift***, consisting of a neck lift, eyelift, jawline recontouring, and liposuction.[67] In a culture that worships youth, it is not surprising that cosmetic surgery has been successful, but it has taken time and effort to convince men that undertaking cosmetic procedures does not negatively influence their masculinity. In a capitalistic culture that instructs men that financial success is an important ingredient in being a man, cosmetic surgery has attracted more men once a connection was established between youthful looks and having a successful long-term career in the minds of men who are looking for ways to extend their careers by years or decades or who are looking for an advantage over those who might challenge them for advancement. But again, a central obstacle for companies in the so-called "beauty industry" looking to profit from men is to get men who have been socialized to shun anything considered to be feminine to purchase and use products traditionally associated with women.

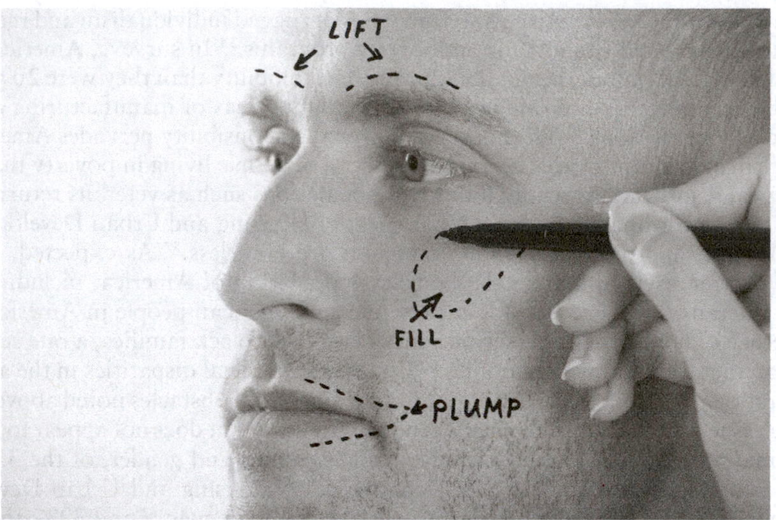

FIGURE 12.4: Elective cosmetic surgery for men

The "male grooming market" is valued at an estimated $6 billion in the U.S. and $33 billion worldwide.[68] This particular market has made inroads into male culture through hair care products, body wash, face wash, and cologne, but getting men to wear makeup is a much bigger challenge. According to makeup expert and founder of Menaji men's line of cosmetic products, Michele Probst, the secret to selling makeup to men is found in the marketing of the products. Probst claims that the greatest sin of marketing makeup to men is calling it "makeup."[69] Instead, words like "power" and "boost" are replacement terms for "makeup" with an emphasis on their undetectability, since presumably other men, and

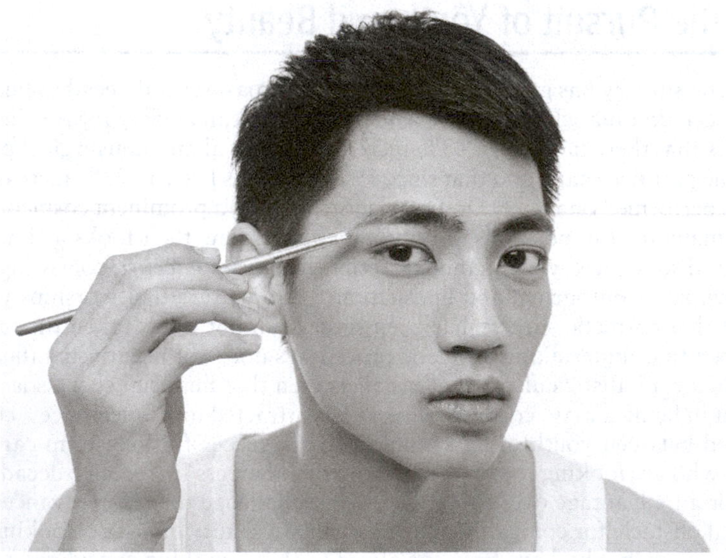

FIGURE 12.5: Makeup for men

women, might mock them for applying cosmetics to their faces.[70] Menaji, in fact, calls their line of men's makeup, "CAMO Urban Camouflage," to give their product a militaristic-sounding, hetero-masculine-friendly association for men who might otherwise cringe at the thought of wearing makeup.[71] Understanding that men are socialized to recoil at being allied with anything remotely thought to be feminine, the marketing strategies have centered around themes considered attractive to men, which includes packaging that marketers believe appear heteronormatively masculine such as cartons for cosmetics that resemble cigar boxes or liquor bottles.[72] Macy's in downtown Philadelphia opened a "men's grooming zone," which they claim, looks like "a men's skin care man cave."[73]

We see this same concern for youthful appearance and aesthetic significance in the ads for hair dye that specifically target men. The ads attempt to appeal to the male insecurity that women will not find them to be sexually attractive if they appear older. In the "Just for Men" ad, ex-MLB star Keith Hernandez (62) and ex-NBA star Walt Frazier (70), both sporting dark hair, taunt a man who is trying to impress a woman, but who is told by Hernandez and Frazier that "he won't get any play" as long as he has gray hair. Once again, an appeal to virility becomes the key to enticing men who might not otherwise care about the graying of their hair or other indicators of age. But increasingly, men are being pitched personal grooming and vanity products as the beauty industry awakens to the fact that there has been a largely untapped market of men who, if approached by an appeal to profitability or sexual ebullience, are open to spending money on their appearances.

THOUGHT BOX

What is your opinion of cosmetics for men? What do the marketing strategies designed to appeal to men tell you about men? Do you think these products will be successful? Why or why not?

FIGURE 12.6: *Just For Men* hair dye ad featuring ex-MLB star Keith Hernandez and ex-NBA star Walt Frasier

At the same time, anorexia nervosa, an eating disorder that historically affects girls and women at much higher rates than boys and men, is on the increase with males. For every ten females that are affected by eating disorders of an anorexic type, one male is affected.[74] When investigating media targeting women versus media targeting men, the explanation for the gender disparity of anorexia and bulimia makes sense. Research conducted by the National Eating Disorder Association discovered that magazines targeting girls and women emphasize weight reduction, while magazines targeting boys and men emphasize fitness, weight lifting, body building, and muscularity.[75] Yet researchers also note that anorexia in men is attended with much higher rates of anxiety over sexual activities and relationships.[76]

EXERCISE

Compare ads in magazines targeting women versus magazines targeting men. Are you able to notice the gender disparity mentioned above? Do ads encourage women to be smaller and men to be more muscular? Are there other notable gendered differences in ads that target women versus men?

In further research, corroborating evidence reinforced the finding that men who suffer from anorexia are significantly less likely to be involved in sexual relationships, while men who suffer from bulimia are more sexually active than males with anorexia.[77] The view is that body dysmorphic disorder, a mental illness where the afflicted person obsesses daily about what they believe to be flaws in their physical appearance, strongly correlates with anxiety, depression, and low self-esteem, which leads many who suffer from it to isolate themselves from others, particularly in terms of forming romantic or sexual relationships.[78] It has also been noted that gay men are more likely to be at increased risk for developing anorexia and were found to be less satisfied with their overall body image than heterosexual men.[79]

In the case of middle-aged men, little is known about the rates of anorexia. Researchers in British Columbia found that men are less likely to be diagnosed with anorexia even when they exhibit classic symptoms.[80] The theory is that the combination of men not seeking treatment coupled with a bias present in some doctors to believe that anorexia is a female disorder lead to decreased cases of anorexia diagnoses in men. These same researchers note that while those who die of anorexia are men in only 10% of overall cases, by age 45 that rate climbs to 21%.[81] If cases of anorexia and other eating disorders increase as men age, some researchers speculate that circumstantial factors such as mid-life crisis, unemployment, divorce, death of a loved one, retirement, and a diminished feeling of power and influence that come with aging may be triggers.[82]

Mascupathy

In 2000, therapists Randy Flood and Charlie Donaldson cofounded the Men's Resource Center of West Michigan, and in 2014 they coauthored the book *Mascupathy*, which takes up a syndrome that afflicts many men.[83] Flood and Donaldson have conducted therapy sessions with hundreds of men who suffer from a host of problems that

FIGURE 12.7: Randy Flood

FIGURE 12.8: Charlie Donaldson

collectively impair men's self-esteem and relational capacities. The specific problems include:

- weak self-concept
- inadequate emotionality
- relational deficits
- externalization

A weak self-concept is described by Flood and Donaldson as either a deficient or grandiose sense of self, neither being healthy. Inadequate emotionality encompasses a range of problems with emotion that include problems experiencing or expressing emotions to governing emotional outbursts of anger. Relational deficits refer to a pattern of men's controlling, distancing, and sometimes needy behaviors that often harm relationships, while externalization describes men's proclivity for addictive, overcompensating, and impulsive behaviors toward work, substances, sex, and aggression.[84] Flood and Donaldson argue that these patterns exist in so many men, in varying degrees, that they uncover a common socializing process that plagues boys and men throughout their lives. Harvard University psychologist Ronald Levant terms this process ***normative male alexithymia*** to describe a common male pattern of suppressing emotion, other than anger, and the resistance to therapeutic treatment for the problems that develop as a result of this emotional silencing.[85] Levant states,

> I believe that a mild form of alexithymia is very wide-spread among adult men and that it results from the male emotional socialization ordeal, which requires boys to restrict the expression of their vulnerable and caring emotions and to be emotionally stoic.[86]

Baylor University psychologist Gary R. Brooks agrees and notes,

> Traditional masculine socialization teaches men to hide private experiences, exert control, maintain stoicism, present the self as invisible, favor action over introspection, avoid relationship conflict, and sexualize intimate relationships.[87]

Flood and Donaldson term this masculine stoicism and the underlying anxiety and feelings of worthlessness it produces *the malaise of men*, which is typified in ordinary men leading ordinary lives by "lacking in empathy, self-recrimination, and the shame of inadequate manhood."[88] Rather than dealing with these feelings in ways that promote healing and transformation, many men turn to alcohol, sex, porn, and work obsessions that allow them to avoid confrontation with their anxieties, insecurities, and feelings. As men avoid their feelings, resist help, and self-medicate with alcohol, a predictable consequence emerges as covered in the next section.

Men and Suicide: The Troubling History of Men and Counseling

While women attempt suicide at slightly higher rates than men, men commit suicide at four times the rate of women.[89] This gender gap in suicide rates has been in place for decades and the question "why?" continues to be a topic of acute investigation and speculation for psychologists and psychiatrists around the world. Answers to this question run the gamut from clinical depression, poor stress-management skills, societal expectations, mode of suicide method, to an alleged suicide gene, SKA2.[90] Men are notoriously taught from boyhood not to show emotion other than anger. When feelings of self-doubt,

FIGURE 12.9:

loneliness, fear, or loss of relevancy or competency arise in boys and men, males are told to "suck it up" or "walk it off," but that it is feminine and therefore unacceptable to openly exhibit these feelings or seek out help.

In his book, *Invisible Men: Men's Inner Lives and the Consequences of Silence*, Clark University psychologist Michael Addis recounts the stories of many men who struggle to cope with their feelings and who face their challenges in solitude and silence.[91] In examining the social rules under which most Western boys are taught to be men, Addis uncovered seven prevalent decrees: [92]

- Keep emotions under control.
- Handle problems on your own.
- Avoid anything considered to be feminine or gay.
- Be physically strong.
- Take control of situations.
- Be a risk taker.
- Be financially successful.

As this script is reinforced over time, Addis notes,

> The ways in which boys and men respond to negative feelings are influenced by culturally prescribed gender norms that discourage expression of "soft" emotions such as sadness and fear and encourage expression of "hard" emotions such as anger.[93]

For many men, it is simply unacceptable to express or communicate feelings of vulnerability, and for some, the stage is then set for rage and violence as appropriate substitutes for sorrow and feelings of losing control. This hostility can take an outward direction in the case of assault or murder, or an inward direction in the case of substance abuse or suicide. There are trigger events, notes Addis, where men and women alike are faced with circumstances that can plunge them into depression. Some of the more notable trigger events include going through divorce, job loss, death of a loved one, prolonged illness, or empty nest syndrome when parents face the reality of their children moving out of the house to start adult lives of their own.[94] But whereas many women are raised to view help-seeking as permissible and preferable strategies for dealing with stressful occurrences, too many men are raised to view help-seeking as a sign of weakness.

Psychotherapist and author Terrence Real agrees and views depression in men as a silent epidemic that goes unchecked much of the time, as men successfully hide their feelings from loved ones to avoid appearing unmanly.[95] Real points to childhood as the time when boys are indoctrinated to abandon their feelings, stating, "The whole point of boyhood is disconnection, severing them from their mothers, severing them from their feelings. The very phrase 'Be a man' means 'Don't feel it.'"[96] According to Real, the key to understanding why so many men keep depressive symptoms to themselves lies in the fact that for many men,

> Depression carries a double stain—the stigma of mental illness and also the stigma of 'feminine' emotionality ... Hidden depression drives several of the problems we think of as typically male: physical illness, alcohol and drug abuse, domestic violence, failures in intimacy, self-sabotage in careers.[97]

Throughout childhood, boys are taught that feelings of sadness are feminine in nature and therefore to be shunned or at least not communicated to others, while mental illness in American culture continues to be viewed with repugnancy and shame, locking many men who suffer from depression into lives of silence, isolation, and feelings of hopelessness. In fact, Flood and Donaldson draw an interesting conclusion about the distinction between the feelings of guilt and shame, writing:

> Guilt is: *I did something wrong*. Shame is: *I am wrong*.[98]

Borrowing from the work of psychoanalyst Helen B. Lewis, Flood and Donaldson note that men internalize shame, which can lead to horrendous consequences beyond emotional distance to aggression, violence, and suicidal thoughts and actions.[99]

In their piece "The Silent Epidemic of Male Suicide," researchers Dan Bilsker and Jennifer White argue that only by "building public awareness, refining explanatory frameworks, implementing preventive strategies, and undertaking research" can the epidemic rates of male suicide be reduced.[100] Bilsker and White note that few explanations and even fewer preventative measures have been offered to address this crisis, and when gender is discussed, it is treated as a static demographic variable rather than as a "culturally-mediated social construction" so that an analysis of how to alter the socialization of boys and men as an avenue of treatment is ignored.[101] One of the changes recommended by Bilsker and White is to disrupt the damaging cultural instruction that men receive as boys not to seek help when dealing with emotional issues and to replace this missive with the healthier advice to share their feelings with those, like parents or counselors, who can provide support and guidance.

One of the problems, according to Bilsker and White, is that research and treatment have focused on teen suicide rates even though the ages when suicide spikes to its highest levels for men are between ages 45 and 49.[102] As researchers search for reasons why men at these ages complete suicide at much higher rates than women, a few factors have begun to emerge. Men who reach the point of suicidal actions are:

- more hopeless
- more clearly resolved to die
- more likely to be intoxicated and thus more disinhibited
- more willing to carry out actions that might leave them injured or disfigured

- more unconcerned with consequences because of a high risk-taking orientation
- more likely to have a greater capacity to enact lethal self-injury[103]

One study showed that men move much more quickly than women between the stage of thinking about suicide to acting on it.[104] One explanation for this phenomenon is that relative to women, men lack a social support network.[105] Men tend to form superficial friend bases that are held together by talk of sports, cars, jobs, and other topics that keep conversations away from more emotionally intimate places. When coupled with the cultural, male instruction to conceal your problems from others, many men bottle up their despair to the point where they feel trapped with no way out. Yet another factor that researchers believe contributes to high suicide rates among men is the addition of alcohol to an already volatile mind set.[106] The view is that alcohol increases impulsivity at a time when being impulsive is the last thing someone contemplating suicide should be. Men who commit suicide are also more likely than women to implement methods that more surely bring about death.[107] The number one method of suicide with men is gun use.[108] This fact has contributed to the ongoing American debate over gun control, as researchers at Harvard University found that states with greater per capita gun ownership had a 400% increase in firearm suicide.[109] If men are more quick to act on suicide and increase impulsivity through higher rates of alcohol use, being in possession of a gun greatly raises the likelihood of suicide.

A further factor thought to contribute to higher male to female suicide rates over the past two decades was the downturn in industrial and construction jobs, which, by 2008, was part of an overall economic recession. In 1981, men committed suicide at approximately twice the rate of women, but, by 2012, that gap increased to four times that of women. With men bearing the bulk of the earning power in many working class households coupled with the sharp downturn in construction work, men internalized the emotional burden of not being able to provide for their families in ways they could when the housing market was strong. For many men, employment, career, and being provider for the family are ingrained parts of the normative male role taught to boys and young men as defining their purpose and meaning as men. In the wake of a career recession or collapse, these men struggle to regain their sense of purpose and can even adopt feelings of guilt or shame for not being able to fulfill what they believe to be their proper role as men even when the factors causing the recession are wholly out of their hands.

In 2003, sociologists formed to research and better understand male suicide patterns.[110] Through researching the patterns of 66 nations, they discovered that those countries that emphasize individualism over collectivism have the highest rates of male suicide in the world.[111] Within the U.S., ethnicity has also been shown to be a factor in gendered suicide rates. African-American females consistently rank lowest in suicide rates, which researchers attribute to better access to communal support and family relations.[112] Conversely, throughout many cultures, and within American culture in particular, men are socialized away from forging strong communal and family support bases, which many view as one of the principal causes of the much higher male suicide rates around the U.S. and the world. Yet even within American culture, male suicide rates vary by race and ethnicity:[114]

TABLE 12.1

White:	26.2
Native American/Alaskan Native:	16.1
Hispanics:	9.4
African-American:	9
Asian/Pacific Islanders:	8.6

(suicide rates per 100,000 residents, Centers for Disease Control)

The steep number of suicides for white men is most prominent as men age. White men age 65 and older commit suicide at much higher rates than any other demographic group.[115] Explanations for why white men commit suicide at much higher rates as compared to African-American and Hispanic men include the notion that African-American men are thought to have developed better coping skills, while both African-American and Hispanic men belong to cultures that tend to promote strong family, community, and church-based support.[116] Another possible explanation is that as many older white men are accustomed to professional lives of greater power than the majority of older African-American and Latino men, retirement presents a starker reality that their days of wielding power over others are behind them. If, on the other hand, one never wielded great power over others during one's economically prime earning years, retirement might not be met with having to make the same adjustments.

One's occupation and level of education also appear to factor into suicide rates. In general, men with more education are less likely to commit suicide than those with less education.[117] However, slightly higher than national average suicide rates have been found in certain non-military occupations that require higher educational levels.[118] In descending order, many of these occupations are careers dominated by men:[119] [120]

1. physicians
2. dentists
3. police officers
4. finance
5. chiropractors
6. construction
7. realtors
8. attorneys
9. veterinary doctors
10. farmers

Among black men, the career that statistically correlates to the highest rate of suicide is police officer and detective.[121] Other high-risk occupations for suicide include maintenance, landscapers, truck drivers, and electricians.[122] [123] A prevailing view is that along with layoffs and fluctuations in the economy that effect some occupations more than others, stress levels of particular occupations correspond to higher rates of depression and suicide.[124] [125] Other researchers warn that regional differences matter and that variables other than occupation need to be considered before jumping to conclusions about the relative risks of occupations in and of themselves.[126] But these same researchers note that when Massachusetts Institute of Technology reported the highest rate of student suicide in the nation, the conclusion "did not take into account the fact that M.I.T. also had a higher proportion than other institutions of male students and older students, both groups with higher suicide rates than college students in general."[127] Similarly, researchers have noted that with a few exceptions, the occupations that document the highest rates of suicide in the nation are occupations where men are found to be in the majority.

Beyond occupational hazards, sociologist Augustine Kposowa of University of California, Riverside, published a large national study that revealed that divorce has a strong impact on suicide rates, but only in men.[128] The study found that divorced

FIGURES 12.10 AND 12.11: Some historically male-centered professions are particularly vulnerable to economic recession

people are twice as likely as married people to commit suicide, but that when the data was stratified by sex, divorced men had a much higher rate of suicide than divorced women.[129] Kposowa speculates that reasons for this disparity include financial obligations:

> If a man loses custody of the children and the woman keeps those children, there are situations whereby she may not allow the man to see the children, and that causes some depression.[130]

In her book, *Divorced Fathers and Their Families*, psychologist Florence Kaslow adds that in the wake of a divorce, many men feel "the sense of having been discarded, rejected, and thrown out ... and for most men this feeling lingered for years."[131] But Kaslow also worries that because there has been a lack of research on divorced fathers, there have been few preventative notions for helping men who are facing or have gone through divorce.

In addition to men avoiding counseling to deal with emotional struggles, men also avoid going to doctors for physical ailments. According to Dr. Rick Kellerman, president of the American Academy of Family Physicians, "One of the biggest obstacles to improving the health of men is men themselves. They don't make their health a priority."[132] The American Heart Association adds that there are a host of reasons why men put off doctor visits, including several excuses that line up well with the ways that males are raised in America to be men: [133]

- I don't have the time.
- I can tough it out; it will pass.
- I don't have anything wrong with me.
- I don't like getting probed.

This final excuse is partly responsible for why so many men die of prostate cancer each year. Prostate cancer is the second leading cause of cancer death to men in America behind only lung cancer, with over 220,000 new cases diagnosed each year.[134] The good news is that most men survive prostate cancer,[135] but for those who resist going to the doctor for tests and treatment, the likelihood of death increases. As prostate cancer goes untreated, the cancer commonly spreads to the surrounding tissue including nearby lymph nodes and eventually to bones.[136] Since prostate cancer is a slow-growing form of cancer in most cases, when it is detected early, treatment can be very effective. But as men put off doctor visits, tests, screenings, and treatments, an easy fix turns into a life-threatening situation. An ongoing challenge, then, for health-care professionals as well as loved ones, is to encourage men to abandon the masculine script that instructs men to be tough or overly self-reliant by avoiding health care, whether physical or emotional, in order to live longer, healthier lives.

Fordham University psychologist and President of the American Psychological Association's Society for the Psychological Study of Men and Masculinity, Jay C. Wade, has focused his research on the intersection between African-American men and self-reliance, arguing,

> The original self-reliance concept as it was developed is, " can do it all on my own. I don't depend on anybody. I don't need anybody." But it may be that the construct isn't necessarily the same for African-American men. Because of the history of discrimination, it may be more like, "I can't depend on others in society to take care of me, so I need to rely on myself. And because others—like my family—are depending on me, I really need to take care of myself."[137]

This desire for self-reliance among African-American men actually works to their benefit, reports Wade, as they are more likely not to delay blood pressure and cholesterol screenings.[138] Wade speculates that possessing a skeptical attitude toward institutional support coupled with the belief that their families are dependent upon them lead more African-American men to seek out preventive health care methods rather than waiting until serious illness overtakes them.

With respect to aging gay men, research has found that two factors negatively affect health: sexual minority stress and marital status.[139] Many older gay men have experienced discrimination throughout their lives, and research as part of the UCLA Multicenter AIDS Cohort Study revealed that the stress of dealing with societal discrimination was a factor in the mental and emotional health of gay men.[140] In addition, the study reported that gay couples who enjoy the benefits of same-sex marriage or who are in long-term domestic partnerships report much higher levels of life satisfaction and overall happiness.[141] However, it was also found that nearly half of all older gay and bisexual men live alone compared to 13.4% of their heterosexual counterparts.[142] At the same time, older gay, lesbian, and bisexual adults are found to suffer from higher levels of chronic physical disorders than their heterosexual counterparts.[143] Older gay and bisexual men, in particular, were found to suffer from higher rates of hypertension, diabetes, and a host of physical disabilities due in part to the fact that one in five gay men in California who took part in the study were living with HIV infection.[144] Other scholars note, however, that much more research is needed to better understand the health challenges that face members of the LGBT community as they age and warn that regional studies (particularly those that do not parse out research across race, ethnicity, and class) may not be good indicators of national trends.[145]

One factor that is thought by some to contribute to depression in older men is a decrease in testosterone, particularly when coupled with other factors such as obesity, smoking, alcohol use, diet, and stress.[146] In some cases, testosterone therapy has been prescribed by doctors to increase the bioavailability of testosterone in older men as part of depression therapy, although there are concerns about adverse effects.[147] A Harvard University study found that for older men who were suffering from depression and who received testosterone treatment, there was significant mood improvement compared to those who received a placebo.[148] Professor of medicine at George Washington University, Dr. Michael Irwig, reports that over half of men who are referred for borderline testosterone levels are also suffering from depression.[149] Most of these men were also overweight with only 16% assessed as being at "normal weight."[150] As a result, many older men who are diagnosed for depression are also placed on a diet and exercise regimen, which causes as a side effect the body's ability to produce its own testosterone.[151] While scientists are still unsure why decreased levels of testosterone in older men correlate to higher rates of depression, the syndrome *partial androgen deficiency* (PADAM) has been named by endocrinologists as a pathology that is found in older men and that supplemental testosterone treatment has been shown to mitigate, which in some cases lessens depressive mood. Researchers, however, are quick to note that evidence is not yet sufficient to claim that testosterone treatment causes a decrease in depression, particularly when other factors such as issues of weight and alcohol use could be more directly tied to depressive mood disorder.[152] Some researchers also believe that it is possible that some older men are being misdiagnosed with depression who also have low testosterone levels, since the symptoms of low testosterone levels (low energy, diminished sex drive, irritability, periods of melancholy, and insomnia) and depression are quite similar.[153] A prevailing thought among mental health professionals is that the connection between depression and low testosterone levels in older men needs more research before replacement therapy becomes an accepted option for treating depression.

Men, the Military, and Post-Traumatic Stress Disorder

One of the more visible and tragic examples of men holding in their feelings and being unwilling to seek help is found in the many soldiers returning from war who suffer from post-traumatic stress disorder (PTSD). Suicide rates in the military have surged in the wake of the wars in Afghanistan and Iraq. A 2012 Veteran's Administration report places the number of veteran suicides at an estimated 22 per day.[154 155] In 2014, congress passed the Clay Hunt Suicide Prevention for American Veterans Act so named after Marine Corp veteran Clay Hunt who in 2011 committed suicide after completing two tours of duty in Iraq and Afghanistan.[156] While in combat, Hunt witnessed the deaths of platoon members who were killed by an IED (improvised explosive device) and soon thereafter was diagnosed with post traumatic stress disorder and depression.[157] When Hunt returned home to America, he was disillusioned by the reaction of people to the war. He believed that people didn't care about what was going on and this was particularly true of the younger students he met when he returned to college. At the same time, he was unable to pay the mounting bills that were accruing due to medical and counseling needs through the Veteran's Administration. In the end, Hunt felt isolated and struggled with his war experiences.[158 159]

Army General Ray Odierno sat down with senior military correspondent David Wood of the *Huffington Post* to talk about the high suicide rates in the military.[160] Wood asked Odierno how the Army deals with military personnel who fear reaching out for help when needed, to which General Odierno replied,

> The Army works against itself sometimes. We want strong, independent people. [This creates a] stigma of saying, I have a problem. Maybe you have a vulnerability, a weakness. [We] have to create an environment where this becomes acceptable ... We have to change the culture at the lowest level.

Odierno finds the cross-purposes of military training to be part of the problem as to why young men and women in the military do not reach out for help when feelings

FIGURE 12.12: U.S. Marine Corporal Clay Hunt, Courtesy of the IAVA

of despair strike them, but that continues to be a problem that must be addressed at the "lowest level," which presumably means at the point of recruitment and basic training. The instruction to be mentally tough no matter what the circumstance along with the prescription for self-reliance is a recipe for bottling up feelings of depression, self-doubt, and fear that may accompany battle fatigue. When soldiers turn to substances to help them cope instead of counseling, the results are often devastating.

Yet, military suicides are much more gender equivalent in terms of percentages than gendered suicide rates outside of the military. Among those who never served in the military, men outnumber women in completed suicides at a rate of 4 to 1. In the military, however, men commit suicide at only a slightly higher 15% rate of women.[161] This may speak to the training military personnel receive whether they are male or female, but it may also speak to the view that depression and suicide are more gender equivalent and that socializing forces are culpable for the gender inequality we witness in nonmilitary rates. The emphasis on being tough, not showing weakness, being completely self-sufficient, and not seeking help for the torment of emotional pain may be a more likely candidate for high rates of male suicide than supposing that there is something biologically inherent in men that accounts for these high rates.

Mid-Life Crisis and the Fear of Losing Relevancy and Independence

Psychoanalyst Elliott Jaques coined the phrase *mid-life crisis* for a phase of human development between ages 40 and 60 when many people question the meaning of their lives.[162] This crisis has received a great deal of attention and is linked more noticeably to men than to women.[163] Psychologist Margaret H. Huyck argues the Freudian view that while many men avoid experiencing a severe mid-life crisis, for those with dominating mothers and perceived weak fathers, the disorder is more pronounced.[164] In what she terms *gender expansion*, Huyck claims that as women become more assertive and men become more nurturing later in life, men become vulnerable to psychological distress.[165] Psychologist Susan Krauss Whitbourne focuses more on a person's job and relationship choices. Whitbourne found that those who change jobs in their 20s or 30s are less prone to mid-life crisis, while those who remain in the same occupation throughout their lives have a greater tendency toward experiencing a more pronounced mid-life crisis, the assumption being that people who feel stuck in their lives, in either a career or relationship context, experience the more severe form of mid-life crisis.[166]

Famed psychologist Daniel Levinson coined the phrase *mid-life transition* as a period in most people's lives that should be viewed as a natural part of aging.[167] [168] Psychologist Dan Jones argues that, for women, the mid-life transition is sometimes associated with the desire to accomplish goals put off in youth, which tend to be professional in nature.[169] Men, however, argues Jones, are thought to reach this stage of life and feel that there is something they need to prove.[170] As a result, an older man may seek out a younger romantic partner, purchase a sports car, wear younger looking clothing, get a tattoo or piercing, or seek out more adventurous hobbies and pastimes. There are triggering events that have been linked to mid-life crisis in men, which are some of the same trigger-events found in those suffering from depression. The most common triggers are divorce, job loss, empty nest syndrome, death of a loved one, and, more specifically, death of one's parents.[171] But for others, the natural process of aging coupled with a nostalgic longing for one's lost youth is enough to trigger a mid-life crisis.

As men age, all of the instruction given to men throughout their lives, that they should be tough, driven, virile, provider, protector, and, above all, self-reliant, works against them. Dr. Martin Seagar of Central London Samaritans argues, "if men have evolved as fathers, protectors and survivors, they are going to feel life is worth living to the extent they can provide and protect."[172] If this evolutionary account is correct, retirement can mean a time of great struggle for men who believe that male relevancy is measured by a man's ability to provide and protect for his family. But even if the explanation for men's desire to provide and protect is cultural in nature, aging represents a challenge to those desires. Aging, for many, represents a time when physical strength and autonomy decrease at approximately the same rate that economic productivity decreases. While some men have prepared financially for the future and therefore may not feel the economic anxiety to the same extent that those who have not prepared are feeling, they may still feel a loss of productivity. While in the prime of their productive years, many men become accustomed to possessing a sense of power and control over themselves and others, or at least feel that their opinions matter so that feelings of worth and confidence are at their peak. Aging, for some, marks a reduction of this confidence and sense of purpose. For those men who have not prepared financially for retirement or have been unable to prepare for the future, the prospect of aging carries uncertainty and fear. If one is no longer employable at a rate of salary required to meet all of one's financial needs and one does not have sufficient resources to meet one's obligations, and, most importantly, one has been taught since childhood that it is a man's role to provide and protect, a guiding precedent has been established that can have severe consequences to a man's self-esteem and sense of relevancy later in life.

A loss of relevancy can be seen when turning to magazines aimed at male audiences. In one study, five men's magazines were investigated (*Esquire*, *GQ*, *Maxim*, *Men's Health, and Zoomer*) where it was found that depictions of older men are largely absent and, when present, usually consist of older, male celebrities who enjoy success and power.[173] The absence of older men in men's magazines mirrors the absence of older women in media in general. But with men, the depictions of older men as being financially successful, autonomous, and powerful reinforces anxieties in older men whose lives do not reflect this archetype. In addition to there being an absence of older men in men's magazines, gerontologist Gabriela Spector-Mersel adds that age is largely absent in the scholarship on men's lives as well.[174] Spector-Mersel theorizes that contemporary hegemonic masculine scripts do not account for aging in men and that media portrayal of elderly people in general is characterized by ungendered individuals who are no longer working and whose lives are more sedentary in nature.[175] A common depiction of older men comes in the form of TV commercials that show an older man gardening, cooking, or simply sitting next to his wife while discussing life insurance or supplemental health insurance options (Figure 12.13). The transition, therefore, from being a culturally accepted, prime-of-life masculine man to an elderly man is, for some, a transition marked for anxiety and feelings of irrelevance. Geriatrician Laurie Jacobs notes that "Men fear retirement because it's [work—profession] how they define themselves and how they fill their time."[176] Retirement also brings about a point in men's lives when their opinions are not solicited as much as when they were younger and this decrease of interest in them equates for many to a lessening of value or what Jacobs terms "becoming invisible."[177] Without new interests and vistas to explore, men can feel insignificant and unnecessary.

As covered in chapter seven and in the section above on the pursuit of youth and beauty, it is also common to see advertisers of pharmaceutical products that promise long-lasting erections exploit older men's anxieties about sex. Drug ads that promise cures for erectile dysfunction (ED) often depict a younger-looking woman, such as the Viagra ad in Figure 12.14, with a slogan that assures older men that they have not lost their virility. This message of virility is often tied to an acknowledgement of competency, a reassurance that, as men age, they gain a level of proficiency that compensates for

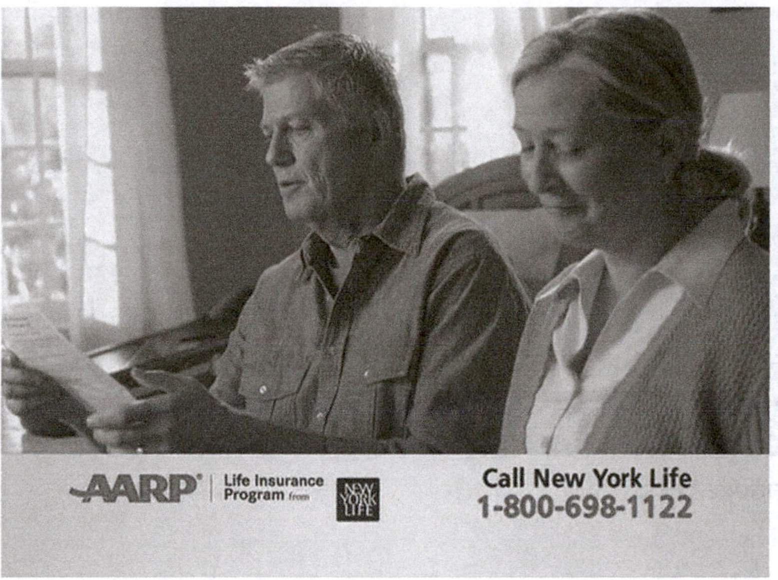

FIGURE 12.13: AARP ad for life insurance

whatever loss in muscularity, agility, and sex appeal they may have possessed when they were younger. By stating "This is the age of knowing what you're made of" in the Cialis ad in Figure 12.15, marketers can assure older men that their age actually places them in an advantage over young men who, presumably, are still trying to figure who they are and "what they are made of." Since virility has long been associated in popular culture with masculine power, there is a direct link in the minds of many men between losing sexual vibrancy and losing masculine identity. In fact, in a survey where older men were asked to prioritize their concerns, impotence came in at the very top of the list.[178]

FIGURE 12.14: Viagra ad

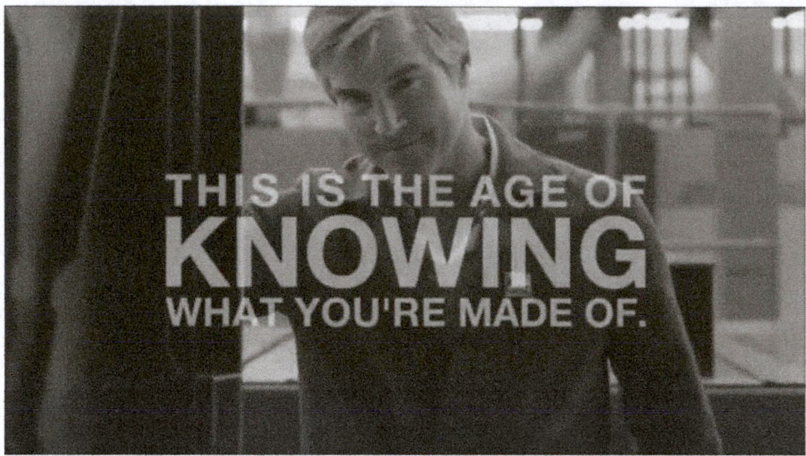

FIGURE 12.15: Cialis ad

In tandem with the fear many older men have about losing sexual relevance, as men age and enter the senior years of their lives, independence and autonomy can give way to dependence and increased limitations. The realization that one will be forced to count on others is to embrace the very thing that men are taught throughout life to avoid. Lurking in the back of the minds of people as they age is the concern about illness and physical incapacity. In fact, in surveys, older men report care more about losing independence than about death.[179] At the same time, self-reports by senior-aged men run contrary to expectations, as older men claim not to have anxiety about their health or impending deaths nearly as much as do middle-aged men.[180] Other studies support the generalization that men of advanced age are less susceptible to anxiety and depression.[181] Speculation for this surprising result includes the notion that advanced age is beset by decreased emotional responsiveness and what researcher A.F. Jorm terms *the psychological immunization to stressful experiences*.[182] As with other results concerning men and aging, researchers agree that much more attention needs to be given to the mechanisms underlying age-related responses to stress, anxiety, fear, and depression.

Summary

The links between capitalistic versions of success and aging create a predictable set of fears and challenges for men as they age. The longstanding male instruction that men are to be the provider for the family places pressure on men from an early age, and in the face of economic downturns, many men assume responsibility and internalize their financial problems as failure. For those who have not been able to set aside resources, the prospect of retirement and aging can be a time of depression and great anxiety. At the same time, depression, while found in high rates in men, is not something many men feel comfortable discussing or treating, making high rates of suicide a foreseeable consequence of such avoidance. The research suggests that this aversion to seeking help is part of a larger problem to get men to open up emotionally. Of course, this means that a revolution in the ways that boys are raised to be men must be undertaken, a revolution that encourages boys and men to report and seek counseling for their emotional pain.

In terms of academics, study after study call for more research into men's health and particularly into the health challenges that face older men. The majority of scholarship that takes up men's health currently focuses on adolescence through the ages of economic productivity. In order to better meet the needs of men as they age, much more needs to be known about health risks, triggering events, and successful treatment options. This is especially true for those men who belong to at-risk populations such war veterans, men in high-stress occupations, and those who are experiencing trigger events such as divorce, death of a loved one, and joblessness.

Notes

1 www.imsdb.com/scripts/Saving-Private-Ryan.html.
2 https://en.wikipedia.org/wiki/History_of_capitalism.
3 www.aneki.com/billionaires.html.
4 www.imdb.com/title/tt0086250/quotes.
5 Gabarino, James, *Lost Boys: Why Our Sons Turn Violent and How We Can Save Them* (Anchor, 2000).
6 Kimmel, Michael, *Angry White Men: American Masculinity at the End of an Era* (Nation Books, 2013).
7 Dyke, Lorraine S. and Murphy, Steven A., "How we define success: A qualitative study of what matters most to women and men," *Sex Roles*, November, 2006.
8 Ibid.
9 Morgan, David, "Class and Masculinities," in *Handbook of Studies on Men and Masculinities*, ed. Michael S. Kimmel, Jeff Hearn, and Robert W. Connell (Sage, 2005).
10 Ibid.
11 Ibid.
12 Ibid.
13 https://en.wikipedia.org/wiki/Fred_Trump.
14 Ibid.
15 Morgan, "Class and Masculinities."
16 www.bloomberg.com/news/articles/2013-12-23/secret-handshakes-greet-frat-brothers-on-wall-street.
17 www.washingtonpost.com/wp-dyn/content/article/2009/01/02/AR2009010202099.html.
18 http://thinkprogress.org/economy/2013/12/23/3100841/wall-street-fraternity-culture/.
19 Kruger, D.J. and Nesse, R.M., "Economic transition, male competition, and sex differences in Mortality Rates." *Evolutionary Psychology*, 5 (2007), pp. 411–427.
20 www.commondreams.org/news/2007/07/01/capitalism-bad-mens-health-study.
21 www.huffingtonpost.com/2012/01/26/overtime-work-depression_n_1234025.html.
22 www.webmd.com/sleep-disorders/excessive-sleepiness-10/10-results-sleep-loss.
23 www.menshealth.com/health/health-effects-working-too-much.
24 www.allbusiness.com/home-based-franchising-is-on-the-rise-14287433-1.html.
25 www.businessweek.com/smallbiz/running_small_business/archives/2010/01/home-based_businesses_increasing.html.
26 www.dol.gov/whd/overtime/NPRM2015/factsheet.htm.
27 www.epi.org/blog/majority-of-workers-who-will-benefit-from-updated-overtime-rules-are-women/.
28 Riska, Elianne, *Masculinity and Men's Health: Coronary Heart Disease in Medical and Public Discourse* (Rowman & Littlefield, 2006).
29 Ibid.
30 www.simplypsychology.org/personality-a.html.
31 Ibid., p. 57.
32 Ibid.
33 www.hardinessinstitute.com/?/page_id=1020.
34 Funk, S.C., "Hardiness: A review of theory and research," *Health Psychology*, 11, 5 (1992), pp. 335–345.
35 Riska, *Masculinity and Men's Health.*
36 Hystad, Sigurd W., "Exploring gender equivalence and bias in a measure of psychological hardiness," *International Journal of Psychological Studies* 4, 4 (2012).
37 www.businessinsider.com/difference-between-men-and-women-managers-rebecca-rockafellar-istock-photo-getty-images-2012-11.
38 www.tuw.edu/business/top-down-vs-bottom-up-management/.

39 Hull, Jay G., Van Treuren, Ronald R., and Vimelli, Suzanne, "Hardiness and Health: A Critique and Alternate Approach," *Journal of Personality and Social Psychology*, 53, 3 (1987).
40 http://fortune.com/2015/09/30/america-wealth-inequality/.
41 Ibid.
42 Hall, Diane M., Cassidy, Elaine F., and Stevenson, Howard C. "Acting tough in a tough world: An examination of fear among urban African American adolescents," *The Journal of Black Psychology*, 34 (2008).
43 www.nytimes.com/1992/04/21/science/black-scientists-study-the-pose-of-the-inner-city.html?pagewanted=all.
44 Ibid.
45 www.healthpovertyaction.org/info-and-resources/the-cycle-of-poverty-and-poor-health/key-facts/.
46 www.who.int/hdp/poverty/en/.
47 www.nih.gov/news-events/news-releases/stresses-poverty-may-impair-learning-ability-young-children.
48 www.usnews.com/news/articles/2012/10/30/americans-in-poverty-at-greater-risk-for-chronic-health-problems.
49 www.npc.umich.edu/publications/policy_briefs/brief16/PolicyBrief16.pdf.
50 Ibid.
51 http://fortune.com/2014/11/04/hiring-racial-bias/.
52 www.npc.umich.edu/publications/policy_briefs/brief16/PolicyBrief16.pdf.
53 http://fortune.com/2014/11/04/hiring-racial-bias/.
54 http://www.npc.umich.edu/publications/policy_briefs/brief16/PolicyBrief16.pdf.
55 Ibid.
56 http://nchv.org/index.php/news/media/background_and_statistics/.
57 Ibid.
58 www.nationalhomeless.org/factsheets/minorities.html.
59 http://nchv.org/index.php/news/media/background_and_statistics/.
60 http://citylimits.org/2012/03/05/homelessness-its-about-race-not-just-poverty/.
61 www.onecpd.info/resources/documents/5thHomelessAssessmentReport.pdf.
62 "Who is homeless?," published by the National Coalition for the Homeless (NCHWIH). Archived April 14, 2010.
63 Ibid.
64 http://goodmenproject.com/good-feed-blog/why-are-men-more-likely-to-be-homeless/.
65 www.inside-man.co.uk/2014/12/12/men-are-nine-times-more-likely-to-die-homeless/.
66 www.washingtontimes.com/news/2015/mar/12/plastic-surgery-43-percent-among-men-report/.
67 Ibid.
68 www.racked.com/2014/11/11/7569603/beauty-products-for-men-dove-lab-series.
69 http://articles.latimes.com/2012/jun/23/business/la-fi-man-makeup-20120623.
70 http://business.time.com/2012/06/25/hey-buddy-got-any-eye-shadow-i-can-borrow/.
71 Ibid.
72 http://articles.latimes.com/2012/jun/23/business/la-fi-man-makeup-20120623.
73 www.wsj.com/articles/SB10001424052702304811304577365902173161004.
74 www.anad.org/get-information/males-eating-disorders/.
75 www.nationaleatingdisorders.org/research-males-and-eating-disorders.
76 Ibid.
77 Ibid.
78 www.adaa.org/understanding-anxiety/related-illnesses/other-related-conditions/body-dysmorphic-disorder-bdd.
79 www.nationaleatingdisorders.org/research-males-and-eating-disorders.
80 www.todaysdietitian.com/newarchives/100713p22.shtml.
81 Ibid.
82 www.todaysdietitian.com/newarchives/100713p22.shtml.
83 Donaldson, Charlie and Flood, Randy, *Mascupathy: Understanding and Healing the Malaise of American Manhood* (The Institute for the Prevention and Treatment of Mascupathy, 2014).
84 Ibid., pp. 40–41.
85 http://nmalex.blogspot.com/.
86 Levant, Ronald, *A New Psychology of Men* (Basic Books, 2003).
87 Brooks, Gary R., *Beyond the Crisis of Masculinity: A Transtheoretical Model for Male-Friendly Therapy*, 1st edition (American Psychological Association, 2009).
88 Donaldson and Flood, *Mascupathy*.
89 www.afsp.org/understanding-suicide/facts-and-figures.
90 www.newsweek.com/2015/02/20/suicide-men-305913.html.
91 Addis, Michael, *Invisible Men: Men's Inner Lives and the Consequences of Silence* (Times Books, 2011).
92 Ibid., p. 50.

93 Ibid., p. 51.
94 Ibid., Chapter 8.
95 Real, Terrence, *I Don't Want to Talk About It: Overcoming the Secret Legacy of Male Depression* (Scribner, 1998).
96 http://community.seattletimes.nwsource.com/archive/?date=19980311&slug=2739068.
97 Real, *I Don't Want to Talk About It.*
98 Donaldson and Flood, *Mascupathy*, p. 71.
99 Ibid. p. 71.
100 Bilsker, Dan and White, Jennifer, "The silent epidemic of male suicide," *British Columbia Medical Journal*, December, 2011.
101 Ibid.
102 Ibid.
103 Ibid.
104 Dombrovski, A.Y., Szanto, K., Duberstein, P., et al., "Sex differences in correlates of suicide attempt lethality in late life," *American Journal Geriatric Psychiatry*, 16 (2008), pp. 905–913.
105 Houle J., Mishara B.L., and Chagnon F., "An empirical test of a mediation model of the impact of the traditional male gender role on suicidal behavior in men" *Journal of Affective Disorders,* 107 (2008), pp. 37–43.
106 www.ncbi.nlm.nih.gov/pubmed/17107255.
107 Schrijvers, Didier, "The gender paradox in suicidal behavior and its impact on the suicidal process." *Journal of Affective Disorders*, 138 ,2 *(2012*), pp. 19–26.
108 www.usatoday.com/story/news/nation/2013/07/21/guns-most-deadly-choice-in-suicide-attempts/2572097/.
109 www.hsph.harvard.edu/magazine-features/guns-and-suicide-the-hidden-toll/.
110 Rudmin, Lloyd Webster, "Questions of culture, age, and gender in the epidemiology of suicide," *Scandinavian Journal of Psychology*, 44 *(2003),* pp. 373–381.
111 Ibid.
112 Goldston, David B., Morlock, Sherry Davis, Whitbeck, Leslie B., Murakami, Jessica L., Zayas, Luis H., and Nagayama Hall, Gordon C. "Cultural considerations in adolescent suicide prevention and psychosocial treatment." *American Psychologist*, 63, 1 (2008), pp. 14–31.
114 www.cdc.gov/nchs/data/hus/2013/035.pdf.
115 www.washingtonpost.com/national/health-science/the-high-suicide-rate-among-elderly-white-men-who-may-suffer-from-depression/2014/12/05/2bad6ea0–222e-11e4–958c-268a320a60ce_story.html.
116 www.psychologytoday.com/blog/reading-between-the-headlines/201305/white-middle-age-suicide-in-america-sky-rockets.
117 www.prb.org/Publications/Articles/2010/suicides.aspx.
118 Ibid.
119 www.newhealthguide.org/Highest-Suicide-Rate-By-Profession.html.
120 www.therichest.com/rich-list/the-biggest/the-10-professions-with-the-highest-suicide-rates/?view=all.
121 www.newhealthguide.org/Highest-Suicide-Rate-By-Profession.html.
122 www.cbsnews.com/media/suicide-in-the-workplace-which-professions-are-high-risk/.
123 http://mentalhealthdaily.com/2015/01/06/top-11-professions-with-highest-suicide-rates/.
124 Cooper, C.L., Rout, U. and Faragher, B., "Mental Health, Job Satisfaction, and Job Stress among General Practitioners," *British Medical Journal*, February, 1989.
125 Margolis, Bruce L., Kroes, William H., and Quinn, Robert P., "Job Stress: An Unlisted Occupational Hazard," *Journal of Occupational and Environmental Medicine*, October, 1974.
126 www.nytimes.com/2002/11/12/science/jobs-rank-low-as-risk-factors-for-suicide.html?pagewanted=all.
127 Ibid.
128 Kposowa, Augustine J., "Marital status and suicide in the national longitudinal mortality study," *Journal of Epidemiology & Community Health*, August, 1999.
129 Ibid.
130 www.cbsnews.com/news/men-wear-divorce-badly/.
131 Kaslow, Florence W., *Divorced Fathers and Their Families* (Springer, 2013).
132 www.webmd.com/men/news/20070620/why-men-skip-doctor-visits.
133 www.heart.org/HEARTORG/Conditions/Heart-Disease---The-Top-10-Reasons-Men-Put-Off-Doctor-Visits_UCM_433365_Article.jsp#.Vjjr8aKdVBw.
134 www.cancer.org/cancer/prostatecancer/detailedguide/prostate-cancer-key-statistics.
135 Ibid.

136 www.cancer.org/cancer/prostatecancer/detailedguide/prostate-cancer-treating-treating-pain.
137 Wade, Jay C., "Traditional masculinity and African American men's health-related attitudes and behaviors," *American Journal of Men's Health*, 3 (2009), pp. 165–172.
138 Ibid.
139 Wright, Richard G., LeBlanc, Allen J., de Vries, Brian, Detels, Roger, "Stress and mental health among midlife and older gay-identified Men," *American Journal of Public Health*, March, 2012.
140 Ibid.
141 Ibid.
142 www.nytimes.com/2011/04/05/health/research/05gay.html?_r=0.
143 Ibid.
144 Ibid.
145 www.ncbi.nlm.nih.gov/books/NBK64800/.
146 Carnahan, R.M. and Perry, P.J., "Depression in aging men: The role of testosterone," *Drugs & Aging*, 21, 6 (2004), pp. 361–376.
147 Borst, Stephen E. and Mulligan, Thomas. "Testosterone Replacement Therapy for Older Men," *Clinical Interventions in Aging*, December, 2007.
148 http://news.harvard.edu/gazette/2003/01.09/01-testosterone.html.
149 www.medpagetoday.com/MeetingCoverage/ENDO/50371.
150 Ibid.
151 Ibid.
152 Amore, Mario, Innamorati, Marco, Costi, Sara, Sher, Leo, Girardi, Paolo, and Pompili, Maurizio, "Partial androgen deficiency, depression, and testosterone supplementation in aging men," *International Journal of Endocrinology*, June, 2012.
153 www.psychology24.org/does-low-testosterone-cause-depression/.
154 www.huffingtonpost.com/2012/06/07/military-suicide-surges-_n_1578821.html.
155 www.va.gov/opa/docs/Suicide-Data-Report-2012-final.pdf.
156 www.cbsnews.com/news/the-life-and-death-of-clay-hunt/.
157 Ibid.
158 Ibid.
159 www.congress.gov/bill/113th-congress/house-bill/5059 and http://iava.org/savact/.
160 www.huffingtonpost.com/2013/09/25/ray-odierno-military-suicides_n_3984359.html.
161 www.latimes.com/nation/la-na-female-veteran-suicide-20150608-story.html.
162 https://en.wikipedia.org/wiki/Elliott_Jaques.
163 www.apa.org/monitor/apr03/researchers.aspx.
164 Ibid.
165 Ibid.
166 Ibid.
167 https://en.wikipedia.org/wiki/Daniel_Levinson.
168 www.webmd.com/depression/features/midlife-crisis-opportunity?page=2.
169 www.webmd.com/depression/features/midlife-crisis-opportunity.
170 Ibid.
171 www.webmd.com/depression/features/midlife-crisis-opportunity.
172 www.newsweek.com/2015/02/20/suicide-men-305913.html.
173 Clarke, Laura H., Bennett, Erica V. and Liu, Chris, "Aging and masculinity: Portrayals in men's magazines," *Journal of Aging Studies*, December 2014.
174 Spector-Mersel, Gabriela, "Never-aging stories: Western hegemonic masculinity scripts," *Journal of Gender Studies*, 15, 1 (2006).
175 Ibid.
176 www.caring.com/articles/5-things-men-fear-about-aging.
177 Ibid.
178 Ibid.
179 www.telegraph.co.uk/news/health/elder/6836648/More-people-fear-losing-independence-in-old-age-than-death-survey-finds.html.
180 McCrae, Robert R., Bartone, Paul T., and Costa, Paul T., "Age, anxiety, and self-reported health," *The International Journal of Aging & Human Development*, February, 1976.
181 Jorm, A.F., "Does old age reduce the risk of anxiety and depression? A review of epidemiological studies across the adult life span," *Psychological Medicine*, January, 2000.
182 Ibid.

Postscript: The Future of Masculinity

To better understand the future of masculinity, it is important to take note of the many changes that have occurred in American culture over the past several decades. In the presence and development of the women's movement in America, some men resisted while others viewed the liberation of women to signal the opportunity for a contemporaneous men's liberation movement. But the concept seemed to be awkward or even preposterous given the fact that men controlled almost every aspect of society. In what way did men need liberating? For some, men's liberation meant the freedom to emote, feel, and embrace the fact that men experience vulnerability, fear, and doubt. For others, it meant that men were no longer required to be the sole financial earners for the family. But for others, the success of women's liberation meant that men would have less power. Some men felt threatened by women's emergence into the workforce, which was viewed as competition with men. Others believed that women's responsibilities in society should remain in the domestic roles of raising children, cleaning house, and tending to meals. These gendered prescriptions were linked to religious pronouncements that God intended the sexes to serve in differing roles, and the notion of *complementarianism* codified these contrasting roles into general rules for men and women. Men, it was argued, were made to assume positions of leadership and authority, while women were created to assume supportive roles to men.

Today, these same gender-bifurcated positions are defended by some, but much has changed since the 1960s and 1970s. Far fewer women believe their destiny is to be deferential and obedient to male authority. Women now make up the majority of college students and are graduating at higher rates than men. Women now enjoy a greater, although still greatly underrepresented, presence in the workforce including management positions. Women are also now present in careers once considered the sole domain of men such as the military, law enforcement, science, law, finance, and government. By every account, women are excelling in these areas of endeavor contrary to the predictions of men of the past who believed that women were incapable of achievement in executive positions of decision-making power. The notion that women were built by nature for supportive and subordinate roles has been revealed to be a sexist myth alongside the many similar myths about race and ethnicity. But this fact does not stop many from continuing the tradition of viewing women in ancillary roles to men. With all this as background, one obvious way that men of the future will have to evolve is in response to the increasing power of women, whether this means more shared responsibilities of parenting or a greater acceptance of the fact that women are going to continue to assume roles of leadership alongside men. Some men will surely embrace these changes with approval, while others will resist and complain.

Even with the acknowledgement of these changes, there is no crystal ball that can accurately predict the future of masculinities. Yet one thing we have witnessed in the early twenty-first century that will almost certainly continue is the increased interest in the study of masculinities, which demonstrates, in part, that men are coming to terms with the fact that men's lives are more complex than the one-dimensional, emotionally constipated, hypermasculine representations offered up in Hollywood action-adventure films or the one-dimensional masculine offerings given to us by our fathers and grandfathers. Yet there is also no indication that forms of hypermasculine, hegemonic masculinity will recede in American culture any time soon. Even so, in the early stages of the twenty-first century, we have witnessed changes to the earlier masculine scripts that dominated the majority of the twentieth century, changes that pluralize masculinity into a multitude of masculine identities, performances, and expressions. Media have contributed both to the reinforcement of old-fashioned hypermasculine standards and to an ever-increasing variety of masculine expression. There is no reason to think that this trend will not continue. Gay and trans-masculinities and femininities will also continue to evolve and enjoy greater visibility in a culture that is opening up to nonconforming gender identities, even as homophobia and transphobia continue to make headlines when hate speech and violence occur.

There is also good reason to believe that masculinity and manhood will continue to be politicized. There are no shortages of conservative pundits today calling for men to be tougher, more aggressive, and to assume greater leadership roles than women. As more progressive voices continue to promote more caring, empathic masculinities, as well as more women entering leadership positions, conservatives are sure to push back against what they view as weak men and powerful women. Conservatives also view these nonconforming masculinities as threats to the nuclear family with men as head of the household, while also insisting that more sensitive men weaken the military and place the U.S. in danger of attack from more manly nations that do not encourage empathy and compassion in men. At the same time, those with progressive viewpoints will undoubtedly continue to call for more empathic and emotionally centered men as a prescription to abate violence, to create more loving and harmonious relationships, and to remedy the notoriously high rates of male incarceration and suicide.

With respect to men's health, the future will almost certainly involve encouraging men to seek out medical and psychological assistance to better combat everything from depression to prostate cancer. There is already movement in this direction with professional sports leagues, including the NFL, advocating for prostate cancer screening and the military urging counseling and increased counseling services. The fight against sexual violence and intimate partner violence will undoubtedly continue to gain momentum with male-centered organizations such as Major League Baseball taking a tougher stance against violators. It would not be surprising to find other professional sports leagues taking similar positions. Pressure will also continue to be placed on colleges and universities to crack down on fraternity hazing and sexual violence. In general, as victim advocacy increases and the visibility of perpetration gains wider audiences, activism that includes legal remedies will be undertaken, which will place pressure on traditional bastions of male-dominant vocations and avocations such as the military, law enforcement, fire and rescue personnel, politics, business, sports culture, journalism, the entertainment industry, and perhaps even pornography.

Because the lives of women and men are inextricably intertwined, no account of men and masculinity can be sufficient that does not take into account the lives of women, particularly as American culture continues to evolve in a variety of ways. As stated above, one of the most interesting questions for the future of masculinities is how men of the future are going to adapt to the increasing power of women. Because women are graduating from college and universities and entering career paths at unprecedented rates, far fewer women will be economically dependent on men. This means that fewer men will be able to get away with mistreating women in the belief that they can do so because women do not have the resources to survive without them. This may be the biggest change to men's lives in the future. Abusive and controlling men will not disappear, but they may find themselves alone in much greater numbers. This fact may push men into adopting more progressive attitudes about themselves and lead to more emotionally connected men, whether or not it was their idea to become more progressive men. With this in mind, there is an opportunity for sexism to be viewed with the same disdain most in contemporary culture view racism. It is not that sexism or racism will cease to exist, or that they will cease to thrive in certain environments, but that more men will join women in condemning sexism and misogyny. The future of masculinities is one of hope and opportunity with only time and future generations to witness whether or not men take advantage of those opportunities.

Index

Page numbers in *italics* refer to figures.